STEPHEN A. DOUGLAS

(From a photograph circa 1858)

The Emergence of Lincoln

VOLUME I ...

DOUGLAS,
BUCHANAN,
AND
PARTY
CHAOS
1857·1859

by ALLAN NEVINS

New York · CHARLES SCRIBNER'S SONS · London

1950

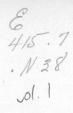
This Chronicle of Lincoln and Douglas
Is Inscribed by the Author
A Son of Their Prairie State
To His Alma Mater
The University of Illinois

PREFACE

THESE TWO VOLUMES are complete in themselves. They are, however, also a sequel to the author's two previous volumes entitled *Ordeal of the Union* —the four covering the history of the United States 1846–1861.

Such a work must necessarily rest upon the firm foundation laid by many previous writers. Although I have worked from the sources, I owe a great debt to the historians who have done so much to lay open the field. No period of the American past has received more careful attention than this era just preceding the Civil War. Two men who lived through it as expert observers of events wrote general histories which no student can neglect: Horace Greeley in *The American Conflict* (appropriately dedicated to John Bright), and Henry Wilson in *The Rise and Fall of the Slave Power*. Antagonistic to these in point of view, George Lunt's *The Origin of the Late War* furnishes at some points a useful corrective. Rather a history of the period than a biography, John G. Nicolay's and John Hay's ten-volume *Abraham Lincoln: A History* is an indispensable compendium of details. Among other treatments of Lincoln, I have specially profited from those of Carl Sandburg, James G. Randall, and Albert J. Beveridge. The lives of Stephen A. Douglas by George Fort Milton (*The Eve of Conflict*) and Allen Johnson, each admirable in its own way, have yielded me much that I could not easily have found elsewhere. Four other biographical studies, Ulrich B. Phillips's *Robert Toombs*, the full-packed *Life of Alexander H. Stephens* by Richard M. Johnston and William H. Browne, the two-volume *Seward* by my oldtime friend and mentor Frederic Bancroft, and the *John Brown: A Biography Fifty Years After* by another mentor, Oswald Garrison Villard, require special mention.

No writer on the period can fail to pay tribute to the general works by four great figures in historical literature: James Ford Rhodes, whose breadth of view, keen sense of what was practically significant, and skill in portraiture give his books enduring merit; James Schouler, who accurately minuted many facts; John Bach McMaster, who wrote on social ferment and Western growth with special felicity; and Edward Channing, who brought a finished scholarship to bear upon a succession of issues and aspects. I have frequently disagreed with their conclusions, but never without hesitation. If I have also frequently disagreed with parts of Avery Craven's *The Coming of the Civil War*, it is with respect for his scholarship, courage, and acuteness, and a concurrence in his belief that we must look behind propagandist distortions to find the realities of the time. As a compactly expert survey of the era, the first ten chapters of James G. Randall's *The Civil War and Reconstruction* are invaluable. I regret that in the large cooperative history of the South now under way, only the able volumes by E. M. Coulter and Charles S. Sydnor (in the later period) were available for my use.

Without the numerous expert monographic studies of the last quarter century, such a work as this could have had little value. Beyond specific debts acknowledged in the footnotes, I owe a great general obligation to scores of writers. It is perhaps not invidious to mention U. B. Phillips, Charles S. Sydnor, Ralph B. Flanders, J. W. Coleman, Charles S. Davis, and W. E. B. DuBois on various aspects of slavery; William S. Jenkins, Robert S. Cotterill, Jesse Carpenter, Clement Eaton, and W. J. Cash on the Southern mind; Arthur C. Cole on the social history of the period; Dwight L. Dumond, Gilbert H. Barnes, Wilbur H. Siebert, and Henrietta Buckmaster on antislavery movements; Carter G. Woodson, John Hope Franklin, and W. E. B. DuBois on the Negro; the books of W. L. Mathieson and Frederic Bancroft on the foreign and domestic slave trade; the studies of Frank L. Owsley, Everett Dick, and Lewis E. Atherton in ante-bellum Southern society; and the writings of Cardinal Goodwin, W. J. Ghent, Robert G. Cleland, and J. W. Caughey on the development of the West. I have leaned heavily on the studies of Roy F. Nichols in Democratic Party history, and especially upon his *The Disruption of American Democracy*. The standard writings of Thomas A. Bailey and Samuel Flagg Bemis upon diplomatic affairs; the investigations of James C. Malin into Kansas history; Philip Foner's treatment of New York businessmen and slavery; the thorough work of Paul M. Angle, David Donald, Jay M. Monaghan, Benjamin P. Thomas, Harry E. Pratt, and Roy P. Basler upon various aspects of Lincoln's career; the admirable volumes by William E. Baringer on *Lincoln's Rise to Power* and *A House Dividing*; the analyses of the campaign of 1860 by E. D. Fite, Reinhard H. Luthin, and Ollinger P. Crenshaw; the work of Dwight L. Dumond on *The Secession Movement, 1860–1861;* and David M. Potter's treatment of Lincoln in the crisis of 1860–1861—all these have been indispensable.

Such a short list omits many writers whom I would like to name. I should add that in my opinion no understanding of the period is possible without much reading in the best literature of the time; in Emerson, Hawthorne, Lowell, Melville, Simms, Longfellow, Whittier, Timrod, Bryant, and Whitman.

The author must give special thanks to three friends who have patiently read all of this work, and who have given him indispensable aid in improving it: Mr. Frank E. Hill, Professor David Donald, and Professor Michael Kraus. He thanks also the men and women who have dealt with special parts of it and offered incisive criticism: Professors Henry Steele Commager, Frank Tannenbaum, Louis M. Hacker, and Joseph H. Dorfman; Mr. Boyd B. Stutler, who not only read the sections on John Brown but opened his rich Brown collection; Mr. Henry Seidel Canby, who read the chapter on literature; Mrs. Laura Roper, who fruitfully criticized the pages on Olmsted; Professors Roy F. Nichols, Charles S. Sydnor, Arthur C. Cole, Herbert O. Brayer, and James C. Malin;

Mr. Kirke Mechem of the Kansas State Historical Society and his associates; Mr. Jay Monaghan of the Illinois State Historical Library; and Mr. Roy P. Basler and Benjamin P. Thomas of the Abraham Lincoln Association. From a circle of friends—George Fort Milton, Merle Curti, Dr. Reinhard Luthin, Holman Hamilton, and Ralph Newman—he derived counsel and encouragement. For help in the early stages of the work he must thank Miss Margaret Clapp, now president of Wellesley College, Professor Basil Rauch of Barnard College, and Dr. W. J. Niven. Mr. Foreman M. Lebold generously admitted the author to his rich private manuscript collection. For aid in dealing with constitutional questions he is indebted to Mr. Charles Warren, Professor E. S. Corwin, Rev. Vincent Hopkins, S.J., and Mr. Frederic R. Coudert.

It would be impossible for the author to thank by name all the librarians and archivists who have assisted him. But he is especially grateful to Carl White, Librarian of Columbia University; to Robert W. Hill of the New York Public Library, and R. W. G. Vail, Director of the New York Historical Society; to Miss Ellen FitzSimons, long the expert and courteous head of the Charleston Society Library; to Robert L. Meriwether and J. G. De Roulhac Hamilton, who have made the collections at the Universities of South Carolina and North Carolina so valuable; to Stanley Pargellis, head of the Newberry Library, and Paul Angle, head of the Chicago Historical Society; to Kirke Mechem of the Kansas State Historical Library; to W. J. Van Schreeven of the Virginia State Archives; and to St. George L. Sioussat and Solon J. Buck of the Library of Congress.

New York, May 15, 1950.

ALLAN NEVINS

CONTENTS

ILLUSTRATIONS

The Emergence of Lincoln

Moods, Attitudes, and Leaders

WHEN AN explorer on an unknown river finds the current quickening under his boat, hears a faint but increasing roar, and sees above the farthest treetops a mist of spray, he knows that he is nearing a cataract. Yet if he is bold, if his craft is strong, and if on a prosperous voyage he has already shot other foaming rapids with success, he may push blithely into the unknown, confident that he can override all dangers.

A bold temperament, a blithe outlook—these we can better understand if we glance at the exuberant American nation in the mid-century.

Few decades in our history are more easily misinterpreted than that between the Compromise of 1850 and the election of Lincoln. An excessive emphasis on politics has led most observers to regard the period too exclusively as one of turmoil and uncertainty. It is true that the mounting antislavery agitation and the problems left by the Mexican War had brought the republic into white waters of political peril. Yet, in any broad view, the period stands conspicuous for a peaceful growth and prosperity greater than any that Americans had previously seen. All the territorial gains of the past decade were being consolidated. The dazzled nation, when the fifties began, was just beginning to realize that it held a permanent frontage on the Pacific and was neighbor to the Orient. By 1860, California had become one of the wealthiest of the States; Oregon had fixed her star in the flag; a frenzied horde of miners (with sober settlers on their heels) had made the name of Colorado familiar. From Montana glaciers to New Mexican deserts, sharp-eyed prospectors were scattering into a thousand mountain pockets. Minnesota, her wheatfields waving red, had pushed into the Union; while the farmers of Kansas were knocking at the door. The industrial revolution was gaining momentum in the North. The South exulted in the apparently insatiable demand of the world for its staples.

This was a more restless period than any before known. The energy of the fast-growing population channeled itself into countless outlets—business, trade, politics, reform, religion, letters, art. But the thrust was strongest toward materialistic objects. Already lusty and opulent, the nation instinctively reached for

3

greater strength and greater riches. Walt Whitman was soon to define in *Democratic Vistas* the two grand preparation stages of America, and to emphasize the fact that the country was in the midst of the second. The first had been "the planning and putting on record the political foundation rights of immense masses of people;" the second (in which these masses were now healthfully immersed) was the creation of "material prosperity, wealth, produce, labor-saving machines, iron, cotton, local, State, and continental railways, intercommunication and trade with all lands, steamships, mining, general employment, organization of great cities, cheap appliances for comfort, numberless technical schools, books, newspapers. . . ."

Critics complained that the land was much too materialistic, too intent on selfish aggrandizement. "We speculate how to get rich; we build railroads and ships, to increase our stores; we spy out the neighboring lands which promise us luxurious harvests hereafter"—so exclaimed a writer in *Putnam's Magazine* in the fall of 1855.[1] Once men had dreamed of a high destiny for the young land, fresh and unpolluted from the hand of its Creator; now, he wrote, the spirit of Timour-Mammon was in the ascendent. But such reflections, however natural to a cultivated New Yorker, did not occur to citizens of St. Paul and Sacramento, which had not existed when the Mexican War ended and were thriving towns in 1860; they did not occur to hustlers who lifted Michigan during the decade to third place in iron ore production; they did not occur to the speculators and toilers who created a new industry in Pennsylvania petroleum. These men were too busy to worry about Timour-Mammon. No such reflections occurred to the Southerners who knew the arguments of David Christy's *Cotton Is King* without reading the book, and who agreed that the $200,000,000 cotton crop of 1858–59 was an indispensable pillar of world economy. "Take from New York, or Boston, or Philadelphia, for one month, Southern exports and Southern trade, and widespread ruin and disaster would follow." [2]

The sunshine of economic prosperity bathed the country throughout the decade, as indeed it bathed the whole Western World. If one brief panic occurred, it was little more than the reaction against too reckless an advance. Great Britain, with her middle classes established in full power, her technological revolution almost completed, and the Peel-Russell system of free trade benefiting manufacturers, merchants, and consumers alike, was enjoying one of the golden ages of her history. Her wealth and prestige had never been greater. Louis Napoleon, proclaiming at Bordeaux in 1852, "L'Empire, c'est la paix," was developing railways, canals, and harbors, half-rebuilding Paris and other cities, encouraging iron mills and textile factories, and by other ostentatious activities assuring

1 *Putnam's Magazine,* "The Kansas Question," October, 1855.
2 New Orleans *Picayune,* September 10, 1859.

employment to artisans and shopkeepers. Prussia and Bavaria, which witnessed an astonishing multiplication of business corporations in this decade, were beginning the creation of industrial Germany. Gold from California and Australia helped force the draught of economic activity. Even the brief wars in which Napoleon, Cavour, and Victor Emmanuel so blithely embarked did something to stimulate production and trade in America.

Vast numbers of people in the Western nations were acquiring wealth; and, in Europe and the United States alike, prosperity bred self-confidence, and egotism engendered an aggressive temper. It was not difficult to measure the arrogance of the British ruling classes which, under the leadership of Palmerston, supported war in the Crimea, applauded Lord Elgin's capture of Peking, and avenged the Sepoy Mutiny, while the arrogance of the French bourgeoisie and the gilt-and-tinsel nobility of the Second Empire was written large in Napoleon's exploits at Magenta and Solferino. Plenty of arrogance was always latent in Prussia. Nor was there any lack of self-assurance and arrogance in the United States. Many Northern businessmen, politicians, and lawyers—the Caleb Cushings, Ben Wades, and Zack Chandlers—after pushing to success in highly competitive fields, deemed themselves capable of solving any problem whatsoever. Their bumptiousness impressed foreign travelers; they were ready to teach the world.[3] Slaveholding planters and politicians meanwhile assured their section that it possessed a superior culture and gentility. Such men as John Slidell, Howell Cobb, and Robert Toombs believed the South the main support of the world's economy. Southerners took pride in Senator James H. Hammond's "Cotton is King" speech—a speech summarized in his boast in 1859 that they were "at this moment unquestionably the most prosperous people on earth, realizing ten to twenty per cent on their capital with every prospect of doing as well for a long time to come;" [4] and their consciousness of material success made them stubbornly insistent on having their own way.

In a period of expansion and explosion, this hardening of temper, this strutting egotism of the self-made and newly rich, carried distinct dangers. Both North and South, large bodies of pushing, successful men were more ready to bluff their way, spurn compromises, and trust to luck than if times had been sterner and failure more frequent. The principal reason why a different outlook was needed lay in the dangerous divisions of the land.

3 Hear D. W. Mitchell on the Northerner: "His mind is always at work, engaged seriously on something useful or profitable; and he wears himself out with unceasing anxious thought about gaining and saving. . . . The most serious faults in his character are too much thought of his own personal independence and dignity, too much jealousy of any superiority, and an unduly excited pride and ambition." *Ten Years in the United States* (1862), pp. 194, 195.

4 James Hammond to W. G. Simms, April 22, 1859, Hammond Papers, LC.

[I]

Silently and irresistibly, the ferments released by the materialistic forces of the time were emphasizing the differences among the three great American sections, the East, Northwest, and South. The industrial revolution was well advanced in the East. From the Penobscot to the Potomac, railroads were scarring the fields, factories banking the streams, streets of offices replacing village lanes. A proletariat, largely immigrant, was being created. The sensational cheap press, the ward boss, the rooming houses and parochial schools, the saloon, the labor union, the baseball nine, the slum, all furnished tokens of a novel culture. Radical leaders, especially after the panic of 1857, were lifting demands for new economic rights, the freedoms earlier preached by William Leggett, George Henry Evans, and Elizur Wright. In New England and the North Atlantic States, the great middle class of yeomen farmers, village artisans and storekeepers, and small professional men was still solidly in control of affairs; but this body was increasingly conscious of the growing number of unpropertied, unrooted, and restless wage earners.

While Atlantic coastal communities were yielding to urbanization and the mill whistle, the sway of the frontier in other parts of the half-empty continent was being extended. The great West, a beckoning terrain in which freemen might plant their farms and shops, was in many essential traits precisely what the West had been since colonial days. It was a region of plentiful opportunity and general prosperity, with unrestrained individual energy, much speculative optimism, faith in the common man (and woman), stubborn insistence on political and social equality, and strong national loyalties. Yet the West was changing. It developed primary and even secondary industries with astonishing rapidity, so that by 1860 many communities from Milwaukee to Cincinnati, from Quincy to Ashtabula, were becoming fairly homogeneous with the factory cities of Pennsylvania and Massachusetts. The second or third generation farmer in the West was much more conscious than his father of the importance of foreign markets. Farming for profit, not subsistence, he was more of a businessman and more alert to see his margin of profit defended. Railways, speedy mails, cheap periodicals, and lyceums placed the Hoosier township in the heart of progressive nineteenth century culture.

The egalitarian radicalism of the frontier had always possessed a strong kinship with the radicalism of the town-bred worker. A highly democratic temper marked the farm and village population of the upper Mississippi Valley in these years. This body of Americans was not at all revolutionary-minded; rather it was distinctly moderate on economic and political issues. Yet it felt itself in the forefront of an advancing western civilization, it disliked aristocratic stratifications, and it was impatient with outworn and obsolescent ideas. The *Prairie Farmer* of John S. Wright well expressed the temper of the Northwest. It carried on incessant campaigns against land speculation, dishonest produce grading, and poor roads. It demanded crop diversification, soil analysis, and better farm implements. It proclaimed its belief in a democratic population of small landholders busy making the most creative use possible of their acres. Farmers of the Middle West might indict slavery mildly as Wright did, or attack it sternly as his fellow leader Jonathan B. Turner did; but all were instinctively hostile to the great planters of the South.[5]

Though the South was by no means static in any absolute sense, it seemed so by comparison with the North and West. The basic elements of its economic life were merely soil, climate, and low-skilled labor. While large bodies of farmers in the border regions and uplands closely resembled their Northwestern brethren, in plantation areas the way of life was hostile to variegation and progress. The ruling class of Southerners (and it was a *class*) clung to the aristocratic and conservative ideals which the North and West instinctively disliked. As Northern capital, technology, and labor-saving machinery forced the pace of industry, the gulf between the sections grew deeper. Those who crossed the Potomac felt they were entering a foreign land. According to his predilections, the traveler might pronounce one side or the other superior; he might agree or disagree with De Tocqueville, who had found the Kentucky bank of the Ohio River ill-populated and half-tilled, while the Northern shore was marked by abundant harvests, elegant dwellings, and the confused hum of industry;[6] he might discover more taste and charm among the slaveholders; but the essential fact was the difference. It grew from year to year. Like the differences between the industrial and rural areas of England depicted in Mrs. Gaskell's *North and South*, it created two sharply divergent populations; the people (when the novelists came to discover them) of Thomas Nelson Page and George W. Cable on one side, and of Howells and Hamlin Garland on the other.

Numerous exceptions to the rule of sectional contrast, and many cross-currents in the broad flow of tendencies, could of course be noted.

Democratic change was by no means wholly victorious in the North, where

5 "I know, and you know, that a revolution has begun. Twenty Senators and a hundred Representatives proclaim in Congress today, sentiments and opinions, and principles of freedom, which hardly so many men, even in this free State, dared to utter in their homes twenty years ago. While the Government of the United States has been all that time surrendering one plain and castle after another to slavery, the people of the United States have been no less steadily and perseveringly gathering together all the forces with which to recover back again all the fields, and all the castles, which have been lost." Seward's Rochester speech, 1858 (*Works*, II, 352).

6 De Tocqueville, *Democracy*, Part 1, Ch. 18.

powerful conservative and aristocratic elements could be found. A landed gentry flourished in the valleys of the Hudson, Genesee, and Susquehanna. In Boston, New York, and Philadelphia the merchant groups were inveterately cautious. From these, and from the new founders of industrial dynasties, millionaires were emerging. Already proud mansions were numerous in the Northern cities. Meanwhile, moderate public men of the type of Edward Everett, Rufus Choate, Hamilton Fish, and John A. Dix strove to prevent the new wine from splitting the old bottles. The North had important elements which preferred the good old ways and the aristocratic approach, which tacitly disliked egalitarianism and the consent-of-the-governed theory, and which took a chilly attitude toward talk of reforms and rights.

Again, in parts of the South, frontier radicalism was as strong as on the borders of Iowa and Wisconsin. Albert Gallatin Brown championed the small farmers of southern and eastern Mississippi against the planting interest of the river country. Reform had its intrepid champions like Daniel R. Goodloe of North Carolina, Cassius M. Clay of Kentucky, and "Parson" Brownlow of Tennessee, while the non-slaveholding whites found numerous voices for their discontent—Hinton Rowan Helper's was only the loudest.

The political and social psychology of the city masses in the North, and especially the Irish and Germans who fell naturally into the Democratic Party, offered an interesting field for study. The followers of Fernando Wood in New York, for example, tenement dwellers without culture or capital, toilers given a reckless temper by their harsh struggle for bread, immigrants resentful of the airs and ease of the richer classes, tended to align themselves against the conservative forces of the North. Yet, just because they hated many features of their environment, they were ready to join hands with aristocratic Southern leaders. Rejecting one form of privilege, they accepted alliance with another.

While confusion, conflict, and incongruity were to be found in every section, and while it would be a fatal error to personify North, South, and West with any idea that they represented unified and unchanging entities, the gulf between free-labor and slave-labor societies was real and deep. What Turner has said of the frontier West was true of the South; it was "a form of society rather than an area." Its special psychology, traditions, and principles ran far back into history. The doctrines of the Virginia school on State Rights and strict construction, crystallized by Madison and Jefferson in the Resolutions of 1798–99, continued to find a wide acceptance. The Richmond *South* affirmed in 1857 that these tenets were still as popular in theory as when first expounded, though in practice they commanded less observance; and the hostile *National Intelligencer* agreed that this was so. Many Southerners felt a deep-seated injury in the "centralizing" tendencies of the national government, and in a long succession of measures enacted since Hamilton had prepared his *Report on Manufactures.*[7] Calhoun's literary executor, R. K. Crallé, and ex-Governor Hammond in 1857 stirred up the Southern Rights Associations of the various slaveholding States to lay before Congress a detailed list of the acts which had operated injuriously on the interests and security of the section; and it was with Hamilton that they began.[8] Aggrieved elements in the South, conscious of their peculiar character and interests, had considered radical action in 1798, more radical action in 1832, and still more radical action in 1850. A belief that consolidated power spelt danger had become deeply ingrained.

North and South had always, from early colonial days, found difficulty in understanding each other. William Byrd of Virginia and John Winthrop of Massachusetts Bay had approached life from totally different points of view. By 1830 the divergent psychologies of the two sections presented the most serious obstacles to mutual comprehension. What an Alabamian meant by "liberty" and "democracy" was something very different from what a New Yorker meant by those terms. The Southerner's liberty was more restricted, and his democracy had to be reconciled with a more patrician leadership. "Self-government" had connotations in the Illinois of Lincoln and Douglas quite unlike those it carried in the South Carolina of Calhoun and Pickens.

Perhaps the word "Union," which a European might have supposed could have but one meaning, best illustrated the differences in state of mind. The Yankee and the Westerner thought of the Union with the high emotional fervor which they had learned from Daniel Webster. They thrilled to the term with an intense spirit of nationality, a passionate attachment to the republic as a whole, a conviction that the people must stand as a unit in defense of national honor and freedom. If Union died, liberty died with it. Jackson, Webster, Benton, and Clay had inculcated an ideal of the Union which imparted a grand devotion to the uprising of the North in 1861. The dominant elements of the Lower South held quite a different conception. Their Union had to be yoked with State Rights; it was, next to their sectional liberties, most dear. As a Southern publicist put it, they clung to Calhoun's definition of the Union: "a peculiar association in which sovereign States were held by high considerations of good faith; by the exchanges of equity and comity; by the noble attractions of social order; by the enthused sympathies of a common destiny of power, honor, and renown." [9]

Naturally, the South thought of itself more and more as a separate nation. By 1857 it *was* in many ways a separate nation. Had secession been crowned with success, historians would have said what John Adams wrote of American

7 Richmond *South*, quoted in *National Intelligencer*, April 30, 1857.
8 R. K. Crallé, Columbia, S. C., to Hammond, December 4, 1857; Hammond Papers, LC.
9 Edward A. Pollard, *The Lost Cause*, 52, 53.

withdrawal from the Empire, that separation was a fact before fighting began. Many Northerners wished to recognize the separation. "So perish all compromises with tyranny!" exclaimed Garrison as at Framingham on July 4, 1854, he burned a copy of the Constitution; and he ceaselessly proclaimed in the *Liberator* that but one honest course was open—"The Union must be dissolved!" Southern radicals talked of the South as if it were another Holland under the Spaniards, another Lombardy under the Austrians. "Ireland *would* be free and independent, if she *could*," wrote one of Senator Hammond's Charleston friends; "the South *could* be, if she *would*. It is because of this opinion, that I would urge the straight and open policy of Disunion, and on its general merits. I only want a pretext to announce and enter upon it—such would be the election of an Abolitionist or protectionist." [10]

The extent to which the South cherished the ideal of separate nationality was demonstrated in the resolutions of the Southern Commercial Convention which met at Savannah in the month following Buchanan's election. Not merely did this body call for direct trade with Europe in place of the "triangular trade" which had enriched New York, and for the construction by the Southern States and Territories of a railroad from the Mississippi by way of El Paso to the Pacific; not merely did it urge the Kentucky legislature to build the final Louisville-Cumberland Gap link in the railroads connecting the Potomac and Mississippi: the Convention went far beyond such measures. It wanted Southern ships built in Southern yards, and Southern seamen trained in large numbers by Southern States. It created a committee of Southern scholars, including William Holmes McGuffey, Augustus Baldwin Longstreet, the historian Gayarré, and the scientist Joseph LeConte, to prepare a series of distinctively Southern texts in every department of study, which Southern legislatures might then order used in the schools. It asked for the encouragement of Southern periodicals, books, and institutions of learning. It exhorted the States to see to the establishment of foundries for casting artillery and arsenals for the manufacture of arms—for the South was to be armed as a separate nation. In the same spirit, it directed Southern Representatives in Congress to inquire whether their States had received due quotas of arms, and to see to it that Southern ports were amply equipped for defense.[11]

Gradually, upon many Southern eyes, had dawned the splendid vision of a republic stretching from Cape Hatteras to the Gulf of California, a nation with a future boundless as the hopes of its people. The South that had produced Washington, Jefferson, and Marshall, whose sons had generally held the Presidency, the chief justiceship, and the control of the Senate, would surely con-

10 John Cuningham to Hammond, Charleston, April 18, 1859; Hammond Papers, LC.
11 *Proceedings*, December, 1856; pamphlet, 48 pp.

tinue to exhibit a rich political genius. This new republic would have a historical tradition, a culture, and an economy all its own. Under the bright sun of independence its dormant gifts would quicken into life. Its harbors would nourish a vigorous commerce, its capital would make laws suiting its peculiar conditions, and its wealth would go to developing its own resources. Architects greater than Latrobe, sculptors more talented than Clark Mills, authors more original than Poe and Simms, orators transcending Henry and Calhoun would arise to express its spiritual greatness. Let the latent energies of the South find outlets under the spur of nationalism—let it show what a defiant people could accomplish. A record equalling that of Greece under Pericles and England under Elizabeth might be written by the free and happy people whose domain embraced the plantations of Virginia and South Carolina, the pine-shaded savannahs of Georgia, the bluegrass farms of Kentucky, the mountains and waterfalls of Tennessee, the iron and coal mines of Alabama, the sugar-cane fields of Louisiana, and the cattle-dotted plains of Texas. Their past role in the political and military annals of America was ample guarantee for accomplishment in the future.

While the South had the dream, the North and West had realities. They had the steady growth of industrial power, which meant wealth and higher living standards; more immigration, and a faster increase in population; the wider areas suited to their free-labor system. The spirit of the modern world was reinforcing their demand for the containment of slavery, which was sure to be followed by demands for its regulation or gradual elimination. For the nation as a whole, irresistible economic pressures were strengthening free society. Resist it as the South might, the movement for tariffs, free homesteads, agricultural education, internal improvements, and a better banking system could not long be withstood; halt the thrust one year, and the next it had enhanced force. By 1860 it was plain that if the country held together, every forward step would strengthen the free society as against the slave society.

[II]

Among the manifold causes of division or divergence of interest—tariffs, public lands, ship subsidies, internal improvements, immigration, the Pacific railroad, Federal powers—the issue of slavery remained fundamental. Could the problems of the labor system and racial adjustment in the South have been solved, all other discords might have proved transient. Year by year the slavery question intensified the conflict, increased the misunderstanding, and heightened the prejudice. By the eighteen-fifties the aura of emotion which surrounded it was so dense that no one could view it without distortion. The emotion was compounded of many elements—suspicion, contempt, anger, but above all fear. In many quarters both North and South it had generated a mass hysteria. No comprehension of the later fifties is possible unless we realize that this emotional tension, this hysteria, magnified every incident to portentous size.

Each side, according to its convictions, was right. The South thought slavery a positive good—and in one sense it *was* a positive good. The Negro was better off on a well-managed Southern holding than anywhere else on earth; better off than in Africa, the West Indies, Brazil, or (arguably) some free-Negro settlements of the North. "Oh, dey ain't no place in de worl' like Ole Virginny for niggers, massa," an intelligent sailor-slave told Olmsted.[12] The North thought slavery a positive evil—and except as a transitional status, it *was* a positive evil. The essence of the dispute between the two sections may be found in Robert Toombs's statement of 1856 in Tremont Temple, Boston. "The white is the superior race," said Toombs, "and the black the inferior; and subordination, with or without law, will be the status of the African in this mixed society; and, therefore, it is in the interests of both, and especially of the black race, and of the whole society, that this status should be fixed, controlled, and protected by law."[13] Most Southerners regarded this as unanswerable logic. Most Northerners would have declared that the moment the major premise, the assumption of racial inferiority, was disproved, the argument collapsed; and even accepting the premise, the question was, *what* status? A fixed status, or an evolutionary status? The latter alone was tolerable.

Logic counted for little, however, in the prevalent hysteria. A deep sense of crisis now pervaded the air. Emotion not merely magnified every collision; it made recurrent collisions inevitable. The Brooks-Sumner assault, the Lecompton battle, the John Brown raid were essentially symptoms, not detached realities. To fasten attention primarily upon them would be as erroneous as to fancy that the rocks in the bed of the Niagara rapids, throwing spray into the air, are the primary force rather than the weight of water pouring torrentially down the gorge. Fundamental loyalties are always a matter of emotion; and these were now so challenged as to create in both North and South a sharp sense of fear— fear among Northerners that slavery would be made universal, fear among Southerners that four million slaves would be suddenly freed amid such scenes of violence and rapine as Haiti had witnessed.

The slaveholding States, a Southern woman resident in Philadelphia wrote in 1851, were slumbering upon a volcano. "It is a truth; every day's information, every paper you take up, teems with the same news—the constant warfare

12   F. L. Olmsted, *A Journey through the Seaboard Slave States*, 107.
13   W. W. Brewton, *The Son of Thunder*, gives the entire lecture of Toombs on slavery, 218-249.

against us from North, East, West; and all the haters, too, they are sending their inflamed missiles against us; all, all about slavery and the slave bill. What are we to do if the South goes on sleeping?" Five years later, even though Buchanan had just been elected, Governor James H. Adams of South Carolina anticipated Seward by declaring the conflict irrepressible:

Slavery and Freesoilism can never be reconciled. Our enemies have been defeated—not vanquished. A majority of the free States have declared war against the South, upon a purely sectional issue, and in the remainder of them, formidable minorities fiercely contended for victory under the same banner. The triumph of this geographical party must dissolve the confederacy, unless we are prepared to sink down into a state of acknowledged inferiority. We will act wisely to employ the interval of repose afforded by the late election, in earnest preparation for the inevitable conflict. The Southern States have never demanded more than equality and security. They cannot submit to less, and remain in the Union, without dishonor and ultimate ruin.[14]

The violence of 1856 in Washington and in Kansas propagated a feeling that violence might soon become general. That common-sense Yankee, Henry Wilson, telling a friend early the next year of the constant threats offered him, said he never left his lodging to go to his Senate seat without wondering whether his papers were arranged as he should wish if he were never to return alive.[15] Wendell Phillips had thought just after the passage of the Kansas-Nebraska Act that the aggressive Slave Power was now in full control of the government. It would seize Cuba within a year or two, annex Mexico within five, and attempt to reopen the slave trade. Indeed, the future unfolded a vast slave empire united with Brazil and darkening the whole Western Hemisphere. Only one remedy existed—disunion: "it is now with nine-tenths only a question of time."[16] Theodore Parker was soon to tell Bostonians that the time had gone by when the great American question of the nineteenth century could be settled without bloodshed, while Thomas Wentworth Higginson was to ask concerning slavery: "Is it destined, as it began in blood, so to end? Seriously and solemnly I say, it seems as if it were."[17] The continuous intensification of fear and hatred came out horrifyingly in the letters exchanged by Lydia Maria Child and Governor Henry A. Wise just after John Brown's raid in 1859. Mrs. Child wrote scathingly of the "slave oligarchy" and its "continual success in aggression," while Wise assured her that he would not let Virginians insult even a woman "who whetted knives of butchery for our mothers, sisters, daughters, and babes."[18]

14 James H. Adams, *Governor's Message*, November 24, 1856.
15 *Letters of Lydia Maria Child*, 88, 89.
16 F. J. and W. P. Garrison, *Wm. Lloyd Garrison*, III, 410–412.
17 *Ibid.*, 472; T. W. Higginson, May 11, 1858; Theodore Parker, May 26, 1858.
18 *Letters of Lydia Maria Child*, 103–116.

The Slave Power, the Freesoil Power—each feared the other, and each mistook defensive postures for aggression. The question of the ultimate source of political power was obviously involved, and it presented a fundamental issue. Edmund Ruffin spoke for a multitude of apprehensive slaveholders when in the spring of 1857 he predicted that Kansas would soon come in free, that other Territories would hold the same complexion, and that, probably within twenty years, three-fourths of the States would be freesoil. Slavery would then be extinguished either directly or indirectly. The North had no such apprehension that increasing population and wealth would make its enemies irresistible. Its fear was that the South, already holding undisputed possession of the official strongholds of government, directing the Executive, managing the Legislative, and keeping in reserve the Judicial department, would continue to rule by intimidation and manipulation—and would use its power in reckless territorial expansion. Charles Francis Adams, a man as moderate as he was shrewd, told the South in 1855 just why his section was deeply worried:

This slave power consists, in fact, of about three hundred and fifty thousand active men, spreading over a large territorial surface, commanding the political resources of fifteen States directly, and, through their connections, materially affecting those of five or six more. These persons, and all their numerous friends and dependents, in and out of the slaveholding region, are held together in interest by a common bond, in the sum of two thousand million dollars worth of what they consider property. For the sake of protecting this against the prevailing tendencies of the age, and the effect of public sentiment created by a large body of their own countrymen, it is impossible that they should escape adopting a system of policy aggressive upon the rights of the freemen. They become, in their action, to all intents and purposes, men of one idea. This idea necessarily includes the extension of their own power, whether they are sensible of its influence in that direction or not. They throw into the public councils their allotted portion of representatives, all equally pledged to be faithful to it, whatever they may think upon other subjects. The unity of policy thus secured for all the time spreads its influence far beyond the limits of its own circle. It is always at hand to wield an umpirage in its own favor, between the contending factions and the rival aspirations of prominent statesmen of the free states. It never relaxes in its vigilance over public events. It never is turned aside by the temptation of an incidental pursuit. The sense of danger overrides every other consideration. Around it have been arrayed, for its protection, alike the conservative and the destructive elements of society in the free States—the richest and the poorest class, the best citizens and the worst: the former from an instinctive dread of anything that looks like an attack upon prescriptive rights to property; the latter from an adhesion to the superiority of caste, the more tenacious by reason of the sense of self-degradation in every other particular.

In addition to all this, it must be admitted that the best abilities of the people in the slaveholding region are enlisted in the defence of their rights. There is no path to distinction but that of public life, and that path leads but one way.

Literature, science, and mechanical invention lag far behind, relatively to the progress they make elsewhere. Commerce and navigation are managed by the citizens of the free States; agriculture, by the slaves. With slaveholders, the mind must either lie fallow in sensuality and indolence, or it must seek its exercise in politics directed to one end—the support of slavery. As a consequence, the representation of the slave power in the federal councils becomes one of more than average capacity, of trained experience, of substantial harmony in the adaptation of means to ends, and last, but not least, of quite flexible public morality.[19]

That Adams's arguments possessed force was admitted by some Southerners. A Louisiana planter who contributed to *De Bow's Review* in 1856 an article deprecating the "artificial" Southern passion of fear and excitement, denied, in correspondence with De Bow, that all the aggression was on the other side. "Well—admit the two millions interested in slavery—shall they give the law to the other twenty-odd millions? Are not the rights of majorities as sacred as those of minorities?" [20] This planter represented the capitalist and conservative groups which, in both sections, were ready to resist terroristic movements and confess that the great issue had two sides. But as the years slipped by, the issue of ultimate political authority grew more burning. In the final paroxysm of 1860–61, large bodies of Southerners were filled with frenzy at the idea that a hostile Freesoil Power, already seizing control of Presidency and House, might soon gain the Senate, the Judiciary, and a sufficient number of States to pass constitutional amendments. Large bodies of Northerners were grimly implacable in resisting the idea that a compact Slave Power could continue to nullify their numerical majority, and could retain the opportunity of expanding their institutions over wide Caribbean domains. Fear was largely the product of ignorance, and ignorance—or misinformation—largely the product of propaganda.

Two stereotypes were created. Readers of even moderate Northern newspapers found them full of articles on Southern aggressions in Kansas, Southern filibustering enterprises against Cuba and Nicaragua, Southern domination in Washington, and Southern cruelties to slaves. Readers of even moderate journals in the South found them full of items about Northern slums and poverty, Northern exploitations of immigrant labor, Northern incitations to slave revolts, Northern aggressions in Washington and Kansas, and Northern desire to reduce the South to a fiefdom. Little thinking of the time was a process of reasoning from fact-buttressed premises to logical conclusions. Anybody who measures the political conduct of the fifties from such a premise is bound to be as confused as if he were a believer in Ptolemaic astronomy making careful observations of the Copernican heavens. The thinking was largely irrational, governed

19 C. F. Adams, "What Makes Slavery a Matter of National Concern?" Lecture in New York, January 30, 1855, pamphlet.
20 R. B. Brashear, February 8, 1856; De Bow Papers, Duke University.

by subconscious memories, frustrated desires, and the distortions of politicians and editors.

When L. W. Spratt reported to the Southern Commercial Convention at Montgomery in 1858 in favor of reopening the slave trade, he argued that the North already had one more State than the South; that it had six million more people; that not only was its native increase far larger, but it gained hundreds of thousands of immigrants each year; and that without some drastic preventive, it would soon control the fortunes of the South. Northern commentators promptly raised their own cries of fear. The South, they said, having won the right by the Nebraska Act and Dred Scott decision to carry Negroes into the Territories, now wished the slave trade so that she might fill the West with Africans and gain a permanent national ascendancy. Each section saw the other as a wanton attacker, itself as an heroic defender.[21]

"Take an extreme case," wrote the editor of the Nashville *Union and American* in 1859. "Take a South Carolina fire-eater who declares himself ready for disunion and the establishing of a Southern Confederacy rather than submit to the unconstitutional wrongs and aggressions of the North, and what is his offence compared with that of the filthy, fanatical abolitionist, who, regardless of all right and justice, is seeking to *usurp* the control of the government, destroy the equality of the States, and trample in the dust the sacred guarantees of the Constitution? The extremist of the South errs upon policy in resisting oppression. The abolitionist in the North violates a principle of right, justice, and the Constitution." With equal sincerity, the editor of the Warsaw (Illinois) *Bulletin* was accusing the South of grasping at Kansas, seeking to seize Cuba, and smuggling in thousands of slaves. "The South is not satisfied with what she is fairly entitled to under the Constitution. She wants more. She aspires to nothing short of absolute supremacy. . . . On behalf of the interests of freedom, the Republicans in self-defense have been compelled to resist; and thus the contest will go on, until one or the other shall have achieved an undisputed supremacy." [22]

These stereotypes were steadily reinforced. Leaders on each side made frantic efforts to propagandize their own people. During the first five months of the Congressional session of 1857–58, with its critical battle over the Kansas constitution, Senators of the free States franked out six hundred and eight thousand speeches, Senators of the slaveholding States one hundred and thirty thousand. And each side paid inadequate attention to the views of the other section. In the North, few men ever saw *Russell's*, *De Bow's*, and other Southern maga-

21 Spratt's report is in *De Bow's Review*, June, 1858. On the danger of exaggerating the rational element in human affairs, see Graham Wallas's *Human Nature in Politics* (3rd ed., 1921).
22 *Union and American*, July 31, 1859; *Bulletin*, July 28, 1859.

zines; still fewer had the liberality of outlook which Lincoln showed in sub-
scribing for the Charleston *Mercury* and Richmond *Inquirer* to learn their
opinions. As for the South, it lay under two great tabus, criticism of slavery and
displays of religious heterodoxy being equally debarred.

A considerable freedom of thought existed in the North, where many Democrats expounded Southern political ideas and Bishop John H. Hopkins and
Charles O'Conor freely defended slavery. Opinion was much more restricted
in the South. Illiteracy, political agitation, and the "black terror" or alleged
danger of servile insurrection were deterrents to freedom of discussion. In
South Carolina, wrote B. F. Perry, Calhoun had "thought for the State and
crushed out all independence of thought in those below him." A Southern
bishop, H. B. Whipple, declared that illiteracy rendered the masses the "dupes"
of designing politicians, the ignorant being obviously more fanatical than the
well-read. Most Southern States had laws which made it a penal offense to circulate any newspaper, pamphlet, or handbill having a tendency to excite discontent among the slaves. Under such a law, even in Maryland a colored minister
was sentenced to ten years in prison in 1857 for possessing a copy of *Uncle
Tom's Cabin*. Humboldt complained that, while his *Political Essays on the
Island of Cuba* was freely read in Madrid, it could not be purchased in the
United States except with the deletion of all passages condemnatory of slavery.[23]

No iron curtain separated the two sections. Travel was free. Southerners by
tens of thousands read Harriet Beecher Stowe, while Northerners discussed the
Southern polemics. But a gauze curtain did exist, more opaque on the Southern
side than the Northern, distorting the vision of all who tried to peer through.

Basically, the struggle lay between two radically different assumptions. The
Northern freesoilers assumed that slavery was morally, socially, and economically wrong, and must therefore be presently circumscribed and ultimately dissolved. The Southern majority assumed that slavery was morally right, economically profitable, and socially indispensable, and must therefore be protected
and allowed to expand. Each side defended its assumption with full conviction
of right. To many Northerners it seemed monstrous that a great people could
believe slaveholding ethical. To many Southerners it seemed equally monstrous
that a great people could forget how recently the North had held slaves, over-
look the immense benefits the Negro had received on American soil, and ignore
the terrible problem of racial readjustment if black men were hastily freed. This
last consideration cut very deep, for many Southerners would readily have
admitted that slavery was unfortunate if they had known what racial controls

23 Clement Eaton, *Freedom of Thought in the Old South*, *passim*; N. Y. *Weekly Tribune*,
May 22, 1858, for franking of Congressional speeches; *ibid.*, June 5, 1850, for Humboldt's
letter. The Maryland statute under which the minister was sentenced is in *Md. Laws of
1835*, Ch. 325.

to put in its place. The South in 1860 had a slave population of 3,949,557. The States of Georgia, Alabama, and Mississippi each had between 435,000 and 465,000 slaves. What helpful steps did the North propose to take in assisting the South to release this ignorant, penniless, and perhaps unruly horde? Massachusetts had a white population about twice as great as Georgia's; for how many liberated Negroes would the Bay State offer homes, employment, and cultural facilities? The answer is that no help whatever was either asked or offered.

In this sectional conflict, as Lincoln said, a crisis had to be reached and passed. The danger point of the crisis would be at hand when one side realized that it must break up the Union, or admit that its basic assumption was no longer tenable. By the late eighteen-fifties, all the forces of the time indicated that the South would have to make this fateful choice. The election of a Republican President, sure to come sooner or later, was the crisis that would have to be reached and passed. If the South reconciled itself to the idea of a Republican Administration, it tacitly accepted the idea that slavery must be contained within the existing limits, and methods studied for its gradual supersedence. The ruling system of the South in 1857 was in the position of the ruling system of France in 1785, or Russia in 1910; it had time for a few more decisions, but it had to think fast and think courageously. A failure to make a decision would be as fatal as an error in deciding.

Yet when the situation demanded the utmost seriousness of thought both North and South, the quarrel over slavery, State Rights, and ultimate power was rendered doubly dangerous by an irresponsible levity among politicians and people. Posturing and finessing were never more recklessly used by leaders than in this period. Senator Hammond, looking about Washington in 1859, found few men who thought for a moment of the good of the country, the maintenance of the Constitution, or even of justice. Shams, filibustering, and crass maneuvering for advantage, he wrote, were the order of the day. "We are not rushing so fast to disunion, as we are to utter anarchy—*at once*." Many a lover of national concord echoed this observation. The genial essayist Donald Grant Mitchell, writing from Connecticut to his Virginia friend, A. Dudley Mann, declared that he would tenfold rather see the country become two distinct nations than continue listening to the mad abuse. "Has it not come to this, that with you a man must villify the North to gain applause and place; and with us, it is equally essential that a politician must depreciate and calumniate the South?" Rufus Choate, Edward Everett, and Hamilton Fish in one section, William Cabell Rives, W. A. Graham, and John Bell in the other, found that a man who undertook to defend conservative positions lost most of his influence. Rives wrote Washington Hunt of New York in 1859 that too many politicians were inflaming public opinion by taking extreme stands on slavery, that the issue was being used to divert attention from flagrant corruptions, and that if this demagogy were not stopped, disaster would ensue. But what could he do? [24]

Levity was equally evident in the popular attitude toward the price of disunion. Americans had never fought a really bloody war. The only conflict which most men recalled, that against Mexico, had furnished drama, heroism, and solid national gains at an absurdly cheap price. As the crisis deepened, both sections indulged the delusion that peace could always be preserved, while if by bad luck it were broken, the struggle would be brief. Northern men thought that slaveholders who talked secession were raising the old cry of Wolf! Wolf! and that the sight of a bayonet would quiet this bluffing. Southern men thought with the editor, J. D. B. De Bow, that the North could not make war for three good reasons: it lived by Southern trade, and would submit to anything rather than lose these profits; it had no means to make war except what it got by preying on the South; and its people were too divided, half of them taking the Southern side. Others believed that the Yankees were cowardly. They accepted Franklin Pierce's private assurances to Jefferson Davis that a Yankee army marching to attack the South would first have to fight a bloody battle with Northern Democrats. Disbelieving in the possibility of war, the two sections drifted into a position that made war unavoidable. But then war itself held no connotations grimmer than those of New Orleans or Palo Alto; a little gallant fighting, and the other side would give in.

In all periods of prolonged peace, the longing of hot-blooded elements for action, adventure, and power is translated into a readiness to spring to war. Not a little jingoism, to use a later term, might have been discerned in America of the fifties. For one evident reason, more of the lust for martial excitement was abroad in the slaveholding area than in the North. The industrial revolution drained off much of the restless demand of Yankee lads for risk and desperate effort. Young men like Rockefeller, Carnegie, Jay Cooke, and Collis P. Huntington had no need to think of the thunder of cannon and shock of charging cavalry. When war came, they were so busy harnessing the industrial forces of the land that it seemed an interruption of larger enterprises. The young blades growing up on Southern plantations and farms, however, found that politics and pioneering by no means occupied all their energies. Having a romantic bent, they romanticized war! Hence it was that Charles Francis Adams, Jr., living with his father in Washington in 1859–61, thought that a good many proud "Southrons"—Keitt, Porcher Miles, and Roger B. Pryor—were

24 Hammond to W. G. Simms, January 21, 1858, Hammond Papers, LC; D. G. Mitchell to Mann, August 15, 1858, Miscellaneous Files, Duke Univ.; Rives to Hunt, May 19, 1859, Rives Papers.

"spoiling for a fight." [25] As he says, they got their bellyful of it—and so did their opponents.

Basically, what light-hearted Northerners and Southerners lacked in regarding the grim face of Janus was imagination. If by some prevision the chief political leaders could have seen the four years of carnage, the million graves, and the devastation of broad States, they would have drawn back in horror. Could they have glimpsed for one minute the reeking field of Chancellorsville or Gettysburg, they would have acted far more responsibly. Hugh McCulloch writes that a Senator who visited the Wilderness at the close of the battle told him: "If that scene had been presented to me before the war commenced, anxious as I was for the preservation of the Union, I should have said, 'The cost is too great; erring sisters, go in peace.'" Secession had to be resisted; but it would never have occurred had Americans realized what a great war meant.

[III]

The divisions of the country bring us to the question of leadership. The sentiment of the American majority had never lain with the extremists. They had proved that fact in 1850 and 1852. They had proved it again in 1856, when all the Presidential candidates professed moderate principles, and Buchanan, Frémont, and Fillmore so divided the vote that the first-named fell far short of a majority. Where could the nation find the moderate and constructive leaders whom it wished to follow?

In the debate on Pierce's provocative final message in December, 1856, two radicals, Wade of Ohio and Mason of Virginia, hurled defiance at each other. The North was determined, said Wade, to confine slavery to the States where it existed, letting it into no Territory whatever. The South, averred Mason, would tolerate no interference with slavery in the Territories any more than in the States; and for that reason it had been ready, if Frémont had won the election, to break up the Union.[26] This exchange defined the immediate ground of difference. What path could possibly be found between these two opposed views, each powerful if not dominant in its section? The answer lay in mollification, reassurance, and delay. Time, however, was running short. "In the next four years is, I think, locked up the fate of the Union," wrote Jefferson Davis on April 9, 1857. "If the issues are boldly and properly met my hope is that the Constitution will prevail; if the attempt is made to postpone them the next Presidential election will probably bring us to the alternative of resistance to oppressive usurpation or the tame surrender of our birthright." [27]

25 C. F. Adams, Jr., *An Autobiography*, 44, 45; R. G. Osterweis, *Romanticism and Nationalism in the Old South*, 90–94.
26 *Cong. Globe*, 34th Cong., 3rd Sess., 16, 26, 27.
27 To E. De Leon, De Leon Papers, LC.

The hope of peaceful adjustment (for, despite fatalistic interpretations of history, in 1857 such a possibility existed) rested on the chance that statesman-like leaders would suppress immediate rancors, plead for patience, lay bare the immense difficulties of race adjustment which underlay the slavery issue, show that time was needed for dissolving them, and bring into the foreground those economic issues which were genuinely pressing. The enveloping national prosperity, the materialistic preoccupations of the people, and the rush of energy into continental development, would assist such leaders. Race adjustment, even though some bold initial steps were vital, was a task for generations. The Pacific railroad, the best use of public lands, a fair compromise between Hamiltonian and Jeffersonian schools on the tariff, and the promotion of scientific agriculture, were subjects of immediate urgency. Could the statesmanship be found which would trace a patient way between exigent and distant problems, teaching the electorate to take long views?

All government is a process of experimentation, full of errors and blind gropings; and the use of government to help evolve a new social and economic order, first in the border States and then in the Lower South, would have been a peculiarly delicate and dangerous matter. Still, it was conceivably not beyond the power of a nation which had produced the Revolutionary Fathers. The eminent Americans of the fifties offered a great variety of character and talent; to what men, if any, could the country look for a leadership paralleling that of its formative period?

On careful examination it becomes clear that the old-fashioned effort to put the leaders in this crisis into radical, moderate, and conservative groups is misleading. To be sure, in 1857 any astute observer would have said that Charles Sumner, Ben Wade, John P. Hale, and Zack Chandler, in the North, and Slidell, Toombs, Henry A. Wise, and R. B. Rhett, in the South, were radicals. He would have said that Seward, F. P. Blair, Sr., Lyman Trumbull, and Douglas, in the North, with Jefferson Davis, Judah P. Benjamin, R. M. T. Hunter, and Alexander H. Stephens, in the South, were moderates. He might fairly have termed J. J. Crittenden, Hamilton Fish, Lewis Cass, and Edward Bates conservatives. But such categories, subject to constant revision, are unenlightening. The essential questions with respect to any leader were three: Did he have a firm grasp on principles—on fundamental realities? Did he possess both tact and courage in supporting principles? Above all (and this was the supreme test before which nearly all failed) was he able to appeal to the nation's imagination, its idealism, its sense of a great historic mission?

Seward, short, rusty-looking, his face and head insignificant, his dress antiquated and badly cut, his only outward title to distinction his quickness of perception and heady flow of talk, possessed talents of a high order. Many thought him the first statesman of the land. He was beloved by all who knew him well;

those who saw his affectionate and unselfish deportment in his family circle, his genuine, hearty fellowship with his Auburn neighbors, who gathered about him as freely as the Marshfield farmers had collogued with Webster, were much impressed. His grasp of mind was unquestioned. Carl Schurz thought that he gave an impression of abilities never fully used, of possessing "hidden, occult powers which he could bring into play if he would." His courage had some-times been conspicuous. Modeling his public career on John Quincy Adams, whose life he had written, he could take large views of public affairs, a trait he had shown as a young governor in promoting public education and legal reform, and would show when an old Secretary of State in buying Alaska. He was an astute politician, quick to measure men at their true worth and subtle in using them. A man of magnanimous heart, he never exaggerated party differences, never sulked under failure (even when he lost the Presidential nomination in 1860), and never showed pettiness. When his constant opponent Jefferson Davis was ill, he was an assiduous and affectionate visitor. "Benjamin," Seward said, as the Louisiana Senator finished some vituperative remarks, "give me a cigar, and when your speech is printed send me a copy." [28] He was always full of talk, badinage, and kindly offices to others.[29] E. L. Godkin thought him in 1859 the best constitutional lawyer in the country, the least of a demagogue among public men, and the clearest-headed statesman.[30]

But Seward lacked the cardinal requisite of steady judgment. For one thing, he was deficient in tact, in sense of timing, and in verbal discretion, so that most people thought this wary politician rash, and many believed this moderate leader (who had been slow to leave the Whig Party) an extremist. In the debate on Pierce's final message, Senator Mason reminded him that he had told a crowd in 1848 that slavery "can and must be abolished, and you and I must do it." So he had, and though the occasion, a speech in favor of the slaveholder Zachary Taylor, and the context, which was mild, had to be considered, the sentence was indiscreet. His "higher law" speech in 1850 was not only poor politics but bad statesmanship, and the "irrepressible conflict" address of 1858 was still more un-fortunate. While rash in the use of words, Seward was also occasionally too com-plicated, devious, and crafty in action; at one time the high-minded statesman, he was at others the partner of the sly Thurlow Weed, who made politics pay in crass ways. His best biographer describes him as a Jekyll and Hyde personal-ity.[31] Save in devotion to the Union, he seemed to lack constancy. He was capable of taking a bold position one day and retracting three-quarters of it the

28 Schurz, *Reminiscences*, II, 34; H. B. Stanton, *Random Recollections*, 204
29 W. R. Thayer, *John Hay*, I, 253–255.
30 Rollo Ogden, *Life and Letters of E. L. Godkin*, I, 258.
31 Frederic Bancroft, *Seward*, I, 200, 201; II, 88.

next, and he frankly told Mrs. Jefferson Davis that he often spoke without conviction.[32]

In short, Seward was erratic. Perhaps an excess of imagination contributed to some of his worst blunders, as when in 1861 he suggested provoking a European war in order to bring back the South; perhaps his emotions sometimes overruled his head. His abundant letters and diary notes show an appealing streak of artistry. Whatever the cause of his instability, this brilliant little Welsh wizard was most valuable when he could lean upon a more massive strength, like Lincoln's.

Jefferson Davis, a man of elegant accomplishments and—despite his humble origin—a gentleman to the core, possessed the dignity of manner and the distinction that Seward lacked. This West Pointer, the son of a Revolutionary veteran, had some of the best traits of a soldier, for he was reserved, self-controlled, and punctiliously courteous, yet plainly not to be trifled with. He was a scholar, who had used his plantation leisure to read widely in military history and the British classics. He was a practical politician, steeped in precedents and instances. Not an orator, he spoke with a finish, lucidity, and force which produced an impression of great logical power—and with a haughty, defiant mien, as one who would not brook contradictions.[33] As Secretary of War under Pierce he showed himself a resourceful administrator, enlarging the army, pushing forward the construction of the Capitol, and experimenting with camels in the Southwest. He was brooding in these years over a plan for saving both the South and the Union; a plan for something like dominion status for the fifteen slave States, making their domestic institutions untouchable.[34]

Those who studied him closely, however, discerned a burning intellectual vanity beneath his impassive exterior, and saw that it was the wellspring of two fatal qualities—selfishness and obstinacy. His future wife, Varina Howell, noted at their first meeting his grim, moody temper, and his way of assuming that when he expressed an opinion, everyone would agree to it. She found him "the kind of person I should expect to rescue one from a mad dog at any risk, but to insist upon a stoical indifference to the fright afterwards."[35] In the Senate, he could never bear contradiction or opposition. When Douglas half-humorously told his Southern opponents on what terms he would admit them to the Democratic Party if ever he gained control of that body, Davis leaped to his feet with blazing passion: " I scorn your quarter!"

Men saw, too, that despite his brilliant public record, his attainments were rather of the study than of practical affairs. Aristocratic, fastidious, self-

32 Gamaliel Bradford, *Union Portraits*, 200–209.
33 E. A. Pollard, *Jefferson Davis*, 33.
34 N. W. Stephenson, *Typical Americans and Their Problems*, 51.
35 Allen Tate, *Jefferson Davis*, 74, 75.

preoccupied, he was Byronically aloof. He disliked meeting men in offhand give and take; he lacked the strong common sense, the practical sagacity, of tamer spirits like Polk or Sam Houston; and his constraint sealed the book of human nature to him. Hence when he attained power, he made grotesque errors in estimating lieutenants, overrating Bragg and underrating Joseph E. Johnston. Having none of the homely, earthy quality which the best democratic leader must possess, he was never willing to place his faith, like Jefferson, Jackson, and Lincoln, in the aggregate wisdom of the people. Moreover, on Southern rights his touchiness led him to hold it "a true maxim to meet danger on the frontier in politics as in war." His stiff sectional feeling estopped him from taking truly national views, and hence long views.

As a parliamentary combatant, the most impressive figure in the country was Stephen A. Douglas. A dozen years younger than Seward, five years junior to Davis, he was still in his early forties when Buchanan was inaugurated; yet he was a political veteran, for he had been elected State's attorney in Illinois at twenty-one, and had been in Congress in Tyler's time. No man excelled him in riding the storm. He had been in the thick of the struggle for the Compromise of 1850, had labored ambitiously for the Presidential nomination in 1852 and 1856, and had given the country the most controversial measure of the decade in his Nebraska Bill. Indeed, ever since the day when, an ill-educated stripling of twenty with hardly enough law to write a simple instrument, he had hung up his shingle in the Morgan County courthouse, he had been ceaselessly fighting his way forward. He had two elementary articles of faith: he believed in the growth of the country—believed that, as it had pushed across the Mississippi, the plains, and the Rockies to the Pacific, it must continue to expand, either north or south; and he believed in popular self-government. When he flung himself into battle it was with tigerish ferocity. In an early run for Congress he had so enraged his opponent, the stalwart John T. Stuart, that this Whig candidate tucked Douglas's head under his arm and dragged him around the Springfield square. John Quincy Adams had stared in amazement when the five-foot Illinoisan, roaring out one of his first speeches in the House, had stripped off his cravat, unbuttoned his waistcoat, and with convulsed face and frantic gesticulation had "lashed himself into such a heat that if his body had been made of combustible matter, it would have burnt out." Schurz had watched him send his sentences like cannon balls, crashing and rending, into his opponents' ranks. Few were the Senators who dared stand against him.[36]

Yet Douglas's limitations were as striking as his gifts. His conduct was sometimes deplorably lax. Charles Francis Adams has left a graphic vignette of

36 Allen Johnson, *Stephen A. Douglas*, 43; Adams, *Memoirs*, XI, 510; Schurz, *Reminiscences*, II, 30–35.

the man invading a sleeping car in 1860, whiskey bottle in hand and half drunk, to try to drag Seward out to address a Toledo crowd. One day Douglas might be leading his party in the Senate, the next be found with his arm about the neck of a crony in a Washington saloon.[37] Deeply versed in political history, he was ill-informed in almost all other fields of knowledge. He had read little but lawbooks, debates, and government manuals, and had seldom found time for that deeper type of reflection which produces statesmen. A marvellously effective floor debater, he had no real power of abstract thought, and no ability to present such general ideas as are associated with Hamilton and Jefferson, Calhoun and Webster. He had never produced a genuine state paper. While he grappled friends to him with hooks of steel, he taught them to act on practical expediency rather than far-reaching principle.

Above all, he was an improviser. His whole genius, backed by irresistible personal force, was for meeting practical situations with some rapidly devised measure, taking little thought of ultimate consequences, and trusting to the country's growth for remedying all defects. He had improvised as State's attorney and judge when he knew little law and no jurisprudence. He had improvised as a young Congressman supporting Polk and the Mexican War. He had improvised policies and bills; above all the reckless measure, the worst Pandora's box in our history, for organizing Kansas Territory. As he improvised he battled implacably, for he loved nothing more than political combat. The great weakness of the born improviser is that he oversimplifies the problem he faces and forgets that remote results are often far more important than the immediate effect. The great penalty paid by the born fighter is that he gradually accumulates a phalanx of enemies. Douglas by 1857 was a doughty champion, famous for his power to give and take blows, but he had still to reckon his final bill of profit and loss.

The best trait of Douglas was his faith in the expansive energies of the American people. Europe, he had said, is one vast graveyard. "Here everything is fresh, blooming, expanding, and advancing. We wish a wise, practical policy adapted to our condition and position." [38] He must be credited, too, with a fervent belief in the masses—in democracy. But he had a number of less happy traits. One was his chauvinism, for he constantly inveighed against the "tyranny" and "aggressions" of European nations, and showed no appreciation of our cultural debt to older lands. Another was his readiness in debate to twist logic, darken counsel, and even misstate facts. Still another was his constant exaltation of material considerations and depreciation of moral factors: the slavery question, he said on the eve of the Civil War, is exclusively "one of climate, of

37 C. F. Adams, *Autobiography*, 65, 66; cf. Milton, *Eve of Conflict*, 258, 259.
38 *Cong. Globe*, 32nd Cong., Sp. Sess., 273.

political economy, of self-interest." [39] Finally, he often suffered from his head-long impetuosity.

In 1857 the brightest pages of his brilliant career lay before him. His success-ful fight against a proslavery constitution for Kansas was to be one of the most gallant episodes of the time; and in 1860 he was to play a more farsighted and heroic role than any other Presidential candidate. But he lacked the capacity to plan, the patient wisdom, and the conciliatory gifts of a great national chieftain.

So we might run down the beadroll of leaders of the time, some of them exhibiting great gifts. How fine in various ways was Charles Sumner, with his broad cosmopolitan culture, his Alpine elevation, his friendship with Brougham, Grote, Macaulay, Longfellow, Prescott, and Tocqueville; yet how petty he could be, too! When he returned to the Senate in 1860, after four years of illness and partial exile, he had an opportunity to deliver a speech full of mag-nanimity, generosity, and Olympian wisdom. Instead, he poured forth a diatribe on "The Barbarism of Slavery," full of erudite venom and personal abuse. Like Douglas, he was incapable of appealing to the highest instincts of the people whom he apostrophized. How able was Salmon P. Chase, who had taken a leading place at the Ohio bar, written for the *North American Review*, helped pioneer the antislavery movement in Ohio, and served with distinction as Senator and governor! Of majestic stature, fine head, and keen eye, he looked like the statesman he was. Unfortunately, he had a touchy self-importance, he let political ambition warp his outlook, he never learned to make friends of national leaders, partly because he could never subordinate himself to others, and he almost totally lacked the arts of popular appeal.[40] He thirsted for the Presidency, yet could never command a large following. How brilliantly capable was Alexander H. Stephens, and how truly national in outlook! High-minded, devoted to principle, well-read and thoughtful, he was the strongest of the Southern moderates. Yet as one of his admirers admits, he was too quick-tempered, too unwilling to yield on details, too eager to score victories for personal prestige or party credit, to carry through any great purpose; while his invalidism made him a bundle of nerves.[41]

[IV]

Where, then, were leaders equal to the crisis to be found—leaders who united intellectual power, moderation of temper, moral earnestness, and the power of lifting the popular heart? All the men named, and others like Lyman Trumbull, J. J. Crittenden, Robert Toombs, and R. M. T. Hunter, seemed

39 *Cong. Globe*, 36th Cong., 1st Sess., 552–559.
40 A. B. Hart, *Salmon P. Chase*, 415–425.
41 Ulrich B. Phillips in *Dictionary of American Biography*.

statesmen *manqués*. And could a fit leader be found in time? For the hysteria, the mounting hatreds and fears made time all too short.

Here and there a new voice of promise was raised. Nobody in the East and few in the West paid any attention to one which was heard at a Republican banquet in Chicago on December 10, 1856. A lanky attorney from Springfield, known only as a man who had served one term in Congress, who had narrowly missed the nomination for Senator that Trumbull got, and who had received some votes for the latest Vice-Presidential nomination, spoke on Pierce's message. He mentioned contemptuously the President's vaunt that the recent election had vindicated "State equality." Then he went on to appeal to the imagination of his hearers and to their high sense of national destiny:

All of us who did not vote for Mr. Buchanan, taken together, are a majority of four hundred thousand. But in the late contest we were divided between Frémont and Fillmore. Can we not come together in the future? Let everyone who really believes, and is resolved, that free society is not and shall not be a failure, and who can conscientiously declare that in the past contest he has only done what he thought best, let every such one have charity to believe that every other one can say as much. Thus let bygones be bygones; let past differences as nothing be; and with steady eye on the real issue, let us reinaugurate the good old "central idea" of the republic. We can do it. The human heart is with us; God is with us. We shall again be able not to declare that "all States as States are equal," nor yet that "all citizens as citizens are equal," but to renew the broader, better declaration, including both of these and much more, that "all men are created equal." [42]

If the Union could yet be saved, if the Ship of State was not to go over the cataract whose thunders ahead shook the air, it would be by some leaders, somewhere, who thus reminded Americans that their republic must be kept the last, best hope of mankind. Lincoln appealed to the older faith in America as "a bulwark for the cause of men." That a deep reservoir of idealistic feeling existed in the nation, and that beneath turbid surface eddies the old moral forces still flowed with pomp of waters, unwithstood, was demonstrated, as we shall now see, by the best literary voices of the young republic.

42 *Complete Works* (Nicolay and Hay ed.), I, 225–226.

2

"Not from a Vain or Shallow Thought"

THE MAIN impression given by American life in the fifties was of health, strength, and constructive force. Slavery was the most dangerous problem of the nation—the more dangerous because of popular self-confidence, the tendency toward regional division, and the mediocre character of most political leadership. But after all, this was only one element in the complex of national affairs. The history of civilization was, as it must always be, more important than the history of politics; when Aristotle wrote of man as a political animal he meant gregarious or social animal, and the busy States cannot be understood if we do not scrutinize many aspects of their life. Some of these aspects were making strong competitive demands upon the country's stock of brains, vision, and character. No part of American civilization in this decade was more arresting than what might be termed the culturally creative element.

We must include among the creative achievements of the time the continued development of government; for the Jeffersonian and Jacksonian impulses were still strong, the bold use of universal manhood suffrage was proving successful, and the world's largest experiment in federalism served as effectively for three million square miles as for two. We must include impulses foreshadowing the distinctively American contributions of the next generations in technology and mass production. America could point to the light suspension bridges of Roebling, the swift slender steamships designed by Jacob Bell and others, the Yankee clippers of Donald McKay, the ingenious balloon-frame house, and the locomotives of basketlike flexibility made by Baldwin or Eastwick. It could point to such feats of invention as the telegraph, sewing machine, and reaper. It could tell of progress in mass production on the interchangeable-part principle, introduced by Eli Whitney and carried forward in Colt's arms works, the Waltham watch factory, and McCormick's reaper works. It could point to a new kind of integrated manufacturing procedure illustrated by the assembly line of meat-packing plants and the planning of elaborate flour mills.

In a different field, Americans could take pride in the high development some States had given to general public education, and in Horace Mann's contributions to teacher-training. They could assert that the lyceum had been a useful path in adult education. In not a few philanthropies and reforms—children's aid, training of the deaf and dumb, prison management—American effort led the world. The nation could claim credit in medicine for one of the great advances of history, the discovery of surgical anaesthesia by W. T. G. Morton, Crawford Long, and others. American theology as represented by Andrews Norton and Horace Bushnell, and American jurisprudence as expounded by Story and Taney, were on a high level; while Henry Wheaton's pre-eminence in international law was widely recognized. In science the United States still lacked names of the highest distinction; but it had bred its own Joseph Henry, naturalized Agassiz, and given oceanography the "pathfinder of the seas," M. F. Maury.

In a variety of endeavors Americans of the fifties made a mark of signal talent or heroic devotion. Now it was the explorer Elisha Kent Kane, scurvy-ridden, driving his *Advance* into yet more perilous Arctic wastes. Now it was the impoverished inventor Charles Goodyear, borrowing money to place his rubber devices in the London and Paris exhibitions of 1851 and 1855. Now it was the critic W. J. Stillman making the *Crayon* one of the best art magazines on the globe.[1] Now it was the topographer Frémont leading his doomed band into the icy fastnesses of the Sangre de Cristo Mountains to prove their midwinter passage feasible. Now it was John Carter Brown of Providence and James Lenox of New York making the first impressive collections of rare books and literary manuscripts. It was Elizabeth Cady Stanton and Susan B. Anthony keeping the flag of women's rights defiantly flying. It was Charles Loring Brace toiling sixteen hours daily on a thousand dollars a year to make his Children's Aid Society effective. It was Francis James Child beginning his lifework of scholarship on the British ballads, and the Le Conte family winning scientific laurels for the South. It was Cyrus W. Field, undaunted by bankruptcy, debt, the burning of his business quarters, and four successive failures, raising funds for the fifth attempt to lay an Atlantic cable. It was the devoted endeavor of John R. Thompson and William Gilmore Simms to give the South magazines for its writers.

In the realms of art and literature, transcendent achievement had proved slow, for it depended upon social and cultural elements which were the growth of time. Something more than large cultivated groups, a clash of minds, and

---

1   Charles Eliot Norton wrote to William Porcher Miles of the *Crayon*: "It is very different from most of our American journals and magazines. There is no claptrap about it, no writing down to the low level of popular taste. It addresses the small audience of true artists and lovers of art. Besides very well written, clearly thought, and high bred essays upon subjects connected with art, it contains much pleasant information upon matters of art both at home and abroad." June 26, 1855; Miles Papers.

accumulations of artistic and literary materials had to be provided. In the soul of a nation, spiritual strength comes from maturity and travail. Americans were for the most part a new people—many had arrived at Castle Garden only yesterday; and most of their travail and social turmoil lay ahead. The best thought and artistry came from old, long-ripened communities, and from areas where layer on layer of troubled history had been laid down. It came, that is, from Boston and its old colonial suburbs, from cosmopolitan New York, from Philadelphia, once the second city in the British Empire, from Tidewater Virginia, and from the basin of the Cooper and Ashley. Yet at last it was coming—particularly in literature. For the first time, men and women throughout the country were recognizing that great writers were among them, and that great writing was being done.

American art, though not attaining the distinction that letters reached, was groping toward it. Here the social basis for achievement was being created: the schools of design, the sales galleries, the fellowship of eager practitioners, the stir of public interest. Italy remained full of American sculptors. Let us call New York the City of Studios, said *Putnam's* in May, 1857, for no fewer than three hundred palettes are set up in Manhattan every morning by as many artists. What was needed was not merely high talent, but a modernized technique and a more spiritual vision. Of the competent, sincere, and commonplace the country had enough in sculptors like Crawford and Story, portrait painters like Chester Harding, and landscape painters like William Hart and Thomas Doughty. It had artists who loved nature as deeply as J. F. Kensett, whose paintings of the Hudson Valley were full of sincere feeling. It had painters of imagination, or at least of a certain grandiosity of outlook, such as F. E. Church of the erupting "Cotopaxi." But as yet, for all its virtues of self-respect, conscientiousness, and skilled craftsmanship, American art had produced no sculptor or painter who united a modern technique with rich distinction of mind and personality.

Art, we say, was groping toward the light. One of the prolific portrait painters, Charles Loring Elliott, several times struck out a work of genius, as in his portrait of Ericsson (1845), called the best American work in the field since Stuart, and that of Fletcher Harper, admired at home and in France. A greater figure, George Inness, with the soul of a mystic and poet, came back from Paris in the middle fifties afire with the lessons taught him by Corot and Rousseau. He began to put into the meticulously detailed canvases characteristic of the Hudson River school a passion which his associates had never admitted. His "Juniata River near Harrisburg" (1856) was full of dryly precise detail. "But," writes Royal Cortissoz, "what a queer thing is genius! This picture cannot die. A mysterious life is stirring in it, the energizing touch of an artist who could not be merely photographic though he tried. . . . All the time that Inness was just taking pains with his subject there was at the back of his mind the generalizing instinct that goes to the making of great works of art." [2] Inness was to do better work—work completely American, as typical of his country as a Vermont hillside in autumn or an upper New York snowscape, executed with the best European expertness. Something of the same freakish touch of genius gave strength to Henry K. Brown's equestrian statue of Washington (1856), making it stand out from the insipid neo-classic sculpture of the period.

As yet it was only dawn in art, but there were signs of sunrise; the sunrise of Winslow Homer, La Farge, Whistler, and Eakins in painting, of Saint-Gaudens and Daniel Chester French in sculpture. In literature, however, the country was well beyond the dawn represented by Irving and Cooper. Letters by the middle fifties were the most noteworthy aspect of the American scene from any cosmopolitan point of view.

[I]

At the beginning of the century the country had possessed little more than the hope of a literature. The work of Franklin, Jefferson, Paine, and Freneau had been special or incidental. But by 1844, when Rufus W. Griswold brought out a large volume on *The Poets and Poetry of America*, it was evident that the country had writers of high and enduring distinction. To be sure, at first there was the usual difficulty in separating genius from talent. Griswold gave inordinate space to such minor authors as Brainard, Dawes, Pike, Ware, Wilde, Peabody, and Sands; while E. P. Whipple, reviewing Griswold in *Essays and Reviews* (1850), devoted as much attention to Sprague, Dana, and Percival as to Holmes, Longfellow, and Whittier. Time, however, quickly separated gold from brummagem metal. Even Griswold pronounced Emerson the country's greatest poet, and by 1855 readers were well aware that Longfellow, Whittier, Emerson, Bryant, and Poe stood far above the Percivals and Spragues. Not a little heart burning accompanied this sieving process. New Yorkers were jealous of New England, while Southerners complained that the work of M. B. Lamar, Philip Cooke, and Simms was unjustly neglected; but the verdict had to stand.[3]

One after another the memorable works appeared. While Taylor and Scott

2 *American Artists*, p. 113.

3 The Raleigh *Register*, replying to an article in *Putnam's*, listed the living Southern writers of renown: "Such names as Simms, Kennedy, Hawks, Grayson, Louisa McCord, Calvert, M. F. Maury, John Esten Cooke, Anna Estelle Lewis, P. H. Hayne, Longstreet, Brantz Mayer, Webber, Benton, Badger, Hammond, Bledsoe, Marion Harland, Gayarré, and twenty others." It recalled Poe's statement that Simms's genius had been neglected because he was Southern. Quoted in Charleston *Courier*, March 10, 1857. Actually most Northern reviewers were quite fair to Southern books; the *Atlantic* was conspicuously generous. Simms complained of Southern rather than Northern neglect. Southern and Northern authors maintained cordial relations to the last. Jared Sparks, for example, sent Caleb Cushing a copy of W. H. Trescot's new book on the diplomacy of the Revolution with high praise. July 29, 1852; Cushing Papers.

were defeating the Mexicans, Lowell published his *Biglow Papers*, Hawthorne his *Mosses from an Old Manse*, Longfellow his *Evangeline*, Prescott his *Conquest of Peru*, and Melville his *Typee* and *Omoo*. The year 1848 found Thoreau printing his *Ktaadn* in magazine form, and Lowell his *Fable for Critics*, while the next year saw Thoreau bring out his *Week on the Concord and Merrimac*. In the twelve months of Clay's last great compromise appeared Emerson's *Representative Men*, Longfellow's *The Seaside and the Fireside*, Melville's *White Jacket*, and Hawthorne's *Scarlet Letter*—books to make any year notable. Whittier, too, was busy; that year he published *Songs of Labor* and *Old Portraits and Modern Sketches*. Yet 1851 was of almost equal importance, illuminated as it was by Melville's *Moby Dick*, Longfellow's *The Golden Legend*, and Hawthorne's *The House of the Seven Gables*. The stream was now flowing full, and we can mention but a few of the outstanding and perdurable titles. In 1854 appeared *Walden*. Another *annus mirabilis* in 1855 gave the country Whitman's *Leaves of Grass*, Longfellow's *Hiawatha*, and the first two volumes of Prescott's *Philip II*. Motley's *Rise of the Dutch Republic* emerged to its resounding success in 1856, the year too of Emerson's *English Traits*. In 1858 Holmes's *Autocrat of the Breakfast Table* divided attention with Longfellow's *Courtship of Miles Standish*.

The political incandescences of the time had no effect upon the great writers save to fire their pens and stimulate their production. Bryant alone, giving his energies to the *Evening Post*, perhaps spent some of his genius unwisely.[4] Irving was still busy, issuing his life of Washington, 1855–59. The stream of Holmes's wit ran on into *The Professor at the Breakfast Table* (1859) and *Elsie Venner* (1861). The year of Lincoln's election Emerson produced what Carlyle thought his best book, *The Conduct of Life*, and Hawthorne one of his greatest romances, *The Marble Faun*, while Whitman reissued his *Leaves of Grass* with additional poems. Where in the history of American letters is another dozen years equal to 1848–60?

[II]

It was of no small moment that these imaginative achievements heightened American pride, proving that the new republic, for all its materialistic pre-

---

4 Bryant brought out his collection *A Forest Hymn* in 1860, the year also of Whittier's *Home Ballads and Other Poems*. But the hot sun of political controversy tended to dry up his fancy. Emerson had written in his Notebooks on March 20, 1842, that the "Humanity and Reform men trample on letters and poetry." Writers of the South suffered from the necessity, as they saw it, of giving half their energies to controversy. The *Southern Literary Messenger* of October, 1856, carried a long article on "The Duty of Southern Authors," urging them to take up their pens against the North and to write a vindicatory history of slavery.

occupations, could touch the finer chords of the spirit. The same Sydney Smith who had asked in 1820 who read an American book, later predicted that when Prescott visited England he would find a Caspian Sea of soup awaiting him. In London in the summer of 1848, young Charles Eliot Norton glowed with pride to see the historian lionized, and to hear people say, even while reading *In Memoriam*, that England had no poet to compare with Longfellow. In the *Athenaeum* he could have found a reviewer who ranked *The Scarlet Letter* among the most powerful, if also the most painful, of all recent books; a work strangely compounded of passion and Puritan reserve, of the allegorical and the real, and shot through with imaginative fire. In *Blackwood's*, long so savage in treating things American, he could have found a discussion of Herman Melville which, highly appreciative of the exotic color of *Typee* and *Omoo*, and of the frank, manly style of *Redburn*, credited the Yankee with introducing a new genre in literature—a combination of Swift, Defoe, the *Arabian Nights*, nautical terminology, and American yarning.[5]

Such praise had real value, for if Americans were anywhere lacking in exuberant self-confidence, it was in cultural endeavors; but after all, large and appreciative native audiences were infinitely more important than the comment of foreign critics. Moreover, much British commendation was coupled with unreasonable demands. Most British critics asked that the rising writers of the West be wildly, shaggily North American, that they bear the stamp of an untamed New World. Why should Longfellow go to Europe for *The Golden Legend* when so much history and folklore lay at home? Why should Bayard Taylor's *Rhymes of Travel* dip into Old World streams when the most magnificent forms of nature awaited description in his own land? Why should Thoreau in his *Week on the Concord and Merrimac* echo Carlyle when a dozen passages made it clear that if he trusted to his genius he might become a prophet

5 The *Athenaeum*, a real power, was conspicuously friendly toward American authors, praising all the great writers of the period—though it gave an adverse judgment upon *Moby Dick*, which it called an ill-compounded mixture of romance and matter of fact (October 25, 1851). In reviewing *Hiawatha* it declared that for many years it had preached "the poetical doctrine of America for the Americans," and it praised that long poem warmly, saying that the tale was beautiful, fanciful, and new, and that the author had given variety even to a metre chosen for its sad and tender monotone (November 10, 1855). Hawthorne was regarded by the *Athenaeum* with marked admiration. *The Scarlet Letter* received praise for its high originality, its delicacy and restraint, its imaginative power, and its touch of the fantastic (June 15, 1850). *The House of the Seven Gables* was greeted as placing Hawthorne "amongst the most original and complete novelists that have appeared in modern times" (May 24, 1851). Of the *Blithedale Romance* the weekly said that it put the seal on the author's reputation as "the highest, deepest, and finest imaginative writer whom America has yet produced" (July 10, 1852). *The Marble Faun* again received warm praise. Melville was done better justice by the reviewer of *White Jacket*, who declared him incomparable in rendering "the poetry of the ship," and placed him high above Marryat. He was credited with "more vivacity, fancy, color, and energy than ninety-nine out of a hundred" of those who understood to poetize monsters of sea or land (February 2, 1850).

of rank in his own right? Let Americans be *national,* insisted Chorley's *Athenaeum* and other periodicals in reviewing books; let them find home themes and develop home ideas. In their great continent they had a wealth of untouched material for song, story, and essay almost as great as that of weary old Europe.

Within limits this was good advice, for it was time that Americans ceased to be imitative. When pushed too far, however, the demand was false and misleading. One reason for its falsity lay in the fact that Americans were not a new stock; they were Euro-Americans and their culture was mainly Anglo-American. Though *The Courtship of Miles Standish* dealt with English folk newly landed on a colonial shore, it was more authentically American, less alien and outlandish, than *Hiawatha.* In every important sense Hawthorne's *Our Old Home* (published a little later, in 1863) was as penetratingly American as Parkman's *California and Oregon Trail.* Parkman's book had high significance in its vivid description of the hunter's and fur-trader's frontier, of the pioneer and the Indian. Who can forget his picture of the dog feast at Fort Laramie, of Jim Beckwourth teaching the Crows how to fight, of the cluttered, smelly Oglalla Sioux village, of the prairies black with buffalo? But Hawthorne's book described some of the enduring roots of Anglo-American civilization. Americans today can name particulars in which they were influenced by Stratford, Epworth, and Cambridge as vitally as they were influenced by the Oregon Trail. It was not for Americans to face West alone or East alone; they naturally faced in both directions.

The larger reason for the falsity of any demand for a *forced* Americanism (and such demands were heard at home as well as in Europe) was that as literature enters the higher realms of feeling, thought, and art it knows less and less of national peculiarities and limitations. Hawthorne, delving into problems of personality, did better with Miriam and Donatello under Italian skies than with Zenobia in a Yankee setting. Emerson's "Saadi" holds a larger measure of American truth, as part of world truth, than his prosaic poem "The Adirondacs." Thoreau's *Walden* dealt with a very American experience, but its value lay in the distinction with which he discussed universal topics. His chapter on "Reading" in that book was not an exhortation to be provincial and national by going through the native works published by Harper's and Little, Brown. On the contrary, he recommended Homer, Aeschylus, Vergil, Dante, and Shakespeare. The important object was not that Americans should strike a cisatlantic note, but simply that they should trust themselves, and look within their hearts and write.

Once they did so, it was inevitable that decade by decade they *would* become more American. As the subsoil of American ideas, folklore, and history grew thicker, as American culture became more satisfying, with better colleges,

THE
ATLANTIC MONTHLY.

PHILLIPS, SAMPSON & COMPANY'S
NEW MAGAZINE,
Devoted to Literature, Art, and Politics.

ITS AIM WILL BE

FIRST: In Literature, to leave no province unrepresented, so that while each number will contain articles of an abstract and permanent value, it will also be found that the healthy appetite of the mind for entertainment in its various forms of Narrative, Wit, and Humor, will not go uncared for. The publishers wish to say, also, that while native writers will receive the most solid encouragement, and will be mainly relied on to fill the pages of the ATLANTIC, they will not hesitate to draw from the foreign sources at their command, as occasion may require, relying rather on the competency of an author to treat a particular subject, than on any other claim whatever. In this way they hope to make their Periodical welcome wherever the English tongue is spoken or read.

SECOND: In the term ART they intend to include the whole domain of æsthetics, and hope gradually to make this critical department a true and fearless representative of Art, in all its various branches, without any regard to prejudice, whether personal or national, or to private considerations of what kind soever.

THIRD: In Politics, the ATLANTIC will be the organ of no party or clique, but will honestly endeavor to be the exponent of what its conductors believe to be the American idea. It will deal frankly with persons and with parties, endeavoring always to keep in view that moral element which transcends all persons and parties, and which alone makes the basis of a true and lasting national prosperity. It will not rank itself with any sect of *anties*, but with that body of men which is in favor of Freedom, National Progress, and Honor, whether public or private.

As an earnest of the material at their command, they subjoin the following list of literary persons interested in their enterprise; wishing it, however, to be distinctly understood, that they shall hope for support from every kind of ability which desires the avenue of their columns, and in the remuneration of which they shall be guided purely by their sense of intrinsic merit: —

WILLIAM H. PRESCOTT,
RALPH WALDO EMERSON,
WM. C. BRYANT,
HENRY W. LONGFELLOW,
REV. F. H. HEDGE, D. D.,
NATHANIEL HAWTHORNE,
JOHN G. WHITTIER,
OLIVER WENDELL HOLMES,
JAMES R. LOWELL,
J. LOTHROP MOTLEY,
GEORGE WM. CURTIS,
HERMAN MELVILLE,
PROF. C. C. FELTON,
PROF. F. J. CHILD,
E. P. WHIPPLE,
EDMUND QUINCY,
    Author of "Wensley,"
THOMAS W. PARSONS,
J. T. TROWBRIDGE,
    Author of "Neighbor Jackwood," &c.

MRS. H. BEECHER STOWE,
MRS. GASKELL,
    Author of "Ruth," "Mary Barton," &c.
MRS. L. MARIA CHILD,
MRS. C. M. KIRKLAND,
MRS. PIKE,
    Author of "Ida May," "Caste," &c,
MISS ROSE TERRY,
WILKIE COLLINS,
    Author of "The Dead Secret," &c.
G. RUFFINI,
    Author of "Doctor Antonio," &c.
SHIRLEY BROOKS,
    Author of "Aspen Court," &c.
E. M. WHITTY,
    Author of "Political Portraits," &c.
JAMES HANNAY,
    Author of "Singleton Fontenoy,"
O. W. PHILLEO,
    Author of "Twice Married."

The Publishers will aim to have each number of the magazine ready in time for distribution and sale, in the more remote parts of the country, on or before the first day of the month for which it is intended.

TERMS. — The ATLANTIC MONTHLY can be had of Booksellers, Periodical Agents, or from the Publishers, at Three Dollars a year, or Twenty-five Cents a Number.

Subscribers remitting three dollars, in advance, to the publishers, will receive the work for one year, *post paid*, in any part of the United States within 3000 miles.

A liberal discount made to wholesale dealers, and to postmasters and others who act as agents, to whom specimen numbers will be furnished without charge.

The Publishers will not be responsible for contracts made by agents. All persons ordering through that medium must look to them for their supply.

All communications for the Atlantic must be addressed to the Publishers.

libraries, newspapers, art collections, and highly literate groups, as American themes supplied a bolder impulse to the imagination, writers would look less to the Old World. Naturally—not in the dogged spirit of Emerson's *American Scholar*—our authors by 1850 were writing more as Americans than ever before.

By that date the eminent authors could be divided into several main groups. Some used foreign themes almost exclusively. That could be said, for example, of Prescott with Spain and Spanish America as his field, and of Motley, devoting his pen to the struggles of Protestant Europe for liberty. Another group chose European or American subjects almost impartially, for education, background, and temperament gave them a cosmopolitan outlook. This was true of Longfellow, whose muse was equally at home in old Norway, Germany, or Massachusetts; true of Lowell, writing his "Legend of Brittany" and lays of Italy with as much gusto as his "Pictures of Appledore"; and even true of Emerson (thorough Yankee though he was), ranging the whole globe and all history for ideas and inspiration. Still another group were so much interested in the American scene and spirit that they seldom forsook the topics of their own land. These writers, Whitman, Thoreau, Whittier, Mrs. Stowe, William Gilmore Simms, Parkman, and others, were instinctively possessed by home subjects. All of Whitman's strength sprang from native ground; Whittier's home ballads and songs of labor were bounded by Monadnock and Cape Ann; Thoreau as a philosopher might belong to the world, but as a naturalist he was all Concord's; Simms had Cooper's own feeling for local scene-painting and indigenous types of humanity; Parkman, haunted from boyhood by images of the wilderness, devoted his life to the history of the struggle for North America. As Lowell grew older, he kept more closely within his national orbit.

Then, too, the question of idiom enters. Some authors, like Longfellow and Hawthorne, wrote with a European tone and accent. Save for its frequent Biblical phrasing, Whittier's language differs little from Tennyson's—even the chant of the fishermen's wives denouncing Floyd Ireson might be by an English poet. But some authors broke frequently into an American vernacular. Lowell did so in the "Biglow Papers" and "The Courtin'," Emerson in many a line of verse ("Drain sweet maple-juice in vats") and many *Journal* entries ("Dumb and unhappy like an Indian in church"), and Mrs. Stowe in the delicious Yankee dialogue of *The Minister's Wooing*. In two writers, Thoreau and Whitman, the American accent is pervasive, lending a homely strength throughout. Nobody could ever believe that Emerson's essays were written by anyone but a firmly planted American using his native idiom.

But the essential fact was that the nation in the fifties could be proud of its authors. If they were not the peers of Dickens and Thackeray, Tennyson and Browning, Hugo and De Musset, Balzac and Heine, they were nevertheless touched with fire by a New World muse. Such authors could be left to follow their own bent.

[III]

The chief values which the country derived from its best creative works in this era were two. They enriched the national scene, transforming its bare landscapes by a multicolored investiture; and still more important, they deepened and invigorated the national spirit. It may be added that although their impact was only beginning to be felt by the late fifties, they also quickened the flow of American ideas. But this was a less noteworthy function. For ideas, readers went not to the imaginative creations, but to books of a tougher, tamer quality. They sought their political ideas in Calhoun, St. George Tucker, and Francis Lieber, and their economic ideas in the Careys, Hezekiah Niles, and Francis Bowen. They found European ideas transmitted by a hundred ready pens—Charles A. Dana, for example, reporting the revolutions of 1848 on the instant. To be sure, Emerson's essays, Thoreau in "Civil Disobedience" and other polemic papers, and Whitman and Lowell as well, were full of ideas. But their best coin was not such silver; it was gold minted with an imaginative and moral stamp.

It is imagination that furnishes and tapestries the national house. As men had looked on the Hudson with brightened eye after "Rip Van Winkle," so they looked with a novel delight on the Plymouth shore after *Miles Standish*, on Louisiana bayous after *Evangeline*, and on the South Carolina uplands after Simms's *The Yemassee*. Most people never fully see their own land until the poet and novelist fit glasses to their eyes. Old New York had been the first to profit largely in this fashion. Readers of Philip Freneau's poems dreamed of the British prison ships firing their evening gun over the black tide of the East River, of Benedict Arnold gloomily sailing for England from the Battery, and of shopkeepers crowding the gallery of Congress Hall. Readers of Drake and Halleck found the "Croaker Papers" mirroring the Park Theatre, the snug bar of Niblo's Hotel, and the busy newspaper offices. Long Island Sound and Montauk Point had been made romantic ground by *Miles Wallingford* and Cooper's other sea tales. As for Otsego Lake, who could see it without thinking of Hutter's "castle," and the rendezvous between Deerslayer and Chingachgook on Otsego Rock? Cooper had done as much for the Lake George country in *The Last of the Mohicans*, and still more for the blood-stained border country of Westchester in *The Spy*. White Plains, Four Corners, and the dales that Harvey Birch, the pretended peddler, fearlessly traversed while the Neutral Ground was being ravaged by miscreants who preyed on both patriot and loyalist, were now seen with an inward as well as outward vision; they had a double existence.

Without these writers, the Empire City and State would have been all foreground, bathed in the hard hot sunlight of the present alone. Irving had done most of all to give them a long cool background. His historian Diedrich Knickerbocker, relating how in the golden reign of Wouter Van Twiller the town of New Amsterdam rose out of the mud to become marvellously polite, how William the Testy carried on the Oyster War, and how Peter Stuyvesant, after leading an army, brimful of wrath and cabbage, to wrest Fort Christina from the Swedes, had to surrender to a legion of British beef-fed warriors, succeeded all too well in lifting the old Dutch regime from the level of realism. As a historian, Irving now had time to repent his grotesque sallies of the imagination. A greater author, Whitman, not only chanted of "Crossing Brooklyn Ferry," but turned his face occasionally to the past, and did his part to give romance to old Long Island, and even to a bloody defeat on Brooklyn ground as recalled by a Revolutionary veteran:

> The years recede, pavements and stately houses disappear;
> Rude forts appear again, the old hoop'd guns are mounted;
> I see the lines of rais'd earth stretching from river to bay. . . .
> As I talk I remember all—I remember the Declaration;
> It was read here—the whole army paraded—it was read to us here.
> *   *   *   *   *   *
> It sickens me yet, that slaughter!
> I saw the moisture gather in drops on the face of the General. . . .

It was New England, however, which by 1861 had fared best in this imaginative transformation. Minor writers were assisting the process; Jones Very of Salem, for example, in verse and essay, and Sylvester Judd in *Margaret*, his fine bucolic study of Massachusetts life just after the Revolution. Yet the great romancers and poets needed no aid. How clearly had Americans seen the Yankee sailor until R. H. Dana, Jr., pictured him in *Two Years Before the Mast*, or the Yankee ports until Longfellow sang of the black wharves and slips, the sea tides tossing free, and the beauty and mystery of the vessels? How well had they known the coastal villagers until Whittier struck out "Skipper Ireson's Ride" and Hawthorne presented the all-too-ordinary facts of tragedy in "The Wives of the Dead?" How vivid had a Northern snowstorm really been to Americans until Whittier told how it came on, the sun rising cheerless and darkly circled over hills of gray to give a noonday light sadder than waning moon; until Emerson described its frolic architecture, with white bastions round every fence stake, Parian wreaths hung on coop and kennel, and swan-like forms investing the hidden thorn—the housemates meanwhile, as the tempest lasted, sitting about the radiant fireplace enclosed in a tumultuous privacy of storm; until Hawthorne touched the very poetry of the new-fallen drifts in his tale of the little snow-sister made by playing children? The Yankee yarn-teller had never been properly identified until Hawthorne's pen caught him—whenafter his counterpart was noted in every grocery and groggery in the land:

One of Uncle Parker's eyes had been blown out with gunpowder, and the other did but glimmer in its socket. Turning it upward as he spoke, it was his delight to tell of cruises against the French, and battles with his own shipmates, when he and an antagonist used to be seated astride of a sailor's chest, each fastened down by a spike nail through the trousers, and there to fight it out. Sometimes he expatiated on the delicious flavor of the hagden, a greasy and gooselike fowl, which the sailors catch with hook and line on the Grand Banks. He dwelt with rapture on an interminable winter at the Isle of Sables, where he had gladdened himself, amid polar snows, with the rum and sugar saved from the wreck of a West India schooner. And wrathfully did he shake his fist, as he related how a party of Cape Cod men had robbed him of that lawful spoil, and sailed away with every keg of old Jamaica, leaving him not a drop to drown his sorrow.

Something much above historical, reportorial, or descriptive talent is needed to people an empty land with living people, and paint pictures of fancy on brown hillsides. The typical Shaker village of the time was lifted out of its evanescent reality into enduring ideality in Hawthorne's story of "The Canterbury Pilgrims." It became as difficult for cultivated Americans to visit the White Mountains without thinking of "The Great Stone Face" as to voyage up the Hudson to Albany without thinking of Irving's "Dolph Heyliger." Not until 1856 was the manuscript of Governor Bradford's great history, miraculously discovered in the Lambeth Palace Library, completely published; good secondary accounts did not exist; and the story of the Pilgrims had never been properly written.[6] All the more marvellous was Longfellow's feat in bringing to bright-hued immediacy the wintry sea, the springtime woods, the village street, the Pilgrim settlers, the little human triangle of Priscilla, John Alden, and Miles Standish. He anticipated history and almost made it unnecessary; no prose writer could overthrow his image of Standish any more than a historian could overthrow Shakespeare's Richard III, for both entered into the heart of the people. The magic of Herman Melville's eye and hand was not so quickly recognized. Yet even in the fifties, if few understood the philosophical overtones of *Moby Dick*, many found in Captain Peleg, who was the very type of

6 The best-known sourcebook until Bradford's history was published was Alexander Young's dry compilation of 1841, *Chronicles of the Pilgrim Fathers of the Colony of Plymouth, 1602–1605*, which contained Nathaniel Morton's *New England's Memorial* and Edward Winslow's *Relation*.

Nantucket Quaker mariner, in Stubb and Starbuck, quintessential whaling men, and in that strangest figure of all, Captain Ahab, with the sea adventures in which they figured, material for understanding the maritime frontier of the United States as they had never understood it before.

BOSTON, 135 WASHINGTON STREET,
MARCH, 1851.

NEW BOOKS AND NEW EDITIONS
PUBLISHED BY

TICKNOR, REED, AND FIELDS.

HENRY W. LONGFELLOW'S WRITINGS.

COMPLETE POETICAL WORKS. This edition contains the six Volumes mentioned below, and is the only complete collection in the market. In two volumes, 16mo, $2.00.

In separate Volumes, each 75 cents.
VOICES OF THE NIGHT.
BALLADS AND OTHER POEMS.
SPANISH STUDENT; A PLAY IN THREE ACTS.
BELFRY OF BRUGES AND OTHER POEMS.
EVANGELINE; A TALE OF ACADIE.
THE SEASIDE AND THE FIRESIDE.
THE WAIF. A Collection of Poems. Edited by Longfellow.
THE ESTRAY. A Collection of Poems. Edited by Longfellow.

MR. LONGFELLOW'S PROSE WORKS.

HYPERION. A Romance. In one volume, 16mo, price $1 00.

OUTRE-MER. A Pilgrimage Beyond the Sea; In one volume, 16mo, price $1.00.

KAVANAGH. A Tale. Lately published. In one vol. 16mo, price 75 cents.

NATHANIEL HAWTHORNE'S WRITINGS.

TWICE-TOLD TALES. A New Edition. In two vols. 16mo, with Portrait, price $1.50.

THE SCARLET LETTER. A Romance. In one vol. 16mo, price 75 cents.

THE HOUSE OF THE SEVEN GABLES. In one volume, 16mo, price $1 00.

TRUE STORIES FROM HISTORY AND BIOGRAPHY. In one volume, 16.o, with fine Engravings, price 75 cents.

Leaf from Ticknor, Reed and Fields catalogue, spring, 1851.

The South, which had produced an immortal in Poe, had its lesser Irving in John P. Kennedy, its lesser Cooper in Simms, and its other minor romancers like John Esten Cooke. That under happier circumstances, with more leisure, better home criticism, and greater freedom from political preoccupation, Simms might almost have equalled Cooper is evident to all readers of his Revolutionary series: *The Partisan, Mellichampe, Katharine Walton, The Scout, Eutaw,* and *Wood-craft.* He could be as interesting a storyteller, and if he totally failed in that work of character creation which made Long Tom Coffin, Hawkeye or Leather-stocking, and Harvey Birch really distinct and memorable personages, he ex-

celled Cooper in his use of historical elements. The six novels named, all delightful if read in the same fashion in which they were written—at headlong, careless
pace—give a fuller, more graphic, and more affectionate picture of oldtime
Charleston and of the Carolina countryside, checkered by Marion's rangers and
Tarleton's cavalry, than Cooper gives of any eastern area. The author write of
Katharine Walton, in which his historical matter is richest, that it was the
product of many different studies pursued for years under the guidance of the
best authorities, that the portraits were mostly of real persons, that the descrip-
tions of manners and social life were drawn from unquestionable sources, and
that the very anecdotes and repartees were often taken from tradition. His
presentation in *Woodcraft* of the prosperous post-Revolution plantation Glen-
Eberley, with its hospitable owner, its loyal, industrious slaves, and its books,
dogs, horses, and boats, and hunting rifles, is a faithful piece of genre painting,
almost comparable to Scott's best work.

On a lower plane, the South had been a fertile field for a broad journalistic
type of humor, which became important in a few literary productions, and
still more important in its influence upon future writers like Bret Harte and
Mark Twain. The *Georgia Scenes* of Augustus Baldwin Longstreet, published
as the 1840's opened, cast its genial rays afar, finding ultimate reflection even in
a few pages of Thomas Hardy's *The Trumpet-Major*. The courtship of Major
Jones, and the adventures of Captain Simon Suggs, as celebrated by William T.
Thompson and J. J. Hooper respectively, were in crude fashion an anticipation
of the local colorists who were to become so abundant in another generation or
two. The best of all these works, Joseph Glover Baldwin's *The Flush Times of
Alabama and Mississippi*, which appeared in 1853, has a special appeal to students
of history. The unsettled, rough, cheerful life of the nearer Southwestern frontier was sketched as graphically in its pages, and with nearly as much literary art,
as that of the Indiana and Illinois frontier was soon to be drawn in Edward
Eggleston's books. The time was the halcyon period 1835–37, when, as Baldwin
put it, shinplasters were the sole currency, bank bills drifted as thick as autumn
leaves in Vallambrosa, and credit could be had for the asking. The crash came,
with personal tragedies aplenty. Both literary and historical values of no mean
sort can be found in the section of the book which describes the ups and downs
of the Virginia migrants to the Southwest, relating how these sanguine, spend-
thrift, genial sons of the Old Dominion were ruined, and how they then turned to
tavern-keeping, school-teaching, or even overseerships for the wealthy planters.

The enrichment of the national scene by the romancer's imagination and the
poet's vision was perhaps the greatest single gain in American wealth during this
period. Scotland before Burns and Sir Walter Scott was one of the poorest of
lands; Scotland after "Tam O' Shanter," "The Cotter's Saturday Night," and

the Waverley novels was one of the richest. By 1860 Americans could feel what they did not in 1840—that they, too, had a picturesque, varicolored social life, a brilliant landscape, a heroic historical background; for the great writers had shown it all to them and to the world. Year by year the tapestry was widened. When Harriet Beecher Stowe in 1858 began *The Minister's Wooing* in the *Atlantic*, Lowell read it with enthusiasm and pronounced it her best work, because it presented with such simple beauty the New England life which she probably knew more intimately than any other author. As yet the realist had not thrown down the gauntlet to the romancer. Tokens of an emerging realism appeared, however, as in the powerful Pennsylvania story which Rebecca Harding Davis published in 1861—"Life in the Iron Mills." In romance and poem, in Whittier's ballads, Hawthorne's allegories, Simms's adventure tales, Whitman's chants, Bayard Taylor's travel studies, and in experimental work by younger hands, America was finding its landscape irradiated and its feeling for social experience vitalized.[7]

[IV]

Americans were learning also that their spiritual life was debtor to the deep underlying seriousness of their best literature. To instruct, to reform, and to elevate were purposes from which the greatest authors were never beguiled by hedonism, paganism, or any cult of art for art's sake. With only one notable exception, Irving, these authors were crusaders. All the eminent New Englanders save Hawthorne enlisted in the antislavery legions; the noble-hearted Simms believed ardently in the cause of Southern nationalism; and Whitman battled for his faith in democracy, brotherhood, and national feeling. The historians, who then had a wider following than at any other period in our national life, felt no desire to be coolly objective. Prescott and Motley dealt with the desperate European struggles in which political and religious liberalism had achieved a partial victory over bigotry and tyranny; Bancroft described with panegyric enthusiasm the growth of democracy in America; and Richard Hildreth, most philosophic-minded and politically conservative of them all, defended the principles of Federalism as exemplified by Washington, John Adams, and Hamilton.

The New Englanders in particular struck two dominant notes: they were unwearying foes of mediocrity and falsity, and they were imbued with a deeply felt moral passion. Emerson, who though he left the church never left off preaching, was the precentor of the group. Always insisting upon excellence—the best

7 Probably never have newspapers reprinted more good poetry than in this period. Indexes to the Burlington (Vermont) *Free Press* show that in 1856–61 it published nine poems of Longfellow, including "Paul Revere's Ride" and long excerpts from *Hiawatha;* twenty of Whittier's; six of Lowell's; seven of Bryant's; and half a dozen of O. W. Holmes's.

that a man, a community, or a nation could do—and always defending the right, he drenched his books in ethical didacticism. This homiletic trait was already recognized by some as his chief title to greatness. As a poet he was uneven, rough-tongued, and short of flight. As a philosopher he made no pretensions to profundity. As a reformer he was too retiring and scholarly to be effective; he had been noticeably tardy in joining the abolitionist movement. As a man of letters he lacked the higher creative gifts. As an ethical teacher, however, he found no equal in his time in America, and no superior anywhere except that more religious, intense, and prophetic genius, Carlyle. He tried always to reach the intellect rather than the emotions, believing that the duty of the preacher "is to convert life into truth." His gospel made a natural appeal to American optimism and individualism, for he minimized evil, urged men to trust in themselves, and extolled the grand intuitive forces in human nature. At the same time, he exhorted his hearers to explore the universe under the direction of thought. His ideal of America was a land intellectually alert and morally earnest; a country impatient of the second-best and ardent in pursuit of the superlative.

Emerson had come home from England in 1848 animated with a warmer love of his native land than ever. Almost as much as Whitman, he took joy in the expansive energy, the variety, and the driving power of the people—their march to the West, their ability to raise cities overnight, their capacity for digesting masses of immigrants. Attending the Concord town meetings, he renewed his faith in democracy as he saw Yankee farmers and tradesmen manage their public affairs with integrity and foresight. He was soon writing passages that Jefferson would have applauded. "Try the rough water as well as the smooth," ran one. "Rough water can teach lessons worth knowing. When the state is unquiet, personal qualities are more than ever decisive. Fear not a revolution which will constrain you to live five years in one. Don't be so tender about making an enemy now and then." The American idea, even in this stormy decade, seemed to him superior to any Old World idea. "I wish," he wrote in his *Journal*, "to cast out the passion for Europe by the passion for America." [8]

Yet the defects of American society did not escape him. The people lacked maturity; they were unripened, like peaches and grapes needing a fortnight more of sun. They were overpractical: "The providing means of living now absorbs them, to the exclusion of the ends. Nothing but the brandy of politics will wake them from brute life." Being ill-educated, they thought too much of machines, of railroads, telegraphs, balloons, and newspapers. Slavery, a reproach in itself,

8 "We have our culture, like Allston, from Europe, and are Europeans. Perhaps we must be content with this, and thank God for Europe for a while yet, and there shall be no great Yankee, until, in the unfolding of our population and power, England kicks the beam, and English authors write to America; which must happen ere long." *Journals*, VI, 264, 265 (1842). See also his essay "Culture" in *Conduct of Life*.

was still more shameful in the way it made cowards among Massachusetts and other Northern men. "Oh for a Roman breath and the courage that advances and dictates!" he exclaimed in the year of Buchanan's inauguration.

It was not until the Compromise of 1850, with Webster's Seventh of March speech and the Fugitive Slave Act, that Emerson had enlisted in the abolitionist crusade. Then he awoke in earnest. He felt infamy in the air; he carried about all day a painful sensation which, when traced home, was "the odious remembrance of that ignominy which has fallen on Massachusetts, which robs the landscape of beauty, and takes the sunshine out of every hour." [9] The Kansas-Nebraska Act confirmed his belief in Southern aggression, so that he later wrote of the crisis as "the years when Southern slavery broke over its old banks, made new and vast pretensions, and wrung from the weakness or treachery of the Northern people fatal concessions." [10] His was a purely moral view of slavery; if it was good, then theft, arson, and homicide were all good. He rejected the doctrine of racial inferiority, quoting Montesquieu's remark that the slaves might be better men than the slaveholders. To determine a nice question of right or wrong, he declared, he would not go to Louis Napoleon, a political hack, or a slavedriver. He did not expect a quick solution of the problem. "Liberty is never cheap. It is made difficult, because freedom is the accomplishment and perfectness of man." Yet he was certain that slavery would be overthrown. "Slowly, slowly, the Avenger comes, but comes surely. The proverbs of the nations affirm these delays, but affirm the arrival. They say, 'God may consent, but not forever.'" And Emerson quoted a verse anticipating the Second Inaugural: [11]

> For evil word shall evil word be said,
> For murder-stroke a murder-stroke be paid,
> Who smites must smart.

Never really at home in politics, Emerson was at his best when he left controversial issues alone and lifted his audiences to a higher plane of thought. He taught self-trust and self-communion as emphatically as Whittier, with his simple Quaker religiosity, taught self-distrust and self-questioning. Emerson's definition of transcendentalism as idealism was derived from Kant; for while Locke had declared that nothing could be found in the intellect which was not previously in the experience of the senses, Kant (and Emerson) held that the mind possessed an important body of intuitive ideas, which did not come by experience, but through which experience was acquired. Emerson's self-communion also owed

---

9 See repeated entries in the *Journals* for May and June, 1850. "This filthy enactment," he wrote in July, "was made in the nineteenth century, by people who could read and write. I will not obey it, by God."
10 See essay on Theodore Parker in *Miscellanies*, Concord ed., 290.
11 For Emerson's opinion of slavery see *Miscellanies*, Concord ed., 179–244.

much to the individualism of the Yankee come-outers. He believed that every man had in his own breast a deity which, intensely personal, yet embraced the world. He distilled this creed into his "Brahma" and still more lucidly into "The Problem," with its assertion that the wisdom of all bibles came from the hearts of peoples, that the litanies of nations rose from a volcanic core below, and that Michelangelo, in rounding Peter's dome, builded better than he knew because he built on the inspiration of an inner power, not on mere knowledge. Countless young Americans found stimulus in Emerson's exhortation to live in the spirit, to seek beauty, to be self-reliant, and to trust to their purer spontaneities.

Countless Americans, too, found a wholesome invigoration in Emerson's optimism. It was characteristic of the Concord seer that he never liked Shelley, whose themes of pantheism, melancholia, and rebellion against the universe repelled him; characteristic also that he disliked *The Scarlet Letter*, pronouncing it ghastly in its gloom and morbidity.[12] To Emerson, one cardinal duty of the poet was to cheer and encourage the soul. He recognized the dualism of nature, all experience finding a double form—good and evil, light and darkness, knowledge and ignorance. But his was what a later critic called a vanishing dualism, for he thought that each man could find in himself the "soul of the whole; the wise silence; the universal beauty; the eternal One." That the ultimate tendency of his ideas was to generate an excessively facile kind of optimism might be argued; that they made spiritual salvation seem too cheap and easy has often been asserted; but that their immediate effect was to brighten the outlook and strengthen the courage of men was unquestionable.[13]

Great as a preacher, he was also great as a teacher of that knowledge which he ranked so much below the inner afflatus. Nearly all his best prose work was cast in the form of the teacher's short discourse, his vocation of lecturer molding his essays. Each paper represented the quintessence of long and wide reading in the master minds of the past and of much ripe thinking, squeezed first into his journals and then refined into his essay. He holds a place with other tremendous readers and quoters—with Montaigne, Bacon, Sir Thomas Browne, Burton, Pascal, and Hazlitt—and his own reflections are as good as the thoughts he borrows from classic lore. Year by year those who heard and read him got the benefit of an encyclopedic explorer of human wisdom from Plato to Comte and Spencer. Oliver Wendell Holmes computed that the essays contained nearly 3,400 quotations from 868 writers; W. C. Brownell has written that the very titles of his discourses are a liberal education. The breadth, the spaciousness, the gem-encrusted wealth of his writings reminded Americans that they were the heirs of all the ages and that they could never afford to lose the culture of past centuries.

12   E. P. Whipple, *Reminiscences of Eminent Men*, 147, 149.
13   Cf. Paul Elmer More's estimate of Emerson, *Shelburne Essays*, First Series.

They spurred ardent minds to further reading, as they spurred ardent spirits to high endeavor.

Yet however much a cosmopolite, a citizen of all ages and all countries, Emerson was not lacking in a deep vein of pure Americanism. The national past was still so new that the question of how to regard it had an urgent importance. The radical instinct was to turn one's back on the past and seek new truth alone. The scholarly instinct was to record the facts, to preserve the more picturesque traditions and legends, and to explain the best ideas of bygone generations. The artistic instinct was to transform old lore and legend by making them more finely decorative and more deeply symbolic. Radical though he was, Emerson had his share of the preservative instinct. He felt the same affection for his national past that Plutarch, Bacon, and Montaigne had shown for theirs. While an illustration from Hindu scriptures or Byzantine story occurred to him as readily as an incident from Washington's career, he was always eager to commemorate the Yankee lares and penates.[14] When the town of Concord began its third century in 1835, he had pronounced his noble Historical Discourse, a summary of the contributions made by one provincial village to the cause of human liberty. He kept a strong sense of the merits of the old Puritanism whose formal creed he had forsaken. Two lines, certain to endure as long as anything he wrote,

> Tis man's perdition to be safe
> When for the truth he ought to die

were transmuted by him from an old Puritan divine writing in the iron year, 1642. His "Historic Notes on Life and Letters in New England" (not composed until 1867) are full of salty appreciation of the past of his section, from William Bradford's day to John A. Andrew's. His study of his witty aunt, Mary Moody Emerson, his sketch of the old Roman-spirited jurist and commissioner to South Carolina, Samuel Hoar, and his essay on Thoreau, all show a fine preservative instinct. His poems "Monadnock" and "Boston" have apt commemorative touches, while the shots of Concord battlefield were made to echo immortally around the world in his stanzas.

[V]

Second only to Emerson in his power as a moral teacher for this era stood Hawthorne. (Not until a later generation was Walt Whitman to come into his own.) Hawthorne had emerged but slowly into general recognition. At first glance this fact might seem difficult to explain. His early sheaves, *Twice Told Tales*, *The Snow Image and Other Tales*, and *Mosses from an Old Manse*, pos-

14 "A good scholar," wrote Emerson in his *Journals* for April, 1847, "will find Aristophanes and Hafiz and Rabelais full of American history."

sessed many qualities to commend them to general readers. Their themes, drawn from the old chronicles and traditions of Massachusetts, were fairly familiar: "The Gentle Boy" echoed the persecution of the Quakers, "The Gray Champion" told of the regicide judges, and the stories of the Province House dealt with important historical episodes. To these materials he gave a beautiful transforming touch. His style, pure, sweet, and graceful, with haunting poetic strains, was as simple and lucid as that of the Bible itself. Yet the moral intensity of the writer made him difficult to accept on his own terms. His pages reflected a lonely, gloomy outlook on life; they had a faint but pervasive subacidity, not quite bitter but at times decidedly misanthropic; they seemed the work of a man who had often probed the sources of spiritual unhappiness but seldom touched the fountains of spiritual joy. Readers who plunged into his tales found themselves shivering in a darker, sadder world. Even his humor had the brightness of Lapland moonlight or December sunshine, for it irradiated without warming.

Then, too, the stories and even the later novels seemed out of touch with active everyday life. As a writer in the *Atlantic* put it in 1860, the fictions suggested a shy recluse, alternately diffident in conduct and bold in thought, whose original and varied gifts "seemed to have developed themselves in the shade, without sufficient energy of will or desire to force them, except fitfully, into the sunlight." [15] He himself often spoke of his creations as unsubstantial or phantomlike, as when he wrote that Hepzibah Pyncheon appeared like someone walking in a dream. His early plaint to Longfellow explains much in his career. Writing from one of the busiest corners of the energetic New World, with a teeming, variegated, hustling life all about him, this self-bound recluse explained that he lived in an owl's nest, never going abroad till dark. He sympathized when Mrs. Longfellow died. "But," he wrote Longfellow, "I assure you that trouble is the next best thing to enjoyment, and that there is no fate in the world so horrible as to have no share in either its joys or its sorrows." Little known, little applauded, he held his pen with numbed fingers. "I have another great difficulty, in the lack of materials; for I have seen so little of the world that I have nothing but thin air to concoct my stories of; and it is not easy to give a lifelike semblance to such shadowy stuff. Sometimes, through a peephole, I have caught a glimpse of the real world; and the two or three articles in which I have portrayed such glimpses, please me better than the others." [16] Though he knew more of the

---

15 Unsigned article, May, 1860.
16 Samuel Longfellow, *Longfellow*, I, 264, 265. But he had another feeling about his long imprisonment in his lonely Salem chamber. It had benefited him in that "if I had sooner made my escape into the world, I should have grown hard and rough, and been covered with earthly dust, and my heart would have become calloused by rude encounters. . . ." Newton Arvin, *Hawthorne*, 91. For another view see Randall Stewart, *Hawthorne*.

world, and played a larger part in its activities, than this plaint would suggest, his early experience was too limited for a full-bodied fiction.

But if his absorption with a shadowy sphere of the imagination, and with the darker aspects of psychology, deprived his work of throbbing vitality, it deepened his moral vision. Hawthorne has been treated by one critic as an author reacting against Transcendentalism.[17] While the view has some justice, he is more accurately to be seen as a latter-day New Englander preoccupied with and reacting against Puritanism, which had an overmastering fascination for him. Indeed, he anticipated a struggle between Puritanism and a freer attitude, to reach its climax early in the twentieth century. When in 1850 he brought out *The Scarlet Letter*, readers saw that he had imparted a deeper feeling than ever before to his work; that putting real passion into it, he had for the first time achieved a true act of creation. His genius shone forth with such power that the book immediately became famous in both Britain and America. Yet its harshness and gloom repelled readers who declared that while it took everybody captive, it captivated nobody. Brooding over the primitive era in New England, in an effort to delineate its spiritual features, Hawthorne seized upon the sternest side of the Puritan ideal of discipline. He presented Hester Prynne and Arthur Dimmesdale as figures sealed into an icy glacier of social condemnation and hostility. They suffered under the concepts of law and justice which Increase and Cotton Mather had stated with such fierce inflexibility; they experienced none of that forgiveness and loving-kindness with which John Winthrop or Samuel Sewall would actually have treated them. The Puritans had their dogmas of grace and love no less than of punishment. New Englanders complained, with justice, that Hawthorne had brought out the iron relentlessness of their forebears in their bleakest moods, but had failed to portray their relieving interludes of humanity, compassion, and gaiety.[18]

Yet it was well for Americans to be reminded of those truths which Puritanism had at times inflexibly enforced. It was well that, in the greatest work of art produced down to that memorable year 1850 on New World soil, they should learn again the power of sin to brand an individual heart with a far more burning stigma than the letter "A" embroidered on Hester's breast. The moral symbolism which gave the book its chill, crepuscular power lifted it to the classic plane.

In *The House of the Seven Gables*, the most variegated, delightful, and lively

17 John Erskine, in *Cambridge Hist. Am. Lit.*, II, Ch. XI.
18 Indeed, Hawthorne delivers himself of iron moralizing: "And be the stern and sad truth spoken, that the breach which guilt has once made into the human soul is never, in this mortal state, repaired. It may be watched and guarded. But there is still the ruined wall, and near it the stealthy tread of the foe that would win over again his unforgotten triumph."

of the American stories, a book which (says Henry James) has a vague indefinable charm, like the sweetness of a piece of music or the softness of a September day, the drama is similarly enacted not so much for its own interest as for its symbolic value.[19] The novel possesses a sunniness unknown elsewhere in Hawthorne. It contains more social observation than the other novels, just as *The Scarlet Letter* contains more history. Several of the characters exhibit a picturesque quality, heightened by idiosyncrasy, which suggests that the author had taken some hints from Dickens. Miss Hepzibah Pyncheon, mistress of the penny shop, a stiff, antique gentlewoman of decayed fortune, spurred on by necessity yet restrained by dignity as she sells gingerbread and toys; her brother Clifford, fresh from prison, dishonored, enervated, collapsing in mind and body; the cheerful, affectionate, efficient country cousin, Phoebe Pyncheon, who comes to succor this forlorn pair, a girl as fresh, sweet, and heart-warming as she is sensible and practical; Judge Pyncheon, that imposing, bland, benevolent-seeming, hard-natured pillar of society, outwardly strong and inwardly rotting—these are the finely imagined members of a sinking family. With lighter touch Hawthorne has sketched the garrulous old wood-sawer, Uncle Venner, and the ethereal little Pearl. But for all its approach to a study of contemporaneous American life, and for all its varied charm, the novel is fundamentally stern and forbidding. Hawthorne has carried out with much fancy, but also with unsparing force, the moral purpose which he frankly avowed: to show how "the wrongdoing of one generation lives into the successive ones, and, divesting itself of every temporary advantage, becomes a pure and uncontrolled mischief."

What power is possessed by the *Blithedale Romance*, a breezy, lively book of less finish and depth, is likewise largely derived from its ethical seriousness. Zenobia dominates the story. In some respects she was unquestionably sketched from Margaret Fuller, a woman imperious, high-spirited, and eloquent; in other respects this beautiful and richly temperamental woman was a creation of Hawthorne's imagination. Almost equally robust is the portrait of Hollingsworth, a typical New England theorist. The novel shows how the flaws inherent in the characters of these two, and of their associates Miles Coverdale and Westervelt, drive them on to an inevitable catastrophe. If the moral conception of the book is narrow, it is nevertheless important.

At the end of the fifties, and near the end of Hawthorne's life, came the grandest though not the greatest of his books, a work of exquisite originality. *The Marble Faun* lacks the four-square strength, the simplicity, the poignant characters of *The Scarlet Letter*. Yet it has a richness all its own. Never has a book depended less upon its plot. It was aptly said at the time that the story began in a mystery and ended in a mist. No small part of its appeal rested upon

19 Henry James, *Nathaniel Hawthorne*, 121.

its ripe appreciation and subtle description of Italian scenery, customs, and social life generally, its acute criticism of ancient and modern art, its illuminating comments upon the architecture, history, politics, and culture of Rome.[20] At the same time, its chief personages, Hilda, Miriam, and Donatello, though types or symbols rather than warm flesh and blood, were the most imaginative and

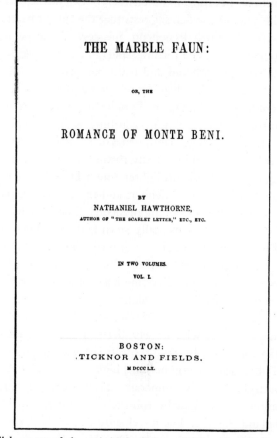

THE MARBLE FAUN:

OR, THE

ROMANCE OF MONTE BENI.

BY
NATHANIEL HAWTHORNE,
AUTHOR OF "THE SCARLET LETTER," ETC., ETC.

IN TWO VOLUMES.
VOL. I.

BOSTON:
TICKNOR AND FIELDS.
M DCCC LX.

Title page of the original edition of *The Marble Faun*.

romantic of all Hawthorne's creations. Once more, as in *The Scarlet Letter* and *The House of the Seven Gables*, the story is overshadowed by a past sin or crime in which one of the characters, Miriam, has some implication. Once more the power of sin to stigmatize and transform a life is studied. The faunlike,

20 As George Edward Woodberry remarks, he looked beyond the Italy of flowers, ruins, music: "The assumption of the myth of the world before sin, the Rousseau-like state of nature, the prehuman, fawn-and-nymph world, is easily made in that land of classical fragments and visible joy; and Hawthorne describes it with his New England pen of light fantasy and wild nature." *Hawthorne*, 185.

innocent Donatello commits an impulsive murder; the dark act matures his character and converts him into a moral being; while the equally innocent Hilda, his companion, finds that her very knowledge of the crime throws a burden upon her conscience, impairs her joy in art and nature, and awakens in her a deeper thirst for rectitude and truth. The once-happy Donatello, who had been able to call furry and feathered creatures to him, is miserable on finding that they avoid his presence. "They shun me!" he cries. "All nature shrinks from me, and shudders at me! I live in the midst of a curse, that hems me round with a circle of fire! No innocent thing can come near me!" The cloudy ending of the story lessens its force as a moral apologue, but apologue it is, and one of wild, haunting beauty.

In all the New England writers this ethical vein was prominent. Whittier was a true son of the Quaker faith in his religious piety, his belief in toleration, his reformative impulses, his abhorrence of violence (which made him condemn John Brown's raid), and his emphasis upon the humbling of self. In many controversial essays, of which "Democracy and Slavery" is the most important, he pressed home his ethical attitude toward public issues. His antislavery poems, beginning with his apostrophes to William Lloyd Garrison and Toussaint l'Ouverture in 1832–33, were destined to rise to a fine climax in such pieces as "The Battle Autumn of 1862" and "Barbara Frietchie." All his poetry was strongly moralized; when he told a tale or pictured a scene, he never let the reader make application for himself. The same could be said of that transplanted New Englander, William Cullen Bryant. His favorite themes were death, to which he wrote more than one hymn, the inexorable march of years, the circle of eternal change in nature, the duty of man to his native land, and the still greater duty of communion with God. Even June reminded him of mortality—it was a happy month in which to be buried, when through the long summer hours the golden light might slant across his grave; even the fringed gentian, fixing its blue eye upon the autumn heavens, inspired a wish that in his fatal hour hope might blossom in his breast. He wrote of American virtues in "O Mother of a Mighty Race," and urged fortitude in "The Battlefield:"

> Truth, crushed to earth, shall rise again,
> Th' eternal years of God are hers;
> But Error, wounded, writhes in pain,
> And dies among his worshippers.

Holmes, touching in the *Autocrat* papers on a multitude of subjects, was affluent in wit, humor, and sagacious insights. His lightness of touch and hints at heterodoxy in religion led many to suspect him of levity. Actually his essays are full of didacticism, and he sometimes preaches as if his ministerial father Abiel were furnishing him a sermon. Jolly as is "The Wonderful One-Hoss

Shay," it cannot be fully understood except in connection with Holmes's essay on Jonathan Edwards; the issue of the *Atlantic* (September, 1858) that carried it also contained his lively piece of moralizing, "The Chambered Nautilus."

Lowell may also be given high rank among the humorists. He had displayed his rare spirits, ebullient humor, and satiric gift in the *Fable for Critics* and the *Biglow Papers*, while he was one of the few genuine epigrammatists that the country has produced. His approach to life was cultivated, genial, and intensely literary; despite his social activity, his journalistic work, and his gay versatility, it was even bookish. He seemed to have read everything of importance in Spanish, Italian, and French, as well as in English literature: he was equally at home in Cervantes, Dante, Molière, and Shakespeare. With the highest standards of classic expression he was thoroughly familiar, and with them in mind he wrote in 1857 an effective condemnation of didactic poetry: "Put all your beauty in your rhymes, your morals in your living." Yet he frequently touched the moral chord—and with resounding force, as his "Sir Launfal" of 1848 had proved.[21]

Heartiest teacher of them all was Walt Whitman, poet of the masses (though they read him but little) and voice of the democratic ideal—a man who sang "the greatness of Love and Democracy" and the song of Companionship; a believer in individualism and "the beauty of all adventurous and daring persons." In Whitman we touch a force far broader, more humane, and more electric than is found in any of his New England contemporaries. He had drawn much from his Quaker forebears, much from Emerson, much from various pagan influences, and most of all from his contacts with the plain people. Out of his experience and reading he painted pictures of the wide national scene and the multitudinous varieties of social action; and he infused his sketches with a sense of American energy, joviality, confidence in the future, and democratic ease. He wrote of Yankee clippers, cutting the sparkle and scud, of clam diggers gathering around the chowder kettle, of the fur-clad trapper marrying a lithe Indian girl in a glade beneath the Tetons, of the foot-bruised runaway slave sinking exhausted at a Northern door, of Texas Rangers massacred by the Mexicans, of an old-fashioned sea fight of the days of 1812. He wrote, above all, of his own appetites, emotions, and aspirations. His *Leaves of Grass* had a surging vitality; it was suffused with a semi-religious feeling for democracy as the very essence of the republic's life.[22]

---

21 Herman Melville, too, a man of deep moral insights, brought them out in *Mardi* and *Billy Budd*; while he had his direct reform objects as well. *Redburn* was aimed at the reformation of bad conditions in the merchant marine, *White Jacket* in the naval service.

22 Emerson writes in his *Journals* that George Bancroft and Bryant were historical democrats interested in dead or organized liberty, not in the work of organizing liberty. This was unjust; for though Whitman was much more concerned with organizing liberty than Bancroft, Bryant's great work for that cause on the *Evening Post* is unforgettable. On Whitman, see Cleveland Rodgers and John Black, eds., *The Gathering of the Forces*.

Whitman's verse was often of a nebulous kind, at its worst harsh and monotonous, and even at its best sometimes seeming to need an alchemic change to precipitate it in true poetic form. His gospel of self-reliance, comradeship, national loyalty, and democracy was sometimes nebulous too, or disjointed and inarticulate—but it was infinitely suggestive; if at times it left the reader baffled and irritated, it usually left him heartened and buoyant. Whitman's faults lay all on the surface, while some of his merits were not fully grasped for half a century. Yet even in 1855 there were many who saw that he was achieving a new and stirring form of verse melody. He conceived it his business to "take hold of muscular democratic virilities without wincing and put them into verse;" and if he frequently fell into prose and even bathos, he also frequently touched felicity. Prophet, mystic, and poet in one, he was willing to speak himself even if he startled others:

> Do you take it I would astonish?
> Does the daylight astonish? Does the early redstart twittering through
> the wood?

And in speaking his broad sympathies ("Whoever walks a furlong without sympathy walks to his own funeral drest in his shroud") he could occasionally convey his feeling with the happiest diction and rhythm. The music of his familiar hymn to earth and night—"Press close, magnetic nourishing night!"—was matched by his pictorial vividness in passage after passage:

> Where the quail is whistling betwixt the woods and the wheat-lot,
> Where the bat flies in the Seventh-month eve, where the great gold-bug
> drops through the dark,
> Where the brook puts out of the roots of the old tree and flows to the
> meadow,
> Where cattle stand and shake away flies with the tremulous shuddering
> of their hides. . . .
> Where band-necked partridges roost in a ring on the ground with their
> heads out,
> Where burial coaches enter the arch'd gates of a cemetery,
> Where winter wolves bark amid wastes of snow and icicled trees,
> Where the yellow-crowned heron comes to the edge of the marsh at
> night and feeds upon small crabs,
> Where the splash of swimmers and divers cools the warm noon.

His gospel of self-reliance, self-release, emotional honesty, and democratic individualism peculiarly fitted the mood of mid-century America. A superbly liberating gospel, it had a foundation of long meditation and self-searching, and it was destined to blow like a fresh wind through the world poetry of succeeding generations. Now he spoke the ideals of the masses—"the dense-packed cities all and the teeming wharves and ways." Now he spoke of the self-realization of

the individual soul, as in his description ("Out of the Cradle Endlessly Rocking";
1860) of the boy listening to a bird-song by the seashore:

> Demon or bird! said the boy's soul,
> Is it indeed toward your mate you sing? or is it mostly to me?
> For I, that was a child, my tongue's use sleeping,
> Now I have heard you,
> Now in a moment I know what I am for—I awake,
> And already a thousand singers—a thousand songs, clearer,
>   louder, and more sorrowful than yours,
> A thousand warbling echoes have started to life within me,
> Never to die.

Whitman was broadening the language of verse by marrying the American
idiom to literature; no other poet in 1855 would have dared to say, "We have
had ducking and deprecation enough." But his greater object was to broaden the
spirit of the nation by a challenge to inert conventionality; by persuading men
to be like himself, one who had "hated tyrants, argued not concerning God, had
patience and indulgence toward the people, taken off my hat to nothing known
or unknown, gone freely with powerful uneducated persons and with the
young, and with the mothers of families."

[VI]

The creation of this resplendent if uneven body of literature had been impossible until various social foundations had been laid. One prerequisite was a
broad measure of freedom of individual expression. The goal stated by Mill in
his *Essay on Liberty*, a goal difficult of attainment under modern conditions, was
within reach of countless citizens in this era. No restrictions checked the spontaneous growth of individuality; no tyrannic forces ground men down to an
average norm. The humanities of the people had full opportunity to develop.
Almost everywhere except in the Deep South a broad freedom of thought and
expression existed. In that area the two before-noted tabus, slavery and religious
heterodoxy, laid a stern restraint upon public utterance. As the tensions of the
decade increased, it is true that intolerance on the slavery issue rose. Even Massachusetts punished Commissioner Loring for merely doing his sworn duty
under the Fugitive Slave Act. But all sections had their courageously independent editors and politicians. The South could point to the brilliant John H.
Pleasants, the tenacious Benjamin F. Perry, the belligerent Cassius M. Clay and
John Minor Botts, speaking unpopular views; South Carolina admired the arch-
Unionist Petigru. And nowhere, North or South, were the religious dogmas of
the time important as restraints upon literature.[23]

23 Clement Eaton, *Freedom of Thought in the Old South*, 162–195.

Northerners enjoyed Hawthorne without repining because he sneered at abolitionism in his life of Franklin Pierce. They delighted in the *Autocrat* without worrying much over Holmes's trenchant rationalism and anti-Calvinism, and in Whitman without resenting his dislike of creeds. The defensive attitude of the South did fetter its writers. But the *Southern Quarterly Review*, praising Longfellow for his gifts of fancy, grace, and taste, merely remarked in passing that he had penned sundry ignorant verses on slavery in a moment of fanaticism, and went on to extol him as one of the most charming of poets in English.[24]

As important as freedom of expression was a wide, appreciative, and growing body of readers. The demand for books in this decade was such as to delight an author's heart. Technical improvements, such as the invention of electrotyping about 1850, had greatly reduced the costs of publishing; book production rose by one-half during the first decade of the fifties; and one publisher estimated that in 1856 Americans bought sixteen million dollars' worth of books published at home, and another million dollars' worth imported from abroad. Harper & Brothers were issuing three million books a year.[25] Anthony Trollope was soon to remark that while an English publisher contented himself with thousands of copies, his Yankee counterpart would deal with ten thousands.[26] Just how many bookstores the country contained it is difficult to say. According to the census of 1860, fewer than nineteen hundred persons reported their occupation as booksellers and stationers; but many shops sold books among their other wares. New York State in 1859 had 422 booksellers, or at least book outlets, in 157 cities and towns; Pennsylvania had 329 in 78 towns; and Maryland had 54 in 13 towns. The *American Publishers Circular and Literary Gazette*, which collected these figures, found that Massachusetts had 237 booksellers, and Connecticut 81. The South, if we may accept the carefully gathered statistics of this journal, did surprisingly well. In 1860 Virginia had 73 booksellers, North Carolina 66, South Carolina 35, Georgia 67, Alabama 80, and Mississippi 70.[27] These figures, North and South, may include general stores which carried a few religious books. But then many books were sold by mail, while book peddlers took orders for standard sets.

The magazines which printed genuinely able reviews, awarding praise and blame with discrimination, were now numerous. The critical pages of *Graham's*, *Russell's*, and the *Southern Literary Messenger* were of fair quality, *Putnam's* was good if uneven, and the *Atlantic*, with Lowell's hand prominent, was excellent, lifting American criticism to a higher plane from the date of its establish-

24 September, 1850.
25 See Eighth Census, Manufactures, cxxxiii; Harper, *House of Harper*, 90, 117, 118.
26 *North America*, 271.
27 *Publishers' Circular*, August 6, September 10, 1859, March 24, 1860.

ment.[28] Newspapers of the time played a greater part in popularizing literature, and especially poetry, than later. They gutted travels and histories, and reprinted verse from all the standard magazines. Lowell's "The Courtin'," Holmes's "Chambered Nautilus," and Bryant's "The Constitution" were thus scattered from the Atlantic to the Pacific. Whittier, however, was the poet most quoted at the North. The newspapers also published admiring articles on the chief literary personages. The *National Intelligencer*, for example, carried in 1856 an essay by a travelling Washingtonian upon "the Athens of America" (Concord), assuming the familiarity of all readers with *Mosses from an Old Manse*, treating Thoreau, Ellery Channing, and Margaret Fuller appreciatively, and lauding Emerson to the skies. "If Emerson has ever written an unimportant word," the writer exclaimed, "I should like to treasure it up . . . as a certificate that Jove sometimes nods." [29]

The professional man of letters could now begin to live by his pen. Prescott and Motley greatly augmented their fortunes by their histories; Hawthorne was lifted out of poverty by his major books; and even so minor a poet as Fitz-Greene Halleck, with three editions of his works published 1848–58, reaped a considerable return.[30] On the day *Hiawatha* was published Longfellow wrote that four thousand out of the first five thousand copies had been sold, and another three thousand ordered. *The Courtship of Miles Standish* was an even greater success. By noon of the day of publication five thousand copies had been sold in Boston alone; two editions of ten thousand copies each were printed or printing. A week later Longfellow wrote that the book had marched steadily on. "Another five thousand are in press; in all, an army of twenty-five thousand— in one week." [31]

The West and South alone failed to offer their writers an appreciative public, the West because it was too new, the South because social conditions were unfavorable. The slave States in the forty years before the war could be said to have two professional writers, and only two. One was Poe, who took refuge in the North and almost starved even there! The other was Simms, who fared nearly as badly.

Early in 1860, poor, in debt, with a dilapidated plantation, torn by care and anxiety, Simms wrote William Porcher Miles a pathetic letter upon the failure

28 Emerson had written in his *Journals* on October 2, 1841, that the country needed severe literary criticism. "I cannot help seeing that Dr. Channing would have been a much greater writer had he found a strict tribunal. . . . It is very easy to reach the degree of culture that prevails round us; very hard to pass it, and Dr. Channing, had he found Wordsworth, Southey, Coleridge, and Lamb around him, would as easily have been severe with himself and risen a degree higher as he has stood where he is."
29 *National Intelligencer*, August 16, 1856.
30 J. G. Wilson, *Halleck*, 478 ff.
31 Samuel Longfellow, *Longfellow*, II, 364, 365.

of his latest volume. "I have been overworked; I have been unsuccessful all my life; my books fail to pay me; I am myself a failure! . . . The labor is wasted upon a people who have seemingly decided that, so far as my labor is to depend upon their favor, I shall die. I shall appear again on no stage. I have heart for nothing, I am resigned to obscurity, and can struggle no more, except to pay off creditors and feed and clothe my poor little children." [32] Three distinguished Southern writers, A. B. Longstreet, John P. Kennedy, and Beverley Tucker (whose *George Balcombe* was called by Poe the best American novel of its time) depended on law, politics, or education for a living. The shy young poet Henry Timrod was a plantation tutor.

Simms prophesied that no Southern literature worthy of the name would ever exist under a slaveholding aristocracy. His views were echoed by Paul Hamilton Hayne, who edited *Russell's Magazine* for two years without pay, and who in 1859 complained that he had sold fewer than two hundred copies of a small book of poems issued two years earlier largely at his own expense. "There's encouragement for you!" he exclaimed. Thanking Lowell for a friendly review in the *Atlantic*, he deplored the unliterary character of the Southern people. To a young literary aspirant, it was hard to learn "that his *very profession* is looked upon with contempt, or at best a sort of half-pitying patronage by those he would fain delight and satisfy." [33] The sparse population of the section, the paucity of large, well-stocked bookshops and public libraries, the preoccupation with politics, and the belief that literature was best regarded either as a proslavery weapon or a proof of elegant leisure, were unpropitious to Southern authorship.

Still another prerequisite for literary achievement was a large and varied body of craftsmen, vying with one another for distinction. By mid-century, America had its swarm of writers. A series of important new types appeared. In the serious field James Parton, with his *Greeley*, *Burr*, and other biographies, represented the hitherto unknown school of journalist-historian; a group which also produced Richard Hildreth. Friedrich Kapp and Francis Lieber led in the column of transplanted European writers of erudition and talent. Artemus Ward and George H. Derby rose to notice in the fifties as newspaper humorists of a fresh kind. Bayard Taylor, George W. Curtis, and others made the light volume of travels more popular than ever before. The painstaking Benson J. Lossing, whose *Pictorial Field Book of the Revolution* was published in 1850–52, showed how interesting the labors of the antiquarian might become. Henry S. Randall set a new standard for scholarly biography in his *Jefferson*, issued in three solid volumes in 1858. On every hand, in fact, authors were hewing out new channels.

32 January 13, 1860; Miles Papers, U. of North Carolina.
33 December 28, 1859; D. M. McKeithan, *A Collection of Hayne Letters.*

Charles Eliot Norton and William Wetmore Story were giving currency to the first really original and incisive art criticism in America, framed in studies of Italian life.[34] It may be said that such figures bear no relation to the masterpieces of Hawthorne, Melville, and Whitman. But if a country does not have a large body of small writers, it is not likely to have a small body of great ones.

The growing swarm of litterateurs made possible the rise of coteries, like the Saturday Club in Boston, the circles that met in Pfaff's restaurant and the Century Club in New York, the friends of the bibliophile Henry D. Gilpin in Philadelphia,[35] and the group that sat in Russell's Bookshop in Charleston. Here, wits were sharpened and spiritual stimuli interchanged. No one can read the letters of Lowell or the journals of Longfellow and Emerson without feeling how immeasurably they profited by the frequent meetings of the whole Concord-Boston group—in the Old Corner Bookshop, at Felton's dinner table or in Harriet Hosmer's drawing room, on the Common, or at the Club; meetings where Prescott was sunny and jovial, where James T. Fields reported on Hawthorne's new book, where Sumner told historical anecdotes, or where Holmes shot out his latest pun; contacts which kept learning and ideas in circulation.[36] No one can read W. D. Howells's account of his meeting with Walt Whitman at Pfaff's on an August night in 1860 without realizing how much a single handclasp from a figure of eminence might mean to a neophyte.[37] And no one can go through the papers of an isolated writer like John Esten Cooke without a poignant understanding of his hopeless craving for literary companionship. Cooke hailed a letter from Simms with joy. "Simms is a hearty, cordial, openhearted man—a capital companion, and as true as steel. It is refreshing now and then to see such a 'high-pressure steamboat,' as he is—it stirs my languid pulse, and wakes me from my indolence." He wrote Thomas Dunn English asking how his New York friends were doing, and what that nice gentleman Aldrich of the *Home Journal* was up to. Alas, the few Southern men of letters had little contact with their Northern fellows or with each other.[38]

We might speak of still other factors in this literary efflorescence. At its roots, no doubt, lay social forces of an indefinable kind. As T. S. Eliot has said, a true culture is not the creation of a special class or set of institutions; it must spring from a way of life, from an ethos that pervades a whole society and embraces all its activities and interests.[39] No complete explanation is possible and none is necessary. The important fact was simply that America did have the

34　As in Norton's *Travel and Study in Italy* (1859).
35　See *Memorial of Henry D. Gilpin* (Philadelphia, 1860).
36　See Edward Emerson, *The Early Years of the Saturday Club.*
37　*Literary Friends and Acquaintance,* 74–76.
38　See letter May 13, 1858, to Edward St. George Cooke, and other letters in the small collection of Cooke Papers in Duke University.
39　*Notes Toward the Definition of Culture.*

vigorous budding of a great literature. This burgeoning of letters was of the first importance to the national mind and spirit. As we have said, it gave the country confidence in its power to contribute to the world's stock of aesthetic treasures; it transformed and enriched the national scene, brightening it with the light never seen on land or sea; and above all, by its high import and moral elevation it fortified the heart of the republic. The soul of a country is best realized in pure literature; here, at last, the American soul was finding expression. Next to its partial demonstration of the value of democratic self-government, America could point to this literature as its proudest achievement.

3

Buchanan Prepares for His Task

THE FIRST DAYS of 1857 found Americans opening the initial number of a bright sixteen-page illustrated magazine: *Harper's Weekly, a Journal of Civilization*. Its leading feature was a first-page, four-column editorial on the recent Presidential election. The result, declared the editor, had proved the strength of the "great conservative element." It was a mandate for preserving the vast national interests by "harmony and concession."

This opinion was generally held, and was borne out by impartial analyses of the returns. The combined vote for Buchanan and Fillmore, an impressive majority of the total, might well be regarded as a conservative vote. In the critical States of Pennsylvania and Indiana, in particular, the electorate had been profoundly moved by apprehensions of civil strife. Union was the controlling desire of the nation, and the Democratic Party had been maintained in power because it was the one chief bond of union. All this seemed reassuring. Did any ground for anxiety still exist? If so, it was not primarily because Mississippi and Georgia were laying down a new "ultimatum," while Greeley's *Tribune* was insisting that the Republicans would never compromise on freedom for the Territories. It was because the main bond of union, the Democratic Party, was itself increasingly disunited.

For the campaign and its results, as viewed by optimists of the day, scarcely reflected the real state of the country. The first issue of *Harper's Weekly* suggested certain sombre aspects of the national scene in touching on polygamy in Utah and a suspected slave insurrection in Tennessee. In the latter State an accused Negro had been whipped, to die after receiving 750 lashes. That episode stood as an unhappy symbol of the tensions between North and South; of rifts that had destroyed the Whig organization, had given birth to the Republican Party, and were now putting a heavy strain on the Democracy. Campaign excitements had thrown a concealing web across the chasm dividing Douglas's popular sovereignty wing from the Southern State Rights wing. While Douglas insisted that the settlers in a Territory might exclude slavery practically from the outset, Jefferson Davis and his associates maintained that the settlers must admit slavery until in forming a new State they gained power to exclude or perpetuate it. The country expected Buchanan to uphold national unity. But the initial question was whether he could restore the unity of his own party. What was his equipment for that task?

[I]

James Buchanan had been so long in public life that neither his character nor his views should have been mysterious. It was forty-three years since he had entered the Pennsylvania legislature, thirty-seven since he had first gone to Congress. Yet he was less understood than many a younger but more salient figure. No great law, no dramatic event, no revealing speech, was associated with his name. The country knew him as a man of dignified bearing, balanced judgment, and conciliatory ways. It knew that, holding many offices—Senator, Secretary of State, minister to Russia and Britain—he had risen in the political firmament by industry, ability, and adroitness. Toiling early and late, he had always mastered his duties thoroughly; he had always spoken clearly and temperately; he was versed in the law, and a learned expositor of the Constitution. But no dramatic act, no gallant episode, had ever revealed the man's soul. His character was unsullied, but it seemed a limited character.

What would latter-day psychiatrists have made out of this stiff, capable, unadventurous man? A toilsome childhood as son of a Mercersburg farmer and merchant; highly ambitious college years at Dickinson, where he would have led his class but for some rule-breaking; an apprenticeship at law, studying hard all day and practicing extempore speeches at night—this is a commonplace story. Within three years of entry to the bar his annual income exceeded $11,000, proof of brains and address. The most striking event of his early life was the sudden death of his fiancée, following a lovers' quarrel between them. The circumstances are not fully known (in his instructions to executors he ordered the pertinent papers destroyed), but he was barred from the funeral, and the tragedy left a scar that forbade all thought of marriage. Though he made warm friends, his life thereafter was lonely. The key to his character, however, is to be found in a quality not easily explained: in a deep irresolution. His deficiency in humor, his meagre imagination, his secretive vein, his tortuous ways, were all connected with this trait. So, too, was his tendency to lean on others; for while in small matters he was reticent, in large affairs he did not trust himself.

To contemporaries, his character seemed strangely at variance with his personal and political antecedents. Of the same Scotch-Irish stock as Jackson, Calhoun, and Polk, he showed hardly a rusty fleck of the iron in these notable men. The typical Ulster Scot was stern, emphatic, and daring, ready for a word and a blow, the blow first. Buchanan had invariably been cautious, peaceloving, and soft-spoken. To be sure, he possessed a few salient traits of his ancestry; he was religious, a man of prayer; he was self-denying and stubbornly tenacious. As Martin Van Buren saltily remarked, he was "amply endowed with those clear perceptions of self-interest and of duties connected with it that are almost inseparable from the Scottish character." [1] He had accumulated a modest fortune, perhaps $300,000, from which he gave generously to charity. But he was totally devoid of stern fighting qualities. It was also plain that, although a Jacksonian, he had little trace of Jackson's unbending devotion to the Union and impatience of sectionalism. Quite ignorant of the trans-Allegheny region, he knew nothing of the Western spirit of nationalism; but he might have displayed as much attachment to national unity as his fellow-Jacksonians of the East, Bancroft and Bryant. On the contrary, he explicitly said that a continuance of the abolitionist agitation would justify the South in seceding. Another contradiction lay in his attitude toward slavery. He had been reared at Mercersburg, educated at Carlisle, and admitted to practice at Lancaster, all in Pennsylvania; he represented a free State; yet he was more partial to slavery than many Virginians.

All these contradictions arose from his irresolution—from the combination of timidity, pliability, and self-seeking in his character. He was too timid to be a fighter; too pliable to stand firmly for the Union; too self-seeking to say a word against slavery when he knew that his political future rested upon slave-State favor. He had thus far tactfully wormed his way through obstacles that had foiled the direct attack of Benton and Webster. His success had sometimes been marvellous. As Jackson's star rose, he had hitched his chariot to it. In 1827, Jackson, insisting on his charges of bargain and corruption in the late election, asserted that Buchanan had been an agent for Clay in the latter's efforts to gain high office for giving up the Presidency. This was untrue, for Buchanan had never been an intermediary in any attempted bargain. He had to deny Jackson's statement. Yet he did it so adroitly that he managed to keep Jackson's favor. During the controversy in Congress over the right of petition, similarly, he somehow managed to take the sound constitutional ground that it must not be abridged, and yet to retain Southern liking by insisting that the petitions be laid on the table without debate. As Polk's Secretary of State, again, Buchanan with one hand made firm demands on Mexico, and with the other offered conciliatory blandishments, leaving it to the President to take the steps which ended in war. He had thus pleased the South without estranging the North. But in managing and leading politicians (as distinguished from placating them), he had practically no experience whatever.

1   Martin Van Buren, *Autobiography*, 406.

Endowed with industry, capacity, and tact, Buchanan was admirably qualified for judicial or diplomatic positions. It was a cruel fate which kept him from
the Supreme Court in 1844 (when Tyler offered him a seat) to raise him to the
White House thirteen years later.[2] As a diplomat, despite the stain left on his
name by the Ostend Manifesto, he had served with high ability. In negotiating
with Russia and Britain, he always showed a firm Americanism, and by his per-
sistence, thorough mastery of facts, and cautious preparation, he usually achieved
success. In his overseas career he again showed his adroitness. Although Martin
Van Buren, spending a month or so with him in London, found that his pertina-
cious Yankee aims had become a subject of general remark, he enjoyed a distinct
social success in England. Oxford had given him a D.C.L. But for an executive
post, especially in a time of grim pressures, he was unsuited. His wariness, his
legalistic temper, his meekness whenever faced by a belligerent associate, and
his taste for shifty maneuvers were heavy disqualifications. Where iron nerve,
decisive action, and a power of bending men to his will were needed, he was
helpless to supply them. Moreover, he totally lacked imagination or inspiration.
No electric spark, no glow of genius, ever lighted up his mind. He had
never coined an epigram or written an eloquent passage; he could not even
quote aptly, for he had no interest in literature. "I do not think he ever
uttered a genuine witticism in his life," states his intimate friend Henry S.
Foote.[3]

President Polk's shrewd eye had perceived the irresolute character of
Buchanan. "It is one of his weaknesses," wrote Polk, "that he takes on and mag-
nifies small matters into great and undeserved importance." William H. Trescot,
who served under him in the London legation, termed him cold, calculating, and
heartless, so devious that he was sometimes false and so circumspect that he was
often crafty; an excessively harsh judgment, but with much truth. His great
admirer, Jeremiah S. Black, speaks of an excess of craftiness. "Even among close
friends," writes Senator Foote, "he very rarely expressed his opinions at all
upon disputed questions, except in language especially marked with a cautious
circumspection almost amounting to timidity." Like other weak men, he could
be a vengeful fighter when attacked; and again like other weak men, he never
confessed himself wrong. Needing the aid of more robust natures, he delighted
in a small circle of cronies, but as Foote remarks, he did not like men of high
intellectual attainments about him. Never very resourceful, he became more stiff
and inflexible with increasing years, as his book *The Administration on the Eve
of the Rebellion* shows. In the final crisis of his term he grew panicky (the word

2 Charles Warren, *Hist. Supreme Court,* II (1926 ed.) 116; cf. *Atlantic,* LII, 708.
3 Foote, *Casket of Reminiscences,* 112.

is endorsed by Jefferson Davis on the basis of their conversations) for both the nation and his personal safety.[4]

In his defense it can be said that he was passionately attached to peace and convinced that appeasement was the one way to stay the South from rash courses. But in iron times our verdict on appeasers must be severe. In a line of mediocre Presidents, not one of whom would be esteemed fit today to head a large corporation, bank, or university, he had more ability than Taylor or Fillmore, more steadiness than Pierce, and more civil experience than the three combined. Yet he was as ill-equipped for a supreme test as they. By half-measures, evasions, and stealthy approaches, by all the arts of weakness, he had gained the Presidency at just the moment when a man of all but superhuman vision and strength was needed.

Since it was natural for him to cling to some strength greater than his own, throughout his career he had shown a strict allegiance to party. He had accepted all the Jacksonian doctrines, good or bad; he had hewn to the Democratic line under Polk. While often statesmanlike in his speeches and papers, he had also often been cheaply partisan. This party constancy, however, was less remarkable than his equally unswerving alignment with the Southern proslavery wing of his party.

The campaign documents of 1856, in appealing to Southern voters, had described this side of his record in detail. During the middle thirties, he had spoken against the abolition of slavery in the Federal District, had declared for tabling the abolitionist petitions in silence, and had pressed for the admission of Arkansas as a slave State. He had espoused a measure making it unlawful for postmasters to distribute printed material touching upon slavery if this was forbidden by State enactment. He had supported all of Calhoun's resolutions of December 27, 1837—the famous resolutions asserting the compact-theory of the Union, assailing the abolitionists, declaring it the duty of the national government to give increased stability to slavery in any State possessing it, and denouncing any Northern attempt to interfere with the acquisition of new lands simply because such annexation would expand the domain of slaveholders. Ten years later, Buchanan had advocated a division of California and New Mexico between slavery and freedom by the extension of the Missouri Compromise line to the Pacific. In the autumn of 1850 he had assured the people of Philadelphia that this Compromise line had "passed away." He had remonstrated against an

---

4 Polk, *Diary*, September 1, 1846; Foote, *op. cit.*, 112. Buchanan's papers contain some striking instances of his timidity when faced by belligerent men. For example, John M. Clayton, his successor in the State Department, wrote him a nasty letter April 6, 1849. Some dispute had arisen over a petty appointment. Clayton wrote that his first inclination had been "to tell you to go to the devil," and called one of Buchanan's statements untrue. Buchanan replied in conciliatory and honeyed terms. Buchanan Papers.

act of the Pennsylvania legislature obstructing the recovery of fugitive slaves. He had supported proposals for the purchase of Cuba at a cost of a hundred millions or more, and had been a ready participant in the Ostend Manifesto upon acquisition of the island.[5]

Each one of these acts was from his standpoint arguably correct. It was nevertheless remarkable that this son of Franklin's State, this fellow townsman of Thaddeus Stevens, had never once deviated from a line congenial to advanced proslavery men.

Buchanan's closest personal friends in Congressional days had been Southerners like John Slidell and William R. King. He had asserted in 1850 that the Compromise was a hard bargain for the South. He wrote in 1851 that he had been fighting the battle of the South on the slavery issue for fifteen years. He had declared in 1856 that a Republican victory would be a decree of outlawry against fifteen slave States, and that disruption of the Union would immediately and inevitably ensue. Taking the view that the North alone was aggressive, he held that the central requirement of the hour was simply that the slave area be left alone. While he never expressed any moral repugnance to slavery (though he had spoken regretfully of its existence), he had uttered some bizarre ideas on its practical aspects. Thus he had assured the Senate in 1844 that the annexation of Texas would be the means of limiting, not enlarging, the slavery domain. "In the government of the world," he remarked, "Providence generally produces great changes by gradual means. There is nothing rash in the councils of the Almighty." (In fact, the Almighty was cautious, evasive, and timid, like James Buchanan.) The acquisition of Texas, he argued, would operate to draw slaves farther south, into a clime more congenial to their nature; and they would probably thus "pass off into Mexico, and there mingle with a race where no prejudice exists against their color." He shared this strange opinion with Robert J. Walker, his Cabinet associate, who likewise believed that Texas would serve as a funnel for draining slavery away, "by diffusion," into the boundless regions of Mexico, Central America, and beyond.[6]

As sectional feeling rose, the dread of secession had become an obsessive idea with the weak-nerved Buchanan. During the recent campaign he had felt that nothing mattered but "the grand and appalling issue of union or disunion."

5 Von Holst, *Calhoun*, Ch. VII; George Ticknor Curtis, *Buchanan*, I, 215–543 *passim*. See the Democratic pamphlet of 1856, "The Agitation of Slavery. Who Commenced and Who Can End It? Buchanan and Fillmore Compared."

6 *Cong. Globe*, June 8, 1844. One caller in these years says he heard Buchanan state again and again that if the two sections separated on the slavery question, it was doubtful with which Pennsylvania would take her stand. W. M. Corry in Cincinnati *Daily Commercial*, quoted in N. Y. *Weekly Tribune*, December 3, 1859. Buchanan requested Sir William Gore Ouseley never to express "abolitionist" opinions in his presence. Ouseley to Buchanan, August 19, 1858; Buchanan Papers.

Republican defeat had stayed the danger, but would it not recur? Another obsession, derived from his Southern friends, was the danger of a servile insurrection. As early as 1826 he had dwelt upon the possibility of Haitian horrors in the cotton States. "There are portions of the Union in which, if you emancipate your slaves, they will become your masters. There can be no middle course. Is there any man in this Union who would for a moment indulge the horrible idea of abolishing slavery by the massacre of the chivalrous race of men in the South? . . . For my own part I would, without hesitation, buckle on my knapsack." He was thus persuaded that slavery represented not a mere political issue, but a question of life or death for the Southern people. "What agony of mind the abolitionist publications are causing!" he exclaimed in 1836. "Many a mother clasps her infant to her bosom when she retires to rest, under dreadful apprehensions that she may be roused from her slumbers by the savage yells of the slaves by whom she is surrounded." As President, he repeatedly touched the same chord. Secession by the South would be justified, he believed, if the antislavery agitation continued; and he held that it would have been justified had Frémont been elected, for the Republican Party was largely made up of abolitionists.[7]

Leaning toward the Southern view of all public issues, sharing the mental processes of his many Southern friends, well aware that but twenty-five miles from his own town of Lancaster lay the slaveholding Marylanders, Buchanan took the Southern position on the great difference in doctrine which divided the Democratic Party. Could the people of a Territory decide against slavery before they formed a State Constitution? He thought not. In his speech to his Wheatland neighbors just after the October elections, he had said that the residents of a Territory should make their decision when about to enter the Union as a State.[8] For various reasons, Buchanan was certain to take an impatient attitude toward Douglas and his popular sovereignty tenets. He had long disliked the "Young America" spirit and its denunciation of old fogies; he disliked Douglas personally, thinking him bumptious, ill-mannered, and aggressive; he thought Douglas's Kansas-Nebraska Act regrettable; he well remembered that if Douglas could have held the whole of the New York delegation at the Cincinnati convention instead of only half, no other man could have been nominated; and he consorted with men who, like Slidell, were enemies of Douglas. Always conservative in his interpretation of the Constitution, he accepted the argument that all citizens had an equal right to carry their property into the Territories. He awaited only the proper hour to trample squatter sovereignty, and with it the Illinois Senator, underfoot.

For if cautious and conciliatory on grim national questions, Buchanan was

7 Curtis, *Buchanan*, I, 317; II, 68.
8 *Ibid.*, II, 176.

harshly unyielding on party discipline. He detested Democratic "guerrillas" and "disorganizers" only less than he detested Republicans. He deemed it the first duty of an Administration to suppress factions. Jackson's imperious attack upon Calhoun, his rough ousting of three Calhounite members, Ingham, Branch, and Berrien, from the Cabinet, his stringent measures to break William J. Duane when that Secretary opposed his Bank policy, and his other acts to marshal his followers into a firm party front, had deeply impressed Buchanan. President Polk's firmness in carrying through his program without regard for the dissent of Benton or any other Democratic chieftain seemed to him equally admirable. Buchanan would not be a fighting President, but he would be an implacable defender of Democratic regularity.[9]

[II]

The making of the Cabinet was a matter of supreme importance, for the Cabinet rather than the President was to determine Administration policies. Throughout the next four years the country was to be governed by a Directory. Not merely was Buchanan cautious, impressionable, ill-trained in executive posts, and readily moved by stronger natures; he believed in the principle of action by a united Cabinet. In his opinion, a President should choose aides who represented like groups, who thought alike, and who would act alike. The Chief Magistrate who tried to conciliate opposing elements by placing determined agents of each in his official family would find that he had simply strengthened discord, and had deepened party divisions. Unity was essential; in Polk's day, he recalled, the Cabinet council scarcely ever failed, after free consultation and discussion, to agree at last—and it was its undivided action "which rendered Mr. Polk's administration so successful." [10] Following this principle, Buchanan often submitted questions to Cabinet vote. But unlike Polk, he was ready to let his own judgment be overruled. In 1859, for example, he and his Postmaster-General were in favor of calling a special session to vote the post office appropriation which the recently adjourned Congress had omitted; the other six members of the Cabinet outvoted these two; and to the disgust of the New York *Times* and the *National Intelligencer*, he yielded.[11]

In short, Buchanan failed to comprehend the vital difference between a unified Cabinet which is managed by the President, and a unified Cabinet which manages the President.

His chief advisers in choosing his official family were the familiar circle of personal friends; Slidell, W. W. Corcoran, Henry A. Wise of Virginia, Jesse

9 Letter to Pierce, December 11, 1852; Curtis, *op. cit.*, II, 69–74.
10 *Idem.*
11 *National Intelligencer*, March 26, 1859.

D. Bright of Indiana, Governor William Bigler of Pennsylvania, and Representative J. Glancy Jones of the same State. They were by no means ideal counsellors. Slidell and Wise were radical slavery men.[12] It was absurd to think of Bright as a spokesman for the Northwest; he was the owner of a slave-stocked plantation in Kentucky, an associate of the slavery circle in Washington, and an enemy of all freesoilers. Corcoran, a genial, philanthropic, and conservative banker whose social relationships were chiefly with Southerners, was deeply concerned lest the nation be disrupted. Bigler, a cautious, phlegmatic man, could furnish nothing but the advice of a machine politician, while Glancy Jones, another political heeler, was useful merely for reporting currents of Washington opinion. Not a single statesman could be found in Buchanan's entourage.

Buchanan moved deliberately, for he believed in the rule (he said it was Washington's) not to decide weighty questions until the final moment for doing so had nearly approached. He believed too that he ought to visit the capital for conferences. The result was that he soon found himself subjected to every variety of pressure, intrigue, cajolery, and wire-pulling. His once-peaceful retreat at Wheatland was overrun with callers, who rapped at the door as he got out of bed at seven and implored his attention as the clock struck midnight. By letters, telegrams, personal visits, and the use of intermediaries, a thousand party manipulators and office hunters beleaguered him. The drain on his larder and wine cellar threatened him with bankruptcy. Buchanan had never possessed a personal secretary; but now he summoned his nephew, James Buchanan Henry, a young man just beginning law practice, and, with many warnings against the temptations he would meet, installed him at a desk. For a confidential assistant he turned to John Appleton of Maine, an experienced man of ready pen—journalist, lawyer, and politician—who had worked with Buchanan before, having been secretary of legation in London. Appleton, a friend of the historian Bancroft, possessed cultivation, wit, and integrity.

Still endlessly harassed, early in January, 1857, Buchanan made a stealthy visit to Philadelphia. His mind was as yet apparently quite open with respect to the Cabinet and other high offices, and politicians flocked to his hotel like bees to an oozing comb. Then on January 27 he dropped quietly into Washington, his arrival unexpected by the most knowing observers.

This Washington trip was a characteristic exhibition of caution. Four years earlier, Buchanan had written President-elect Pierce that he ought not to make his final decisions on his Cabinet without visiting the capital, the best place to

---

12 Wise had been one of the leaders in threatening secession and military action if Frémont were elected; Nevins, *Frémont*, 451. He and John B. Floyd led one of the two main factions of the Virginia Democracy, R. M. T. Hunter the other.

consult disinterested Democratic leaders. He knew that he could see a wide range of men in Washington, especially Southerners. The sojourn was more eventful than he had expected. Arriving the day of Preston Brooks's sudden death, he attended the funeral ceremonies in the House, and watched Republican members, when Representative Savage of Tennessee declared that the world had applauded the justice of Brooks's chastisement of Sumner, leave the chamber in abrupt dudgeon. At the National Hotel he contracted the mysterious "disease" connected with that place, apparently amoebic dysentery, attributed by many to its bad plumbing. But above all, he carried out his main purpose; he made certain that the conservative appointments upon which he was fixing would find favor among the Southern groups whom he so deeply respected.[13]

The cardinal question was whether Robert J. Walker or Lewis Cass should be Secretary of State. Both were old-time friends; both were staunch Jacksonian Democrats; both had agreed with Buchanan in publicly supporting but privately disapproving the Kansas-Nebraska Act; both were strong Unionists and sternly conservative on the slavery question. Both were expansionists. It was at Walker's house in Washington that Buchanan had been staying when he was appointed minister to Great Britain. The President-elect had been intimate with both men in the Senate, and he remembered pleasantly his association with Walker in Polk's councils. On personal grounds he could readily have accepted either, and on grounds of fitness there was little to choose; the question therefore must be left to party pressures.

Such active groups pressed Walker's claims that for a time it seemed almost certain that he would become Buchanan's chief lieutenant—and probably his controlling guide. Some radical Southern expansionists, like C. C. Clay of Alabama and Alfred Iverson of Georgia, who believed that he would take steps to annex Cuba and other Gulf areas, threw their weight behind him. Jefferson Davis was said to regard him favorably. The familiar agents of "Young America," including George N. Sanders and Daniel Sickles, deemed him their best hope. Senator Douglas, though very friendly to Cass, seemed to incline toward him. Every possible plea for Walker was presented by Buchanan's young newspaper friend, the ebullient, mercurial John W. Forney, whose activities had been vital the previous fall in carrying Pennsylvania. As the author of the tariff of 1846, Walker was naturally a favorite of the anti-protectionists.

Yet as the weeks passed, antagonism toward the baldish little Mississippian gained ground. This bustling, courageous, highly ambitious politician had cheerfully made many enemies in his long climb to eminence. An excitable man with a taste for the melodramatic, he had for years written hard-hitting newspaper

13 N. Y. *Herald,* February 8-17, 1857.

articles on a wide variety of issues. Essentially independent, he was no en-
thusiast about slavery, and some Southerners recalled how heartily Calhoun
had condemned his lukewarm attitude toward its expansion. His ventures into
land speculation and railroad promotion had convinced many that he was a
reckless, perhaps even an unscrupulous, business plunger. In the New York
Herald, James Gordon Bennett raked him with a withering fire, blasting his
connection with Pacific Railroad schemes and his intimacy with greedy New
York politicians who might use the new Administration to fatten their pocket-
books. Even Slidell shared this view. "While I have great respect for Walker
and high appreciation of his talents," he wrote Buchanan, "I do not like the
men by whom he is surrounded and to a great degree controlled. . . . I fear
that from his extreme facility of temper he may be led to say and do things
that his own judgment would disapprove." [14] Obviously, many Northern conservatives would be aghast at the choice for Secretary of State of a Manifest
Destiny man, who in 1846 had wished to annex all Mexico, and who had since
been an open abettor of filibustering; and Europe would take alarm.

Various other considerations helped incline Buchanan to Cass. It seemed
important to place Howell Cobb in the Treasury. Not only did he have energy
and brains, but he combined political boldness with a talent for administrative
system. The proud Georgian made it clear, however, that he would play
second fiddle to no man of his own station or years; he would take a lower
Cabinet appointment than the venerable Cass or Marcy, but he would not sit
below Robert J. Walker.[15] The North, too, must be given some places, and
the appointment of Cass would help to supply a sectional balance.

If we may believe various newspapers and G. P. R. James (the acute British
consul in Richmond), the Russian and French legations, well aware of Cass's
Anglophobic views, did their utmost to rally the press behind him. The *Herald*
spoke of their sleepless "intrigues." A correspondent of the Albany *Argus* declared that the Russian envoy was spending large sums to fill Southern and
Western newspapers with laudatory articles and items, even corrupting many
small country weeklies. "I have every reason to conclude," James wrote the
Foreign Office early in the year, "that one-half the newspaper paragraphs,
stating General Cass's appointment and acceptance to be certain, proceed from
Russian sources; the object being to work up a popular feeling in favor of his
appointment, and thereby influence, if not control, the President-elect." He
thought Russia very adroit. "She used the newspaper press of America with
great skill and success during the late [Crimean] war; and if she can now raise a
general expectation that Mr. Cass is to be Secretary of State, it might puzzle
Mr. Buchanan to avoid making him so." James knew many American politicians,

14 He thought Sanders the chief operator; February 14, 1857, Buchanan Papers.
15 William Bigler, December 29, 1856, to Buchanan; Buchanan Papers.

heard much political gossip, and believed that he had a correct estimate of Cass; the man was incompetent from age, full of vanity, and swayed by foolish antipathies.[16]

The result of all the arguments and pressures was that Buchanan, on his return to Wheatland, determined to appoint Cass to the State Department—under certain rigid conditions. He would not take the corpulent, constitutionally indolent, ailing old Michigan leader, now in his seventy-fifth year, unless Cass accepted an efficient aide: John Appleton, with his experience as chief clerk in the State Department, chargé in Bolivia, and secretary of the London legation, must be made Assistant Secretary. Obviously, he would be expected to guide Cass's hand. Moreover, Cass must explicitly renounce his anti-British views. These stipulations, embodied in a formal letter, were unhesitatingly accepted by Cass. The State Department was counted the post of highest dignity and greatest ease in the Cabinet; he could enjoy its honors without being crushed by its burdens, and it would save him from a humiliating retirement to Detroit. Michigan was now a Republican state, and Zachariah Chandler was about to take Cass's seat in the Senate. The way was thus opened for the appointment of Howell Cobb to the Treasury. He too accepted with alacrity—for his would clearly be the post of chief authority.[17]

The lesser Cabinet places were filled without great difficulty, although the Attorney-General and the head of the Navy were not selected until after Buchanan went to Washington for his inauguration. It would be tedious to rehearse all the factional squabbling and personal intriguing which attended the bestowal of the various places, and we may content ourselves with a statement of results. A proffer of Cabinet seats to Wise, Bright, and Slidell was politely rejected. Wise desired to serve out his four-year term as Governor of Virginia; Bright and Slidell preferred to continue in the Senate. "There is no respectable office in the United States that I would not rather take than a Cabinet place," wrote Bright, who told friends the apocryphal story that he might have been Secretary of State had he chosen. He thought of himself as a Senatorial viceroy for the Northwest, dispensing Administration patronage in that quarter, and he had dreams of the White House.[18] When Wise, who also had dreams, declined a place, his Virginia friends rallied about John B. Floyd,

---

16 N. Y. *Herald*, January 14, 1857; F. O. 5/677, G. P. R. James to Lord Clarendon, January 9, February 28, 1857. The *Herald* remarked that if the hardheaded Lord Elgin came over as minister, "we suspect that the intrigues of the Russian and French embassies would be very rapidly brought to a close, and that the course of opinion in Washington would not be, as it has been lately, persistently hostile to England."

17 Nichols, *Disruption of the American Democracy*, 66; A. C. McLaughlin, *Lewis Cass*, 377.

18 Bright, April 16, 1857, to Wm. H. English; English Papers. N. Y. *Weekly Tribune*, February 27, 1857. Bright liked to go to his Kentucky farm, living "in my log Cabbin (very much such a one) as Genl Harrison was described as living in in 1840," and companioned only by "Niggers and Dogs." May 5, 1857, to Corcoran; Corcoran Papers.

a former governor who was best remembered by most Americans as the man who had advocated laying a tax on the products of those Northern States which would not return fugitive slaves to Virginia. He was formally designated by a meeting of Virginia members of the electoral college, and Buchanan gave him the War portfolio.

Since in Howell Cobb the Cabinet would have a leader who had supported the Compromise of 1850, the timid Buchanan thought it advisable to include some Southerner who had opposed it. Jacob Thompson of Mississippi, a Southern Rights man who had served in Congress from 1839 to 1851, was less objectionable to the nation at large than Pickens, Quitman, and Soulé, simply because he had done less to lift his radical views into notice. He was given the Interior Department; a logical place, for he had once been head of the House committee on public lands and Indian affairs.

The Post Office Department went to A. V. Brown of Tennessee, a former law partner of Polk and an able governor of his State in Mexican War days. He was a stump orator of rough hard-hitting qualities, and a proslavery expansionist who had been a delegate to the Nashville Convention. Now an elderly man of infirm health, he was destined to die in office. As the Post Office and Interior controlled a great part of the appointments and contracts of the government, and as the latter department did much to regulate the pace at which the Western areas were converted into free States, the South was pleased to have both in its hands.

Because New England had to be recognized, the Navy Department was assigned to an elderly political hack of Hartford, Isaac Toucey. He might earlier have gone into the Supreme Court, but he too, almost incredibly, had dreams of the Presidency! [19] At the last minute Buchanan bestowed the Attorney-Generalship upon his faithful friend, Jeremiah Black.

[III]

It was not a brilliant Cabinet, as Pierce's had been. Indeed, it was distinctly mediocre. Cass compared ill with the sagacious Marcy, Floyd with the energetic, far-sighted Jefferson Davis; Cobb was less of a practical financier than Guthrie, and Black less learned in the law than Caleb Cushing. Still, in routine ability it would do well enough.

19 Senator Dixon, December 2, 1858 to Welles; Gideon Welles Papers. Welles's opinion of Toucey was scorching. "Cold and selfish by nature and by calculation, Toucey was never known to make a sacrifice for his friends, his party, or the state, but would readily sacrifice either or all to promote his own aggrandizement. . . . In past conflicts the Southern States . . . had usually been successful; he therefore made it a point to identify himself with that section, without considering that it involved a reversal of principles." Papers Relating to Gideon Welles, LC.

The strongest criticism of the Cabinet naturally came from Republicans, who regarded it, in Greeley's words, as proslavery to the hub. Of the seven places, the South took four. And how much could be said of the aged Cass and the meek, time-serving Toucey as Northern representatives? The Michigan Polonius meant well, but he had long been inert, and was now subject to attacks of vertigo and incapable of prolonged concentration. Only a month before inauguration he had fallen on the Interior Department steps, and been picked up insensible and bleeding.[20] His appointment gave him a new lease of life, and for a time he showed heightened briskness and industry. Donning a new brown wig, shaving more closely than before, dressing with greater care, and taking a daily constitutional, he performed ordinary duties with promptness, and entertained with seeming pleasure.[21] However, a lover of ease and a man of conciliatory temperament, hesitant in taking any stand, he was certain to avoid home controversies. It was significant that although chosen a member of the Senate committee on the Brooks-Sumner assault he had failed to say a word against that outrage.

As for Toucey, he had long shown himself aware that his political bread was buttered on the Southern side. Every Northern freesoiler knew that he had urged a stern enforcement of the Fugitive Slave Act, had attacked the constitutionality of the Missouri Compromise, and had espoused the Nebraska Bill. He was destined to play an equivocal part in the early drama of secession. In fact, his role was to be such that Montgomery Blair called it treason, that E. M. Stanton secretly urged his arrest, and that the Connecticut legislature indignantly removed his portrait from the gallery devoted to ex-governors. Cass and Toucey could make no stand against such strong-willed Southerners as Cobb, A. V. Brown, and Jacob Thompson. It was a Cabinet controlled by slavedrivers, scornfully commented the New York *Tribune*.[22]

Of course Buchanan cared nothing for Republican censure. He cared little that conservative Whigs complained bitterly of their exclusion; that members of the Pierce Administration resented his failure to consult with them in Washington; and that New York Democrats felt left out in the cold. Much more important to the nation's future was the offense taken by the popular sovereignty Democrats of the North.

Buchanan's chief error in dispensing offices was his needless estrangement of the most powerful leader of the Northwest, the very man whose timely withdrawal at Cincinnati had made his nomination possible—Stephen A. Douglas. In these early weeks of the Administration we find the germ of a quarrel pregnant

20 *National Intelligencer*, February 9, 1857.
21 MS Journal of Samuel Ryan Curtis (Ill. State Hist. Lib.), January 1, 1860; *National Intelligencer*, March 31, 1859.
22 N. Y. *Tribune*, February 18, 1857.

with the direst consequences to party and nation. Douglas had believed that the Northwest was entitled to two places in the Cabinet. He was anxious that William A. Richardson of Quincy, Illinois, defeated for Congress the previous autumn, should get one seat, and willing that Cass should get the other. He had hoped that his friend Judge Samuel Treat of St. Louis might represent the border States. But it was soon plain that neither Treat nor Richardson stood a chance. Buchanan, determined to apply his principle that faction must be crushed, was going to form an Administration that would stand as a unit behind the Southern antipathy to squatter sovereignty. When the President-elect made his unexpected descent on Washington, Douglas visited him, got a frosty reception, learned that his enemies would drive the Administration chariot, and departed glowering with anger. He wrote Judge Treat:

Under all the circumstances the inference is irresistible that the patronage of the North West was disposed of before the nomination. Bright is the man who is to control it if they dare to carry out their designs. Slidell, Bright, and Corcoran (the banker) assume the right to dispose of all the patronage. If this purpose is carried out and I am the object of attack I shall fight all my enemies and neither ask nor give quarter. I do not decline to urge friends, provided the opportunity is presented to do so under any prospect of success. At present, I am an outsider. My advice is not invited nor will my wishes probably be regarded. I want nothing but fair play. I want only a fair show for my friends. I desire the brave true men who fought the battle to be sustained. If this can be done I am content. If on the contrary, the power of the Administration is to be used for plunder or ambition I shall return every blow they may give.[23]

Never was resentment more justifiable. Douglas was the ablest man in the party, its most formidable speaker in the Senate, the author of its most important legislation during the past decade, a leader who had borne the heat and danger of conflict while Buchanan was safe in a foreign haven. He should have been the nominee in 1856, for his Nebraska Act was the chief plank in the party platform. Had New York's Soft Delegation been seated and had Tennessee stayed in line, he might well have been chosen.[24] He was the champion of a host of Northern Democrats whose aid would be indispensable to future victory. Now he was not merely ignored; his enemy Bright, the Indiana slaveholder, the man whom Wise called a "money pimp of Corcoran's" and "a land-whore in the Northwest," the Midwestern tool of Southern leaders, was preferred over him.[25] It is no wonder that Douglas exploded in open hatred of Bright, that he showed Slidell, when they met, a front of suspicion and dislike, and that this alarmed gentleman reported that the Illinoisan was ready to run amok like a

23 February 5, 1857; Treat Papers. On the hostility of Buchanan and Slidell to Douglas, see P. G. Auchampaugh, *James Buchanan and his Cabinet*, 36, 37.
24 Milton, *Eve of Conflict*, 226–230.
25 Wise to Buchanan, January 5, 1857, Buchanan Papers.

maddened Malay.[26] He was not a man to sit tamely inert while he and his section were being wronged.

The three most vigorous figures of the Cabinet, Howell Cobb, Jacob Thompson, and Jeremiah S. Black, were the men who with Senator Slidell would control Buchanan at critical moments. Of these, the ambitious and active Cobb, still in his early forties, was the most attractive figure. He knew how to season his labors with jollity and wit. Sunny-tempered and generous-spirited as well as able, he was a delightful conversationalist, with just a dash of Falstaffian coarseness. It is not strange that Buchanan grew fond of him, and that whenever Mrs. Cobb's domestic responsibilities (she was a Lamar, sprung from one of the wealthiest and most aristocratic families of Georgia) kept her at home in Athens, he became an inmate of the White House. He had a high reputation for personal honor. When his father, plunging into land speculation, went bankrupt in 1837, the son, as an endorser of his notes, scrupulously paid every penny, although the act cost him a large estate and embarrassed him for years. He also had a reputation for hard, painstaking work. At the bar he had neglected no point in preparing his cases; in office he was careful, methodical, and a firm disciplinarian. With his Assistant Secretary Clayton and his law officer, Junius Hillyer, he placed the Treasury on a high level of efficiency. It could be said that he was first and always a politician, and, with patronage and contracts absorbing much of his time, took party rather than national views; but it could never be said that he neglected his duties.[27]

As a great planter-lawyer, with more than a thousand slaves calling him master, Cobb naturally held the opinions of the ruling class in the Lower South. He was a conservative by taste and habit, but his conservatism was all for the welfare of his own section. In 1850 he had been for the Compromise because it meant Southern peace and safety; he was presently to be for secession because he thought that it alone could give the South security. For good or ill, this imperious Georgia grandee was now to be Buchanan's chief personal guide.

Jacob Thompson had a prosaic name, and with his clean-shaven, rugged, rather homely face and stocky figure looked as prosaic as a butcher; but his career, with its alternations of wealth and ultimate ruin, honor and final exile, was to prove romantic enough for any novel. Compared with the aristocratic Cobb, he belonged to the newly rich of the South. A poor graduate of the University of North Carolina, he had gone west to practice law and had rapidly coined wealth out of raw Mississippi land. Now he held, besides minor tracts, a "home place" of 550 acres at Oxford with a fine mansion, another plantation

26 February 14, 1857, Buchanan Papers.
27 Samuel Boykin, *Howell Cobb*, *passim*. Boykin says that he knew from personal contact that Secretary Cobb enjoyed the unbounded confidence of Buchanan, and was really prime minister of the Administration.

in the same county of 2,720 acres, and a third on the Mississippi River of 1,783 acres. As a chairman of the trustees of the State University, he had lent its strongest men, Augustus B. Longstreet and Frederick A. P. Barnard, a shoulder in their progressive policies, aiding them also in trying to reclaim nearly a million of State-guaranteed funds which had been lost in bank crashes. Living at the university seat, Oxford, he profited from his intimacy with the professors, who temporarily included Longstreet's brilliant son-in-law, L. Q. C. Lamar.[28]

One singularly romantic episode had lighted up Thompson's early life. He had fallen in love with a poor girl of fourteen; had married her in 1840; and without consummating the marriage, had hurried her off to Paris for four years of schooling. Mrs. Thompson, a gay, beautiful woman in her early thirties, was now to shine as one of the social ornaments of Washington.

Another striking episode of Thompson's early life, destined to have important national consequences, was his quarrel with Robert J. Walker. It happened that Thompson and James K. Polk, both educated at Chapel Hill, were long-time friends. The spring of 1845 found Polk making up his Cabinet, and Thompson, a Representative from Mississippi, urging him—successfully—to make Walker head of the Treasury, instead of Attorney-General as first planned. Walker thereupon perpetrated an act of bad faith. When he resigned his seat in the Senate, the governor appointed Thompson to fill out Walker's term. He sent the commission to Walker for delivery to Thompson, so that the latter might remain on hand for special session after March 4, 1845. Walker received it. But he wished to be succeeded by his friend William M. Gwin, and though he saw Thompson several times, he never handed him the commission! The result was that Thompson returned to Oxford and accepted a renomination for the House before he learned of his appointment, which then went to a man named Chalmers. Walker never came back to the State, while Gwin migrated to California. For years Thompson loathed both men; and, though he was ultimately reconciled to Gwin, his detestation of Walker persisted. He thought Walker an unprincipled fellow, of flighty weathercock views, likely to be controlled by any man of strong will. Before the year 1857 expired, this opinion was to have its bearing on grave Cabinet decisions.[29]

Thompson himself, a ruthless, ambitious leader, ready for anything—during

28 The memoir of Thompson in the first volume of Claiborne's *Mississippi as Province, Territory, and State,* was dictated by himself to his niece.
29 See Dorothy Z. Oldham, MS Life of Thompson, Univ. of Mississippi Library. Jefferson Davis was a close personal friend of Thompson's. As head of the House Public Lands Committee, Thompson had learned much about the deficiencies of the Interior Department. Its important bureaus (public lands, Indian affairs, patents, census, pensions, and public buildings and grounds) worked independently of each other. Thompson resolved to unify the department and make himself the controlling head; and against not a little opposition, he did so.

the Civil War he supported a scheme for burning Northern cities—was not excessively troubled by principle. He meant to manage his department efficiently while looking out for the main chance. More than a year earlier, while standing for the Senate before the Mississippi legislature, he had tried to bribe the editor of the Washington *Sentinel*, a journal of some Southern influence, to support him; so, at least, that editor assured Jefferson Davis. He had offered "pecuniary favors to any reasonable amount." [30] On the slavery issue he was frankly radical. "You Illinoisans," he told one Congressman, "ought to concede that slaves are property, and treat them as such." "That," replied the Representative with asperity, "is the very point at issue." [31]

A third member of the ruling Directory, Jeremiah S. Black, stood out in craggy relief from the other appointees. Grim, intense, prejudiced, narrow, he could throw his powerful but unimaginative mind behind the most exasperatingly partisan doctrines. He scolded, fought, and jested like John Knox. And like that greater Calvinist, he was rigidly honest according to his lights, while he never tired of battle. A product of the Pennsylvania frontier, he had managed to attend an academy and had broadened his education by diligent reading. Steeped in the English classics and religious literature, he spoke with thunderous precision, and wrote with signal effectiveness. His was a fine mind, but a very legalistic mind. As a lawyer, he showed a passion for reducing the complexities of codes and statute books to first principles, which he expounded with learning. He displayed an unalterable devotion to justice, and an unchallengeable integrity. As member and head of the Supreme Court of Pennsylvania, he had handed down decisions of marked power, especially on points of corporation law. His oration on the character of Andrew Jackson and his speech of 1856 in defense of religious liberty were fine examples of his championship of the fundamentals of democracy.

This keen-witted, argumentative Scotch-Irishman, able to quote Shakespeare, St. Paul, and John Marshall with equal appositeness, always biased and sometimes excessively emotional, loving a saturnine jest, could be more voluble than discreet. Eccentric in appearance—tall, loose-jointed, and subject to spasmodic jerks—he was highly temperamental in spirit, giving rein to exaggerated loves and hates. His friends worried over his notorious forgetfulness of engagements, his carelessness of details, and his tactlessness. But his intellectual power and stubborn will made him refreshingly independent. For a time he was curiously subservient to Buchanan, whose experience and rank awed him; then, as if suddenly recognizing the President's weakness, he brusquely asserted himself. While Cass dozed, and Toucey yielded, Black was

30 H. J. Harris, August 16, 1856; Davis Papers, Duke University.
31 Samuel Ryan Curtis, MS Journal, Dec. 26, 1859.

not the man to let the Southern leaders hoodwink or intimidate him. In the ultimate crisis he stood up courageously for the Union, and when Buchanan showed his lack of backbone Black was ready to supply plenty of it.[32]

These men, together with Slidell, would help the President sway the rod of government. And Slidell, though outside the Cabinet, was a power. Now sixty-four, he had behind him lucrative years at the New Orleans bar, service in Congress, the use of fraud in Plaquemines parish to carry Louisiana for Polk, and an abortive mission to Mexico; he was the ruling boss of Louisiana, and one of the Senate leaders. Firm and unscrupulous, a shrewd wire-puller who had contributed much to Buchanan's nomination and election, he could count on the President's gratitude. For all his New York birth, Slidell was a Southern nationalist, anxious to acquire Cuba, and full of zeal for all the Gulf State demands.

Little need be said of Cass, who, after giving public assurance that he would drop his Anglophobe tendencies, contributed no ideas and no vision to the Administration. Buchanan blocked out the main foreign policies. Most of Cass's dispatches were written or rewritten for him by Appleton, Black, or the President.[33] He made a firm stand against British claims to the right of visitation and search on the high seas, and he cooperated with Buchanan in an aggressive policy in the Western Hemisphere.

Secretary Floyd proved equally clumsy and hapless. Scion of an old Virginia family, elected governor because his father had been one, he was an amiable cipher. Shrewd men soon saw that his dullness and laziness made him easy to victimize, and an odor of corruption rose from the War Office.

As for Toucey, a stiff, dignified gentleman, he exercised more vigilance. Naval officers and bureaucrats generally ran his department for him, but he prevented thefts. Postmaster-General Brown was interested in distributing offices and in securing his wealthy second wife a high social position. He took an elegant mansion, and an entertainment there, with his consort presiding in rose-colored brocade and his stepdaughter showing her white arms at the harp, was an occasion to delight the social reporters.[34]

It took time for the great defects of the Cabinet to show themselves. The general view was that it would serve well enough, and the South, with Virginia, Georgia, Tennessee, and Mississippi all represented (Kentucky might be added for Bright) purred with complacency. To be sure, the Cabinet represented the

32 See W. N. Brigance, *Jeremiah S. Black*; biographical sketch in C. F. Black, *Essays and Speeches of Jeremiah S. Black*.

33 "The real Secretary during the four years preceding the Civil War was President James Buchanan, who directed the foreign affairs of the United States with great ability." Lewis Einstein, in S. F. Bemis, ed., *American Secretaries of State*, VI, 297.

34 Mary J. Windle, *Life in Washington*, 249, 250.

moderate rather than the radical South. Duff Green, the fearless old Jacksonian editor, now engaged in railway promotion, thought Buchanan should be warned that the fire-eaters were dissatisfied and hostile; warned, too, that Calhoun in his grave was no less potent than in his senatorial chair.[35] The Calhounites hoped to convert or cow the Southern members. Some Northern freesoilers also waited hopefully for disaster. Lincoln's partner Herndon assured Lyman Trumbull that this group of moderate slavery men, ground between two extremes, could never withstand the pressure of the revolutionary times. A soft, fat, good-natured parcel of men, it would soon split. "Buchanan and his Cabinet must go north or go south, or perish." [36] The majority of Americans, however, were (as always) optimistic.

Howell Cobb and Jacob Thompson were less good-natured than they looked, and Slidell, the Senate whip, was not good-natured at all. Buchanan was justified in choosing a predominantly Southern Cabinet—if he used it. The South was losing ground; all the great social and economic forces were against it; it must adjust itself to painful concessions. A President could better reconcile it to the inevitable surrenders, as in Kansas, if upheld by a Southern Cabinet. But he must dominate his Cabinet and employ it to persuade the South. The grand error of Buchanan was that, having chosen a Southern Cabinet, he did not use it; he let it use him.

[IV]

On the eve of taking office, Buchanan sustained a serious blow in his own State. His editorial friend Forney, thwarted by party enemies in his desire to gain control of the Washington *Union*, eagerly coveted a place in the Senate. The President-elect was duly grateful for the man's twenty years of devotion. He therefore intervened openly, expressing a hope that the legislature would give Forney the seat about to be vacated by the mediocre Richard Brodhead. In doing so he took distinct risks. Many Pennsylvania Democrats disliked Forney, and some men in Washington and Harrisburg thought that Brodhead was entitled to a reelection. Jefferson Davis, related by marriage to the Brodhead family, was reported "mad as fury." For a time the situation looked so hopeful that veteran politicians predicted the victory of Forney, who was jubilant. Then as a little group of Democrats in Western Pennsylvania showed a rebellious temper, the astute Simon Cameron saw his chance.

If there was a man on earth whom Buchanan hated, it was this devious intriguer, once a Democrat but now a Republican. "Cameron, after having be-

35 To G. M. Dallas, September 1, 1857; Duff Green Papers, LC.
36 March 4, 1857; Trumbull Papers.

trayed me at the Baltimore convention, has since been moving heaven and earth to destroy me," Buchanan had written in 1851. "His election to the Senate would be a disgrace to the State, and would inflict a most serious blow on the Democratic party." [37] After Cameron's change of party and his warm espousal of Frémont, Buchanan's enmity toward him intensified. Yet the aggressive Harrisburg politician stepped into the confused hurly-burly of the legislature with the ease of a gallant in a ballroom, deftly blocked his rival, and bore off the prize. He was chosen Senator for six years—six years in which he would take charge of the Republican organization in Pennsylvania and make eager preparations for his party's victory in 1860!

How did Cameron do it? The chagrined Democrats, counting the vote (67 for Cameron, 58 for Forney, 8 scattered), hardly knew. They talked of bribery, and forty-four members of the House petitioned Congress for an investigation, alleging corrupt and unlawful acts. In Schuylkill County the Democrats held a public meeting to condemn the "atrocious" conduct of two Representatives who had inexplicably violated their solemn party pledges. Everybody knew that Cameron was not above the purchase of votes. But in this instance it may not have been necessary. He still had some warm personal friends among the Democrats. His papers show that for years he had been in the habit of lending legislators small sums on their notes, with the understanding that these would never be presented for payment if the beneficiaries furnished some *quid pro quo*. He was president of the Lebanon Valley Railroad, with offices at Reading, and prominent in other business enterprises—coal, banking, insurance —which offered possibilities in the way of pressure or reward. In short, he could wave his hand with fair confidence that a number of Harrisburg Democrats would instantly fall into line.[38]

The essential fact was that Buchanan had received a sharp rebuff in his own State, and that the Republicans had gained a dexterous new political leader in the Senate. Greeley, Thurlow Weed, and the allied Republican editors rent the air with their huzzas. Slidell and other Democrats in Washington were dumfounded. And the President-elect, smarting from the blow, was worried to find Forney behaving with childish petulance. The editor began drinking heavily, demanded impossible offices, inspired his wife to ask for the Post Office

---

37 January, 1851; American Autograph Shop, Merion Station, Pa.
38 Pennsylvania House-Senate Journal, January 9, 1857. The Cameron Papers contain much matter on this election. They also contain other curious data. For example, one C—— writes from Carlisle, July 13, 1857, that Cameron contributed $200 toward his election to the State Senate, that he gave a note which he understood to be a receipt, never to be presented for payment, and that he also agreed to "do a certain thing." Another correspondent wrote on August 4 that he had been given a "loan" of $300 by Cameron in return for supporting the sale of the main line of the Pennsylvania public works. Both were indignant when Cameron's son tried to collect on the notes.

on his behalf, and indulged in wild fits of scolding. He was momentarily a case for a neurologist if not an alienist. For a time Buchanan put up patiently with his querulous rages and his officious advice on appointments. Then, in the presence of a tittering company at Wheatland, he uttered a rebuke that the editor never forgot;[39] and thereafter he simply brushed Forney aside. The mercurial journalist felt crushed. "I go to Washington at the Inauguration to sell my furniture and to retire to a country newspaper," he wrote.[40]

Some other changes in the Senate were of national interest. It is not often that a prosperous middle-aged dry-goods merchant can be converted into a political chieftain of force, but Zach Chandler, the former mayor of Detroit who had organized the overthrow of Cass, was an exception. A rough-spoken, imperious man, who expected to rule Michigan as an honest, iron-fisted boss, he was quite fearless. He would face the Southern fire-eaters with anger as quick and a roar as dogmatic as their own. He had been the dominant figure in the Buffalo convention of 1854 to concert plans for promoting the freesoil migration to Kansas. The recent Presidential canvass had revealed him as one of the most effective of stump speakers.[41]

Another businessman, the yarn manufacturer James F. Simmons, came forward from the Rhode Island Republicans to replace a Democrat; he was a devotee of tariff reform and a man of some expertness in finance. Wisconsin sent a brilliant attorney, James R. Doolittle, to Washington. He had proved his independent stamp when in 1848, a rising young politician of western New York, he had cast aside his Democratic allegiance to become a Free Soiler. His powerful frame, Hobart College education, and trenchant personality had quickly brought him to the front in the Northwest. Still another former Democrat turned Republican, the sagacious Preston King, appeared from the northern border of New York to occupy Hamilton Fish's old seat. These men added much to Republican power. They showed how rapidly the new party was gaining in talent as in numbers. Missouri did little to offset them when she put one of the bitterest anti-Bentonian Democrats, James S. Green, into the Senate.[42]

But just before Buchanan took office, a sharp trick in Indiana gave the Administration one Senator to whom it was not entitled. The story behind this maneuver illustrates the low political morals of the State. In 1854 the Republicans, carrying Indiana by about 12,000, had won a decisive majority on joint ballot of the two houses. They were entitled to elect a Senator for the term expiring March 4, 1855. The Democrats, however, kept a majority of two in the upper chamber, refused to go into joint session, and thus caused a vacancy.

39 Forney, *Anecdotes of Public Men*, II, 421.
40 February 18, 1857; *Toombs, Stephens, Cobb Corr.*, 397.
41 George Frisbie Hoar, *Autobiography*, II, 75, 76.
42 N. Y. *Weekly Tribune*, January 17, 24, 1857.

When the election of 1856 came, the Democrats carried the lower chamber but fell short of success in the upper. It was now the turn of the Republicans to play an obstructionist game. They stubbornly refused to go into joint session, demanding one of the two senatorships. Jesse Bright's term expired March 4, 1857, and the possibility loomed up that he might lose his place—that Indiana would have two vacancies until the election of 1858. Some chicanery was necessary. The Democratic minority in the Senate therefore joined the House majority in an irregular session. Though they had less than a quorum of either body, they reelected Bright; and they chose as his colleague Dr. G. N. Fitch, a Logansport physician. This was on February 4, 1857, and the two at once claimed their seats in Washington.

The irregular election of both men, under the rule just laid down by the Senate in debarring James Harlan of Iowa, a Republican chosen by a rump legislature, should have been voided. But an investigation would take some time. Indiana Democrats counted on having the inquiry prolonged until after March 10, 1857, when the State legislature was constitutionally required to adjourn, not to meet for two years. This plan was duly carried out. When the two doughfaces took their places under the unfinished Capitol dome, Lyman Trumbull urged immediate action to debar Fitch. But Toombs, arguing that his credentials were in proper form, asked for a leisurely inquiry by a select committee. Fitch was sworn in, and Bright shortly entered on his new term. The Indiana legislature had adjourned, and the two men were temporarily safe. From Republican newspapers arose a chorus of wails and denunciations. In equity, Bright should have been reelected, but the Republicans should have been given the other seat.[43]

[V]

The debates of the expiring Congress on Pierce's last message, with its denunciation of Republicans, exhibited the feverish rancors of section and party. Republican leaders, denying that they had fomented disunion, carried the attack into the enemy trenches. It was Pierce's party, they said, which by introducing the Nebraska bill had blown flame into dying sectional embers. The recent election had not endorsed this Democratic action; it had repudiated it. The Democrats had nominated Buchanan because he was unconnected with the Kansas-Nebraska iniquity. They had carried Pennsylvania, Indiana, and the election on the slogan, "Buchanan, Breckinridge, and Free Kansas." Even so, they had barely won; and Pierce, thrust into outer darkness by the North,

43 N. Y. *Weekly Tribune*, February 7, 14, 21, 1857; review by "Amicus" in *National Intelligencer*, December 2, 1858; *Cong. Globe*, 34th Cong., 3d. Sess., 774–776.

was but venting his spiteful bile. "I hope he may live to a hale old age," snapped John Sherman, "and have time to reflect that in politics, as in morals, honesty is the best policy." [44]

The Republicans scored heavily when they pointed out how utterly the Northwestern and Southern Democrats differed on the interpretation of their own platform. The Douglas wing believed that settlers could exclude slavery from a Territory almost from the beginning. The Slidell-Toombs men held that slavery could not be excluded until the Territory was adopting its constitution for statehood. "Behold," said Humphrey Marshall of Kentucky, "the crack behind the smooth Democratic facade!" Their spokesmen had been boastfully speechifying, he said—and then some cruel outsider asked whether they believed in popular sovereignty. The question was devastating. "It told upon that portion of the House as though a 24-pound shot had fallen into a battalion. You could *see* its effects." [45]

Quite visibly, Congress had two Democratic parties. While the Cass-Douglas Democrats reiterated that a territorial legislature might interdict slavery, most Southern members vehemently asserted that neither Congress nor a legislature could touch slavery in any Territory. Some men hoped for a judicial determination of the issue. "Well, sir," complacently remarked Keitt of South Carolina, "if the Supreme Court decides that this power is not conferred upon the territorial legislature, then the Northern portion of the Democratic Party do not claim the power, but are satisfied with the decision." [46] Preston Brooks echoed him, saying that the Supreme Court would hew a channel through "the shoal which is threatening us with wreck." With this view English of Indiana agreed. John Sherman asked him whether Southerners might carry their slaves into a Territory, even if the settlers objected. That, said English, is purely a question of constitutional law; it would probably soon be decided by the Supreme Court; and he would acquiesce in the decision.

Would all Northerners, however, be as ready as English to accept an adverse ruling? Already some leaders were stating the view later elaborated by Douglas in his famous Freeport Doctrine. Ex-Speaker Orr of South Carolina declared, in effect, that no court decision would have much practical significance. The people alone would establish the character of popular sovereignty. Personally, he did not accept the theory of squatter sovereignty, but it was of little consequence what anybody in Washington thought:

In every slaveholding community of this Union, we have local legislation and local police regulations appertaining to that institution, without which the

44 *Cong. Globe*, 34th Cong., 3rd Sess., 53 ff.
45 *Ibid.*, 100.
46 "The Democratic Party," added Keitt, "makes this a judicial question." *Ibid.*, 100.

institution would not only be valueless, but a curse to the community. Without them the slave-holder could not enforce his rights when invaded by others; but if you had no local legislation for the purpose of giving protection, the institution would be of no value. I can appeal to every gentleman on this floor who represents a slaveholding constituency to attest the truth of what I have stated upon that point.

Now, the legislative authority of a Territory is invested with a discretion to vote for or against laws. We think they ought to pass laws in every Territory, when the Territory is open to settlement, and slaveholders go there, to protect slave property. But if they decline to pass such laws, what is the remedy? None, sir. If the *majority* of the people are opposed to the institution, and if they do not desire it engrafted upon their Territory, all they have to do is simply to decline to pass laws in the Territorial legislature for its protection, and then it is as well excluded as if the power was invested in the Territorial legislature, and exercised by them, to prohibit it.[47]

As the statements of Keitt, English, and Orr indicated, the case of Dred Scott was now exciting close attention. This humble Negro had been born a slave in Virginia about 1795. Taken by his master to St. Louis, he was sold to an army surgeon, Dr. John Emerson. As a household servant he accompanied Emerson to Rock Island in Illinois and to Fort Snelling in Wisconsin Territory, thus dwelling on free soil during most of the years 1834-38. Carried back to St. Louis, he was transferred on Emerson's death to the widow and her brother, John F. A. Sanford, as part of a trust estate. Mrs. Emerson tried to make some use of Dred, hiring him to various families, but he was infirm and inefficient, and became increasingly dependent on his owners and those who befriended him. In 1850 Mrs. Emerson married a Massachusetts physician, Calvin G. Chaffee, who had political ambitions and in due course was elected to two terms in Congress as a Know-Nothing; the ownership of Dred thus becoming a greater embarrassment than ever. Since neither Mrs. Chaffee nor Sanford wanted him, and he was a drain on the charity of the sons of his original owner —one of whom, the able businessman Henry Taylor Blow, was a strong supporter of the freesoil cause and was later, in 1860, to become a supporter of Missouri Republicanism—it is not remarkable that the idea of giving him freedom gained currency. As early as 1846 Dred and his wife brought suit, perhaps at the instance of some lawyer who hoped to share in the collection of fourteen years' wages, perhaps on the prompting of some humane friend, for their liberation. The Blow family then lent their assistance.[48]

47 *Ibid.*, 103, 104.
48 See John D. Lawson, *American State Trials*, XIII, 220 ff.; Helen T. Catterall, "Some Antecedents of the Dred Scott Case," *Am. Hist. Rev.*, XXX, 56-71; and the pamphlet "Case of Dred Scott in the Supreme Court of the United States." H. T. Blow's letters in the E. D. Morgan Papers throw light on his freesoil fervor. His papers are in the Missouri Hist. Soc. Vincent Hopkins, in "The Dred Scott Decision," a doctoral dissertation completed at Columbia University in 1949, shows that under Missouri law Mrs. Chaffee, after her re-

The decisions in the State courts had been contradictory. First a circuit court, following the general line of Missouri decisions, held that Dred's long residence on free soil had made him a free man. An appeal was prosecuted, however, and the Missouri supreme court in 1852 reversed the lower tribunal.[49] In doing so it made a curious acknowledgment of influences not pertinent to law or equity. The times, it said, "are not as they were when the former decisions on this subject were made. Since then not only individuals, but States, have been possessed by a dark and fell spirit in relation to slavery, whose gratification is sought in the pursuit of measures whose inevitable consequences must be the overthrow and destruction of our government. Under such circumstances, it does not behoove the State of Missouri to show the least countenance to any measures which might gratify this spirit."

The suit was then remanded to the circuit court of St. Louis County, where it was continued. It was shortly decided, however, that the case, still continued, should be taken to the Federal district court. Full control over Dred, since Mrs. Chaffee's new marriage, now rested in Sanford, who at this time was a citizen of New York. Dred, averring himself to be a citizen of Missouri, brought a totally new action in the Federal district court; and thence an appeal was entered on the docket of the Supreme Court in Washington in the closing days of 1854. Delays ensued. Finally an initial argument of the case early in 1856 was followed by an order for a reargument.

This reargument opened in December, 1856—and at once the crucial importance of the litigation became evident. It involved the very point which Northern Democrats and Southern Democrats were so sternly debating in Congress; the question whether either Congress or a local legislature had power to exclude slavery from territorial confines. The eminence of the counsel engaged showed that the case was meant to settle issues immeasurably greater than the ownership of a Negro whom nobody wanted to own. On Dred's side appeared Montgomery Blair of St. Louis, scion of the most powerful border family, and George Ticknor Curtis, one of the leaders of the American bar. On the owner's side appeared a former Attorney-General of the United States, Reverdy Johnson of Maryland, and Senator Henry S. Geyer, the oldest and most distinguished attorney of St. Louis. Such giants did not plead in minor cases. They were on their mettle, too. The argument of Reverdy Johnson, delivered before a crowded courtroom, had defects of style and temper but

---

marriage, could not act in any capacity with respect to Emerson's estate, which had been left in trust to a daughter, Henrietta Emerson. Her brother and his St. Louis agent looked after matters. Dr. Hopkins also shows that the usual statement that Blow instigated the suit of 1846 is erroneous. But after the inception of the suit, some member of the Blow family appeared in it at every stage.

49 Scott . . .vs. Emerson, 15 Missouri, 577–592.

exhibited him at the height of his powers, while that of Curtis was pronounced by one associate justice of long tenure, Catron, the best plea on a question of constitutional law that he had ever heard.[50]

Before Christmas arrived, Washington was full of speculation and discussion on the case. Interest was particularly keen, as James S. Pike told readers of the *Tribune*, among those who realized the transcendent importance of the coming decision. To be sure, the bench might evade a broad pronouncement. "Yet the urgency of the Slave Power is so great—the temper of the slaveholders within the bar and without the bar, to say nothing of the bench, is roused to crush the rebellious spirit of the North, and a decision of the Supreme Court is eagerly desired which shall promote this end." The depth of feeling among the contestants was disclosed when Reverdy Johnson made two astonishing statements to the court. In one he said that slavery promised to exist through all time; in the other that the expansion of slavery might prove the only means of preserving the constitutional freedom of the nation.[51] While Southerners applauded such doctrine, freesoilers held up their hands in horror.

Various newspapers, including the New York *Commercial Advertiser*, urged the judges to hand down a broad decision, not failing to rule on the constitutionality of the Missouri Compromise.[52] Senator Lyman Trumbull asked a friend if it was really possible that the Court would decide that slavery followed the flag everywhere outside the free States. Indeed it is, replied his correspondent; it may yet go further, plant its heel on the neck of the North, and claim for slavery a place within the States themselves.[53] Gossip was soon busy with reports upon the positions taken by the nine justices. One rumor had it that Curtis of Massachusetts, Nelson of New York, and McLean of Ohio were for upholding the constitutionality of laws excluding slavery from a Territory; that Campbell of Alabama, Wayne of Georgia, and Daniel of Virginia wished to deny the constitutionality of any restriction; and that Taney of Maryland, Grier of Pennsylvania, and Catron of Tennessee were undecided. "Thus it will be seen that the division is geographical and sectional," wrote James S. Pike; "of the three judges who hold the balance of power, two live well up to the Ohio River, and Mason and Dixon's Line."[54] He added that Grier was well known to be proslavery in sentiment. Such gossip was worthless except as an

50 Warren, *History of the Supreme Court*, II (1926 ed.), 287.
51 N. Y. *Tribune*, December 23, 1856. George Ticknor Curtis said on the occasion of Johnson's death: "It was the forcible presentation of the Southern view of our Constitution in respect to the relation of slavery to the Territories and of the Territories to the nation, that contributed more than anything else to bring about the decision that was made in this case." B. C. Steiner, *Reverdy Johnson*, 38.
52 *Commercial Advertiser*, January 17, 1857.
53 D. L. Phillips to Trumbull, January 18, 1857; Trumbull Papers.
54 N. Y. *Tribune*, December 24, 1856.

indication that Washington was eagerly forecasting a decision, that the judges seemed inclined to give it a sweeping character, and that most people expected the panel to divide along lines of sectional sympathy.

By mid-January, reports were thickening that the Supreme Court would soon deny the power of Congress to exclude slavery from a Territory. This, said indignant Republicans, was a naked scheme to use the judicial power in a political maneuver. "If the Supreme Court were today to decide that Congress had no power over slavery in the Territories," wrote Pike, "the decision would be simply a majority decision, carrying no moral power with it in the North, and if a speedy change were possible in one or two individuals composing the court, such a decision would be unceremoniously reversed at the very next session." [55] Many Southerners were obviously thirsting to have the question resolved in their favor by the Court; so were many freesoil Northerners, who wanted to keep up the sectional agitation. Sooner or later, thought Greeley's Washington correspondent, the Court would give slavery men what they wanted. He hoped they would do it at once, while the Northern mind was still excited, and when Congress, Court, and President could be identified by the people as fellow conspirators in the work of extending the slavery domain.[56]

[VI]

Meanwhile, the nation was exuberantly prosperous. Its interests were many and diverse. Sectional animosities seemed to dwindle as the debate on Pierce's message wore itself out. The country was reading about war in China, Richard Burton's expedition in East Africa, and the desperate troubles of William Walker in Nicaragua as overwhelming forces hemmed in his little army. General Scott and Jefferson Davis were conducting a newspaper quarrel with such ferocious epithets as "falsehood" and "hypocrisy." A report that the Empress Eugénie had appeared without hoops aroused vast feminine excitement.

From such topics the nation turned at the beginning of March to Buchanan's inaugural ceremonies. Pomp and glitter attended the great day. The President-elect came down from Lancaster in a special car. A huge concourse poured into the capital, the Baltimore & Ohio alone bringing more than thirty thousand from the north.[57] Attired in a well-advertised suit of homespun, and escorted by a colorful parade of regulars, marines, and militia from various States, Buchanan rode to the Capitol with Pierce, and received the oath from Chief Justice Taney —a reception at the White House following.[58]

---

55 *Idem.*
56 N. Y. *Weekly Tribune,* January 10, 1857.
57 N. Y. *Express,* March 6, Washington *Union, National Intelligencer,* March 5, 1857.
58 MS Recollections of Mrs. C. C. Clay, Duke University.

That night, in a large building erected on Judiciary Square, a ball offered the grandest spectacle of the kind yet seen in Washington. From outside, the impromptu structure looked like a huge railroad-constructor's shanty; but the interior, lined with glazed cambric and handsomely beflagged, with chandeliers lighting its ceiling of white cloth and golden stars, was attractive. Buchanan, his niece Miss Lane, and Breckinridge made a brief appearance. Members of Congress attended, Slidell and Douglas being prominent. It was recorded that Gautier, the caterer, provided 500 gallons of oysters, 800 chickens, huge quantities of venison, beef, turkey, pheasants, ham, and lobster, and 100 gallons of ice cream. Ladies predominated, for they entered free while men paid ten dollars. As guests drove home through the clear moonlight, they agreed that the ball promised a brilliant social future for the Administration.[59]

But if the ceremonies were imposing, the inaugural address was uninspired. No eloquence of phrase or glint of original thought lighted up its turgidity. Buchanan reiterated his determination to serve only one term. This was an error, for his political authority would have been far greater had he concealed his intent. The one striking passage of his discourse dealt with the Supreme Court and might better have been omitted. It was now widely believed that the judges would soon present a decision annulling the Missouri Compromise. The Chicago *Times*, for example, on February 26, 1857, had accurately predicted that the Court would declare the Compromise restriction unconstitutional, with only Justices Curtis and McLean dissenting. The new President should prudently have avoided the subject. Instead, after pointing out that men differed as to the time when the people of a Territory should decide for slavery or freedom, he went on:

This is happily a matter of but little practical importance, and besides, it is a judicial question, which legitimately belongs to the Supreme Court of the United States, before whom it is now pending, and will, it is understood, be speedily and finally settled. To their decision, in common with all good citizens, I shall cheerfully submit, whatever this may be, though it has ever been my individual opinion that, under the Kansas-Nebraska Act, the appropriate period will be when the number of actual residents in the Territory shall justify the formation of a constitution with a view to its admission as a State into the Union.

For the rest Buchanan expatiated upon the importance of maintaining the Constitution and the Union; proposed to use the Treasury surplus in extinguishing the national debt, increasing the navy, and strengthening the coast defenses; declared against squandering the public lands; and recommended a military road to the Pacific. Though he spoke of expanding the American realm, he stipulated that new territory should be acquired only by honorable means. All this was

59   N. Y. *Times*, March 6, 7, 1857.

commonplace. The central defect of the American governmental system at the moment was that it had no policy-making agency other than the President. In Britain, the Cabinet did consider long-range policy, and did sometimes lead Parliament effectively in implementing it; in America, the Cabinet merely dealt *ad hoc* with exigent issues, while Congress had no planning machinery. The problem which now required planning was slavery—and Buchanan showed that he did not understand its nature.

For the most significant part of the address was his denunciation of the long slavery agitation and his expression of a fatuous hope that it would soon cease. During the whole previous twenty years, he remarked, the agitation had done no positive good to any human being, but had been a prolific source of evils to the master, the slave, and the nation. This was partially true. It was equally true that no fever resulting from an inner malady, no riot provoked by a social maladjustment, and no depression caused by economic blunders ever produces much positive good. They are not, however, to be regarded as detached phenomena. If weighed in connection with their causes, it becomes plain that only a removal of the source will eliminate their "great evils." Buchanan remarked that by letting slavery severely alone in the States, and remitting it in the Territories to the principle of popular sovereignty, the matter might easily be settled. Since no other question would then remain for adjustment, the protracted controversy might speedily become extinct.

When the new President said this, he knew that the Supreme Court was about to decide that slavery should range freely through any Territory until the moment came for its admission to the Union. His statement thus amounted to a cool proposal that the Republican Party, built on a demand for the exclusion of slavery from all Territories, should disband; it amounted to an equally cool proposal that the Douglas, or squatter sovereignty, wing of the Democracy, built on a demand for early territorial autonomy, should give up its basic tenet. Nor was Buchanan's statement a mere rhetorical flight. The amazing fact is that he really believed that his proposal might be realized.

4

The Dred Scott Decision

FORTUNATELY for the country, few administrations open with a thunder-clap. Usually the new President and Cabinet find a few quiet months in which to settle routine affairs, and to take their bearings, before they have to deal with controversial problems. Buchanan was unfortunate when his long courtship of political quiet ended only two days after his inauguration, and the Dred Scott decision broke upon the nation with a confusing crash. His friends assured the country that the Supreme Court bolt had scattered his enemies and cleared his path for a successful term of office. It was quickly evident, however, that the thunder had brought not victory and peace, but a furious political storm.

The full implications of Dred Scott can be grasped only if we remember to what a savage pitch Pierce's recent castigation of Republican doctrines had raised the dispute upon the constitutional position of slavery in the Territories, and with what fierceness the defenders of the three main views had sprung to arms. During December and January, Congress had quivered with the debate. Senator Cass expounded his and Douglas's view that the settlers of a Territory alone had definitive power over slavery. Lyman Trumbull and John P. Hale argued that Congress possessed full power to regulate it, like other domestic institutions, throughout the public domain. Alexander H. Stephens and Senator Mason of Virginia declared that neither Congress nor the territorial legislatures had any authority to limit slavery, and that the late election had sustained the principle that the institution could not be prohibited in lands belonging to the whole nation. Perhaps the ablest speech was by Collamer of Vermont, reviewing the many historical instances in which Congress *had* acted to interdict or restrict slavery in certain Territories; but it made no Southern converts.

Everybody knew that this issue of the Negro in the Territories was the central question before the country; and the Congressional debates, running concurrently with the courtroom arguments on Dred Scott, were caught up by the press. Justice McLean's essay, arguing that Congress certainly had no power to institute slavery in a Territory where it did not exist, had lately been reprinted. Many people remembered Attorney-General Cushing's extended opinion of

November, 1855, on the subject, written at Pierce's request. He had held that the United States never possessed any "municipal sovereignty" in the common territory, and that the Missouri Compromise of 1820 must have been declared by any court to be null and void because it gave certain new States a position unequal with the old States; that is, it deprived the States north of 36° 30′ of the right to decide on slavery for themselves. Editors now worried the topic as dogs chew a juiceless bone.[1] Yet for all the debate, the Court decision, far more sweeping than had been anticipated, took the country aback.

[I]

March 6, 1857: Another bright, clear day. The sunlight filtered through even into the cool, dim apartment of the Capitol basement which, beneath the throbbing discussions of Senate and House, was reserved for the Supreme Court. At eleven exactly, the procession of black-garbed judges moved from their robing room to the chamber, the younger members, as they kicked up the long gowns with their heels, adjusting their gait to that of the tremulous chief, Roger B. Taney. They found the tiny courtroom jammed. Indeed, it had been packed the previous day in expectation of the great decision, which was deferred. By this time the crowd of distinguished public men, the reporters with pad and pencil, were not disappointed. The judges bowed to the lawyers, the lawyers bowed to the judges; the crier opened the session with the immemorial "Oyez! Oyez!" that had echoed through English-speaking courts since Plantagenet days; and the Chief Justice, gathering his papers before him, began reading in a high, thin voice. He continued, with signs of ebbing strength, until half-past one, though his words became almost inaudible long before he had finished.[2]

The general tenor of the decision was no surprise, for word of it had confidentially passed around Washington. The correspondent of the New York *Commercial Advertiser* had explicitly stated on March 5 that the Court would give judgment seven to two against the Missouri Compromise. James S. Pike had simultaneously written the *Tribune* that the judges would declare slavery coextensive with the nation outside of the free States, and would rule that its expansion must keep pace with every gain of territory. As Taney pronounced the Compromise restriction on slavery invalid, disappointment gathered on the face of John J. Crittenden of Kentucky, Clay's disciple, and indignation on the brow of Henry Wilson of Massachusetts, Webster's successor. Reporters caught a gleam of exultation on Caleb Cushing's visage, and watched anger deepen in Lewis Cass's eyes. As Justices Nelson and Catron followed Taney, the audience

1 Claude Fuess, *Caleb Cushing*, II, 153, 154.
2 Full texts of the decisions are in 19 *Howard*, 393–633.

melted away. By midafternoon the wires were humming with the news which fell upon Northern readers next morning like a bludgeon-stroke: "Slavery Alone National—The Missouri Compromise Unconstitutional—Negroes Cannot Be Citizens—The Triumph of Slavery Complete."

The questions caught up in Dred Scott's suit for freedom were now familiar to all well-informed citizens. One issue in the case was whether any man of Dred's color, descent, and status could be a citizen of a State and hence entitled to sue in the Federal courts. Another issue was whether Dred's residence at Rock Island and Fort Snelling, on free soil, had given him a title to liberty which continued to hold good when he returned to Missouri. Bound up with this, obviously, was the third issue: the question whether the Missouri Compromise restriction, which made slavery illegal in the Territory embracing Fort Snelling, was constitutional. To everyone but Dred the third issue overshadowed all the other considerations. With some bitterness, freesoilers pointed out that the Supreme Court had once included two justices who, when members of Congress, had voted for the Compromise: Philip P. Barbour of Virginia, and Henry Baldwin of Pennsylvania. What would these men have said of the constitutionality of the law they had helped to pass?

On the question whether Dred, or any other Negro of slave ancestry, could be a citizen (the question of jurisdiction), only three judges pronounced a broad and explicit negative. They were Judges Taney, Wayne, and Daniel, who found grounds for stating that citizenship was impossible to any such person. Not one of the three cited any apposite precedent, for, while Taney mentioned that the issue of citizenship had been raised in the famous Prudence Crandall case in Connecticut, he noted that no final opinion had then been handed down upon it. Indeed, no precedent was to be found in any work of reference known in 1857, though one has since been discovered: in 1793 the Federal circuit court in Connecticut had decided that a free Negro of Massachusetts possessed the right to sue.[3] Of the other judges, John McLean and Benjamin R. Curtis firmly asserted that a free Negro *was* a citizen, while the four others avoided the broad abstract question. Justice John A. Campbell, for example, held that Dred was a slave and hence not a citizen; but he skirted what seemed to him the academic issue whether the man, had he been a freeman, would have possessed citizenship.[4] It was an important fact that only three judges found that no Negro, even when free, could be a citizen—that is, that the Federal courts were closed to all such persons. If five or more judges had so held, the case would have been halted then and there. As matters stood, it had to be pushed one step further.

This step was to determine whether Dred Scott's residence at Rock Island

3 *Columbian Centinel*, May 15, 1793; information supplied by Charles Warren.
4 H. G. Connor, *John A. Campbell*, 63.

and Fort Snelling had freed him from bondage. In most of the Missouri cases bearing on this point the removal of the slave to free soil had been with a view to *permanent* domicile, something quite different from Dred's temporary sojourn. A majority of judges, led by Taney, held that the status of the Negro with respect to freedom or slavery was fixed, not by the law of areas in which he held transitory residence, but by that of the State in which he lived when the question was raised. As Judge Campbell put it: "The claim of the plaintiff to freedom depends upon the effect to be given to his absence from Missouri, in company with his master, in Illinois and Minnesota, and this effect is to be ascertained by reference to the laws of Missouri." The action of the Missouri Supreme Court was therefore upheld.

One justice, Daniel of Virginia, stated his opinion as to the controlling influence of Missouri law with vituperative emphasis. He pointed out that various slaveholding States had passed acts which limited the power of masters to set their slaves free. The arguments in behalf of Dred, he remarked, would permit any owner to emancipate his slave without reference to those legal restrictions; he need only take the slave to free soil and then bring him back: "At assumptions anomalous as these, so fraught with mischief and ruin, the mind at once is revolted." Judge McLean, on the other hand, held that the rule of interstate comity required Missouri to give due effect to the constitution and laws of Illinois. He noted that, as lately as 1851, the South Carolina Court of Appeals (following precedents in other Southern States) had recognized the principle that a slave when taken to reside in a free State lost his condition of bondage.[5]

Since, of the nine judges, a majority concurred in holding that the Missouri law did control Dred's status, that he remained a slave, and that he therefore had no right as citizen to maintain a suit in a Federal court, the case might have been halted at this stage. Why go on to explore the constitutionality of the Congressional enactments making the Territory of Wisconsin and the other Territories free?

This, however, is precisely what the Court did. Only one justice, Nelson of New York, stopped short with the judgment that Dred had no right to come before the tribunal. Concurring with the verdict that the plaintiff was a slave, and that the Federal circuit court therefore had no jurisdiction, he halted at that point. Chief Justice Taney and the other seven associate justices went further. They dealt with the whole field of Congressional power. Six, including the Chief Justice, held that Congress had no right to exclude slavery from any Territory,

5 In *Commonwealth* vs. *Pleasants*, 10 Leigh Reports 697. Chief Justice Gamble of the Missouri Court, in his dissenting opinion, had written: "In this state it has been recognized, from the beginning of the government, as a correct position in law, that the master who takes his slave to reside in a state or territory where slavery is prohibited, thereby emancipates his slave." J. D. Lawson, *American State Trials*, Vol. XIII. But one question was whether Dred had really been taken to "reside."

and that the Missouri Compromise was therefore unconstitutional. (Of these six, Taney, Wayne, and Daniel held that a Negro like Dred could not be a citizen; Grier, Catron, and Campbell left the issue of citizenship untouched.) Two judges, Curtis and McLean, dissented from the decision *cum ira;* they argued that Congress had ample power under the Constitution to debar slavery from any Territory. The vagueness and ambiguity of the instrument gave full room for an honest difference of interpretation.[6]

Taney's judgment on this constitutional issue was read by Americans with emotions varying from white-hot indignation in parts of the North to jubilant rejoicing in most of the South. Whenever new areas were acquired outside the limits of the United States, he reasoned, they were held for the common benefit of the people of the whole nation. The general government must act simply as trustee for the people, administering the areas for them until made part of the Union. It was undoubtedly necessary for Congress to establish some local government over the Territories, but it must not be on a discretionary or discriminatory basis as regards persons and property. The Georgian with his slave must have equality in the Territory alongside the Vermonter with his horse. He argued that what authority Congress did possess was derived, not from the clause empowering it to make necessary rules and regulations for the Territories (this being a mere emergency provision for the lands ceded to the Confederation), but from the power to create new States and to acquire land by treaty. It was therefore a power to acquire territory and prepare it for statehood; it was not a broad internal police authority. His language was emphatic: "No word can be found in the Constitution which gives Congress a greater power over slave property, or which entitles property of that kind to less protection, than property of any other description." Congress could not exclude slavery, for as Taney broadly construed it, this would violate the "due process of law" clause of the Fifth Amendment. It had "only the power coupled with the duty of . . . protecting the owner in his rights." [7]

The five judges who concurred with Taney in holding the Missouri Compromise unconstitutional were Wayne, Daniel, Grier, Campbell, and Catron—

6 The power of Congress over Territories had been exhaustively discussed by George Ticknor Curtis in his *History of the Constitution* (1854), II, 351–358. For the hasty way in which the Constitutional Convention, near the end of its work, wrote the territorial clause, see Charles Warren, *The Making of the Constitution*, 598–600.

7 Taney's reasoning is analyzed by E. S. Corwin in "The Dred Scott Decision in the Light of Contemporary Legal Doctrines," *Amer. Hist. Review*, XVII (1911), 52–69. The stands taken by the various judges (a tangled and in part obscure set of opinions) are lucidly summarized in G. T. Curtis's *Constitutional History of the United States* (prepared at the end of his long career and published in two volumes in 1896), I, 266–278. The "due process" clause had hitherto been generally held to limit governmental procedure, but not substantive legislation. Taney's dictum stands with the New York decision in *Wynehamer* vs. *New York* (13 N.Y. 378) as the first notable attempt to apply it to legislative acts.

Southerners, all but one. The position of James Catron of Tennessee was somewhat peculiar, While in his brief, crudely expressed opinion he joined the majority in pronouncing the Missouri Compromise restriction invalid, he declared that Congress was invested with a broad authority to make needful regulations concerning the Territories. Having hanged men under the power of Congress to pass laws for the western domain, he was anxious to insist that Congress and he had acted properly. He held, in short, that the national government had large powers—but not quite large enough to permit the interdiction of slavery. Justice Daniel once more used improper language. Some groups, he wrote, in attempting to exclude slavery from Territories, had "asserted a power in Congress, whether from incentives of interest, ignorance, faction, partiality, or prejudice, to bestow upon a portion of the citizens of this nation that which is the common property and privilege of all—the power, in fine, of confiscation." This, likes his use of the terms "iniquity" and "absurdity," was undignified name-calling.

To sum up, three Southern judges declared that no Negro of slave ancestry could be entitled to citizenship; five Southern judges, with Nelson of New York, decided that Dred's status depended upon the laws of Missouri; five Southern judges, with Grier of Pennsylvania, maintained that any law excluding slavery from a Territory was unconstitutional; and two Northern judges, McLean and Curtis, held that Dred was a citizen, that Missouri law did not control his status, and that Congress had a constitutional right to pass laws debarring slavery from any Territory.[8]

The majority having made its decision, all territorial restrictions on slavery were dead; wherever the flag advanced into new regions, it carried slavery with it. The doctrine of squatter sovereignty seemed equally dead. So long as any area held the status of a Territory, its people were theoretically as helpless as Congress to bar out the slaveholders with their slaves. But what would be the actual force of the decision? Would all good citizens, as Buchanan had predicted in his inaugural, cheerfully submit to it, or would the Northern people, legislators, and courts, as several freesoil members of Congress had threatened in advance, disregard it? The answer was not left in doubt for a single day. The greater part of the North instantly rejected the judgment on the ground that, handed down by a bench overwhelmingly biased in favor of one section, one party, and one slaveholding interest, it had no moral validity, and would retain legal validity only until a truly national bench overruled it.

8 The five men who joined Taney in holding the compromise restriction unconstitutional had various approaches. Writes Corwin, *op. cit.*, 52–69: "When the student finds six judges arriving at precisely the same result by three distinct processes of reasoning, he is naturally disposed to surmise that the result may have induced the processes rather than that the processes compelled the reasoning."

[II]

The storm of anger which instantly swept the North emphasized first and foremost the moral argument. Freesoilers believed that the fathers of the republic, anticipating a sentiment of the civilized world which by 1857 had become well-nigh irresistible, had regarded slavery as an evil which must eventually wither and die. It was therefore important to circumscribe and weaken it.[9] The Constitution ought to be interpreted in the light of this basic principle; instead, it had been interpreted in such wise as to diffuse and strengthen slavery. Greeley called for the creation of an enlightened public opinion to place all departments of the government in "the hands of men who love the Constitution and the Union much, but Liberty, Eternal Justice, and the Inalienable Rights of Man, still more."[10] A number of editors raised the cry that if the Constitution recognized no difference between slave property and other property, then a State legislature was as powerless as Congress or a territorial legislature to deprive any slave owner of the full use of his property. The Lemmon case, an appeal from the New York appellate court involving the status of a slave carried into that State, was pending. The Supreme Court, said these alarmists, had now indicated what would be its decision. Let its doctrine be established by law, and Toombs's reputed boast that he would yet call the roll of his slaves under Bunker Hill Monument might be realized. Meanwhile, William Cullen Bryant was denouncing Taney's decision as morally intolerable:

Hereafter, if this decision shall stand for law, slavery, instead of being what the people of the slave States have hitherto called it, their peculiar institution, is a Federal institution, the common patrimony and shame of all the States, those which flaunt the title of free, as well as those which accept the stigma of being the Land of Bondage; hereafter, wherever our jurisdiction extends, it carries with it the chain and the scourge—wherever our flag floats, it is the flag of slavery. If so, that flag should have the light of the stars and the streaks of morning red erased from it; it should be dyed black, and its device should be the whip and the fetter.

Are we to accept, without question, these new readings of the Constitution —to sit down contentedly under this disgrace—to admit that the Constitution was never before rightly understood, even by those who framed it—to consent that hereafter it shall be the slaveholders' instead of the freemen's Constitution? Never! Never![11]

9 George Mason had said in the Constitutional Convention: "He held it essential, in every point of view, that the general government should have power to prevent the increase of slavery." Elbridge Gerry had said: "He thought we had nothing to do with the conduct of the states as to slaves, but ought to be careful not to give any sanction to it." Madison Papers, Rives ed., 1391, 1394.
10 N. Y. Tribune, March 18, 1857.
11 Nevins, New York Evening Post, 254, 255.

The Northern revulsion against Taney's judgment was deepened by several passages which suggested a certain harshness of outlook. In building a historical foundation for his doctrine that Negroes were ineligible to citizenship and hence could not sue, he, like Daniel, exaggerated the public antipathy to Negroes in colonial days. History, he wrote, showed that for more than a century prior to the adoption of the Constitution they had been regarded as "beings of an inferior order, and altogether unfit to associate with the white race, either socially or politically; and so far inferior that they had no rights which the white man was bound to respect." The black man might be reduced to slavery, bought and sold, and treated as an ordinary article of merchandise. "This opinion at that time was fixed and universal in the civilized portion of the white race." A substantial inferiority had indeed existed. Charles R. Ingersoll had said in the Connecticut legislature in 1787 that Negroes in that State were "universally regarded as a servile, subject, exceptional class, in no sense fitted for . . . American citizenship." Yet Taney painted the situation too blackly. All the chief British colonies contained free Negroes who held property, made contracts, sued and were sued. Many Negroes served valiantly in the Revolution, Taney's own Maryland gladly accepting their services. Many were highly respected. As for the opinion of the "civilized portion" of mankind, everyone knew that in 1773 Lord Mansfield had forever established the rule that no Negro could be held to slavery within the realm of England; and that Jefferson's first draft of the Declaration of Independence had contained a reprobation of slavery which was omitted only in deference to Georgia and South Carolina.

In another unhappy passage, Taney asserted that the decision to abolish slavery in the Northern States had not resulted from any changed opinion upon the Negro, but from the fact that the North had found slave labor unsuited to its climate and productions. This was an untenable simplification of a complex process, its emphasis on materialistic elements doing injustice to salient moral considerations. A truer statement would be that moral opposition to slavery, increasingly strong in both sections during the Revolutionary period, was promoted in the North but checked in the South by economic factors. The contribution of reformative idealism to Northern emancipation was decisive; the labors of John Woolman, Anthony Benezet, and Franklin in America and of Granville Sharp, Wilberforce, and Clarkson in Britain had nothing to do with dollars or pounds. Numerous followers of these reformers were actuated by justice and philanthropy to the detriment of their pockets. Taney also remarked that Northern unregeneracy was illustrated by the continued activity of slave-traders plying from Northern ports, their traffic being "openly carried on and fortunes accumulated by it, without reproach from the people of the States where they resided." It was well known that the few Northerners who engaged

. in the slave trade after 1800 were held in bad repute, and their business had sullied the name of their descendants.

Next to the moral argument, indignant Northerners emphasized a belief that the decision constituted a flagrantly improper intrusion into the political domain. Men declared that while the supreme bench must sometimes touch political issues, a body of judges so predominantly Southern and sympathetic with slaveholding culture had no right to present a decision so manifestly sectional and partisan. Had they vindicated their impartiality by a decision adverse to their personal predilections, a different view might have been taken of their course. But in a great national crisis, said freesoilers, they had stooped, with political motives, to an act which all too obviously favored their own half of the country. Bryant's *Evening Post* on March 7, and James Watson Webb's *Courier* on March 13, set up the cry of "political conspiracy"; it spread throughout half the Northern Press; and its wide acceptance is indicated by the fact that Abraham Lincoln soon took it up. A political motive was believed even where the idea of a conspiracy was rejected.

Throughout the North and West, the dissenting opinions of Curtis and McLean (particularly Curtis's, which contained much the greater panoply of historical and legal facts) exercised a profound influence. They had weaknesses of evidence and logic. But taken together, they offered a large body of evidence to rebut Taney's findings on Negro citizenship and on Congressional power.

Nothing could be more erroneous, urged Curtis, than this denial of the Negro's historic status. The Constitution spoke of "citizens of the United States at the time of adoption" of the instrument. It was therefore clear that citizens of the several States under the Confederation were citizens of the United States under the Constitution; and it was a fact that in 1787 free native-born Negroes of five States (New Hampshire, Massachusetts, New York, New Jersey, North Carolina) were not merely citizens, but held suffrage rights on equal terms with white men. Curtis cited the opinion of Judge William Gaston of North Carolina that free Negroes had voted in his State for years until a constitutional amendment deprived them of the ballot.[12] Both McLean and Curtis pointed out that under the Treaty of Guadelupe Hidalgo the United States had given citizenship to persons of color in the lands annexed from Mexico. It had done the same,

12 At a later date, free Negroes were allowed to vote in Tennessee until the Constitutional Convention of 1834 deprived them of the right. P. M. Hamer, *Tennessee: a History*, I, 468. When James Monroe was minister to Great Britain, he gave a passport to Essex White, a slave of John Randolph of Roanoke, describing him as a "citizen of the United States." Passports were given to free Negroes of the United States, as citizens, until Franklin Pierce's Administration in 1856 issued instructions to legations abroad stopping the practice (Amer. Antislavery Soc., *Report, 1860*, 220, 221). But Curtis and Taney did not meet squarely. Curtis argued that citizenship, for persons born in the republic, came through the States. Taney held that "a citizen of the United States" gained his status through some form of Federal intervention; and he regarded Curtis's historical instances as irrelevant.

they argued, in treaties covering Louisiana, Florida, and the Cherokee and Choctaw domains. Nor was it true, asserted Curtis, that the Constitution was made
exclusively for white people. Its preamble declared that it was to secure to the
people of the United States the blessings of liberty, and "people" certainly included the free Negroes voting in five States.[13]

As for Congressional power over slavery in the Territories, McLean and
Curtis offered arguments based both on theory and on precedent. In theory,
McLean contended that the power to acquire carries the power to govern; that
Congress had always exercised this authority; and that if it deemed slavery in-
jurious to any Territory, it had a right to prohibit it. In this argument he was
able to cite Chief Justice Marshall, who had described the right of governing as
"the inevitable consequence of the right to acquire." It necessarily followed, he
believed, that when the United States gained a new area by conquest or purchase, Congress might govern it in any manner and for any length of time it saw
fit, so long as it remained a dependency external to the Union. Curtis laid down
the same doctrine still more emphatically. Chief Justice Taney's contracted
interpretation of the powers of the general government was inconsistent, he held,
with the nature and purposes of the Constitution. That instrument gave Congress authority "to dispose of and make all needful Rules and Regulations respecting the Territory or other property" of the nation; it could deal *both* with
jurisdiction and soil; and so long as the laws were "needful" (that is, not arbitrary, capricious, or unnecessary), their scope could be left to Congressional
discretion.[14]

In citing precedents, Curtis found that Congress had passed two classes of
acts. In eight distinct instances, beginning with the first Congress and coming
down to 1848, it had excluded slavery from various Territories. In six distinct
instances, beginning with the first Congress and coming down to 1822, it had
recognized slavery in a Territory and contained it therein. These laws had been
signed by seven Presidents, including all who were in public life when the Constitution was adopted. This fact, he believed, should have much weight in interpreting the Constitution, while it was difficult to resist the force of the acts
themselves. (When the Missouri Compromise became law, all the Southern
Senators, a large majority of Southern Representatives, and the whole executive
branch deemed it constitutional. President Monroe, as J. Q. Adams's diary
shows, propounded to the Cabinet—Adams, Calhoun, Crawford, McLean, and

13 *I Peters,* 543.
14 Curtis cited Marshall's famous opinion in *American Insurance Co. vs. Canter* (1828)
as showing that Congressional power did come from the rules-and-regulations clause as well
as from the power to acquire land. Edward S. Corwin concludes that on the question of
citizenship Taney's argument was the stronger; "The Dred Scott Decision in the Light of
Contemporary Legal Doctrines," *Amer. Hist. Review,* XVII, 52–69.

Wirt—the question of power and they unanimously concurred with him as to its existence.) Indeed, for a half-century the Congressional power was hardly challenged.

If it could be shown by the Constitution itself that when it gave Congress authority to make all needful rules and regulations slavery was excepted, then, said Curtis, he would give due weight to that fact; but no such demonstration was possible. He must find something more than Taney's theoretical reasoning to make him believe that the Constitution did not mean *all* when it said all; especially as the Court had repeatedly balked efforts to introduce exceptions not found in the Constitution. Under the power to regulate commerce, Congress had embargoed all ships, thus prohibiting the use of a special kind of property belonging mainly to citizens of the Northeastern States; yet the Court had held this constitutional. If the power to govern commerce extended to an indefinite prohibition of the use of vessels, did not the power to make all needful rules respecting the territory of the United States extend to a prohibition of slavery?

[III]

Would the prestige of the Court, which for sixty years had been gathering dignity and influence, override all opposition? "Mr. President," Senator Cass had exclaimed in the Senate two years earlier, "it is an impressive spectacle, almost a sublime one, to see nine men . . . establishing great principles essential to public and private prosperity and to the government; whose influence is felt throughout the whole Union, and whose decrees are implicitly obeyed. It is the triumph of moral force." [15] Yet Cass knew that the interpretation of the Constitution was a human process, and that the conclusions of the nine judges must in the last analysis harmonize with the will of the people, or they would be swept aside; he acknowledged this fact when he said that the Court "lives and breathes upon public confidence," and that "it cannot carry into effect a single decree without calling upon the other departments of government to aid it." For two main reasons all Republicans and many freesoil Democrats were quite unwilling to acknowledge the finality of the decision; one being the biased composition of the Court, the other the widespread suspicion of some political maneuvering or even conspiracy behind its decision.

Northern spokesmen had for years repeatedly declared that public confidence in the Supreme Court was impaired by the lack of balance in its membership. Of the nine judges who heard the Dred Scott case, five, including the Chief Justice, were Southerners, and four Northerners. Of these four, Grier of Penn-

15 *Cong. Globe*, February 8, 1855; see *Ordeal of the Union*, I, 171.

sylvania was as pronouncedly Southern in his sympathies as Buchanan.[16] So far as sectional inclination went, the Court stood six to three. As for party affiliation, seven of the nine were Democrats, McLean was a Republican, and Curtis still called himself a Whig. The Court plainly had an excessive party and sectional bias. Representative Stanton of Ohio, early in 1857, had introduced a resolution calling on the House Judiciary Committee to inquire into an equalization of the population and business of the judicial circuits. As critics pointed out, the seventh circuit (Ohio, Indiana, Illinois, Michigan), with four and a half million people, had more white inhabitants than three Southern circuits combined.

The bias would have been excessive even had the times been perfectly calm. But the Court had been called upon to decide the constitutionality of the Missouri Compromise restriction just when President Pierce, Attorney-General Cushing, and Secretary Jefferson Davis were condemning that law as a monumental error, and just when President-elect Buchanan and the Southern leaders were hailing the late election as a sweeping verdict against any restrictions.

The character of the judges, whose attainments ranged, as always, from consummate ability to mediocrity, offered no guarantee that party and sectional pressure would be withstood. Of the intellectual power and profound learning of the Chief Justice no question could exist. Strength of mind and elevation of spirit were stamped upon Taney's face. Tall, thin, bent with his eighty years, his skin a parchment yellow, his features deeply furrowed, his hair drooping over his high forehead, his plain black garb ill-brushed, his long arms and bony fingers giving him a spidery look as he took nervous notes, he was not an attractive figure.[17] Yet fire dwelt in his eyes, and intensity marked his movements. From the time in 1836 when Henry Clay had violently denounced his appointment, political opponents had spoken of him harshly. Counsel familiar with the Court, however, paid tribute to his spotless character, his sagacity, his vast legal erudition, his serene dignity as presiding officer, and his painful conscientiousness in holding the scales of justice even between litigants.[18] Deploring slavery, he had long since freed all his bondsmen. A devout Catholic, he made it a daily custom to implore heaven for guidance. Even hostile editors admitted that in the sincerity of his convictions and his intellectual authority, he was no unworthy suc-

16 There may or may not be significance in the fact that Grier was a distant relative of the mother of Alexander H. Stephens, and that his daughter married a Kentuckian who became a Confederate officer. J. Z. Rabun, "Alexander H. Stephens, 1812–1861," MS Dissertation, Univ. of Chicago; N. Y. *Tribune*, September 27, 1870.

17 Born the year of the battle of Saratoga; March 17, 1777.

18 Caleb Cushing in due course penned a glowing tribute to Taney. He spoke of the Chief Justice's erudition, masterly style in written opinions, and kind deportment toward members of the bar. "He was one of those men who possess such tenacity of vitality as half to suggest that the human body may sometimes endure to extreme old age by the mere force of a great mind within it, as the will may have power to withstand physical decay, and repel the attacks of death." Undated MS; Cushing Papers.

cessor of John Marshall; while "affectionate reverence" was the term used by Judah P. Benjamin for the feeling which he inspired among friends.[19] To his trenchant power as a political thinker, later generations would do full justice.

It could nevertheless be said that, penetration and not breadth being his chief mental attribute, he sometimes displayed a narrow stubbornness; that he was strongly molded by his early Calvert County environment, the tobacco-planting, slaveholding tidewater strip of Maryland, and was deeply sympathetic with Southern ways and manners; and that his conduct as a judge had not been un-tinged by partisanship. As a member of Jackson's Cabinet, helping make war upon the Bank of the United States, he had developed an anti-monopolist feeling which expressed itself on the bench in a desire to restrain mercantile and financial concentrations. The tendency of his decisions was to a strict construction of national powers conferred in the Constitution, and to a protection of the States in a full and unfettered use of their retained authority.[20] His judgment in the Charles River case was one of several which almost caused Justice Story to resign, and inspired James Kent's indignant protest.[21] Even sympathetic biographers admit that his opinion in one case involving the Bank and his own previous action as Attorney-General went to the verge of impropriety.[22]

It might be noted that, in the famous Prigg case, he and Justice Daniel had stood together in holding that States could pass laws for the surrender of escaped slaves, but not laws which impaired the master's right to recover them. A champion of human rights in the economic field, he had an agrarian instinct, a feeling for the rural South as against the wealthy, partially industrialized North, which was bound insensibly to color his judicial thought. He felt that the South, and with it the Union, were in imminent danger.

Of the four other judges from slaveholding States, John A. Campbell, only forty-six this year, was easily the ablest, and had gained national reputation as an attorney before Pierce lifted him to the Supreme Court. The son of an eminent Georgia lawyer, he grew up in the same aristocratic town as Toombs —Washington—and graduated from the University of Georgia. Removing to Montgomery, Alabama, he distinguished himself by studious tastes, a remarkable memory, and undeviating regard for principle. His charge to the grand jury in New Orleans in 1854, denouncing William Walker and other filibusters, was a long-remembered exemplification of his courage. Genial, gentle, and philosophical, a close and accurate reasoner, he was never strongly partisan. He labored

19 Cong. Globe, 35th Congress, 1st Sess., 1065–1072.
20 G. W. Biddle in T. M. Cooley et al., Constitutional History, 195 ff.
21 Appleton's Cyc. Amer. Biography, VI, 29.
22 Bank of Augusta vs. Earle; C. B. Swisher, Roger Brooke Taney, 380–386.

nearly to the last against secession, although he believed it a right.[23] Unhappily, his three Southern associates had a less rigid impartiality.

James M. Wayne of Georgia, an intelligent, hard-working, and in no way brilliant man, who bore his sixty-seven years sturdily and who had been a member of the Court since Jackson's Presidency, was deeply attached to the Union; a fact proved in 1861 when, unlike Justice Campbell, he stuck to it. But he was also sternly positive in defense of Southern institutions. His specialty was admiralty law. Another judge of Jacksonian antecedents, John Catron of Tennessee, was a big, forthright, awkward frontier lawyer who spoke his common-sense (and commonplace) mind in a booming and unmelodious voice. A shrewd politician, he had won his place on the bench by helping Jackson in his Bank contest, and a politician he remained. There was much that was likeable in a rough western way about Catron; he had shouldered a rifle at New Orleans and had resented insults to his honor with duelling pistols. The stamp of Nashville, not as the Athens of the South but as the capital of slaveholding Tennessee, with her old interest in western expansion, was upon him.

Equally picturesque was Peter B. Daniel, a tall, thin, sharp-visaged, fidgety Virginian of aristocratic family, who had studied law under Washington's Attorney-General, Edmund Randolph, and married his daughter. While he had a fine library, read widely, and cultivated music, he made few pretensions to legal learning. He was simply an old-school gentleman of taste and logical intellect. His weakness lay in his fanatical temper, for if Wayne was an extremist in defending slavery, Daniel was a bigot. He told his grandnephew, Moncure D. Conway, that the antislavery men were "monsters," and his language in the Dred Scott case was so intemperate that his friend W. W. Seaton gravely rebuked him in the *National Intelligencer.* The portrait of Daniel reveals a wild gleam in his eye, an intolerant set about his mouth.[24]

These five members from the slaveholding region constituted a majority of the Court. Of the two judges from the Middle States, Samuel Nelson of New York was the more easily appraised. He was a conservative up-State Democrat who, while chief justice of the State Supreme Court, had been raised to the national tribunal by Tyler. Plodding, blunt, honest, and hard-working, he was perfectly trustworthy. His interest was in technical questions of maritime, patent, and international law rather than in broad constitutional issues. While his views might be limited, he stuck to them without regard for politics, personalities, or public opinion.[25] The other, Robert C. Grier of Pennsylvania, one of

23 E. I. McCormac, "Justice Campbell and the Dred Scott Decision," *Miss. Valley Hist. Review,* XIX (1933), 565–571, shows that Campbell wrote Calhoun in a long and careful letter, March 1, 1848, that Congress had a full right to exclude slavery from the Territories. He suggests that this was Campbell's real view, changed in 1857 for political reasons.
24 Conway, *Autobiography,* I, 223; *National Intelligencer,* June 18, 1857.
25 *The Green Bag,* June, 1907.

Polk's appointees, had of late been ceaselessly attacked in his own section as a fickle tool of slavery. Like Taney (class of 1795) and Buchanan (class of 1809), he was a graduate of Dickinson College (class of 1812) at Carlisle. During recent years his zeal in upholding the Fugitive Slave Law had evoked Southern praise and freesoil wrath.[26] "He succumbs to touch and returns to shape upon its removal," wrote James S. Pike of this rotund, cheerful jurist. "He is ardent and impressible." A neighbor and friend of Buchanan, he was eager for the success of the Administration and the party. It was to Grier that the President-elect had written just after his triumph the previous fall that he meant to destroy the dangerous slavery agitation, strengthen the Democratic Party, and thus restore peace to the distracted nation.[27]

Grier's pliability was coupled with an inadequate instinct for propriety and dignity. The Buchanan Papers contain some curious letters showing that at this very time Grier's family affairs were embarrassed; indeed, he was always heavily burdened, for he had toiled hard to support his mother and help educate ten younger brothers. To mend his circumstances, he was anxious to install a relative as clerk of the circuit court in Philadelphia, a position held by an efficient party lieutenant, George Plitt. The justice first asked Buchanan to give Plitt another office, which the President coldly refused to do. Grier then brought pressure upon Plitt to resign. The clerk declined. "You and I and the public too," he wrote Grier, "if aware of all the facts, would know that by resigning I should make myself party to an apparent traffic in official trusts, which . . . the President, when it was hinted to him, promptly rebuked." Yet Grier persisted, and in the face of a memorial signed by numerous members of the Philadelphia bar brought about Plitt's removal.[28] This improper act was much resented. Grier, to be sure, had certain good qualities; a former head of Northumberland College, he was broadly cultivated, while his Civil War record was to prove creditable. But he was a weak man.[29]

Altogether, it is not strange that countless Northerners regarded the Dred Scott decision as the political stroke of a sectional, proslavery majority of judges. Many press reports were highly colored. Describing the panel on March 6, some Northern journalists pictured them as guilt-haggard conspirators. The general air of the majority, wrote Pike of the *Tribune*, was one of "nervous exultation over their attempt to garrote the free States."[30] He presented a series of caustic vignettes of the Southern members. Daniel, he wrote, was a palsied, fretful old gentleman in glasses, with the politics of a Virginia slaveholder and abstraction-

26 Castner Hanway, correspondence, *National Intelligencer*, November 10, 1853.
27 November 14, 1856; Buchanan Papers.
28 Letters, January-February, 1858, Buchanan Papers.
29 See obituaries, N. Y. *Tribune*, N. Y. *World*, September 27, 1870.
30 J. S. Pike in N. Y. *Tribune*, March 8, 1857.

ist who still swore by the resolutions of 1798. Catron's errors would more often spring from obtuseness than from original sin. Campbell was more Southern than the extreme South from which he hailed. Wayne, who had shown his ill temper by uttering loud comments while Curtis read his judgment, would dispute the right of any Northern man to an opinion on slavery or its relations. But Pike's sharpest barbs were reserved for Taney. Not content with saying that the inverted step, narrow forehead, sunken eyes, and "sinister expression" of the Chief Justice made him look like a man of malign disposition, he impugned his honor. Reverdy Johnson, he declared, had overcome the opposition in the Senate when Jackson appointed Taney head of the Court, and Taney was duly grateful. Hence the eagerness of the slavery men to hire Reverdy Johnson to argue the Dred Scott case! [31]

While such calumny was deplorable, Northern insistence that the one-sided decision would shortly be rectified by a truly national court was perfectly defensible. Freesoil men held that the decree was valid insofar as it affected Dred Scott, but not in its more sweeping pronouncements, and that as soon as a freesoil President could change the list of judges, the Court would restore the old reading of the Constitution. Every Republican editor caught up the cry. "The remedy," stated the Chicago *Tribune*, "is union and action; the ballot box. Let free States be a unit in Congress on the side of freedom. Let the next President be Republican, and 1860 will mark an era kindred with that of 1776." [32] The Springfield *Republican*, Albany *Journal*, and other sheets pointed out that the judgments of the Court were always reversible. If the Court had affirmed the constitutionality of the Alien and Sedition Acts, the people would nevertheless have annulled them and paid back the penalties exacted under them. The Court had pronounced the Bank of the United States constitutional, but the people had made a contrary decision. The tribunal of final jurisdiction was the American nation massed at the polls.

Declaring that six million whites of the South had more weight in the Supreme Court than sixteen million people in the free areas, the New York *Tribune* called for a reapportionment; "Make the judicial districts equal, let judges be fairly selected therefrom, and the Dred Scott decision will soon be overthrown and effaced." [33]

The conviction of Republicans upon the bias of the Court was enhanced by their belief that more "national" nominations to the bench had been defeated

31 N. Y. *Weekly Tribune*, March 21, 1857; for the close friendship between Taney and Reverdy Johnson, begun when they were young lawyers together in 1815, see B. C. Steiner, *Reverdy Johnson*, 10, 11, 31. Ex-Senator J. W. Bradbury of Maine told Rhodes that Northern Democrats in 1857 had said that Johnson prevailed on Taney to give his decision; Rhodes, *United States*, II, 269, 270. No evidence exists for this piece of gossip.
32 Chicago *Tribune*, March 19, 1857.
33 N. Y. *Tribune*, March 18, 1857.

mainly by Southern votes. President Tyler had nominated John C. Spencer and Chancellor Reuben Walworth, both New Yorkers of high standing and both Whigs, but the Senate had refused confirmation. When Polk had nominated George W. Woodward of Pennsylvania, he had been rejected because of his alleged nativist views, because of the dislike of Simon Cameron, then a Democrat, and because some Senators feared Woodward would be hostile to slavery. Fillmore had nominated George E. Badger of North Carolina, a Whig, twice a Cabinet member, and a distinguished Senator. The Democratic press had deluged him with abuse, one editor terming him worse than an abolitionist because he believed the Wilmot Proviso constitutional, and the Senate blocked him. Had these four men gone into the Supreme Court, its character in 1857 would have been very different.[34]

[IV]

While charges against the Court's impartiality were serious, those against its probity were far graver. The theory that the majority decisions had originated in a conspiracy between Buchanan and Taney was bitterly asserted by several newspapers, and caught up by Republican politicians. Eminent leaders soon adopted it. In a resounding speech of March 3, 1858, Seward declared that before entering office Buchanan had approached or been approached by the Supreme Court; that his reference to the decision in the inaugural was proof of a coalition between Court and President "to undermine the national legislature and the liberties of the people;" and that the plot culminated in dishonorable "whisperings" between Buchanan and Taney just before the new President took his oath.

Taney was revolted by this charge. He long afterward told his first biographer that if the scoundrel Seward had been chosen President in 1860, he would have declined to administer the oath of office to him. That Seward wronged the Chief Justice, in bringing so harsh an accusation, there can be no doubt. While there had been a most improper exchange of views between the President-elect and two associate justices, there had certainly been no collusion between Taney and Buchanan.[35] But, setting aside the misstated charge of conspiracy, we must

34 A House Committee of the Vermont legislature brought in a report early in 1858 which sternly indicted the Court: "The judges, without check or control except by the President, combine with him and with the Government to legalize oppression and wrong. Instead of judges they become tyrants . . ." Report of the Select Committee on Slavery and the Dred Scott decision (pamphlet).

35 Buchanan left among the papers used by his official biographer an uncandid document. He spoke of "the infamous and unfounded assertion of Mr. Seward that in a conversation with Chief Justice Taney, he [the Chief Justice] had informed him what the opinion would be." Curtis, Buchanan, II, 306, 307. Virtuous indignation! But Seward's statement was erroneous merely in detail. Buchanan's information came in writing from Grier and Catron, not orally from Taney.

still ask why the Court entered so unnecessarily upon the dangerous question of Congressional power in the Territories. When it was decided that Missouri law controlled Dred's status, it was beside the point to explore the validity of the Missouri Compromise. Did the Southern members of the Court wantonly intrude upon this political terrain, or did the fault lie elsewhere? Conflicting evidence requires the closest possible analysis.

Let us review what had happened. From the moment Congress met in December, 1856, and found the Court ready to hear argument, Southern and Democratic pressure was brought upon the judges to make a clear-cut decision on the Compromise. Alexander H. Stephens, a close friend of his fellow-Georgian Wayne, vigorously urged a broad judgment on this controverted issue. He wrote his brother Linton in mid-December that he was active and hopeful.[36] The Washington correspondent of the New York *Express*, a Know-Nothing organ which prided itself on the best capital intelligence in the country, stated that a comprehensive decision was expected by those who knew the situation. "The Democracy is especially anxious that the bench should relieve them from the territorial issues of the slavery question, and it is understood are bringing whatever influence they may to bear upon the court." [37] On New Year's Day, another of its correspondents added that some of the judges had made up their mind on the territorial issue. "Their opinion has found partial expression in the Dred Scott case, and you will find that, before six months shall have expired, the unconstitutionality of territorial legislation upon the question will be regarded as settled, both by the North and the South." [38] The Washington *Union*, precentor of the Administration press, simultaneously prophesied that the Court would find the Compromise restriction unconstitutional by a vote of seven to two, McLean and Curtis dissenting.[39] It and other Democratic sheets were patently anxious for a sweeping decision.

When reargument began in mid-December, the Chief Justice had carefully framed the two main questions to be treated *de novo:* (1) Whether a Negro of Dred's position and lineage could be a citizen of the United States and entitled to sue, and (2) Whether Congress had constitutional authority to exclude slavery from the Territories. It was noteworthy that counsel dealt with the whole range of issues. Reverdy Johnson, with much undignified gibing at "Sambo" and "Cuffee" combined with sarcasm, partisan prejudice, and appeals to South-

36 The day set for the second argument of the case was December 15, 1856. That very day Alexander H. Stephens wrote his brother: "I have been urging all the influence I could bring to bear upon the Sup. Ct. to get them no longer to postpone the case on the Mo. Restriction before them, but to decide it. They take it up today. If they decide as I have reason to believe they will that the restriction was unconstitutional . . . then the . . . judicial question as I think will be ended. . . ." Stephens Papers, Manhattanville College. Taney and Stephens had been members of the same Congressional mess, 1844–46.
37 Washington correspondence N. Y. *Express*, December 19, 1856.
38 N. Y. *Express*, January 3, 1857.
39 Quoted in N. Y. *Express*, January 5, 1857.

ern emotion, covered the widest possible ground. He held that slavery, as a beneficent institution, should be perpetual and should be given the right to expand.[40] On Dred's side, Montgomery Blair argued the right of the Negro to citizenship, and George Ticknor Curtis the right of Congress to prohibit slavery in the Territories. Indeed, Curtis, the first of whose two learned volumes on *The History of the Origin, Formation, and Adoption of the Constitution of the United States* had appeared three years earlier, furnished a searching examination of the use Congress had made of its authority to devise "all needful rules and regulations" for the Territories. Geyer also argued the constitutionality of the Missouri Compromise.[41] Press reports and editorial comment covered the whole subject, and with Democratic papers confident and Republican journals apprehensive, the public gained the impression that a broad decision impended.[42]

Alexander H. Stephens, who was in touch with Justice Wayne, thought that such a decision was about to be rendered. On New Year's Day he wrote a friend that he felt a deep solicitude over the judgment. "From what *I hear sub rosa* it will be according to my own opinions upon every point as abstract political questions. The restriction of 1820 will be held to be unconstitutional. The Judges are all writing out their opinions I believe *seriatim*. The Chief Justice will give an elaborate one." [43] Montgomery Blair, who was on the alert to pick up every grain of news, also expected a sweeping decision. He informed ex-President Van Buren on February 5 that it seemed to be the impression that the Court would decide against Dred, and also against the power of Congress over the Territories.[44]

At this point an extraordinary correspondence began between the President-elect and Judge Catron. Buchanan, aware that he would be expected to say something about popular sovereignty in his inaugural, and that any explicit statement would anger either the Cass-Douglas or the Southern wing of the party, wished with characteristic caution to fall back on the Supreme Court. He wrote his old Jacksonian friend on February 3, asking whether he might say that the Court would soon decide the question. Catron immediately replied (February 6) that it rested with Chief Justice Taney to move in the matter, and that so far he had said nothing to him about it. A conference might have been held earlier, he thought, but for the prostration of Judge Daniel by the tragic death of his beautiful young wife, whose clothing had accidentally caught fire. This delay was really unnecessary, for Daniel "will surely deliver his own opinion in the case, *at length*." Probably Catron knew how profoundly Daniel's feelings were stirred.

40 N. Y. *Weekly Tribune*, March 21, 1857.
41 Correspondence, N. Y. *Times, Herald, Tribune*, December 16, 17, 18, 1856. Curtis's second volume appeared in 1858.
42 Curtis, *Const. Hist. U. S.*, I, 266–278.
43 January 1, 1857; Stephens Papers, Manhattanville College.
44 Warren, *Supreme Court* (1926 ed.), II, 293.

He promised to keep Buchanan informed. Four days later, February 10, he wrote again:

The Dred Scott case will be decided next Saturday [that is, would be discussed in conference on Saturday, February 14] but it is not at all probable that you will be helped by the decision in preparing your Inaugural. Some of the judges will not touch the question of [Congressional] power, others may, but that it will settle *nothing*, is my present opinion.

No opinions can be expected to be announced before the end of this month.[45]

Catron went on to make it plain that he himself believed the Missouri Compromise unconstitutional, simply because the Louisiana Purchase had guaranteed slavery in that region. His letters must have provoked Buchanan. They made it evident that Daniel would surely express his fanatical opinions at length, that other judges might touch the Compromise issue, and that Catron himself had fixed views on the subject—but that he doubted whether the decision would settle the matter. On February 14, however, Glancy Jones, who operated his own listening post in the capital, sent Buchanan a different view. "The Supreme Court will give their decision soon and the reasoning of the opinion will cover Squatter Sovereignty. To anxious inquirers on this subject in your inaugural I have answered I believe you would rest on the decision of the Supreme Court." [46]

What, meanwhile, was the Court actually doing? Rules of secrecy and judicial reticence envelop the subject in a murky haze through which we can peer but dimly, and dogmatic assertions on the critical point are impossible. It appears that when conferences began on or about the fourteenth,[47] the majority wished to stop short with the decision that after Dred's return the Missouri law determined his status as slave, and he had no right to sue in a Federal court. Judge Nelson was deputed to prepare the majority opinion on the subject, and did so; the question of Congressional power would lie untouched. It also appears that various members contested this majority action, and a series of stormy debates began. What members? Catron had mentioned Judge Daniel's wish to express himself *at length;* evidence exists that Judge Wayne, pressed by Stephens, had already begun to write a broad opinion. Indeed, Judge Campbell later stated that several opinions had been begun before the first conference, and that Wayne shortly urged Chief Justice Taney to write a full decision instead of letting Nelson pen a brief judgment.

"The instruction of the majority, in reference to the preparation of this opinion," writes Campbell,[48] "was to limit the opinion to the particular circum-

45 Catron, February 6, 10, 1857; Buchanan Papers.
46 Glancy Jones, February 14, 1857; Buchanan Papers.
47 Warren says the fifteenth, but that day was Sunday.
48 In Samuel Tyler, *R. B. Taney*, 384; Campbell's letter is dated November 24, 1870.

stances of Dred Scott; and Mr. Justice Nelson prepared his opinion, on file, under this instruction, to be read as the opinion of the Court. Subsequently, and before it was read, upon a motion of Mr. Justice Wayne, who stated that the case had created public interest and expectation, that it had been twice argued, and that an impression existed that the questions argued would be considered in the opinion of the Court, he proposed that the Chief Justice should write an opinion on all of the questions as the opinion of the Court. This was assented to; some reserving to themselves to qualify their assent as the opinion might require." [49]

If we accept this statement, Wayne apparently convinced Taney, Catron, and Campbell that a broad verdict was needed—Daniel already taking that view. But Judge Grier, as a Northerner who had been under heavy fire for "subservience," was reluctant to act. If he held to his position, the Compromise restriction would be declared unconstitutional by five slave State judges. This, from the Southern point of view, was undesirable; at least one Northern judge should join the others. Something must be done!

For the Southern majority, Catron took action. Resuming his correspondence with Buchanan, he asked him to bring pressure upon his close friend Grier. Writing February 19, he stated that the omens were better, that the case had been before the judges several times since Saturday the fourteenth, and that Buchanan could safely pass responsibility to the Court. "You may say in your inaugural that the constitutionality of the Compromise is now before the tribunal," he wrote, "and you may add, 'It is due to its high and independent character to suppose that it will settle and decide a controversy which has so long and uselessly agitated the country, and which *must* ultimately be decided by the Supreme Court.'" But would the President-elect please lend a hand? "A majority of my brethren will be forced up to this point by two dissentients. Will you drop Grier a line, saying how necessary it is, and how good the opportunity is, to settle the question by an affirmative decision of the Supreme Court, the one way or the other? He ought not to occupy so doubtful a ground as the outside issue—that admitting the constitutionality of the Missouri Compromise law of 1820, still, as no domicile was acquired by the Negro at Fort Snelling, and he returned to Missouri, he was not free. He has no doubt about the question on the main contest, but has been persuaded to take the smooth handle for the sake of repose." [50] Catron knew that Grier readily yielded to manipulation.

Buchanan was quite ready to act. In fact, he had a special reason for doing so; for if Catron stuck to what was apparently his original position, that the

49 Wayne in conversation corroborated this; Curtis, *Benjamin R. Curtis*, I, 234, 235.
50 Buchanan, *Works*, X, 106,

Missouri Compromise was void merely because of the Louisiana Purchase treaty, then only a minority of four judges (Taney, Wayne, Daniel, Campbell) would declare that Congress had no power over slavery in the Territories in general. The President-elect sent Grier a letter, since lost, which urged him to join in quashing the slavery agitation. Grier replied on February 23 with all the expected complaisance. He had at once shown Buchanan's letter to Taney and Wayne, he wrote. "We fully appreciate and concur in your views as to the desirableness at the time of having an expression of the opinion of the Court on this troublesome question."

Indeed, he explained, they had already reached this conclusion. At first, Nelson had been commissioned to write an opinion leaving the difficult issues of citizenship and Congressional power untouched. "But it appeared that our brothers who dissented from the majority, especially Justice McLean, were determined to come out with a long and labored dissent, including their opinions and arguments on both the troublesome points, although not necessary to a decision of the case. In our opinion both the points are *in* the case and may be legitimately considered. Those who hold a different opinion from Messrs. McLean and Curtis on the power of Congress and the validity of the Compromise Act feel compelled to express their opinions on the subject." [51]

Grier was anxious, he continued, that no line of latitude should seem to have determined the Court's decision; anxious, too, that the majority opinion should have a general unity of view. Conversing with Taney, he had agreed to concur with him, while he had also agreed to labor with Wayne to get Daniel, Campbell, and Catron to do the same. He feared that some Southern members might throw out extreme views. But at any rate, six judges would declare the Missouri Compromise unconstitutional. "We will not let any of our brethren know the *cause of our anxiety* to produce this result." [52] This missive greatly relieved Buchanan and Catron. But they continued under some anxiety. As late as February 21, eleven days before the inauguration, Buchanan was writing Catron again to urge prompt action, and two days later Catron was replying that he had hoped to have the opinion delivered before the third of March, that most of his colleagues were ready, and that "I want Grier speeded." [53]

What does all this come to? On the letters of Grier and Catron many writers have founded a dogmatic statement that the dissenters, McLean and Curtis,

51 *Ibid.*, 106–108; C. B. Swisher, *Taney*, 499.
52 What was "the cause of our anxiety"? Obviously, Buchanan and Grier were anxious to annul the compromise restriction so as to cripple the Republicans and to destroy Douglas's doctrine, thus (as they hoped) unifying the Democratic Party. They were also anxious that at least one Northerner join in the annulment. Grier may have referred to either anxiety, or both. In any event, he was assuring Buchanan that he and Wayne would work upon their fellow judges, from a secret motive, for a political end.
53 Catron to Buchanan, February 23, 1857; Buchanan Papers.

forced a broad decision; [54] but hastily written letters usually give but a partial view of the truth. One curious contradiction in these epistles is evident at a glance. Catron asked Buchanan to induce Grier to support a sweeping judgment; Grier wrote Buchanan that he would try to get Catron to agree to one! The two men did not clearly understand each other. For half a dozen reasons, which are discussed in the first appendix of this work, we may doubt their accuracy in placing the main responsibility for the broad decision upon McLean and Curtis; for this oversimplifies a very complex transaction.

[V]

Rosy hopes of benefit and prestige from the decision danced before the Administration eyes. The truculent Douglas would have to "cave in"; Republicans would find themselves battling the Constitution and the Union. "There was but one thing needful to give to the result in the presidential contest the force of an absolute and final settlement of the sectional issue," exulted the Washington *Union.* "That thing was the judgment of the Supreme Court in confirmation of the Democratic doctrines which had received the popular endorsement. . . . The people have decided that sectional agitation must cease, and the highest judicial authority has declared that the people have decided in accordance with the Constitution." The attacks of Republicans on the decision it stigmatized as "the last dying fit of fanatical sectionalism." [55]

In the minds of Buchanan, Taney, Wayne, and wishful-thinking leaders of the Southern Democracy, a certain confusion existed. The Supreme Court "settled" great national questions. When it handed down its decision in *Marbury* vs. *Madison,* the right of judicial interpretation was "settled"; men ceased to contest it. When it spoke in *Gibbons* vs. *Ogden,* the jurisdiction of the national government over navigation was "settled"; thereafter none denied it. When it decided the Dartmouth College case, the sanctity of certain contracts was "settled"; acceptance was general. It was natural to believe that when the Court gave explicit judgment on the position of slavery in the Territories, that too would be settled. Good citizens would cease to hold an adverse view. Multitudes of Republicans would say, resignedly: "Well, I had thought we possessed some ground for believing slavery could be excluded from the Territories. I see now that it cannot. We shall have to pull our party over to the tariff, or some other new dogma."

The fact that a deep and insuperable difference existed between a demand that individuals should abandon a legal theory, and a demand that a great party

54 For example, F. H. Hodder in "Some Phases of the Dred Scott Decision," *Miss. Valley Hist. Review,* XI (1929), 3–22.
55 Washington *Union,* March 11, 1857.

should abandon a basic conviction, escaped these observers. Men could be persuaded by the logic of the Court to give up an interpretation which touched only property interests or the mechanics of government. They could not be persuaded to give up a party doctrine upon which they believed the whole destiny of the republic—nay, its very position as the hope of mankind—depended. Points of law could be determined by a decision from the Capitol basement; main lines of national development could not. Even had the Court in 1857 been a body of Olympian majesty, its purity unquestioned, millions of Republicans would have said: "Some issues can be decided only at the polls—only by the masses."

Thomas Hart Benton, now dying of cancer, expressed this conviction with characteristic vigor. Filled with indignation, he was determined to give his last energies to a long and minute exposé of the errors of the Court. He objected to its decision, he wrote, not so much because it was mistaken as because it violated a great principle. Recalling the failure of two efforts in Congress in 1848-49 to pass a bill carrying the Constitution (and slavery) into the Territories, he exclaimed: "And this is what the Supreme Court has decided—the judicial power deciding a political question!—and in a way which the political power had twice repulsed!" [56]

The wave of denunciation that swept across the North and West was long in subsiding. Lincoln dealt with the decision in a widely reported speech in Springfield on June 12, 1857, notable for its appeal to first principles. The position of the slave, he declared, had grown worse. Masters had largely been prevented from emancipating them. Provisions had been written into State constitutions to prevent legislatures from abolishing slavery. The Supreme Court now decided that Congress could not keep slavery out of the Territories. Once the Declaration of Independence had been held sacred, but now it was assailed, construed, and hawked at until its framers would not recognize it—and all to make the bondage of the Negro universal and eternal. "All the powers of earth seem rapidly combining against him. Mammon is after him, ambition follows, philosophy follows, and the theology of the day is fast joining the cry. They have him in his prison-house; they have searched his person and left no prying instrument with him. One after another they have closed the heavy iron doors upon him; and now they have him, as it were, bolted in with a lock of a hundred keys, which can never be unlocked without the concurrence of every key—the keys in the hands of a hundred different men, and they scattered to a hundred different and distant places; and they stand musing as to what invention, in all the dominions of mind and matter, can be produced to make the impossibility of his escape more difficult than it is." He appealed to the rightful meaning of the

56 T. H. Benton, *Hist. and Legal Examination of Dred Scott Case*, 120.

Declaration. Its authors intended to apply it not to Americans and Britons alone, but to all peoples—they contemplated a progressive improvement in the condition of all men everywhere:

They meant to set up a standard maxim for free society, which should be familiar to all, and revered by all; constantly looked to, constantly labored for, and even though never perfectly attained, constantly approximated, and thereby constantly spreading and deepening its influence, and augmenting the happiness and value of life to all peoples of all colors everywhere.

The New York legislature adopted savagely condemnatory resolutions. After declaring that the Court had lost the respect and confidence of the State, it announced that New York would never permit slavery within its borders in any form, under any pretext, or for any space of time. Any slave brought to New York would instantly become free, and any person trying to hold a slave, even in transit, would be liable to imprisonment for two to ten years.[57] A committee of the Pennsylvania legislature reported that the decision was a gross misconstruction of the Constitution, inoperative on any point save Dred Scott's own status.[58] John A. Andrew assailed the Court in a speech to the Massachusetts legislature which became famous; and the Massachusetts, Maine, Connecticut, and Rhode Island houses all acted to condemn the decision. So did the Vermont legislature, a committee terming the majority judges "tyrants." Much of the press and pulpit did not hesitate to hit below the belt. The New York *Tribune* called Taney jesuitical, thought it fitting that he sunk his voice to a whisper, and spoke of his "atrocious" doctrine that Negroes had no rights which white men were bound to respect—though what he had actually said was that before 1787 this doctrine was universal.[59] Personal liberty legislation received a strong impetus.

Copies of Benton's book, his final testament to the American people, were soon sown broadcast. "I will die upon the truth and justice of what I wrote," exclaimed the old Roman, who confessed that the annulment of the Compromise "is the heaviest political blow that ever fell upon my heart." Another telling indictment was presented by George Robertson, former chief justice of Kentucky, who had been a Congressman when the Compromise passed. In three articles in the *National Intelligencer* he arraigned the majority decision and rebuked the Court. Such a tribunal, he wrote, could retain public esteem

---

57 *National Intelligencer*, April 11, 1857.
58 *Idem*, May 5, 1857.
59 The N. Y. *Tribune* issued in July a compact pamphlet "The Case of Dred Scott," containing the full dissenting opinions of Curtis, vital portions of the other justices' opinions, an analysis, and the legislative resolves of New York. It sold large quantities. For Dr. Cheever's sermon see N. Y. *Express*, March 16, 1857.

only by showing rare learning and complete impartiality—"and by never tampering with political questions or any others which its duty does not require it to decide." [60]

This antagonism to the judgment of the Court never subsided. It soon crystallized, for Republicans and Douglas Democrats alike, in a simple refusal to accept the decision as binding upon anyone save the poor black man whose plea had evoked it. Lincoln, speaking for Western freesoilers, declared that he would refuse to obey it "as a political rule." Benton crisply remarked that such political decisions could not be enforced. "No mandamus can be directed to Congress and the people; no process of contempt can issue against them." This was true. When the Republicans took control of the government, the decision was set aside quietly, completely, and forever.

[VI]

Events soon made it clear that Chief Justice Taney and his associates felt themselves upon the defensive. His half-inaudible decision had been very imperfectly reported by the press, and early and complete publication of the judgment was impatiently awaited. The custom was that judges should file their opinions with the clerk immediately after the delivery, whereupon they became accessible to anyone who applied and paid the costs of copying. The press soon carried reports, however, that Taney's judgment was being drastically revised.[61] The New York Assembly committee, in reporting its condemnatory resolutions, stated that it had been unable to obtain authenticated copies of any of the majority decisions.

Meanwhile, behind the scenes, a remarkable controversy was taking place between Taney and Justice Curtis. Filing his opinion with the clerk, Curtis gave a copy to a Boston journal for publication, and left for his vacation in Pittsfield. Learning there that Taney's opinion had been revised and materially altered, he wrote the clerk for a copy. This was refused him, the clerk stating that Taney had directed that nobody should be allowed to see his opinion until it was published in *Howard's Reports*. The fact was that three majority judges, Taney, Wayne, and Daniel, had agreed on a rule, after their colleagues left Washington, which sealed up the Court's judgment on Dred Scott until published in the term volume.

Curtis then applied directly to the Chief Justice for permission to see the opinion. He received a reply tinged with acerbity. Taney censured Curtis for the publication of his opinion, which, along with McLean's, had been widely

60 *National Intelligencer*, October 24, 29, November 3, 1857.
61 *National Intelligencer*, June 18, 1857.

used by assailants of the Court; he spoke of the use of such documents by "political and partisan newspapers, for political and partisan purposes"; he objected strongly to a proposed pamphlet issue of Curtis's and Taney's opinions,[62] implying that Curtis would take the profits "for his own emolument"; and he showed himself hurt because Curtis had announced from the bench that he regarded Taney's judgment on Congressional power as extrajudicial and not binding. Curtis made a vigorous rejoinder. He denied any connection with the scheme of pamphlet publication, censured the arbitrary rule laid down by the three judges, and deplored the delay in publication. Above all, he implied a strong criticism of Taney's course in revising his opinion after its delivery. Stung by this, the Chief Justice affirmed that he had not altered one statement of fact or principle in his opinion, but had merely inserted some new proofs and authorities. When Curtis saw the document, however (*19 Howard* appearing at the end of May),[63] he took a different view, commenting that Taney had added at least eighteen printed pages, with new factual and theoretical matter, in rebuttal of Curtis's dissent.[64]

Filled with disgust, Justice Curtis announced his resignation in September. His ostensible reason was the inadequacy of his salary; his real compulsion sprang from the fact that he could not again feel that confidence in the Court and that willingness to labor harmoniously with its members which were essential to a just discharge of his duties. He should have sat through one session more, declared his friends, to prove that no intimidation by slave State members could shake the firm seat of a judge of the Supreme Court.[65]

The significance of Taney's tart replies to the more polite letters of Curtis lies in their revelation of the bitterness of the Chief Justice over the public reception of his decision. His feelings were lacerated by the hostile analyses of his argument, the Northern denunciation of the "pro-slavery judges," and above all, the painful fall in the prestige of the Court. He soon realized, moreover, that the majority opinions had not strengthened slavery in the Territories by one iota, that they were rejected as sharply by the Cass-Douglas wing of the Democracy as by the Republicans, and that they had thrown oil and not water on the flame of sectional dissension. Would not posterity arraign him as critically as had the mass opinion of the North?

The novelist G. P. R. James, British consul in Richmond, found Taney sunk in depression when in May the Chief Justice visited that city on circuit duty. The two, as old friends, spent a number of evenings together. Domestic affliction, in the recent death of his wife and the loss of a daughter by yellow fever,

---

62 C. P. Curtis, former partner and distant kinsman, had suggested this.
63 Publication of opinions began in *National Intelligencer*, May 30, 1857.
64 Swisher, *Taney;* Curtis, *Benjamin R. Curtis,* I, 211–230.
65 R. C. Winthrop, September 21, 1857; Kennedy Papers.

had contributed to the melancholy of the aged jurist. The sad state of the nation, however, weighed most heavily upon his spirits. He spoke of the evils of the spoils system and rotation in office, and of the bad effect of the frequent election of all officers, great and small, so that public servants became too timid to do their duty. He feared that a bloody national convulsion impended. As James wrote to Lord Clarendon of the Foreign Office:

He believes that the unity and power of the Democratic Party have alone saved the Union from being torn in pieces by two conflicting factions—North and South—and that the growing dissolutions in that Party must end in arraying North and South in actual hostility against each other.

The Chief Justice expatiated largely upon the anarchical tendencies evident in various parts of the United States—upon the organized riots in Baltimore, the anomalous condition of New York, the apathy of the Magistracy, the system of lynching, the Filibustering spirit in all Southern cities, the fanaticism of the North, the corruption in Congress—even, as he asserted, in the Senate; and the disregard of law, and want of respect for authority, evident everywhere.

This, he said, might all be amended, and probably would be, did not the evils arise from sources, not only still acting, but daily increasing in force, and so deeply fixed in the new constitutions of the various States, and in the minds of men, that there was no hope of their peaceful removal.

Their conversation touched upon the recent decision:

A war on the subject of Slavery between the North and South, he thought very probable, and not remote; and he spoke freely of his late decision in the Dred Scott case, saying that he was fully aware, at the time he pronounced it, of the dangerous consequences which might ensue, but that he was on the Bench to announce the law and the Constitution, and not to make them; he was disinterested, too; for nobody could either promote or displace him, and all his own slaves he had emancipated twenty years ago.[66]

Taney must undoubtedly be credited with high and patriotic motives; but no man is ever as impartial as he thinks, and he, as much as any Chief Justice in our history, had been shaped by a special environment and a distinct set of allegiances. He wrote ex-President Pierce late in the summer that he felt an abiding confidence that his decision would stand the test of time and the sober judgment of the country.[67] This statement, itself a disclosure of uneasiness, has not been justified by events. Instead, the verdict of history has been enunciated by one learned jurist and endorsed by another: "The Dred Scott decision cannot be, with accuracy, written down as a usurpation, but it can and must be written down as a gross abuse of trust by the body which rendered it." [68] The

66 G. P. R. James to Lord Clarendon. May 30, 1857; FO 5/677.
67 August 29, 1857; *Am. Hist. Review*, X.
68 E. S. Corwin, *Am. Hist. Review*, XVII, 52–69; cf. Warren, *Supreme Court* (1926 ed.), II, 316.

same authority remarks that its worst result was simply that it dealt a shattering blow to the influence of the judicial branch, so that during neither the Civil War nor Reconstruction did the Supreme Court play anything like its due role of supervision. But this is erroneous: the worst result was to appear in 1858–60 in the fateful Southern demand that the Democratic Party should be placed upon a Dred Scott platform. The party should be moved, that is, from the old position that Congress had no right to legislate slavery *out* of the Territories, to the new position that it must protect slavery *in* them.

Not one of the results expected from the decision appeared. It did not affect Dred Scott. It did not strengthen slavery in a single Territory. It did not unite the Democratic Party. It did not discomfit the Republicans. But it did give Southern extremists a judicial basis for that positive-protection demand which contributed so much to rend the Democracy and the nation in twain.

As for President Buchanan, he may have read with satisfaction the editorial in the Philadelphia *Pennsylvanian* which dogmatized: "There are certain points which are settled and beyond the reach of the fanatics of the nation. . . . The decision is a closing and clinching confirmation of the settlement of the issue." [69] He may have helped John Appleton or Jeremiah Black write the leader in the Washington *Union* which sang a requiem over the slavery quarrel: "We believe it is settled, and that henceforth sectionalism will cease to be a dangerous element in our political contests. . . . Of course, it is to be expected that fanaticism will rave and clamor against the decision of the Supreme Court. But fanaticism ceases to be a formidable enemy, when it seeks to measure strength with the Union-loving spirit of the people, sustained or confirmed by the great arbiter of constitutional opinions." How completely these statements misread the situation the next stormy year was to show. Taney, who knew his Milton, could have pondered over applicable lines:

> Chaos umpire sits,
> And *by decision more embroils the fray*
> By which he reigns; next him high arbiter
> Chance governs all.

69   Quoted in Warren, *Supreme Court* (1926 ed.), II, 311.

The First Months

THE SPRING SUN, first warm, then hot, shone down resplendently on the little capital sprawled along the Potomac. It shone on the long marble colonnade of the new Treasury Building and the gleaming front of the White House hard by; on the fantastic red towers of the Smithsonian Institution in its embowered grounds; on the truncated monolith rising to the memory of Washington, with inscribed stones piled about its base; on the handsome Post Office Building and yet incomplete Patent Office staring at each other across F Street. On the imposing lines of the Capitol, broken in the center by the unfinished dome, cobwebbed with scaffolding, the black arms of several cranes pendant from the rim, and on the surrounding waste of mud and sand, dotted with wooden shacks and huts, Greenough's conception of Washington as a half-naked Jupiter looming up on the east front. On the ailanthus trees along Pennsylvania Avenue, bursting into sudden foliage; on the National, Willard's, and other hotels, some dingy, some gaily decorated, but all crammed with politicians, lobbyists, and newspapermen; on the compact shopping center, putting out its awnings; and on the curious conglomerate of handsome big residences, little red-brick houses flush with the uneven sidewalks, and squalid wooden shanties. On the silvery Potomac, the dense woods lining Rock Creek, and the rim of high hills to the west.

Washington, though mainly unpaved, unsewered, slipshod, and dirty, grew livelier year by year. Steadily it gained better railroad facilities, more hotels, a larger number of wealthy residents, and a fuller stream of visitors. Till recently, said Senator Seward in 1858, it had been only the mockery of a capital, but now it had become a seat of magnificent public edifices and gardens. This was extravagant. Half a dozen buildings at most deserved the adjective magnificent, while the public grounds should have been much better kept. Washington seemed to lack focus and plan; it was all suburb and no city, observed W. H. Russell a little later.

Still, that it was interesting nobody could deny. Indeed, some aspects were almost fabulous in character. At Willard's, twenty-five hundred people sometimes dined in the main refectory, doubtless the largest assemblage of hotel guests to be found in any capital in the world. Slaves and free Negroes lent an exotic touch: liveried servants running errands, nursemaids proudly wheeling their charges, maids in bright cotton-print gowns and gay shawls marketing or attending their mistresses. Officers in uniform, back from western posts, strutted along. Hunters from beyond the Missouri lounged by in buckskin, with bowie knives at side. More rarely, a few Wyandottes or Sioux stalked the streets, their feathered headdresses setting off impassive copper faces and greasy black hair. Europe and even Asia lent color to the scene: a Frenchman with the now fashionable imperial, a ruddy Englishman, a Turk with a fez. Everywhere billowy crinolines, swaying singly along the pavement or clustering at shop doors; everywhere parasols lifted against the sun. By day, vehicles clattered over the cobbles. By night, under flaring gas lamps, the hotel doors sucked in and poured out streams of people; men with cloaks, canes, and starched linen escorted white-shouldered women to carriages, and if several parties were being given, wheels drummed over the few paved streets with a steady rumble.

Buchanan, who despite his years and dignity unbent enough to let friends call him "the old Squire," had social tastes. He loved a good dinner, good wines, the sparkle of pretty women, and the conversation of well-informed men. He himself was a good talker, for, if lacking in saltiness, he had sense, geniality, and a wonderful store of reminiscences. His niece, Harriet Lane, who had made a success in English society while he was minister, rose to her opportunities as mistress of the White House. A robust young woman of more than medium height, now in her late twenties, with golden-brown hair, deep blue or violet eyes, faultless complexion, and regular features, she was handsome rather than beautiful. As Nathaniel Hawthorne tactfully put it, she bore an English rather than American look, "being of stronger outline than most of our young ladies." [1] Extremely well poised, quietly conscious of her rank, and inclined to avoid small talk in favor of a close-textured exchange of ideas, she seemed to many observers a stately woman. But she liked gaiety, could be vivacious in small gatherings, and played whist well. Her elegance lighting up any room, she made the White House a brighter place than it had been since Dolly Madison's time.

Dingy and faded under Pierce, the thirty-one-room mansion was given enough redecoration and refurnishing to make it glisten. Miss Lane insisted upon adding an inviting conservatory. While Buchanan settled into his office on the second floor, with its black walnut desk, table, and sofas, and its mantel clock telling the day, hour, temperature, and barometric pressure, she placed more books in the library, the mahogany cases of which had been installed by

1 Nathaniel Hawthorne, *English Note Books*, January 9, 1855.

Fillmore. The President sometimes used this room for receiving visitors. Immediately, with the aid of Buchanan's private secretary, J. Buchanan Henry, a systematic mode of entertainment was instituted.

Once a week, some member or members of the Cabinet, with ladies and perhaps an extra guest or two, were invited to dinner; these were informal occasions marked by cheerful merriment. State dinners were managed with more formality than under President Pierce, Miss Lane and Mr. Henry issuing invitations and assigning seats with care. So liberal was Buchanan's hospitality that his expenses, despite savings in summer when he stayed at one of the cottages of the Soldiers' Home, exceeded his salary of $25,000. At receptions, the contrast between the tall, snowy-haired, black-garbed old President, standing with head slightly awry, and the statuesque, golden young woman by his side, was appealing. Guests were soon remarking that the chief executive had brought Washington a touch of the formal elegance of St. Petersburg and St. James's; while one observer long afterwards pronounced Miss Lane's regime as hostess the best combination of good cheer and good taste that the capital had thus far known.[2]

The punctilious courtesy of the President, a gentleman of the old school, was refreshing. He toiled hard. It was his custom, rising early, to breakfast, read the newspapers, and reach his desk by eight in the morning. Mr. Henry briefed all the letters received; Buchanan replied to a few of the most important, and the rest were answered by Henry or referred to the departments. Not until five was the President ordinarily through with callers and other business, then (if possible) going for an hour's walk before dinner. He lamented to a friend that the duties of the office had grown so heavy during the past twenty years that he scarcely had time, in his good Presbyterian fashion, to say his prayers.[3] Jeremiah Black complained that he deputed too little business to others. He had suffered greatly under the late hours of London society, and White House entertainments usually broke up at ten. But he tried to be as polite to Northern Republicans as to Southern Democrats, while he combined dignity with democratic frankness, saying that what he had seen of British class feeling made him more appreciative of the manly equality of American life. He liked a good joke —in London he and Lord Clarendon, the congenial foreign minister, had indulged in much jesting—and in Washington he delighted in facetious raillery with Howell Cobb or Jere Black. He liked rapid-fire conversation; once, when the wife of the Mexican minister, a handsome woman of rare intellectual gifts, was at table, a friend found that he was "perfectly kindled by her genius and fascinations, and indulged himself in a flow of spirits and anecdote very rare

2 Ben Perley Poore, *Sixty Years in the National Metropolis*; M. C. Ames, *Ten Years in Washington*, 175, 234; Louise Quitman, January 23, 1858, Quitman Papers; Buchanan-Lane Papers, *passim*.
3 October 8, 1858; Buchanan Papers.

for him." [4] On official matters, however, he was reticent. He had once written his niece, "Be quiet and discreet and say nothing," and this was his own rule.

Miss Lane at first followed this advice, studiously ignoring party strife. She was nationally popular. Clubs, cravats, and flowers were named for her, as was a small government vessel; the song "Listen to the Mocking Bird" (one of Lincoln's favorites) was dedicated to her. With suitors both American and British, she might have wedded a title. But Buchanan admonished her not to act in haste ("I have witnessed the long years of patient misery which fine women have endured from rushing precipitately into matrimonial connections without sufficient reflection"), and it was not until 1866 that she married a Baltimorean of wealth, Henry Elliott Johnston.

[I]

In the social life of the Administration, Southerners continued to play the chief roles. Not only was the South politically dominant, but Southern gentry found attractions in Washington which it lacked for Northerners of equal distinction. Itself a town of Southern atmosphere, it offered more entertainment and intellectual stimulus than any center farther south except New Orleans. Planters, merchants, and politicians from all over Dixie found it in winter a beguiling social and political metropolis. They brought troops of black servants whose use they counted the chief of luxuries; they regarded as the height of splendor balls and dinners which patrician New Yorkers thought rather tame. Strongly social in tastes, they enjoyed the variety given to Washington by the uniforms, manners, and ideas of the personnel from the various legations. It was not until the city cast off its semi-rural character, the Senate became a millionaires' club, and a large number of expensive residences were built, that Northerners were strongly attracted to Washington.

Of the Cabinet members, Howell Cobb gave the most elaborate parties. He and his wife were both wealthy, and their house at the corner of Fifteenth and I Streets cost $1,800 a year, while their furnishings represented a small fortune. They could seat nearly fifty guests at table, and their fine silver, monogrammed Bohemian glassware, and china adorned with the Georgia coat of arms attracted much attention. Five wine glasses were sometimes set for each place.

Cass and Floyd, whose homes were less than two blocks apart, entertained much.[5] The old Secretary of State, who had grown wealthy with the increasing

---

4 See Buchanan to Marcy, August 25, 1854, Buchanan Papers; Joseph Holt to wife, August 26, 1859, Holt Papers.

5 *Georgia Historical Quarterly*, VI, 233; N. U. Gannon, *Howell Cobb*, MS dissertation, University of California. By contrast many public men lived with great simplicity. Senator Zach Chandler, complaining of high living costs, was content with hotel rooms. In 1857 the Avenue House, where Senator Crittenden lived, offered Chandler a parlor and two bedrooms, commanding a fine view of the Smithsonian grounds, with board for four persons, for $200 to $300 a month. A. S. Kellogg, October 20, 1857, Chandler Papers.

value of a tract he owned near Detroit, possessed a fine library, and many curios and *objets d'art* gathered during his residence in Paris. He valued intercourse with scholarly people as well as politicians, for he had written historical and political essays of lasting value, while he showed a kindly interest in young men. His granddaughter, Miss Ledyard, was highly esteemed as a cultivated hostess. Secretary Jacob Thompson and Postmaster-General Brown, who had houses in the same block near the corner of Eighteenth and G Streets, also used their fortunes in generous hospitality. And if a New England chilliness clung about Secretary Toucey, his wife was socially popular.

Of necessity, many official entertainments were appallingly heterogeneous and crowded. Buchanan at his levees suffered under the necessity of pumping two thousand arms. The houses of Cabinet members, Senators, and such grandees as Speaker Orr, who had a place on Lafayette Square, often burst at the seams. At small parties, guests moved in increasing fear of some sudden explosion between Northerners and Southerners. Yet the contacts between the two sections were often pleasant. One of General Quitman's daughters tells us how, at a White House dinner, it was arranged that Senator Collamer of Vermont should take her in, and Senator Dixon of Connecticut, her sister. "I could not but think, What extremes!" she writes. "However, my partner seemed to be a man of information and intelligence, and made himself quite agreeable." [6] Her sister has amusingly described the crush which she encountered the same season at "Auntie Cobb's." Two of the Quitman girls, with escorts, were ready when the hacks arrived at half-past nine:

I, dressed in my best, with Father in his handsome new suit, took possession of one, while Tonie, dressed in her new blue silk, with lace berthe, pink bows, and her chenille headdress, stepped into the other, escorted by Mr. Wright, member from Tennessee, and our radiant young friend Cluskey. When we arrived at the lighted-up mansion of the Secretary, we were quite terrified at the tremendous crowd in the hall and on the staircase. It was a terrible business getting up those steps to the dressing room. I am sure we were blockaded on the stairs midway for more than half an hour. Mr. Wright and I went forward, while Tonie and her *glowing* friend followed. Finally, after making desperate exertions, we reached the top, and after due patience . . . succeeded in getting into the ladies' room, and divesting ourselves of mantles and hoods, set out to meet our gentlemen in order to go to the drawing room. Mr. Whitely and Mr. Wright seized upon us and just as I was entering the crowded reception room I spied [my sister] Louie in front of me, shawled and hooded, within a few feet of our hostess, Mrs. Cobb, hair tumbling down and altogether having quite a battered look. I immediately caught her and carried her back to the dressing room and arranged her troubled cheveux. At last we were ready and with our attendant beaux worked our way up the stairs to the drawing room, which was on the second floor. We were presented to the Secretary and his *dignified* partner as the daughters of General Quitman. The old gentleman would come

6 Louise Quitman, January 23, 1858, Quitman Papers.

under Old King Cole's category of being a "jolly old soul." We passed along or rather squeezed along through the rooms, Father presenting us every few steps to some of the dignitaries. We at length took up our stand at the opposite end of the room, where there was a small breathing-space. You cannot conceive what a crowd it was! There stalked the grave statesman, the fiery politician; then came the gallant officer and the quiet citizen. Many persons were brought to our corner and introduced, among them Mr. Orr, the Speaker . . . a fine old South Carolina gentleman. Father and General Scott promenaded arm in arm. The gallant old general nearly shook our hands off and said that he felt as if we were his daughters. . . . Unfortunately we did not reach the refreshment room.[7]

In the circle of old-time residents, including W. W. Seaton, Joseph Gales, Benjamin Ogle Tayloe, and George Washington Riggs, the most important place was taken by W. W. Corcoran and his daughter Louise. This retired banker, of Irish extraction, great wealth, and Democratic leanings, held such a position that when Lord and Lady Napier left London to take the British legation, Minister Dallas gave them a letter of introduction to him. Corcoran's house on Lafayette Square, rich in works of art, some good, some as dubious as Powers's "Greek Slave," was a favorite meeting place of diplomatists, national leaders, scientists like Joseph Henry and young Spencer F. Baird, and distinguished visitors. Their host was by no means generally popular, for he had a Dombeylike stiffness and showed poorer men a displeasing condescension. Nevertheless, William Appleton of Boston, Slidell of Louisiana, Hunter of Virginia, and Daniel S. Dickinson, all wrote him in terms of warm friendship, while Edward Everett, who frequented the house, assured Louise that an entertainment for Reverdy Johnson, which he attended, had been the most memorable event of his recent years.[8] Corcoran kept a French *chef*, and his dinners (which Jenkins of the New York *Herald* called banquets) were worth eating. Senators Bright and Hunter were among the numerous politicians who owed him financial favors. Jefferson Davis shared his interest in the improvement of Washington, and in 1857 they were exchanging ideas on the unfinished landscape work undertaken by A. J. Downing. The marriage of Louise Corcoran in April, 1859, to a member of the Eustis family of Louisiana, was one of the social events of the Administration.[9]

7 "Darling" Quitman, January 8, 1858, Quitman Papers.
8 Edward Everett to Louise Corcoran, May 30, 1857, Corcoran Papers.
9 Prior to this marriage Miss Corcoran had a blighted romance with a handsome attaché of the Spanish legation, Sr. Muruaga. The two fell in love, Corcoran interposed, and a dramatic episode resulted. While Corcoran was dining with Slidell, word was brought him that Muruaga, defying strict orders, had come to the banker's house to see his daughter. Corcoran rushed home. The luckless attaché, dragged from behind a piano, was literally kicked out of the house. The diplomatic corps, indignant over this affront to a member, met, deliberated, and sent Corcoran word that it would hold no social relations with him until the matter had been adjusted. The banker's partner, Riggs, of course took a stand with him.

Somewhat different was the status of ex-mayors W. W. Seaton and Joseph Gales, editors and owners of the staid *National Intelligencer;* men not so rich, public-spirited rather than philanthropic, and of Whig, not Democratic, connections. Buchanan liked to pay an informal call on Corcoran, but never appeared at the editors' houses. Yet they maintained all their old-time leadership in the life of the community. Both Seaton, member of an old Virginia family, and Gales, who was English-born though educated at the University of North Carolina, were now past seventy, and their journal had been a political landmark since the War of 1812. They liked to talk of the great times of Jefferson and Madison, while one of Gales's treasures was the original of Webster's reply to Hayne, full of erasures and corrections.[10] They worked side by side, attended the same Unitarian church, and maintained until death a common bank account. Mrs. Seaton, a sister of Gales, and a witty, cultured woman who had once translated Spanish documents for the *Intelligencer*, gave frequent small dinner parties at their home in the city. Mrs. Gales, a daughter of Theodorick Lee and a niece of "Light Horse" Harry, entertained at her husband's country estate, "Eckington," two miles from the center of town. Here Gales had his library (he was a good Latinist), cellar and hunting trophies. The two men threw all their influence on the side of moderation, compromise, and the Union.

Great had been the sensation among the old families, when in 1856 Stephen A. Douglas became engaged to Adèle Cutts, grandniece of Dolly Madison and niece of the talented Rose O'Neil Greenhow. Married on Thanksgiving Day, Douglas and his wife returned to the large stuccoed house at New Jersey Avenue and I Street before Christmas. Mrs. Douglas refurnished it in elaborate style and was at once recognized as one of the arbiters of fashion. Douglas, who since the death of his first wife, Martha Martin, had been careless of dress and bearing, suddenly grew well-groomed, sober in deportment, and correct in habits. The extent of Adèle's influence became evident when, despite the protests of political friends, she entered his two boys in a Jesuit school in the city. A portrait of Mrs. Douglas by the second Benjamin West soon adorned their

For a time the two mansions were boycotted; but the pleasures of the Corcoran and Riggs cuisine were too much to forego, and the corps soon forgot its grudge. N. Y. *Tribune*, July 21, 1858.

10 See biography of Gales, *Appleton's Cyc. Am. Biog.*, II. The press mirrors many social changes of the time. Beards were steadily coming in; chin beards, cheek beards, mustaches, and bushy beards that covered half the face. One correspondent deplored the way in which young women plucked their eyebrows and used rouge and powder as well as jewels. Hoop skirts were in their glory. Husbands, it was said, were requested to ride on the box with the coachmen so that wives might arrive uncrushed; but in crowded gatherings women were quickly reduced to natural size. The early winter season in Washington was always gay, but when Lent began, small dinners and receptions took the place of large balls. See N. Y. *Express*, February 14, 20, 24, April 5, 1857, and the Washington notes in *Harper's Weekly* under "Domestic Intelligence."

dining room, and one of Douglas by G. P. A. Healy another apartment. For a time, Mrs. Douglas, richly dressed, as gracious as she was beautiful, and with the prestige of old family connections, held her own in rivalry with Miss Lane. Her dances, dinners, and Saturday afternoon receptions were bright affairs, and her house was besieged by callers. In the gay winters of 1856–57 and 1857–58 she exercised a charm that was all her own.[11] Visitors knew not which was the more fascinating, the tall, chestnut-haired lady of the house, with her beautiful figure and expressive brown eyes, or Douglas himself, his abundant hair now touched with gray, but his domelike brow, glowing black eyes, and combative bearing as impressive as ever.

Though the French minister, the Comte de Sartigues, was dean of the diplomatic corps, and though his American-born countess made their house on Georgetown Heights a brilliant place, leadership among the legations was quickly assumed by Lord and Lady Napier, who arrived a few days after Buchanan's inauguration. They took Hamilton Fish's former residence at 245 H Street and greatly enlarged it. Napier, a descendant of the discoverer of logarithms, was connected with the Scottish family of military and naval renown and with the historian of the Peninsular War. Not yet forty, with diplomatic experience at Vienna, Naples, and Constantinople, he meant to make his Washington appointment a success. At the dinner of St. George's Society in New York on April 23, 1857, his intimation that Britain would look with favorable eyes upon further American expansion made many friends. "His Lordship," wrote Edward Everett's naval son-in-law, Henry A. Wise, after an evening with the minister, "seems to be a man of enlarged views, and with a pretty fair knowledge of what constitutes the real interests of this country. Withal he is very undiplomatic, and expresses his opinions freely and openly. I judge he has a strong slavery tendency; that is to say, he regards the institution as a necessity under the circumstances. Jamaica seems to have sickened him for any further yearnings toward negro philanthropy. I feel pretty well assured, too, that his lordship *advocates* the acquisition of Cuba by these United States." [12] At the same time, Napier won the heart of William H. Seward. Before he had been in Washington a month, the two were talking of Anglo-American cooperation in opening China to foreign commerce and bringing her into the family of civilized states. He associated so intimately with Seward, in fact, that some Democrats complained that he did not show them equal favor.[13]

At the minister's house, however, all parties stood on an equal footing. Lady Napier, a sturdy Scotswoman interested in educating her four chubby boys, disliked ostentation. Her gowns, carriage, and furniture were all simple; her

11   Milton, *Eve of Conflict*, 255–258; Johnson, *Douglas*, 336, 337.
12   Henry A. Wise to Governor Wise, May 23, 1857; Wise Papers.
13   Seward, *Seward at Washington*, II, 299, 345.

receptions were remarkable only for their informality and the frequent appearance of some good singer to help entertain the guests. The Napiers' dinners were marked by good company, good food, and good music.[14] On exceptional occasions the pair displayed splendor enough. Lady Napier could be superb in satin embroidered with pearls, and a Juliet cap of pearls or a diamond and emerald tiara; Lord Napier shone in court dress; dinner was served upon gold and silver plate; and the guests admired paintings brought from England.[15] But it was the homely good sense of the Napiers that made Cabinet members and Senators their fast friends, and their stay a long-remembered page in Washington history.

[II]

As North and South confronted each other with growing bitterness, social decorum was often difficult to maintain. The White House, the Cabinet parlors, and the homes of the old Washington families were theoretically neutral ground —yet the atmosphere in all became too Southern for many a freesoil man. Nobody knew when a burst of temper might rip through etiquette. Mrs. Greenhow, a friend of the President and other prominent men, invited Representative and Mrs. Charles Francis Adams to dinner just after John Brown's execution; and when Mrs. Adams tactlessly spoke in praise of Brown, the hostess angrily bit her lip and retorted that he was a scoundrel. The episode illustrated the fact that the ladies of Washington, both Northerners and Southerners, showed more incandescence than their husbands.[16]

Southern radicals had various meeting places. Slidell's house on H Street near Sixteenth and Senator Hammond's at Third and C were favorite resorts. Mrs. Slidell, once Mademoiselle des Londes of New Orleans, and Mrs. Hammond, once the South Carolina heiress Catherine FitzSimons, were hostesses devoted to the South. No one knows just how much intrigue clustered about the unscrupulous Slidell, but it was plenty. W. H. Russell later described him as one of the most consummate masters of political machination alive. "He is a man who unseen moves the puppets on the public stage as he lists, a man of iron will and strong passions, who loves the excitement of combinations and who in his dungeon . . . would conspire with the mice against the cat rather than not conspire at all." Three of the men who took the Southern Rights creed most fervently lived, bachelor style, in a private house at 148 F Street, near Twentieth: Representatives Lawrence Keitt, W. Porcher Miles, and Muscoe Garnett. In 1858–60 this trio used to meet, after the House adjourned, at the home of

14 Clay, *Belle of the Fifties*, 117.
15 Pryor, *Reminiscences of Peace and War*, 57, 58.
16 Leech, *Reveille in Washington*, 19, 20.

Roger A. Pryor on New York Avenue. Mrs. Pryor has told us how, following a supper of ham, oysters, biscuits, and tea, they and such other radical Southerners as Lamar, Boyce, Barksdale, and Hunter would hold midnight conferences in the study. Sometimes, with the aid of bourbon, hot water, and lemons, they would talk out the night, the dawn finding them "again and again with but one conclusion—they would stand together." [17] Two, Garnett and Keitt, ultimately stood together in giving their lives for the South.

At the other extreme, radical freesoilers continued to gather at the house of Gamaliel Bailey, editor of the *National Era*. This devoted abolitionist was used to breasting a storm. He had been a ship's doctor on a China voyage in the eighteen-twenties and hospital physician in Cincinnati during a savage cholera epidemic. Turning to antislavery journalism at the time of the revolt in Lane Seminary, he had thrice seen mobs in Cincinnati attack the office of his *Philanthropist*. His *National Era*, which since its publication of *Uncle Tom's Cabin* possessed a household fame, celebrated its tenth anniversary just before Buchanan entered the White House. Bailey, a man of wit, culture, and common-sense judgment, with a real literary gift, was a genial host. He made his Washington home a distinguished intellectual center, where freesoilers of all parties, and especially those whose views verged upon abolitionism, conferred with each other and with outsiders like Horace Greeley, Samuel Bowles, and Moncure D. Conway. Here, such former Democrats as Hannibal Hamlin and Salmon P. Chase mingled with former Whigs like Tom Corwin and Ben Wade, and veteran Free Soil Party men like Joshua Giddings. Many were social outlaws elsewhere. Great was the regret when Bailey's death in the late spring of 1859 put an end to his Saturday night receptions.[18]

Another and more moderate club for freesoilers was Seward's house, a roomy three-story brick mansion on F Street near the business center, with his study on the basement floor. The New Yorker was not one of those who "entertained lavishly." He had Webster's liking for small suppers of turkey, venison, or broiled shad with ham and eggs, a half-dozen friends passing the bottle. He enjoyed a game of whist and was ready to invite any comer to make a *parti carré* with himself, his wife, and his son or daughter. Naturally he saw most of his Republican colleagues. But as a moderate, even-tempered man, he remained on pleasant terms with the Southerners. However spirited his public response to attack, in private he was always kindly and good-natured. Hence it was that he often took the role of peacemaker between politicians thirsting for a duel. "Nobody can apologize for insults but I, who never give any," he once wrote. Within a single month in 1858, he reconciled Jefferson Davis with the

17 Pryor, *Reminiscences*, 102, 103.
18 Hamlin, *Hannibal Hamlin*, 275 ff.; Grace Greenwood, **Cosmopolitan Magazine**, February, 1890.

irascible Zack Chandler, and Henry Wilson with the hotheaded William M. Gwin. People had feared street encounters or a formal exchange of shots, but, by scurrying to and fro and writing enough notes to make a bonfire, Seward composed these quarrels.[19]

Yet in the first two years of the Administration the general gaiety was not greatly troubled by the rising political storm. One Jenkins, the New York *Herald's* social correspondent in Washington, rose to ecstatic heights in the winter of 1857–58. He wrote of Miss Lane in mourning for a brother, her purple silk gown trimmed with black velvet; of Attorney-General Black at a Presidential reception with his pleasant wife and pretty dark-haired daughter; of a dinner at Postmaster-General Brown's attended by "Prince" John Van Buren, Vice-President Breckinridge, and Colonel John T. Heard of Boston; of a ball given by Sir William Gore Ouseley, the Queen's special envoy to Central America, at which Miss Cass was magnificently attired in pearl-colored satin, while Mrs. Thompson was dressed in rich pink silk, with lace flounces, and a coiffure of pink flowers; of the crush at Senator J. R. Thomson's and of diplomats airing their French at Mrs. Slidell's. If the Republicans seemed on the fringe of the social swirl, they comforted themselves by reflecting that their time might soon be at hand.

[III]

The first stern problem before Buchanan's Directory, the disposition of offices, was attacked with resolution. These leaders decided that the rule of rotation should apply in most States of the North and West; that is, that men who had held place for four years should go out unless a Senator or other power specially interposed. For one entire week in March the Cabinet met daily at nine and sat till three, giving most of its attention to the mass of demands before it. People with public business complained that department heads, including even Attorney-General Black, neglected all routine work for the first month.[20]

It was not strange that they did. The spoils system was now at its apogee, and the city was crowded with applicants. From Pennsylvania alone came a devouring horde. The President was incessantly besieged; he could not stir from his desk without being assailed, and the press reported that his very bedroom was invaded. As May ended, some two hundred gentlemen were said to be settled in Washington seeking foreign missions. Greeley's *Tribune* seized the opportunity to call attention to the British Civil Service Commission, which had

19 Seward, *Seward at Washington*, II. Chs. 43–45. Seward's house in 1855–57 was at the corner of G and Twenty-first.
20 N. Y. *Weekly Tribune*, March 28, 1857.

begun work two years earlier, remarking that it was high time the United States followed this example.[21]

Though Buchanan was more adroit than his predecessor Pierce, the distribution of patronage inevitably made more enemies than friends. In New York, where harmony was essential if the State were to be regained from the Republicans, a half-dozen factions squabbled and grabbed. The brazen demagogue Fernando Wood, just reelected mayor of the metropolis, headed one; Augustus Schell, a highly successful lawyer and a director in important corporations, of late the national committeeman for the State, captained another; various silk-stocking leaders, including August Belmont, formed a third; while an up-State group was led by Dean Richmond and Erastus Corning of the New York Central, and another by that narrow, selfish veteran of politics, Daniel S. Dickinson.

All insisted upon places, and all descended upon Washington to get them. At the end of a month it was announced that the "Hards," who had supported Buchanan before the Cincinnati convention, had got the best of the struggle. Their chieftain Schell was made collector of the port, controlling the populous Custom House; the position of Naval Officer was given to George N. Sanders of "Young America" fame; while the Federal marshalship went to a whilom "Soft" of gangster affiliations, Isaiah Rynders.[22] From the point of view of the public weal, these were all wretched appointments. Schell, the ablest of the three, was presently caught in a shameless piece of spoils-mongering. He addressed a circular letter to the Administration Congressmen of New York City, asking each to furnish a list of persons in his district whom he wished given subordinate posts in the Custom House, or protected in existing jobs there.[23] From the political point of view, the important fact was that Buchanan's appointments left nearly everyone dissatisfied. James Gordon Bennett, editor of the Herald, called them "horrible." Fernando Wood was bitterly resentful. An acrid quarrel broke out between the mayor and his old friend Daniel Sickles. So general was the dissension that Buchanan's faithful servitor "Chevalier" Wikoff—that incredible dilettante of politics and diplomacy—stayed in hot New York most of the summer trying to arrange a truce.[24]

In dealing with Pennsylvania, the President naturally took the advice of Senator William Bigler, Representative Glancy Jones, and Jere Black. Here his task was less difficult. He filled the chief positions, such as the Philadelphia

21   Harper's Weekly, March 21, 1857; N. Y. Tribune, May 13, 1857.
22   Nichols, Disruption of the American Democracy, 84, 85; Harper's Weekly, April 4, 1857.
23   National Intelligencer, September 24, 1858.
24   Henry Wikoff to Buchanan, August 6, 1857, Buchanan Papers. Wikoff, who for a short time had been editor of the Democratic Review, had a connection with Bennett's Herald that was useful to Buchanan.

collectorship, postmastership, and marshalship, without arousing any burning jealousies. His great misfortune in his own State lay in a final rupture with John W. Forney. That resentful editor was not at all placated when Buchanan offered him the Liverpool consulship or the second place in the Philadelphia Custom House. Neither post was sufficiently important or well paid: the Liverpool office, now divested of its rich fees, would mean political exile, and the Philadelphia office would place him beneath a Lancaster nonentity who had been made collector. Declaring himself "utterly disenchanted" with Buchanan, Forney cast about for other employment. He thought of taking charge of the *Daily Pennsylvanian* if the President would guarantee that paper a profitable share of the public printing. But Buchanan hesitated, having greater matters to think about and supposing that he could ignore so helpless a person as Forney. Little did he think that the volatile and vindictive journalist would soon be in a position to deal him the heaviest blows; little did he reckon that the *Pennsylvanian*, kept alive only by subsidy, would soon be rendered more unprofitable than ever by a rival journal under Forney's alert management.

The foreign service, taken up with deliberation, was for the most part filled respectably. The conciliatory, dignified George Mifflin Dallas, who had succeeded Buchanan in London, was left there. He had his full share of foibles, including vanity, of which the secretary of the legation, Moran, sent Buchanan vivid accounts. But this former mayor, Senator, and Vice-President kept a personal following in Philadelphia which it was well to conciliate, while the President meant to manage all British negotiations himself. John Y. Mason was retained in Paris, to continue enjoying his table, sideboard, card games, and occasional colloquies with Napoleon III. The President had an indulgent fondness for him as an old associate in Polk's Cabinet and in the Ostend Manifesto affair. South Carolina was favored with the Russian post, which went in 1858 to Francis W. Pickens, a confirmed nullifier and secessionist. The more respectable of the two warring Democratic factions in Indiana was recognized by the appointment of ex-Governor Joseph A. Wright to Berlin. It was to Buchanan's credit that he continued the novelist Theodore S. Fay as minister to Switzerland. Still more to his credit was the appointment of the brilliant Virginia editor, John M. Daniel, the friend of Poe and the man who had made the Richmond *Examiner* famous, as envoy to the court of Victor Emmanuel at Turin. Daniel's unconventional ways and fiery Americanism rendered him a focus of controversy, but he made even the great Cavour respect his views.

Once more that sensitive capital, Madrid, was treated frivolously. August Belmont would have welcomed a transfer thither from The Hague. But circumstantial stories were afloat that Belmont had managed affairs in Holland to his own business profit, and that of his old employers, the Rothschilds. Buchanan kept Pierce's recent appointee, the rough-hewn A. C. Dodge, a son of the frontier who had lost his senatorship when Iowa became Republican. Dodge, who had boasted to the Senate that he sawed his own wood and did his own marketing in Washington, showed an ignorance which inspired Greeley to remark that whereas his predecessor Soulé, with all his faults, had spoken six languages, the new envoy could not even talk one correctly. However, he soon gave way to a cultivated scion of patrician stock, the Kentuckian William Preston. For the rest, the diplomatic appointments were remarkable chiefly for the favor shown to annexationists and newspapermen. One apostle of Manifest Destiny, John L. O'Sullivan, became minister to Portugal; another, Joseph W. Fabens, was planted as consul in Cayenne; and a third, Edwin DeLeon, was made consul-general at Alexandria. Courting the favor of Bennett's *Herald*, Buchanan appointed two of its staff members to minor positions. Beverley Tucker, whilom editor of the Washington *Sentinel* and printer to the Senate, became consul in Liverpool.

In his treatment of the patronage Buchanan did nothing to soothe the resentment of Stephen A. Douglas. Northwestern foes of the Little Giant had marked with glee his failure to obtain a Cabinet post for any of his lieutenants. "Lincoln and I," wrote William H. Herndon just before the inauguration, "are glad to death that Douglas has been crushed." [25] His feelings might have been assuaged by a few timely gifts. He had hoped that John A. McClernand, the Shawneetown lawyer who had served four terms in Congress and been a faithful leader of the Illinois Democracy for a quarter century, might receive a good ministership—but he got nothing. He had hoped that his friend W. A. Richardson of Quincy might get a handsome appointment—but he received only the governorship of empty Nebraska Territory. He had hoped that Henry M. Rice of Minnesota might have a position; he was passed over. With the Dred Scott decision in mind, Douglas had ground for concluding that the Buchanan Directory really wished to "crush" the Northwestern Democrats. Meanwhile, one of Douglas's friends was equally incensed. Senator David Broderick had expected to control most of the California appointments. The former stonecutter's apprentice and New York fireman, wresting a senatorial seat from John B. Weller, had extorted from his colleague William M. Gwin an agreement that he should manage the Federal patronage while Gwin controlled the State offices. Buchanan, however, was an old friend of Weller, whom he had known as an officeholder under Polk. He did not like the agreement. Gwin dexterously gained the ear of the Directory, swayed their Far Western choices, and shouldered Broderick out into the cold.

The two fundamental political emotions are jealousy and fear. As Douglas

25 Herndon to Trumbull, March 2, 1857, Trumbull Papers.

saw Jesse Bright enjoying Administration favor and Broderick watched Gwin bask in Administration sunshine, as they thought of their unrequited services, and as they looked to the perils of the future, their wrath smoldered.

[IV]

Meanwhile, the unsolved Kansas problem haunted the pillow of all thoughtful Americans and demanded Buchanan's immediate attention. The President and Cabinet took office to find a new crisis convulsing the long-racked Territory. A volcano was rumbling on those Western plains which made the ground tremble even in Washington. Fighting, to be sure, had virtually ended. No longer did panoplied bands of settlers and border Missourians make intimidating raids and forays; no longer were immigrants waylaid on lonely prairie trails or along cottonwood-shaded creeks. Nevertheless, the spirit of violence still reigned. It would continue until the two rival authorities — the irregular regime of the free State men with their Topeka constitution and legislature, dominated by honest "Governor" Charles Robinson, and the regular regime headed by blunt John W. Geary—were somehow replaced by a single administration.

Geary, sent out by President Pierce in the late summer of 1856, had arrived determined to show no favoritism to any faction and to make himself the governor of the entire people. He efficiently stopped the disorders. Meanwhile, he discussed a secret agreement with Robinson; they would try to effect a merger of the Topeka and Lecompton regimes, with Geary as governor and the Topeka constitution the basic instrument. But the proslavery extremists in the Territory had not wanted a governor who would act with even-handed firmness. Friends had warned Geary in advance of the dangers he ran. "What you say suits us first rate," said the free State leader Captain Samuel Walker, "but mark my words, you'll take the underground railroad out of Kansas in six months." [26]

The new crisis was produced by the effort of the proslavery forces in Kansas to gain two great objects. They had resolved, first, to force Geary, the strongest governor Washington had yet sent out, to quit office, and second, to arrange a constitutional convention which by hook or crook would bring Kansas into the Union, at least nominally and temporarily, as the sixteenth slave State. Radical freesoil men were equally ready to block a fair solution.

To understand the audacious and unscrupulous course of the proslavery leaders we must recall the atmosphere of emotion which enveloped Kansas, so

26 Malin, *John Brown and the Legend of '56*, 643–690; Spring, *Kansas*, 197–210; Robinson, *The Kansas Conflict*, 337 ff.

lately a land of robberies and ruffianism. Many settlers who came from Missouri believed that it would be disastrous to their State to have the new Territory colonized by "slave-stealers." If fugitives were to be helped to freedom east, north, and west, in Illinois, Iowa, and Kansas, slavery would not last long in Missouri. Not a few settlers from farther south believed that the Yankees of the emigrant aid societies had used unfair tactics. We must recall, too, that it seemed an apt moment to achieve the goal of a new slave State. The election had momentarily stunned the Republican Party. Southerners would dominate the incoming Administration. Buchanan, like Pierce, had hotly condemned the free State Topeka regime under Robinson. About realities in Kansas he knew little. He had been in England during the worst troubles, had come back to associate with men who denounced the emigrant aid companies and the Topeka regime, and had read the *Pennsylvanian, Union,* and other newspapers which gave colored accounts of territorial affairs. In a speech to his Lancaster neighbors in the fall of 1856 he had displayed a strong bias. The abolitionists of Massachusetts and Vermont, he said, must not be allowed to prescribe to the people of Kansas their course on slavery; he did not say that Missourians must not be allowed to interfere. "Abolition fanaticism," he declared, had made the Kansas question acute; he said nothing about border-ruffian aggressions. Condemning the Topeka government as a body of lawless men, he threatened the use of military force to sustain the regular authorities. A President of such views might well support extremely partisan measures in Kansas.

Leadership of the slavery forces in the Territory had passed into more desperate hands. While ex-Senator Atchison was now confining himself to Missouri affairs, three men had arisen who seemed ready for anything; ready, said Geary, for revolution. They were John Calhoun, the surveyor-general, L. A. Maclean, his chief clerk, and A. J. Isaacs, lately district attorney. The land offices were natural citadels of power in Kansas. Calhoun, with several hundred employees, could exert a powerful influence on the settlement and development of the Territory. All settlers came to the offices to have preemptions confirmed; all speculators eyed them hungrily. Calhoun and Maclean could hold out an attractive bait; they could say that once Kansas was admitted, Indian titles to new tracts would be extinguished, and liberal grants of land would be made to the new State for schools, colleges, asylums, and railroads—especially a Pacific Railroad. These men expected to manufacture future governors and Senators, and shape State policy.

That they, and their Southern backers in Washington, expected to keep Kansas a slaveholding State for long is unlikely. But even a few years would be of practical help to the South; it would enable Southern politicians to save face;

and it would humiliate the free State men whom proslavery Democrats detested. Calhoun and Maclean were born fighters and speculators. The former had long dwelt in Springfield, Illinois, where Lincoln and Douglas knew him well and where he rose to be mayor; the latter was a tall, tough, hot-tempered frontiersman. Isaacs was a schemer. The trio worked in close cooperation with Chief Justice Samuel Lecompte—"Jeffreys" Lecompte, the free State press called him—and Judge Sterling G. Cato, who controlled the courts. They were pleased when Buchanan gave office to such men as J. W. Whitfield and Daniel Woodson, connected with old proslavery frauds in the Territory.

The expulsion of Governor Geary was a deplorable occurrence. If ever an executive deserved full support it was this Pennsylvania engineer and soldier who, after helping shape the new governments of San Francisco and California, had answered Pierce's call to duty. Arriving when partisan gangs scoured the country, towns were fortified like medieval strongholds, and agriculture was half abandoned, he had quickly grasped the situation. Kansas was the daughter not of New England, but of the Ohio Valley. The great majority of the small farmers who made up the population did not want the negro (the Topeka Constitution men had voted three to one to exclude free negroes), and hence did not want slavery. Geary restored peace. Finding the courts idle, the laws disregarded, and the government almost paralyzed, he put energy into the administration. The treasury was bankrupt, and Kansas, without adequate Congressional appropriations, seemed to lack financial resources; but partly from his own purse, partly from other channels, he supplied funds. A man of action, he made rapid, sagacious decisions; a hard worker, he toiled until even his strong frame broke down. At the outset he had naturally leaned toward the proslavery groups which upheld the regular government, but intercourse with the settlers and shrewd observation quickly brought him to an impartial course.

Not all the credit for the pacification could be assigned to him. Some of it belonged to the Federal troops under Persifor F. Smith, some to the growing strength of the freesoil elements, some to Democratic Party necessities in 1856, and some to a general desire to get on with peaceful industry. Nevertheless, he had succeeded—and he should have had the consistent help of Washington.[27]

But beneath the surface ran heady currents. The Free State Party had resolved to maintain its policy of watchful non-cooperation. Immediately after the Presidential election in 1856, "Governor" Robinson, A. H. Reeder, and other leaders, conferring with Amos A. Lawrence and various Easterners, had decided that, while they must avoid a conflict with Federal authority, they would never surrender to the regular territorial government and accept its proslavery legislature. They would gather support in the North, continue

27 Gihon, *Geary and Kansas, passim.*

passive resistance to the obnoxious code of laws still in force, and bide their time. On Christmas Day, Robinson had resigned his office to serve the cause of freedom in a private capacity. One large section of the population, therefore, regarded Geary with watchful coolness. Another section, as he became impartial, grew rancorously hostile. The proslavery men, seeing in his strength and honesty an insuperable obstacle, resolved to pick a quarrel and drive him out. John Calhoun, late in 1856, removed his office from Wyandotte to Lecompton to direct the campaign. He and his associates filled the Lecompton *Union* with venomous articles. A considerable group (Geary later thought fifty sworn men) were ready if necessary to murder the governor.[28]

As a result of these machinations, hardly had 1857 begun when Geary was involved in a desperate series of struggles. He had demanded the removal of Chief Justice Lecompte, accusing him of neglect of duty, for he had held court only two or three weeks in six months; of partisan entanglements which destroyed the standing of the court; of dealing harshly with freesoil prisoners while neglecting the cases of proslavery men; and of releasing an indicted murderer on straw bail. Beyond doubt, Lecompte had been lazy and inefficient, while his party sympathies made him an agent of the proslavery interest. A small, fair-complexioned man, keen-eyed, indolent, and kindly, he was later to find his proper place as a routine attorney.[29] But he struck back on January 9, 1857, in a letter of thirty-five closely written foolscap sheets, defending himself and assailing Geary. And he naturally found support in Washington. While Secretary Marcy called on the governor for further explanations, the Senate failed to confirm Pierce's half-hearted nomination of a successor to Lecompte.

The fact was that President Pierce, irritated by the extralegal Topeka government, moved by Southern influences, and soured by failure, turned a hostile shoulder toward the governor who had served him so well in Kansas. His lukewarm course in nominating a successor to Lecompte without removing that judge had simply invited senatorial obstruction; and though Geary on January 12 sent him a convincing exposition of his policies, Pierce paid no attention to it. Naturally Judges Lecompte and Cato did all they could to thwart and weaken the governor. Geary wished to keep on amicable terms with the free State legislature which met early in the year in Topeka, and with whose leaders he had an understanding that it would transact no business. His hopes for general peace and amity were dashed, however, when a deputy marshal appeared with a writ from Judge Cato and arrested seven of the legislators.[30]

28 Gihon, 158–162; Geary to Pierce, January 12, 1857, Pierce Papers; N. Y. *Weekly Tribune, Herald, Times;* Topeka *Kansas Tribune,* January-March, 1857.
29 Gladstone, *Englishman in Kansas, passim;* Holloway, *History of Kansas,* 409, 410.
30 *National Intelligencer,* January 15, 1857; N. Y. *Weekly Tribune,* January-March, 1857.

Worst of all, the recognized territorial legislature, chosen the previous fall in a one-sided poll, came into open conflict with the governor. It met in Lecompton on January 12, ready for a desperate series of acts to maintain Kansas as fighting ground for slavery. Geary had prepared recommendations for a statesmanlike course. The time had come, declared his message, to purge the statute books of the intolerant laws which, denounced throughout the North, had been admitted wrongful even in the South. Specifically, he recommended the elimination of all test oaths; reform of the election laws with due safeguards for the ballot; repeal of the provisions which entrusted the choice of county officers to the legislature instead of to the people; and removal of all pretexts for the use of the militia against settlers. In fact, he wanted a wholesale overhauling of statutes which were full of inconsistencies, intolerance, and injustice. Let men forget the bloody clashes of the past year, he urged. "The dead, whom the madness of partisan fury has consigned to premature graves, cannot be recalled to life; the insults, the outrages, the robberies, and the murders, 'enough to stir a fever in the blood of age,' in this world of imperfection and guilt, can never be fully atoned for." The legislators should look solely to the future. They should cultivate a jealous regard for the sanctity of the ballot box, for the principles of self-government guaranteed in the organic act, for the election of all officers by the people, and for unqualified submission to the will of the majority.

Unhappily, the Lecompton leaders had determined to strike boldly and lawlessly for a slave State. Calhoun, Whitfield, Lecompte, and others were in touch with such national leaders as Senator Slidell, Speaker Orr, and Jacob Thompson. A slight gesture was made toward modification of the obnoxious statutes, not because Geary requested it, but because it was feared that Congress would act if the legislature did not. But it was very slight; the abolition of the test oath was the only important reform effected. All the legislation protecting and fostering slave property, all the inhuman penalties prescribed for writing, printing, or speaking against the institution of slavery, were kept intact.[31] Having made this gesture, the leaders turned to their plan for a census of inhabitants, a registry of voters, and an adroitly controlled constitutional convention. Action had to be expedited, for the incoming migration would soon swamp the proslavery element. On February 14, the legislature finished its work and sent Governor Geary a bill which horrified him and all other fair-minded persons.

A bill which made a mockery of democratic self-government, its purpose was to guarantee the proslavery forces a thoroughly packed and partisan constitutional convention. It must be remembered that nearly all county officers, having been chosen by the dishonestly elected legislature, were proslavery men. The measure provided that the county sheriffs and their deputies, predominantly

31 See Topeka *Kansas Tribune*, February 16, 1857.

proslavery agents, should enumerate in March the white residents, including all free male citizens of the United States over twenty-one. Thereupon the sheriffs should file in the office of the probate judges complete lists of qualified voters in the various counties. Following this, the boards of county commissioners, also mainly proslavery men, should choose judges of election. Then, on the third Monday in June, delegates should be chosen to the convention; and, finally, this body should sit at Lecompton in September. Everybody knew that the provision that none but men resident on March 15 could vote would exclude a multitude of new settlers, mainly antislavery, who were expected that spring. Everybody knew that the sheriffs who enumerated the settlers, the probate judges who helped prepare voting lists, and the county commissioners who chose election judges were for most part Democrats who wanted to see Kansas a slave State.

Most objectionable of all, perhaps, was the fact that the convention was to be given a completely free hand; for the measure made no provision for submitting the constitution to the people. Indeed, when the bill was passing through the Council, one member admitted that the design was to avoid submission; for he suggested a clause to provide for the contingency that Congress might return the constitution for a popular vote.[32]

In this and other legislation the proslavery men showed their eagerness to flout Geary's wishes. Their speeches were full of defiance and insult. When in mid-February the governor paid a visit to the house, one excited sheriff, W. T. Sherrard of Douglas County, a florid young man of reckless character, waylaid him in the antechamber, cursed him, and, when Geary, ignoring his presence, walked past, spat twice on his back. Had the defenseless governor, who was unaware of the indignity until told of it, showed resentment, Sherrard would have killed him. Citizens of Lecompton promptly held a meeting to denounce the insult offered to Geary. Sherrard attended and grew violent. Suddenly he and others began firing, and, when the smoke cleared, he was dead. "I saw Sherrard leap into the air as a bullet struck him in the forehead," said one spectator. Next day Geary vetoed the convention bill.

The governor's arguments against it were unanswerable. He declared the whole movement premature. For twenty-five or thirty thousand Kansans—burdened with heavy debts, their public buildings unfinished, their schools, courthouses, and jails mere blueprints, the very title to their lands in great part insecure—to cast off the fostering care of the national government, ready to furnish financial and military assistance, was folly. Though Minnesota had become a thriving Territory of 180,000 people, it was only in recent weeks that her governor had urged steps to form a State constitution. Michigan had re-

---

32 The text of the bill and of Geary's veto are in the N. Y. *Tribune*, March 14, 1857. See also files of St. Louis *Missouri Democrat*, January-March, 1857.

mained a Territory for five years after she gained a population equal to that of a Congressional district. Why the haste in Kansas? And even if the movement for statehood was accepted, the pending bill was flagrantly defective. It left all the preliminary activity to county officers who were chosen by and subservient to one party. It contained no such precaution as the provision in the Toombs bill that five impartial commissioners should correct the census of voters and take additional measures to secure a fair election of delegates. Its failure to authorize a popular vote on the constitution was unforgivable, for, with scarcely an exception, State constitutions which had been made in controversial circumstances had been submitted to popular ratification.

The legislature quickly passed the bill over Geary's veto; and as it did so, the atmosphere in the frowsy, muddy river town of Lecompton, its streets full of rough men, grew more threatening than ever. Tough rowdies with bowie knives and revolvers profanely boasted that if the governor remained they would take his life. Citizens laid bets that Geary would be assassinated within forty days.[33] As the Lawrence *Herald of Freedom* said, the fire-eating leaders of the proslavery party, anxious to be rid of so troublesome an obstacle, "coveted his life's blood, and sought every opportunity to take it." The alarmed governor had written General Persifor F. Smith at Fort Leavenworth on February 9, requesting two additional companies of dragoons to meet a conspiracy to breach the peace. But Smith, who regarded Geary with jealous antagonism, and who at the moment bubbled over with gratitude to President Pierce for his recent promotion to brigadier, thought that his orders gave him discretion to deny armed support, and did so. In a sharp letter, he scoffed at Geary's fears. Thus left without Presidential support or proper military assistance, the governor felt powerless. Overwork and overstrain had brought him to the verge of collapse, and on March 4 he mailed his resignation to Washington.

Though some observers thought that Geary should have stood his ground, the more sensible view is that he did well to think of his safety and return east to arouse public sentiment to the critical situation in the Territory. He penned a manly farewell address to the citizens of Kansas.[34] Then, gathering his books and papers, and accompanied by his secretary, Dr. Gihon, he set out for Washington. On March 21 he was at Willard's, where he found himself the lion of the freesoil element in the city, his room thronged with visitors. He had paused in St. Louis to give the *Democrat* an interview, and that journal promptly sounded the tocsin in a widely reprinted warning to the nation. Proslavery intransigence, it declared, had undertaken to pack the approaching convention, and to drag a manacled Kansas before Congress with a slavery constitution:

33 N. Y. *Weekly Tribune*, March 28, 1857.
34 *National Intelligencer*, March 21, 1857.

Every contingency is provided for in this compact and complicated scheme. From the taking of the census by the county sheriffs to the organization of the convention, through the graded surveillance of election judges, probate judges, etc., the felon legislature has provided as effectually for getting the desired result as Louis Napoleon did for getting himself elected Emperor. . . .

In our humble judgment, the Kansas question has never worn the ominous aspect and the colossal proportions which it is now beginning to assume. It is impossible to conceive that the people of the North will acquiesce in the final triumph of a system of fraud, violence, and ruthless tyranny—equally impossible to conceive that the slavery extensionists will forego their purposes; and therefore the prompt and vigorous intervention of the President is demanded by the most serious considerations.[35]

[V]

During late March, excitement ran high in Washington over Geary and his revelations. The proslavery leaders of the South, delighted to have him out of the way, treated him with cool contempt. Buchanan, who knew that he was a political liability and who had already determined to send out a new governor, was pleased to have his resignation. But Republican members of Congress, free-soil journalists, and not a few old Democratic friends made the most of him. The Kansas ordeal, they noted, had laid a heavy imprint upon the man. A heavy brown beard covered his face; his high forehead and sharp-cut, handsome features were blanched with a pallor which told of overwork, worry, and confinement; he complained of ill-health.[36] Secretary Cass gave him a cordial private interview. On March 23, he sat with the Cabinet for two hours, making a detailed report on Kansas affairs. His antagonists, Calhoun, Maclean, and others, however, had hurried from Lecompton to give the Administration a different view, while Lecompte and Cato were busy writing letters to their Southern friends.[37]

Although Geary made no impression on the Directory, his repeated interviews did tell heavily with Northern opinion. He reiterated that the great majority of Kansans were conservative, peace-loving folk; that small combinations of crafty, passionate, unscrupulous men had deliberately fomented discord; that the fieriest proslavery leaders were actual foes of the Union; and that their scheme to use Kansas to disrupt the nation, while thwarted for the time being, was still alive and dangerous. General Smith, who had agreed with this, had written Buchanan on February 3 that the disunion plot had been laid in the capital: "A plan was organized in Washington to force Kansas to be a slave

35 St. Louis *Missouri Democrat*, March 18, 1857. The editor, declaring that the main features of the new constitution had already been devised in the proslavery Blue Lodges, urged honest Kansans to boycott the convention.
36 N. Y. *Evening Post*, March 23, 24, 1857.
37 N. Y. *Weekly Tribune*, March 28, 1857.

State, but if the effort to do it in the manner there proposed failed, it should at least produce a civil war ending in prompt dissolution of the Union." [38]

President Pierce, added Geary, had promised to support him with the Treasury and the army. Instead, Geary had been compelled to pay $12,000 from his own pocket to maintain his government; his request for two cavalry companies to meet an emergency had been scornfully denied; the judges had been allowed to thwart him at every step; and his life had been in constant jeopardy. Even his mail had been opened by proslavery officials, and letters to him frequently destroyed. Calhoun's liege-tool Maclean had boasted of suppressing two bushels of correspondence! Geary related that his letter of resignation, a profound secret between himself and his secretary, had not been in the post office an hour before its contents were the gossip of every Lecompton barroom. He warned hearers of the grave danger that Kansas, before snow flew again, would have a slavery constitution.[39]

These statements made Geary appear to most Northerners a deeply wronged man, and to most Southerners a prejudiced, malicious foe. Dr. Gihon's vividly written book on their joint experiences was shortly selling briskly. His denunciations of the Calhounite plot to dominate Kansas were the more telling because he had gone to that Territory with his sympathies on the slavery side. A fresh wave of alarm spread across the free States. It was nowhere felt more strongly than among Geary's fellow Pennsylvanians, who knew enough of him to respect his honesty. Even staunch Democrats are irritated, wrote one of Jere Black's correspondents. "It is manifest that unless 'order reigns in Kansas' we may soon add Pennsylvania to the domains of Northern fanaticism." [40]

Nobody was placed in a more difficult predicament by the new Kansas crisis than Senator Douglas and his squatter sovereignty allies. Their doctrine had been made a judicial nullity by the Dred Scott decision. Was it now to be made a practical absurdity by Calhoun and his schemers? This was a question of burning import to Douglas, for with a new election for his Senate seat coming on next year, his political future depended on the answer.

Inevitably, Douglas and his school had received the Dred Scott opinions with outward complaisance but inward irritation and antagonism. The principle subsequently termed the Freeport doctrine, the doctrine that the local police must control any system of labor, was already widely accepted by Northern Democrats. Geary had espoused it. In a letter of January, 1857, defending his record, he remarked that, the disunionists having been foiled, "the people here will soon be in the complete enjoyment of their sovereign rights, and 'sovereignty of the

38 Smith to Buchanan, February 3, 1857; Buchanan Papers.
39 N. Y. *Weekly Tribune*, March 28, N. Y. *Evening Post*, March 28, 29, 1857.
40 J. R. Jones to Black, March 26, 1857, Black Papers.

people' will hereafter be . . . the brightest jewel of the Democratic crown."
He had added that from a thorough acquaintance with every part of Kansas, he
knew that at least three-fourths of the actual settlers wished Kansas to be a free
State.[41] Buchanan's friend William Bigler had also enunciated the Freeport idea.
Writing Buchanan as 1856 closed, he had declared that sooner or later the popular will would decide the slavery issue in the Territory, and that the longer the
decision was deferred, the more certainly it would be for freedom.

Then, again, whatever diversity of opinion may exist as to the right of a
territorial legislature to reject or embrace the institution, all concede that there
is no power on earth to make a territorial legislature pass laws, or make police
arrangements for the protection of slave property—and that without such protection it cannot exist. . . . Hence I have said that I believe the people can *control* the subject. I have never used the terms *establish* or *abolish*.[42]

If, however, Calhoun, Maclean, and Lecompte packed a convention and
foisted a proslavery constitution on unwilling Kansas without a referendum, how
could Douglas ever talk of popular sovereignty again? How could he hold up
his head before the Illinois voters?

Douglas was therefore deeply alarmed by the reckless course of the Kansas
legislature. He had wished to see the obnoxious laws on the statute book re-
pealed, and had made this plain to Calhoun as an old Springfield friend, long
under his influence. Calhoun had sent him an explicit promise that it would be
done, yet some of the worst laws were left untouched.[43] Again, Douglas had
been in no hurry to see Kansas write a constitution and apply for statehood. He
believed the population as yet insufficient for this step. When the proper time
came, the instrument should be drafted by a truly representative body, and
submitted to the people. Instead, the legislators, rushing into premature action,
had driven a forty-mule team through all representative principles. With much
uneasiness, Douglas felt himself betrayed by Calhoun. This headstrong fellow,
after going to Kansas as a moderate, and taking some sensible steps to procure
the abandonment of a slavery party in favor of an Administration party which
should include freesoil Democrats, slavery Democrats, and former Whigs, had
yielded to his associates and rapidly grown violent and vindictive.

For the Senator to aid and abet such defiance of the popular will would be
political suicide. He had staked his future on the Kansas-Nebraska Act; he had
given the North a solemn pledge that the voice of the people would be held
sacred; he had warned the South that Kansas would almost certainly become
free. He was the last man in the world to let himself be duped by Calhoun and

41 Geary to Buchanan, January, 1857, Buchanan Papers.
42 William Bigler, December, 1856, Buchanan Papers; Bigler had just toured Kansas.
43 John Calhoun, January 26, 1857, Douglas Papers; he wrote that the legislature "has the
subject in hand."

Lecompte, or to be made the tool of the Southern leaders advising them from Washington.

While Geary boldly placed his views before the country, Douglas and his fast ally, Senator Charles E. Stuart of Michigan decided that the legislature's work ought to be repudiated. Congress should take charge anew, pass an enabling act, and scrupulously supervise the whole process of State-making. Stuart, visiting New York late in March, was impressed by the exasperation of intelligent Democrats in the metropolis. If the scheme for a packed convention went through, multitudes of them would turn to the Republicans. Kansas could probably never be admitted under a constitution framed by such a body, but whether it was admitted or not, the outcome would be disastrous. Utter destruction awaited the Democratic Party in the North and Northwest unless his and Douglas's plan for heading off Calhoun and his crew by an enabling act was carried. The wisest and most prudent men in New York, wrote Stuart, agreed on this:

You and I can do this thing. We can bring our party in the Senate to the support of this ground, if we unflinchingly stand by it ourselves.

There are two reasons why I shall do it. The first is that it is right in itself, which ought always to be reason enough. And the other is, that *it is the only mode in which, what is left of the party in the northwest,* can be saved. The success of this measure, or our political burial, will be the certain result.

I have seen several from our section, and they all say that the excitement is increasing both in amount and intensity in consequence of the . . . inaugural and the Dred Scott decision. . . . I know there is strong feeling in certain quarters of the great strength of the Administration. I hope it may prove so. But at the same time I am forced to the opposite conclusion by past and passing events. My wish is otherwise, but my *opinion* is, it cannot sustain itself, throughout its term. . . .

But, sir, it will prove true as holy writ . . . on one side there is salvation, on the other inevitable ruin.[44]

Immediate action, however, was beyond Douglas and Stuart. Congress was not in session—the Senate, held for confirmations, adjourned March 13. Would the proslavery men in Kansas stay their hand? Douglas, returning to Illinois, had to content himself with a speech at Springfield (June 12) in which he interpreted the Dred Scott decision in his own way. A master's right to take slaves into any Territory was now unassailable, he said. Yet "it necessarily remains a barren and worthless right unless sustained, protected, and enforced by appropriate police regulations and local legislation, prescribing adequate remedies for its violation. These regulations and remedies must necessarily depend entirely upon the will and wishes of the people of the Territory."

44 Stuart to Douglas, March 29, 1857, Douglas Papers.

Alas for Douglas! In this same speech, for partisan reasons, he declared that the law under which Kansans three days later were to elect a constitutional convention "is believed to be just and fair in all its objects and provisions." [45]

[VI]

The new President, many men were saying, could write a bold and honest record in Kansas. But would he and his Cabinet insist on fair measures, or would they accept the scheme for a fraudulent census, a one-sided election, and a controlled convention?

Before Geary reached Washington, the President had found his successor in Robert J. Walker of Mississippi, the man who had almost been made Secretary of State. Doubtless Jacob Thompson, remembering the suppressed letter, grimaced over the appointment. This versatile, ambitious, skillful man, always restlessly self-assertive, accepted the governorship with some reluctance. Kansas was a political graveyard where three governors had failed; the meagre salary was less than Walker could make from a single legal case; life on the Kansas border was uncomfortable and risky. Mrs. Walker, of a prominent Pennsylvania family, related to the Baches and Dallases, was equally inclined to shrink. Buchanan held out the prospect, however, that Walker could perform a great national service, could soon return to Washington as Senator from Kansas, and could even gain laurels which would enhance his claims to the Presidency. Douglas and others seconded the plea. Finally, after making several conditions, Walker—who had a truly patriotic zeal in public service—accepted on March 26. One stipulation was that his friend, former Representative F. P. Stanton of Tennessee, should be made territorial secretary, and that General William S. Harney, then in Florida, should be placed in command in Kansas, to remain while disorder threatened. Another, of the first importance, was laid down in his letter of acceptance; he took office on the understanding that Buchanan and the Cabinet "cordially concur in the opinion expressed by me, that the actual bona fide residents of Kansas, by a fair and regular vote, unaffected by fraud or violence, must be permitted, in adopting their State Constitution, to decide for themselves what shall be their social institutions."

No better man could have been chosen. Most people liked Walker's personality: an indefatigable, wide-awake, nervous little man, he had a soft-spoken, ingratiating address that was almost feline and that lent itself to his gift for finesse. Though sometimes fussy and excitable, when aroused he had the heart of a lion. Nor did anybody ever question his abilities. The precocious son of a well-known Pittsburgh jurist, head of his class at the University of Pennsylvania,

45 Milton, *Eve of Conflict*, 260; N. Y. *Times*, June 23, N. Y. *Tribune*, June 25, 1857.

and a leader at twenty-two in the convention which placed the Keystone Democracy behind Jackson in 1824, he had once seemed destined to a career in his
native State. Then in 1826 he had followed a brother to Mississippi. Combining
law, land speculation, and politics, he had quickly made his mark in that still
untamed State. He was a strong Union man in nullification days. In the middle
thirties, by virtue of President Jackson's endorsement, the astute campaign management of William M. Gwin, and his own magnetism, he won a seat in the
Senate. A tireless worker and a ready speaker, unafraid to cross blades even with
Clay, he had achieved national prominence before Polk lifted him to the
Treasury. Despite chronic ill-health, he had proved his ability to solve difficult
problems. Nobody had done more to make Polk President; nobody had labored
more shrewdly for the annexation of Texas. The principal author of the tariff
bill which bore his name, he had penned in its defense the best state paper on
commerce and revenue since Gallatin's day. He had devised astute measures to
finance the Mexican War.

It was too much to expect that radical freesoilers would welcome the appointment of a Mississippian of such marked expansionist views. The New York
Tribune grumbled because all of the territorial officers—the governor, secretary,
and judges—would now be Southerners. Schuyler Colfax believed that Walker
would accept the Calhoun scheme and send a slave State constitution to Washington, while Amos A. Lawrence was certain that his real aim was to let Kansas
go and to create a new slave State south of it.[46] Objective comment, however,
approved of the choice. As a Northerner by birth, a Southerner by adoption,
and a Union man by conviction, Walker seemed as likely to take statesmanlike
views as anybody. The ever-fearful freesoilers should have remembered that
Southern radicals had barred his appointment to a high Cabinet place because
he had always been a strong nationalist and a believer in gradual emancipation.
The Washington correspondent of the New York *Times* printed an accurate
estimate:

He is a thinking machine which works badly sometimes, and which has once
or twice been turned to awkward uses; but his power, industry, and discrimination, keen insight into the motives of men, and laudable ambition to stand well
before the country cannot be questioned. I urged in conversation today with a
gentleman who stands high in Mr. Buchanan's confidence his identification with
the ultra-Southern interests. . . . "You do not know," said he, "of whom you
are talking. I predict that if Mr. Walker goes to Kansas, he will unravel the
whole Atchison web, and pave the way for the admission of Kansas as a free
State in such a manner that the mouths of those who have hitherto sympathized
with border ruffianism will be effectually and forever stopped."

46 Colfax, April 8, Lawrence, May 16, 1857, Robinson Papers, Univ. of Kansas. For a
succinct appraisal of Walker, see H. Donaldson Jordan, "A Politician of Expansion: Robert
J. Walker," *Miss. Valley Hist. Review*, V (1918), 158–189.

Mr. Walker disowns all partisanship with Davis and men of that clique and calibre. He has professed a determination, since November last, as I am told by his intimate associates and friends, to sustain the Administration in its endeavors to build up a Union party in antagonism to the *per se* secessionist doctrinarians, who have flourished so gloriously under the regime of President Pierce.[47]

As a matter of fact, before his appointment Walker had placed on record his belief that Kansas was certain to become a free State. In his widely circulated *Appeal for the Union*, a campaign pamphlet dated six weeks before election day in 1856, he had based this prediction on several distinct grounds. Soil, climate, and production favored free labor. So did the flow of population, the North possessing superior numbers, greater human mobility, a steady European immigration, and freedom from any apprehension as to the safety of its property. Finally, he wrote, slavery could not long persist in any State against the constant agitation of even a powerful minority. It was also an important fact that a special tie existed between Walker and Douglas.

"You must go, Bob," Douglas had said, in effect. "I feel intensely on this. The whole success of the Kansas-Nebraska Act in that Territory is to a great extent dependent on your consenting to go. I beg it of you." [48]

Nor could Walker's emphasis in his letter of acceptance on the right of Kansans to decide their institutions by fair popular vote be overlooked; an emphasis which was echoed by Buchanan in the instructions he gave to the new governor. "The institutions of Kansas must be established by the votes of the people of Kansas," wrote the President, "unawed or uninterrupted by force or fraud." All alien voters must be excluded. When the new constitution was submitted to the people, "they must be protected in the exercise of their right of voting for or against that instrument, and the fair expression of the popular will must not be interrupted by fraud or violence." [49]

Meanwhile, in Kansas a free-state gathering on March 10 had adopted a policy on non-cooperation with the regular territorial government, which meant abstention from the polls in territorial elections; although some conservative freesoil men inside and outside Kansas condemned this decision. The Lawrence *Herald of Freedom* declared that the gathering should at least have waited to see how the course of the Administration would develop. It believed that the freesoil men would have done better to fling their full strength into the elections, rigged though they were. The opposite course gave the proslavery conspirators a clear field; "a proslavery constitution will be submitted to Congress as a result of that action, when, had a different policy prevailed, a different result might

47 Washington corr. N. Y. *Times*, March 26, 1857.
48 Walker's testimony, Covode Committee; 36th Cong., 1st Sess., House Report No. 648, pp. 105, 106.
49 Walker's instructions received May 17, published *National Intelligencer*, July 16, 1857.

have been attained." But in view of the way in which proslavery leaders had ridden roughshod over Geary's veto, and in view also of their patent determination to manipulate both the census of voters and the election of convention delegates, the refusal of most freesoil men to participate had been inevitable.

Summer heat and humidity closed down on the Potomac. Congress had gone home; most of the great houses were shuttered; the President and Cabinet toiled on with appointments and routine business. After the thunderclap of the Dred Scott decision, the season promised to be quiet. Most people forgot about the dark plot of Calhoun, Maclean, and Lecompte, and the outraged protests of Geary. The New York *Herald* and *Times* were busy praising Buchanan's Kansas policy, and together with the Washington *Union* were predicting its success. Only the doubters waited anxiously for news from the valley of the Missouri.

6

Melodrama in Kansas

HUNDREDS of people, a tense, expectant throng, had gathered in front of the Cincinnati House in Lawrence. The sun, just sinking in the west, threw its level rays on grimy farmers, wagoners, and blacksmiths in checked shirts and blue jeans, on storekeepers wearing aprons, on black-coated doctors and lawyers, and on women in sunbonnets holding children by the hand. Many stalwart fellows had knives in their belts or revolvers strapped to their waists. An impatient murmur arose, until "Governor" Robinson emerged upon the hotel steps with a portly, dignified gentleman of middle age—Frederick P. Stanton, former Congressman from Tennessee, now secretary and acting-governor of Kansas. He had preceded Robert J. Walker to the Territory, coming by steamboat to Kansas City and Lecompton. Thence he had ridden down to Lawrence, taken tea with Robinson, and let it be known that he would make a speech. With the ease of a practiced orator, he began talking of Walker, the Union, and the territorial government.

Suddenly a fierce shout burst from the crowd: "Never! Never!" Stanton faced them defiantly. He had said that he meant to enforce the laws of the much-hated "legitimate" legislature (to free State men the "bogus" legislature) and to collect the taxes it had levied. Tactfully retreating a little, he remarked that what he really had at heart was the enforcement of Federal law and Federal authority. An assenting murmur arose. "We're ready to obey the United States," shouted some. "Always have been," came other voices. But a few minutes later Stanton declared again that they must accept the territorial laws, and again a thunderous clamor checked him: "Never! Never!"

Then Stanton began to recite an appropriate passage from *Hiawatha*: the speech of the Great Manitou exhorting the Indians to cease their battling, wash the war paint from their faces, carve pipes from the redstone quarry, smoke the calumet of peace, and live together as brothers. Halfway through it, his memory failed and he broke down. Mrs. Gates, keeper of the hotel, hastily brought forth her copy of Longfellow. She held a candle to the page, and he went on:

I am weary of your quarrels,
Weary of your wars and bloodshed,
Weary of your prayers for vengeance,
Of your wranglings and dissensions;
All your strength is in your union,
All your danger is in discord;
Therefore be at peace henceforward,
And as brothers live together.

At nine o'clock Stanton sat down with the free State men to a bounteous meal, and the rest of the evening passed harmoniously.[1]

Stanton represented as happy a choice as Walker; shrewd, alert, courageous, he had just been described by a group of Tennesseans recommending him for a Cabinet post as the most prompt, reliable, and skillful attorney in the State. An honest man, he believed in the right of Kansans to a free and fair charting of their own course. Like Walker, he meant to insist on a square deal. Even more than Walker, he was ready to fight a crooked deal. Though he supported slavery and had voted against the abolition of slave-trading in the District of Columbia, he had often said that the institution could never flourish on the Kansas plains. Even while he was explaining that Governor Walker and he would enforce territorial laws, he declared that he would protect the ballot box as the remedy for all evils and would demand that both sides grant a political amnesty. Calhoun and Maclean had returned in a truculent frame of mind from Washington, where they had conferred with Jacob Thompson, Jefferson Davis, and other Southerners; but Stanton faced them coldly—he meant to be neutral and fair.[2]

Taking up quarters at Lecompton in the building formerly occupied by Governor Geary, Stanton began to urge free State voters to take part in the June election for a constitutional convention. His arguments were promptly challenged by "Governor" Robinson and fourteen other free State leaders in a letter explaining how unfair that election would be. The census and registry of voters already carried out had omitted large numbers of free State settlers, while including many names of non-residents. The freesoil men would participate in the election, therefore, only if certain conditions were met. First, in each township or district, two persons, one chosen by the free State and one by the slavery party, should act together in correcting the registry. Second, in each precinct,

1 MS address, J. C. Horton, December 2, 1903; Lane Papers, Univ. of Kansas; *National Intelligencer,* May 7, 1857; N. Y. *Tribune,* May 9, 1857.
2 Stanton reached Kansas on April 15. See his letters, Sen. Exec. Doc. 8 (35th Cong., 1st Sess.); L. W. Spring, *History of Kansas,* 210 ff.; *Missouri Republican,* April-June, 1857. Stanton and Maclean had a conference on April 24. Maclean justified the interference of Missourians in the spring election of 1855, demanded that the free State men be made to submit to the regular or "bogus" legislature, and intimated that Walker and Stanton should be guided by Calhoun and himself. Lawrence correspondence, N. Y. *Evening Post* dated April 24; *Missouri Republican,* May 5, 1857.

four election judges should act, two named by the free State and two by the slavery party; and at least three must sign the election certificate of every delegate to the convention. Stanton replied that as acting governor he had no authority to meet these conditions. He had no power over the probate judges who alone were authorized to correct the voting lists, and he could not appoint four election judges, for the law provided that the county commissioners should name three. Admitting that the registry was defective, he blamed the free State men for boycotting it, and called upon them to help correct the lists by sending in sworn statements.[3]

In this attitude Stanton agreed with Senator Douglas, who, after saying at Springfield that the election arrangements seemed fair, added that if any group of voters avoided the polls, the responsibility must rest "on those who, for partisan purposes, will sacrifice the principles they profess to cherish." Both men later rued their hasty statements. They had reason to learn just how grossly unjust the census and registration were. What were the facts? Kansas then had thirty-eight counties. The partisan officers deputed for the task took no census at all in nineteen counties, so that no apportionment of delegates could be made for them. In fifteen counties they made no registry of voters, so that these areas, including some of the oldest organized counties in Kansas, were entirely disfranchised.[4] No voting precinct was established in the town of Lawrence. Any citizen of that free State center who wished to follow Stanton's advice would have to ride twelve miles to vote. In such places as Leavenworth, prominent free State men were left off the registry lists. To be sure, radical freesoilers helped to block a proper enumeration; but the proslavery men were chiefly to blame.[5]

Walker soon followed the secretary westward. On his way, he stopped in New York long enough to attend a dinner given by Henry J. Raymond of the *Times*, George N. Sanders, and other friends. He told them he was determined that Kansas should have a full, free, and solemn referendum upon any constitution that might be framed, after a fair census of all the true inhabitants of the Territory at the time; and to this he pledged himself both as an officer conscious of his duty, and as a gentleman sensitive of his honor. Any attempt by a special group to impose upon the Territory a constitution unsanctioned by popular vote would be a usurpation and wrong which could not be tolerated for a moment. His statements got into the press and were applauded.[6] At the end of May he reached Kansas and made his first important public appearance there in strange company. He had landed at Leavenworth. Clattering into Lawrence with his staff on May 26, he rejoined in that town three New Englanders who had been

3 Kansas correspondence in N. Y. *Weekly Tribune*, May 16, 1857.
4 See details in Walker's letter of resignation, December 15, 1857.
5 Quindaro correspondence, *Missouri Democrat*, April 24, 1857.
6 *National Intelligencer*, May 16, 1857.

on his steamboat coming up the Missouri—Senator Henry Wilson, the venerable poet-preacher John Pierpont, and the abolitionist and philanthropist Samuel Gridley Howe. All three were to speak in the Unitarian Church, and some two thousand men and women, with a band, gathered to do them honor. Governor Walker consented to attend and spoke briefly, saying that his Kansas policy would be outlined in his inaugural next day.

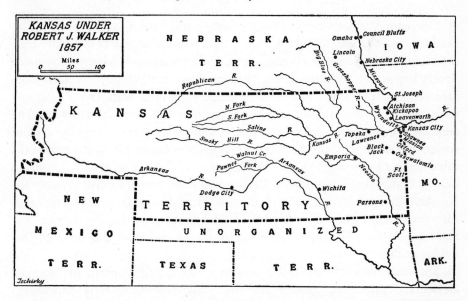

That inaugural address, long, well-written, and conciliatory, was delivered at Lecompton. Walker necessarily recognized the enactments of the regular legislature, and said that all of them that were constitutional would be enforced. Urging participation in the imminent election of a constitutional convention, he expressed confidence that its handiwork would be submitted to the people for a fair vote. He pointed out the importance of removing the slavery issue from Congress and the Presidential elections. Most striking of all, he declared that the entry or exclusion of slavery would ultimately be determined by climatic law, for an isothermal line, regulating labor, productions, and profit or loss, seemed to have made Kansas unsuitable for slavery. If it was found that the institution could not exist there, Kansas must nevertheless recognize that she had a constitutional duty to other States, and particularly Missouri; she must yield up their fugitives. The address had been prepared with patient care (parts of it being rewritten many times), and had been shown to numerous friends. Buchanan had seen at least some sections of it, and Walker had let Douglas read it as he passed through Chicago.[7] This fact lent special significance to his emphatic warning

7 N. Y. *Weekly Tribune*, June 6, 1857; Nichols, *Disruption of Amer. Democracy*, 108.

that "in no contingency will Congress admit Kansas as a slave state or free state, unless a majority of the people shall first have fairly and freely decided this question for themselves by a direct vote on the adoption of the Constitution, excluding all fraud or violence."

[I]

Governor Walker's main intent was simple and logical: to bring Kansas by peaceful steps to the position of a freesoil but Democratic State. He rapidly confirmed his impression that climate, crops, and conditions of immigration made slavery impossible. As he wrote Buchanan, perhaps four hundred slaves had been held there the previous fall, but, since the severe winter with its icy gales and temperatures of twenty below zero, about half had been taken away. The permanent existence of slavery was preposterous; a very large majority even of settlers and investors from the South were against it because it would reduce the value of their holdings.[8] Walker hoped, however, that Kansas would become as heavily Democratic as California. Thus it might forge a strong link between the Northern freesoil Democrats and the Southern slavery Democrats, and thus Missouri would escape the calamity of finding an aggressive new abolitionist State as neighbor. He knew that Douglas shared his views, and believed that Buchanan did so.

His immediate aim, therefore, was to create a middle party of "national Democratic principles," neither ardently proslavery nor bitterly antislavery. This was a sensible aim, which harmonized with actual conditions. The great majority of Kansas settlers, drawn from the border and middle States, were freesoil on an anti-negro rather than antislavery basis; they did not want black men in Kansas. They were naturally conservative in temper.[9] Such a middle party would stand equally against the Calhoun-Lecompte faction who wanted to make Kansas slave soil, and the Jim Lane men who talked abolitionism and defied Federal authority. Upon this party, wrote Walker's private secretary to the New York *Times*, the destiny of Kansas must ultimately rest.[10] Talking with citizens and shrewdly appraising the situation, Walker found the prospect encouraging. A month after his arrival, he sent Buchanan a perceptive sketch of the political forces:

That a vast majority of the people of Kansas are with me is certain, but there are restless men on both sides who desire revolution. . . .

There are several parties here: First, Free State Democrats composed of men who supported your election; second, Proslavery Democrats who supported

8 June 28, 1857; Buchanan Papers.
9 See Malin, *Legend of '56*, Ch. 30, on the conservative triumph.
10 Dated Lecompton, June 3, 1857.

your election; third, Slavery men (a small party, mostly Know-Nothings) who opposed your election and supported Fillmore; fourth, Republicans who supported Frémont. With me, are, first, all the Free State Democrats, constituting a plurality of the settlers; second, a majority of the masses of the Proslavery Democrats, but a considerable portion of the leaders are against me, on the point of submitting the Constitution to the people. The Proslavery Know-Nothings [are] against me generally. The Republicans [are] against me generally, but three of their papers including the most influential are against the Topeka movement if the convention will submit the constitution to the people.

The relative strength of the respective parties is: First Free State Democrats, second Republicans, third Proslavery Democrats, fourth (very small) Proslavery Know-Nothings. Supposing the whole number of settlers to be 24,000, the relative numbers would probably be as follows: Free State Democrats 9,000, Republicans 8,000, Proslavery Democrats 6,500, Proslavery Know-Nothings 500.[11]

His initial success in handling the free State men encouraged Walker in his undertaking. On June 9, their "legislature" was to meet at Topeka under the guidance of Robinson and reckless Jim Lane. Governor Walker visited the town three days earlier to deliver a warning speech. If this pretended legislature should pass laws and try to put them into force, he said, the upshot would be a direct collision with the national government. If the free Staters behaved sensibly, peace would be preserved, and he would see to it that actual residents of Kansas managed territorial affairs—that is, he would exclude Missouri interlopers. In particular, he promised that if the constitutional convention tried to evade a popular vote on its work, he would take spirited action. "I will join you, fellow citizens, in opposition to their course. And I doubt not that one much higher than I, the chief magistrate of the Union, will join you." [12] But for this fresh pledge of popular submission, Walker assured Buchanan, the Topeka "legislature" would assuredly have passed a complete code of laws, and put them into operation in a large majority of counties. This would have united the freesoil Democrats and Republicans, and brought on a sanguinary civil war between them and proslavery Democrats.[13]

As it was, the free State "legislature" took a lenitive course. It met on a lovely spring morning, the sun flooding the rolling prairies and turning the little Kansas River to silver. Robinson delivered a long message, reviewing events since the pillage of Lawrence a year earlier, answering the governor's inaugural, and pointing out that no isothermal line could stop the machinations of infatuated slavery propagandists.[14] Jim Lane made an astoundingly conservative

11 Lecompton, June 28, 1857; Buchanan Papers.
12 Spring, *History of Kansas*, 213; George W. Brown, *Reminiscences of Gov. R. J. Walker*, 42–44.
13 Walker to Buchanan, June 28, 1857; Buchanan Papers.
14 For complete text see N. Y. *Weekly Tribune*, June 27, 1857.

speech. The gathering then passed resolutions denouncing the approaching constitutional convention, and adjourned. Nothing was done to harass Walker, who, with a carriage full of aides and ladies, bustled diplomatically from group to group on the initial day, trying, said critics, to emasculate the freesoil cause with wily cunning.[15]

Even without Walker's tactful mixture of promises and warnings, the free State men would not have dared to erect their government to full stature. They knew that they would have met implacable hostility from the Executive and Congress. They knew, too, that since Frémont's defeat, opinion among their Republican supporters in the east had altered. As Schuyler Colfax wrote Robinson, a multitude of Northerners believed that if two-thirds the people of Kansas were freesoilers, they should rely upon their own strength, try voting at least once, and attempt to capture the regular machinery of government. You will be playing against loaded dice, declared Colfax, but most Republicans do not know it, and will hesitate to act as auxiliaries to a Topeka government in defying Washington.[16] A collision might fatally weaken the free State cause.

Such New England conservatives as Amos A. Lawrence took this view. Raymond vigorously expressed it in his New York Times. While old Whig organs like the National Intelligencer and Boston Courier scolded the free State leaders for their contumacious non-cooperation with the Federal government, the redoubtable Whig leader Thomas Ewing denounced them as actuated by folly and ambition. If they provoked civil war, they would be overthrown by Federal arms. They had nothing to do but take possession of the government in legitimate fashion, he wrote, but this would not suit Horace Greeley and others who wished to capitalize on continued trouble-making. In Kansas itself, a majority of free State newspapers were against efforts to put the Topeka government into active operation.[17] The strongest journal in the Territory, the Herald of Freedom, which claimed a weekly circulation of about 8,000 copies, wanted to drop the free State or Topeka constitution in favor of determined action to take control of the regular government; and it declared that at least five-sixths of the free State settlers north of the Kansas River favored this conservative policy.[18]

While the fiery Lane and stubborn Robinson were not yet ready for cooperation with the regular government, they knew they had to stop short of obstruction. They must not resist the regular authorities. Their program was to wait and see. Walker nevertheless deserved credit for the firmness and skill with which he had brought their irregular legislature to its milk-and-water conclusions.

The governor's real difficulty lay with the other extreme—the proslavery

15 Topeka correspondence, N. Y. Tribune, June 9, 10, 12, 1857.
16 April 8, 1857; Robinson Papers, Kansas State Hist. Soc.
17 Thomas Ewing to his son, July 23, 1857; Ewing Papers.
18 Lawrence Herald of Freedom, July 18, 1857.

men. He had written Buchanan that some restless leaders desired revolution; and this meant Calhoun, Maclean, and Lecompte as much as Jim Lane and other violent freesoilers. He had written that a considerable number of leaders were against him on popular submission of the new constitution; and this was stating the situation mildly.

Actually they were belligerently defiant, and they meant to have their own way. The evening after Walker read his inaugural in the straggling village of Lecompton, placed on the bluffs looking north over the Kansas River, a banquet had been held for him at the best hotel. He sat at table with Calhoun on one side, Maclean on the other, and a roomful of proslavery Democrats in front of him. Whiskey-drinking, which had filled the day, continued. When toasts began, Calhoun spoke courteously. Maclean, however, was of the quarrelsome Highland breed, another Glencairn or Lochiel. He had heard with anger Walker's statement that he believed Congress would not admit Kansas until a majority of the people had fairly passed the constitution. To him the governor was simply a frail, bald, red-eyed little politician who could be kicked back to Washington like Reeder and Geary. Gigantic in stature, he glowered down at Walker:

"And do you come here to rule over us?—you, a miserable pigmy like you? You come here with ears erect, but you will leave with your tail between your legs. Walker, we have unmade governors before; and by God, I tell you, sir, we can unmake them again!"

So runs the report of an auditor.[19] Maclean even bade Walker tell the President to mind his own business—they cared not a fig for Buchanan. This might have been passed over as bibulous bluster but that on June 11 a formal deputation of "law and order" Democracy trooped into the governor's office in Lecompton with an ultimatum. Declaring that they were not going to let the people pass on the constitution, they demanded that he stop talking of a vote. They had their plans and meant to carry them out. At first Walker was aghast. "Gentlemen," he said, "today for the first time I have learned what is your real course and policy, and you have taught it to me." But with fire in his eye he showed his Jacksonian mettle. "Gentlemen," he declared with quiet determination, "you cannot force *me* into that policy." Freesoilers heard of the collision without surprise. The inevitable crisis had come a step nearer. Walker would have to face the political crookedness, corruption, and threats that had been too much for his predecessors. "He is getting into the breakers," wrote one observer, "and it is to be seen whether such a crafty bark can ride out the storm in so rough a sea." [20]

19 J. H. St. Matthew, *Overland Monthly*, December, 1870; A. B. Morris, "R. J. Walker in the Kansas Struggle," MS Dissertation Univ. of Chicago.
20 Topeka correspondence dated June 12, N. Y. *Weekly Tribune*, July 4, 1857.

[II]

With the western land boom at its height this spring, migration to Wisconsin, Minnesota, Iowa, and Kansas eclipsed all precedent. Beginning a month earlier than usual, the tide was flowing strongly by March 1. Week after week it swelled. During April, May, and June, newspapers published along the travel routes described a veritable torrent of humanity. The country seemed swarming with groups and individuals excited by the rich, virgin land available at low prices. "Yesterday morning," noted the Cleveland *Herald* early in April, "the train from Buffalo numbered thirty-four cars, and this morning twenty-six, all crowded. Our hotels are full; the second class even filling their floors full every night." It told of emigrant wagons rolling in long, white-topped files down every turnpike. Railroad men estimated that a fourth of the people passing through Cleveland were bound for Kansas, and the remainder for the West generally.[21] The Toledo *Commercial* spoke of hundreds daily pouring through that city. Many were from New England, with a solid, go-ahead, Bunker Hill look about them; many from the Pennsylvania German country with plenty of baggage; and many from Europe, clutching their savings.[22] Though more steamboats were running on the Ohio, Mississippi, and Missouri than ever before, every night dozens of passengers slept on the cabin floors. "Still they come!" exclaimed the Keokuk *Whig*:

By railways and steamers, the flood of immigration continues pouring into the great West. The lake-shore roads are crowded to their utmost capacity. . . . The Ohio River steamers are crowded in the same way. On Friday last, two steamers brought into St. Louis some six hundred passengers. And "still they come," from Pennsylvania, from Ohio, Indiana, and other States, until, by the side of this exodus, that of the Israelites becomes an insignificant item.[23]

Kansas, with land warrants selling for eighty to ninety cents an acre, and new Indian holdings about to be auctioned, got more than its share of the spate. People seemed converging from all parts of the map, but chiefly from the middle and prairie States. In Ohio, a veritable fever of speculation in Kansas lands was raging, men selling homes, giving up well-paid positions, and even borrowing money at ten percent to purchase farms.[24] Seeing trains of the Chicago & Alton and Ohio & Mississippi disgorge hundreds of prospective settlers in St. Louis daily, the Missouri *Republican* was almost ready to believe men who expected Kansas to increase by seventy thousand people that year. All the old sense of risk and experiment was passing away; men now came with families and imple-

21   Quoted in *National Intelligencer*, April 16, 1857.
22   Quoted *idem*, April 7, 1857.
23   N. H. Parker, *Iowa As It Is in 1857*, 60.
24   Cleveland *Herald*, Warren *Chronicle*, quoted in *National Intelligencer*, March 18, 1857.

ments. Railroads from the eastern seaboard to Chicago and St. Louis were advertising a reduction of one-fourth in rates, and promising settlers a safe, easy transit across Iowa or Missouri. A considerable number of emigrants winterbound in Illinois and Iowa the previous fall had resumed their march as soon as roads and rivers were passable. Teamsters swore and pushed on every muddy road; Missouri River towns marvelled to see every boat struggling upstream crowded till its decks were black.[25]

Between the opening of river transportation and the end of March, it was estimated that seven thousand settlers had arrived in Kansas City, and nearly as many more in neighboring towns. The Leavenworth *Herald*, boasting early in May that the population of that city had leaped to almost four thousand, told of seeing a hundred houses completed within the past fortnight. Indeed, Leavenworth grew with fairy-book rapidity. By midsummer it had seven or eight thousand people, lots that had been valued at $500 the year before were fetching $4,000, and many merchants had sold out and replenished their stock four times since early spring. Plans were afoot for a railroad to connect with the Hannibal & St. Joseph.[26] While the *Herald of Freedom* estimated in April that settlers were arriving at the rate of a thousand a day, the Kansas City *Enterprise* predicted that the Territory would have a population of one hundred thousand by October.[27] In areas recently known only to the prairie dog, crow, and cottontail, villages leaped into existence. "Four months ago," said the Emporia *Kanzas News* of August 15, "there was not a house where Emporia now stands, and from the town site none were to be seen. Now . . . as far as the eye can reach in every direction, every quarter-section is occupied. In every bend of the Neosho and Cottonwood is a dwelling, and one or more fields of grain. . . . The country around this is as thickly settled as many parts of the West that have been open for years." [28]

25 N. H. Parker, *Kansas and Nebraska Handbook, 1857*, 24 ff., 27; Leavenworth *Herald*, May 9, 1857. "Everybody is full of hope," E. B. Whitman had written Samuel Gridley Howe on December 6, 1856. "Real estate is rising rapidly. If peace continues there will be life and vigor beyond precedent. Land! Land! is the cry. . . . I am maturing some land operations of great importance, and hope to interest you and some of your friends in them." Howe Papers. Thomas Ewing, Jr., descended on Kansas late in 1856, and invested $11,300 for the family in lands near Leavenworth, declaring the property worth $100,000. E. L. Pierce, later the biographer of Sumner, wrote letters to the N. Y. *Evening Post* predicting that the huge spring migration would make Kansas a free State. See letter of Thomas Ewing, Sr., January 1, 1857, in Ewing Papers; Pierce to J. Q. Adams, September 10, 1886, in Charles Sumner Papers, Kansas State Hist. Soc.

26 Leavenworth *Herald*, May 9, 1857; N. Y. *Evening Post*, July 6, 1857.

27 Lawrence *Herald of Freedom*, April 11, 1857; Kansas City *Enterprise*, April 16, 1857. Actually the census of 1860, three years later, showed 107,206 people in Kansas, of whom 627 were Negroes.

28 A number of freesoil Kansans had lectured or written in the East during the winter of 1856–57 to stimulate emigration. For the activities of one former New Yorker, O. C. Brown, who induced "hundreds" to meet him in Buffalo this spring, see G. G. Smith, *Spencer Kellogg Brown*, 102–107.

Settlement continued to follow the streams, not for transportation but for alluvial soil and timber. With the Kansas River valley the principal attraction, Lawrence and Topeka became two of the liveliest bases for newcomers. The roads leading into them had a blithe holiday air, for they were filled with rattling stages, white Conestogas, buggies, carry-alls, lumbering oxcarts, and travellers afoot and horseback. Lawrence had rapidly repaired all the damage suffered in the previous spring; Topeka had become the third town in size (led by Kansas City and Leavenworth), and boasted a society of refinement and hospitality.[29] Three main government-protected highways opened up the interior. One was the Fort Leavenworth-Laramie road in the north; a second the Fort Riley-Bridger's Pass road near the center; the third, the Santa Fé road in the south. Along the eastern boundary a passable north-south highway ran from Leavenworth to Fort Scott. While the earliest settlers had flocked to the northeast corner of Kansas, many now pushed far to the south. Indeed, men hunting desirable claims had scattered over half the Territory.

With the whole country standing this spring at the apex of a precarious boom, Kansas had its full share of promoters, gamblers, and their get-rich-quick dupes. New towns were being laid out, with paper churches, opera houses, city halls, and colleges; ambitious railroads and factories were being projected; lots in cities only four years old sometimes brought $10,000. Attractive Indian lands, suitable for farming and dairying, were going on the market—some two hundred and fourteen thousand acres of Wea holdings, and some two hundred and forty-five thousand acres of the Delaware Trust property. The Neosho Valley lands, still distant from any market but pronounced by some the best in the Territory, had become preemptible, and settlers were turning eagerly to them. Everywhere, with prices rising, money seemed easily made. Senator Bigler of Pennsylvania had a partner in Fort Scott who beat the big drum with the ardor characteristic of his kind. Invest! invest! was his cry—by which he, like others, meant speculate. "I wish you would hunt up *money*," he exhorted Bigler. "It is sad to see so many chances—fortunes—passing into other hands because I need the 'stinko.' There will be a glorious opportunity here to get timber lands etc. with warrants if you could make arrangements with Drexel, Clark & Co., or some of the Washington City men. Timber lands here will be worth from $20 to $100 in a few years." One of his friends had purchased for $650 a quarter-section claim on which stood timber worth $16,000. This partner was interested in town lots, and had bought the principal Fort Scott hotel; in railroad building, for he thought the city would become the principal railway center of southwestern Missouri and northwestern Arkansas; in banking, for money could be lent at high rates;

29 Leavenworth correspondence, N. Y. *Evening Post*, dated March 29, 1857; M. J. Parrott et al., *Kansas*, 1856.

in furs and buffalo skins, which he got from the Indians in winter; and in mining, for he shipped Fort Scott coal to Westport at 35–45 cents a bushel.[30] Kansas was alive with such eager, pushing men.

As the boom grew, only a few observers saw the true facts. One was shrewd Amos A. Lawrence, who wrote "Governor" Robinson that spring: "There must be a collapse in the land speculation all over the West. Now is the time to sell a large half and lend the money to those who think differently." [31]

Most newcomers, however, were hard-working farmers, craftsmen, and merchants, vigorous, primed for hardship, and determined to establish prosperous homes. They meant business, even if many were greenhorns. The cost of settlement staggered poor men. To break the raw prairie cost $2.50 an acre; lumber for houses was $20 a thousand feet; fencing was often needed to keep out cattle, and that meant posts and rails; wells had to be dug down from twenty to fifty feet to reach water. Tools, horses or oxen, seed, all cost money.[32] Stoves were landed at Leavenworth and Kansas City in hundred- or two-hundred-lot consignments. Already one distinctive feature of the Kansas landscape was appearing— the windmill. Winter or summer, the plains nearly always had a breeze or a gale, and windmills were advertised to furnish from one to a hundred horsepower in a moderate wind.[33] The bright hope of most arrivals was that a single good crop year would pay for the initial investment.

The freesoil ascendency in this Great Migration to Kansas (not unlike the Great Migration of Puritan days to Massachusetts) was marked. The correspondent of the New York *Evening Post* thought that at least nine-tenths of the

30 G. A. Crawford, June-August, 1857; Bigler Papers. One of Thomas Ewing's sons was in Leavenworth when the sales in the spring of 1857 began. These sales, he writes, "attracted speculators and settlers by thousands from all parts of the Union. All the Indian reservations had been broken up and divided into sections and subdivisions of sections down to forty acres. The treaties solemnly promised the Indians that the lands would be sold at auction to the highest bidders for cash and the entire net proceeds should be placed to the credit of the tribes respectively. But the doctrine of squatter sovereignty had not been taught to the white settlers in vain. They organized in settlers' societies to secure the several selections at the appraised values; and to prevent speculators from forcing up prices on them at the public auction sales. The Indians protested and appealed to Commissioner Manypenny, a man of ability and courage who assured them that every acre of their lands should go to the highest bidder." Regular army troops were present, with cannon shotted and primed. So were a host of speculators loaded down with money. So were a thousand squatters armed to the teeth. Norman Eddy, the Federal Land Agent, appeared at ten, and announced that the first bidder would be expected to bid the appraised price, and that higher bids would then be received from others. The first quarter section was called. The settlers' representative then announced that John Doe was settled on that tract and that he bid the appraised price. As the auctioneers called for other bids, the squatters, glowering at the speculators, significantly fingered their revolvers. No bid came. "So the sale went on—one bidder to each quarter-section, and he the settler; and then the indignant and despairing speculators left the scene." Unsigned, undated memorandum in Ewing Papers, Vol. XI.

31 May 16, 1857; Robinson Papers, Univ. of Kansas.

32 Atchison letter in Warsaw, Illinois, *Bulletin*, August 4, 1859.

33 Lawrence *Herald of Freedom*, January-August, 1857.

spring settlers were from the free States; the correspondent of the Missouri *Democrat* said almost all; and the proslavery correspondent of the Missouri *Republican* put the proportion at fifteen freesoil emigrants to one slavery man. All observers agreed that they were a superior body, with a higher average of brains, character, and physical strength than could be found in old communities.[34] It was significant that the "border ruffians" had given up all attempt to interfere with the flow of population. For one reason, the very numbers of the freesoil men compelled respect. For another, the partial stoppage of Missouri River traffic in 1856 had cost various interests large sums, the steamboat owners alone reckoning that they had lost half a million; and western Missouri, suffering from a shortage of money, hoped for friendly relations with Kansas buyers of flour, meat, and other goods.[35]

Most proslavery men on the spot now knew that they had lost all hope of a preponderant voice in Kansas affairs. Ex-Senator Atchison wrote a significant letter this spring to the mayor of Columbia, S. C. Some of our Southern friends in Kansas have become apathetic and despondent, he wrote, while others have turned their attention to money-making. "I would therefore suggest that no more money be raised in South Carolina. The people of that State have been liberal above all others of the Southern States. Yet I fear that the North has and will raise and expend in Kansas, to effect their unholy purposes, ten dollars where we can raise one." [36] Actually subsidized emigration was but a small part of the whole. The National Kansas Committee, meeting early in the year in New York, had disclosed receipts of about $90,000 since the previous June, but it had sent out only about two thousand emigrants. Its chief usefulness had been in getting transportation rates reduced, selling low-cost tickets (fares from the eastern seaboard to Kansas City were now only $20–$25), and furnishing food and clothing to needy settlers. At the South, Captain A. B. Biland of Alabama was leading a new company to the Territory.[37] It was the volunteer efflux from the free States, spontaneous and unorganized, the same human torrent that had already given Iowa half a million people, that was determining the future character of the land.

Representative William Barksdale of Mississippi, sadly admitting to a British tourist that Kansas would probably be a free State, put his finger on one reason. While true settlers poured out from the North with their families, the South sent young adventurers who went for the frolic, and came home when they got tired. Men who wanted to take their slaves to new lands kept farther south. From Missouri itself a considerable migration of men, slaves, and cattle

34 Leavenworth correspondence, N. Y. *Evening Post*, dated March 29, 1857; Parker, *Kansas and Nebraska Handbook, 1857–58.*
35 Lawrence *Herald of Freedom*, January 10, 24, February 21, 1857.
36 Columbia *Times* quoted in *National Intelligencer*, July 7, 1857.
37 *Alabama Journal*, April 11, 1857.

was reported, but it was moving into Arkansas and Texas.[38] One token of the times was the sale of that stalwart proslavery journal, the Atchison (Kansas) *Squatter Sovereign*, to men who made it an antislavery newspaper. Of eighteen weekly sheets published in Kansas in the summer of 1857, thirteen were free-soil, and some of the others neutral.[39]

Yet the new freesoil immigration sweeping into Kansas all spring and summer would have no voice, under the law, in determining the State constitution. That privilege was confined to the voters registered in March. And unfair as this arrangement was, the proslavery element had stolen other advantages. The lands of the Shawnee Reserve were not yet legally open, but early in the year an association of men from Jackson County, Missouri, invaded them and pre-empted large tracts. They were divided among some two thousand seven hundred claimants, many of whom merely drove stakes and laid down four logs, while others left no token of ownership at all. Most of these bogus settlers at once went home, but many made a special return trip for the census and the election of delegates. Week by week, as summer came on, evidence accumulated of the gross injustices which had accompanied the census-taking, carried out by sheriffs' deputies paid four dollars a day. It was easy to understand why Calhoun, Maclean, and Lecompte wanted no fair referendum on the constitution. The rigged convention, arbitrarily foisting its handiwork on the people, represented the last hope of making Kansas a slave State.

[III]

The election of the convention took place on June 15 amid the scoffs and jeers of such antislavery citizens as took time from field and shop to look up. A little more whiskey-drinking than usual in Lecompton, a few more Missourians than ordinary riding into boundary-towns—these were the only signs of activity.[40] At least half of the antislavery men could not vote, and most of the

---

38 London *Daily News*, January 24, 1857; *National Intelligencer*, July 9, 1857. Yet some Southern spokesmen maintained their confidence. "That Kansas will be a slave State is now near to a settled question," declared Henry Clay Pate, publisher of the Westport, Mo., *Star of Empire*. He expected the coming Lecompton convention to deliver a slave State constitution. Then the South would say, "Let Kansas come in, and we shall not keep Minnesota out." Some men feared that even if admitted as a slave State, it would not remain so long. But, declared Pate, "the history of slavery in the United States goes to show that it is not so easily uprooted." Quoted in *Kanzas News*, June 6, 1857.
39 One slavery center after another, in fact, was either dying or being conquered. Douglas and Benicia had perished; Tecumseh had been taken over by freesoilers; and now many believed that Lecompton itself contained a majority of free State men. Lawrence *Herald of Freedom*, May 9, 1857.
40 Lawrence *Republican*, June 19, 1857; St. Louis *Democrat*, June 22, 1857. The free State men had issued an address to the nation (*National Intelligencer*, May 7) saying they would take no part because thousands of freesoil men had been disenfranchised, and other frauds committed.

remainder would not. They felt abundantly justified in boycotting an election so unfair. Though there were probably twenty thousand adult males in Kansas, only nine thousand two hundred and fifty-one had been registered—and a goodly number of these were outlanders. Moreover, the delegates had been apportioned on a basis of brazen gerrymandering. Of the sixty members, the three river counties of Doniphan, Atchison, and Leavenworth, easy of access from Missouri and supposed to be strong in slavery sentiment, were given twenty-four. Johnson County, which held the Shawnee Reserve and had not fifty legal voters, was allowed three delegates. Linn, Lykins, Bourbon, and McGee counties were given ten in all. Thus eight river and border counties were allotted thirty-seven of the sixty delegates; the other thirty counties, including thickly populated freesoil areas, were granted twenty-three.[41]

As an expression of territorial opinion the election was a farce, for only about twenty-two hundred men, out of the nine thousand two hundred and fifty-one registered, cast ballots. In Douglas County, containing the town of Lawrence, only two hundred and forty votes were polled; it had been announced that a voting place would be open in the Lawrence post office, but reporters searched every nook and cranny without finding it. Leavenworth County recorded only about five hundred votes.[42] No free State candidates had been put up. But certificates were immediately issued to the sixty proslavery men; and the Calhoun faction, now showing open enmity to the governor, hailed them as fit agents of the sovereign people of Kansas.

When this election took place, the Southern press and politicians were already savagely denouncing Governor Walker for a course much too impartial to please them.[43] On what ground? He was toiling hard at his duties, inquiring into a murder at Leavenworth, visiting land sales at Paoli, and urging the whole people to join in a new territorial election in the fall. The Washington *Union*, in an editorial which Jere Black wrote, was defending him and maintaining that his advocacy of popular submission of the constitution was just and statesmanlike.[44] Why was he bitterly assailed?

He had offended Southerners when, in his inaugural, he had said that if the instrument were not submitted to the people, he believed it would be and should be rejected by Congress. What right had he to dictate to the convention? This was "intervention." What right had he to prescribe what Congress should or should not do? This was more "intervention." He had likewise outraged many Southerners when he seemed to prejudge the result. His talk of an isothermal law, his statement that the "elevated plains" and "chilling blasts" of

41 *Kanzas News*, June 6, 1857; this paper was edited by Preston B. Plumb.
42 Lawrence correspondence, June 25, in N. Y. *Weekly Tribune*, July 11, 1857.
43 N. Y. *Express*, quoted in *National Intelligencer*, June 25, 1857.
44 Washington *Union*, July 7, 1857; Black Papers.

Kansas, reducing the average temperature nearly as low as that of New England, might well make slavery impossible, was another bit of "intervention." He was taking sides. Keitt of South Carolina accused the little governor of treachery. John A. Quitman thought this a misnomer, for Walker, more Pennsylvanian than Mississippian, had never been a proslavery man. "Like most Northern politicians, he desired Kansas to come in as a 'free State.' They esteem the ascendency of the party of more importance than the rights of the South, and believe the former would be best served by Kansas coming in as a free State. When Walker was selected, I anticipated some ingenious plan to effect that object. Even the inaugural of Buchanan squinted at it. Neither of these gentlemen have deceived me." [45]

By mid-July the entire Southern Rights press had opened fire on Walker. The New Orleans *Delta* raked him as the pet and tool of the North. The Jackson *Mississippian* declared that he now stood unveiled before the outraged South, a self-convicted traitor to her constitutional rights. The Richmond *South* was equally violent. The Augusta *Constitutionalist* published a letter suggesting assassination; his conduct "makes one think of the dagger of Brutus and the axe of Cromwell." The Montgomery *Advertiser* adopted a threatening tone, saying that the Administration must repudiate the governor, or the South would turn against the Administration: "Southern hopes in Kansas shall not be easily dashed; Southern efforts in that Territory shall not be easily defeated." [46] Dozens of Southern editors took the view that Walker was trying to cheat their section in order to keep the Northern and Southern Democrats united. This was the opinion of Quitman, who expected an effort to proscribe State Rights men. "When the war opens, how many will have the courage to stand and fight?" he demanded of Keitt. "The test struggle is before us and nigh us. It will soon be seen whether we will maintain our equality, or sink into a degrading subserviency to political masters." [47]

Both the anger and fear of the South, feeding on many supposed grievances, were rising steadily. It must be remembered that, with sixteen free and fifteen slave States in the Union, Southerners saw the balance tipping heavily against them. Minnesota and Oregon must soon enter as free States. Indeed, six or seven new free States loomed on the horizon, each with two Senators and a lengthening list of Representatives; whereas Kansas was the one Territory which *might*

45 To Keitt, July 23, 1857; Quitman Papers, Univ. of N. C.
46 All quoted in Lawrence *Herald of Freedom*, July 11, 1857. Many Southerners said that they did not object to a decision by the constitutional convention to submit its work; they did not even object to seeing Kansas become a free State. But they did object to intervention by the Federal government, or the governor it appointed, to compel submission. This, they said, violated popular sovereignty even as Douglas understood it. See Mobile *Daily Register*, June 17–26, 1857.
47 Quitman to Keitt, *ut supra*.

become slave. Many believed Republicans had made a test case of Kansas, vowing that on no account must an additional slave State be admitted, anywhere, anyhow, anytime. If the South lost Kansas, it would feel that a seal had been placed on this decree. Innumerable Southerners had now been led to believe that the freesoil inundation of Kansas was a bought emigration, an influx of hirelings, an artificial maneuver which might fairly be fought by any weapon. "I will venture to say this much," fulminated Senator Mason, "that if African slavery be ultimately excluded from Kansas, it will be effected by the numerical force of organized majorities, operating against the usual laws which govern emigration, and will present a new and most instructive lesson to the Southern States." [48]

Another potent consideration was the manifest peril in which Missouri, the northwestern bastion of slavery, now stood. Early this spring an avowed emancipationist, John M. Wimer, was elected mayor of St. Louis over a proslavery candidate by a plurality of one thousand seven hundred and twenty-eight votes. The issue had been clearly stated and the result was decisive. It had long been evident that the growing German and Northern-born elements were converting St. Louis to an antislavery sentiment. For a variety of reasons—popular sensitiveness, old Southern ties, the desire of newcomers to behave tactfully, fear of isolating the city from the rest of the State—little had been done to assert a policy of doubtful strength. Now, however, the blow had been struck. For the first time in the nation's history an emancipationist party had given overt battle in a slave State and made conquest of its chief city. The lesson to hardy leaders in Wilmington, Louisville, Baltimore, western Virginia, and eastern Tennessee could not be missed. In Kansas, cried the St. Louis *Intelligencer*, "the effect will be strikingly manifest, no doubt. The Free State party will grow doubly strong in moral courage, and the proslavery party must cringe under such an 'attack from the rear.' " [49]

But most of all, the election result seemed to threaten the loss of Missouri to slavery men. A freesoil Whig, James S. Rollins, was entering the lists this summer for governor. He stood a good chance to win. If Kansas, Iowa, and Illinois surrounded Missouri on three sides by free soil, if St. Louis became a freesoil fortress, and if more Germans and Yankees rolled in, how long would the State stand firm? For immediate abolition, to be sure, there was little sentiment. But this was largely because many believed with Edward Bates that, since force of circumstances must soon extinguish slavery in the State, it was unwise to force the pace.

Many Southerners were in a mood of defiance—they had always meant to gain Kansas, and they would not be cheated of it; many were in a mood of

---

48 Letter in Richmond *South,* quoted in N. Y. *Weekly Tribune,* August 8, 1857.
49 St. Louis *Intelligencer,* April 8, 1857.

apprehension—the free States were growing too strong; many were in a mood of recklessness—Buchanan's victory and the Dred Scott decision had made them arrogant. Disunionists had sown their seed broadcast in the campaign of 1856, and it had taken root. An ebullition of wrath, verging on hysteria, swept

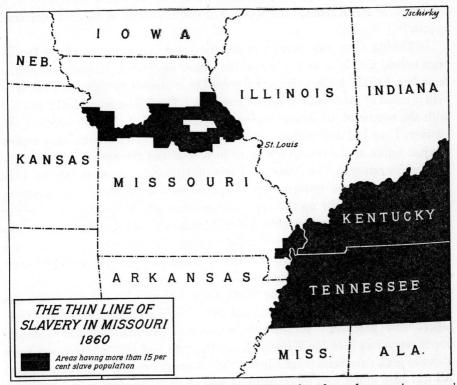

This will help explain why slaveholders in Missouri and southerners in general worried over the situation in Kansas. (Kentucky and Tennessee are colored black without reference to the density of slave population.)

the Lower South in particular as editors pictured Walker handing Kansas over to the abolitionists. The South Carolina *Times* agreed with the New Orleans *Crescent* that the governor was "probably the most unscrupulous, heartless, and unprincipled man in the United States."

Georgia was the first State to speak. Her Democratic convention, meeting at Milledgeville late in June, showed a radical temper, nominating Joseph E. Brown, Southern Rights lawyer and judge, for governor. Turning to Kansas, the members emphatically condemned Walker's course. They stigmatized the popular-submission section of his inaugural as "a presumptuous interference in matters over which he has no control"; declared his isothermal doctrine "a gross departure from the principles of non-intervention and neutrality"; and demanded that Buchanan recall him. Even the moderate Alexander H. Stephens was filled with indignation. Toombs felt the same. Walker was not expected to give advice, he wrote; much less to utter his insolent and arrogant threat that unless Kansas carried out *his* will, Congress would not admit the State. "It is this which so much aroused the South. The condemnation of him is as universal as just."

In Florida, Governor Perry was declaring that, unless the Northern Democrats upheld the rights of the South, the Union was ended. Mississippi took the same line. Of the leaders there, Jefferson Davis aspired to Calhoun's baton as field marshal of the Southern Rights host, while Jacob Thompson hated Walker with the rancor of his inveterate feud. Extremists ruled the Democratic Convention. They laid their malison on Walker's conduct as a discrimination against the just rights of the proslavery party in Kansas and the nation, and they demanded his removal. The American Party of Mississippi, meeting July 13, likewise condemned the governor in savage terms. Forthwith all the Southern Rights journals caught up the cry: Walker must go. As early as July 11 the New York *Evening Post* concluded that Buchanan would find the cotton kingdom implacable against him unless he recalled the governor. Not since the nation began, wrote R. B. Rhett, had any question brought the South into more complete union than Walker's course.[50]

The sudden bellicosity of the South amazed those who did not realize the sad fraying of slaveholders' nerves, the intensity of their conviction that free-soilers were practically abolitionists and mortal enemies, and the passionate hopes many had held for Kansas. (Even Stephens had said in 1855 they were about to get a slave State there.) It was their Brenner Pass, their Alsace-Lorraine. All had been going well there. Why should Walker interfere so suddenly and wantonly to their disadvantage?

Albert Gallatin Brown told a crowd on July 4 that if Buchanan suffered Walker to remain governor, the South would rise up against the President as false to the principles of the Nebraska Act. Judge T. W. Thomas, a Georgia lawyer-editor, seized his pen the moment he read Walker's inaugural. "If the document I have seen is genuine," he wrote Stephens, "it is clear that Buchanan has turned traitor." A crisis was upon them; "if Kansas is admitted as a free State we are ruined"; and unless the governor was dismissed within a month, they must repudiate the Administration. Toombs declared that ruin faced the government. It was the concern of the delegates alone whether the convention submitted its work to popular vote. His threat of hostile action if no referendum

50 N. Y. *Evening Post*, July 11; *National Intelligencer*, July 28, 1857; Toombs to W. M. Burnell, July 11, 1857, Toombs Papers, LC; Stephens in Augusta *Constitutionalist*, August 18, 1858.

were permitted should have emphatic answer: "The convention ought never under any circumstances to comply with his demand that it be submitted to all the people who happen to be in Kansas when the ratification takes place, and I trust they will give him a chance to carry out his threat and join the freesoil traitors." [51]

For Charleston fire-eaters the *Mercury* was declaring that Buchanan, Walker, and all the national spoilsmen might go to perdition together. In Virginia the Hunter faction caught up the agitation as a possible means of crushing Buchanan's friends Wise and Floyd, using Pryor's Richmond *South* as an organ. Their splenetic attacks on Walker were part of an effort to align the Old Dominion with the Lower South. The Jackson *Mississippian* and New Orleans *Delta* were vitriolic. That summer the Springs, always a favorite resort of irritable aristocrats, hummed with execrations of the Administration. George Sanders's son, prowling about White Sulphur, concluded that the States of Georgia, Alabama, Mississippi, and Virginia were in open arms against Walker—and his letter went to Buchanan's desk. H. W. Pickens at the same resort found sentiment insistent that Walker must be recalled, or at any rate that the Administration must disavow his utterances; otherwise the South would believe that he had been sent out to overawe the convention just as President Taylor had sent T. B. King to California to help mold its constitution. He wrote Buchanan warningly:

Since my arrival here I have seen and conversed with gentlemen from all parts of the South and West, not politicians only but planters and private gentlemen, and I find there is universal condemnation of Gov. Walker's extra-official conduct and speeches. I thought at first some weeks ago the extreme feeling against him was perhaps more stimulated by the partisan press than otherwise, but I now think there is a settled and deep feeling of disappointment and distress. It is a great mistake to suppose that the democracy of Virginia even sustains him, and the feeling in Georgia and Mississippi is running into excitement against the Administration too. . . .

I am sure that no moderation or conciliation on your part will ever appease your opponents of the free soil party or black Republicans of the non-slaveholding States. However much they may appear to acquiesce in your course, whatever it may be, they in reality intend war to the knife. With the loss of sympathy in the South your Administration would lose half its moral power to resist them and to mould conservative measures, so essential to save the Constitution, and preserve the real power and integrity of the Democratic Party for the future! [52]

---

[51] N. Y. *Weekly Tribune*, August 1, 1857; *Toombs, Stephens, Cobb Correspondence*, 400–404.

[52] Pickens to Buchanan, August 5, 1857; Buchanan Papers. See the Richmond *South*, July 28, 1857, for an excoriation of Walker.

The President's intimate friend Slidell, too, lounging away some August days at the Virginia Springs, found their Southern habitués unanimously castigating Walker, and he thought they took it for granted that Buchanan equally disapproved of the governor's foolish speeches and was only biding his time to reveal his condemnation. Slidell intimated, in a letter to the President, that he shared this view of Buchanan's duty.

[IV]

To a strong Executive the situation would have presented few difficulties, but to so weak a man as Buchanan it offered a cruel dilemma. On the one side he had to think of his recent pleas to Walker to go to Kansas, his pledge of support, and his written assurance that "the institutions of Kansas must be established by the votes of the people," and that when the constitution was submitted "they must be protected in the exercise of their right of voting for or against that instrument." He had to think of the fact that Governors Reeder and Geary had been broken because they stood up against what they deemed outrageous proslavery frauds and threats, and that it would produce the most painful impression if Walker were broken for the same reason. He had to think of Cass, Douglas, and the uneasy Northern Democrats. On the other side, he had to think of the pressure from the Southern majority in his Directory, from Slidell, Davis, and other Senators, and from the State conventions. He had to think of the peril to his legislative program. Above all, he had to think of threats of Southern secession.

Senator Bigler, who could speak with authority, for he had lately returned from a visit to all the principal towns of Kansas, exhibited unusual zeal—even impassioned feeling, the more impressive because he was a phlegmatic man—in trying to stiffen the President's backbone. The bad temper of the South, he assured Buchanan, sprang from a misunderstanding of the real state of Kansas parties. All probability of Kansas becoming a slave State had long since vanished; the leading proslavery men from St. Louis to Leavenworth had confessed as much; even Stringfellow, Whitfield, Jones, and others once so active for Kansas slavery now admitted that they did not have one-third the votes. It would be outrageous, declared Bigler, to let two thousand out of twenty thousand or twenty-four thousand voters make a constitution. The real question on which the South should fix attention was whether Kansas should come in as a Democratic or a Republican State. "Let Gov. Walker be sustained and all will be well," exhorted Bigler.[53]

At first Buchanan, while maintaining a Delphic silence in public, seemed

53　Senator Bigler to Buchanan, July 9, 1857; Buchanan Papers.

inclined to take this sensible attitude. On July 12 he was still firm—at least in the letter he wrote Walker that day. He told the governor that he had read the latter's long account of the party situation to the Cabinet, and that they hoped for the best in making Kansas a Democratic State. "The point on which your own success depends is the submission of the constitution to the people of Kansas; and by the people I mean, and I have no doubt you mean, the actual bona fide residents, who have been long enough in the Territory to identify themselves with its fate." He thought three months might be a reasonable period. "On the question of submitting the constitution to the bona fide residents of Kansas, I am willing to stand or fall. It is the principle of the Kansas-Nebraska Bill, the principle of Popular Sovereignty, and the principle at the foundation of all popular government." If it were applied, all would be settled harmoniously. "The strictures of the Georgia and Mississippi conventions will then pass away and be speedily forgotten." [54] This was at almost the same time as Attorney-General Black's editorial in the *Union*, supporting Walker's demand for submission. It was about the same time that ex-Senator Henry S. Foote, the staunch Mississippi Unionist, who visited Washington full of indignation over the wild talk in Georgia, Mississippi, and South Carolina, was assured by one Cabinet member that the President would never waver. Alas, that Buchanan did not nail his colors to the White House flagpole by a few public hammerblows! [55]

For almost at once he began to waver. The consideration which counted most heavily with Buchanan was fear of Southern secession, and the wish uppermost in his mind was to end his Administration with the Union intact. Throughout his later political career he had identified himself with the South. He agreed with Southern leaders that their section stood in genuine danger and should be supported and sheltered. The threats which came from the Lower South— threats pronounced by some of his correspondents to be the beginning of a new secession movement—terrified him. During the late summer he continued to hear such warning voices as Slidell's and Reid Sanders's. He continued to get vehement letters from such Southern Rights leaders as Governor Robert G. Wickliffe of Louisiana, who tartly censured any delay in dealing with Walker.[56] He continued to see the new shibboleth "nonintervention" bandied through half the Southern press, with a growing implication that Buchanan himself was guilty of intervention if he countenanced the governor's interference with the Kansas convention. Doubtless he heard the report that Jefferson Davis had drawn up the Mississippi resolutions. How far were Davis, A. G. Brown, Pickens, Rhett, Wickliffe, and their like going in the organization of the

---

54 This letter was first published in the N. Y. *Tribune*, April 21, 1860.
55 Foote, *Casket of Reminiscences*, 114 ff.
56 August 21, 1857; Buchanan Papers.

Southern Rights men? Quitman had written Keitt that they *must* organize.[57] How far would they go toward secession?

Great new forces were at work in the South, making much of it a one-party area. In August the Democrats swept three States, Kentucky, Tennessee, and North Carolina, in which the Whigs had long been dominant, carried Missouri (though narrowly), and made a net gain of ten House seats. The opposition, whether Whig, American, or what not, seemed collapsing throughout the slavery area. Buchanan might feel more than ever that the party's whole strength lay in maintaining Southern confidence.

Above all, as his Directory moved, so moved Buchanan. From Howell Cobb's letters we can gain some knowledge of what was occurring in Cabinet circles. Cobb himself was so hopeful of Southern victory in Kansas that he at first supposed that Walker's inaugural was simply intended to make her admission as a slave State more palatable to the North. He tells us that Jere Black *wanted* Kansas to be a slave State. The Cabinet, he informs us, thought Walker a selfish opportunist, a man who, strongly backed in New York, was playing a bold game for the Presidency. He also states that the Cabinet and Buchanan had discussed the propriety of submitting the constitution, that they had agreed on this, but without any view of "affecting the result," and that they had planned no action if the convention did *not* place its work before the voters. He believed that the President did not want Walker or any other official to use his position to affect the decision on the slavery question one way or the other. Buchanan, he thought, was really indifferent to that decision, so long as it was fairly and honestly made by the people of Kansas; and this was the position of all members of the Cabinet. Cobb's writings suggest that the Directory had a rather high opinion of the convention elected on so preposterous a basis.[58]

And as the summer passed the animus of the Cabinet against Walker became marked. Jacob Thompson, who had long detested him, was affected by the angry upheaval in Mississippi, and Cobb by that in Georgia. Jere Black's position was shaped in part by his narrowly legalistic mind, which rejected everything beyond the letter of the law, and was hence quick to condemn any bold action by Walker on behalf of the law's spirit; in part by his venomous hatred of all Republicans. Ever since he had fought the Wilmot Proviso he had regarded freesoilers much like rattlesnakes. Addicted even more than Floyd to intemperance of thought and utterance, he spoke of the free State men in Kansas as "abolitionists," who had "insulted and blasphemed the laws" made by the legitimate territorial government. All adherents of Robinson and the

57 Quitman to Keitt, July 23, 1857; Quitman Papers, Univ. of N. C.
58 *Toombs, Stephens, Cobb Correspondence*, 401–408. Cobb says that one of the Northern members of the Cabinet wished to see Kansas adopt slavery, and this must have been Black, not Toucey.

Topeka legislature he regarded as rebels and even traitors. Republican critics of the Administration he dismissed as "miserable hypocrites" who resorted to "vulgar abuse and brutal vituperation," their editors penning "daily slanders" packed with "lies." [59]

The three most active, vigorous spirits in the Directory could hardly reconcile themselves to the thought of a Republican conquest of Kansas. Calhoun, Maclean, and Isaacs, in their spring visit to Washington, had consulted at great length with Cobb, Slidell, and Jacob Thompson, and it is quite probable that letters (which have since disappeared) were now exchanged. It was common talk in Kansas that the Calhoun group were urging the Administration to dismiss Walker, and it was to Cobb and Thompson that they would naturally write.[60]

When, in mid-July, Walker fell into a controversy with the people of Lawrence, Cabinet feeling against him was plainly manifested. The dispute concerned an independent municipal government which a minority of voters, drawing up their own charter, had rashly instituted. To Walker, always given to excitement and melodrama, this attempt to organize the city in defiance of the regular territorial authorities was incipient rebellion. After issuing a proclamation against the movement and marching dragoons to a point near the town, he informed the President that he wanted a total force of two thousand men (more than twice the number on hand) to keep the peace in the Territory. At the moment Buchanan was resting at Bedford Springs, Pennsylvania. The Cabinet held two meetings, decided that no new force was necessary, and wrote the President in sharp terms about Walker's acts.

"We do not like Governor Walker's letter," declared Cass, "and I am satisfied this will be your opinion. . . . We all fear that Governor Walker is endeavoring to make a record for the future." Floyd was blunter. The Cabinet had concluded, he wrote, that the governor was alarmed by the Southern denunciation of his course, wished to retrieve lost ground, and desired to throw the blame for his "failure" upon either the Administration or the War Department. "I doubt, now, whether the investment in Gov. Walker is going to turn out very profitable, notwithstanding we all thought, and I in particular, that his mission to Kansas was to prove a perfect political California for the Administration." [61]

Walker had become such a political liability that when Buchanan returned from Bedford Springs, he found several Cabinet members ready to advocate dismissal. Jere Black in particular was in a violent frame of mind about the

59   All quotations are from Black's letters, 1857; Black Papers.
60   Lawrence correspondence, N. Y. *Weekly Tribune*, July 9, 1857.
61   Both letters July 31, 1857; Buchanan Papers. For the situation in Lawrence, see G. W. Brown, *Reminiscences of R. J. Walker*, 53–68.

whole Kansas situation. His advice to the President was to take drastic measures to crush the free State opposition to the existing territorial government. War, unfortunately, could not be levied against these traitors and murderers. But what the President could do was to arrest the ringleaders, bring them to trial, sentence them to jail, and thus force a crisis; the free State men would have to fight, with the certainty of being whipped, or give up forever.[62] This was dangerous counsel which Buchanan was too wise to accept, and which nobody heard about. It showed that the Attorney-General wanted the freesoil organization of Kansas smashed, and was not at all queasy about the means so long as they had a veneer of legality.

Ex-Senator Foote had meanwhile gone to Memphis, Jackson, and other Southern cities to speak in favor of what he thought was the Administration policy in Kansas. When he returned to Washington at the end of summer he got one of the shocks of his life. He found that Buchanan had "already become thoroughly panic-stricken." The firm policy had been abandoned.[63]

[V]

While the cotton States thus boiled with excitement, the hour for the constitutional convention was approaching. No man in Kansas or Washington knew whether Calhoun and his associates would yield to Walker's demand, or force a constitution on an unwilling people without a vote.

The Democratic "State" convention, which had met in Lecompton in July, had leaned strongly toward popular submission of the instrument. Amid tumultuous cheering, it rejected a resolution pledging support of the constitution even if *not* laid before the voters; and the correspondent of the St. Louis *Republican* thought that this made a referendum certain. The delegates-elect to the constitutional convention talked of an instrument modeled loosely on one of the Southern constitutions, with a section sanctioning continued ownership of

---

62 See Black's draft letter, proposed instructions to Walker, August 1, 1857; Buchanan Papers.

63 Foote, *Casket of Reminiscences*, 114 ff. In Memphis, writes Foote, his earnest plea to a large crowd to support Buchanan in this perilous conjuncture had elicited many evidences of public approval. He sent Buchanan newspapers showing what a cordial reception he had met. In Jackson he answered Senators Davis and Brown, who had just denounced Buchanan unmercifully; and again he obtained many testimonials of approval of the President and his supposed policy. All the greater was his astonishment to find that the President had abruptly surrendered. "The howlings of the bulldog of secession had fairly frightened him out of his wits, and he ingloriously resolved to yield without resistance to the decrial and villification to which he had been so acrimoniously subjected." Foote became deeply alarmed. "I knew well that a scheme for the destruction of the Union had been long on foot in the South. I knew quite as well that the leaders of the movement were only waiting for the enfeebling of the Democratic Party in the North, and the general triumph of Free-soilism as a consequence thereof, to alarm the whole South into acquiescence in their policy." See also D. Harmon, "Buchanan's Betrayal of Governor Walker," *Pa. Mag. of Hist.*, 1929, 51 ff.

the two hundred-odd slaves in the Territory, but forbidding the entry of more negroes whether free or slave. They talked, too, of providing for rigid execution of the Fugitive Slave Law, for the right of appeal to the Supreme Court in all constitutional cases, and for strict oaths of allegiance to the Federal Constitution by all officers. This would please the South. According to the *Republican* correspondent, the constitution would probably not be submitted entire to popular vote, but the section authorizing or forbidding the future introduction of slaves would be presented separately. Governor Walker, however, wrote Cass in midsummer that submission of any type was still uncertain.[64]

The nation's eyes were upon the delegates when they met at Lecompton on September 7 for a brief preliminary session. John Calhoun, who was elected president, made a speech notable for its avoidance of any explicit statement on the vital issue. They must present to Congress, he said, a constitution so framed and endorsed that they could not merely petition for admission, but demand it. Committees were appointed to draft various sections of the constitution, and the delegates adjourned until October 19.

Before that date arrived, a new demonstration of the recklessness of the proslavery leaders in Kansas startled the North. The very important election to choose a new legislature (and a Congressional Delegate) was held on October 5 and 6. Everyone expected this election, coming just as it did before the final convention session, to be decisive of the slavery issue. Accepting Walker's promise of a fair poll and eager to prove their overwhelming strength, the free State voters, both Democratic and Republican, turned out en masse. With a dismal rain to damp excitable men, and with Federal troops in troublesome precincts, the day passed with nothing worse than a few fistfights.[65] Returns came in slowly over the muddy roads. When all were counted, they showed an amazing outcome: the Republican candidate for Delegate had won by a majority exceeding four thousand, but the legislature was apparently proslavery. Careful inspection revealed that McGee County, in the extreme southeastern portion of Kansas, made up of Cherokee Indian lands not yet open to preemption and hence one of the most sparsely settled of all the counties, containing fewer than a hundred qualified voters, had returned 1,266 proslavery ballots! Still more remarkable was the showing of Johnson County, where the six-building hamlet of Oxford on the Missouri line reported 1,628 votes! Walker and Stanton visited both areas, made certain of the impudent frauds committed, and threw out the returns. If their action stood, the legislature would have a clear free State majority.[66]

64 July 15, 1857; Cass Papers. See also full Walker-Cass correspondence in *Kansas Hist. Colls.*, V, 321 ff.

65 N. Y. *Weekly Tribune*, October 17, 1857.

66 F. P. Stanton's "Letter to the People of the United States," January 29, 1859. Walker's proclamation is in *Kansas Hist. Colls.*, V, 403.

In two prompt and forcible proclamations, Walker presented full evidence of the illegalities, and pointed out that a victory gained by frauds so monstrous would be more fatal to the Democratic Party than any defeat. On his return from Oxford he halted at Lawrence, and, taking out of his portfolio a large roll of paper, told the crowd that he would exhibit a curiosity. He then unrolled the Oxford returns, consisting of sixteen hundred and one names all in the same handwriting on a roll fifty-four feet long, nearly fifteen hundred of them copied in consecutive order from Williams's Cincinnati Directory.[67]

Stanton and Walker felt a burning resentment. They had been put in the position of having to expose their whilom political associates, or of rendering themselves accomplices in a disgraceful trick. They had been compelled to face a revival of the dangerous party excitement of former days—for the freesoilers quivered with anger. They saw their hope of collecting the moderate groups into a dominant free State Democratic Party struck down, and hosts of voters so outraged that they would turn their faces toward the Republican fold. The governor took care to explain the validity of his action. "In rejecting these papers, *we do not go behind the returns*, because no legal or valid returns were made." [68]

Once more the fat was in the fire, which blazed up furiously. When Walker and Stanton took their decisive action, they knew that a storm would ensue. The immediate sequel was a furious mass meeting of proslavery Democrats, a mandamus (happily futile) from Judge Cato, and an effort by the hotheaded Sheriff S. J. Jones of Douglas County to obtain his legislative credentials by threat of violence. The governor's chagrin over the death of his hopeful plan for a strong "middle party" was intense. That had been the principal object of his mission, and his whole policy since his inaugural address had been designed to promote it. But he was a man of spirit, and by now was utterly sick of the machinations of the proslavery extremists. When he heard of Jones's gross outrage on the law, he caught up a pistol, bade Stanton follow him to beard the "Bengal tigers," and, visiting the saloons and gaming dens scattered along Lecompton's single straggling street, denounced the border ruffians there with all the expletives he had learned on the Mississippi frontier.

In Washington, Southern leaders were filled with consternation and anger. There and in Kansas, a long wrangle over returns, certificates, and forgeries, with control of the legislature in the balance, loomed up. The episode heightened sectional feeling throughout the nation. Walker wrote that he did not doubt that this disreputable assault on honest government would meet the reprehension of honest men of all parties. This was certainly true of the North, where repre-

67 *National Intelligencer*, November 5, 1857.
68 Proceedings, October 22, 1857; *National Intelligencer*, November 5, 1857.

hension was a mild word for the condemnation loudly expressed. In much of the South, however, a different response was visible. Multitudes, swayed by the prevalent excitement, concluded that Walker was again acting unfairly, and the clamor for his recall was simply accentuated.

Meanwhile, the final session of the Lecompton convention was beginning. As delegates gathered for it, a peremptory warning came from the great voice of the Democratic Northwest. Stephen A. Douglas had been profoundly affected by the emphatic free State vote. He knew well that if chicanery thwarted the will of the true residents of Kansas, he and his party were lost in Illinois, while the future of the Democracy throughout the North would be ruined. Speaking through the Chicago *Times*, he declared that the late Kansas election proved that the voters wanted a freesoil State; "that nothing less than a constitution which shall exclude and prohibit slavery will be accepted by the people of this Territory." In terms read as an ultimatum throughout the land (for half the press republished the editorial),[69] the Douglas organ went on:

What that Convention will do or what it will not do we have not the means of knowing. But we know that any attempt to force a pro-slavery constitution upon the people without an opportunity of voting it down at the polls will be regarded, after the recent expression of sentiment, as so decidedly unjust, oppressive, and unworthy of a free people, that the people of the United States will not sanction it. It would add thousands to the vote of the Republican party in every State of the Union. . . .

As Kansas must be a free State, even those persons in the Territory who are known as pro-slavery men must recognize in the late election a decision which must not be slighted or put at defiance. To that expression of the popular will there should be a graceful, if not a cheerful submission. Kansas is to be a free State. That fact being ascertained, let the Convention frame a constitution to suit her best interests, upon all other questions, and let *the prohibition of slavery be put into it*, clearly and without quibble, plainly, without disguise, explicitly, broadly, and firmly. Let the Convention then submit that constitution to the people.

But we have outrun part of our story. While the political skies were growing stormier, those of the financial and commercial world had also suddenly darkened.

69 Quoted in *National Intelligencer*, October 22, 1857.

7

Panic and Recovery

ON THE morning of August 24, 1857, the financial community of New York was horrified by the announcement of president Charles Stetson that his city branch of the Ohio Life Insurance & Trust Company had suspended payments. Men quickly learned that the house, which did a heavy business in western investments, had liabilities of from five to seven millions—and that its assets had been largely embezzled by the cashier. The economic situation had been uneasy. A panic now struck, sudden and devastating as a tornado. Stocks fell to incredible levels; commodity prices sank; bankruptcy followed bankruptcy.

This panic of 1857 ranks among the lesser financial convulsions of our history. Yet it may be doubted whether any other, in its implications and consequences, was so fateful. The most important of its results were psychological, and were felt during the next three years throughout both North and South. The eve of the panic had seen the North striding toward almost irresistible strength. Railroads were being hammered down, factories were rising, new cities were springing up, old cities were doubling in size. While immigration streamed in through the ports, British, Dutch, and German capital was being freely invested. The morrow of the panic saw railroad building stopped, factory doors locked, blast furnaces cold, and immigration almost paralyzed. The Northern giant had been brought to his knees—he was but a Goliath after all, and the pebble of a few bank failures had almost slain him. It was now the agricultural South, relatively but by no means absolutely unharmed, which appeared the stronger. How profound an effect this seeming revelation had upon the Southern leaders was quickly made evident in pamphlets, newspaper articles, and political speeches.[1]

[I]

The roots of the panic ran deep into the period of expansion and prosperity which had opened in 1846–47 with the repeal of the British Corn Laws, the

[1] Cotton prices of eleven and twelve cents or better, which had softened the discontent of the cotton kingdom in 1850, accentuated Southern self-confidence after 1856.

victories in Mexico, and the discovery of California gold. Already the operation of the business cycle was partially understood. The *National Intelligencer* quoted an English economist on the periodic oscillation: "First quiescence, next improvement, then growing confidence, then prosperity, then excitement, then overtrading, then revulsion—followed in turn by pressure, stagnation, and distress, until the equilibrium of quiescence is again attained." [2] All these phenomena, in a long rising and falling curve, could be found in the exuberant era of the eighteen-fifties. Happily, the panic (the only one in our nineteenth-century history on a currency of approximately specie value) never struck deep into the productive powers of the nation.

The ten-year boom, beginning with the Corn Law repeal and our own liberal Walker Tariff of 1846, had gained impetus when the Irish potato famine of 1846–47 and the continental revolutions of 1848 had started heavy waves of emigration to America. The growing web of railroads in both America and Europe stimulated production and commerce. Steam navigation on ocean, lake, and river was rapidly increasing. The broad new conquests in the Southwest fed a spirit of confidence. When gold was discovered in California and Australia, small armies of adventurous men migrated to both lands, new cities arose, a speculative export trade to San Francisco and Sydney developed, and in return large quantities of the yellow metal flowed into the world's reservoirs of capital. New credit institutions to help handle the transfer of capital sprang up in all the Western nations. The St. Louis *Prices Current*, in its review of the year 1851, remarked upon the way in which California bullion and the multiplication of new banks in the North had made money and credit abundant. "Loans and banking facilities were obtained readily. The bankers and banking institutions were anxious to do business and make money." So rapid was the expansion of banks and banking operations, in fact, that in 1848–56 the credit resources of the country (in banknotes, loans, and deposits combined) rose from $538,000,000 to $1,042,000,000.[3]

California gold for a time seemed an Aladdin's lamp with which Columbia could make any coveted object her own. The new State, according to the Secretary of the Treasury in 1852, was producing at least seventy-five and probably one hundred millions annually, and the government had warrant for believing that this total would not diminish for many years to come. His estimate proved exaggerated. The five-year product for the first half of the eighteen-fifties was slightly under $300,000,000, while for the second half it was about $250,000,000. Even this output, however, then seemed immense. It inspired Americans with dreams of vast national wealth, and led multitudes to

2 *National Intelligencer*, October 22, 1857.
3 Cochran and Miller, *Age of Enterprise*, 82, 83.

believe that the currency system possessed such a strong metallic basis that it could not be seriously shaken. These notions were quite erroneous. The fact was that a large part of the gold was immediately exported to meet the unfavorable balance of trade, and more than the whole of it would have been required for that purpose had it not been for the sale of many million dollars' worth of railroad and other securities in Europe. Such large issues of State bonds were marketed overseas that the Treasury, replying to a Senate inquiry, estimated that on June 30, 1853, about $73,000,000 in State obligations was held by foreigners. Other estimates ran much higher; Winslow, Lanier & Co. of New York placed the true figure at more than $110,000,000.[4] By 1857, about $400,-000,000 in American securities of all types were held in Europe.[5]

The United States, in short, from 1850 to 1857 was laying railroads, opening factories and mines, and buying large quantities of manufactured staples and luxuries by the combined export of gold, farm products, and securities. The balance of trade was unfavorable in 1850, when the country's total exports, including specie, were $151,898,000, well below the total imports of $178,-138,000. The next year imports and exports almost balanced. The margin was slightly unfavorable in 1852, and very heavily so in 1853 and 1854.[6] Then in 1855 and 1856, thanks to the Crimean War, it became favorable again. If specie is excluded, however, the balance of trade was unfavorable in every year.[7] Borrowing abroad on stocks and bonds met the deficiency, and of course built up a huge mortgage on the future production of the country.

The sharp check administered to the boom in 1854 had turned out to be temporary and unimportant. With banks closing and stocks cascading, the recession was bad enough for a few months. Many men who owed money suffered severely. Horace Greeley, for example, lost good Pennsylvania lands which had cost him $5,000 because he was unable to raise one-tenth that amount.[8] The European demand for cotton and foodstuffs, however, remained high, railroad earnings on the main trunk lines were much better than in the previous autumn, and the steady supply of four or five millions a month in California gold furnished a basis for bank credit.[9] It soon became evident, too, that the Crimean War would heighten, not lessen, American prosperity. Throughout 1855–56, therefore, the flush times continued. Orders for grain, livestock, textiles, and metals rolled in from embattled France and Britain, filling the pockets of farmers, planters, and mineowners. Under rolling factory smoke, wages and profits rose.

4 *National Intelligencer*, March 4, 1854.
5 W. G. Sumner in *First Century of the Republic*, 254.
6 *Statistical Abstract*; E. R. Johnson et al., *Commerce of the U. S.*
7 See table in Van Vleck, *Panic of 1857*, 9.
8 James Harrison Wilson, *Dana*, 128.
9 *Journal of Commerce*, quoted in *National Intelligencer*, November 23, 1854.

As prices of foodstuffs and cotton touched high levels, speculation in land naturally increased. The Graduation Act of 1854, reducing the charge for some classes of unclaimed lands as low as twelve and a half cents an acre, helped persuade investors to buy large tracts. The Kansas-Nebraska Act, of course, lent its impetus to western settlement and speculation. The great land boom reached its peak in 1855–56, the government in each of these years parting with title to more than seventeen million acres, an area absolutely unprecedented. While the greater part of this was sold for cash, a good deal was purchased with military bounty and other warrants, which anybody could buy up cheaply.[10] As colonizers swept westward by train and steamboat, town-planners unrolled more gorgeously imaginative maps and sold wilder dreams of the future. Illinois, Iowa, Kansas, and Minnesota positively swarmed with promoters, who laid out more cities than already existed in the eastern and middle States, and sold "choice locations" at prices higher than good lots brought in Boston, Philadelphia, or Cleveland. By June 30, 1857, the outstanding railroad bonds totaled about $400,000,000 in face value, and the stocks about $500,-000,000. How much had been sunk in land was anybody's guess. A shrewd British observer, D. W. Mitchell, estimated that by 1857 more than $800,000,000 had been invested in idle western land and lots, held for a speculative rise, and but one-quarter paid for.[11]

At its apogee, this era of expansion, gambling, and lavish consumption of luxuries was as spectacular as all such periods are. The spend-and-splurge years under Buchanan did not differ essentially from the similar frenzies of boom-and-bust in the Jackson, Grant, and Coolidge-Hoover eras. In the North, moralists bewailed the heavy importations of diamonds, laces, silks, and fine wines. In the South, William Gregg protested against similar extravagances. "Ladies are seen dashing about the streets and watering places again with their $500 dresses and $1,500 shawls; merchants are seen pulling down princely buildings to vie with each other in the erection of stores, at an expense of three to five hundred thousand dollars; men are seen running to and fro, to find employment for money that has been borrowed at ten to fifteen percent premium; every railroad project, however visionary, may make bonds and find purchasers." [12] These were the years of Miss Flora M'Flimsey of Madison Square, who made three journeys to Paris, and on each

> Spent six consecutive weeks, without stopping,
> In one continuous round of shopping. . . .
> For bonnets, mantillas, capes, collars, and shawls;

10 The rapid disappearance of the public domain in parts of the West naturally heightened the demand for homestead legislation. In Illinois the westernmost land office, at Quincy, was closed in the summer of 1855. Cole, *Irrepressible Conflict*, 116–118.
11 Mitchell, *Ten Years in the United States*, 328.
12 "Speech in the South Carolina Legislature, 1857," pamphlet.

Dresses for breakfasts, and dinners, and balls,
Dresses to sit in, and stand in, and walk in;
Dresses to dance in, and flirt in, and talk in;
Dresses in which to do nothing at all;
Dresses for Winter, Spring, Summer, and Fall—
All of them different in color and shape,
Silk, muslin, and lace, velvet, satin, and crepe.

And yet this same Miss M'Flimsey:

The last time we met was in utter despair,
Because she had nothing whatever to wear!

These were the years of Mrs. Fitzdazzle, who did her own "expanding" in diamonds at Tiffany's, laces at Stewart's, bonnets at Ferrero's, and a summer tour at Newport: "like a watch, she ran on tick, until her husband found himself wound up." [13] They were the years in which fashion and gaiety ran riot at Saratoga, Cape May, and the Virginia Springs. They were the years of the new marble Fifth Avenue Hotel, of W. W. Corcoran's resplendent entertainments in Washington, of the "nabob turnouts" of Commodore Vanderbilt, Robert Bonner, the Grinnells, and other lovers of fast trotters, of the height of antebellum luxury in Charleston and New Orleans. They were the years in which Emerson expressed a fear that the swift increase of great fortunes might "upset the balance of men, and establish a new, universal monarchy more tyrannical than Babylon or Rome." [14]

[II]

No feature of the boom had excited more comment than the novel vogue of speculation in securities. Stock-gambling, scolded the *National Intelligencer*, has grown to "an incredible extent" in the chief cities; "the parties to it are called the Bulls and the Bears." [15] Society, grumbled the New York *Evening Post*, must comprehend the dangers of a system that throws the faro table into the shade. While numerous journals printed sharp exposures of nefarious operations of brokers,[16] the New York *Observer* defended them. The public, it argued, had an incorrect estimate of the New York Stock Exchange. "It is not a gambling-house; and although many desperately risk their all on the rise and fall of the market, yet a large part of the business is as legitimate as any other commercial transactions." [17]

13 *Belle Brittan on a Tour* (Anon.), 60.
14 *Journals*, V, 285, 286; and see essay "Manners" for condemnation of a moneyed aristocracy.
15 August 18, 1857. The New York Stock Exchange dated from 1817.
16 An old topic; cf. O. G. Villard, *Early History of Wall Street*.
17 N. Y. *Observer*, quoted in *National Intelligencer*, May 12, 1857.

More than sixty years old, the New York Stock Exchange still conducted its business on the "call system" of trading. Members were elected, any person who had been a stockbroker for a year, or a clerk to a broker for two years, being eligible; seventeen votes sufficed to elect, though three blackballs might exclude; and the entrance fee was but $400. Brokerage charges were strictly regulated, fictitious sales were forbidden, and brokers who could not surrender a responsible principal were held personally responsible. The members met twice daily, the quarters in 1842–54 being in the Merchants' Exchange on Wall Street, and thereafter in Beaver Street near William. Their morning session, which all were expected to attend (though many members commuted fines for absence on a yearly basis) lasted from ten-thirty to a little after noon; the afternoon session opened at two-thirty and closed at three. Each member had a regular chair, whence arose the practice of referring to a "seat" on the exchange, while at the end of the long room the officers and secretaries sat on a dais. The method used was to call the roll of stocks and bonds, the sellers naming their prices and the buyers offering bids. Transactions in bank and insurance stocks were usually sedate, but railroad shares often produced a wild hubbub. The presiding officer would call out "Erie Railroad" or "Illinois Central":

First broker, "At 41⅝, seller 3" [that is, an offer to sell]. Second broker, "I'll give 45⅝, buyer 60, for 100." Third broker, "I'll sell 100 at 41⅝; I'll sell 100 at 41½." Broker, "Done!" Second broker, "Another hundred." Fourth broker, "I'll take 'em." Second broker. "Fifty more." Fifth broker, "Here, here, done!" By this time twenty voices are going at once; "I'll give 41½ regular"; "41¼, seller 10"; "43⅜, seller 3"; "done"; "take 'em"; "sell 'em"; "seller 10, 5 up"; "fifty more"; "one hundred more"; "I'll take your lot, buyer four months." A dozen men are on their feet, their arms swinging above their heads . . . and the scene is a perfect Babel to the uninitiated.

The Vice-President has seen everybody; heard everybody; above the din has distinguished the peculiar expressions denoting the closing of sales, and has rapidly repeated them, so that the secretaries have recorded them.[18]

To John Bigelow, the sale of more than $22,000,000 worth of stock in one fortnight of 1857 seemed ample basis for an *Evening Post* editorial denouncing "A Growing Evil"—overspeculation. The mania for playing the market had attacked everybody, he wrote; lawyers, merchants, doctors, and even clergy were abandoning a safe seven percent to gamble for twenty.[19] If the speculation was deplorable, the secret manipulation of stocks by insiders was far more reprehensible. Michigan Southern in the summer of 1857, at the apex of the boom, was a bone of contention between bulls led by the Litchfields and bears captained by young Leonard Jerome. Having learned the power of the press in

18 *Ibid;* cf. J. E. Meeker, *The Work of the Stock Exchange.*
19 N. Y. *Evening Post,* August 3, 1857.

Rochester, Jerome began an attack in the *Herald* on Wall Street security prices in general and the Michigan Southern stock in particular. Exhuming old railroad reports, he found facts which undermined public confidence. He was soon joined by Bigelow, who forced an admission from the railroad that it had printed and pledged several hundred thousand dollars in shares for a bank loan, trusting to future profits for a quiet retirement of the stock.[20] The immediate drop in the value of its securities cost the Michigan Southern a loss of about half a million.[21]

Commodity speculation was equally reckless. The press in 1856 and 1857 was studded with items on fortunes quickly conquered by bold Napoleons of the market. Chicago wheat brokers who bought at $1.40 and sold at $1.85, pork dealers who secured prime mess at $16 a barrel and parted with it at $20—these men were objects of admiration so long as prices rose.[22] Guano speculations, sugar speculations, even poultry speculations enlisted thousands. By midsummer of 1857, declared the New York *Herald*, commodity prices had increased forty percent in four years. Ignoring the effects of gold production, the Crimean War, and rising population upon prices, the *Herald* laid this disastrous rise to speculation. It made a particular point of cotton. Despite an estimated American crop in 1856–57 of about three million bales, with a large carry-over in European warehouses, raw cotton had gone so high that textile interests were being crushed between excessive costs and an overladen market.[23] Within a year, declared the *Herald*, speculators had forced it up nearly forty percent, while sheetings and other goods had risen only twelve to fifteen percent.

There was manifest truth in this statement. By mid-August in 1857, before the panic began, about six thousand looms had been stopped in New England because of the high price of raw cotton and the low price of goods, and orders had been given to stop many more as fast as the yarn was exhausted. In England, meanwhile, thirty thousand looms had been halted.[24] In other fields, commodity prices remained exorbitant while finished products were falling. The British consul in Chicago thought that grain speculation had become a mania. "The great increase of the exports of cereals both in quantity and value during the years 1855, 1856, and 1857, over the aggregate of the seventeen preceding years since Chicago had become an exporting port," he wrote his government, "produced a state of prosperity which ended in speculative excitement somewhat akin to

20 *Idem*, August 12, 18, 1857.
21 Margaret Clapp, *John Bigelow*, 111 ff.; J. K. Medbury, *Men and Mysteries of Wall Street*, 174, 175.
22 *National Intelligencer*, May 14, 1857.
23 July 18, 1857; quoted in Van Vleck, 35.
24 Providence *Journal*, N. Y. *Journal of Commerce*, quoted in *National Intelligencer*, August 18, 1857.

that which existed in Australia and California during the early development of the Gold Fields." [25]

Speculative ventures in lands, railroad building, and slaves kept pace and were closely interrelated; the rise in grain, meats, and cotton, and the westward movement of the population, maintaining all three. The "negro fever" was now rife in the South. Cotton planters found that the cost of hands soared out of all proportion even to rising prices for their staple. Prices in the Lower South were rising to $1,800 and even $2,000 for prime field workers. The two possible remedies were a reopening of the African slave trade, and a utilization of cheap lands.[26] Since the former could not be attained except after prolonged agitation, if at all, planters bought lands in Arkansas, Texas, and unsettled parts of the older States with avidity. If they could only get the labor, they might pay for their holdings with one or two crops. Similarly, in the Northwest, where McCormick's reaper and other machinery made labor a minor problem, high prices for foodstuffs and meat turned prosperous farmers and immigrants into land buyers, while speculators crowded in eagerly upon their heels. The Graduation Act of 1854, reducing the price of public land in proportion to the length of time it had been fruitlessly offered for sale, played into the hands of would-be monopolists; for it placed no limit on the amount of land one purchaser might take. Some bought large areas.

The London *Economist* in the summer of 1857 predicted a money panic as a consequence of this attempt by speculators to obtain a partial monopoly of the soil.[27] Banks were ready to lend large sums on land mortgages which, grossly overvalued in boom days, collapsed utterly when the panic came.

At the height of the inflation, town lots in nascent western cities might pass through a dozen hands within sixty days, rising in price with every sale. Unbroken farm lands in the Northwest were sold and resold in great tracts, neither buyers nor sellers having precise facts about location, fertility, or transportation facilities.[28] The land speculation in Kansas, conducted with Northern money, affected national history.[29] Greeley distrusted "Governor" Robinson because he was too much a speculator; Eli Thayer's Emigrant Aid Company was half an enterprise in land speculation; and Reeder owed his downfall as governor to his

25   R. Wilkins, April 30, 1859; FO 111/216.
26   Cf. Bancroft, *Slave Trading in the Old South*, 339–364.
27   London *Economist*, July 4, 1857.
28   For three years large sums of money had been sent into the West to buy land; for a similar period great numbers of young farmers had poured westward. A rational demand for land would have kept close to ten millions of acres a year; half again as much was being sold by the government, including land warrants. When it came to town lots, the speculation was fantastic. The Cincinnati *Railroad Record* in the spring of 1857 protested against the craze. The bursting of the bubble, it warned, was at hand. Quoted in *National Intelligencer*, May 19, 1857.
29   Malin, *Legend of '56*, 177.

inability to resist a chance on land. One of Walker's first concerns on going to the Territory was to oppose the grabbing of the best tracts, especially along projected railroad routes, by greedy monopolists. By the panic, half the people East and West had a share of God's earth which they fondly hoped was rising in value by twenty to one hundred percent yearly.[30]

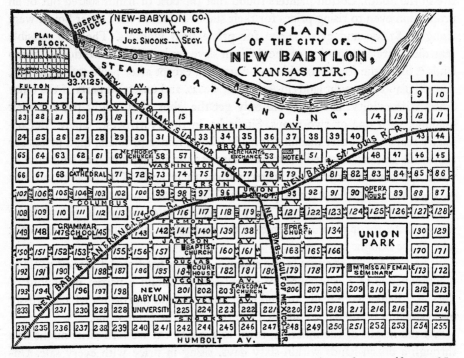

Satire on land speculation: An imaginary town promotion scheme. About 1857.

[III]

Another element in producing the crash of 1857 was the grave weakness of the country's banking system. Its excessively rapid expansion, as State after State passed general banking laws, was alone a source of peril. In 1850 the United States had eight hundred and twenty-four banks, with an authorized capital of $217,000,000; in 1855 it had one thousand three hundred and seven, with an authorized capital of $332,000,000. This rate of growth far exceeded that of the population and far outpaced industry. The aggregate immediate liabilities of the banks in 1855, according to the Secretary of the Treasury, were about three times their aggregate immediate resources: $422,500,000 to $155,000,000. Their

---

30 Mitchell, *Ten Years in the United States,* 328.

total specie resources fell short of $54,000,000.[31] The general belief that profits would be large had much to do with the rapid multiplication of banks. One writer declared in 1856 that the net annual profits on the banking capital of the land averaged at least ten percent,[32] which was far more than railroad stocks paid. As Secretary Guthrie had pointed out, the profits of banks in the large cities were derived principally from the creation of deposit accounts through loans to merchants, industrialists, and country banks; while the profits of rural banks were gained chiefly from the substitution of their banknotes for money— that is, from circulation. In Wisconsin, for example, anybody could set up a bank by investing $25,000 or more in State or Federal bonds, and depositing them with the bank controller. He received banknotes equivalent to the market value of his bonds; and these banknotes he could lend to clients. A banker who bought $25,000 worth of Missouri State bonds got seven and a half percent on them, while on his $25,000 of banknotes he got ten percent more; a total of seventeen and a half percent without any real commercial service.[33]

Most incorporated banks were prohibited by law from engaging in any business other than banking. Unincorporated banks, however, were free to employ part of their capital in outside operations, and frequently did so. They sometimes made prodigious temporary gains at the sacrifice of safety. Banks of large capital were likely to have a more prudent management than lesser institutions, for they could employ more skillful and experienced officers, and command better means of credit investigation. Yet even large, incorporated banks were sometimes grossly misconducted. Much indignation was aroused in New York when in 1855 the cashier of the Mechanics' Bank, who had been forced to resign after a quarrel with the president, published a pamphlet containing amazing disclosures. It showed that the bank had contributed to political parties out of a secret drawer, that it had paid "assessments" by the City Chamberlain without keeping any account of them or making any report to the directors, and that it had permitted other shocking laxities in expenditure and bookkeeping.[34]

The banking heart of the nation was New York. "Every beat of this great financial organ is felt from Maine to Florida, and from the Atlantic to the Pacific," said the Louisville *Courier* on October 14, 1857. By 1855 the metropolis had fifty-three banks, of which seven were specially chartered, and the others established under general law; the aggregate capital falling just short of fifty millions. Boston, which as the center of industrial New England received most of the accumulations of capital in that section, fell into second place, with forty banks in 1854 capitalized at about thirty-seven millions. Her banking business,

31 Secretary of the Treasury, *Annual Report*, December, 1855.
32 "State Rights" in *National Intelligencer*, January 5, 1856.
33 Secretary of the Treasury, *Annual Report*, December, 1856.
34 "Defense of F. W. Edmonds, Late Cashier, Mechanics Bank"; pamphlet.

like that done in insurance, was actually not far behind New York's, a city four times as populous and enjoying about three-fourths of the import trade of the country. The Middle Atlantic States in 1855 had four hundred and sixty-four banks with a paid-in capital of $120,750,000; the New England States had four hundred and forty banks with a paid-in capital much larger, $191,804,000. Other areas lagged far behind.[35]

Far behind!—a reason for much heartburning. The Southern States had only one hundred and twenty-four banks in 1855, with a paid-in capital of about fifty millions, and the Southwestern States but ninety-six banks, with a capital of about forty-six millions. The Western States had one hundred and eighty-three banks, with the low capital of less than twenty millions. In short, the Eastern States possessed about nine hundred banks with a capital of $312,000,000, while all the rest of the country had but four hundred banks with a capital of $116,000,000. New York City in particular was already regarded as a financial tyrant. "Look at its functions," exclaimed a Virginia editor. "It regulates stocks, determines the value of produce, estimates the worth of State bonds, elevating or depressing them in the public estimation, without regard to their intrinsic value, and thus regulating the monetary affairs of the United States. The great heart of American commerce becomes diseased from a plethora of trade or a stagnation in the arteries of traffic and speculation, beats in unhealthy throbs, and every State in the Union . . . instantly feels the effects of its morbid action." [36]

In most new, fast-growing countries, and most flush periods, interest rates are high. Millions of Americans in the fifties, paying heavily for capital, thought that New York and the East were profiteering in the most exorbitant fashion. Though the year 1855 was not one of exceptional stringency, the United States loan maturing in 1862 at six percent a year stood in the autumn at only 112 and 113. The six percent bonds of Virginia sold at 96–97, and the seven percent bonds of California at 86–87. The six percent loans of a long list of cities, such as Pittsburgh, Cincinnati, St. Louis, and New Orleans, were well below par. As for railroads, despite the high profits of the Baltimore & Ohio its six percent bonds maturing in 1885 sold at 83–85.

With the West and Southwest hungry for capital, borrowers there had to pay from ten to twenty percent a year. State usury laws were utterly ineffica-cious. When Ohio in 1851 made the experiment of relaxing hers to allow a ten percent interest rate, that figure became practically the minimum, and in Cin-cinnati during 1852 money fluctuated upwards to twelve, sixteen, twenty and

---

35 *Special Report* of Treasury Department on Banks, February 27, 1855; *National Intelli-gencer*, April 11, 1854, October 25, 1855.
36 Bedford, Virginia, *Sentinel*, October 16, 1857.

even twenty-four percent. Yet in New York, distant hardly two days' travel, the ruling rate for good borrowers was only five percent. In semi-frontier areas, the demand for cheaper credit was always emphatically expressed. In Wisconsin, the Whig convention in 1852, for example, called for "a sound, specie-paying home currency" which would give farmers and merchants capital "without a resort to loans at exorbitant rates" from Eastern banks and brokers.[37]

Nothing irritated the West and South more than unexpected fluctuations in the money market, with the frequent sudden tightening of credit and interest rates. In 1851, for example, the year opened with flattering prospects of an easy supply of money. In St. Louis, loans were made on first-class security at five and six percent. Then the heavy imports of European goods made it necessary during the spring and summer to ship increasing quantities of specie to Europe. The New York bankers took alarm, and at the beginning of August determined to arrest the shipments of money by curtailing discounts and accommodations. This sudden contraction of the money market produced a wave of public apprehension. Confidence in all financial circles became impaired. For a time, eastern banks feared a suspension of specie payments, and interest rates in St. Louis and other outlying centers rose to eighteen and twenty-four percent. Gradually the country recovered from the shock. But the interior snarled resentfully. The mischief had been done, it said. The West had been robbed of the capital and credit it needed, while losses on the great Southern staple, cotton, had been so enormous that many firms in New Orleans had failed.[38]

Viewing the banking system of the country as a whole, men could see that it contained too many new and immature units; in the ten years preceding 1857, no fewer than six hundred and seventy-eight new banks had been set up. They could see that ready assets were much too small in proportion to liabilities; in 1856, deposits and circulation came to $407,000,000, while specie was only $53,000,000.[39] They could see that bank management was sometimes dishonest, often incompetent, and still more often reckless. The ablest bankers of New York, Boston, and Philadelphia, eager to increase their deposits, fell in with an unfortunate trend. Not content with being mere passive recipients of funds from country banks, they actively solicited deposits, even sending out circulars. On the floating capital thus obtained, they paid as much as four percent for sums up to $5,000, and as much as five percent for sums beyond that amount. These funds they then lent to brokers and others, often on dubious security, at profits of one to three percent a year. The brokers then used the money in ventures of a more or less speculative hue. As the nation's load of debt from railway con-

37 *National Intelligencer*, May 15, 1852; N. Y. *Tribune*, October 4, 1851.
38 *St. Louis Prices Current and Commercial Record*, January 10, 1852.
39 William Gregg, Speech in S. C. Legislature, January, 1857; pamphlet.

struction, the expansion of mills, factories, and stores, town promotion, and speculation in commodities rose, the sums owed to banks, brokerage houses, and private lenders became more and more disproportionate to the supporting assets.

The banking system was the weaker, moreover, because it was subject to great seasonal strains. At certain periods—chiefly late summer and early fall—the importers and country bankers were likely to bring heavy pressure on the large city banks for cash, and, if a crisis developed, their joint pressure might become catastrophic. Year after year the importers needed money to meet the unfavorable balance of trade. Their needs were likely to be greatest from midsummer on. Exports of cotton, wheat, and other agricultural products in winter and spring sufficed to square the accounts. In August, September, and October, however, before cotton-picking began and while the grain was merely being harvested and moved to elevators, the insatiable gulf had to be filled. Importers therefore drew many millions in coin or bullion. The movement of crops, meanwhile—the payment of farmers and planters at primary markets—caused country bankers in the West and South to make exigent demands upon the East. They had placed large deposits there, partly for the four percent interest, partly because eastern bankers refused to take and hold their bank notes at par unless such deposits were maintained. The annual strain was serious enough in good times; in a crisis it would become far worse. For the country banks were chronically short of cash; they based their circulation not on specie but securities, and when securities fell, their reserves were mainly in the East. These reserves were their most liquid assets, and, the harder the times became, the more frantically they demanded them.[40]

New York—much used, much hated New York—was certain to be hardest hit in a crisis. There were the chief importing interests, the stock speculators using borrowed funds, the busy land agencies and commodity markets. The city was the main money reservoir of the country—its money subject to calls which might make it dry up like a lake when the dam goes out. When debt reached the saturation point, the dam began to tremble.

[IV]

Still another factor in ending the boom and bringing on depression lay in foreign strains and stresses which originated, for the most part, in armed conflicts. The Crimean War, like all wars, was an international calamity. While it scattered gold among American farmers, planters, arms-makers, cloth manufacturers, and others, its long-term results were unfavorable. By its heavy costs, the shock it gave European production and trade, and the tax loads it imposed, it

40 Kettell, *Southern Wealth and Northern Profits, passim;* N. Y. *Tribune,* October 4, 1851, for description of the system.

drained European funds from the American market. Huge quantities of specie had to be shipped from Western Europe to the Near East during the Crimean operations. The military campaigns of the British in China and Persia in 1856–57, the French operations against the Kabyles in Algeria, and the Indian Mutiny of 1857 also required large expenditures. From the spring of 1854 to the summer of 1857 Europe exported an estimated $700,000,000 in specie to the Near and Far East, much of which stayed there. The Bank of France, in the four years preceding 1857, lost more than $200,000,000 in specie, while the Bank of England, its reserves ebbing, had to raise its discount rate in 1856–57 to six and at times seven percent.[41]

By the fall of 1855, American observers in Europe were expressing fears of a financial crisis. The Bank of France was drawing large sums of gold from London; the Bank of England, irritated by the drain, was unable to stop it. Silver was growing steadily scarcer in France, where it was the legal tender. "There is a sort of war between the two great banks of London and Paris," wrote one American from the French capital.[42] When the Bank of England raised its discount rate to seven percent, other London banks began to charge borrowers eight. European capitalists who could get up to eight percent on good British mortgages, or five percent on Indian railway bonds guaranteed by the East India Company, felt little incentive to invest in American securities. Not merely did the flow of capital to the United States dwindle; as European interest rates advanced, many holders of American stocks and bonds sold them and called home the money. These sales did much to force a decline in the winter of 1856–57 in the price of American obligations—and a steady weakening of the banks, insurance companies, and other firms which relied on them as assets.

Nor was Western Europe herself guiltless of speculation and overexpansion. In France the Crédit Mobilier bubble was blown up to portentous size. That reckless trading bank, which under the encouragement of Napoleon III collected the savings of peasants, workingmen, and shopkeepers, using them to build railroads in Austria, to work mines in Spain, to dig canals in Belgium, and to carry on multiform enterprises in France, had for a time enjoyed a grandiose success.[43] Its stock had risen to dizzy levels. Its semi-annual reports, penned in bombastic language, had intoxicated the French public. It had whipped up a spirit of speculation which led British onlookers from Lombard Street to conclude that the French public was half mad. Even before the American crash, two large defalcations had created alarm, caused a rapid fall in shares, and forced most of the governing board to resign.[44]

41 A slight reduction took place in the summer of 1857; London *Economist,* June 20, 1857.
42 *National Intelligencer,* November 8, 1855; letter dated October 18, 1855.
43 In 1855 it declared a profit of 44 percent, and in 1856 of 25 percent.
44 Clapham, *Econ. Hist. of Modern Britain,* II, 367–372; *National Intelligencer,* October 1, 1857; London *Economist,* September 26, 1857.

[V]

The history of the panic itself, a world-wide convulsion, may be briefly dismissed; it is the results which concern us. During the spring and summer of 1857, talk of an imminent financial crash had spread throughout the country. Bankers and tradesmen discussed it; the press was full of it. "A Coming Crash" —such was the title of an editorial in the New York *Tribune* of June 25. The London *Economist* echoed the dark prognostications of the New York *Shipping List*.[45]

Yet to most Americans, confident in their resources and energy and encouraged by favorable crop reports, the blow that fell in August was stunning. Till the middle of the month the stock market remained fairly vigorous. At home, hopes of peace in Kansas remained high; abroad, the only serious trouble was the Sepoy revolt. On August 11, one of the oldest flour and grain houses of New York, N. H. Wolfe & Co., failed. Then came the Ohio Life & Trust crash, and alarm became universal. The largest purchaser of uncurrent bank notes in the city immediately failed. On the twenty-sixth, men learned that Jacob Little, prince of speculative investors, could not meet his debts, and that several important railroads were bankrupt. Stocks fell precipitately, distress spread like a cloud of poison gas, and money grew so tight that New York bank loans dropped by four millions in a week. The panic was on.

As merchants, factories, and country banks closed their doors, the universal cry was, "Who goes next?" A brief rally took place at the beginning of September; then the panic worsened. On the ninth a run on the banks for note redemption began, and on the thirteenth depositors came in crowds to demand their money. Before the fifteenth, all the New York banks but one had suspended specie payment, while those of New England and Pennsylvania, with many in the West and South, had fallen or were tottering. Credit was reduced to a minimum; bank loans in New York City, which stood at $120,000,000 on August 22, were down to $67,000,000 by October 17. During the autumn the situation became steadily darker. The seven hundred and four-mile Illinois Central, whose stock had recently sold at $140, and whose last yearly return had shown net receipts exceeding a million, went down—a staggering blow. Other great roads confessed bankruptcy. As security prices collapsed, financial houses toppled. John Murray Forbes wrote that William Appleton and W. Sturgis—the two best names in Boston—could not raise $100,000 within forty-eight hours at three per cent a month.

British and American interests were so closely connected that a blow to one

45 London *Economist*, July 4, 1857.

struck the other with almost equal weight. More than a fifth of the British exports in 1856 had gone to the United States, while more than a third of the foreign government securities ordinarily listed on the British exchanges were American. When business with America was half paralyzed, American stocks and bonds dropped to abysmal levels, and New York paper became unsaleable, then British merchants, bankers, and investors were hard hit. In October and November a dismal succession of failures was chronicled by the British press. Scottish banks were smitten as by a plague. One London brokerage house failed for five million pounds. In France the Crédit Mobilier bubble was pricked. French failures in the autumn of 1857 were even more numerous and calamitous than British. Norway, Sweden, and all the Baltic ports suffered heavily. Hamburg, one of the principal trading links between North Europe and America, was brought to her knees. As far east as Poland and Austria, the battering impact of the panic was felt.[46]

As Disraeli said, the business mismanagement of half Europe was suddenly exposed. "All the bubbles, blunders, and dishonesties of five years' European exuberance and experiments in credit were tested or revealed."[47]

In the United States, the successive strokes of the panic left many businessmen utterly bewildered. As their notes were thrust in their faces, they tried to sell assets at half price and failed. Their feet became sore with running about town for unobtainable loans; their friends were out on the same errand—all borrowers, no lenders. Neighbors failed, banks failed, customers failed. They gazed sadly at drawers full of bills receivable (all worthless), attempted in desperation to sell their paper at any price, and went home sick with despair. The blackest rumors flew about every city. Talk of dishonesty was rife, and some of it was true.[48]

"Conceive," wrote Amos A. Lawrence from Boston in mid-October, "conceive of the rate of interest here being fifty per cent, and for large sums! Our manufacturing interest is for the present completely broken down and discredited." Two months later he reported that Boston was still prostrate. "Many men who have possessed handsome properties for thirty or even fifty years have become dependent on friends."[49] In Washington, Seward, for the first time in years, was unable to pay his current bills on demand, and ended the year more deeply in debt than he began it. "Money is a mere name," wrote a well-known Virginian, R. K. Crallé. "No one can safely sell anything except for specie—and there is no specie to be had."[50] Propertied people in Philadelphia were at first

46 *National Intelligencer*, November 17, 1857; London *Economist*, November-December, 1857.
47 Clapham, *Econ. Hist. of Modern Britain*, II, 370.
48 *Hunt's Merchants' Magazine*, XXXVII, 462.
49 A. A. Lawrence, October 19, December 17, 1857; Robinson Papers, Univ. of Kansas.
50 Frederic Seward, *Seward*, II, 327; R. K. Crallé, October 19, 1857, Brock Collection, HL.

sanguine, and the Bank of Philadelphia gave generous aid to distressed commercial houses. But on September 25 a sudden run forced this institution to close its doors. The news, spreading as on a gale, brought people thronging from every part of town into Third Street, which became jammed. Lines radiating from this vast but orderly mob poured into every downtown bank; the banks soon ceased paying on deposits, and their heads, hastily consulting, announced their suspension. Most banks of Pittsburgh, Reading, Baltimore, and various Jersey cities followed suit, and money rates were soaring.[51]

The chief western centers—Cleveland, Chicago, Milwaukee, St. Louis, and other cities—displayed the same distress and ruin. Western merchants had made large purchases of goods on notes which they expected to pay when the crops went forward. This year the western grain crops were good and the quality high. Wheat was just pouring freely to market, when the panic forced a heavy contraction in rediscount operations and prevented any large remittances from New York, Philadelphia, and other seaboard centers on produce account. By the end of September, harassed western merchants had to pay eight to twelve percent for sight exchange on New York, and a fortnight later could hardly get it at any price. Market quotations on grain and livestock dropped with a crash.[52] By November, western red and mixed wheats were selling at the seaboard for ninety-eight cents to $1.27 a bushel, while the general average for beeves in New York was eight cents a pound. In many Mississippi Valley communities, money disappeared so completely that little business was done save by dicker.

"You can have no idea of the troubles here," William Tecumseh Sherman wrote from St. Louis early in the fall. "We have correspondents as far up as Omaha City and all through Iowa who say the money has quit and gone they know not where." His neighbor, Frank Blair, bore the same testimony, though he believed that Benton's sound-money views had saved them from the suffering encountered in other cities. In Illinois, the stringency caused many people to cry for a special session of the legislature and a debt moratorium. "The most of us are determined to stand firm," wrote Lincoln's partner Herndon.[53]

One of the many who suffered from dire hardship in the St. Louis area was a former army officer who, after serving in the Mexican War and the Northwest, was living in pinched fashion on a small farm near the city. Two days before Christmas he realized that he was without money to buy gifts for his small children. He possessed a gold hunting-case watch. Placing it on a pawnshop counter, the shabby farmer took $22 from the pawnbroker's hand and signed his name on the ticket—U. S. Grant. He little thought that this ticket, with all its

51 N. Y. *Weekly Tribune*, October 3, 1857.
52 Report of Brit. Consul, Chicago, September 30, 1857; FO 5/678.
53 W. T. Sherman, September 22, 1857, Ewing Papers; F. P. Blair, Jr., October 16, 1857, Blair-Lee Papers; W. H. Herndon, October 5, 1857, Trumbull Papers.

associations of poverty and struggle, would in time become a cherished possession of the State of Illinois.

Within a few months, however, the storm had largely died away. "There never was a more severe crisis nor a more rapid recovery," observed the London *Economist*.[54] Before Christmas the New York banks voluntarily returned to specie payments, and with them up-State and New England banks. Those of Philadelphia and Baltimore resumed at the beginning of February, 1858, while all other banks not hopelessly insolvent were operating again by midsummer. Wise measures by New York financial leaders had helped the country banks accumulate funds which were in large part redeposited in the city coffers. Meanwhile, a steady flow of gold from California and Europe had reached the eastern centers—though the loss of the *Central America* off Cape Hatteras with more than four hundred passengers and $2,000,000 in treasure was one of the heavy blows of this dark year. These circumstances, which had made redemption possible sooner than had been expected, encouraged many to believe that the economic fabric of the nation was essentially sound and possessed a healthy recuperative power. The strong State banks of Indiana, Ohio, and Kentucky had stood erect throughout the tempest. The national credit was less shaken than might have been expected from the diminution in revenues.

But if the panic was over, the inevitable aftermath of depression had to be faced. It closed down over the country like a chill mist, filling the next two years with slowly diminishing misery and discontent. A painful readjustment in values had to take place. The price of land, for example, sank to a level bearing a far closer relation to tillage returns. Not merely speculators, but farmers who had mortgaged themselves to buy excessive tracts, paid a sad penalty. As late as 1860 Greeley wrote from Prairie du Chien: "The West is poor. The collapse of the railroad bubble . . . has spread desolation over the land." [55] Consumers' goods were a drug on the market. Europeans, estimating that they had lost hundreds of millions of dollars in worthless securities bought during the previous five years, were in a morose mood, and it gave them little comfort to think that Americans had lost more.

Buchanan wrote an inadequate analysis of the panic into his message of 1857, dwelling upon the stale theme of vicious systems of paper currency and bank credits. He said nothing about extravagant railroad construction, reckless speculation in land and commodities, or swollen imports. The London *Economist* characterized it as "a cloud of dust to cover a disgraceful retreat—a great scapegoat for the rash and impudent speculations—and in some cases, we regret to say, for the impudent frauds practised upon the too-gullible and too-avaricious

54 London *Economist*, January 2, 1858.
55 N. Y. *Weekly Tribune*, February 4, 1860.

people of the Old World." No action was expected of the general government in dealing with the depression, and except for certain palliative measures by the Treasury, nothing in particular was done.[56]

[VI]

The social misery of the winter of 1857–58 was even greater than that following the panic of 1837. Throughout the country, railway construction halted. In New England, textile mills stood lifeless amid scenes of poverty and discouragement. In Cincinnati, of some twenty-five thousand employees in clothing establishments fully half were discharged. More than half of the furnaces and iron mills of the country were idle, those of Pennsylvania being especially hard hit. The lumbermen of Wisconsin and Michigan, discharged with hardly a day's warning, were soon on the verge of starvation. In St. Louis, more than a mile of smokeless funnels lay frozen at the wharves. While New Bedford whalers and Gloucester fishermen commiserated with each other on the failure of their markets, Boston reported that two hundred and fifty ships were tied up. Frightened immigrants turned homeward in such numbers that the outgoing Boston and New York packets were soon full.[57]

The situation gave its opportunity to demagogues. Mayor Fernando Wood of New York lost no time in sending the Common Council a message which, mingling good proposals with bad, might have had a friendlier reception from the press but for its violent language. Pointing out that two hundred thousand New Yorkers depended directly or indirectly on manual labor, and that midwinter would find fifty thousand men out of work, he suggested a resort to public projects. Central Park needed improvement; a new reservoir had to be built; enginehouses were needed; and streets required paving. The city might well buy fifty thousand barrels of flour and corresponding quantities of corn meal and potatoes to be used in part payment of wages. This would be better than placing the unemployed on pauper relief. The proposal was sound, but unfortunately Wood made a venomous appeal to class feeling, and seemed to the propertied classes to be inciting men to violence. Multitudes, he wrote, "labor without in-

---

56 London *Economist*, December 26, 1857. Secretary Cobb began using some of the gold in the sub-treasuries to redeem government bonds, thus furnishing the banks with much-needed specie, while he speeded the mints to increase the circulation of coins. Government revenues fell, and when Congress met in December, 1857, a deficit clearly impended. Under emergency legislation, Treasury notes were issued, while later a loan of twenty millions was floated. Government expenses were somewhat reduced; indeed, Buchanan thought that Cobb and Jacob Thompson had done marvels in this direction. Buchanan, *Works*, XI, 243.

57 N. Y. *Times*, *Tribune*, October-December, 1857; Providence *Tribune*, October 23; Chicago *Journal*, November 7; Boston *Transcript*, November 9; Nevins, *Hewitt*, 171; Cole, *Era of the Civil War*, 203.

come while surrounded by thousands in selfishness and splendor who have income without labor."

Throughout the land, observers noted that workingmen did not bow to summary discharges and cruel pay reductions with the spiritless docility they had exhibited after the panic of 1837. They had learned fast in the interim years; the ideas of Owen, Fourier, and George Henry Evans, the writings of Leggett and Greeley, had taught them much. Philadelphia had its "hunger meetings," where thousands passionately implored Mayor Vaux to provide public works. "We will loan our labor, and our labor is capital," they declared, "if you will assure us that the scrip of the city, which we are willing to accept, will be taken for bread and butter, tea and sugar." In New York, noisy demonstrations were staged in City Hall Park and Tompkins Square, while long processions marched under banners inscribed "Work" and *"Arbeit"* to present the authorities with petitions declaring that work was a right. These ebullitions were orderly. When sharp pay cuts were imposed by some New England textile mills, the employees struck. Nor did they stay quietly at home; they thronged the streets, jeering their comrades who remained at the looms. New York, Philadelphia, Chicago, and other cities undertook some special municipal enterprises. But they were inadequate, and a defiant spirit was shown by workers all winter.[58]

The depression was most severe in the Northern industrial areas, and in the Middle West where an indifferent crop year in 1858 prolonged its effects. Of course a considerable part of the losses in the deflation of western land values fell upon the East. The border States, and particularly the tobacco kingdom, were also hard hit. Tennessee and Kentucky tobacco-growers found that, as most of the banks serving them suspended, they could not sell their product at all, and, when the eastern ports resumed buying, it was at halved prices. Many a trader went down and many a fortune melted away. Seven-eighths of the Virginia manufacturers of tobacco had to give up operations for the winter, for, with their drafts on the banks returned unpaid and with prices of cigars and plugs falling heavily, they could not meet their running expenses. Many of the factories returned their hired slaves to the owners. It was a dark season which followed in large parts of Virginia and North Carolina.[59]

The cotton kingdom suffered least of all. It by no means escaped scot-free, for the staple suffered a gradual but in the end a serious fall. Cotton quoted in September at sixteen cents a pound had dropped by Christmas to nine cents. While the largest crop yet known was being gathered, it became clear that both New and Old England would furnish a lighter demand than usual. The South, however, had not run into debt in the reckless fashion of the North. It had not

58 Pleasants, *Fernando Wood, passim.* At Chicopee this winter, women operatives earned an average of only $1.40 a week; Vera Schlakman, *Econ. Hist. of a Factory Town,* 143.

59 W. P. Titus, *Picturesque Clarksville,* 388, 389; J. C. Robert, *Tobacco Kingdom,* 227, 228.

imported so many luxuries, built so much railroad mileage in excess of need, or speculated so much in stocks and commodities. "In no respect are we the worse off than we were twelve months ago," boasted the Lynchburg *Virginian*.[60] The weak price of cotton might worry some planters as they sat down to their Christmas turkey. But, as various leaders assured them, they had only to store their bales under their own sheds and wait until prices grew better—as they did by spring of 1858.

The Southern banking system, moreover, stood up more sturdily than that of the North. The important houses of New Orleans came through the ordeal almost unscathed. In this busy commercial center the specie reserve against liabilities was one-third, or more than twice as great as in the country at large. Then, too, Louisiana law limited credit operations of each bank to twice its capital, prohibited banks from paying out at their counters any but their own notes, and laid down strict requirements as to the security basis for loans. Charleston banks which had suspended made a rapid recovery. Even where the banks stopped specie payment, as in North Carolina, the blow was less felt because the South depended less on specie. In Mississippi, for example, all the banks suspended. But there were only two of them; and as Governor McRae told the legislature, they had but small capital and circulated only a moderate amount of notes.[61]

Proud Southerners lifted exultant voices. The North is tottering with paralysis, declared Herschel V. Johnson of Georgia; but the South, with three million cotton bales, "stands calm and unmoved, poised upon the consciousness of her capacity to outride the tempest."[62] Our wealth, boasted *De Bow's Review*, is permanent and real, while that of the North is fictitious.[63] Senator Hammond called attention to a circular from a New York commercial agency, Tappan & McKillop. Listing the failures of 1857, it computed that the free States, with one hundred fifty-five thousand, five hundred and twenty-six business firms, had lost 3.24 percent, while the slave States, with sixty-one thousand, four hundred and ten business establishments, had seen only 1.21 percent go under. This agency estimated the total loss to the commercial community in the free States, after allowing for probable payments, at $142,000,000, and that in the slave States at less than $17,500,000. The liabilities of failed banks and mercantile houses in Massachusetts during 1857–58 were $6,115,000 against only $3,800,000 in Loui-

---

60 Quoted in *National Intelligencer*, October 3, 1857.
61 Annual Message, November, 1857. The admirable Louisiana law, which grew out of the depression of 1837–42, is discussed in W. O. Scroggs, *A Century of Banking Progress*, 132–135. Loans of capital had to be separated from loans of deposits; deposit loans were restricted to ninety-day paper; and a large specie reserve was required against all liabilities. A State supervisory board was created, which had to examine each bank four times a year. Louisiana pointed the way to other States, which in time followed her example.
62 N. Y. *Weekly Tribune*, November 7, 1857.
63 *De Bow's Review*, December, 1857.

siana. Similar liabilities in Virginia were lower than those in Michigan, while in Georgia they were less than half the Ohio totals.[64]

By the spring of 1859, the whole country seemed fast recovering. Pennsylvania iron mills and New England textile plants, though still depressed, were resuming activity. The South, with crops abundant and prices high, was notably prosperous—perhaps more prosperous than ever before. Railroad stocks were rising and railroad construction was being restored. Settlement and trade were flowing briskly into the West, where only the poor harvest had prevented a rapid liquidation of debt. Imports had fallen off so steeply that in 1858 they were little more than three-quarters of their value the previous year; and as a result the balance of trade favored the United States. The three chief elements in the nation's recovery were the rich revenues from cotton, the keen foreign demand during 1858 for foodstuffs (European harvests in 1857 having been poor), and the continued flow of California gold into world markets. Many communities, however, were still debilitated.

The psychological, social, and political consequences of this swinging economic blow were certain to be important. Some had been foreseen at once. A check to immigration; a marked accentuation of social discontent and radical agitation; a drop in the prestige of the Administration, were all immediately noted. As government revenues fell, without any effort to tap important new sources of revenue, the national debt was rising fast; it went from about twenty-nine millions in 1857 to almost sixty-five millions in 1860. As the American correspondent of the London *Times* wrote, many signs indicated that this financial deficit would be the groundwork of an attempt to revive the policy of protection.[65] "I look now to see matters of finance, the tariff, and so on become the leading topics in Congress," predicted Frank Blair, Jr. Most important of all, however, was the increased self-confidence of the South, its faith in its economic impregnability, its belief that its products were indispensable to the world.

64 See letter of J. M. Leitch, March 17, 1858, Hammond Papers, LC; table, *Bankers' Magazine*, XIII, 641–643.
65 Quoted in London *Economist*, August 21, 1858.

New Wine in Old Bottles

ALL MEN, according to an old maxim which rests on ample authority, derive a subtle pleasure from the misfortunes of their associates. While we would wrong the South to say that it was pleased by the heavy stumble of the industrial North in the panic of 1857, nevertheless many Southern people did feel that the event justified some of their criticisms. To understand the psychological effects of this economic disaster, we must realize that the waters of social and political controversy were boiling furiously, and that each section was assailing the fundamental basis of the others' civilization. No Communist of 1950 could have seized more eagerly on an economic depression in Western Europe as proving the vulnerability of democratic institutions than Southerners seized on the depression of 1857–58 as proving Northern weakness. Seldom in our history have two parties flung at each other weightier polemics—books, pamphlets, review articles—than the slave State and free State publicists were discharging in these years. Inevitably, any major social disturbance would be interpreted in very different fashions on the two sides of the Potomac.

[I]

Already, Southern writers had stated in both verse and prose the thesis that Northern wage-earners toiled in constant danger of that misery which actually filled the streets of Boston, New York, and Chicago in the winter following the panic. In 1854, William J. Grayson, postmaster of Charleston, a man in his middle sixties, had issued through the press of his friend John Russell a ninety-page poem in heroic couplets, after the style of Pope, called *The Hireling and the Slave.* Running through two small editions, it was republished with additional verse in 1856. The author threw his exposition into two parts. The first contended that the state of the slave and that of the hireling were substantially identical in that each was compelled to labor, and each got the same reward, a subsistence:

How small the choice, from cradle to the grave,
Between the lot of hireling and of slave!
To each alike applies the stern decree
That man shall labor, whether bond or free;
For all that toil the recompense we claim—
Food, fire, a home, and clothing—is the same.

But the hireling, declared Grayson, could not always find the employment he sought, nor obtain the subsistence, whereas the slave never lacked food and care. The versifier paused to explain how slavery had improved the lot of Africans lifted out of the cannibalism and idolatry of Africa.[1] He passed into invective against the meddlesome abolitionists who would ruin the South as their British brethren had ruined the West Indies:

There, chief and teacher, Gerrit Smith appears,
There Tappan mourns, like Niobe, all tears,
Carnage and fire mad Garrison invokes,
And Hale, with better temper, smirks and jokes;
There Giddings, with the Negro mania bit,
Mouths, and mistakes his ribaldry for wit. . . .
There supple Sumner, with the Negro cause,
Plays the sly game for office and applause.

In the second, longer, and better part of his poem, Grayson contrasted the comforts, sports, religious enjoyments, and security of the slave with the precarious position of the industrial hireling. Turning to the rural life he knew so well, he presented scenes of hunting, fishing, and picnicking with a gusto worthy of Cowper or Thomson. What worker would not choose the bounties of Carolina—the fruits, the game, the wholesome toil amid moss-bearded oaks— over the squalid city slum? So, too, wrote the poetess Millie Mayfield:[2]

Your laborer is white, *and your equal*—yet he
Is a sufferer in a much greater degree

1 Wrote William J. Grayson later: "The question of negro slavery in the United States had been discussed for many years. It had assumed all garbs except the garb of verse. I thought the subject possessed aspects both of argument and description which admitted a poetical dress. In a broad view of the transfer of the African to America it may be regarded not merely as an act of commercial enterprise or avarice but as an emigration of the Black to a new country. It was an emigration hardly more forced than that of the starving Irish peasantry and not attended perhaps with greater suffering. The negro was brought to a country where he could be trained to those habits of industry which alone constitute the foundation of civilization and make it possible for a people to improve. The advancement of the Black in all relations, civil, social, or religious, must come from the white race. The negro has never been able to originate a civilization. The white man cannot live in the negro's country. The negro must therefore be brought to the home of the white. This has been accomplished by slavery only. The benefits bestowed on the negro are obvious. The slaves of North America are the most civilized of the African race." William J. Grayson, MS Autobiography, edited by Robert Duncan Bass, South Caroliniana Library.

2 Millie Mayfield, *Progression; or, The South Defended*, 199.

Than his ebony rival . . . tho' this till doomsday
Perhaps you'll contend; but I've this much to say:
Let 'crises,' 'panics,' 'suspensions,' invade
And break down the barriers guarding all trade;
Let banks go to ruin and stocks sink to naught,
The whirlpool, to one class with misery fraught,
Glides light past the other as singing brooks play
In the beams of the sun on a calm summer's day . . .

Simultaneously, George Fitzhugh of Virginia had likewise carried the war into Northern territory with the contention that free society was a monstrous growth, the natural result of whose competitive cruelties was the corruption of public morals, the sapping of domestic affections, the oppression of the laboring poor, and the accumulation of a mass of pauperism and crime. His *Sociology for the South; or, The Failure of Free Society*, issued from Richmond in 1854, admitted that slavery had its imperfections, which as far as possible should be corrected—and the South would correct them if the abolitionists would let the section alone, or advise with it as friends, neighbors, and gentlemen. But he concentrated his attention upon the defects of the free labor system of Europe and the North. In proof of their gravity, he quoted the *Latter Day Pamphlets* of Carlyle, who had influenced him, and the writings of Fourier and Robert Owen. The white slave trade, he declared, was far more cruel than the black slave trade, for it exacted more from its slaves without protecting or governing them. The irresponsible capitalism of free society, exploiting its hands as factory fodder, pursued the hireling from the hovel to the poorhouse, the prison, and the grave. He characterized free society as a bag of cats tied up together; and he, too, contrasted the safety, comfort, and solidarity of the Southern slaves with the disintegration of Northern communities which followed the old maxim of the devil take the hindmost.

While Grayson used *Russell's Magazine* for vigorous press attacks on industrialism and defenses of slavery,[3] Fitzhugh continued to press his ideas in essays for the *Southern Quarterly Review* and *De Bow's Review*.[4] In the year of the panic, he published *Cannibals All!; or, Slaves without Masters*, an expansion of the earlier book and a bolder statement of its principles. One feature of the work was a rough eviction of Jefferson from his pedestal.[5] Fitzhugh frankly declared his belief that slavery suited the masses; that the duty of protecting the weak always involved the necessity of enslaving them; and that Northern com-

---

3 See especially "The Dual Form of Labor," *Russell's Magazine*, VI.
4 See his "Centralization and Socialism," *De Bow's Review*, XX.
5 Fitzhugh's most direct contradiction of Jefferson is his statement: "Men are not born entitled to equal rights. It would be far nearer the truth to say that some were born with saddles on their backs, and others booted and spurred to ride them; and the riding does them good. They need the reins, the bit, and the spur." See Harvey Wish, *Fitzhugh, passim.*

munities might be much better off if they adopted slavery as a form of communism. Let men look realistically at the cruelties of Northern society, he declared, and they must see how inferior it was to the kind paternalism of the Southern institution, which he termed the oldest, commonest, and best type of socialism:

Capital exercises a more perfect compulsion over free laborers than human masters over slaves; for free laborers must at all times work or starve, and slaves are supported whether they work or not. Free laborers have less liberty than slaves, are worse paid and provided for, and have no valuable rights. Slaves, with more of actual practical liberty, with ampler allowances, and constant protection, are secure in the enjoyment of all the rights which provide for their physical comfort at all times and under all circumstances. The free laborer must be employed or starve, yet no one is obliged to employ him. . . . His wants and other men's capital make him a slave without a master, or with too many masters, which is as bad as none. It were often better that he had an ascertained master, instead of an irresponsible and unascertained one.

Fitzhugh's proposals for the universal establishment of some form of slavery were justly derided,[6] but his picture of the cannibalistic tendencies of raw industrialism—which anticipated Marx's chapters on capitalist production—did not lose force in the months of depression and unemployment.[7] This middle-aged, self-taught Virginia attorney had really convinced himself that the competitive life of mankind, when not mollified by human servitude, tended toward degradation. He had seen little of free communities. His only visit to the Northern States took place after he had gained some reputation by his writings, when he lectured in Boston, went to see his kinsman by marriage, Gerrit Smith, and met Harriet Beecher Stowe. Alas that we have no record of the conversation of these hostile authors! Fitzhugh clearly owed much to those earlier panegyrists of slavery as a positive good, Calhoun, T. R. Dew, and William Harper, but he had hammered out some notions all his own.

The chief of these ideas was that the free labor system had never been more than an experiment, and had already proved a dismal failure. The ordinary workingman, he wrote, with insecure employment, no fixed abode, and few if any savings, was almost certain in the end, through disease, accident, or old age, to come to penury. Such hopeless men had few incentives to virtue and many to

6 See the long review in *National Intelligencer*, June 9, 1857. For Congressional attention to him see Harvey Wish, *George Fitzhugh*, 275–288.

7 Thomas Carlyle ("Ilias Americana in Nuce," *MacMillan's Magazine*, August, 1863) wrote that the difference between North and South was simply this, that Northerners wanted to hire their labor by the day, Southerners by the lifetime. Karl Marx, in *Das Kapital*, Pt. II, quotes the London *Times* of July 2, 1863: "Very many of us think that, while we work our young women to death, using the scourge of starvation instead of the crack of the whip, as the instrument of compulsion, we have scarcely a right to hound on fire and slaughter against families who were born slave-owners, and who at least feed their slaves well, and work them lightly."

vice and crime; life gave them little happiness and abundant misery. Mankind must reorganize itself on a positive gradation of human levels. The State must compel the idle to work, assigning every person his or her place in the labor field; it must place toilers under the most rigid discipline and direction. In Old England, New England, and other industrial areas, unskilled hands ought to be converted into slaves of the capitalists, forbidden freedom of movement, and kept efficiently busy. At the same time the State should guarantee them what they had hitherto lacked, ample food, shelter, and old-age care. In the West, broad tracts of land might be granted to an aristocratic class under entail, and landless, unemployed men might be attached to these estates as life tenants or serfs, again under guarantees of full security. Thus the nation would become one great family, while idleness, poverty, and social strife would disappear.

It will be seen that Fitzhugh's dream had a distinct resemblance to that of subsequent totalitarian theorists in Nazi Germany and Soviet Russia: freedom and poverty would vanish together. While the dream was both absurd and vicious, the writer's explicit criticism of capitalist recklessness and *laissez faire* toleration of poverty had a trenchancy which gave it wide influence in the South. He and many of his readers exaggerated the evils incident to freedom of contract and personal liberty, underestimated the benefits, and ignored the evidence that free society was steadily restricting *laissez faire* for the general good. Like the future totalitarian leaders, Fitzhugh made his ideas more palatable by drafting a constructive program for the benefit of the ruling class. He urged better public education, more diversification of industry, and a protective tariff to foster Southern manufactures. Altogether, his books and his articles in *De Bow's* gave comfort to many Southerners who, facing the rising storm of world disapproval of slavery, wanted some answer, however flimsy, to the increasingly searching attacks made upon their system by able Northern and British writers.

[II]

Some of these attacks linked themselves with the great economic changes of the time. That could not be said, of course, of such polemic works as Frederick Douglass's *My Bondage and My Freedom*, Solomon Northup's *Twelve Years a Slave*, or Benjamin Drew's *The Northside View of Slavery; the Canadian Refugees' Own Story*, which had appeared in 1855. It could not be said of Mrs. Stowe's *Dred*, or C. E. Stevens's *Anthony Burns: a History*, or the numerous books on the Kansas struggle, all brought out in 1856. It could not be said of Harriet Martineau's *Manifest Destiny of the American Union*, or the Rev. G. B. Cheever's *God against Slavery*, issued in 1857. But it could emphatically be said of the writings of Frederick Law Olmsted, who did more than any other man of the time to make the discussion of slavery realistic by examining in detail its practical workings, and describing all its concomitants in the life of the people.

Few books of economic and social observation ever written in any land possess the enduring interest of Olmsted's *A Journey in the Seaboard Slave States*, published in 1856, and *A Journey Through Texas; or, A Saddle-Trip on the Southwestern Frontier*, issued in 1857. In due course a third title was added: *A Journey in the Back Country* (1860). Olmsted was exceptionally well equipped for his work. A son of Hartford, Connecticut, he was of adventurous tastes, as he had shown in his boyhood wanderings all over the Connecticut countryside, in four early journeys with his elders of more than a thousand miles each, and in shipping before the mast for Canton at twenty-one. By vocation he was a farmer, though he had taken courses at Yale, and had served for a time with a mercantile house in New York. He had managed a small place in Connecticut and a much larger farm on Staten Island, and he had written a book called *Walks and Talks of an American Farmer in England*. Only thirty when he accepted a commission from Raymond of the *Times* to explore the South and report on its condition, he had a shrewd, flexible mind, a tolerant outlook, and an intense sincerity.

It should be added that he belonged to the moderate school of Northern thought, being quite untouched by abolitionism. He resented and opposed all talk of political interference by the North to extinguish Southern slavery. Regarding slavery as an unfortunate circumstance for which the Southern people were in no way to blame, and an institution which could no more be summarily abolished than prisons or hospitals, he rejected the Garrisonian abuse of slaveholders as highly mischievous. It was his opinion that Southerners possessed certain peculiar virtues. But he did think that a thoughtful demonstration of the economic disadvantages of slavery and a tactful encouragement of Southerners to move toward a free labor system might be useful. The first step was to analyze slavery on the spot; and he resolved to scrutinize the situation "carefully and fairly, but cheerfully and kindly." [8]

Equipping himself for his horseback expedition with a general letter of credence from the governor of New York, and with supplies ranging from emergency rations to gunpowder, from quinine to pocket classics, Olmsted in his first journey traversed Virginia, the Carolinas, Georgia, Alabama, and Louisiana.[9] He took careful notes on every aspect of life, white or colored: dress, diet, rural scenery, inns, barrooms, religious conditions, methods of making tar, hoeing cotton, and rolling tobacco, slave-hunting, Christmas jollities, Creole balls,

8 Olmsted, preface to *Back Country;* Mitchell, *Frederic Law Olmsted,* 45.
9 Mitchell, 84–86; Olmsted, *Seaboard Slave States, passim.*

land values, crimes of violence, the sand-hillers and other poor whites, roads, overseers, and the prevalence of malaria. He even recorded the songs of river roustabouts and the inscriptions on slave tombstones. Innumerable scraps of conversation are set down verbatim. Frequently, Olmsted supplemented these notes with material drawn from newspapers, farm journals, or books. When he described the diet of slaves, he collected facts on the fare of Eastern and European laborers by way of comparison.

The second book, that on the Texan journey, contains more of the Western frontier, wild and rough to a degree, and less of the tame, settled South. Olmsted and his brother, after traversing Kentucky, on which he wrote a valuable chapter, explored about one-third of the huge State, covering the region east and south of a line drawn from Nacogdoches through Fredericksburg to Eagle Pass; a region embracing ranching country, farming areas of good soil, the old American settlements of central Texas, the main sugar district, the town of Houston, and the German or half-German counties around New Braunfels. A novel range of topics demanded description: frontier military posts, Indian camps, Mexican towns, the character of the peons, the Alamo, cattle drives, Kendall's famous sheep ranch, deer and bear hunting, vigilance committees, alligators, and organized emigration. Again he missed nothing, from the price of wild turkeys to the number of mechanics in New Braunfels and the make-up of a California cattle-train.

Had Olmsted written systematic treatises instead of travel journals, he would have conveyed scantier information and produced books of far less human interest. The charm of his *Seaboard Slave States* and *Texas*, like that of his subsequent *Journey in the Back Country*, lies in the constant flow of diverting incident, the spirited dialogues, and the brisk alternation of scene-painting and human sketches, all interspersed with bits of vigorous analysis. On one page we find an account of a stage-coach journey over muddy North Carolina roads, on another a report of a talk with a Louisiana slaveholder about *Uncle Tom's Cabin*, on a third the story of his dangerous predicament when his horse stampeded and disappeared on a boundless Texas prairie. He could etch a little picture with expert touch, as in his night-study of some wagoners near Fayetteville:

I walked out, about eleven o'clock . . . and found, upon the edge of an old field, near the town, a camp of wagoners, with half a dozen fires, around some of which were clustered groups of white men and women and negroes cooking and eating their suppers (black and white from the same kettle, in many cases), some singing Methodist songs, and some listening to a banjo or fiddle-player. A still larger number appeared to be asleep, generally lying under low tents. . . . There were thirty or forty great wagons, with mules, cattle, or horses, feeding from troughs set upon their poles. The grouping of all among some old sycamore trees, with the fantastic shadows and wavering lights, the free flames and black brooding smoke of the pitch-pine fires, produced a most interesting and attractive spectacle, and detained me long in admiration.[10]

He could report a conversation with Borrow's fidelity. On a river boat he fell in with a tall, thin, awkward planter, with a knife hilt protruding from his waistcoat:

"Stranger," [the planter] asked me once, "did you ever come up on the *Leweezay*? She's a right smart pretty boat, she is, the *Leweezay*; the best I ever see on the Alabamy river. They wanted me to wait and come down on her, but I told 'em time was in the objective case to me. She is a right pretty boat, and her capting's a high-tone gentleman; hain't no objections to find with him—he's a high-tone gentleman, that's what he is. But the pilot—well, damn him! He run her right out of the river, up into the woods—didn't run her in the river at all. When I get aboard a steamboat, I like to keep in the river, somewar, but that pilot, he took her right up into the woods. It was just clairin' land, clairin' land and playin' hell ginerally, all night; not follerin' the river at all. I believe he was drunk. . . . They hev good livin' aboard of her, too. Haan't no objections on that score, weddin' fixins all the time; but I won't go in a boat war the pilot's drunk. I set some vally on the life of two hundred souls. They wanted to hev me come down on her, but I told 'em time was in the objective case." [11]

And while he was so exact that he sometimes halted to measure the precise distance between cornstalks or the inches in a ploughshare, he could also impart a picturesqueness to his narrative which verged upon the poetic. On the Cumberland River:

As we lay quiet one evening in the fog, we heard and listened long to the happy wordless song of the negroes gathered at firelight work, probably corn husking, on some neighboring plantation. The sound had all the rich and mellow ring of pure physical contentment, and did one good to hear it. Like the nightingale, the performers seemed to love their own song, and to wait for its far-off echo. It was long before we discovered that this was artificial, and came in response from the next plantation. No doubt, had one the tender and ubiquitous ear of a fairy, he might hear, of a fine evening, this black melody, intermingled with the whippoorwills' notes, all the way from Carolina to Kansas, resounding, as the moon went up, from river to river.[12]

The fundamental preoccupation of Olmsted, however, was with the economic condition of the South. As he wrote later, he found the position of both white and black races worse than he had anticipated, and the more thoroughly he studied the section the darker did the picture appear.[13] White mastership over the Negroes he believed a necessity, and emancipation undesirable for the exist-

10 Olmsted, *Seaboard Slave States*, 357, 358.
11 *Ibid.*, 562, 563.
12 Olmsted, *Journey through Texas*, 34, 35.
13 Olmsted, *Back Country*, preface.

ing generation. But on economic grounds alone eventual emancipation was highly desirable, and the way should be prepared for it by organized action. He constantly emphasized a few cardinal economic doctrines. "Servile labor must be unskilled labor, and unskilled labor must be dispersed over land, and cannot support the concentrated life nor amass the capital of cities." [14] Slavery meant ignorance—in fact, a vast apparatus was set up to keep slaves ignorant. The result was constant misapplication of labor, constant waste and breakage, constant exhaustion of the land. He saw stock maimed, crops ruined, topsoil swirling down rivers, because of the enforced ignorance of the labor corps. On Carolina rice plantations the Negroes would dislike and break any improved implement; they were happiest with a clumsy iron hoe. "It is a common thing, I am told, to see a large gang of negroes, each carrying about four shovelsful of earth upon a board balanced on his head, walking slowly along on the embankment, so as to travel around two sides of a large field, perhaps for a mile, to fill a breach—a job which an equal number of Irishmen would accomplish, by laying planks across the field and running wheelbarrows upon them, in a tenth of the time." [15] Lack of capital accumulations, skilled tillage, machines, and factories was tragically retarding the South, and these benefits could be obtained only through free labor.

At no point did Olmsted condemn the slaveholder as a type; at every point he deplored the slaveholding system. Of cruelty he saw little. The contentment shown by many slaves pleased him, and he was quick to praise the paternal kindliness of numerous masters. He found the slaves in general not merely well fed but more abundantly fed, in all probability, than the proletarian class in most other parts of the world. But the social and economic effects of the slave system upon the Southern community as a whole he thought extremely pernicious. It kept the millions of Negroes far below their potentialities for usefulness; it banished free white labor, discouraging the artisan, the mechanic, and the manufacturer; it numbed the ingenuity, skill, and enterprise of the white population; it applied to the land a slovenly, ignorant labor force; and too often it depended on a ruinous exploitation of the soil.[16] He attacked the slaveocracy which defended this scheme of things. "The present agitation of the country," he wrote in the preface to his Back Country, "results less from the labors of abolitionists than from the conceit, avarice, and folly of wealthy owners of slaves. These

14 Olmsted, Journey through Texas, 37.
15 Olmsted, Seaboard Slave States, 481.
16 Idem, 146–148, 286 ff., 195 ff., 208 ff., etc. It should be added that Olmsted did condemn the typical slaveholder of a few areas, such as Eastern Texas, where he met special brutality. These Texas planters, he writes, seemed to wish to work the "damned niggers" with a sole eye to cash profits; they constantly said, "Damn 'em, give 'em hell," as if they meant it; and they were determined to make the slaves' life infernal if they did not submit abjectly. Journey through Texas, 123.

constantly, and by organized action, endeavor to reverse the only line of policy by which safety and peace can, in the nature of things, be secured to the people of the South; for there are moral forces, as well as material, in nature, and there is the same folly in expecting to overcome the one as the other."

The system also struck him as hostile to democracy, fostering the sway of small patrician groups, restricting education, and in many places (most notably South Carolina) inculcating among the superior caste a contempt for the masses.[17] The large body of poor whites, a group whom he defined as those who brought nothing but their labor to market, he regarded as economically and politically the victims of the slave system.

Olmsted was in fact deeply depressed by the squalor, ignorance, and social degradation which he found in large parts of the South. The great mass of Southern whites he described as ill-clothed, ill-fed, and uneducated. Talking with everyone as he jogged along the roads and put up at night at farmhouses, he found that most common people did not know the elementary facts of geography: they thought Virginia south of Carolina, and Indiana somewhere between Georgia and Texas; they believed New York, then a city of seven hundred thousand, a town in which Olmsted must know everybody and see every Southern visitor; they talked in 1856 of the recent annexation of Nebrasky, which they thought as large as the original thirteen States. Many of them read nothing and knew nothing outside the affairs of their locality. He found their tables spread with coarse, ill-cooked food. He travelled almost the length of the South without finding a farmhouse which boasted of two sheets to a bed. He saw white women and children laboring in the fields, often beyond their strength. The scattered homes of the large planters of course bespoke prosperity, and sometimes elegance; but the great majority of Southerners dwelt upon a level of poverty. Indeed, he declares in *A Journey in the Back Country* that he honestly believes that the average free Negro in New York or New England lived in greater comfort than the average white man of the Lower South.

This does not mean that Olmsted failed to perceive the variegated class structure of the South, or to note that many families which lived in discomfort really had considerable capital. He was aware that a large part of the Southern population was composed of small slaveless farmers who owned land, houses, and implements, and that another large part was made up of farmers and small planters each of whom held from one to twenty or thirty slaves. Indeed, in his *Back Country* he states that nine-tenths of the planters were small planters and small slaveowners. What struck him was that many families which possessed a capital that Northerners would have thought substantial had a standard of living that the Northern farmer or mechanic would have despised.

17 *Seaboard Slave States*, 500 ff.

What was the cause of this low standard? In the hilly areas it was attributable to physiographic circumstances: poor land, inaccessibility of markets, and like factors. In Texas, frontier conditions played their part. In the old cotton area, however, Olmsted found the root of bad living standards in the institution of slavery. This region, which had the most favored soil, in the most favored climate, with the cheapest natural facilities of transportation to market for that product which commanded the most urgent commercial demand, should have been far richer than it was. Slave labor was by no means always unprofitable. To many individuals it yielded a very high return indeed, making the great planters opulent. But to the South as a whole, he wrote, it was a relatively unprofitable form of labor. It produced gains only in the sense in which the practice of rolling tobacco a hundred miles to market in casks had once yielded gains in Virginia, and only in the sense in which the harvesting of wheat with sickles and threshing it with flails had once yielded gains. Slave labor was in itself inefficient; the necessity of investing most of the free capital of the South in it, so that funds could not be used for better buildings, livestock, roads, bridges, and increased soil fertility, was calamitous to the section. The constant increase in the slave investment arose largely from the special feature of the Southern economy —its dynamic, expanding character. As Southerners viewed slavery, it was not merely a labor system but a system of colonization as well.

In the distant future Olmsted looked forward to the abolition of slavery as an unprofitable, anachronistic institution. Meanwhile, as the best step for the immediate amelioration of the South, he advocated its restriction to a definite territorial area. The result would be beneficent. The natural increase of the negroes would make them more abundant within this area and provide more and cheaper labor. Land would then rise in productiveness. This rise would bring about better transportation facilities; and, as more goods were exported, so a richer assortment of wares would be imported. Articles of use and comfort, including tools and machinery, would become more accessible, and with them the methods of agriculture would improve. Mines would be opened, textile mills be built, and other factories established—and thus poverty might slowly give way to prosperity. At the same time, the South ought to take some immediate steps toward ultimate emancipation. That is, it should educate the Negro; give him an incentive to perform larger tasks and more skilled work by compensating him for unusual achievement; let him save money, and respect his family relationship:

When he desires to marry, and can persuade any woman to marry him, let the two be dealt with in partnership. Thus a young man or woman will be attractive, somewhat in proportion to his or her reputation for industry and providence. Thus, industry and providence will become fashionable. Oblige them to purchase food for their children, and let them have the benefit of their children's labor, and they will be careful to teach their children to avoid waste and to honor labor. . . . When any man has a balance to his credit equal to his value as a slave, let them constitute him a free man. It shall be optional with him and his employer, whether he shall continue longer in the relation of a servant.[18]

Olmsted was as eager to see the South assimilate its society to a free labor system as Fitzhugh was to convert the North to a rigid caste system based on servile labor; and Olmsted really knew both sections well, while the untraveled Virginia theorist knew neither. The Northerner, who includes facts on the earning power (expressed in food, shelter, and comforts) of the Yankee wage-earner, tells us frankly his opinion of those writers who believed slavery a "positive good." Virginia in 1832 had come near to emancipation; in 1857 she was further from it than ever. "Like a poor man rendered prematurely imbecile by his long endurance of pain, and who, conscious that every pretext against the application of the surgeon's relieving knife has long since been exhausted, finally, in unconquerable cowardice . . . throws himself, in a flood of grateful tears, into the embrace of some contemptible, bragging quack, who pretends that his disease has hitherto been entirely misunderstood . . . ; so Virginia now insultingly spurns from her counsels all who suggest that slavery is *ever* to be eradicated, and not one man is allowed to enter her legislature who dares to declare and demand 'the rights of the middle class.' "[19]

[III]

Another attack upon slavery, this time from the pen of a Southern-born journalist, Hinton Rowan Helper, was still more intimately connected with the economic changes of the time. It let some light—of dubious quality, to be sure—into a dark situation. Such Southern apologists as Harper, declared Olmsted, persistently ignored the poorer class of the white population.[20] As a practical student of all sides of Southern life, Olmsted paid close attention to them, and was distressed by their ignorance, indigence, and helplessness. Intelligent representatives of the underprivileged whites voluntarily told him that slavery laid a heavy incubus upon their folk. The sand-hillers of South Carolina, gaunt, cadaverous, and listless, living in shanties on rice and milk, their women sometimes working at hand looms for a wage of sixteen cents a day; small subsistence-farmers on the Congaree, superstitious and idle, their dress the coarsest

18 *Seaboard Slave States*, 444. For a brief account of the complex social structure of the South and the predominance of the small farmer and small planter of substantial capital see *Ordeal of the Union*, I, 468, 469.
19 *Idem*, 287, 288.
20 *Idem*, 357.

cloth, their chief sustenance a porridge of cow-peas; [21] the illiterate folk of the frontier regions of Louisiana and Arkansas, the wretched starvelings and wild men of the pine woods in Georgia, the backward hillbillies of north Alabama—these were all victims of slavery.[22] He noted that white artisans were constantly made to feel themselves engaged in a degrading competition with slave labor. He commented upon the lack of educational facilities for the poor in most slaveholding communities.[23]

Unexpectedly in 1857 appeared a forcible appeal to that great majority of Southern whites who possessed no slaves. "The Resurrection of the Dry Bones" was the title which the New York *Tribune* placed above its eight solid columns of summary and comment, for if Helper's *Impending Crisis* were read, Ezekiel's prophecy of an exceeding great army risen from the valley of skeletons might be realized. The book soon picked up with enhanced interest because of the concern with all economic subjects generated by the panic.

The few who had heard of Hinton Rowan Helper knew him as author of a disillusioned, prejudiced book, *The Land of Gold*, on a three years' unprofitable sojourn in California. A North Carolinian, the son of a poor blacksmith named Helfer, he had from boyhood reflected upon the pernicious effects of slavery on the white race, and his residence in the North and Far West had crystallized his convictions on that subject. He had no interest whatever in the moral aspects of slavery, and no feeling for the colored people but dislike. To the end of his life he regarded Negroes, Indians, Chinese, and other colored folk as obviously inferior races of mankind; in his work on California he had lumped the Digger Indians and the blacks together as degraded groups, and had attacked the abolitionists.[24] His family had possibly owned slaves (he mentions three by name), and he was convinced that the Negroes could not exist in the United States without becoming subordinate to the will of the whites, or else dropping to a very low level of life.[25] He believed fervently in a white America. The coexistence of these other peoples was a calamity on any terms, but he thought it particularly a calamity when fostered by the crippling institution of slavery, which enriched a few white men and injured all the others. What he had seen of the rapid progress of the North and West had convinced him that the South was being tragically outdistanced, that the blindness of its own citizens to its terrible handicaps was appalling, and that the non-slaveholding majority must be awakened to the evils from which they were suffering.[26]

---

21 *Idem*, 505, 506, 507.
22 Olmsted, *Journey through Texas*, 61, 62.
23 Olmsted, *Seaboard Slave States*, 296, 297.
24 Helper, *The Land of Gold*, 276; T. V. Theobald's MS Life of Helper, Columbia Univ.
25 In *Nojoque: a Question for a Continent*.
26 Southerners had frequently uttered precisely Helper's sentiments. C. J. Faulkner had told the Virginia House of Delegates on January 20, 1832, that the once fertile Common-

Helper resolved to address a warning not to the illiterate "poor whites" in the specialized meaning of that unscientific term, but the great body of self-respecting, thoughtful small farmers, artisans, shopkeepers, and clerks of the South—the millions who had no slaves but held a deluded loyalty to the devitalizing slavery system. If the more primitive whites of the hill-billy type heard his arguments, all the better; but he had sprung from the yeoman and mechanic groups himself, and knew they constituted the real strength of his section.

He was shrewd enough to realize that he must buttress his argument at every step with facts, figures, and influential testimony. Though only in his mid-twenties and mainly self-schooled (he speaks of getting his early education from some half-dozen old books which had found their way into his Davie County neighborhood, and which he read by the light of pine knots at his father's hearth), he was master of a clear, vigorous English style. His *Land of Gold* proves that, and so do his surviving letters of the period.[27] Spending about two years in study, travel, and writing, he completed his manuscript in Baltimore early in 1857. When he sought a publisher there, he was shown a Maryland law which made it a criminal offense to print anything that tended to excite discontent among colored people. The disgusted Helper caught a train to New York. Established publishers like Harper and Appleton rejected his volume, for they had no mind to anger their Southern customers. Finally, after Helper had guaranteed costs of paper and printing, A. B. Burdick of Nassau Street issued the 420-page volume in midsummer. It was at once reviewed far and wide, even in England.[28]

"Non-slaveholders of the South! farmers, mechanics, and workingmen, we take this occasion to assure you that the slaveholders, the arrant demagogues whom you have elected to offices of honor and profit, have hoodwinked you, trifled with you, and used you as mere tools for the consummation of their wicked designs. They have purposely kept you in ignorance, and have, by moulding your passions and prejudices to suit themselves, induced you to act in direct opposition to your dearest rights and interests." So cried Helper, emphasizing the fact that among the six million one hundred eighty-five thousand whites of the slave States in 1850 there had been only three hundred fifty thousand slaveowners or slave-hirers. His book contained much denunciation of "the bloodhounds of slavery." Speaking of the necessity for uprooting

---

wealth had become "barren, desolate, and seared," and that the change was to be attributed solely to the withering effects of slavery; to that unfortunate state of society in which freemen regarded labor as disgraceful, and slaves shrunk from it as a burden tyrannically imposed on them.

27 Notably those in the Blair-Lee Papers.
28 Greater part of N. Y. *Weekly Tribune*, July 4, 1857.

the institution, he wrote that men who wished to perpetuate it were on a level with the basest criminals. At one point he suggested that slaveholders might become the objects of vengeance from non-slaveholders by day and of attacks by the negroes at night. At another he remarked that it was for the poorer

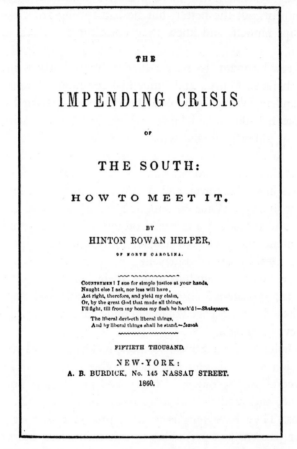

whites to decide whether they should gain justice from the oligarchs, the "slaveocrats," peaceably or by violence. He accused "the slave-driving Democrats" of "almost every brutal outrage that ever disgraced our halls of legislation." This rhetoric defaced the book and was to make trouble for its sponsors. But the main tenor of the volume was sober to the point of dullness.

Negrophobe though Helper was, he did not make the tactical mistake of ignoring the moral and humanitarian argument against slavery. He devoted nearly a hundred pages to showing how Washington, Jefferson, Madison, Marshall, Randolph, and Monroe had condemned or deplored it; how eminent Northerners like Franklin and Jay had bewailed it; how England and other nations bore testimony against it; and how Catholic and Protestant leaders had long regarded it with aversion. Much the greater part of the text, however, was given to economic and social data. With the inflaming scalpel of sectional comparison Helper probed beneath the Southern skin. By census reports, State figures, and letters from mayors he tried to show the vast superiority of the free North in wealth, trade, production, libraries, education, churches, and literature. Slavery, he exclaimed, was ruining the South. Particularly was it ruining the poorer whites, a people who in "deplorable ignorance and squalid poverty" seemed to him below the serfs of Russia.

To what end did Helper print his arid rows of statistical tables, his dull facts on books, schools, and factories North and South? To arouse the non-slaveholding whites to thrust aside the "slaveocrats," to convince them that the Negro must be emancipated, and to urge the nation to transport the blacks back to Africa. "Why will you not see realities?" Helper demanded in effect. "Why will you yeomen and artisans not throw off your thraldom? Do that and you can insist on emancipation followed by African resettlement; the preludes to Southern progress, wealth, and cultural distinction." Essentially, he was appealing to the small farmers and laborers of the South to conduct much the type of revolt which, when great political and economic changes had prepared the way, Ben Tillman, Cole Blease, Huey Long, and others led a generation or two later.

Always specific, Helper laid down an eleven-point program for the slaveless whites. They should begin by a thorough organization for independent political action. Then they should move forward to exclude slaveholders from office, to boycott slaveholding merchants, hotelkeepers, and professional men, and to stop proslavery newspapers. They should end by taxing owners $60 for every slave, the money to be used to carry negroes to Africa, Latin America, or some distant part of the United States. Once the yeomen gained control, they should enforce a general liberation within a reasonable time. "Then let us charter all the ocean steamers, packets, and clipper ships that can be had on liberal terms, and keep them constantly plying between the ports of America and Africa." It was a program as harsh as it was impracticable.

The immediate impact of Helper's book was considerable in the North, but very slight in the South. While Northern journals caught it up, sometimes critically but more often with elation, Southern newspapers tended to ignore it. Gradually, however, it gained sufficient Southern currency to make some notice imperative. Edmund Ruffin early in 1860 was reading it for the second time, and marvelling over Helper's delusion that any real hostility existed between slaveholders and non-slaveholders in the South.[29] Senator James H. Hammond devoted a speech in the spring of 1858 to its blunders, the least of which,

29 Edmund Ruffin, MS Diary, March 1, 1860.

he remarked, was the omission to point out that the three hundred fifty thousand slaveholders represented not individuals but families, and must be multiplied by five or six.[30] Hostile publicists gave it prolonged scrutiny, and in such books as Samuel M. Wolfe's *Helper's Impending Crisis Dissected*, and Gilbert J. Beebe's *Review and Refutation*, contended with many apt illustrations that the poor man enjoyed a better chance in the South than in the North, and insisted that the Negro, stamped with a permanent mental and physical inferiority, held precisely the place where he was most happy and useful.

The non-slaveholders whom Helper specially addressed read the book least of all. Nevertheless, Southern leaders manifestly dreaded the spread of its arguments. The small farmers and poorer whites had so many real grievances in unfair taxation systems, uneven representation, wretched schools, and other social and economic injustices that the call to a class war—the war that Ben Tillman, Jim Ferguson, and Huey Long subsequently led—was dangerous.[31] The race issue could as yet be used to maintain solidarity. Albert G. Brown of Mississippi, representing those rough frontier planters who particularly valued slavery as the quickest means to wealth, sounded the already familiar note of warning. Slavery equalized all white people by assigning to slaves the degrading labor, he wrote. If the slaveless whites let themselves be misled by Helper, they would sink to a lower level. While the rich saved themselves, the poor man would have to submit to Negro competition:

> The negro will intrude into his presence—insist on being treated as an equal —that he shall go to the white man's table, and the white man to his—that he shall share the white man's bed, and the white man his—that his son shall marry the white man's daughter, and the white man's daughter his son. In short, they shall live on terms of perfect social equality.[32]

Yet if a really serious and protracted economic depression ever overtook the South, the suffering yeomanry would be unlikely to remain insensible to some of the arguments which Helper used. These would be expounded with greater force by more skilful men. It was significant that 1858–59 witnessed

---

30 *Cong. Globe*, March 4, 1858. See *National Era*, July 23, 1857, on impact of the book.
31 See the fiction of Faulkner and Erskine Caldwell for pictures of the gulf between the poor whites and aristocracy of the South—and the ill-feeling.
32 A. G. Brown, "Letter on the Interest of Non-Slaveholders in the Perpetuation of African Slavery," 1860 (pamphlet). Most non-slaveholders feared abolition even more than slaveholders. They believed they would suffer the most. The wealthy classes could lift themselves above the harsh results of emancipation; the poor would have to bear the competition of the liberated Negroes and adjust themselves to the new equality. They would have to live in a country delivered back to barbarism—so at least some of them reasoned. What an appalling fate would be theirs, wrote Daniel R. Hundley to the *Southern Advocate* (December 12, 1860): "What social monstrosities, what desolated fields, what civil broils, what robberies, rapes, and murders of the poorer whites by the emancipated blacks would then disfigure the whole fair face of this prosperous, smiling and happy Southern land."

the rise in the border States, including Virginia and North Carolina, of powerful "Opposition" movements, which we shall describe later; movements based
largely on the inequalities in taxation, representation, education, and other
matters from which the small farmers of few or no slaves suffered. The keen-
eyed journalist E. L. Godkin, after travelling widely on horseback in the South
in 1856–57, wrote that the world had long rung with the wrongs and miseries
of the Irish peasant and the Turkish rayah; that he had seen much of both
classes; and that he believed the poorest whites of the South were worse off
than either. Some kind of revolt could not forever be prevented.

[IV]

An inevitable result of the depression was the heightening of economic and
class antipathies. The old, deep-seated animosity of the frontier toward the
metropolis, the suspicion the West always held of eastern banking and trading
interests, were touched to new life. "Who but Eastern jobbers and speculators
are responsible for the panic?" demanded the Chicago *Press and Tribune*.[33]
Farmers from Ohio to Kansas, suffering from frozen markets and beggarly
prices, laid the blame on the manipulations of Boston, New York, and Philadelphia. The many settlers who lost their land through the foreclosures of
eastern mortgages were filled with resentment. The hardship imposed by high
interest payments to lenders, and by the refusal of railroads to make any material
reduction in freight charges, brought down many a curse on the head of Boston
plutocrats and New York Shylocks. Farmers of Central Illinois in 1858 held a
convention which passed severe resolutions against "trading combinations,"
banks, and railroads for depressing prices and lifting interest rates and transportation levies. They urged that every community form a Farmers' Club to
strengthen the economic position of the tillers of the soil, and give them that
class equality which they had lost by their own neglect. A Farmers' Congress
at Centralia later in the year went further. It was angrily convinced that stock-
yards and grain-market rings were robbing the agriculturist. Resolutions were
passed, declaring that the producing class should assert not merely its equality
but its supremacy, condemning rules for trading made by non-producers, and
calling for the establishment of cooperative buying and selling agencies. This
was plainly a forecast of the Granger movement.[34]

Even in Cleveland, Chicago, and Milwaukee, surly mutterings were heard
over the ten or fifteen percent which these cities had to pay for New York
exchange; a cruel imposition, thought many. Throughout the upper Mississippi

33 Chicago *Tribune*, quoted in N. Y. *Tribune*, November 4, 1857.
34 Beveridge, *Lincoln*, II, 569, 570, fn.

Valley, too (as in the South), an intensified demand for home manufactures was heard. Five-sixths of the Wisconsin and Iowa farmers wore shoes made in Massachusetts and hats made in New York; and this gear was paid for by corn which the Iowan sold for twenty-five cents a bushel and which cost the eastern workman seventy-five. Why not bring the shoe factory to Burlington and the hat factory to Oshkosh, saving freight both ways?

Even if manufacturing could not be transplanted in a hurry, the commercial system certainly might be modified to bring its center of gravity farther west. Horace Greeley, visiting Davenport, Iowa, the winter after the panic, prophesied that fewer merchants would thereafter make semi-annual pilgrimages to the seaboard for goods. Why should five thousand men take a costly journey of two thousand miles when two hundred agents could buy for them more judiciously? An expansion of jobbing businesses into the thriving western towns —into Dubuque, Racine, Burlington, Rock Island, Quincy, Springfield, Peoria, South Bend, Jackson, and Kenosha as well as Chicago, Milwaukee, and Indian-apolis—would benefit everybody. Local merchants, replenishing their stocks more frequently, could pay for smaller and more numerous orders in cash or short-term notes; the goods would be fresher; and the east would have a more stable business.

Indeed, Westerners manifested a widespread feeling that henceforth they ought to stand more sturdily on their own feet, and pay less heed to eastern speculators, land sharks, railroad promoters, and boomers generally. (They forgot how many of these breeds were their own.) We need fewer dream cities, fewer surveyors, lithographers, and auctioneers, wrote Illinois and Iowa editors. But, they added, never has such an opportunity existed for Easterners to come out with a few thousand dollars and buy good prairie farms at rock-bottom prices.

Many poor men, caught in the depression, turned wistful thoughts to the old idea of free homesteads. Farms, in the boom days, had cost altogether too much. An Iowa correspondent of the New York *World* declared that the government's stubborn insistence on selling its land at high prices had been the primary cause of the northwestern depression.[35] It was a quaintly fallacious view, but not a few adopted it. Similarly, a demand arose for more competition in the transportation field. Was it not exorbitant rail charges that made wheat sell in the West for seventy cents when it brought $1.20 in New York? asked farmers. The government should develop rivers, canals, and harbors. On these points, said midlanders, the East and South must give way.[36] If the industrial

35   Iowa correspondence, N. Y. *World* quoted in *Weekly Illinois State Journal*, July 25, 1860.

36   Madison Kuhn, "Economic Issues and the Rise of the Republican Party in the North-west," MS dissertation, Univ. of Chicago.

East was to receive the benefit of higher tariffs, then the agricultural West must have homestead legislation, and western shippers must have internal improvements.

A bargain on this basis could obviously be struck within the new Republican Party; but such a compact would just as obviously be regarded by the South as a hostile movement. Appropriations for internal improvements, A. G. Brown had told the Senate in 1856, are "a tribute levied upon the labor and wealth of one part of the country for the benefit of the other!" [37]

[V]

The most unfortunate of all results of the depression was the deepening of the chasm between North and South. Angry sectional recrimination began at once. Herschel V. Johnson laid the troubles of the Georgia banks to "the assaults from the commercial centers of the North." Greeley retorted with a peremptory summons: "Pay Up!"—if Georgia would only meet her commercial debts, the North would be more solvent.[38] The fact that the South escaped the worst evils of the depression strengthened the arrogant self-confidence of the Hammonds and Slidells. It was *our* cotton, Southerners were soon boasting, which when shipped abroad at good prices lifted the prostrate North Atlantic region to its feet. When the North and West began demanding reform and readjustment, the South, complacent in the rich yield of its main staples, was content to maintain the *status quo*. Its labor system, its steady expansion of cotton production, its well-tested principles, said Southerners, gave it economic, social, and political stability; why alter them? Only its excessive dependence on the Yankee manufacturer, banker, and shipper needed to be changed. Will the South, asked Johnson, "break the only chain that now fetters her giant limbs?"

More than ever, after 1857, the South chafed under the burden of its real and fancied tribute to Northern capitalists and middlemen. When the Boston *Post* estimated that New England sold sixty million dollars' worth of merchandise annually to the South, editors below the Potomac asked how much profit the Yankees extracted. When New Englanders boasted that their large fleet was the common carrier of the South, cotton shippers inquired just how much wealth it had taken from Southern pockets. Above all, Southern producers denounced Northern factors, bankers, jobbers, and exporters as leeches battening upon their hard-earned income.

The panic helped convince cotton-growers that their sales had become altogether too heavily dependent on eastern financial interests. Whenever Wall

37 Debate of May 6, 1858; *National Intelligencer* report. Cf. *Cong. Globe*, 34th Cong., 1st Sess., 1118, 1119.
38 Both quotations in N. Y. *Tribune*, November 4, 1857.

Street so mismanaged its affairs (as by delaying to pay its just debts to Europe) that no demand for sterling bills existed, then the cotton market sagged. And not merely did Southern staples pay a large profit to legitimate agents through whose hands they passed; they yielded—so the complaint ran—another large

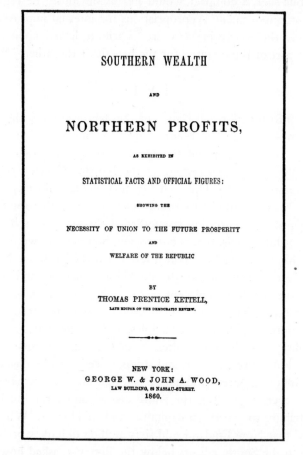

SOUTHERN WEALTH

AND

NORTHERN PROFITS,

AS EXHIBITED IN

STATISTICAL FACTS AND OFFICIAL FIGURES:

SHOWING THE

NECESSITY OF UNION TO THE FUTURE PROSPERITY

AND

WELFARE OF THE REPUBLIC

BY

THOMAS PRENTICE KETTELL,
LATE EDITOR OF THE DEMOCRATIC REVIEW.

NEW YORK:
GEORGE W. & JOHN A. WOOD,
LAW BUILDING, 69 NASSAU-STREET.
1860.

profit to mere speculators and manipulators. Before long, Thomas Prentice Kettell, former editor of the *Democratic Review*, was bringing out his effective book on *Southern Wealth and Northern Profits*, which set forth in some one hundred and seventy pages of text and tables the thesis that, while the South produced vast wealth, the North grabbed most of it.[39] His argument boiled down to the old physiocratic doctrine that all profits of manufacture and trade come out of the land; and he estimated the annual Northern profits taken from the South at $231,500,000.[40] Like Helper, he made careless and emotional use of

39 New York, George W. and John A. Wood, 1860.
40 Kettell, *Southern Wealth and Northern Profits*, 127.

statistics. At one point he compared the wealth of New York and New Orleans, implying that the Northern city had a bloated prosperity, when his figures actually showed that their ratio of wealth to population was about the same.[41] The inevitable rejoinder promptly came in Samuel Powell's *Notes on Southern Wealth and Northern Profits.*[42] But Kettell found a public already burning with indignation.

Here, said some slaveholders, was the answer to Helper's fallacious analysis. In early days, Virginia and South Carolina had been busy, opulent States, boasting a vigorous leadership. Now wide areas were in decay, once-smiling farms were used for cattle ranges, and stately mansions were falling into ruin. Why? It was nonsense to point to slavery as the reason. The Tidewater South had possessed slavery at the height of its power and glory; Brazil and Cuba, possessing slavery, yet flourished. The true reason, wrote Richmond and Charleston editors, was that the North placed unequal burdens on the Southern people. The protective tariff, the fishing bounties, the charges of brokers, bankers, and shippers, all wrung a vast tribute from the South. The national system, wrote E. A. Pollard, has been "made a conduit of wealth and power to the North, while it drained the South of nearly every element of material prosperity."[43] The same view was expounded with still greater vigor in the articles, lectures, and letters of George Frederick Holmes, an omnivorous scholar of English parentage who became professor in the University of Virginia in 1857.

The South, according to its leaders, was wealthy and powerful, but might be far stronger if the North would but do it economic justice. Events of 1857–58 seemed to prove how completely dependent the world was on the great Southern staples. In Great Britain cotton manufacturing stood third in the list of occupations, employing more than half a million people directly and hundreds of thousands more indirectly. Shipments of cotton goods and yarn in 1856 had constituted one-third the value of the kingdom's exports. The welfare of countless British families and the prosperity of the country seemed bound up with the cotton-textile business; and the South supplied about four-fifths of the entire British consumption.[44] Fear that war might suddenly cut off this supply haunted the pillows of innumerable Britons, and spurred Manchester men in 1857 to form an association to promote cotton in other parts of the globe. India, where American seed had been planted, was the chief hope of British mill owners; but nobody pretended that Surat cotton approached in quality the

41 *Ibid.*, 132, 133.
42 Philadelphia, C. Sherman and Son, 1861. See also Wolfe, *Helper's Impending Crisis Dissected.* I have treated Kettell in another connection in *Ordeal of the Union*, I, 470, 471.
43 In *The Lost Cause*, echoing many early editorials.
44 London *Economist*, April 25, June 20, 1857.

"Uplands," "Bowed Georgia," or "New Orleans" grades from the South.[45] Lancashire had built on American fibres one of the most remarkable industrial edifices in the history of mankind; her two thousand factories, with twenty-one million five hundred thousand spindles and three hundred thousand power looms, had filled England with fortunes and raised Lancashire workers to the head of the European laboring class.[46] How could Lancashire exist without the South? For that matter, what could the cotton industry of the North, with nearly five million spindles, do without Southern production? And how would the world fare without Southern sugar and tobacco? [47]

While the panic increased the confidence of Southerners in their resources, it sharpened their resentment over tariff burdens which Kettell estimated at forty millions a year. Secretary Cobb, Senator Hammond, A. Dudley Mann, and others labored to establish direct trade with Europe and direct mercantile and banking connections with England, as the one way to lift the South to economic independence. Our drawbacks, declared Hammond, have not been inferior energy or intellect, and certainly not slavery, but our shallow bars, yellow fever, want of capital (for we use our money to settle fresh lands and thus clothe and feed the world)—and Northern exactions. Give the South direct trade, give it a fair tariff, land, and taxation system, and it will yet lead the world.[48] As Northern workers clamored for free homesteads and Northern manufacturers for higher tariffs, Southern opposition became more determined. "We must separate," Edmund Ruffin was writing in 1857, "and the sooner it is done, the greater will be the relative strength of the Southern party, and the more sure will be the success of the movement." [49]

[VI]

The tariff—this, on the morrow of the stinging blow from the panic, suddenly became a party and sectional issue. With the object of cutting down an unwelcome surplus,[50] Congress had just finished (in the last month of Pierce's Administration) a slight reduction of the rates of 1846, passed almost without debate, without visible relation to sectional interests, and without arousing any popular feeling. Now, however, the sleeping tiger of tariff controversy awakened, to ramp and roar his way through the next three generations of history.

45 *Ibid.*, May 23, 1857.
46 Henderson, *The Lancashire Cotton Famine, 1861–1865.*
47 Clark, *Hist. Manufactures in U. S., 1807–1860.* 552–558.
48 James Hammond to Cobb, March 29, 1859; Hammond Papers, LC.
49 Edmund Ruffin, February 2, 1857; C. C. Clay Papers, Duke Univ.
50 Stanwood, *Amer. Tariff Controversies in Nineteenth Century*, II, 83–109.

As a matter of fact, the tariff had been a subject of occasional contention in the press and in local politics, for the old Whig demand for increased duties had been inherited by a powerful wing of the Republican organization. Until now, however, the debate had been languidly intermittent, for most Whigs had been as moderate as sucking doves. Such men as Tom Corwin, J. J. Crittenden, and even Horace Greeley stood not for head-high but merely breast-high protection. The United States, they declared, ought industrially to be more self-sufficient, and less a British appanage. They quoted the words of the London *Times* in 1851: "For all practical purposes the United States are far more closely united with this kingdom than any one of our colonies, and [with us] the United States keeps up a perpetual interchange of the most important good offices; taking our manufactures and our surplus population, and giving us in return the materials of industry, of revenue, and of life." [51] A moderate, well-graduated set of import duties, helping the nation's nascent industries attain strength, would be the shortest road to genuine free trade; for with maturity these industries could fearlessly meet world competition. [52] To this postulate, such low-tariff statesmen as Robert J. Walker, supported by editors like William Cullen Bryant and Henry J. Raymond, had replied that the Treasury did not need more revenue, that it would be iniquitous to tax the many to benefit the few, and that our industries were already great and growing. "What has a giant to do with swaddling clothes?" [53]

The basic argument of the Whig-Republican protectionists was that the United States ought to produce its own iron, cloth, and most other manufactured commodities; that this could not be done while European wares came in unchecked floods; and that, when home manufactures once gained vigor, they would benefit American producers of raw materials far more than any European markets could. No nation, they argued, had ever grown rapidly in wealth, power, intelligence, and arts while exporting raw materials and importing finished goods. On the contrary, such nations had always been impoverished.

The United States, many said, had rolling mills, but they were very poorly utilized; for, without a tariff, profits were impossible. Yet one great iron mill in Chicago would open a market for more Illinois foodstuffs than ten such mills in England. Look at Germany! By a wise policy of protection she had created a textile industry which supplied her with cloth more cheaply than any other nation in the world. Before 1820, German cloth was seldom seen in America, but by 1850 it sold in New York on equal terms with British

51 London *Times*, June 4, 1851.
52 N. Y. *Weekly Tribune*, June 28, 1851.
53 Robert J. Walker quoted in N. Y. *Tribune*, June 26, 1851.

cloth. On the other hand, Italy had no protection and, except for silks, almost no manufactures; and the poverty of her people was proverbial. Not even in Ireland, another unprotected country, was there a more irregularly employed, wretchedly paid, shabbily clad population. The United States was exporting grain, meat, cotton, and lumber; it was importing rails, clothing, china, and hardware; and it had to redress the adverse balance of trade by pouring California gold into British pockets, and in addition filling them with bonds and stocks.[54]

In the spirit of Hamilton, the moderate Whig-Republican protectionists had pleaded for a balanced economy; and Henry Carey, who wrote many of the New York *Tribune's* editorials on the subject in the fifties, entitled one of his most effective volumes *The Harmony of Interests, Agricultural, Manufacturing, and Commercial*. Protection had benefited the German farmers, declared Carey, for not only did the industrial population of Germany consume large quantities of food, but the mills furnished agriculture with implements, garb, and household wares at prices as low as those in Manchester, Sheffield, and Leeds. The seaboard merchants of the United States were assured that tariffs, while not lessening foreign commerce, would greatly increase domestic trade. On every hand the protectionists found facts to illustrate their views. Certain Fall River manufacturers in 1850 made nearly half a million shawls, supplying the Canadian as well as American market; and this was held to prove the value of the thirty percent duty—the American shawl industry had become sturdy, and was furnishing goods at lower cost than if no duty had ever been laid.[55] Charles A. Dana, making a vacation tour of the Adirondacks, found that the Saranac Valley, which under the tariff of 1842 had promised to become a thriving ironmaking area, had been blighted by the low rates of 1846. Out of sixty-six furnaces and bloomeries, only three were left running, and they at only one-third their capacity.[56]

But the great body of Americans had seemed content with the Walker Tariff. Why not, when the national revenue was rising to unprecedented heights and furnishing a broad Treasury surplus? Why not, when in the first seven years of the fifties the nation's exports rose from $137,000,000 to $338,000,000; the imports from $178,000,000 to $360,000,000; and the shipping in foreign trade from one million four hundred thousand tons to two million three hundred thousand? When business in nearly every field was expanding, and with it banking and credit? To protectionists demanding a balanced economy, Douglas for the West and Walker for the South replied that a steady, healthy develop-

54 N. Y. *Tribune*, September 24, 1851.
55 N. Y. *Tribune*, August 8, 1851.
56 N. Y. *Weekly Tribune*, September 6, 1851.

ment was providing it. A forced growth of manufacturing at the expense of agriculture and the consumer was rejected by men satisfied with the existing system. "The result of that system," wrote Walker in 1853, "has been to double our exports and imports, and also our revenues; whilst the taxes imposed on our people have been diminished one-half. At the same time the increase of our tonnage, foreign and coastwise, has been unprecedented. These are great results, but I assure you, the good work is only fairly begun." [57]

But now, in 1857–58, to many the results seemed apples of Sodom. "That an efficient Protective Tariff would have kept our country out of the vortex of this mad whirlpool . . . we most earnestly believe," declared the *Tribune*.[58] Most Republican journals in the East opened fire on the low tariff breastworks, with the *National Intelligencer* and other Whig journals joining the bombardment. Friends of Seward recalled that in a speech of March 1, 1855, on iron rail duties, he had foretold the panic, and even the year of its occurrence, with signal precision. The government was stimulating importation, he said, when it should stimulate production, and the result would be a disastrous revulsion in 1857 or soon after.[59]

In the debates which filled the winter of 1857–58 the Democrats found the readiest scapegoat for the panic in banking errors. Buchanan told Congress that such calamities were inevitable so long as the amount of paper currency and the management of loans and discounts were left to fourteen hundred irresponsible State banks; and Nathan Appleton of Boston, echoed by a thousand voices in the South and West, laid the principal blame on the New York bankers, greedy manipulators who had expanded too much in fair weather, and contracted too harshly when the tempest lowered.[60] Most Republicans, however, found the scapegoat in the Walker Tariff of 1846, and the more recent tariff reductions.

Their demand for higher duties was posited on two main grounds. Pointing to the sudden stoppage of iron mills, textile factories, and other establishments under sharp European competition, they showed that these businesses suffered doubly from foreign goods when falling prices made the *ad valorem* duties a weaker defense than ever. Again, they argued that the country had imported too lavishly, spending its money recklessly for foreign merchandise, and letting an adverse trade balance drain off gold bullion and specie sorely needed at home. We have indulged in wild luxuries, said the Cincinnati *Times*; only California gold saved us from earlier disaster; yet a prudent tariff would have

57 Robert J. Walker, February 7, 1853; Cushing Papers, LC.
58 N. Y. *Weekly Tribune*, January 30, 1858.
59 *Cong. Globe*, March 1, 1855.
60 N. Y. *Weekly Tribune*, October 24, 1857; see Appleton's *Remarks on Currency and Banking*, enlarged edition, 1858.

made us the richest people in the world.[61] The foreign exchange brokers, lamented the *National Intelligencer*, have shipped money abroad in floods:

During the last fiscal year ending June 30, 1857, these brokers have sent out of the United States to pay for drygoods, cotton, and woolen cloths, hardware, glassware, cutlery, jack-knives, and domestic wares; saws, gimlets, axes, and chisels; rolled iron, hammered iron, bar iron, railroad iron, and other like things which should have been made by our own people, the sum of $69,136,922 in solid gold and silver.

Yet the *South* naively wonders at the scarcity of *specie*.[62]

With a Democratic Congress in power until at least March 4, 1859, and a Democratic President until at least March 4, 1861, no merely spasmodic demand for higher tariffs could accomplish anything. A sustained crusade was needed. Were any economic constituencies sufficiently strong and earnest to make a ten-year uphill fight? The answer lay primarily with the iron and textile industries.

Little by little, a compact, able, and well-to-do body of ironmasters had arisen in the East—and 1857 found them bitterly incensed. The United States was obviously suited to a great iron industry. It had iron ore, coal, and the necessary fluxes in close juxtaposition; it had capital, skill, and labor. Iron was demanded in ever-greater quantities for rails, farm implements, and articles of popular use. Inevitably, ironmasters and consumers of cheap British iron had clashed along a widening front. Walker, James Guthrie, and other low-tariff leaders believed that a just balance could be struck between the two interests, with iron manufacture growing steadily but slowly under moderate duties as the national needs increased. Production of iron, steel, and articles made from them was greater in proportion to population in 1850 than in 1840; greater in 1855 than in 1850. Secretary Guthrie had written in 1856 that considering this growth, the rising cost of freights from abroad as the interior population moved westward, and the constant home improvements in iron and steel manufacture, "Americans would be justified in expecting home supply for their own consumption before the year 1870 was reached." [63]

This slow, low-profit growth, however, often interrupted by setbacks and losses, did not suit aggressive industrialists. The *ad valorem* duty on iron, they declared, offered an inadequate protection. Fixed under the Walker Act at roughly thirty percent of the invoiced value of foreign iron, it fell whenever prices were lowered, giving lessened assistance to American mills just when they needed it most. When the Act was passed, a ton of railroad iron had paid

61 Cincinnati *Times*, October 7, 1857.
62 *National Intelligencer*, October 24, 1857.
63 Secretary of the Treasury, *Annual Report*, 1856.

about $15 in duty, and domestic production seemed rapidly overtaking consumption. But the British ironmasters in various ways reduced costs and prices, so that by 1850 the effective duty had fallen to half what it was in 1846; and many American furnaces were sold under the sheriff's hammer. A period of rising prices, under the influence of gold from California, then began. Iron quotations rose, and the duty went up once more to the point of protection, so that in 1852–54 American iron output steadily increased.[64] Railroad building was active not only in the United States and Britain, but all over Europe, in India, and in South America. The rolling mills of the entire globe in 1852 could produce enough rails for only some six thousand miles of track. Under the eager American demand for rails at $70–$80 a ton, the domestic mills (which of course added the duty to their charges) prospered. But a new era of cruel competition was at hand. British geologists found extensive ore deposits in the Cleveland area of Yorkshire, where fifty or sixty new mills instantly sprang up.[65]

By the end of 1854, plethoric imports had dispelled what Abram S. Hewitt called "the delusion that Great Britain could not supply all the iron required by the world at the present time." British rails had fallen in a year from $70 to $50, the *ad valorem* duties dropping with them. Stocks of iron were accumulating in every market in the world, and a majority of American mills had closed. As they faced ruin, the agonized ironmasters had once more raised a clamorous demand for higher duties.[66]

Yet in the South and West, the great Democratic areas, this demand still met the sternest opposition. Much of the press teemed with articles insisting that *all* duties on railway iron be abolished forthwith. Every railroad, declared one writer, must pay at least $1,500 a mile in tariffs, a hardship felt by new sections struggling to reach an ordinary standard of prosperity.[67] Why, demanded another, should hard-working communities, intent upon improving their transport facilities, pay tribute to selfish eastern millowners? Let the easterners show enough efficiency to meet the British price for rails, and let them build new mills in the West, where they would find abundant materials and an eager market.[68] In 1852, Hewitt, lobbying in Washington for better duties on iron, wrote a friend that no tariff bill could be passed without Southern and Western votes, and that concessions on railway iron would have to be made to obtain higher rates on other shapes. When the tariff of 1857 actually reduced iron duties, the struggling mill owners were deeply resentful.[69]

64 N. Y. *Tribune*, July 10, 1854.
65 Nevins, *Hewitt*, 108–111.
66 *Idem*, 112.
67 "Memphis" in *National Intelligencer*, May 6, 1856.
68 "Indiana" in *National Intelligencer*, May 17, 1856.
69 Nevins, *Hewitt*, 154, 155.

Textile manufacturers insisted as loudly as ironmasters that the Walker Tariff was grossly unfair, and indeed disastrous. Most woolen mills had been reduced to utter ruin, one observer complained in 1857. A steep duty on raw wool, and a lack of any correspondingly high duty on finished woolens, had placed them at the mercy of British competitors. Either raw wool should be made free (and free raw materials was classic Democratic doctrine, often stated by Guthrie), or satisfactory tariffs should be imposed on woolen goods; and though some sheep-growers might protest against the former step, efforts to increase sheep-farming by tariffs had accomplished nothing.

As for cotton textiles, manufacturers grumbled that Walker's abolition of "minimums" had stopped all efforts to make the finer fabrics and invited a torrent of British goods. In ten years, 1846–56, the imports of British printed and dyed cottons had leaped from thirteen million yards to one hundred four-teen million; those of plain calicos from ten million to ninety million. By partial use of cheap Bengal fibre, Lancashire was able to produce low-priced goods more cheaply than Lawrence and Lowell. These plaints fell on deaf ears.[70] The tariff of 1857 slightly reduced cotton duties, and placed only the lowest grades of raw wool on the free list, while reducing the duty on finished woolens. Textile manufacturers, too, were sullenly indignant.[71]

All these resentful interests had money to fight their battle. The capital invested in cotton manufacturing by 1860 approached a hundred millions. Woolen manufactures, situated mainly in New England and the Middle States, by that year had an annual value exceeding sixty millions. Northwestern Penn-sylvania and northeastern Ohio alone then counted sixty-six furnaces.[72] And ironmasters and textile men found potent allies in other industries. Even the South had one important group of tariff claimants—the sugar growers. Com-peting with the West Indies and Brazil, they too grumbled over the *ad valorem* system. In the spring of 1857, a spokesman for the Louisiana planters asserted that the thirty percent levy upon the high valuations then ruling was double the amount needed to satisfy sugar producers if made a permanent and specific duty. It came to two and a half cents a pound on fine sugar, which was at least a cent more than growers wanted. What they did ask was a fixed protection against heavy imports when a large home crop (as in 1853–54) brought prices to a ruinously low level. It is significant that J. D. B. De Bow, editing his *Review* in the sugar metropolis, and wishing to see industries developed in the South, held that protection was frequently desirable.

All the manufactures of the country taken together in 1860 had an invested

70 *National Intelligencer*, January 29, 1857.
71 Dewey, *Financial Hist. U. S.*, 262, 263.
72 Eighth Census, Vol. III (Manufactures); Clark, *Manufactures, 1807–1860*, I, 498, 499.

capital exceeding a billion. The iron men had already learned the value of a regularly employed lobbyist, John L. Hayes, in Washington. In the period of depression, many industrialists rallied to wage a determined campaign.

They knew that they had a hard struggle ahead of them. Intermittent and lackadaisical effort had accomplished nothing against the insistence of the rural South and West upon cheap rails to extend their trackage, cheap implements for farms, and cheap cloth for yeomen and slaves. It could accomplish nothing, so long as a host of merchants, railroad builders, and land speculators took sides with the agricultural interests. The opening-up of the Mississippi valley and the Southwest seemed more important, for the nonce, than developing the seaboard industries by artificial stimulants. In the debates on the tariff of 1857, Representatives from three sections, Norton of Ohio, Boyce of South Carolina, and Bennett of New York, had agreed that the great mass of the American people should not be required to pay an indirect tax in favor of the manufacturers, while every Massachusetts member had voted for the downward revision. Garnett of Virginia had expressed the hope that America, the greatest democracy in the world, would take the leadership in a grand movement for unfettered commercial intercourse among all nations.[73] The same hope was expressed by Raymond in the New York *Times*. It was an alluring ideal, closely connected with some of the most idealistic currents of the time. Many of those who espoused the low-tariff policy were obedient to the bright vision of a freely interconnected world, first painted by Adam Smith and now eloquently defended by John Stuart Mill.

It would take time, labor, and money to make headway against these convictions. But the campaign was at once opened. While the *Tribune, National Intelligencer,* and Philadelphia *Press* pleaded for higher duties, members of Congress from industrial districts began to raise their voices. Senator Simmons of Rhode Island was quick to answer Buchanan's message blaming the State banks. Not so, he said; productive home labor had been unable to compete with foreign dumping, and an upward revision of the tariff would both fill the Treasury and revive industry.[74] Certain circumstances favored the protectionists. The old obstacle of the constant Treasury surplus was gone. New York was now a Republican State, while Pennsylvania, with her iron interests prostrate, had become doubtful.

[VII]

New wine had been poured into old bottles, and they were cracking. Through all the political movements after the panic, disputation on economic

73 *Cong. Globe,* February 10, 1857.
74 *Idem,* December 18, 1857.

9

The Sixteenth Slave State?

ANY CRITIC of democracy who wished to indict its American workings would have done well to attend the constitutional convention which sat at Lecompton in the fall of 1857. Destiny waited upon this body. The fate of the Administration, of the Democratic Party, and of the nation itself was to be mightily affected by its acts. And what was it? The sixty delegates, forty-eight of them from slave States, had been chosen by a small minority of voters in a rigged election; they met under the shadow of fresh election frauds committed by their supporters; they were regarded with open hostility by the majority of citizens. Four-fifths of them were ignorant, semi-illiterate, and prejudiced men, totally unrepresentative of the Kansas population. One of President Buchanan's correspondents wrote that he had not supposed such a wild set, with hardly six fit debaters in the lot, could have been found even on that frontier.[1] They began with three days of struggle to get a quorum, and ended with a shout from one prominent member: "Now, boys, let's come and take a drink!"[2]

Newspapermen from far and near had gathered in the picturesque hamlet, beautifully situated on a low bluff above the Kansas River, the hills and valleys bright with autumn foliage. They watched the evolutions of the several hundred Federal troops, horse, foot, and a brass field-battery, who had pitched their tents and stood ready to keep order. They examined the two hotels, the American and National, the heavily stocked barrooms, and the three shops—a hardware store, drugstore, and Leamer's general store. They lounged about the office of the weekly *National Democrat*, and some had their pictures taken by the ambrotype artist who had come in for the convention.[3] They climbed the steps of the two-story, clapboarded hall as the delegates gathered, and collected

1 Findley Patterson to Buchanan, November 10, 1857; Buchanan Papers.
2 Lecompton Correspondence, dated November 7, 1857, N. Y. *Weekly Tribune*, November 28, 1857.
3 See files of Lecompton *National Democrat*, October, November.

opinions on the vital issue: Would the constitution be submitted to popular vote? [4]

When debate began, the Northern correspondents could hardly believe their ears. If any fact in Kansas was plain, it was that an overwhelming majority of residents wanted a free State. Yet a preponderance of the convention was resolved to adopt a proslavery constitution and send it direct to Congress for acceptance. And if this preponderant body was, in the words of the Emporia *Kanzas News*, a set of "broken-down political hacks, demagogues, fire-eaters, perjurers, ruffians, ballot-box stuffers, and loafers," they had some shrewd leaders. Their managers included J. H. Danforth of Georgia, a tall, well-built man of piercing eye and stern countenance, who spoke little but showed consummate skill in maneuver; the dashing and persuasive young Colonel W. H. Jenkins, of South Carolina origin; and A. W. Jones, a lawyer from Virginia who was an accomplished wire-puller. At times they were reinforced by Lucius S. Bolling, an attorney from Georgia, who had oratorical force, and by Captain J. W. Martin of the reckless band called the Kickapoo Rangers. They gained encouragement from the Southern press, now in full cry for direct transmission of the constitution to Congress. Some of them exhibited letters from important Southern leaders, R. M. T. Hunter of Virginia having written two widely published arguments for this course.[5] Both leaders and followers knew that the one last chance of a slave State lay in writing an adroit instrument and avoiding any popular vote. All were influenced by hatred of Governor Walker—grown greater since his denunciation of the recent frauds.[6]

The moderate minority in the convention, who knew that some type of popular submission was almost imperative, were led by John Calhoun, Rush Elmore, and John D. Henderson; supported, of course, by Governor Walker, who was absent, and Secretary Stanton, who was present. Unfortunately, they lacked the single-minded determination of their enemies. Calhoun, with his record of activity among Illinois Democrats and his personal friendship with Douglas, was an honest believer in popular sovereignty. But his limited moral stamina had been weakened by whiskey—the Chicago *Tribune* reporter wrote of his

4 The Cincinnati *Gazette*, N. Y. *Tribune*, *Herald*, and *Times*, St. Louis *Republican*, and *Missouri Democrat*, all had correspondents present. According to Dr. Gihon, Lecompton had been a sort of moral plague spot, shunned by good citizens. The personnel of the convention was not unlike that of the regular Lecompton legislature. Gihon in his book on Geary in Kansas tells of a stage-driver who, falling into bad company in a Lecompton barroom, slept off his excesses in a shed. Roused the next morning by a man who wanted his vote for a bank charter, he flew into a passion, ejaculating: "It is bad enough to get drunk and make a fool of myself, but no man shall insult me by mistaking me for a member of the Kansas legislature!"

5 Nichols, *Disruption of the American Democracy*, 122.

6 See full characterizations of convention membership, Emporia *Kanzas News*, November 7, 14, 21, 1857.

florid face, swinish eyes, and Bardolph nose—and by association with proslavery Kansas politicians. He gave battle, but not with the temper demanded by the crisis. When the struggle ended the freesoil citizens bitterly indicted him as villain and traitor.[7] Rush Elmore, of a distinguished Southern family, had been appointed Federal judge by Pierce and was now esteemed the ablest attorney in the Territory. A stalwart six-footer of massive frame, his large head set squarely on his shoulders, his jaw firm, he was vigorous, conservative, and unscrupulous.[8] He spoke effectively for submission. Henderson was editor of the Leavenworth *Journal*. The trio were given assistance by Hugh Moore, vice-president of the convention, a former Georgian living in Leavenworth and a stump speaker full of Union-saving oratory, who after some hesitation came over to their side.

Sundry speakers for the majority made it plain that they still hoped to see a Southern type of society dominate Kansas. John W. Randolph of Atchison, a stonemason out of Kentucky, proposed that the upper age for militia duty be fixed at forty. "I think," he said, "that a man of forty-five is too old to be run about over the prairies at the will of some boy of eighteen who mought be captin. I expect we air goin' to make a slave State, and if we air most of the spectators will be children and niggers, and I object to makin' such a spectacle of an old man jist to make laughin' for niggers." [9] Warmer debate was evoked by a proposal that the legislature be empowered to stop the importation of slaves for sale. This paralleled the statutes of Georgia and some other Southern States. The object, said Randolph, was to prevent negro-traders from bringing in the scrapings of the Southern communities: "all the old, blind, halt, and lame niggers, so that they would get all the mean niggers. It would be so if the African slave trade was opened. The country would be filled with mean niggers." On motion of Bolling, who wanted no interference whatever with slavery, the restriction was eliminated.

The convention really began work, taking up draft sections prepared by various committees, on October 28. Most of the instrument, conventional in form and based on older State constitutions, was readily disposed of. The critical points were the slavery article and the issue of submission or non-submission; and the culminating battle took place November 6–7, the convention finally adjourning at one o'clock Sunday morning, November 8.

This final battle was a tensely exciting contest. As the convention for two days debated into the small hours, newspapermen reported bitter wrangling and the gloomiest uncertainty as to the outcome. The radical non-submissionists were determined to win, and fought like tigers. They were united behind the

7 Leavenworth *Times*, January 9, 1858.
8 Elmore family papers, University of North Carolina; Emporia *Kanzas News*, November 21; N. Y. *Weekly Tribune*, November 14, 28, 1857.
9 N. Y. *Weekly Tribune*, November 14, 1857.

demand that the constitution be sent direct to Washington as the will of Kansas, while the submissionists were divided on various schemes of reference. At one moment the ultras seemed to have won completely. On the night of November 6, taking advantage of dissensions in the opposition and the absence of a few moderate delegates, they passed a clause sending the constitution straight to Congress, with no popular vote whatever. The utmost excitement ensued. Moderates at once gave notice of a motion for reconsideration. The anti-submissionists, denouncing it, resolved not to adjourn until they had finished the text of the constitution and won the final vote. The battle then waxed violent. At last, early in the morning, the radicals gave way, permitted an adjournment, and trooped wearily to bed. But the moderates gathered at once in caucus, organized more firmly, and when the convention reopened later on the morning of the seventh, were able, 26 to 25, to reconsider the vote for direct transmission to Congress.[10]

In the final clash, an important part was played by an agent sent West by two Southern members of the Cabinet. Howell Cobb and Jacob Thompson, anxious to make their views known, first tried to enlist L. A. Gobright, a Southerner connected with the Associated Press, and then sent out a land-office clerk, Henry L. Martin of Mississippi.[11] His ostensible errand was to investigate charges of land-office corruption, his real mission to help guide the convention. It need not be said that Cobb and Thompson wanted Kansas to become a slave State. Just what instructions they gave Martin we do not know. At a later date when Governor Wise of Virginia, hearing sinister rumors, queried Buchanan about it, Thompson was evasive.[12] But we do know that Secretary Cobb wished the constitution to say nothing about slavery (which would leave it in existence); that he, like Thompson, wished the instrument submitted to the voters; and that he wished the voting list confined to those who recognized the existing government, which would leave out a great body of free State men. This, he wrote Alexander H. Stephens on October 9, "presents the only fair mode that I see of making Kansas a slave State, a result most desirable if it can be brought about on the recognized principle of carrying out the will of the majority." [13]

---

10 Lecompton correspondence dated November 7, 1857, N. Y. *Weekly Tribune*, November 28, 1857; some observers gave the vote as 27 to 24.

11 L. A. Gobright, *Men and Things*, 170.

12 See letter of C. J. Wise, December 17, 1857; Buchanan Papers.

13 Cobb to Stephens, *Toombs, Stephens, Cobb Correspondence*, 424. In the Covode Investigation of 1860, Martin, Thompson, and Cobb all testified. Their evidence shows that the two Cabinet members were in favor of submitting the constitution to popular vote, and asked Martin to make representations to that end in Lecompton. It also shows that the two men were by no means rigid in the matter. Martin quoted Jacob Thompson's words to him: "We are in favor of the submission of the constitution, when made, to the popular will of Kansas for ratification or rejection; but I am not willing to take the converse of that proposition; that is, I am not prepared to take ground against the admission of Kansas if a pro-

Probably Martin was instructed in this sense. He took up his quarters in the basement of the convention hall, where the land records were stored. He conferred with John Calhoun; and both supported Hugh Moore, chairman of the committee on the subject, in demanding a referendum. However, Martin wished this vote taken in a fashion which would allow a strong chance for the State to preserve existing elements of slavery; and he conveyed this idea to Calhoun.

Out of the conferences of Martin with Calhoun, Elmore, Moore, and others in the final two days emerged a compromise plan. The constitution proper would not be submitted to the people, but they would be allowed to vote on a separate section permitting a choice between "the constitution with slavery" and "the constitution without slavery." Moreover, the constitution would preserve existing slave ownership. The scheme, matured by November 6 and brought forward on the seventh when direct transmittal to Congress was barely defeated, was hailed with satisfaction by proslavery observers. One Southerner pronounced it the best proposition yet offered for making Kansas a slave State, while the correspondent of the proslavery St. Louis *Republican* praised it with a tribute to Calhoun's "profound talents." [14] It was open to two strong objections: first, that it was a transparent device for preserving the shreds of slavery already in the Territory; and second, that it fell far short of the full and fair submission promised by Buchanan and demanded by Walker and Stanton.

Calhoun should have realized that it would never satisfy his friend Senator Douglas. But his drink-fogged mind was not what it had been; he had written Douglas for advice but received no answer; and what caution he possessed was overborne by Martin, Isaacs, and other associates. He read the Chicago *Times*

---

slavery constitution should be made and sent directly to Congress by the convention. I am not prepared to say that the convention have not the right to make a constitution and demand admission under it." When Martin reported this in Lecompton, as he must have done, he doubtless encouraged the radicals. Martin also quoted Jacob Thompson as taking up the question of the future status of slavery in the area, it being generally agreed that no reasonable hope existed of making Kansas an out-and-out slave State. The Secretary "made several suggestions as to how the constitution might be shaped to protect the rights of owners of the slaves then there, and their natural increase, and indicated that all fair-minded men ought to be willing to go a step further than this; that young men from the southern States had gone there in considerable numbers and established themselves homes for the future; they may *inherit* negroes, family servants that they would not be willing to dispose of, and all just men ought to be willing to allow them to bring such servants to Kansas and keep them rather than force them to abandon their homes or sell them." Howell Cobb testified that he asked Martin to press upon the convention the propriety of submitting the constitution. He awaited the event eagerly. Then, "when the news was received it was considered that, as the only question at issue—the slavery question—had been submitted, the material point had been attained; and it was regarded as virtually carrying out the policy of submission." Covode Report (36th Cong., 1st Sess., Report No. 648, pp. 157-171, 314-323).

14 See long letter dated Lecompton, November 7, in Jackson *Mississippian*, November 27, 1857; Dispatch of November 6, 1857, in St. Louis *Republican*.

editorial of October 14, and thought he found warrant there for a separate vote on the mere question of slavery. Had he read it more carefully, he would have seen that it said in conclusion: "Let them, if they desire to vote in favor of a slave State, have the opportunity; but let the constitution be submitted to the popular vote, and at an early day." This plainly meant the whole constitution.

On the last day the compromise plan was carried. A few radical slavery men, struggling to the last for direct transmittal to Congress, resigned rather than take it. On the final passage of the whole constitution the vote was 28 for, and about a dozen against.[15] The convention, returning from dinner, remained in session to deal with some last items of business. As midnight arrived, the smoke-filled hall, dimly lighted by a dozen guttering candles, presented a strange scene. Some delegates stood, some sat with feet cocked at an angle of forty-five degrees, and some who were half intoxicated stretched themselves on the cloth-covered tables. Rough horseplay interspersed the last resolutions and complimentary speeches. Outside, the gloom was relieved only by the twinkling lights of the scattered grogshops, from which now and then came a boisterous shout.[16] As President John Calhoun brought down his gavel and proclaimed the termination of the convention, few would have thought that such a cheap, disorderly assemblage had carried the nation a long step nearer to civil war.

[I]

What kind of a constitution had been drawn up? And who would be allowed to vote on the separate slavery question? The North was eager for news on these points.

Vital parts of the instrument at once aroused the hot indignation of free-soil circles. They represented an attempt to fasten at least partial toleration of slavery upon an antislavery population. The preamble of the first section declared: "The right of property is before and higher than any constitutional sanction, and the right of the owner of a slave to such slave and its increase is the same and as inviolable as the right of the owner of any property whatever." The legislature was forbidden to emancipate slaves already in Kansas

15 Forty-five members signed the engrossed document. Nichols, *Disruption of the American Democracy*, 124. Martin relates (Covode Report, 163) that after he and Calhoun had fought to the last for out-and-out submission, and been defeated, they feared that all was lost and the constitution would go straight to Congress. "Colonel Isaacs and myself induced Mr. Blair, who had voted with the majority, to move a reconsideration, on the assurance that if we could get a reconsideration, the plan of partial submission, for which he had expressed his willingness to vote, should be brought forward. . . . They voted for a reconsideration, which was carried. The plan finally adopted was then brought forward and carried by a majority of three votes."
16 Lecompton correspondence of N. Y. *Weekly Tribune*, November 28, 1857.

without the consent of the owner and payment of a full money equivalent. Stringent enforcement of the Fugitive Slave Law was required. Still other parts of the constitution seemed objectionable on general grounds. Know-Nothing influence appeared in a provision that governors must have been citizens for twenty years before election, while radical agrarian influence was evident in a stipulation that the State might have only one bank, with not more than two branches, to be incorporated only after popular consent. Free negroes were excluded. A peculiar provision forbade amendment of the constitution prior to 1864—this apparently to prevent any change of the clauses upon slavery.

And what of the vote? By an outstanding "schedule" attached to the constitution, the convention ousted Governor Walker and other Federal office-holders on December 1, 1857, and devolved their authority upon a provisional government. The head or "regent," John Calhoun, was to order an election for State officers and legislators. He was to appoint all judges of elections until the legislature took jurisdiction, was to have charge of the counting of returns, and was to decide who was entitled to legislative seats, issuing certificates of election. He was also to convene the legislature by proclamation. As the New York *Express* remarked, this was a Parisian *coup d'état*. On December 21, the special referendum was to be held on the "constitution with slavery" or "constitution without slavery." Calhoun was to appoint three election commissioners for each county, who were to name three judges for that county, with power to establish precincts and open polls. This gave the regent complete authority over the referendum—and the Oxford and McGee frauds were in recent memory!

But how much real choice would be permitted in even a fairly conducted election? If the "constitution with slavery" carried, the institution would be planted in Kansas with no possibility of eradication prior to 1864, and then only if two-thirds of each house submitted the question of a new convention to the people, and a majority of qualified voters (not merely of those voting) approved the call. If "without" carried, even then some two hundred slaves might remain in the State. Would their progeny also be held in servitude? Many believed that they would; that this servile population would facilitate the smuggling of new slaves across the border; and that Kansas would have a slavery atmosphere. True, the number of slaves would be small. But then the number in Delaware was small, and yet Delaware was a most tenaciously slave State. True, again, the importation of slaves would be illegal. But various slave States had laws prohibiting any such importation, and yet somehow large numbers were fetched in. This conditional and partial choice was a trick, declared free State men. The question was, *Heads I win, Tails you lose;* you may vote for slavery unlimited or slavery limited, but you may not vote for freedom. As one Kansan expressed it, the doctor had said: Vote to take this arsenic with bread and butter, or without bread and butter.

An angry outcry instantly arose throughout Kansas. "The Great Swindle," trumpeted the Emporia *Kanzas News*.[17] "Act or Be Slaves" was the caption over an editorial of the Topeka *Kansas Tribune*. As Governor Walker presently stated, only one of the twenty Kansas newspapers supported the instrument. Charles Robinson and "Jim" Lane were ready to lead an organized resistance. Meetings were soon being held all over the Territory, with freesoil Democrats prominent in many of them, expressing their indignation at this latest trick. Leaders like young Preston B. Plumb, fearful that all was lost and that the constitution would be rapidly carried through Congress, called upon the people to rise in their wrath, let the country know of their condemnation, and if necessary resist by force.

Particularly impressive was the protest of the Democratic editors. The pending scheme is an infringement of the people's rights, an outrage upon the spirit of republicanism, and a violation of the intent of the Nebraska Act, said the Kickapoo *Pioneer;* it has not only done the Democratic Party great harm, but the injury is of a permanent nature, declared the Leavenworth *Journal*.[18] These papers accurately reflected public sentiment. Intense excitement reigns, a friend wrote President Buchanan. "The instrument itself, the manner of its submission, and the means by which it was adopted, are the subject of emphatic condemnation all over the Territory, and none but the ultras, most of whom are Know-Nothings from the South, endorse it. The true Democracy both from the North and the South repudiate it." [19]

As was to be expected, the Republican press throughout the North echoed this Kansas uproar. One plot follows another, the editors declared; outrage is piled upon outrage. The columns of the Chicago *Tribune*, Cleveland *Leader*, Albany *Evening Journal*, Springfield *Republican*, and the newspapers made famous in New York by Bryant, Greeley, and James Watson Webb, with dozens of less prominent dailies, blazed with denunciation. The *National Intelligencer*, for surviving Whigs, pronounced a more measured condemnation.

What was hardly more surprising, but profoundly significant, was the instant verdict of the popular sovereignty organs of the Northern Democrats.

17 Emporia *Kanzas News*, November 7, 1857.
18 Leavenworth *Journal*, November 27, 1857.
19 J. F. Schroder, November 22, 1857; Buchanan Papers. Arkansas in 1836 had been the last State to adopt a constitution without popular vote. Her people were homogeneous, no sharp issues existed, and the constitutional convention was trusted. Beginning with Massachusetts in 1780, and ending with Ohio, Iowa, and Minnesota in 1857, twenty States had adopted or amended their constitutions by popular vote. As Douglas said, those which had not resorted to popular submission were States where the utmost harmony prevailed.

Their chagrin was natural. Here was a constitution which, apart from slavery, was studded with controversial provisions. The bank restriction, the twenty-year residence clause for the governor, the bar against free negroes, the provision for a tax system which had been tried and abandoned in Illinois, were all debatable. To put such a constitution into force without a general vote was to make popular sovereignty a farce. As early as November 18, the Chicago *Times*, Douglas's mouthpiece, recalling the solemn promises of 1854, declared that all action by the Democratic Party must have in view the faithful redemption of that pledge. The Quincy, Illinois, *Herald*, speaking for Douglas's friend W. A. Richardson, termed the Lecompton stand an insult to all intelligent Kansans and all honest Democrats. The Columbus, Ohio, *Statesman* called for rejection of the constitution, a flagrant outrage which could not be tolerated without disorganizing the Democratic Party. The Detroit *Free Press*, the leading Democratic journal of Michigan, predicted that any Northern Democrat who lent himself to this scheme to evade the popular will would be visited with political annihilation. The Northern wing of the party, it announced, "will not recede one inch from the preservation of the integrity of the great principle of the Kansas-Nebraska Act." [20] Equally emphatic was the Milwaukee *News*, leading Democratic organ of Wisconsin.

And in Pennsylvania a defiant new voice was lifted. John W. Forney, bitterly resentful of Buchanan's neglect, had returned to Philadelphia, collected a fund from his many friends, and on August 1 launched the *Press*. This independent Democratic journal scored an astonishing success. Within a short time it had a larger daily circulation than any other Philadelphia paper except the *Ledger*, and was distributing thirty thousand copies of its weekly edition. Animated by a trenchant fighting spirit, it lost no time in declaring that the Lecompton convention had shown a cool disregard of the people, an impudent deceit, and an utter shamelessness, which made it unique among representative bodies. Congress should reject its work by unanimous vote; and "we trust that the Senators and Representatives from Pennsylvania will boldly and at once put their feet upon it, and spurn it as it deserves to be spurned." [21] It kept up its fire. Its vehement words created a sensation. "The streets of Philadelphia this morning are filled with people speculating on the course of the *Press*," wrote J. C. Van Dyke to the President on November 21.[22]

All over the North, in hotels, barrooms, clubs, stores, and where farmers met on country roads, men were shaking their heads: "A dirty piece of work!" Did the Kansas gang really think they could get away with it? Forney shortly

20 Quotations in Phila. *Weekly Press*, December 5, 12, 17, 1857; Lawrence *Herald of Freedom*, December 12, 1857.
21 Quoted in N. Y. *Weekly Tribune*, November 25, 1857.
22 J. C. Van Dyke to Buchanan, November 21, 1857; Buchanan Papers.

listed fifteen local Democratic papers in Pennsylvania which roundly denounced the Lecompton plot, while a longer roster might have been made in New York. A suggestion of the Chicago *Times* that Congress should authorize the Kansans to assemble a new convention and write a new constitution was widely echoed. The handful of Democratic newspapers which sustained the Lecompton scheme in the North were viewed with suspicion. Two were the Albany *Argus* and Rochester *Union*, whose editors were said to hope for postmasterships; two were Pittsburgh papers; and one was the Dubuque *Northwest*, whose head had been promised the clerkship of a Senate committee.[23]

In the South, however, the story was different. The editorial fire against Walker as a traitor and renegade had never slackened, and now the convention's work was greeted as the richly deserved defeat of the governor. Inflamed with a suspicion and hatred which drew little distinction between freesoilers and abolitionists, most Southerners believed that the freesoil pronouncements against any new slave State were a challenge which must be emphatically answered. Many of them regarded Kansas as rightfully their own. Did the North think itself entitled to take every trick in the game? to seize Kansas as well as California, Iowa, Nebraska, Minnesota, and Oregon? to allow the South nothing? If the Yankees had placed more settlers in Kansas, it was by the forced and unfair measures of the emigrant aid societies. To Southerners, the Lecompton delegates were not ruffians but dauntless paladins, making a gallant last-ditch stand. The Yankees declared their tactics were fraudulent; this was not so—they were entirely legal; but if some sharpness did appear, it was a just answer to the chicane and arrogance of the North.

Even the sober Richmond *Enquirer* greeted the Lecompton constitution as the promise of a final settlement of the Kansas troubles, predicting that of course Congress would accept it. The Washington *Union* was jubilantly confident of the future. "The vexed question is settled—the problem is solved—the dead point of danger is passed—all serious trouble about Kansas affairs is over and gone," it rejoiced. "Kansas comes into the Union on the principle of the great act which organized her and Nebraska as territorial Governments. Another star is added to the republican constellation." Not a hint was breathed in half the Southern editorials that the constitution would ever be called into question. Yet some journals were frank as to its central design. "You see," wrote a Lecompton correspondent to the Jackson *Mississippian*, "that while it seems to be an election between a free-State and proslavery constitution, it is in fact but a question of the future introduction of slavery that is in controversy."[24] And the Charleston *Mercury* proclaimed:

23 J. W. Sheahan to Douglas, November 30, 1857; Douglas Papers.
24 Jackson *Mississippian*, November 27, 1857.

We do not think that the question of slavery or no slavery is submitted to the vote of the people. Whether the clause in the constitution is voted out or voted in, slavery exists, and has a guarantee in the constitution that it shall not be interfered with; whilst, if the slavery party in Kansas can keep or get the majority of the legislature, they may open wide the door for the immigration of slaves.[25]

The Northern and Southern wings of the Democratic Party were openly at odds. To add to the suspense, news came that Governor Walker, his health and his personal affairs both needing attention, would leave Kansas on November 17 for a visit to the East. The Northern public had applauded his firm stand against the Oxford and McGee frauds; the South had denounced this tampering with election returns as another piece of "intervention." What authority, Southerners asked, had *he* to go behind the returns? None whatever.

Walker was going east on what he considered a vital mission. He had never been confirmed as governor, and he realized that Southern extremists would give him no quarter. He could explain that he had not gone behind the Oxford-McGee returns, but had thrown them out because the judges had not taken the proper oaths, the poll books had not been sent to the territorial secretary in proper form, and the votes had been recorded in an impossibly brief period of time. He could place the Kansas situation before the President and the entire country.

[II]

Seldom in the history of the nation has a President made so disastrous a blunder as Buchanan was about to commit. Within a few weeks, Pierce's old secretary, B. B. French, was to write: "I had considerable hopes of Mr. Buchanan—I really thought he was a statesman—but I have now come to the settled conclusion that he is just the d——dest old fool that has ever occupied the Presidential chair. He has deliberately walked overboard with his eyes open—let him drown, for he must." It is misleading, however, to speak of his policy. It was rather the policy of the Directory; of the Cabinet junta (Howell Cobb, Jacob Thompson, and Jere Black), and of the gray-eyed, thin-lipped Slidell, persevering, subtle, and in W. H. Russell's words, "full of device." [26]

From the moment the Lecompton gathering adjourned, these men began to exert a tremendous pressure on Buchanan. Secretaries Cobb and Thompson were committed to the Kansas scheme by their wishes and the work of their agent Martin. Jere Black was filled with detestation of freesoilers everywhere

25 Quoted in Phila. *Weekly Press,* December 26, 1857.
26 B. B. French, December 17, 1857, to brother, French Papers; Russell, *My Diary North and South,* Ch. 30.

but particularly in Kansas, the men who controlled the extra-legal Topeka "government." He hated the Black Republicans, and he specially hated those who had been ready to defy the recognized territorial legislature. His manuscripts contain a draft paper in which, defending the Lecompton instrument, he wrote: "Lane and the godless crew of fanatics and knaves that followed him have lived in open rebellion against the laws, and not one of them has yet been punished. The convention that framed the constitution was threatened by the tools and hirelings of the abolition aid societies and was saved from their attack only by a military force." He tried to imbue Buchanan with these passionate and distorted views. Floyd and Toucey lent their aid. The President knew that Jefferson Davis and other Senators were ready to open a raking fire on the Administration if Governor Walker were not forced to resign; and even before the Lecompton result he was privately condemning the little governor.[27] Buchanan's pliability in Southern hands was a matter of jest. It was reported that Howell Cobb, on being asked once why he bore a transiently worried air, replied: "Oh, it's nothing much; only Buck is opposing the Administration." [28]

Buchanan knew that the hot blood of the South was up; he knew that the more rabid politicians of the cotton States were denouncing him along with Walker as a turncoat. Threats of secession were growing more numerous. Believing that party discipline would hold the Northern Democrats in line, he regarded the South as the prime point of danger. He was affected by his old Southern bias, his deep dislike of freesoil agitation, his belief that popular sovereignty was a delusion, and his personal antipathy for Douglas. Above all, however, he was swayed by timidity: he quailed before the Southern menaces transmitted to him by Cobb, Thompson, and a hundred others—before the jealousy and resentment which for the time, as the Columbia *South Carolinian* remarked a year later, "seemed to have inflamed the whole South." [29] Appeasement appeared the best course.

Undoubtedly, when Governor Walker left for the East he believed that, inasmuch as Buchanan had pledged himself to a popular submission of the

27 Undated paper, end of 1857, Black Papers; N. Y. *Express*, November 2, 4, 1857.
28 Greeley, *Recollections*, 335, 356.
29 Quoted in *National Intelligencer*, November 18, 1857. Southern extremists were partly influenced by political reasons. The Washington *Republic* declared, just before the convention adjourned, that nothing was so vital to the union of the Southern Democracy as a proslavery victory in Kansas. "In truth, it is not merely the union but the very existence of the Southern Democracy which is staked upon making Kansas a slave State. . . . If Kansas comes in as a free State, the black Democratic ascendency at the South is ended, and the next House will be overwhelmingly in opposition to the Administration. From whatever motives Mr. Buchanan was voted for at the North, he was supported at the South simply and solely from the belief that his election would fix slavery upon Kansas." Quoted in Chicago *Tribune*, November 11, 1857.

constitution, instructing Walker that the people must be protected in their right of voting for or against that instrument, he could bring the President to take a stand against Lecompton. The doughty little governor was deeply exasperated. He regarded Calhoun, Isaacs, Elmore, and the other ringleaders as a set of scoundrels who had ruined all hope of Democratic ascendency in Kansas, had tried to ruin him, and might yet ruin the Democratic Party throughout the North. He believed that his own career, the future of Kansas, and above all, the vital Democratic principle written into law by Douglas, were at stake. He would tell the President what all fair-minded Kansans knew, that the people of the Territory would never submit to Lecompton. He would confer with Cass, Douglas, and others on means of vindicating the great rule of popular sovereignty upon which they had staked their honor. He would remind Buchanan how explicitly he had promised a full and fair vote on the institutions of Kansas. He would fling his defiance in the teeth of his old enemy Jacob Thompson and the other Southern ultras.

Walker did not know that on the very day he left, November 17, the Administration organ, the *Union*, had come out with its complete endorsement of the constitution. Nor did he know that in Virginia the moderate Henry A. Wise had just withdrawn from the senatorial contest, apparently under pressure from the Directory, in favor of the radical R. M. T. Hunter. This was an ominous event. Wise was a warm friend of the President. The Directory had overruled Buchanan, and the event was interpreted as making the Senate's rejection of Walker almost certain.[30]

Amid fervent farewells from admiring friends, Walker strode up the gangplank of the steamer *Oglesby* at Leavenworth. "The Governor leaves here," the former Pennsylvanian John F. Schroder wrote Buchanan, "with the endorsement of nineteen-twentieths of the friends of the Administration, and of all the good people of the Territory."[31] But he took all his books and papers, well boxed, and his other movable property. Cheerful but determined, he talked with fellow passengers, as the boat swung downstream, in a vein which showed that he did not anticipate returning.[32] Like Reeder and Geary, he had been worsted by the proslavery fanatics of the border.

Arriving in Washington, Walker on November 26 had a long talk with the President. After several hours they parted in friendly spirit. Immediately thereafter the governor appeared before the Cabinet and stated his position emphatically. Word quickly spread about Washington that irreconcilable differences had appeared. Southern Senators, arriving for the new session, heard with pleasure that Walker's resignation or dismissal seemed a certainty. Dozens

30 N. Y. *Evening Post*, November 19, 1857.
31 J. F. Schroder, November 22, 1857, Buchanan Papers.
32 Chicago *Tribune* correspondent aboard *Oglesby*, November 20, 1857.

of newspapermen, avid for news, were soon able to tell the country what had happened behind the White House doors.[33]

Walker had sworn the oath of John Hampden against the Lecompton constitution; the Cabinet majority and the President were immovable in its defense. Walker declared that the Administration was bound by the Nebraska Act, and by solemn pledges the previous summer, to see the entire instrument submitted to a popular vote. The Directory replied that the convention was at liberty to submit its whole work to the people or send it direct to Congress, as it pleased; and that they had not deemed submission advisable, chiefly because of the feverish state of opinion in the Territory. A fundamental principle is involved, said Walker. Not at all, rejoined the Directory; for the convention is submitting that part of the constitution which bears on slavery, the only serious question at issue. All that was required by the principles of the Nebraska Act, the Cincinnati platform, and the President's inaugural was that the problem of slavery should be submitted to popular vote; as this is done, no ground for objection exists. The attempt to jam through such a constitution will cause bloody strife, explained Walker. "I doubt if three hundred men wish to fasten slavery on Kansas; no party stands for slavery; the people will fight before they let this cheating document, which means slavery both ways, go through." So much the worse for them, declared Cobb and Black. If these lawless freesoilers fight against a legally drawn and legally adopted constitution, we shall quell their resistance. "They will not submit, and they ought not to submit," exclaimed the governor.[34]

The Southern wing of the Democrats, having Buchanan's ear, placed him under an adroit and insistent pressure to drop Governor Walker, forget his pledges, and make a fight for Lecompton. "The people are so tired of Kansas that they will sustain your settlement," wrote Robert Tyler, in effect. "If you can convert Walker, well and good; if not, I trust you will remove him without hesitation."

Leading Southern politicians, crowding into the capital, saw a golden opportunity to check the Presidential aspirations of Walker and Douglas and suppress the freesoil elements in the party. They talked earnestly with the President.[35] A hasty canvass indicated that five Northern Senators—Bright,

33 The N. Y. *Herald, Times, Evening Post* accounts are good; November 28–December 5, 1857. The *Herald* quotes Walker as telling Buchanan in their first interview that slavery was no longer the issue in Kansas—that was settled; but all the questions respecting their government were involved in the constitution, and the people would resist at all hazards the attempt to force it upon them. So intense was the feeling that he could not influence a single man to vote for it. He suggested that Congress should pass a bill similar to the Minnesota Enabling Act.

34 Wash. correspondence, *Express, Herald*, November 28, 30, 1857.
35 Wash. correspondence, N. Y. *Tribune*, dated December 1, 1857.

Bigler, Fitch, Thompson, and Wright--would support the Administration's Kansas policy, and that some Northern members of the House would follow their lead. Senator Slidell lost no time in carrying this news to the White House. Bigler was anxious to see a vigorous policy pursued. If you will put the full power of the Administration behind Lecompton, he wrote the President, the people of Kansas will knuckle under, vote quietly on December 21, and thus end all our troubles. J. C. Van Dyke lent his strong personal influence to the same end. And two soldiers with some claim to expert standing (both Southerners) put in their word. General Persifor Smith was for admitting Kansas forthwith under the Lecompton plan. General Harney assured Buchanan that he need not worry about disturbances in the Territory, for winter was coming on, troublemakers on both sides would be kept busy getting fuel to burn and food to eat, and the existing forces could meet any contingency; moreover, many Northerners, after a bad crop season, were going home from sheer necessity.[36]

Most important of all were the continued threats from the South. The well-informed Washington correspondent of the New Orleans *Picayune*, "Tiber," later described just how aggressive this *démarche* was:

The President was informed in November, 1857, that the States of Alabama, Mississippi, and South Carolina, and perhaps others, would hold conventions and secede from the Union if the Lecompton constitution, which established slavery, should not be accepted by Congress. The reason was that these States, supposing that the South had been cheated out of Kansas, were, whether right or wrong, determined to revolt. The President believed this. Senator Hunter, of Virginia, to my knowledge, believed it. Many other eminent men did, and perhaps not without reason. The President determined in November, four or five months after his famous letter to Gov. Walker, to submit the Lecompton constitution to Congress, and recommend its acceptance. . . .

I was myself at the time [November, 1857] disposed to go with Governor Walker, Mr. Douglas, and others, but became convinced, from facts presented to me, that the course of the President was expedient, and I supported him in it. It was not worth while, as I thought, to provoke a quarrel with the South, or any part of it, upon a matter of opinion, which was of little practical importance. Everybody knew that the danger in Kansas itself had passed over. It remained to concede an abstract question to the South.[37]

Since the Cabinet had now taken Buchanan's measure, its bolder spirits—Cobb, Thompson, Floyd—were growing arrogant in their treatment of him. A few episodes indicated just what the relation of the Directory to the weak Executive was. Early in September, weeks before the Lecompton decision, the

---

36 J. C. Van Dyke, November 29, Persifor Smith, December 14, W. S. Harney, November 29, 1857; Buchanan Papers.
37 "Tiber" in New Orleans *Picayune*, April 29, 1860.

President, anxious to shield himself against Southern attacks, had asked two Kansans in Washington, General Whitfield and Dr. Tebbs, to send the *Union* a letter explaining that Walker's policy pleased the people of Kansas, a majority of whom favored a free State. The letter was in type, with an editorial endorsement of Tebbs as a veracious observer, when a Southern member of the Cabinet ordered its suppression. Howell Cobb had countermanded the President's action.[38]

A little later the accurate head of the Associated Press in Washington, L. A. Gobright, who was on intimate terms with Cobb and Thompson, heard from a Cabinet member that Walker and Stanton would be removed or forced to resign. He sent out an A.P. dispatch to this effect, reporting that the governor's rejection of the Oxford and McGee returns had been condemned, that the Cabinet believed the legislature alone was competent to pass on the election of its members, and that both the offending officers would soon be ousted. This was published under date of October 30, just as the Lecompton drama was nearing its climax. Buchanan, taken aback, wrote a paragraph denying the story, and had the contradiction telegraphed over the country. Summoning Gobright to the White House, he unavailingly tried to learn who had supplied the information. Then he questioned the Cabinet about the leakage. At once the Cabinet officer responsible (doubtless Cobb or Thompson, though Gobright does not say) boldly avowed his responsibility. He did this, as he told the journalist, not merely to protect the Associated Press, but to remind Buchanan of their previous understanding upon the removal of Walker! The incident unpleasantly illustrates two facts—the President's malleability and the whip-cracking attitude of the Southern Cabinet members toward him.

Even Jere Black, who combined his attorney-generalship with editorial writing for the *Union*, now did not hesitate to override Buchanan. The private papers of that bitter partisan contain a note which he received just after the Lecompton convention ended, a distinct indication of Presidential weakness.

> My dear sir: In reading your article this morning which was excellent in its original form, I deeply regret to observe that the notice of Governor Walker has been stricken out, whilst the praises of the Convention remain. What is the reason for this? It will give just cause for offence to Governor Walker's friends; and I confess I am much worried myself at the omission.
>
> Your friend, very respectfully, James Buchanan.[39]

Several Southern governors in their annual messages were calling for the admission of Kansas under the Lecompton scheme. Governors Perry of Florida

---

38 See N. Y. *Weekly Tribune*, November 6, 1858, for Stanton's story of this incident.
39 Buchanan to Jeremiah S. Black, November 18, 1857; Black Papers.

and Wickliffe of Louisiana rumbled threats against the Union. Other politicians in the South were predicting that the party there would go to pieces unless Buchanan forced the scheme through Congress. We have quoted the statement of a Washington newspaper that if Kansas came in as a free State, Democratic ascendency at the South would be ended, and the next House would be overwhelmingly in opposition to the Administration. Day after day the leaders and articles of the Washington *Union*, controlled by the Cabinet, fixed a semiofficial stamp of approval on Lecompton.[40]

In vain did George Bancroft, as a fellow-Jacksonian, send the President an eloquent plea. You occupy a position which is inexpugnable if you choose to make it so, he wrote. Pierce's Administration had died of Jefferson Davis and Caleb Cushing, and you should not listen to similar men. "I entreat you, as one who most sincerely wished honor and success to your Administration, not to endorse the Lecompton Constitution." That document, he continued, had not been submitted to the people because it was obvious they would reject it. He should put aside this arrogant usurpation, and ask Congress for an enabling act and a new convention. "Justice, the peace of the country, the present strength of your Administration, its standing with posterity, all point to the same policy. Jackson resisted the nullifiers when they had a real ground of grievance from the excessive tariff of the day; now the nullifiers rally on a ground which, if they are resisted with firmness, will sink under them and compel them to fly to you for shelter." [41]

But what of his explicit pledges to support Walker in insisting on popular submission? Clamorous voices assured Buchanan that Walker lusted for place and power. The governor was acting in bad faith, Robert Tyler declared; he had chosen a line which he thought might make him a great man, "and this outside the Democratic Party perhaps." [42] Roger A. Pryor brought the same accusation against Walker in the Richmond *South*, alleging that the governor was scheming to revolt and put himself at the head of an opposition party in the North. "He thinks he holds the Administration by the throat." [43] Far out in Leavenworth, the wily A. J. Isaacs had caught up the same insinuation. The governor, he assured the President, has been "against your friends, and he is doing all in his power to secure the Northern support for 1860." [44] While

---

40 Washington *Union*, November–December, 1857. The message of Governor Allston of South Carolina spoke of Kansas in moderate terms, while Governor Winston of Alabama made no reference whatever to the subject. But the Alabama legislature passed resolutions attacking Walker, deploring the failure of the government to remove him from office, and endorsing the convention system of adopting a State constitution. N. Y. *Herald*, December 2, 1857.

41 George Bancroft, December 5, 1857, Buchanan Papers.

42 Robert Tyler, November 16, 1857, Buchanan Papers.

43 Quoted in Chicago *Tribune*, November 10, 1857.

44 A. J. Isaacs to Buchanan, November 16, 1857.

Buchanan knew the honest, hard-working, loyal Walker too well to accept these malicious insinuations, he may have let them color his mind. At any rate, that mind was now made up—as the Southerners desired.

The error of Buchanan was in not clinging to principle. He had enunciated a wise principle—the people of Kansas must have a full, free, and fair opportunity to pass on their constitution; a true statesman would not have abandoned so just a line. Of course, it was easy (as he soon did) to cite all kinds of expedient arguments. The Lecompton convention was quite legal; the country, struggling out of a depression, needed peace; a Southern uproar would hurt business; if Kansas voted for the constitution "without slavery," the institution would gradually wither there as in other free States; and once in the Union, Kansans could change their constitution and laws as they pleased. Such pleas had a plausible ring. But for all that, they represented an abandonment of a clear public pledge and of the high ground of principle.

That the President knew this is evident from an interview with Forney, who called at the White House to expostulate. Relations between him and the President were now strained. While getting his *Press* upon its feet, Forney had penned the harshest letters upon Buchanan. After spending two years and sacrificing $150,000 to make his old friend the Chief Magistrate, he wrote, he had found the man an utter ingrate. Buchanan had first tried to balk the new journal; now that it had made a dazzling success, he was patronizing a gang of men who, with the *Pennsylvanian* office as headquarters, were systematically attacking the *Press*.[45] Forney had sent some of his bitter letters to Jere Black, who was just the man to show them to the President. No doubt the talk took place in a tense atmosphere. Its date is uncertain, and the details rest only upon the editor's recollection nearly a year later, perhaps overdramatized.

"Mr. Buchanan," he said, "for the first time in our lives we are at variance. I find myself standing by one principle, having followed your lead—and you have deserted it."

"Well," Buchanan rejoined, "cannot you change too? If I can afford to change, why can't you? If you, Douglas, and Walker will unite in support of my policy, there will not be a whisper of this thing. It will pass by like a summer breeze."

Forney replied that he could not go back to Pennsylvania to eat his own words, and that he possessed a conscience. He suggested that Buchanan ought at least to let dissenting Democrats have their own way: Jackson had tolerated large differences of opinion, while Polk had suffered Buchanan to remain in the Cabinet despite his objections to the Administration's tariff policy. But

45 J. W. Forney to Black, July 24, 30, August 2, 1857; Black Papers.

Buchanan was angry with the *Press* for fomenting dissension among the Penn-sylvania Democrats.

"Sir," he grimly avowed, "I intend to make my Kansas policy a test."

"Well, sir," rejoined Forney, "I regret it; but if you make it a test with your officers, we will make it a test at the ballot box." [46]

[III]

That Buchanan's surrender to Lecompton would precipitate a terrible schism in the Democratic ranks was clear to all observers. The Washington correspondent of the *Evening Post* was quick to prophesy "a bitter contest between the two wings of Democracy"; that of the *Times*, "open hostility"; and that of the *Herald*, a warfare involving "disaster to the country and perfect annihilation to the Democratic party." Why did not Buchanan see this? For one reason, never understanding the freesoil sentiment of the North, he nat-urally underrated its force. For another, as a thick-and-thin party man, always talking about unity and well remembering how Jackson and Polk had outridden temporary factional storms, he believed that the Administration could quell any revolt. As he had no nerve, so he had no imagination. And the fact was that he had so completely placed himself in the hands of the Cobb-Thompson-Slidell group that he was their prisoner. He had let them encourage instead of quell the Southern storm; he had allowed them to commit the Administration to a false policy by condemning Walker's rejection of the Oxford-McGee ballots and by sending Martin to Kansas; he could not turn back. Timid and vacillating, he feared the wrath of the strong men about him more than the calm judgment of the people. A truly courageous man, a President with the courage of John Adams in 1798 and Grover Cleveland in 1887, might have stood on principle—but not Buchanan.

"If the back-track is taken—if the Administration reconsiders its decision, and sides with Walker and Douglas—the South will justly feel humbled and trifled with," wrote one of the ablest Washington observers. "There are men in the Cabinet, too, who will hardly consent to such a course. It is well known that a portion of the Cabinet have incessantly labored to check and thwart Mr. Douglas, and they are not likely, except from sheer necessity, to allow him such an advantage as the credit of guiding the policy of the Democratic Party in the just and liberal direction, and of compelling a reluctant Administration to follow him." [47]

Congress fully organized itself on Monday, December 7. The Senate elected

46 See Forney's Tarrytown Speech, September 2, 1858; N. Y. *Weekly Tribune*, September 11, 1858.
47 Washington correspondence, N. Y. *Weekly Tribune*, December 5, 1857.

an Alabaman of ability and high integrity, Benjamin Fitzpatrick, its President *pro tem*; the vote of 28 to 19 over Hannibal Hamlin accurately indicated the party strength.[48] The House chose the Democratic caucus slate for its various offices, James L. Orr of South Carolina becoming Speaker. A large, powerfully built man, Orr was well equipped for his post. Not yet forty, he had graduated from the University of Virginia, from newspaper work, and from a leisurely career as lawyer in the upland town of Anderson, center of a Scotch-Irish population. His frank, ruddy countenance, his straightforward, business-like air, his common-sense, logical speeches in debate, had inspired general confidence. He was far removed in opinion from the fire-eating radicals. In fact, his whole career was to demonstrate his moderation, for in Reconstruction days he was to become a Republican governor, and he was to die in St. Petersburg as President Grant's minister to Russia. He was familiar with the rules, patient but authoritative, and gifted with a loud ringing voice (like a locomotive whistle at a crossing, somebody said) which could instantly quiet confusion on the floor.

Next day Buchanan's message was read to the intent Houses. It contained some excellent recommendations, including an espousal of the Pacific Railroad and a condemnation of filibustering. But on the Kansas issue Buchanan showed a subtlety in word-juggling which was all his own, combined with a bold defense of the "dodge" which smacked of Cobb and Thompson. He upheld the Lecompton arrangement, urged the voters to go to the polls on December 21 to choose between "with" and "without," and scolded the country for its excessive preoccupation with the Kansas question. Trying to slip adroitly over his instructions to Walker, he declared that when he had written that the voters must be protected in a full and fair expression on the constitution he was thinking only of a vote on the slavery question! The Nebraska Act, he argued, had not provided for a popular vote on the entire constitution; it had merely declared that the people should be free to "regulate their domestic institutions" in their own way. Since the phrase "domestic institutions" had a meaning "limited to the family," wrote Buchanan, it embraced the relation of master and slave, but no other institution whatever. This word-juggling was worthy of the worst of sophists. As if the tax system, or banking, or the mode of elections were not domestic institutions in the time-honored sense!

Buchanan declared that citizens of Kansas had been "fairly afforded" an opportunity to register and vote for convention delegates, which was simply not true. He asserted that the election of December 21 would give the inhabitants a "fair" opportunity to decide the slavery issue, which was also false. He remarked that the only alternative to the protection of slaves already in

48 Hamlin voted for Seward.

Kansas was their confiscation, ignoring the fact that they might be taken else-where. Finally, he failed to state that, under the Nebraska Act, Congress had given the people a right to decide on the immediate existence of slavery, whereas the Lecompton convention gave them only a right to decide whether additional slaves should or should not be introduced.

As the gauntlet was thus thrown down, nobody could doubt that Douglas would pick it up. The climactic years of his career were opening. He was about to find his true role on the national stage. Hitherto, compromising with the Lower South, he had appeared in a dubious light to most freesoil North-erners; now, standing up to give battle for principle, he was to take on heroic stature. Two parts politician and one part statesman, he found in this new crisis a challenge to powers previously unknown even to himself. Always an essen-tially honest man, he thought no longer of the main chance but of the public weal. Anger at the malice of his Southern assailants, scorn for Buchanan's cowardice, apprehension for the future of party and nation, abhorrence of disunion schemes, all united to give him a stern determination. He had been a great Democratic chieftain; now he was to be a great American leader.[49]

49 Albert J. Beveridge, in a curiously myopic passage (*Lincoln*, II, 533), assumes that Douglas had a choice between supporting the Administration's Lecompton policy and break-ing with it; and writes that if Douglas had stood with Buchanan probably no resistance would have been made to Lecompton by any but Republicans, and it would have been adopted with little difficulty. He is wrong on both heads. The fact is that Douglas had no choice. His political future was bound up with the Northwestern Democracy, and the Northwestern Democrats were instantly in arms against Lecompton. The newspapers and Douglas's personal files, full of letters urging him to act, show this. Had Douglas played the part of Dr. Trimmer, the vengeance of Illinois would have fallen upon him in the Senatorial election of 1858 and the Presidential election of 1860. But no man was less likely to be a trimmer than Douglas. And what if Douglas had broken with his popular sovereignty vows, with principles, and with the Northwestern Democrats? Would only the Republicans have opposed Lecompton? Walker and Stanton were against it; Senator Stuart was against it; Forney and the Philadelphia *Press* were against it; George Bancroft and many like him were against it. These Democratic spokesmen would have made a fight even without Douglas; and while they were being defeated, a host of plain Northern Democrats would have moved *en masse* into the Republican ranks.

10

Douglas in Revolt

THE DISRUPTION of a great party, as the Whigs could have told any inquirer in 1857, is a pitiable spectacle. To keep a victorious party harmonious and unified is, for obvious reasons, a severer test of leadership than to maintain the integrity of a defeated party. Had the Buchanan Administration possessed statesmanlike attributes, it would have realized that the very life of the republic might depend upon meeting this supreme test; for the Democracy was the one great organization left which united the North and South with tenacious bonds. But how accurately did Buchanan read the omens of Kansas?

As Douglas in late November packed his bags to return to Washington, word that he was determined to resist the Lecompton scheme was spreading far and wide. He made no public announcement, for he had seen no copy of the constitution and did not wish to speak hastily on the basis of mere newspaper reports, but his private utterances were emphatic. The intention of Buchanan and the Cabinet to support what the Senator called "treachery and juggling" filled him with contempt. "We must stand on the popular sovereignty principle," he wrote his old friend John A. McClernand, "and go wherever the logical consequences may carry us, and defend it against *all assaults* from whatever quarter."[1] To a caller, he stated his resolve to maintain the fundamental principle he had laid down. "I will show you that I will do what I promised. By God, sir, I made Mr. James Buchanan, and by God, sir, I will unmake him!"[2]

Upon the issue of justice against fraud, said his organ the Chicago *Times*, the Northern Democracy will offer an undivided front. Douglas's mail was full of assurances of this fact. From every northwestern State during November came pledges of support. J. D. Eads wrote from Iowa that the party pledges were

[1] November 25, 1857; McClernand Papers. A Representative in Congress 1843-51, McClernand had just removed from Jacksonville to Springfield, where he worked hard for Douglas. As early as 1850 he had thought that the Southern radicals were trying to break down the Democratic Party, and he insisted sternly on the popular sovereignty doctrine. Milton, *Eve of Conflict*, 40, 41.

[2] C. H. Ray, November 24, 1857; Trumbull Papers.

sacred, and that all true men looked to him as the champion of squatter sovereignty. Four-fifths of our people, declared Samuel Crawford of Wisconsin, oppose nonsubmission as a violation of the Nebraska Act. "You alone," asserted Daniel Mace of Indiana in essence, "have the power to vindicate popular rights in Kansas, and you will stand forth with the fearless boldness which is your nature." "We do not doubt your course," exclaimed W. N. Coles of Urbana, Illinois, "and every Democrat in Champaign County will sustain you." A stream of such letters, soon augmented by eastern mails, poured in upon the Little Giant.[3]

Douglas knew that with the Old Democracy of the South and the New Democracy of the West at a complete rupture, he had a fight to the finish before him. He knew that proslavery politicians were making a tool of the pliant Buchanan, and he believed—with Henry S. Foote of Mississippi and other Southerners—that many of these politicians hated free government and meant to break up the Union. For politic reasons he made no public threats. He intended, as soon as he reached Washington, to try to persuade the President to drop Lecompton, ask Congress for an enabling act modelled on the old Toombs bill, or the Minnesota bill, and thus bring into existence a new and fair constitutional convention. To the Federal Attorney in Kansas, William Weer, who was resigning in disgust, he wrote that while he would battle for all his well-known tenets, "I shall do this in a kind spirit towards the Administration and all my friends."[4] Actually, however, he knew that a kind spirit would be impossible. He told Chicago friends that one object of Cobb, Thompson, and other Southerners in the Kansas proceedings was to ruin him, that Buchanan was too pusillanimous to interfere, and that the conspirators hoped to run Buchanan again as their tool in 1860. As for himself, he would never rest content with less than a fair vote on the whole Kansas constitution: "Depend on me to carry out the principle or fall in the attempt," he exclaimed.

With his eye for strategy, he instantly saw how vital would be the question of Republican aid or passivity. He knew that the party which had been defeated just a year earlier would watch the civil war in Democratic ranks with incredulous joy; that they would ask whether they could make the most of it by alliance with Douglas or by cheering from the sidelines. He knew that in Illinois, where most freesoilers regarded Douglas as an adroit and unscrupulous politician, and where the glittering prize of the senatorship would be contested in 1858, the Republicans were all suspicion. Douglas took pains to call a number of leaders to his house and tell them how implacably he meant to fight the

3 J. D. Eads, Fort Madison, November 19, Samuel Crawford, Mineral Point, November 28, Daniel Mace, Lafayette, November 28, 1857; Douglas Papers.
4 November 22, 1857; Wyandotte, Kansas, *Western Argus*, October 22, 1860.

Administration. He sent a friend to C. H. Ray's office at the Chicago *Tribune* to protest that the paper ought to desist from its attacks now that he was doing just what it wanted done. Several of the Northern Illinois chieftains were impressed by his bellicosity. "He really made some of their eyes stick out at his zeal," Norman B. Judd reported to Senator Trumbull. The general view among Illinois Republicans, however, was that Douglas bearing gifts was nearly as dangerous as Douglas bearing arms, that he could not gain forgiveness for past blows by an act which after all was one of political self-preservation, and that the party should cheer on his assault but stick to its own banner. If they relaxed their discipline, some of their recruits from the former freesoil Democrats would drop away and disorganization ensue. Hearing Douglas talk of an enabling act for Kansas similar to that of Minnesota, several Republicans urged Trumbull to get in first with such a bill.[5]

While still in Chicago, Douglas talked with the irate Governor Walker, and, en route to Washington, tarried briefly in New York to confer with adherents. He perhaps saw George Bancroft there. That honest Jacksonian, who had sat in Polk's Cabinet alongside Buchanan, was intensely aroused. The trickery in Kansas seemed to him abominable; the path out of the difficulty, an enabling act in the words of Douglas's Minnesota Act, was so simple that the President could hardly miss it. If they did talk, Bancroft urged the Senator to try persuasion first and then offer relentless battle, the advice he shortly put into a letter full of historical instances.[6]

Reaching the capital on December 2, Douglas was received with huzzas, bonfires, and a serenade. He found the city filling with Congressmen, office-hunters, and newspapermen, and hotel lobbies buzzing with speculation on the impending fray. Votes were already being counted. Coincident with Douglas's arrival, the combative secretary of Kansas Territory, Stanton, withdrew the resignation which for business reasons he had recently offered. Since Walker was battling for justice and right, he wrote, he would stand with his chief. The Cabinet that day once more discussed Kansas, and gossip reported that it once more resolved to support Lecompton.

On December 3, Douglas called at the White House. His bosom was filled with fresh anger, for friends had told him that Southerners were spraying Washington with venomous attacks on his and Walker's "lies," "contumacy," and "treason," and uttering dire threats of ruin. The Northern Democrats, he felt, were being pushed toward the abyss and must struggle for their lives.

5   E. Peck, N. B. Judd, C. S. Wilson, M. W. Delahay, November 26–December 1, 1857; Trumbull Papers.
6   George Bancroft, December 2, 1857; Douglas Papers.

[I]

One of the historic scenes of the period was enacted as Douglas confronted the tall, white-haired President. They had never liked each other, and doubtless shook hands in frigid fashion.

The Senator advised Buchanan, as a friend, not to recommend acquiescence in the Lecompton constitution. He gave his reasons for a new enabling act. Buchanan, whose message—the Directory's message—lay written in his drawer, declared that he would urge acceptance. "If you do," Douglas replied, "I will denounce it the moment your message is read." Despising Buchanan, he was probably at little pains to conceal his contempt, while the President responded to his dark scowl with ill-restrained resentment. At last, Buchanan terminated the interview with an abrupt threat. Glaring down at the short, powerful, defiant Senator, he exclaimed: "Mr. Douglas, I desire you to remember that no Democrat ever yet differed from an Administration of his own choice without being crushed." This was inaccurate, for John Randolph of Roanoke, William H. Crawford, and Calhoun had all dared to differ, and none had been crushed. On the other hand, the Barnburner revolt had actually crushed Cass in 1852. Buchanan added: "Beware the fate of Tallmadge and Rives." Opposing Jackson's policies, N. P. Tallmadge and William C. Rives had been forced to take refuge with the Whigs.

But Douglas was not to be read out of the Democratic Party by a man he regarded as a pigmy. He tossed his mane of black hair angrily:

"Mr. President," he said, "I wish you to remember that General Jackson is dead."

To that doughface member of the Cabinet, Toucey, the Senator was still more scornful. With bland assurance, Toucey urged upon Douglas the evils of a split in the Democratic Party; a calamity which would sink the combatants so deep that it might take a generation to raise the party again. Douglas declared that this was quite true. "Why, my dear sir," cried the delighted Secretary, "you agree with me in everything—I don't see how we can disagree at all."

"Certainly not," said Douglas, wringing Toucey's hand with excruciating grasp. "We *can't* disagree, Mr. Toucey; it's impossible; for you are always right on a constitutional question, and while the Constitution declares that *Congress* may admit new States, it hasn't a word in it about *Cabinets* admitting them!" [7]

7 N. Y. *Express*, December 9, 1857. Douglas later wrote that Southerners at this time were threatening that unless Lecompton passed, four States would immediately secede. *Cong. Globe*, 35th Cong., 1st Sess., 1865.

As Douglas stalked out of the White House, the President knew that a terrific internal upheaval awaited the party; but he believed it would be short. His faith in party discipline was always great. The fall elections had just shown that despite Dred Scott, the Kansas troubles, and the panic, the Democratic Party was well organized and vigorous in the North.

New York, which the Republicans had swept in 1856, now ran up a Democratic margin of nearly twenty thousand for minor State offices, while the Republicans lost control of the legislature. Wisconsin, which the previous year had given Frémont a plurality of more than thirteen thousand, was almost recaptured. The Republicans elected a governor by only a few hundred votes, and saw the impassioned Carl Schurz defeated for secretary of state. In Ohio, another Republican stronghold of the previous autumn, the Democrats carried the legislature and almost placed an able young Cleveland leader, Henry B. Payne, in Chase's chair as governor. In Pennsylvania, the Democrats had nominated for governor an exponent of the coming industrial order, the railroad organizer William Fisher Packer, against the doughty Republican champion David Wilmot. In a three-cornered contest Packer overwhelmed both Wilmot and the American or Know-Nothing nominee, getting more votes than the two combined.[8] Kentucky elected eight Democrats to Congress, and only two Americans; Tennessee similarly filled eight of her ten Congressional seats with Democrats. In both States the legislatures were Democratic, with the result that Kentucky would soon elect one and Tennessee two Democratic Senators. North Carolina, too, witnessed a Democratic sweep.[9]

The Know-Nothing Party was manifestly going to pieces, and the Democratic organization seemed the chief beneficiary of its breakup. It was true that the Americans could take some comfort in Maryland, where they elected the able and popular Thomas H. Hicks governor, while the Republicans could rejoice over the victory of N. P. Banks in Massachusetts. But on the whole, the results tended to increase Democratic confidence. They indicated to many that the Republican effort in 1856 had been spasmodic and impermanent, that any third party was certain to be short-lived, and that the ingrained conservatism of the American people favored the Administration. Various Democratic newspapers trumpeted their hope of the approaching dissolution of the "Black Republican" gang, and the New Orleans *Bee* expressed the hope of many old Whigs for a revival or reincarnation of their truly national and patriotic organization.

Buchanan's faith in party strength and party discipline, however, was short-sighted. No matter how favorable the result of the fall elections, everyone knew

8 Packer's vote was 188,890; Wilmot's 146,147; Hazelhurst's, 28,132.
9 Andrew Johnson and A. O. P. Nicholson were the two Tennessee Democratic Senators.

that the Democrats could not win in 1860 without important Northern States, and close observers were aware that these States would respond sensitively to the new Kansas issue. The Lecompton game was not understood when voters went to the polls; it was a burning topic of discussion by the opening of Congress. Douglas was not a mere Rives or Tallmadge, but one of the most powerful leaders the Democratic Party had ever produced; he had an appealing principle on which to stand; and he was the fiercest and most tenacious fighter since Jackson himself.

Most important of all, many Northern Democrats were increasingly irritated by Southern domination, increasingly aware that doughface policies would mean loss of power to the Republicans, and increasingly jealous of their own rights. Despite the Dred Scott decision, most Northwestern Democrats clung to popular sovereignty; and if the Administration tried to ram Lecompton down the throat of a gagging Kansas, popular sovereignty would seem more than ever a weapon against governmental injustice. Party discipline as Jackson had interpreted it meant the will of the Administration against a small, well-scattered economic minority; party discipline as Buchanan was interpreting it meant the will of Southern Democratic leaders against the great majority of Northern Democrats. Jackson had always used party discipline in behalf of national cohesion; Buchanan was doing the precise opposite. He was risking the division of the Democratic Party into hostile Northern and Southern wings. He was risking, that is, the worst possible threat to the Union, for such a schism would overthrow the last barrier to a disruption of the nation itself.

Douglas was right. In more senses than one, Andrew Jackson, the President who had said, "Our Federal Union: It must be preserved!" was dead.

"The Lecompton Constitution will pass both Houses, though after a terrible fight," predicted Laurence Keitt of South Carolina.[10] So Buchanan and the Directory thought—perhaps sharing Keitt's faith that Douglas would return to the fold after the battle. In the Senate the Democrats had an easy majority, counting 39 members against 20 Republicans and 5 Americans. Their House majority was similarly substantial—131 Democrats against 92 Republicans and 14 Americans. With a majority of fourteen in the Senate and twenty-five in the House, the President believed that the use of the whip with one hand and some office taffy with the other would produce an early victory.[11] By the hour Congress opened, he knew that at most only four Democratic Senators would stand against the Lecompton constitution; after defeating Douglas in his own chamber, he hoped to carry the House with a rush.

It was quickly evident that the Directory meant to force the fighting. The

10 Keitt to Hammond, December 18, 1857; Hammond Papers, LC.
11 John G. Nicolay and John Hay, *Abraham Lincoln*, II, 127.

tone of Buchanan's message was uncompromising. Immediately after sending it to Congress, he removed Stanton, the acting governor of Kansas, and nominated General J. W. Denver, Commissioner of Indian Affairs, in his stead. Stanton's offense was that, yielding to the demands of the great majority of Kansans, he had called the newly elected legislature to meet at Lecompton on December 7, four weeks in advance of its regular date, so that it might give legal direction to the resistance to the Lecompton constitution. The Senate at once confirmed Denver, who was hurried west with all speed. In the secret-session debate, according to one correspondent, "the tone and manner of the Southern Senators indicated unmistakably that they felt they had full possession of the government, and meant to put down with the strong hand Walker and Douglas, and all who dissent from their policy with regard to Kansas." Jefferson Davis was declaring that he would mangle Douglas in the Senate debate.[12]

Already it was evident that the Administration would use its patronage to keep men in line. Douglas reported that in their conversation Buchanan had threatened to decapitate every friend of his who held office. One of those friends, the Ohio editor James B. Steedman, called at the White House with reference to an appointment. If a newspaper story can be believed, Buchanan frostily remarked, "Sir, you did all you could against me at the Cincinnati Convention." Steedman retorted: "True, sir, I *did* support Judge Douglas in that convention because I believed him the ablest and fittest man presented. I am of the same opinion still. I wish you good morning."[13] The tale was probably invented. It is certain, however, that when Douglas was asked if he had counted the cost of the battle, he replied: "I have taken a through ticket and checked all my baggage!"[14]

[II]

Since Administration control of the Senate was incontestable, the decisive struggle would be waged in the House; but the effect of the Senate speeches and of events in Kansas might prove of critical influence. Douglas intended to appeal to Northern sentiment, to effect a temporary alliance with the Republicans, and, in unison with Walker and the free State delegate from Kansas, Marcus J. Parrott, both of whom he called into protracted conference, to encourage the resistance of Kansas settlers to Lecompton and the regency government of John Calhoun. He meant to force a long delay. By the time the House voted, he hoped to have the North fully aroused.

---

12 Washington correspondence, N. Y. *Tribune,* dated December 10, 14, 1857.
13 N. Y. *Weekly Tribune,* December 12, 1857.
14 Washington correspondence, N. Y. *Evening Post,* May 10, 1858.

The day after Buchanan's message was read, Douglas rose for one of the most honest, impassioned, and therefore greatest speeches of his life. A skillful dissection of the tricky Lecompton scheme, its inconsistency with Democratic promises, and its impolicy on national grounds, the address had a compact force that was masterly. While his language was courteous, his manner was haughty and defiant, the mien of a man who meant to brave all the consequences of his perilous stand. Even the hostile Washington *Star* called the speech the ablest forensic effort Douglas had ever made in Congress.[15]

His first thrust pierced a weak spot in Buchanan's armor. With irrefutable evidence, he denied the President's assertion that the Nebraska Act had carried merely an obligation to submit the slavery question, and not the whole constitution. "Sir, permit me to say, with profound respect for the President of the United States, that I conceive that on this point he has committed a fundamental error—an error which lies at the foundation of his whole argument on this matter." He showed that during the debates of 1854 he and others had argued that the people of a Territory should decide for themselves their type of judiciary system, school system, tax system, and banking system. The Nebraska Act did not make a stipulation in behalf of slavery alone in giving the people a free and full voice on their institutions; it abolished the old stipulation in order to make self-government universal and complete. Douglas corrected a widespread misapprehension when he pointed out that the Lecompton convention had never been recognized by Congress as legal, for on the contrary, Toombs's enabling bill for a convention had been defeated. The only authority behind the convention was a territorial enactment. It had no legal power to establish a government—indeed, no power, except to petition Congress for a redress of grievances; and while this petition might take the form of a draft constitution, it ought not to be endorsed by Congress unless it expressed the popular will.

Douglas pointed to the President's own pledges on popular submission, to Governor Walker's repeated assurances on the point, and to the fact that numerous delegates had been directed by the people to lay the constitution before the voters. The election now arranged, he said, offered Louis Napoleon's choice: Vote *yes* and be protected, vote *no* and be shot. Those in favor of the instrument could vote for it, and those opposed could not vote at all. Why?

I have asked a very large number of gentlemen who framed the constitution —quite a number of delegates and a still larger number of persons who are their friends—and I have received the same answer from every one of them. . . They say that if they allowed a negative vote, the constitution would have been voted down by an overwhelming majority, and hence the fellows shall not be allowed to vote at all. [Laughter]. . . . I believe it would have been voted

15 Washington *Star*, December 10, 11, 1857; N. Y. *Tribune*, December 10–12, 1857.

down by a majority of four to one. I am informed by men well posted there—Democrats—that it would be voted down ten to one; some say twenty to one.

In conclusion, he proposed a return to the Toombs bill, on which all Democrats had agreed at the previous session. Discard both the Lecompton and Topeka constitutions, he urged; attach to the Toombs bill a clause providing for a general submission; or take the Minnesota Enabling Act, which contained such a clause, and apply it to Kansas. This course would give Kansas and the nation peace within ninety days. "But," exclaimed Douglas with solemn emphasis, "if this constitution is to be forced down our throats, in violation of the fundamental principle of free government, under a mode of submission that is a mockery and insult, I will resist it to the last." [16] As he sat down, the crowded galleries burst into applause so loud that Mason of Virginia angrily moved they be cleared.

The twenty-five Southern Democratic Senators listened to this speech with grim hostility. Already it was known that at least eight of their Northern colleagues would stand with them. Douglas's inveterate enemy, that Kentucky slaveholder Jesse Bright who had been elected from Indiana, would take sides against him, and so would his associate Fitch. John R. Thomson and William Wright of New Jersey (though Thomson might better be called Senator for the Camden & Amboy Railroad, of which he had been a director some twenty years) were sound Administration men. Gwin, formerly of Alabama and now of California, George W. Jones of Iowa (a college mate of Jefferson Davis at Transylvania) whose term had little more than a year to run, and Allen of Rhode Island, also near the end of his term, were equally regular. Both Jones and Allen hoped for diplomatic posts from Buchanan. Bigler of Pennsylvania was closely attached to Buchanan. The only two allies on whom Douglas could count were Charles E. Stuart of Michigan and David Broderick of California, neither very effective in debate. For a short time the position of George E. Pugh of Ohio was doubtful. He belonged to the popular sovereignty school, knew that Lecompton would cost the Ohio Democrats dear, and had a warm personal liking for Douglas. But, a conservative of staunch party feeling, he could not yet support a factional revolt. It was not strange that Slidell and Jefferson Davis counted on humiliating and crushing Douglas, and that Buchanan said openly that the Illinoisan had ruined himself.[17]

Yet the Administration front was by no means the unfaulted granite it seemed. The party was splitting not into two, but three or four groups. Such Southern extremists as Toombs, Davis, and Hammond assailed Douglas with

16 *Cong. Globe*, 35th Cong., 1st Sess., December 9, 1857.
17 Washington correspondence, dated December 9; N. Y. *Courier and Enquirer*, December 11, 1857.

epithets of which traitor and scoundrel were the mildest; excommunicating him and his followers, they hailed the breach as final. To them, he was as hateful as Seward and Chase. A very different tone prevailed north of the Potomac. While Buchanan and Jeremiah Black showed intense bitterness, old-time leaders like Cass were saddened and taciturn. Pugh would have preferred to follow Douglas, and when he bowed to expediency it was with deep regret and foreboding. Bigler was uneasy, while even Fitch, no such minion of slavery as Bright and well aware of Indiana's feeling, would have inclined toward Douglas's standard had he not needed Administration support to hold his contested seat. It was quickly noted that two prominent up-State New Yorkers, Horatio Seymour and Daniel B. Dickinson, were exceedingly reluctant to express themselves on the painful question. Seymour, in fact, said he could make no statement until he consulted his friends.[18] Not a few old eastern Jacksonians, men of George Bancroft's stamp, who had long distrusted Douglas, decided that he was essentially right and that they must either go with him or cross into the Republican camp.

The short interval between the opening of Congress and the Christmas recess on December 23 witnessed a hot running debate between Bigler, Fitch, and Green of Missouri on the Lecompton side, and Douglas as a one-man opposition. Not until December 23 did Stuart and Broderick speak, and then unimpressively. But Douglas was in superb fighting form. Repeatedly he harried Bigler as an Elizabethan ship-royal would outsail and harry a Spanish galleon. The slow, clumsy Pennsylvanian was helpless against his charges. On the twenty-first, after summarily disposing of both Mason and Bigler, he let off a sudden broadside against his Southern enemies and the newspapers they controlled; newspapers like the Montgomery *Advertiser* for W. L. Yancey, the Jackson *Mississippian* for Jefferson Davis, and the Richmond *South* for R. M. T. Hunter:

There are men here personal enemies of mine—men who would be willing to sink an Administration if they could kill off northern men, and get them out of the way in the future; such men are getting their tools to denounce me as having abandoned the party. Why? Because I do not desert my principles as freely as the masters of these editors desert theirs. I have seen this attempt—not sanctioned by the President; he scorns it; but there are men under him busy at work to convince every one that I have betrayed my party and my principles, in order to see if they cannot crush me among my Democratic friends. That every press which can be controlled, is thus controlled, is beyond denial or dispute. Nineteen twentieths of all independent Democratic presses— those who do not depend on certain departments of the government for support —are with me in sustaining the credit of the Democratic party. . . .; but the few who are not allowed to speak for themselves are endeavoring to drive me where they cannot drive me—to desert the [party] principles. . . .

18 Daniel Sickles, December 21, 1857; Buchanan Papers.

Next day Fitch of Indiana drew another destructive volley. He had delivered an elaborate defense of Lecompton, combined with a harsh attack on the Topeka faction; his discourse being distinguished by malignant, personal innuendoes against Douglas. He held up *in terrorem* a picture of the tragic fate of Burr and Van Buren when they treacherously attacked the Democratic Party. During the latter part of the speech, the Little Giant lay perfectly motionless in his chair, his back to the orator; but he knitted his brows angrily, and his deep-set eyes took on smouldering fire. When Fitch sat down and Douglas rose slowly to his feet, a murmur of expectation ran through the hall. His rejoinder was magnificent in itself. It was compressed, epigrammatic, and forcible. And its effect was doubled by the proud, fierce energy of the speaker, who presented a striking picture of physical and intellectual strength as, pacing to and fro across the Senate floor, tossing his shaggy locks, and indulging in dramatic gestures, he threw out his arguments in a ringing voice. Several times he turned with sudden fury toward his assailant. Stamping his foot, he demanded what Fitch had meant when he compared him with Aaron Burr? What did he mean by accusing him of a selfish ambition to destroy the Democratic Party? What was behind his dark insinuations and vague innuendoes? "What if I do differ from the President? I have not become the servile tool of any President to receive and obey his instructions against my own judgment and sense of right." [19]

This was no teapot tempest; this was a party earthquake. Nobody who listened to Douglas's speeches could doubt that he would fight to a Waterloo end. His manner, his tone, his promise that he would repel every blow struck, bespoke irrevocable determination. He showed a bitterness toward his former brethren, too, which animated gestures and bearing. When he mentioned the "returns" of Kansas votes, it was with scorching contempt; when he spoke of the men behind Lecompton, it was with a mingled venom and disgust which proved that he would never again strike hands with Southern radicals. He accused the Administration of sending agents west by express to snatch the slavery clause out of the constitution so as to win doubtful Congressional votes. Walker showed the same temper. Returning to Washington on December 11, he shortly met Jeremiah Black, and the fire flew. He came to Douglas after that talk with a firm conviction that the Cabinet were determined to ruin both of them politically and financially. As for the Southern "ultras," they knew that they must conquer or forever lose control of the party which they had dominated, except for Cass's brief summer of candidacy, since 1840.

The Administration had used its light guns first. It reserved its heavy artillery until after the Christmas recess: Davis, Slidell, Hammond, Hunter, and Toombs.

19 N. Y. *Weekly Tribune*, December 23, 1857; for a slightly different version see *Cong. Globe*, 35th Cong., 1st Sess., 140.

But the Republican chieftains were now ready to move reinforcements to the aid of Douglas. As Seward, Fessenden, Lyman Trumbull, and others polished their weapons, the outlines of a strange alliance emerged. Douglas began talking confidentially of a Constitutional Union party to save the nation from Southern secession, such a coalition of Union Democrats and Republicans as actually appeared in 1864.

[III]

The Illinoisan was quick to renew in Washington the overtures which he had made to Republicans in Chicago. On December 14, he called Schuyler Colfax and Anson Burlingame to his house for a long conference.

"I believe," he said in effect, "that Jeff Davis and other Southern ultras are ready for disunion. I believe they want an opportunity to break up the nation. If they go on, we must form a grand Constitutional Union party to stop them. I confess, I never expected to meet such opposition to the simple demand for justice that I made on behalf of the people of Kansas. I shall stand my ground inflexibly; I shall uphold the principle of popular sovereignty even if this means my enemies will drive me from public life." He was confident that he could keep the bulk of the Northern Democracy behind him and that, if the Republicans gave full aid, he could defeat the Southern radicals.

"Our strategy is clear," he told Colfax and Burlingame. "The Administration will try to rush Lecompton through. They will say that Kansas must come in at once. If they succeed, all is lost. We must fight a delaying game. We must insist that Minnesota, with her unanimously adopted constitution, be admitted first. Let the South resist that if they dare! If they oppose Minnesota, we can block the appropriation bills in the House, and stop Cobb's Treasury note issue there. After Minnesota comes in, we must press for the admission of Oregon. As for Kansas, I shall present the Toombs bill with a hard and fast clause for popular submission added." When Colfax pointed out that many Republicans were so committed against the Toombs bill that they could not change front, Douglas said he would be glad to use a copy of the Minnesota Enabling Act. "I will go for any measure of any kind that provides for a full and fair vote of the people of Kansas on the whole constitution." He agreed to meet Banks to arrange a joint plan of action.

"Our true policy," continued Douglas with a far look into the future, "is to put the disunionists in their real light before the country. We must put them in such a position that when the break comes, as come it must, they will be in the position of insurgents; instead of letting them create a situation, as they wish to do, in which *we* must revolt. We will let them be the rebels. Then the army and the power of the nation will be against them." [20]

The Republican leaders, exultant but suspicious, were ready to effect a temporary alliance on the clear understanding that it involved no permanent commitment. Ben Wade, who had hailed Douglas's initial speech as "the first slave insurrection I ever saw," gladly went to his house for a friendly talk. He would concert plans with alacrity. Nevertheless, he thought Douglas actuated only by selfish motives, for the man knew that if he followed Buchanan's lead, Illinois would defeat him for reelection to the Senate. "You are driven into our port like a ship by stress of weather," he crowed to his host.[21] Lyman Trumbull was equally distrustful. At first he thought the Democratic schism mere shadow-boxing; Douglas would be allowed to vote against Lecompton if his ballot was not necessary to carry it, and would then quietly return to the fold.[22] Even after hearing the Little Giant's angry speeches, he was uncertain how far the revolt would extend. Trumbull would neither embrace nor assail the new ally, but simply accept him so long as his course was right. "Douglas does not mean to join the Republican Party, I presume," he wrote Lincoln, "and yet if the Kansas question should be kept open for a few months, he may be forced into that position." [23] Seward, too, was for a cautious, mistrustful alliance. Douglas could never be consistent, he wrote. "After making a bold stroke for the defense of Kansas, we shall soon see him making a demonstration for the acquisition of Cuba." [24]

This cautious position suited Douglas; he, too, wanted only an emergency coalition. Colfax, anxious to encourage him in the fight, bade him look to the distant future. He probably underestimated the power of the Administration, which by use of patronage, prestige, and party press could wear down and defeat any rebel; but he must remember that defeat within the party was not defeat in the nation. "You have an opportunity," said Colfax in essence, "to place yourself in the most commanding position held by any statesman in the country; you can make yourself the Silas Wright of your party and conquer the prejudices of your old freesoil opponents." Colfax could promise nothing for the Republicans if Douglas was forced into their fold; he could not pledge Republican support for the senatorship in 1858, much less the Presidency in 1860. But he could say that the Republicans agreed that popular sovereignty in Kansas was the ques-

---

20 Schuyler Colfax, "Memorandum of Interview," December 14, 1857; Colfax Papers, Ind. State Lib.

21 December 20, 25, 1857; Wade Papers. "We must treat him with friendship, but not hunt him."

22 Trumbull to Lincoln, December 5, 1857; Trumbull Papers, Ill. State Hist. Lib.

23 *Ibid.*, December 25, 1857.

24 Frederic Seward, *William H. Seward*, II, 322; December 22, 1857.

tion of the hour, and would cooperate in maintaining that principle wherever it protected free men on free soil.

"You are right," responded Douglas, "I ask no support except in this present contest. If this issue is settled aright, new issues will come up hereafter, and we shall divide again. If it is not settled rightly, and remains the dominant question, we can let the future determine our duties and positions." Douglas introduced his bill to give Kansas a new enabling act on December 18, and the same day N. P. Banks for the Republicans offered a new enabling bill in the House.[25]

Spending the Christmas holidays with his wife in New York, Douglas was received by Democratic leaders, Republican editors, and the public with a hearty good will which elated him. He found members of Greeley's staff cordial. Greeley himself, delighted that the Senator had "broken the backs of the Democrats," was writing leaders to say that the Little Giant had the popular side, that he must win, and that the Administration could never turn him out of the party. Douglas found the *Herald* conducting a mere sham fight against him, which helped rather than hurt his cause; he found Raymond and the *Times* strongly on his side. Many Federal officeholders in New York were secretly with him. Talking freely, he told John Bigelow and Parke Godwin of the *Evening Post*, whom he met in N. P. Banks's room at the St. Nicholas, all about his plans. He was confident of defeating the Administration by preventing a House vote on Lecompton until late spring or summer, meanwhile mobilizing public sentiment and marshaling his Congressional forces so that he could either force an adjournment without action or destroy the measure. He left no doubt of his earnestness. Banks thought that he was almost ready to become a Republican convert—that he realized that no halfway house could be found between the Administration and the Republican Party. This was wishful thinking. But, testified Bigelow in a note to Bryant, his bitterness was extreme:

"Douglas does not disguise his conviction that he can never be forgiven by the South if he were ever so much disposed to ask forgiveness, and I thought I could perceive by the way in which he talked abundant evidence of an old hostility rankling in his bosom of which this outbreak about the Lecompton Constitution was as but the flash of the priming to the discharge."[26]

Republican suspicion of Douglas went far deeper in Illinois than in New York and the East generally. Let the party profit by the treason without taking the traitor to its embraces, recommended Illinoisans; Douglas may be capable of

25 *Cong. Globe*, 35th Cong., 1st Sess., 65, 84. The Washington correspondent of the *Herald* wrote of the Republicans, December 19, that "the case is by no means settled whether they will work for him [Douglas] or merely avail themselves of his labors to advance themselves and their interests." N. Y. *Herald*, December 23, 1857.

26 John Bigelow, December 28, 1857; Bryant Papers.

good, but his long fellowship with wrong and outrage should inspire misgivings.[27] Greeley, Preston King, Bigelow, and N. P. Banks, however, began to cherish hope that Douglas would follow in the path of the Blairs and Lyman Trumbull. A Democrat asked Banks if the Republicans would take the Little Giant into the party.

"Yes, sir," replied Banks, whom Massachusetts friends liked to call "the little iron man." "We will take all who want to come; the church is large and the door wide."

"Very well," rejoined the Democrat, "but are you willing to make him your leader?"

"We are willing, after they all get in," replied Banks, "to let the smartest man lead the column." [28]

Events played into the hands of Douglas in his struggle for delay. When Congress resumed work after New Year's of 1858, it was deemed wise to await the result of the January elections in Kansas, while financial problems, the arrest of the filibuster William Walker by Commodore Paulding of the Navy, and the Mormon question all urgently demanded discussion. February found the able Republican platoon in the Senate—Seward, Trumbull, Fessenden, Collamer, Doolittle, Wade, Henry Wilson—all alongside Douglas on the firing line. "You are great and strong," cried Seward to the Southern members, "but you can never, never conquer Kansas."

[IV]

That Territory was furnishing proof of the statement, and helping arouse precisely the Northern feeling that Douglas desired. In a series of dramatic moves, the free State settlers of Kansas defied the regency government of John Calhoun, provided for a plebiscite on the entire Lecompton constitution, and showed that the people overwhelmingly repudiated the instrument. These acts sealed the fate of Lecompton in the national House.

Much evidence exists that the Administration hoped to sweeten the Lecompton pill by having the constitution accepted at the December 21 election "without slavery." We have noted Douglas's charge that agents were hurried west to arrange this. Schuyler Colfax learned, early in December, that a dozen men had been sent to Kansas to insist that the slavery clause be voted out, or taken out by a falsification of the returns.[29] Buchanan, indeed, told his friends that he was sure the "constitution without slavery" would triumph. Most Senators seem to have supposed this.

27　C. S. Wilson of the Chicago *Journal*, December 14, 1857; Trumbull Papers.
28　N. Y. *Evening Post*, December 19, 1857.
29　Colfax, "Memorandum," December 14, 1857; Colfax Papers.

But the Administration erred in two respects. It failed to realize how completely free State voters would boycott the Hobson's choice election. Still more egregiously, it failed to comprehend that the little proslavery faction in Kansas, hardly a thousand men out of sixteen thousand voters, were determined to get the "constitution with slavery" even if the heavens fell. As Thomas Ewing, Jr., wrote his distinguished father, this group under John Calhoun were utterly reckless. "They are composed of those of the Ruffians who figured conspicuously in the arsons and murders of the past two years, and who have not yet died of delirium tremens. That is, honestly, the character of the men who are likely to have the control of the State government and to have the power of the General Government to back them in subjugating the people. But Kansas cannot be forced like a bastinadoed elephant to kneel to receive the paltry riders." [30]

The Administration failed, also, to reckon with the intrepid Stanton, secretary and acting-governor of Kansas until supplanted by Denver. The Oxford and McGee frauds, and the Lecompton convention, had incensed this former proslavery man. He had discovered, as he put it later, why the great mass of the Kansans were so dissatisfied with their government that they were ready to rebel to throw it off.[31] The Territory naturally boiled with indignation after the convention broke up. Settlers in scores of communities swore that they would fight to the death before submitting. A call went out for a free State convention in Lawrence to determine what action should be taken to meet the new contingency. Demands poured in upon Stanton to convene the recently elected legislature that it might deal with the situation. He sympathized with the popular feeling, for he regarded the whole convention scheme for a regency government as outrageous. This regency government, under the Lecompton "schedule," was to reign supreme until a new legislature and other officers were chosen on January 4, 1858. In view of the unjust apportionment clause which gave a heavy preponderance to counties on the Missouri border, of the special powers conferred on Calhoun to manage the new elections, and of the grant of suffrage in these crucial elections of December 21 and January 4 to every white male "in the Territory on that day," fair balloting was impossible.

"It was apparent," Stanton later wrote, "that all the machinery had been artfully prepared for a repetition of gross frauds, similar to those which had been attempted in November." While Congress fastened the Lecompton constitution on the new State, a rigged election would furnish a new Lecompton legislature which would prevent any interference with the obnoxious instrument.

Stanton cut through the regency scheme with his call of December 1 for a

---

30 Leavenworth, January 18, 1858; Ewing Papers.
31 F. P. Stanton, Philadelphia speech, February 5, 1858.

special session of the recently chosen legislature. He acted none too soon. The next day the Cabinet dispatched a messenger westward with that part of Buchanan's forthcoming message which related to territorial affairs. Cobb, Thompson, and Floyd wished to paralyze Stanton. That next day, too, the free State convention opened in Lawrence, with "Governor" Robinson and Jim Lane in charge. The delegates, meeting in soft Indian summer weather, filled the town to overflowing. Angered as never before, they pledged the freesoil majority to implacable resistance to Lecompton. Eighteen thousand men, said Lane, were ready to shoulder arms. If Stanton had not given the people due legal means for protecting themselves from imposition, the elections of December 21 and January 4 would doubtless have witnessed a reopening of civil war. As it was, when the legislature convened December 7, the acting-governor laid before it a message which not only spoke of the "profound agitation" and the "sense of wrongs and injustice," but recommended definite action. He asked for legislation to punish election frauds. But above all, he urged the legislature to fix an election date when qualified citizens might vote for the constitution in either of the forms provided by the convention, and also might vote against it *in toto*. He believed that Congress could not disregard the voice of the people, thus legally expressed.[32]

The legislature immediately took this sage advice. It was anxious to fortify the freesoil settlers before Washington could send out a new governor to harass them. While the members had promised Stanton that they would not try to set the Topeka government in operation, they were nevertheless able to inaugurate a new era. Hitherto the free State men had acted extra-legally; now they wielded a legitimate authority. They provided for an investigation of the Oxford and McGee frauds, and prescribed effective penalties for such acts—with the result that some offenders fled the Territory. They also submitted the Lecompton constitution to popular vote on January 4. Ballots might be cast "For the constitution with slavery," "For the constitution without slavery," and "Against the constitution."

Three elections were now impending: the partial plebiscite on December 21, the full plebiscite January 4, and the election of a new legislature and other officers on the last-named date. It was thus possible for Kansans to prove themselves overwhelmingly against the instrument in all its parts. Republican leaders in Washington kept in close touch with "Governor" Robinson and other free State leaders. Using B. Gratz Brown of the Missouri *Democrat* as intermediary, they advised that the legislature stay in session to await Washington events, repeal the act authorizing the Lecompton convention, and make preparations

32 Full message in Emporia *Kanzas News*, December 19, 1857.

for regaining full possession of the Territory if necessary.[33] No rash steps, however, were taken.

Beyond question, Stanton's call of the special session was a statesmanlike act. It diverted public attention from schemes of violent resistance, substituted debate and investigation for angry personal collisions, and enabled representatives of the people to devise methods of counteracting the wrongs planned against them.[34]

The Administration was taken aback by the acting-governor's spirited course. The Cabinet, in sending him an advance copy of part of Buchanan's message, had instructed him to follow the President's views.[35] He was to encourage voters to accept the Lecompton formula; instead, he had assisted them to reject it! His instant removal came too late. Long before Denver could arrive to take his place, the legislature had completed its work, passed a militia bill over Stanton's veto, and adjourned. For a few days, Administration leaders were fearful lest Walker make a hurried trip to Kansas to supersede acting-governor Denver. But Walker thought he saw a more effective mode of helping the Territory than by beginning a contest which would end in his swift decapitation. After hurried conferences with Douglas and other friends, he spent several days composing a long appeal to the country. Under date of December 15, he sent this to Cass as a letter of resignation which the freesoil press gleefully published in full. It produced a public sensation, brought about an extra session of the Cabinet, and gave Lecompton a heavy new blow. He should not have resigned—he should have gone down with his flag nailed to the mast; but his parting shot did heavy execution.

Disgust, chagrin, and burning resentment mingled in the letter. Abandoned by the Administration, stigmatized by Southern epithets, laboring under a sense of betrayal, Walker spoke with devastating frankness. He branded "my Southern opponents" as cheats. He reiterated the familiar facts showing that the Lecompton convention had not represented one-tenth of the people. He warned Congress that an attempt to force the constitution upon Kansas would require coercion of an overwhelming majority, would settle nothing, and would, "I fear, be attended by civil war, extending, perhaps, throughout the Union." He declared that he would not play the part of a mute in a pantomime of ruin. Most stingingly of all, he told the nation that the President had been victimized by a Southern conspiracy. All had been going smoothly; the peaceable entry of Kansas had seemed assured—and then "my Southern opponents interfered . . . and by denunciation, menaces, and otherwise, aided at a critical period by several Federal officeholders in Kansas, including the Surveyor-General, and the Presi-

33 N. P. Banks and F. P. Blair, Jr., telegraphed B. G. Brown thus December 14; Brown to Robinson, December 15, 1857, Robinson Papers, KHS.
34 F. P. Stanton, "To the People of the Union," January 29, 1858.
35 Cass was the mouthpiece; *Senate Exec. Docs., No. 8*, 35th Cong., 1st Sess., 112, 113.

dent of the Convention with his immense patronage, embracing many hundred employees, intervened, and as I believe without the knowledge or approbation of the President of the United States, produced the extraordinary paper called the Lecompton Constitution."

Ex-Secretary Stanton was ready to add his voice to Walker's. In a long letter, written as soon as his hands were free, he laid bare the frauds in the Territory, defended his own conduct there, and warned Congress not to force upon the Kansans an instrument which four-fifths of them condemned; not to commit the supreme folly of defending "so wicked and dishonest a contrivance as the Lecompton Constitution." His detailed speech in New York on the subject was soon being sold by the *Tribune* as part of an eight-page extra.[36]

The men who had gone out as proconsuls of the Directory to make Kansas a Democratic State had come back as surrogates for the freesoil settlers who were soon to make Kansas one of the most rock-ribbed Republican States of the Union. Walker was concluding his service under Buchanan; his next great public role would be under Abraham Lincoln.

Meanwhile, all eyes were fixed upon the three Kansas elections. The Administration accepted the *fait accompli* of the legislature's arrangement of a plebiscite on January 4, instructing Denver to see that the election was held as freely and fairly as the two ordered by the convention. Just before Christmas, therefore, the new acting-governor issued a proclamation in which he certified to the legality of the plebiscite and also recognized the validity of the law passed to punish election frauds. While Denver was not so strong a man as Geary and not so able as Walker, he was honest and impartial. A Virginia lawyer who had made a sterling record in the Mexican War and in California, and who had lived on the Missouri border before Kansas was opened to settlement, he was resolved to yield no improper ground to any party or group. Announcing that he would carry out Walker's policies in good faith, he soon won the regard of conservative freeholders.

The first election, the "with slavery" or "without slavery" contest of December 21, followed the old farcical pattern. An alleged vote of 6,226 was cast for the constitution with slavery, and 569 for it without. Proof was later adduced that many ballots were fraudulent, a legislative committee which inspected them declaring that at least 2,720 should be annulled.[37] Most free State men of

---

36   Priced at $15 per thousand; N. Y. *Tribune*, February 25, 1858.
37   Spring, *Kansas*, 228, 229. President C. W. Babcock of the Council, present at the counting of the votes, believed that about 4,000 of them were fraudulent; see Douglas's report for the Committee on Territories, 1858. Walker also declared about 4,000 of them invalid. This was the conclusion reached by the State officers elected January 4. They pointed out that 3,012 of the votes for the constitution "with slavery" were polled in three sparsely settled districts on the Missouri border, Oxford, Shawnee, and Kickapoo; and from personal knowledge of these settlements they knew the great bulk of the vote to be fictitious. They believed that not more than 2,000 true citizens cast their vote for the Lecompton constitution on December 21. See text of their protest, Phila. *Weekly Press*, February 13, 1858.

course ignored the election. In the contest for officers on January fourth, 6,545 votes were allegedly cast, of which 2,458 were later pronounced fraudulent. Freesoil settlers largely boycotted this, too. Once more the proslavery element perpetrated grave frauds, and the result was uncertain, both sides claiming the victory. The referendum on the constitution as a whole, held without disorder on the fourth of January, was much more impressive. No fewer than 10,226 voted against the constitution, while 138 were ready to accept it without slavery and 24 with slavery. This emphatic result, proving clearly how Kansas stood, brought John J. Crittenden's influential voice in the Senate over to Douglas.

Most Southerners accepted the vote of December 21 as final; Kansas had asked for entry with a slave State constitution, and must be admitted. Most Northerners accepted the vote of January 4; Kansas had rejected slavery, and must be allowed to write a new constitution. Acting-Governor Denver felt no doubt whatever that the free State men had carried both the election of State officers and the only valid test on the constitution. On January 16, he wrote Buchanan that Congress would commit a vital error if it accepted Lecompton. The free State men constituted a large majority; feeling was high—an organization had been formed sworn to kill every man who took office under the Lecompton constitution; and the people simply would not submit to that instrument. Denver recommended that Congress pass an enabling act and let a new constitutional convention be held. "As for the Democratic party here it cannot be worse off than it is at present, and this course will afford them an opportunity to organize a strong conservative party which will be able to control the Territory."

Bitter it would have been for a truly sensitive President to review the events of these six weeks in Kansas; to see how Stanton had outmaneuvered him, to read of the overwhelming repudiation of the constitution by more than ten thousand voters, and to find the new acting-governor recommending substantially Douglas's proposal. But no one doubted that Buchanan would prove obedient to the voice of his masters. He pressed forward with the tenacity not of courage but of timidity. Having chosen his path, he felt it would cost him too much to make honest confession of error; while he was afraid to turn against the Directory.

The Cabinet had discussed a compromise plan, under which Congress would approve of Lecompton with a solemn stipulation that the first State legislature must submit the whole constitution to popular vote. Buchanan, Cass, and Toucey, three Northerners, had favored it—and the time had been when a President backed by his Secretary of State would have had his own way; but Cobb, Floyd, Brown, and Jacob Thompson were sternly opposed, and Buchanan yielded to the strong men about him.[38] When Denver's letter was brought to

38 H. Von Holst, *United States*, IV, 204; Nichols, *Disruption*, 156.

him by Rush Elmore, a former judge and a man who, although the largest slave-holder in Kansas, held moderate, sagacious views, the President was ready to renew his championship of Lecompton. He was ready, that is, to tell Congress that the burlesque vote of December 21 constituted good ground for accepting Kansas as the sixteenth slave State.

What he said to Elmore we do not know. He had the effrontery to write Denver that he regretted he had not received the information sooner, for having prepared a special message re-espousing Lecompton and having shown it to several Senators, he could not withdraw it.[39] On February 2, 1858, he sent the Lecompton constitution to Congress with a long message urging immediate admission of Kansas—"at this moment as much a slave State as Georgia or South Carolina." He knew that more than 10,000 Kansans had voted against the constitution and not more than 3,000 for it. The peculiar features of the message were two: a vitriolic denunciation of the Topeka organization under Robinson and Jim Lane as treasonable, disloyal, and revolutionary, its very existence constituting "a state of rebellion"; and an argument that if Kansans did not want slavery, they need only enter the Union, and then they could remake their government immediately. But could they really do so? A constitutional clause would forbid it; and even if this were disregarded, the accomplished fact would be hard to reverse.

[V]

The important fact was that the course of events in Kansas, with the vigorous letters of Walker and Stanton, had greatly strengthened Douglas and his Republican allies. Another broad ebullition of public sentiment, akin to that of 1854, was visible from the Kennebec to the Kaw. The moral position of the Douglas-Seward coalition was invulnerable, for only the most extreme Southerners denied that the constitution should have been submitted to popular vote, and Buchanan's instructions to Walker had placed the President in a role where he must eat his words. The political position of the coalition was also strong. The entire Republican Party, almost the whole Know-Nothing Party of the free States, and a heavy majority of Northern Democrats, stood behind Douglas on this issue. In the Northwest in particular, Democratic newspapers seemed ten to one on his side.[40] The ablest editors of the land were embattled against the Administration. In all the larger cities from Boston to Chicago, and in country districts everywhere north of the Ohio, public meetings testified to the groundswell of feeling. The fighting power of Douglas, Walker, and Stanton, their defense of popular rights, their dramatization of a bold cause, aroused general admiration.

39 *Kansas State Hist. Publs.*, I, 170.   40 N. Y. *Weekly Tribune*, December 26, 1857.

They were for the New Democracy against the old; they were the people's men against privilege and power. Douglas, wrote Greeley, "would carry this State for President tomorrow, as against Buchanan, Dickinson, or anybody that could be started to compete with him in the Democratic convention." [41]

Day after day, a snowfall of approving letters from every free State whitened Douglas's desk. Many were from prominent men. Governor Henry A. Wise was with him, declaring that this legerdemain scheme, if Buchanan pushed it through, would raise the Black Republican flag above Capitol and White House; George Bancroft applauded him, writing that every student of history knew that Lecompton must leave the Administration helpless with the people.[42] It pleased Douglas to receive from the owner of the Gloversville, New York, *Standard* a belligerent anti-Lecompton editorial with the assurance that it yielded but a faint indication of the feeling in that area.[43] He was still better pleased by word from Lanphier of the *Illinois State Register* that a Democratic convention in Springfield, representing all parts of the State, had shown almost complete unity and a belligerent spirit.[44] Humble party workers sent their testimony as to popular support. A citizen of Reading, Pennsylvania, who circulated five thousand German translations of Douglas's anti-Lecompton argument, declared that if Governor Packer's inaugural had not been sound on Kansas, he would have been left without a Cabinet twenty-four hours after he took office.[45] A lieutenant in Scioto County, Ohio, wrote that he did not know a Democrat in that region who was not heartily behind Douglas's party. Another in Lawrence, Massachusetts, declared that the Senator was on the floodtide of popular enthusiasm. A third in Trenton, New Jersey, sending a fiery speech by a local politician, estimated that nine hundred and ninety-eight voters in every thousand were with the Little Giant.[46]

Particularly striking were the expressions welling up from the border States. Virginians sent numerous letters: R. H. Glass of Lynchburg, father of a future statesman, for example, praised Douglas's courage and fairness.[47] A Marylander

---

41   December 20, 1857; Greeley-Colfax Correspondence.
42   Bancroft to Douglas, December 2, 1857; Douglas Papers.
43   January 24, 1858; Douglas Papers.
44   C. H. Lanphier, January 22, 1858; Douglas Papers.
45   G. M. Sanman, January 23, 1858; Douglas Papers.
46   J. Enslow, January 24, G. W. Harland, January 26, F. F. Patterson, January 22, 1858; Douglas Papers.
47   R. H. Glass, January 21, 1858; Douglas Papers. Some Southerners of course wrote their disapproval. J. J. Quarles of Carthage, Texas, informed the Senator that if he did not drop his fight against Lecompton he would not get a corporal's guard to support him in Texas for the next Presidential nomination. But such letters are comparatively few, and the impression to the contrary given by A. L. Venable in his article "The Conflict between the Douglas and Yancey Forces" in the Charleston Convention (*Southern Hist. Review*, May, 1942) is misleading.

wrote that Ogle County gave the Senator strong adherence.[48] A citizen of Mt. Vernon, Kentucky, who had hoped to see Kansas a slave State, declared that his section was against any constitution not popularly approved. Simon B. Buckner, destined for a distinguished career, wrote that a majority of Louisville people gave Douglas their full approbation. Another Kentuckian put local sentiment crisply: "We would rather Kansas would come into the Union as a slave State. But we are opposed to trickery and all such abominations as the Lecompton Constitution." [49] The Louisville *Democrat*, oldest and ablest Democratic paper of the State, thought that Lecompton would fare worse there than in Kansas.

Early in 1858, the legislatures of New Jersey, Rhode Island, and Michigan passed resolutions denouncing Lecompton; the New York Assembly invited Stanton to address it; and the Ohio legislature instructed Pugh to vote against admission. In Buchanan's own State, Governor Packer said that he believed he expressed the conviction of the people in declaring that if the people of a new State wished to vote on their constitution after it was framed, they should have an unqualified right to do so. Forney's *Press* and George W. Child's *Public Ledger* were attacking Buchanan in every issue, while the *Pennsylvanian* offered but weak resistance. An anti-Lecompton meeting in Philadelphia on February 8, where Forney presided and Stanton made a rousing address, elicited letters from a long roll of Democrats—Douglas, Walker, Stuart, Representatives T. L. Harris of Illinois and S. S. Cox of Ohio, and Governor Wise. Characterizing Lecompton as undemocratic and oppressive, Wise contradicted Buchanan's assertion that admission would speedily end the agitation outside Kansas. Instead, he wrote, it would have the worst effects. It would create a border war, arouse Northern bitterness, drive multitudes of honest Democrats from the party, and ensure Republican triumph—thus raising the last dread issue of disunion.[50] Only by heroic efforts, using officeholders present and expectant, did the Administration prevent the State convention at Harrisburg early in March from passing hostile resolutions.[51]

Walker and Stanton, throwing their private business aside, were maintaining an effective crusade. They were able orators. Both spoke at an anti-Lecompton gathering in New York. Stanton addressed another in the capital of Ohio for three hours,[52] while in Philadelphia he caustically arraigned Buchanan's timidity. It was the well-understood design of certain Southern leaders in Washington, he said, to break up the Union if Lecompton failed. Their threats had caused

48   J. A. Ettinger, January 25, 1858; Douglas Papers.
49   W. R. Thompson, January 24, 1858; Douglas Papers.
50   *National Intelligencer*, February 11, 1858.
51   N. Y. *Weekly Tribune*, March 13, 1858.
52   *Idem.*

the President to surrender, when, if he had only defied them, the true-hearted Democracy of Tennessee, Kentucky, Virginia, North Carolina, Louisiana, and possibly other Southern States would have rallied to the national standard, and he could have crushed the conspirators.[53] If any man knew the upper South, it was Stanton.

In Michigan, Wisconsin, and Iowa, no less than Illinois, most Democrats were reported for Douglas; the Detroit *Free Press* (still regarded as Cass's organ), the Columbus *Statesman*, Cincinnati *Volksfreund*, Milwaukee *Wisconsin, Illinois State Register* and Chicago *Times* heading the roll of anti-Lecompton papers. Senator-elect Shields of Minnesota was doubly indignant, because he thought the admission of his State was being made dependent on the passage of the Lecompton scheme. In California the party was rent asunder, Broderick as head of the San Francisco machine and close friend of the Illinois leader fighting tooth and nail against Gwin, who had executive patronage to aid him. Governor Weller was on Douglas's side, while the Democratic *Globe* and *Herald* in San Francisco, with the well-edited *Alta California* and Sacramento *Union*, took the same position. California had good historic reasons for believing in popular sovereignty.[54] When the legislature instructed Broderick to support Lecompton, the Senator defied it, saying he was satisfied that four-fifths of the people of the State repudiated the Lecompton fraud.[55]

The most remarkable evidence that the tide was running against the Administration was furnished by the revolt of the Indiana Democrats—a "majestic uprising," as the New York *Tribune* called it, against which the two Senators fought in vain. Bright and Fitch believed that they could use the postmasters, Federal marshals, swamp-land commissioners, and other officeholders to maintain the line against Douglas. They were aided by Governor A. P. Willard, one of Bright's lieutenants. The State convention had been fixed for January 8, 1858, and for weeks beforehand the Administration machine promised offices right and left, strained every sinew to pack the county conventions, and even when those bodies condemned Lecompton, tried to choose Buchanan delegates. The result was that despite fairly plain evidence of popular sentiment, the convention was so closely divided that the outcome was uncertain.

The Bright-Fitch faction, blanched but determined, played all its best cards. By nominating Willard for president of the convention, they gained the vote of counties which would have rejected any other Lecompton man, and the gover-

---

53 Philadelphia *Weekly Press*, February 13, 1858.
54 *National Intelligencer*, March 4, 1858. Every Democratic newspaper but one in Iowa was on Douglas's side. J. D. Eads, Des Moines, December 12, 1857; Douglas Papers. Of the fifty-nine Democratic newspapers in Illinois, only four supported Lecompton; Lewiston (Illinois) *Fulton Democrat*, March 13, 1858.
55 Jeremiah Lynch, *A Senator in the Fifties: David C. Broderick of California*, 180.

nor then shut out all Douglasites from the platform committee. Bright, so apprehensive that he trembled, made a speech which even his supporters pronounced a failure. When his faction by desperate exertions averted a flat condemnation of Lecompton and passed inconclusive resolutions on Kansas, the body was thrown into a perfect bedlam. It broke up in an uproar, many delegates swearing that not a constable or justice of the peace could be elected on such a platform. The dissenters at once launched a movement for a new mass gathering of Democrats in Indianapolis the following month. Fresh county conventions were held and delegates chosen. "In no other way can the State be saved," wrote one leader; and many agreed that feeling was so intense that unless the party was brought over to the right track, the State would go Republican.[56]

When the mass convention crammed into Masonic Hall, it represented every part of the State. Letters from Walker and Henry A. Wise were cheered. Henry B. Payne of Ohio spoke. Resolutions passed arraigning the Lecompton movement, thanking Douglas for his exertions, and proposing a convention of Northern Democrats. From end to end of Indiana, it was clear that candidates for Congress must take an anti-Lecompton stand or face almost certain defeat.[57]

And Indiana was typical of a long list of Northern States where the Administration had the party machinery but the anti-Lecompton men had public sentiment. When the Connecticut convention, after stormy scenes, adopted a straddle endorsing both Buchanan and popular sovereignty, the chairman of the platform committee uttered a blunt warning. The party had met defeat ever since the Nebraska Act, he said; it had been decimated in the past five years; if it now passed a Lecompton resolution, it would sink in ruin. In Rhode Island, a collision between Federal officeholders and anti-Lecompton spokesmen resulted in similar predictions.[58] Most ominous of all was the spring election in New Hampshire. The Democrats went down with a crash. Again, said the Concord *Patriot*, leading Buchanan organ of the State, the Kansas question has crushed us with its blind ponderous weight. "Before the Lecompton constitution question was brought before the country, our prospects for success were highly flattering: our triumph seemed to be certain; that matter, with the course of the Administration upon it, fell like a wet blanket upon the rising courage and earnest zeal of our friends, and from that day we were doomed." [59]

Nowhere did Democrats look to the coming elections with more dread than in New York. The Administration forced to heel every adherent it could; not only good party mastiffs like Dan Sickles and D. S. Dickinson, but the more

56 A. May, December 1, 1857, Ezra Reed, January 21, 1858, to Douglas; Douglas Papers.
57 Indianapolis *Journal*, February 24, March 1, 1858.
58 *National Intelligencer*, March 6, 1858.
59 Concord *Patriot*, March 10, 1858. The Boston *Herald* and the Augusta, Me., *Age*, both supported Douglas.

independent John A. Dix, who told a Tammany mass meeting that, while he had at first condemned Lecompton, he now supported it on the ground that admission of Kansas would leave that State free to remake its constitution immediately in freesoil form. This easy reasoning was rejected by Bancroft and other former Barnburners, by Raymond of the *Times,* and by a great body of Know-Nothings led by the Brooks brothers of the *Express.* Representative John B. Haskin of Westchester, a staunch anti-Lecomptonite, became a popular hero. The Democrats here, too, adopted a preposterous straddle by declaring for both Buchanan and popular sovereignty—and their candidates made as much of Douglas and as little of Buchanan as possible.[60]

[VI]

It was a perplexed, harassed Buchanan who thus saw revolt sweep the North and Northwest, corrode the border States, and find voice even in the New Orleans *Delta,* which spat contemptuously on Lecompton. Alexander H. Stephens was touched to find the President worn out with official cares. "He is now quite feeble and wan," reported Stephens on February 3. "I was struck with his physical appearance; he appears to be failing in physical health." [61] The Directory, however, quite undaunted, was beginning to use the patronage to enforce its will. Forney, visiting Washington early in March, found the capital full of gloom and apprehension. "What is the aspect now?" he exclaimed. "One wide Reign of Terror." A test had been erected, and those who would not crawl through it went to the guillotine. He described a typical piece of discipline: Maxwell McCaslin of western Pennsylvania, who had worked for Buchanan's advancement during fifteen years, who had been given an Indian agency in Kansas by Pierce, and who had discharged his duties capably, was summarily dismissed when it was found that he agreed with Walker instead of Jacob Thompson. "An army of spies are on the alert, hunting for victims," warned Forney.[62]

The outcome in the Administration-controlled Senate was certain. Had Douglas and Seward possessed the logic of Burke and the eloquence of Cicero, they would have made no converts in that chamber. About fifty set speeches were delivered, which changed not one vote in Congress and not a thousand outside. Southern leaders delivered attorney-like pleas on the legality of the Kansas convention; Douglasites reiterated their defense of popular sovereignty; and Republicans proclaimed their freesoil views.

60 N. Y. *Express, Tribune;* D. S. Alexander, *Pol. Hist. New York,* II, 248–250.
61 R. M. Johnston and W. H. Browne, *Alexander H. Stephens,* 329.
62 Phila. *Weekly Press,* March 20, 1858.

A handful of Senators, however, made contributions of some originality to the debate. Jefferson Davis uttered a plaintive defense of disunionist tendencies in the South while avowing his own love of the Union. A stranger in the Senate gallery, he said, might suppose that he was watching a conference of representatives of two belligerent nations. The South was being arraigned day after day as an aggressive power. Yet what aggressions had it committed? The sum of its offense was a wish to let slavery expand into those parts of the common territory where the people wished to have it. Why should the South care about such expansion? "Simply because of the war that is made against our institutions; simply because of the want of security. . . . You have made it a political war. We are on the defensive. How far are you to push us?" So long as the Southern people were violently denounced, and so long as institutions which they inherited and intended to transmit were being undermined, he added, the Union was truly in danger.[63]

Peculiar weight was given to John J. Crittenden's speech on March 17 by his venerable years, high impartiality, and position as spokesman for the borderland. For two hours he held the attention of one of the largest audiences of the debate. Lord Napier, Baron Stoeckl, and many Representatives were given seats on the floor. The question, he said, was whether Lecompton was the constitution of the *people* of Kansas. He described the chicanery in the writing of the instrument, the election frauds, and the popular disgust. He scoffed at the idea that Kansas could first accept and then immediately rewrite the instrument: "It cannot be abolished, except in the manner prescribed and pointed out in the constitution itself, if any manner is prescribed." Better take twenty votes, better hold twenty elections, than force a misshapen, ill-begotten fundamental law upon a resisting people.

In Clay's spirit, the aged Senator appealed for a decision above bitter sectional antagonisms. "Look at our great country, and the great subjects which claim our attention as her legislators; look at them in all their majesty and their magnitude, and then say how little, how pitiful, in comparison, is the question about which we are making so much strife and contention." [64] With the aid of anti-Lecompton Representatives, Crittenden shortly framed a substitute for the Lecompton bill. It provided for the admission of Kansas on condition that the Lecompton constitution should *first* be submitted to the voters in a carefully guarded election; a new constitution to be drawn up if the old one were rejected.

63   Robert McElroy, *Jefferson Davis*, 176. The N. Y. *Herald* in an editorial of February 4, 1858, pointed out that Southerners who thought that Lecompton would permanently give them a slave State were deluded. But, it declared, the South is frightened by the growing preponderance of free States in Congress, and by the concurrent increase in antislavery sentiment in the North. Appeasement of Southern fears, it argued, was merely common sense.
64   *Cong. Globe*, 35th Cong., 1st Sess., 1153–1159.

This substitute was to be brought forward in the House as soon as the Senate bill was taken up there.

Extremists on both sides made the Senate walls resound with their challenges. Toombs paid tribute to the "sublime spectacle" presented by Buchanan and Black in defending Southern constitutional rights. James H. Hammond, the wealthy grandee of "Redcliffe" in South Carolina, a quiet-mannered but impetuous man, made his famous "cotton is king" speech, which bore only slightly upon the questions in hand. It provoked the angriest rejoinders from Republican seats. Altogether, the long debate was lively—but it altered no opinions.

Throughout the struggle, Douglas by physical and mental force dominated the scene. A host in himself, he was always ready to meet any onslaught, to answer any argument. The incessant strain bore heavily on him. He was harassed by financial worries (for he had overextended his realty purchases and suffered cruel losses in the panic); he was exhausted by sixteen hours of labor a day without exercise, and anguished by his wife's illness. But, determined to protract the contest until national feeling was fully aroused, he was always in the thick of the battle. An able new Republican Senator, scholar, poet, and lawyer in one, James Dixon of Connecticut, expressed his admiration for the Little Giant:

Douglas is quite unwell. He came into our night session about midnight on Monday, but we sent him home. He was not fit to be there. He is very nervous, though he does not show it at all in his looks or appearance. His wife was dangerously sick for some days—say about three weeks ago; and from this cause and the anxiety natural to his position, he became nervous and sleepless. For ten days and nights he did not sleep at all, and for four days last week he was confined to his bed. He now wishes to be able to speak on Monday next. The design of the majority was to force the Kansas bill to a vote on Monday night—but they found the minority determined and resolute. About half-past six on Tuesday morning they gave up the effort. . . .

I am more and more impressed with admiration for the man. I see more and more what a struggle it cost him to sever all personal and political ties, and take his stand on the foundation of eternal truth and justice. All sorts of blandishments and fascinations were applied in vain—and when promises proved unavailing, resort was had to threats. He could have had the assurance of fifteen States at the next Presidential election, with a good prospect of Illinois, Pennsylvania, and perhaps others. But he was decided and resolute. He is now calm and hopeful—and says he has no personal wishes; is willing to throw his influence for the cause.

The South never made a greater mistake than in provoking his opposition. He will prove a terrible foe.[65]

The best single contribution by Douglas lay in his minority report from the Committee on Territories; one of three, for Green brought in the majority

---

65 James Dixon to Gideon Welles, March 17, 1858; Welles Papers, LC.

Lecompton report, and Collamer and Wade the Republican report. Douglas refuted Buchanan's contention that the Kansans could forthwith revise their constitution. It is only when public sentiment approaches unanimity, he stated, that constitutions and governments can be radically altered without violence. Did the character of John Calhoun's gang of slavery men furnish any prospect that, once they had put the constitution in force, unalterable until after 1864 and then only by two-thirds vote, they would "permit it to be subverted and abrogated by a revolutionary amendment, when they will have acquired the right under the Constitution of the United States to demand of the President the use of the Federal Army, to . . . protect the State 'against domestic violence'?" [66]

The Little Giant was never more combatively irresistible than in his final speeches. The admission bill he termed a deathblow to State rights and popular sovereignty. "Reverse the case," he challenged the Southern Senators. "Would Southern men, if a convention of freesoilers should make a constitution, and allow you to vote for it, but not against it, and then attempt to force that constitution on a slaveholding people against their will, would you Southern gentlemen have submitted to such an outrage?" He scornfully attacked the Washington *Union* and the editorials that Attorney-General Black was writing for it. With savage defiance, he warned the Administration that its proscriptions were forcing the party to ruin. Every officeholder was being asked if he were Douglas's enemy, and if he said *no*, off went his head. Men might vote as they liked on the Pacific Railroad bill or Army bill, but on Lecompton no tolerance was extended. Did Cobb, Thompson & Co. intend to expel from the party every man who did not vote for admission? If so, "how many will your Democratic Party number in Pennsylvania? How many in New York? How many in Ohio? How many in any other Northern State?"

Dramatic scenes attended the final debate on March 22. Long before the Senate met at ten o'clock, hurrying crowds, anxious to hear Douglas, had blocked the corridors and gallery. Stuart spoke for three hours. Broderick indulged in scathing language; the attempt to carry this indefensible measure sprang, he said, from the petulance, failing intellect, and trembling dotage of an old man on the verge of the grave. Still Douglas reserved his fire; he would be heard at the evening session. As this drew near, the crush became greater than ever. Veteran observers thought the crowd unprecedented in Capitol history. To rescue many ladies, a motion was carried to admit them to the floor, and in a twinkling the aisles were jammed. Messengers trying to carry copy from the

66 Full text in Phila. *Weekly Press*, February 27, 1858. His wife's illness had delayed Douglas in composing his report. Receiving notice from Green that it was needed at once, he toiled for two days and two nights, pausing only to snatch three hours' sleep and a little food. Two clerks copied the sheets as they came from his hand.

press correspondents to the telegraph offices were unable to fight their way through. As Douglas took the floor, he looked worn and ill. Yet he spoke for three hours with unsurpassable resolution and vigor. When Toombs replied with arrogant insults, even terming Douglas's supporters hypocrites, Stuart rebuked him with the statement that his language and manner befitted a barroom, and moved adjournment.

Next day, only a few desultory exchanges preceded the vote, on which Lecompton carried 33 to 25. Houston reluctantly yielded to the instructions of the Texas legislature and voted *aye;* Pugh, who had a futile compromise plan of his own, followed those of the Ohio legislature by voting *no*. Administration men hailed the victory as decisive. The Douglas-Seward forces pointed out that, if Allen of Rhode Island and Jones of Iowa had obeyed *their* instructions, if Wright and Thompson of New Jersey had followed the clear wishes of their constituents, and if Indiana had been represented by truly elected men instead of Bright and Fitch, the bill would have been defeated. Some Republican comment, following a still more caustic line, recalled that it was almost four years to a day since the Kansas-Nebraska Act had passed Congress; that the fruit of this legislation was now implacably opposed by Douglas himself; that the seats of eight Senators who had voted for the Nebraska bill had been filled by men who were antagonistic to Lecompton; and that not a single Senator who had voted against the bill had been superseded by a Lecompton supporter—though Pugh, chosen by a legislature elected before the Lecompton issue arose, was half hostile to the manifest sentiment of his State.

But the real battle lay ahead. The House offered the crucial test—and the House was more responsive to tides of public feeling than the Senate.

"Yield Not One Inch"

BURKE'S REMARK upon "the mischief of not having large and liberal ideas in the management of great affairs" might well have been remembered by the chief officers of the nation early in 1858. When the Lecompton bill passed the Senate, the most fateful crisis in the history of the Democratic Party since the rivalry of Jefferson and Burr was nearing its climax. The next few weeks would see momentous and irrevocable decisions taken. Would Douglas be crushed, or would the South be beaten and humiliated, or would some final face-saving compromise be arranged? It must be repeated that since the party was the last powerful link binding North and South together, the impending decisions might involve the life of the Union itself.

Senator Crittenden was right when he said that the situation of the republic was fantastic. Although the panic had confronted the country with complex economic difficulties, and although a dozen other problems, from the contumacious Mormons to public lands legislation, demanded attention, the government was half paralyzed by the slavery issue; and no less paralyzed because the disproportion between the immediate quarrel and its effects was ludicrous. Because a few score slaves dwelt in the wide, empty spaces of Kansas, the nation was in an uproar. Their presence was repugnant to four-fifths of the thirty or forty thousand white people dwelling with them; climate and products were hostile to their stay; sensible men knew that these faint dewdrops of slavery would swiftly evaporate under the western sun. A little realism, a little readiness to accept the equities of the situation, would apparently cut through the mesh, for the nation seemed a Hercules entangled in packthread.

To contrast the hundred slaves of Kansas with the frenzied commotion in Washington was, in one sense, to demonstrate what trifles control history. A few words in a treaty, a disputed mile in a boundary, or a bullet in an archduke's body can detonate mighty human explosions. Actually, of course, the hundred slaves were but symbols; and ghostly armies fought in the clouds above Kansas, while legions with flaming swords stood in her red sunrises and purple sunsets. Both North and South, millions had now entered the sphere of hysteric emotions; prejudice warped and passion inflamed their minds; they were influenced by the memory of old affronts and the fear of future wrongs. Above all, fear actuated them. Because each section imputed aggressive designs to the other, every proposal became a plot and every act a menace. Northerners saw the "slave power" already in control of the Presidency, Congress, and Supreme Court; saw it ready to grasp Kansas, cut Texas into five States, and send ten new proslavery Senators to Washington; saw it scheming to annex Mexico, Cuba, and Central America; saw slavery, in short, dominating the continent. Southerners, meanwhile, conjured up a vision of equal perils. They saw Oregon, Kansas, Nebraska, and Minnesota all coming in as free States, Northern population and wealth gaining with ten-league strides, a sectional party taking control of the government, and arrogant majorities rewriting the Constitution to extirpate slavery.

As fear, antagonism, and irrational hostility grew, only statesmanlike action could keep the Northern and Southern wings of the Democratic Party in patient collaboration; and how much statesmanship was at hand in the early months of 1858?

[I]

When Buchanan sent Congress his special message in support of Lecompton, Southern opinion had almost completely solidified. In the Lower South particularly, the arguments of Buchanan, Jefferson Davis, and Alexander H. Stephens (the two latter managing the cause in Senate and House) were accepted at face value. The South was convinced that the Kansas convention, legally elected, possessed full power to form a constitution and prescribe how it should take effect; that interference by any officer of the national government was intolerable; and that so long as the constitution was republican, Congress must accept it. Nor was this all. The South also believed that the Northern assault on Lecompton was in effect a proclamation that no new slave State, anywhere, should ever be admitted. It believed the Republican Party had declared in 1856 that it would never consent to another slave State; Kansas was demanding entry as one; and therefore all who opposed her were upholding this Republican dogma. Sooner than consent to any such prohibition, the cotton States would leave the Union.

It was useless to point out to incensed Southerners the flaw in their syllogism. They did not listen even to Crittenden when he declared that, readily as he would assent to a new slave State, he would never force a constitution on Kansas which three-fourths of her people abhorred. As for the Douglas Democrats, many already half identified them with the Republicans. Linton

Stephens expressed the view of a multitude of Southern men when he declared with passionate energy that if Kansas were excluded, it would not be because of any flaws in the process of constitution-making, but because the canting, holier-than-thou North considered her unworthy company. "The true issue is, and Congress ought to be held to it, and it ought to be so proclaimed to them with a united defiance, whether a State with slavery is fit to be admitted into the Union. If it be decided against us, honor leaves us but one course, and that is, for all the slave States to walk out of the Union, and fling their defiance behind them; and if no other will, I hope Georgia will do it, solitary and alone."[1] The pride of the slaveholders, deeply wounded by Northern utterances on the moral degradations of the peculiar institution, was too hotly inflamed to let them make nice distinctions. Many of them failed to distinguish between a "Black Republican" and an abolitionist; both were enemies, and that was that. Many were hostile, moreover, to arguments based on an appeal to the rights of popular majorities. Preferring government by an elite, they attached no weight to mere numbers in Kansas or elsewhere—to an irresponsible mob or a despotic democracy, as they put it.[2]

It must be remembered that the South was ill-informed. It was not addicted to newspapers, magazines, and books like the North; illiteracy was commoner, and travellers like Olmsted not only found homes bare of reading matter but were thunderstruck by the ignorance of farmers and shopkeepers. The semi-organized campaign against Walker's policies in the summer of 1857 had diffused a general idea that Kansas was being prevented from realizing her desire for slaves only by the plots of emigrant aid men and antislavery governors. "Our people here, and especially the Democrats," wrote F. P. Stanton's brother from Maysville, Kentucky, "are kept in lamentable darkness in regard to the facts and principles involved in the Kansas question"—and this could have been said of many areas.[3] Being more and more on the defensive respect-

1   J. D. Waddell, *Biog. Sketch of Linton Stephens*, 138.
2   *Ibid.*
3   February 17, 1858; Douglas Papers. And not the South only, but Washington as well. Democratic newspapers North and South, including the Washington *Union*, had suppressed much news about Kansas and distorted more. The *National Era* had told the truth, but while it had a wide Northern circulation it was little read in Washington and never seen in the great hotels. The *National Intelligencer* was honest in what it did print, but timid in publishing news that would offend the mass of Washington, Maryland, and Virginia subscribers. In consequence, Southern Senators and Representatives (who would as soon pick up a rattlesnake as a *Tribune*) actually did not know what was going on in Kansas. When the "law and order" foray against Lawrence took place late in 1855, Administration Democrats were as much taken aback, one of them remarked, as if they had heard that a Russian fleet had occupied San Francisco. Not a single Democratic newspaper in the free States had maintained a regular correspondent in Kansas throughout the eventful years 1855-57. The N. Y. *Tribune* of August 20, 1857, declared that if the Philadelphia *Public Ledger* had only stationed an honest reporter there and printed his letters, Pennsylvania would have sent Frémont to the White House.

ing slavery, the South was also more and more intolerant—and no intolerant community, applying restrictions and censorships, can face realities clearly.

It must also be remembered that not a few men both North and South, desiring and planning disunion, hoped that Kansas would furnish an adequate pretext. If they could bring on civil war in Kansas in such fashion that the other side would seem the aggressor, so much the better.

In the South, Robert Barnwell Rhett, W. L. Yancey, William Gilmore Simms, and other private citizens could count now on the cooperation of such Congressional radicals as Keitt, Porcher Miles, Milledge L. Bonham, and Alfred Iverson. To be sure, it was only a small minority as yet who delighted in the idea of party disruption as leading up to national disunion; but their ideas had infective quality. A good many men talked about separation with apparent revulsion but secret attraction. "We cannot remain with honor in the Union if Kansas is thrown out as the issues are now made," exclaimed Senator Hammond. "I have given my ear to every suggestion for a peaceable arrangement of this rotten business that would not compromise the South. I now say Lecompton or Separation, and I will go out, if we can do no better, with South Carolina, Georgia, Florida, Alabama, and Mississippi—three and a half million people and two and a half million cotton bales." [4] Simms, to whom he sent this statement, knew just how much weight to give to Hammond's talk of a peaceable arrangement. The Senator, he informed his fellow conspirator, Porcher Miles, is friendly to Buchanan and will aid him while he is useful. "In brief, Hammond will support the Democratic Party only while it is tributary to the interests of the South." [5] There were an increasing number of Hammonds.

The forces behind this rising disunionist sentiment were numerous. Bright as the vision of the ancient Athenian democracy, so rich in poets, historians, philosophers, and scientists, the dream of a separate Southern nation floated before the eyes of thousands. Casting off the shackles of the dour, jealous, commercial-minded North, they would erect a republic as opulent, as confident of the future, and as full of great men as Virginia and South Carolina just after the Revolution. Others thought of practical commercial advantages. The South produced the wealth of the nation, and the North wrung it from her. Once separate, Southerners could keep the vast sums exacted by Yankee jobbers, manufacturers, bankers, export merchants, and shippers; could use it to fill the land with plenty. Still other Southerners believed that the only hope of peace, of a cessation of the constant antislavery agitation, lay in secession. The very churches had divided on the subject; how, then, could publicans

4 To W. G. Simms, February 7, 1858; Hammond Papers, LC.
5 December 28, 1857; Miles Papers, Univ. of N. C.

and sinners cease to quarrel while tied hand to hand? "No, sir, there is no hope of peace, for there is no peace now—nor will there be until we separate," wrote one Georgian to Alexander H. Stephens.[6]

More and more, however, one feeling dominated all others: the feeling of inevitability. We must eventually separate, men reasoned; the sooner the better, for we are far stronger now than we shall be hereafter. The South was actually in the midst of a revolution, declared Judge Magrath of South Carolina, and it must be hurried on lest the Southern mind become distracted.[7] "The issue will come sooner or later," wrote James H. Taylor of Montgomery, "and the sooner we stand to arms the better for the South."[8] W. H. Trescot spoke for the most thoughtful of these inevitable-secessionists when he told his friends that since disunion was coming, the quicker it came the better, and they should maneuver to throw the onus on the North. If Kansas were admitted under the Lecompton constitution, if Dred Scott were maintained, and if party discipline were enforced in the North, they could carry the election of 1860. This was not important as a mere Democratic victory. It was important "as a means to force the great Republican party into open antagonism with the government and compel them to threaten dissolution etc. when if circumstances favor we can take them at their word or force them to put their principles into the extremest practise. With such a state of parties I think the next four years would give us a good practical issue and one made by the opposition."[9] This was truly Machiavellian.

Honest Quitman was proposing a much more direct procedure. He wrote, as the vote on Lecompton approached:

We are now on the eve of the solution of the great questions: 1. Whether the Northern Democrats will stick to the principles laid down on the slave question in the Cincinnati platform? and 2. Whether any new slave State can ever be admitted? These are the issues involved in the vote on the Kansas constitution. All other questions are mere pretences, flimsy as the mazy sophistries by which they are attempted to be sustained. . . .

Well, suppose we carry the constitution! National democracy will almost cease to exist in the free States. Every man who votes with us will be swept off in the next election. The Black Republicans, or the anti-slavery party under some other name, will sweep every free State at the next contest for President. Parties will become purely sectional, and no remedy [be] left to us of the minority, but separation.

On the other hand, should the constitution be rejected, the South must regard the plighted faith of the Northern Democracy [as] violated. It will assure us that no more reliance can be placed on them to aid us in protecting

6 M. C. Fulton, March 30, 1858; Stephens Papers, LC.
7 To W. P. Miles, February 18, 1858; Miles Papers, Univ. of N. C.
8 To Hammond, March 23, 1858; Hammond Papers, LC.
9 To Hammond, March 20, 1858; Hammond Papers, LC.

our rights; that National Democracy is worthless. We must also see in the act, a fixed and inexorable determination on the part of the majority never to admit another slave State, to stop forever the extension of slavery, and thus to bind the South to the triumphant car of an antagonistic majority.

Who can doubt what under such a state of things the South ought to do? If she waits for the border States, Virginia, Maryland, Kentucky, and Missouri, or either of them, to move, she will never act, but gradually become the willing slave of an insatiate master. The cotton States must move first. . . .

Let but five States determine upon secession, and separate to preserve their social systems, and all the other States having similar systems must sooner or later unite with them.[10]

The most striking single speech of the Senate debate, Hammond's "cotton is king" address, was essentially a bombastic piece of disunionist propaganda, the full flower of Southern nationalism flaunting its petals more gaudily than ever before. Hammond was one of those grotesque figures, like Wade, Sumner, and Wigfall, who if transferred to the pages of Dickens would have been pronounced incredible. Short, plump, with a domelike brow and pleasing manners, this master of broad reaches of rice and cotton, herds of blooded stock, and four hundred slaves, was as temperamental as Randolph of Roanoke, as inflated with vanity as Thomas Hart Benton, as crotchety as John Tyler. He actually dreamed of a Presidential nomination; as if any party could nominate a man who declared that "God created negroes for no other purpose than to be the subordinate 'hewers of wood and drawers of water,'" and who expressed the hope that slaves would populate every spot on earth where their labor would benefit the whites.[11] He preened himself on all his public utterances. Withal, he was kind, shrewdly independent (he disliked the Lecompton constitution because it demanded an exorbitant body of public land, some twenty-three million acres in place of the four millions that would normally be allowed, while he believed the slavery clause worthless), well-read, and able. He was a brilliant novice in politics. As he wrote to the Charleston *Mercury*, he had never acquired much practical experience of public service, had lived for thirteen years immersed in plantation affairs exclusively, and had felt no desire for political battle.[12] But now, suddenly elevated to the Senate, he meant to strike a heavy blow for the South and slavery.

Why, he asked the Senate, should his section not become a great independent power? The slave States covered eight hundred and fifty thousand square miles, an imperial domain, rich in every natural product; their population was four times that of the colonies when America had become independent; a million brave men, familiar with the arts of war, were registered on their muster rolls.

10 February 1, 1858; Quitman Papers, Mississippi Dept. Arch. and Hist.
11 J. H. Hammond, *Letters and Speeches*, 338 ff.
12 Letter dated October 2, 1857; Hammond Papers, LC.

Athwart the South ran the mighty artery of the Mississippi, holding in tributary affiliation the rich Northwest. It was idle, he declared, to talk of checking the spread of slavery throughout the valley of the Mississippi and along its affluents. Above all, he boasted of the impregnable economic strength of the South. That region had a monopoly of two or three staples which controlled the commerce of the world; above all, a monopoly of cotton. Cotton could bring Europe to its knees; for, cut off the supply, and within three years Britain would topple headlong from her seat of power. Cotton had just rescued the North from bankruptcy. When in the great industrial cities a speculative bubble burst and business sank in ruin, the South, selling her cotton crop for $65,000,000, had saved the country. Inasmuch as, but for the panic, she could have gotten a hundred millions, she had put $35,000,000 into her charity box for the textile lords and merchants of the North. No power on earth dared make war on the fleecy bolls. Cotton *is* king, said Hammond. It was far stronger than that other potentate, the Bank of England.

The greatest strength of the South, however, he continued, lay in the harmony of her social institutions. Every society required a menial class, characterized by strength, docility, and recognition of its own lack of skill; those menials upbore the class which led progress and civilization; they were the mudsill of society. The South had a race happily adapted for that very end. Did the North boast that it had abolished slavery? "Aye, the *name*, but not the *thing;* all the powers of the earth cannot abolish that." [13] Naturally, this sally infuriated many Northern champions. Hannibal Hamlin pointed out that the value of Northern manufactures far exceeded the hundred millions in cotton annually exported by the South. Ben Wade drew a scathing contrast between Northern democracy and Southern aristocracy. Henry Wilson, stung by the mudsill image, declared that his father had been a manual laborer all his life; that for years he himself had been farmhand and shoemaker; and that he gloried in the sturdy character of the Northern workers. But Hammond's speech etched a proud impression on the Southern mind. "The rank and file of Southern men are delighted," the Senator informed his brother; "over twenty-five thousand copies have been subscribed. . . . I have changed the programme." [14]

Many Southerners held with Hammond that cotton was king; that as Simms put it, the North, boasting perpetually of its prosperity, owed everything to the South. Southern officials continued to rumble threats of secession. The Alabama legislature spoke; the governor of Texas penned a scolding message. In Washington, a shrewd Representative, T. L. Harris of Illinois, thought the atmosphere alarming. "There is a worse state of feeling here than there was in 1850,"

---

13 *National Intelligencer,* April 13, 1858, full text differing slightly from *Cong. Globe.*
14 To Colonel M. C. M. Hammond, March 9, 1858; Hammond Papers, LC.

he wrote McClernand. "There are less open outside threats than were made then—but there is in fact a more sullen hostility and bitterness than I ever saw before. The truth is that there are many earnest disunionists in the South who see no obstacle to their wishes but the destruction of the Democratic Party— and they think the passage of Lecompton will effect that." [15]

[II]

Because the House was the crucial arena, much of the bitterness was concentrated there. Everybody knew that the contest would be close. At the outset, Administration leaders boasted they would carry the bill by ten or fifteen votes, but impartial observers doubted that. By the time the Senate acted, Buchanan's supporters had lowered their probable margin to five.

The tempers of Southerners in the House had been strained by Commodore Hiram Paulding's sudden seizure of William Walker (who, overthrown in May, 1857, had returned to Nicaragua with a new expedition late in the year) for violating the neutrality laws of the United States. When Walker and his fellow prisoners were landed at Norfolk on January 1, 1858, the South buzzed like a mutinous ship. Chairman Clingman of the House Foreign Affairs Committee called on the President for information; Quitman demanded a special committee to revise the neutrality laws; and Stephens made a speech in which he used the word "outrage" eight times. The South was not mollified when Buchanan, in a special message to the Senate, declared that Paulding had committed a grave error, but also expressed the Administration's hostility to filibustering. Stephens wrote his brother on January 20 that the whole ground for Buchanan's opposition to Walker in Central America was the fear that "if successful he would introduce African slavery there." To such an unreasonable pitch had even this calm man's emotions led him! Many Southerners were more determined than ever that, if they could not have Central America, they should at least have Lecompton.

The tempers of Northern Democrats, too, were wrought up to a high pitch. A caucus of twenty-three anti-Lecompton members had sent a deputation of three, Haskin of New York, S. S. Cox of Ohio, and James B. Clay of Kentucky, to expostulate with the President. They had found Buchanan courteous but firm. He knew that the Northern Democrats faced ruin if the bill passed—but he insisted on passage. When he sent his special Lecompton message to Congress, his opponents tried to refer it to a select committee with power to investigate, while Stephens moved to refer it to the Committee on Territories. A gruelling struggle that lasted until two in the morning ensued. The Republicans, seeing

15 February 16, 1858; McClernand Papers.

that they had a temporary majority, attempted to force a vote. The Administration leaders, sending out urgent calls for men absent at dinner parties, used every tactic of delay. Nerves began to snap. Finally, when Galusha A. Grow stepped over to the Democratic side, an affray began.

Keitt of South Carolina shouted at Grow: "Go back to your side of the House, you Black Republican puppy!" Grow retorted with a sneering defiance of "nigger drivers." They grappled, Grow knocked Keitt down, and excited members rushed into the melee. For two minutes, about thirty Representatives engaged in a free-for-all fight. Finally order was restored. Though nobody was hurt, the damage to tempers was serious. Remarking that this was the first sectional fight in the House, Stephens wrote that if weapons had been at hand blood would probably have flowed. "All things here are tending to bring my mind to the conclusion that the Union cannot or will not last long."

Others took the shindy more lightly. It had a droll look, commented one reporter. "There were some fifty middle-aged and elderly gentlemen pitching into each other like so many Tipperary savages—most of them incapable, from want of wind and muscle, of doing each other any serious harm." [16] *Punch* did the event justice. In a long poem beginning, "Sing, O Goddess, the wrath, the untamable dander of Keitt," it told how the debate had raged long and late; how "plugs were becoming exhausted, and Representatives also"; how Keitt the clear grit, Reuben Davis the ra'al wild hoss of Mississippi, and others lunged at their enemies; how "fiercely they gathered around Grow, catawompously up as to chaw him"—

> But without Potter they reckoned, the wiry from woody Wisconsin,
> He, striking out right and left, like a catamount varmint and vicious,
> Dashed to the rescue, and with him the Washburnes, Cadwallader, Elihu . . .
> Well was it then for Barksdale, the wig that waved o'er his forehead,
> Off in Cadwallader's hands it came; and the wearer releasing,
> Left to the conqueror nought but the scalp of his worthy opponent!

On the question of reference to a special committee, the anti-Lecomptonites won, 114 to 113. Their majority comprised ninety Republicans, twenty-two Douglas Democrats, and one Know-Nothing, Henry Winter Davis. The select committee of fifteen, however, did the opposition no good. Speaker Orr gave it eight men opposed to any investigation; Alex Stephens, as chairman, directed the majority astutely, and it brought in a report, eight to seven, endorsing the Lecompton constitution. The anti-Lecomptonites lost that skirmish.

With every vote precious, both sides lobbied frenziedly, while the Administration used patronage and pressure. Strange scenes were enacted in Washing-

---

16 N. Y. *Weekly Tribune*, February 13, 1859. The long night sessions were conducive to disorder, for the exhausted Congressmen resorted to stimulants.

ton as spring came on. The city seemed full of Kansas men, come partly to argue for Lecompton and partly to beg for offices; an *Evening Post* correspondent counted about a hundred who made the Kirkwood Hotel their headquarters.[17] John Calhoun was brassily laying siege to Congress, for if Kansas were admitted, he hoped that a proslavery legislature would elect him Senator. Judge Cato seconded him, while J. J. Clarkson, who had fetched the constitution to Washington and wished to be made Superintendent of Indian Affairs, buttonholed unwary members. Calhoun had with him the returns of the election of January 4 for State officers and a legislature. By virtue of the extraordinary powers given him under the Lecompton schedule, he was entitled to hold these returns; and as yet he had not decided whether the free State or proslavery tickets had been elected! It was evident that he would manipulate the result in whatever manner best suited his own interests and those of the Administration.

To impartial onlookers it seemed preposterous that one man, the agent of a discredited convention, should have arbitrary power to determine the complexion of the Kansas government. "Why Does He Not Decide?" demanded the *National Intelligencer* in an unwontedly belligerent editorial.[18] In Kansas itself, no doubt existed that a free State legislature and State officers had been chosen. Citizens swore to numerous depositions of proslavery fraud. The president of the council and speaker of the house, who had assisted at the counting of the votes, proclaimed the victory of the free State forces. Calhoun, however, rejected some votes which these men declared valid, while he stated that late returns from the Delaware Crossing precinct seemed to elect the whole proslavery ticket. At once a blaze of publicity was fastened upon Delaware Crossing, Kickapoo, and other points where the free State men alleged fraud. Calhoun spoke of several hundred votes from Kickapoo; the judges of that precinct testified that only forty-three had been cast. Still, Calhoun kept his strategic seat astride the fence; he would decide in his own good time.[19]

Soon after reaching Washington, Calhoun was ushered into Douglas's handsome mansion. The two had been close Illinois friends for years; now they were enemies. The Senator, receiving his guest coldly, chatted about general matters. Then he suddenly fixed his intensest gaze on the visitor. "What about Delaware Crossing?" he demanded. Calhoun stuttered out that the return had been properly certified. With quick step Douglas crossed to his desk, drew out the depositions of fraud, and slapped them on Calhoun's knee. "Then how about this evidence?" he thundered. Calhoun turned pale and left the house.[20]

Not since the great Bank war of Jackson's time, if then, had Federal patron-

17 Letter dated February 14, 1858.
18 February 16, 1858.
19 *National Intelligencer*, February 9, 13, 16, *et seq.*, 1858.
20 Washington correspondence dated February 9, 1858, Phila. *Press.*

age been used so brutally as Buchanan's Directory used it now. The President himself may have averted his gaze and stopped his ears; but he unquestionably knew that contracts, jobs, perquisites, and even army commissions were being traded for much-needed votes. In the name of discipline, Douglas's friends were struck down right and left. J. W. Gray, editor of the Cleveland *Plain Dealer*, was postmaster of his city and a warm friend of Douglas. Caught by his dilemma, he wriggled lustily for a time but finally gagged over the Lecompton bolus. Off went his head. The Chicago postmaster was a Douglas Democrat named William Price. He was summarily dismissed, and Isaac Cook, a particularly tough-hided liquor dealer, land speculator, and machine politician, was reappointed in his stead despite the fact that during Pierce's regime Cook had allowed subordinates to steal several thousand dollars. In fact, special efforts were made by the Directory to weaken Douglas in Illinois. The efficient mail agent for the State was removed, and Dr. Charles Leib, another liquor dealer and machine hack who had flirted with Mormonism, was installed in his stead. Leib, traveling freely on his railway pass, was able to twist the screws on postmasters. The marshal for northern Illinois lost his place, and a Lecompton man seized it. By the middle of March, Cook, Leib, and Nye were busy organizing Lecompton demonstrations and plotting against the Little Giant.[21]

All over the North, officeholders were put in terror of their poor livings; editors of papers like the Pittsburgh *Union* were rewarded with government advertising; Congressmen deemed approachable were told of position and pelf which might be theirs. Cornelius Wendell, with his large revenues from the public printing, was called upon to finance weak newspapers like the *Pennsylvanian*, and to put up money for still more dubious purposes. Evidence exists that he offered one capable Ohio lobbyist $5,000 for every Ohio Congressman whom he won over to the Lecompton side.[22] Representative Montgomery of Pennsylvania was assured that he could have almost anything he desired if he would sell out his constituents.[23] Because the New York *Sun* denounced Lecompton, the publishing of lists of letters was taken from it and given to the more amenable *Herald*.[24] In Indiana, decent party leaders protested publicly against the despotism of the Administration and its use of what one disgusted man called a venal press, and a horde of dirty officeholders or expectants.[25] Postmaster-General Brown made lists of all the Douglas postmasters he could find, and had letters sent them of which the following is typical:

21 Cleveland *Leader*, index for 1858, *passim*; Havana, Illinois, *Democrat*, March 13, 20, 1858.
22 Covode Report, 120 ff.
23 J. L. Dawson to Jeremiah S. Black, May 12, 1858; Black Papers.
24 N. Y. *Express*, February 3, 1858.
25 W. W. Wick, April 2, 1858; English Papers.

Sir: Complaints are made against you that you are unfriendly to the present Administration, and circumstances are detailed in confirmation of this fact. An opportunity is now offered you to present such evidence as you may deem proper in refutation of the charges.

Respectfully, etc.

Horatio King, First Assistant Postmaster-General.[26]

Buchanan's opponents charged, late in March, that several million dollars in army contracts for the Utah expedition, let at prices that would make a dozen fortunes, had been awarded by Secretary Floyd himself to men whose political aid was needed. They charged, with evidence, that Cobb was using the rich patronage of the Treasury in the most shameless way; that Jacob Thompson was even more shameless with the benefits of the Interior Department; and that Toucey was letting politics creep into his contracts for new naval vessels. They accused Representative Burns of Ohio, originally an anti-Lecompton man, of coming to a new perception of his duty under a pledge that his son-in-law should remain postmaster of Keokuk and that he himself should be made marshal of northern Ohio when his term ended. Greeley's *Tribune* declared that, if Lecompton passed the House, it would be only because a sufficient number of members had been paid directly or indirectly to support it. Everyone knew that, as was proved by the current case of Orasmus Matteson, a New York Republican expelled for corruption, a few Representatives were venal.[27]

[III]

Despite all this pressure, together with the blandishments of Administration hostesses in as lively a social season as Washington had seen, the anti-Lecompton Democrats held their House lines almost intact. Five Illinois members led by T. L. Harris, six Ohioans led by S. S. Cox, and three Indianians led by William H. English constituted the solid Middle Western heart of the phalanx. Pennsylvania supplied three men of unshakeable fiber, and New York two. At the beginning, this block counted twenty-four members. If it could keep at least twenty, and could gain the support of half a dozen or more Know-Nothings, then, with the ninety-two Republicans, it could win the day. The group organized in caucus, with Harris as chairman and John B. Haskin of New York as secretary. Douglas conferred steadily with the members; Forney's *Press* and the Washington *States* applauded them heartily; and Greeley wrote editorials

26 Phila. *Press*, March 13, 18, 1858.
27 N. Y. *Tribune*, February 11, March 28, 1858; *Cong. Globe*, March 4, 1858; Nichols, *Disruption*, 165, 166. It was said that Glancy Jones was armed with blank invitations to White House dinners which he was empowered to use in enlisting doubtful Congressmen. London *Daily News* (American correspondence), January 11, 1859.

assuring them that, if they stood firm, they would have wide Republican support for reelection in the fall.

All efforts to arrange a compromise between Lecompton and anti-Lecompton Democrats broke down. The Crittenden plan was unacceptable to most Administration supporters. As taken up and slightly amended by the anti-Lecompton caucus (becoming the Crittenden-Montgomery amendment), it provided that Kansas should be admitted on condition that the constitution was submitted to the voters in its entirety, at a carefully controlled election, and approved by them; but that if they rejected it, a new constitutional convention should be called. Toombs helped sponsor another proposal which was quite unacceptable to most anti-Lecompton men. Declaring that nothing in the act of admission should be construed to abridge the right of the people of Kansas at all times to alter, reform, or abolish their form of government as they thought proper, it fell far short of the positive provision for a popular vote which the opposition demanded. But could not a formula be invented midway between the two extremes? [28]

As March drew to an end, Stephens, floor manager for the Lecomptonites, made a supreme effort, enlisting William H. English in the formation of a conference committee. English, still in his middle thirties, was precocious, adaptable, and cultivated. The son of an Indiana pioneer, a graduate of Hanover College, he had been admitted to the bar at eighteen and to practice before the Supreme Court at twenty-three, and had held a variety of minor posts in Indiana and Washington before being chosen for Congress in 1852. While a loyal Douglas man, his residence in southern Indiana and friendship for Bright gave him a moderate outlook. On March 27, the Democratic Representatives held a night caucus. Stephens made a speech imploring the anti-Lecompton men to be reasonable, and English moved that each side appoint ten men to a conference committee. When this body met on the twenty-ninth, the anti-Lecomptonites brought forward what they thought a generous offer. They would vote for the Senate bill if it were amended to declare that the people of Kansas then had, and might at all times exercise, the right of altering or rewriting their constitution at will.[29]

28 See Toombs to Buchanan, March 2, 1858; Buchanan Papers.

29 Washington correspondence, N. Y. *Tribune*, March 28, 29, 30, 1858. Buchanan evidently talked the situation over with English soon after the middle of March; for on March 22, Buchanan sent him a memorandum "according to promise," saying that it might contain some ideas useful to him. He buttered up English: "I repeat that I consider the present occasion the most fortunate of your life. It will be your fate to end the dangerous agitation, to confer lasting benefits on your country, and to render your character historical." English Papers. The feeling of southern Indiana came out strongly in English's subsequent statement that he and his friends believed Negroes "inferior by nature," had no "sickly sentimentality" upon slavery, and regarded free Negroes as "a great pest." *Cong. Globe*, January 3, 1860, 312 ff.

Garnett of Virginia and other Southerners, making no proposal of their own, instantly objected to this as a Federal intervention in State affairs. A large body of Southern Senators and Representatives, in fact, had consistently opposed any weakening of the slavery clauses in the Lecompton constitution, and had deplored Buchanan's suggestion that Kansas might immediately amend that instrument. Thirty-five men had agreed in conference to stand against any dilution. Iverson had been vehement on the subject; Keitt had proclaimed that the Kansas instrument could not be altered before 1864. The committee of twenty broke up in dispute, and thereafter the Douglas bloc was more determined than ever to kill the measure. This deadlock, they and their Republican allies exulted, sealed its scroll with defeat. They believed that many Southerners did not care if they were beaten so long as they could keep their records straight for the fall elections—and that some actually courted defeat as a step toward disruption of the party.[30]

Even yet, it was with great difficulty that Buchanan and the Directory reconciled themselves to a fiasco. They had hoped to the last to hew their way through. With fully a hundred Democratic votes in their pockets, they had counted on buying or bullying a dozen members and on gaining most of the fourteen Know-Nothings from Southern districts. They remembered how effectively Stephens, in 1854, had beaten down the House opposition to the Kansas-Nebraska bill. Day after day, Howell Cobb appeared in the House lobby, rotund, smiling, and talkative, expending charm and promises on doubtful men. Night after night, Jacob Thompson feasted Congressmen at his sumptuous table. Buchanan invited dozens of Congressmen to the White House, where he argued, expostulated, and, as the outlook grew darker, even pleaded. By last-minute solicitation, following the advice of George Sanders to change his bill-of-fare from lemon salad to orange, and from vinegar to champagne, he won the votes of Dewart and Reilly of his own State, being somewhat assisted in this by a timely endorsement of Lecompton at Harrisburg.[31] The experienced Sanders labored with such Know-Nothings as Marshall of Kentucky, Campbell of Ohio, and Harris of Maryland—as it turned out, in vain. The eve of the final House vote found almost the entire Cabinet sitting up with doubtful cases and trying to nurse them into compliance.[32]

In this uphill struggle the Administration suffered from the antics of John Calhoun. Had that marplot stayed in Kansas, made a fair count of votes in the

30 Washington correspondence Phila. *Press*, March 29, N. Y. *Express*, *Herald*, March 31, 1858.
31 Sanders to Buchanan, March 25, 1858; Buchanan Papers. The Washington correspondent of the N. Y. *Express* wrote April 2 that Buchanan had in one instance shed tears, salt tears, to get a member to change his vote.
32 N. Y. *Weekly Tribune*, April 10, 1858. Campbell called himself a Whig.

January election, and given prompt notice of the free State victory, he might have contributed much toward the success of Lecompton. Northern Democrats would have been readier to vote for admission if assured of a free State legislature and State officers to interpret the new constitution. Having come to Washington, however, Calhoun lingered with the undecided election totals in his breast pocket. The East was much impressed by news of flagrant frauds unearthed by a Kansas investigating committee; in one issue, the *National Intelligencer* spread before its readers full columns of depositions on the subject.[33] Proof of the irregularities was clinched when the committee, hearing that bogus returns had been secreted, obtained a search warrant, went to the suspected spot, and found the Delaware Crossing vote in a candle box under a wood pile.[34] At first, Calhoun did nothing except declare through the Washington *Union* that he awaited full evidence and would sanction no frauds. But after a Kansas investigator brought to Washington sworn copies of proof that the returns had been crooked and that Federal officers in Kansas had connived at the cheating, Calhoun had no choice. On March 19, he announced that he would certify the choice of a free State Republican majority in the legislature—but said nothing about the other State offices.

If we may believe Calhoun's brother, he had been under intense pressure to deliver the election to the proslavery ticket. When he announced his decision, writes the brother, it "gave great umbrage to the Democratic party, and to President Buchanan in particular. That functionary gave him the cold shoulder at once; and very soon afterward evinced his disapprobation by superseding him in the office of Surveyor-General. . . . It was well understood that he was to have been reappointed, and had he connived at the fraud . . . no one doubted that his name would have been sent to the Senate." [35]

The Charleston *Mercury*, Richmond *Whig*, and other newspapers exploded in denunciation of Calhoun, terming him a traitor who had invalidated proslavery votes while accepting fraudulent free State ballots. His decree, they agreed, made Kansas a thoroughgoing abolitionist State, and there should be no hurry about admitting it to send Jim Lane and some equally rabid Black Republican to the Senate.[36] Senator Iverson declared that the decision was a cheap political trick, forced by Cobb, Toombs, and Stephens in a desperate final effort to gain over a few anti-Lecompton Democrats. Whether Cobb & Co. had intervened or not, many passion-blinded Southerners agreed with R. B. Rhett that Northern fanaticism, placing an intolerable sectional pressure

33   February 9, 1858.
34   With other returns; for details see Ewing Papers, February, 1858.
35   A. H. Calhoun, MS "Vindication of John Calhoun," Kansas State Hist. Lib.
36   Quoted in *National Intelligencer*, March 27, 1858.

on the party and Administration, had pushed Calhoun into a base betrayal of the South.[37]

The decisive factor in the final Congressional vote was certainly Northern sentiment. No experienced politician could mistake the trend of opinion. Every weathervane—newspapers, pulpit, mass meetings, letters—pointed in the same direction. Shrewd Congressmen forecast the result shortly announced in the spring elections. The Republicans carried New Hampshire in April by some five thousand majority, electing governor, council, and legislature. Franklin Pierce, who viewed Buchanan with jaundiced eye, found something to please him in this overturn in his State. They similarly swept Connecticut in the largest vote in years, electing William A. Buckingham in opposition to a popular and active Democrat who had handled Lecompton as gingerly as he could. They confirmed their grip on Rhode Island. Still more significant were certain western decisions. The Republicans again carried Chicago, where *both* parties were anti-Lecompton. They seized Toledo from the Democrats, won a large majority in Michigan towns, and with a People's ticket carried Dubuque, usually Democratic two to one. In Cincinnati an anti-Lecompton opposition overthrew the Democrats, while St. Louis chose a freesoil Democratic ticket by about twelve hundred majority.[38]

Douglas's tactics of delay had succeeded; the popular will had made itself felt. As the final test of April 1 approached, many Northern Democrats knew that a Lecompton vote meant political suicide.

At a little past noon, the galleries jammed, every member was in the House but two: Caruthers of Missouri and Harris of Illinois, the latter gravely ill. Administration lobbyists, among whom Senator Bigler was prominent, were urging a last word. Speaker Orr had to rap thunderously and threaten to call members by name if they did not come to order. Still the buzz continued; knots of Lecompton men gathering for final instructions about Stephens, anti-Lecomptonites about Montgomery, Republicans about Grow, and Know-Nothings about Gilmer of North Carolina. Only Joshua Giddings gazing contemplatively from his seat, Quitman reading quietly as usual, and Eli Thayer with hands in pockets, seemed unperturbed. As business commenced, Harris, pale as death, was carried in and assisted to his seat. This hero of Cerro Gordo, who would not outlive the year, was determined to vote against the bill if it

37 Rhett to W. P. Miles, April 7, 1858; Miles Papers, Univ. of N. C. It appears that Stephens and Toombs did advise Calhoun to make his announcement. They saw that it would have to be made some time, and they thought it would be best to let the South know the true state of affairs before the vote on Lecompton, so that if the bill were defeated radical Southerners would take the disappointment more calmly. See a letter dated Milledgeville, April 6, illegibly signed, in Stephens Papers, LC.
38 Summaries in N. Y. *Weekly Tribune*, April 10, 17, 1858.

killed him. Stephens moved to take up the Senate measure, and the grapple began.

First, a majority of Administration men voted to strike out an amendment originating from Senator Pugh and guaranteeing Kansas the right to change its constitution immediately. Then a vote was taken on the Crittenden-Montgomery amendment, which, providing a popular vote on the constitution, was really a substitute measure. Men totalled the names one by one. The amendment passed, 120 to 112. A wild shout rang through the galleries. Keitt rose, shaking with rage, to move that they be cleared, but was mollified. The amended bill was put on its final passage and carried by the same vote. A coalition of ninety-two Republicans, twenty-two anti-Lecompton Democrats, and six Know-Nothings had defeated Lecompton.

"This Crittenden substitute," said Douglas, "carries out those principles to which I have given my life, and it should now pass the Senate." Forney called the vote a magnificent Democratic triumph. Republicans struck a fuller note of joy. The oppressor's rod is breaking, wrote Greeley. "Champions of Freedom and Honest Rule—Let us rejoice and take courage!" In New York a great crowd, gathering at the Battery to celebrate, heard a hundred and twenty guns fired—one for every vote.[39]

[IV]

The Administration was now in a dilemma. It could not possibly accept the Crittenden substitute. Southern pride would not swallow it; while Buchanan, though willing to acquiesce in the clause which provided for submission of the Lecompton constitution, would not agree to the other section which authorized a new convention if the popular vote were unfavorable. This he deemed unconstitutional, and he said he would veto it. Yet some kind of admission bill had to be passed. It had become a political necessity. Upon Stephens fell the unhappy task of arranging a face-saving measure—Stephens, discouraged, disillusioned, disgusted. The able Georgian, who knew well that Buchanan was

39 The elder Blair called on the dying Thomas Hart Benton on the morning of April 6, finding him unable to talk above a whisper. They spoke of the compromise of 1850. Benton dwelt on the immeasurable service Clay had then rendered in preventing disunion. According to a record which Blair set down that very day, the great Missourian was intensely aroused by the new crisis. "In energetic whispers," wrote Blair, "he told his visitor that the same men who had sought to destroy the republic in 1850 were at the bottom of this accursed Lecompton business. Among the greatest of his consolations in dying was the consciousness that the House of Representatives had baffled these treasonable schemes and put the heels of the people on the neck of the traitors. Few events in our history had given him so much satisfaction as the defeat of Lecompton. He warmly praised the intrepid and incorruptible Douglas Democrats who had resisted the power and the wiles of a corrupt and deluded Administration." N. Y. *Semi-Weekly Tribune*, May 28, 1858; W. E. Smith, *Blair Family in Politics*, 1, 435, 436. Blair's report aroused a violent controversy, but it rings true.

weak and Howell Cobb shortsighted, and who had begged both not to make war upon Douglas, had now to help them out of the pit they had digged.[40] He was vexed at his fellow Congressmen of the South. Half a dozen slave State men had voted against Lecompton, others would have done so if they had dared, and still others had been so drunken, disorderly, and lazy that it took herculean labor to keep them in the House for a vote. Even before the defeat, Stephens had concluded that he was wearing his life out for nothing. He desired nothing so much as to get home to peaceful Liberty Hall and stay there.

Yet he resolutely set to work; indeed, foreseeing the defeat, he had laid some plans before it took place.[41] The Administration majority in the Senate of course refused to heed Douglas's plea for a swift passage of the Crittenden substitute, thus (Douglas suggested) ending the Kansas excitement forever and letting the Kansas people shape their own institutions. The Senate rejected the substitute, and a deadlock between the two chambers ensued. Both the Republicans and anti-Lecompton Democrats were quite ready to let Buchanan languish in his self-made predicament. When the Senate requested a conference committee, the House majority was loftily reluctant. Buchanan, the Directory, and the Administration whips in Congress had to use every conceivable form of magic—more offices, more contracts, more army commissions, more money—to gain over the three or four anti-Lecomptonites they needed to save the President from utter humiliation. They suggested that two Ohio regiments might be included in the expedition to Utah; they promised that when the conference took place, they would accept some modification of the Crittenden substitute. William H. English, genuinely anxious to repair the broken Democratic unity, lent efficient aid. Two other Representatives joined him. One was Lawrence W. Hall of Ohio, and it was later shown that Wendell, as party bursar, paid Hall's roommate $5,000 just before he came over.[42] The three men sufficed; the vote for a conference stood 108 to 108; and Speaker Orr turned the balance for the President.

The way was thus open for a juggle, masking the Administration's defeat. Green, Hunter, and Seward acted for the Senate; Stephens, English, and Howard of Michigan for the House; four Democrats and two Republicans. Within a week the ingenious Stephens and the brilliant English had a scheme ready.

This so-called English bill, reported to the two houses on April 23 with Seward and Howard dissenting, had one all-important provision: it gave the people of Kansas a chance to vote upon the Lecompton constitution in its entirety. It did so, however, under very curious conditions. The greedy authors

40 Johnston and Browne, *Stephens*, 329, 428.
41 Nichols, *Disruption*, 168.
42 *Idem*, 170.

of Lecompton had asked for land grants larger than had ever been given a State on admission—23,592,160 acres, or nearly 37,000 square miles, about the area of Indiana. The English bill (substantially a bill, though in form it was an amendment) cut the grant to 3,988,868, the same proportion of land given to all the States recently admitted and the same amount named in the Crittenden substitute. If the people of Kansas accepted the Lecompton constitution, they were assured of this amount, and, in addition, of five percent of the net proceeds from about two million acres which were to be sold by the government at the beginning of July. If they rejected the land grant and constitution, Kansas might not enter the Union until a census had proved that she possessed the population required of a Congressional district, about ninety thousand. The probability was that she would thus be kept waiting for at least two years longer. A curious measure, and made the more curious by the fact that Stephens, Hunter, and Green, asserting that the vote would be primarily upon the land grant, denied that any popular submission of the constitution lurked in the measure.[43]

Actually it did submit Lecompton to popular vote, and for this reason alone the Administration expected to be able, with an immense renewal of pressures and cajoleries, to carry it. Henry Wilson attacked it as carrying a bribe in one hand and a threat in the other. To a limited extent this was true; a minor cash reward was held out on one hand, and a penalty of delay offered on the other, to a poverty-stricken, uneasy, ambitious frontier community. It was also true that if Kansas was fit to come in under a slave State constitution with but forty thousand people, she was fit to come in under a free State constitution with that many.

The vital fact, however, was that the bill allowed Kansans a fair opportunity to crush the Lecompton iniquity; and only a few deluded men doubted that they would seize it. Do not worry over the measure, Greeley wrote Colfax. "It is a vicious blunderbuss, and will kick over those who stand at the breach. Of course the earnest anti-Lecomptonites must all oppose it, but if it is passed I shall not shed a tear. The Kansans will dispose of it." [44] This view was confirmed by all experts on Kansas sentiment. The Leavenworth *Daily Ledger* declared that the English proposal had the chance of a snowball in a prairie heat wave; the government did not own land enough to buy up the Kansas people, who would rather live in eternal poverty than be the instruments of their own degradation.[45]

---

43 Nominally, the land grant alone was submitted to the people, with the implication that if it were accepted, the Lecompton constitution would go into effect; if it were rejected, Kansas would remain a Territory and Lecompton would pass into oblivion. The collateral consequences were infinitely more important than the direct question. Five percent on public land sales had been given to other States on admission; see statement by Senator Green, *Cong. Globe*, 35th Cong., 1st Sess., 1824.

44 April 21, 1858; Greeley-Colfax Correspondence.

45 May 7, 1858.

The exciting question was whether Douglas would come around to support so disagreeable a measure. Once more the Administration exerted every ounce of its strength. It was later shown that from $30,000 to $40,000 was spent in helping wavering members see the light; three men, including a government clerk and a newspaperman, being almoners of the fund. It was not denied that from $10,000 to $15,000 was paid for a single vote.[46] The honest anti-Lecompton member from New York, Haskin, was put to the trouble of rejecting a proffered grant of a township of land.[47] Cobb, Thompson, and other Cabinet members used their personal influence unstintedly. So did Slidell, who felt no scruple in offering bribes. One by one, for good reasons or bad, the House anti-Lecompton Democrats fell away until only twelve remained. Pugh of Ohio endorsed the bill. So did Robert J. Walker, declaring that it laid Lecompton before the people and that the odious constitution, baptized in forgery and perjury, would be slain by an overwhelming vote. F. B. Stanton also, while declaring some features very objectionable, wrote that he was willing to accept it.[48] After all, party unity was worth a mass—particularly just before an election.

Still, Douglas held out. He was torn between detestation of the shabby expedients of the bill, and realization that after all it would permit a popular vote; torn between his hatred of Buchanan and the malicious Directory, and his honest desire for Democratic harmony; torn between apprehension that in the impending Senatorial election in Illinois the freesoil Democrats would turn against him if he acquiesced in the bill, and fear that Administration men would knife him if he did not. He was torn, in short, between conflicting ideas of duty and expediency. In his agony of mind he wavered. For one brief day he seemed about to yield. Stephens and Slidell expected to carry the bill through the House on Wednesday, April 28, and to take it up in the Senate immediately. On the previous Saturday evening, Douglas held a conference with Forney, Stanton, and Walker. Their influence had just weight with him: all three were men of great ability and high patriotism, who had suffered heavy indignities from the Administration and had battled courageously against injustice. When Walker argued persuasively for compromise and was supported by Stanton, the Illinois

---

46 Covode Report, 138–159, 184–197. Wendell testified that he had several interviews about carrying the Lecompton bill; that "I paid some money to outsiders to aid" in that process; that he drew checks "pay to politics," "pay to Kansas," and "pay to bearer"; that using sums up to $20,000, "it was a matter that I tried to banish from my mind as soon as possible, and I intentionally disguised my books." He did not deny that he might have authorized a payment of as much as $15,000 for a vote.

47 Wilson, *Rise and Fall of the Slave Power*, II, 565.

48 May 2, 1858; to *National Intelligencer*. Representative Harris of Illinois wrote Lanphier that nobody liked the miserable English scheme; that they could beat it by twenty votes but for Administration pressure; and that Southern men were alarmed by Buchanan's stubborn folly. When the bill passed, he reported that the Administration had bought men "like hogs in the market." April 20, 29, May 7, 1858; Lanphier Papers.

Senator was reluctantly moved by their pleas. Finally he assented, and agreed to advance $100 to have a statement of their position and reasons telegraphed over the country.[49]

But next day he had to break the news to the irreconcilable anti-Lecompton Democrats; to Senators Stuart and Broderick, and to Representatives Montgomery, McKibbin, Haskin, and their associates. He met a group at Broderick's rooms in the Kirkwood House. They received his statement with stark hostility. As he proceeded, the atmosphere grew heated. Broderick, a man of intense feelings, was furious. Passion was running high in California on several political issues, Senator Gwin and Representative Scott taking the Southern side while Broderick and McKibbin assailed the Administration machine. Feeling wronged by Buchanan's use of the patronage, and resenting the haughty airs of Southern aristocrats, Broderick was athirst for revenge. He had replied to Hammond's remarks about mudsills and white slavery with the proud statement that for five years he had been an apprenticed stonecutter, that his father had been a stonecutter, and that he never looked at the beautiful capitals supporting the Senate roof without thinking of his father's talent. All his Irish temper inflamed, he stormed at Douglas: [50]

"I can't understand you, sir. You will be crushed between the Administration and the Republicans. I shall denounce you, sir. You had better go into the street and blow out your brains!"

Others present said nearly the same. Simultaneously, Douglas's mail was filled with appeals to stand firm. "Yield not one inch," wrote an Illinois friend. "For God's sake, put your foot on every proposition looking that way," implored an Ohioan. To the State Democratic Convention in Illinois on April 21, ninety-seven of the ninety-eight counties represented had sent anti-Lecompton delegates; and the convention had adopted resolutions of the most spirited character on Kansas. How would these delegates feel if Douglas let them down? He turned back decisively.

On April 27, Crittenden opened the brief Senate debate, and next day Douglas followed. Many of his friends had besought him to compromise, he said; he desired no personal triumph over the Administration; but he could not sanction a measure which made admission contingent on a set of unfair conditions and offered only an indirect popular submission of the constitution. Stuart and Broderick attacked the bill. While these three Democrats stood out to the last in the Senate, thirteen party associates did the same in the House. On the thir-

---

49 See memorandum in the Buchanan Papers stating what Walker had told Gwin of the meeting.
50 P. G. Auchampaugh, "The Buchanan-Douglas Feud," *Ill. State Hist. Soc. Journal*, XXV, 5-48; "Journal of Milton S. Latham," *Calif. Hist. Soc. Quarterly*, XI, 14 ff.

tieth, however, the English bill carried by 112 to 103 in the lower chamber, and 31 to 22 in the upper.[51]

In effect, Kansas had been thrust back into territorial vassalage, with Buchanan's nominee Denver as governor, and Pierce's nominees Cato and Lecompte as judges. But the Republicans and Douglas Democrats rejoiced in the certainty that the people would now show their utter scorn of Lecompton, a lethal blow. They did. When the vote was taken August 2, it stood 11,812 to 1,926 for rejection of the constitution. Most of the people of Kansas were willing enough to continue in territorial status if only they could have peace, security, and fair elections. The troubles of the land now practically ceased, for though slavery was permitted under the Dred Scott decision, it was practically excluded by force of determined freesoil control.

Buchanan showed heartfelt relief at the partial measure of face-saving that he had achieved. He wrote English that it was painful even to think what would have been the alarming condition of the Union had Congress adjourned without passing his compromise, and that he wished he had a thousand votes to cast for the reelection of the Indiana Congressman. Southern men exhibited mixed feelings.[52] Stephens, who justly claimed most of the credit for the scheme, having prompted English and managed the passage, was in a triumphant frame of mind; out of defeat he had snatched a cup of balm. Not a few associates were pleased to reflect that Kansas, which had manifestly been ready to send two Republican Senators and one Representative to Washington, would be kept on the doorstep indefinitely. The most radical Southerners, however, felt mingled grief and anger over the loss of the one new slave State that might have been theirs.

[V]

The dark Kansas chapter in the chronicle of intersectional conflict was now closing. As the country looked back upon it, a number of lessons were distinctly visible. Foremost among them, the most glaring and the most painful, was the lesson of the gross miscalculations involved in the Kansas-Nebraska Act. Intended to quiet sectional antagonisms, it had increased them; designed to furnish a relatively quick, automatic, and natural solution of the slavery issue, it had produced delays, artificial interventions, and endless conflicts; presented as the embodiment of justice, it had fostered fraud, chicanery, and outrage. The gallant role of Douglas in the final scenes of the drama could not conceal the fact that it would have been infinitely better for Kansas, for the Democratic

51 Senator John Bell of Tennessee also voted against the bill, defying instructions from his State.
52 July 2, 1858; English Papers.

Party, for the South, and for the nation, had he insisted in 1854 on respecting the Missouri Compromise. He could say that he was not to blame for the raids of the border ruffians, the heated propaganda of the Kansas aid societies, the frontier clashes, the stuffed ballot boxes, the trickery and tyranny; certainly not. But he could be blamed for not foreseeing the false arousal of Southern hopes, the Northern sense of outrage, and the angry contest on the western plains.

Almost equally evident was the failure of two successive Presidents to show candor, vision, and above all courage in dealing with Kansas affairs. Pierce and Buchanan had appointed a succession of good governors—Reeder, Geary, Walker, Denver. These men had all grappled with their problems manfully and reported upon them honestly; they had tried to punish fraud and extirpate violence. The betrayal of Geary by President Pierce was a tragic episode. Still more inexcusable was the betrayal of Walker by President Buchanan. After making every effort to entice this able and highly experienced man to accept the governorship; after giving him explicit promises of support, in which the Cabinet joined; after endorsing and underlining his insistence upon fair elections and a popular submission of the new constitution, Buchanan had abandoned him and let his enemies drag him down.

The one excuse that can be made for Buchanan was that he became terrified in the summer of 1857 under Southern threats, and thought the sacrifice of the sturdy little Kansas governor preferable to the risk of a cotton-State secession.[53] But a President should not become terrified. Georgia, Mississippi, Alabama, and South Carolina had no ground for disunion in the admission of Kansas as a freesoil State. The business of the President in that crisis was to stand by his pledges and his governor; to use every possible means (even a speechmaking tour would have been warranted) of driving home to the Lower South the fact that a heavy majority of Kansans were freesoil men and had fairly won the right to a freesoil constitution; to force Cobb, Thompson, and Floyd to join him in stating the true facts, and to await the result. If the four States had tried secession, which is highly improbable, they would have been brought up short. We cannot doubt how a Washington, a Jackson, a Cleveland, or a Theodore Roosevelt would have acted that fateful summer.

But a still deeper failure was involved—the failure of the American people. Both North and South, Republicans and Democrats, had at critical moments shown deplorable partisanship and excitability. The feverish beating of tom toms by the emigrant aid societies and the editors and politicians back of them

53　Henry S. Foote writes: "But he had, in some way, learned to dread the fierce audacity of the Southern fire-eaters, as he was accustomed to call them, and it several times became obvious to me, long before he fell under their domination in 1860, that his fear of the leaders of this boisterous and menacing faction was not wholly unmixed with something of a respectful admiration." *Casket of Reminiscences*, 113.

was as needless as it was provocative. As events proved, the freesoil settlement of Kansas was effected not by artificial inducements but by a natural flow of small farmers, artisans, and shopkeepers from the Middle Atlantic, Border and Middle Western States. Many Republican leaders were anxious to keep the Kansas excitement alive to strengthen their party. Had they accepted the Toombs bill in the summer of 1856, the subsequent embroilments might have been avoided and Kansas quietly brought into the Union as a free State. The Republicans and abolitionists who extolled Jim Lane and John Brown incurred a heavy responsibility. On the other hand, Southerners who cheered on Atchison, Stringfellow, Sheriff Jones, and the border ruffians were equally culpable. The willingness of proslavery men to profit by the brazen swindling of John Calhoun and his fellow delegates at Lecompton was saddening. Southern Cabinet members were *particeps criminis* in that shabby juggle; Southern Senators abetted it by hollow arguments; even Stephens, admitting that Lecompton was a cheat, regretted its failure because he thought the South entitled to another slave State.[54] Had the level of political morality in America been higher and that of political excitability lower, the worst Kansas pages would never have been written.

If Kansas ceased to haunt the dreams of the nation, it left a sinister general heritage in the enhancement of sectional ill-will, and a specific legacy of evil in the Democratic schism. The refusal of Douglas to assent to the English compromise had hardened the hearts of Buchanan and the Directory against him. Even had he acquiesced, many Southerners would have been reluctant to pardon him. Now that he had stood recalcitrant to the last, Cobb, Jacob Thompson, Floyd, and the fire-eaters of the Deep South were implacable. They meant to ruin him even if this meant party ruin. Some hoped to ruin him, the party, and the Union together. "We shall treat Judge Douglas," said the Nashville *Union* on June 24, "just as we should treat any other Democrat who, in an emergency, abandoned his principles and made common cause with the enemy."

How great the change in the short fifteen months since Buchanan was inaugurated! The Democrats were broken, leaderless, bitter; the Republicans were filled with confidence. Frank Blair, actively organizing his party in Missouri, threw out an exultant prophecy: "There is now no earthly doubt of the overthrow of the Administration party in the next Congress and Presidential election." [55]

Meanwhile, it became evident to Americans that the rapid growth of Kansas was but one chapter in an astonishing story of trans-Mississippi development In this magical tale, unmatched at the time in any other part of the globe,

54 R. M. Johnston, *Autobiography*, 151.
55 April 19, 1858; Brodhead Papers.

12

And Still the Country Grew

ONE LATE summer day in 1858, an unusual stir was noticeable in the streets of Leavenworth. A roughly dressed man named E. Y. King, an Ohioan turned prospector, had arrived from the Rockies with important news. He had accompanied a party of Kansas men led by John Easter, a Lawrence butcher, who had gone to the Pike's Peak region some months earlier to investigate stories of gold brought by two Delaware chiefs. Though reticent to strangers, King told his friends that the group had found pay dirt.

"It is on Cherry Creek," he said in effect, exhibiting a little store of dust and nuggets. "You go west along the South Platte, up and up; Cherry Creek forks to the south. Long's Peak is almost in front of you, and Pike's Peak away off to your left."

He was certain of gold in that region. A party of Georgians under one Green Russell, equally positive, was remaining there. It was seven hundred miles from Leavenworth, but King was going back in the spring.[1] And in the ensuing months, other prospectors arrived in eastern Kansas bringing reports which filled the towns with a glow of interest and were speedily telegraphed east. While some of the returning men were disillusioned and intended to take up Kansas farming, others set to work to form companies, buy tools, and launch systematic operations. Any man, they said, could make five to ten dollars a day, and with luck twenty, in panning gold; but capital, skill, and some organization were desirable.

Iowa and Missouri quickly caught the fever, while workless men in Atlantic cities listened hopefully to the reports. Kansas City, Lawrence, and Omaha were soon full of adventurers planning a spring expedition to the mountains. Thousands, all the way from Maine to Illinois, were eager to join the search. "Never," wrote a lad who was lifted out of a dull general store in Iowa, "have a great boom, a fabulously wealthy mining district, and a new civilization been started on slimmer realities. It was all talk and dream, and yet in Iowa we were hotter about it than a prairie fire." [2]

1 King reached Leavenworth September 10; *National Intelligencer*, September 18, 1858.
2 Robert Claiborne Pitzer, *Three Frontiers*, Ch. 3.

Don't go if you have a job or a farm, exhorted Greeley's *Tribune*. But if you have neither, possess strength and grit, and can gather $50, we do earnestly advise you to set out *toward* Pike's Peak. You can reach Chicago, St. Louis, or Lawrence before winter, can find work somewhere, and when spring comes can decide whether to get your gold riskily along Cherry Creek, or safely and easily by farming, trading, or hauling in the West.[3] Some bold gold-hunters pushed through to Cherry Creek during the winter of 1858–59, and the first bakery, carpenter shop, watchmaker's, and saloon were opened, along with the Eldorado Hotel. As spring came, lines of Conestogas rolled across Iowa and Missouri, while the boats up the Missouri River were thronged with adventurers. The stampede, irrational and irresistible, was on.[4]

Minnesota had been admitted to the Union on May 11, 1859, with a population stated by the last territorial census at about one hundred and fifty thousand. Oregon stood knocking at the door, to be admitted February 11, 1859. Now the future Colorado was being born. The star of fortune rising over the Rockies attracted a swarm of those whom Henry Villard called masters of the ready Anglo-American art of town-making.[5] Near the site of the future Colorado Springs, a hamlet named El Paso sprang up and withered. Boulder City was laid out and survived. Central City (at first Mountain City) and Golden City were established. But a preeminent place was taken by the two settlements on Cherry Creek—that on the west bank called Auraria after a Georgia mining town, and that on the east Denver after the recently retired governor of Kansas. By the first snowfall of 1858, the two had about a hundred and twenty-five cabins, dugouts, and tents, and by May the habitations had increased to two hundred. Denver-Auraria became the commercial center of the gold-hunting district. The principal founder of the Denver Town Company, William Larimer, had arranged with W. H. Russell, planner of the Central Overland California & Pike's Peak Express Company, to make it a terminus of the stage line. Goods from the East were trans-shipped at Denver-Auraria to all the mining camps about.

The situation was superb. More than five thousand feet in altitude, Denver-Auraria lay within fifteen miles of the eastern base of the Rocky Mountain chain, visible through the crystal atmosphere for two hundred miles. Bold bluffs rose abruptly from the sandy bed of Cherry Creek which flowed into the South Platte hard by; the countryside was dotted with little lakes; cottonwood groves lined the streams. The first settlers lived in rude comfort, sleeping on buffalo robes and rising to a breakfast of antelope meat, trout, and flapjacks.

3 N. Y. *Tribune*, September 16, 30, 1858.
4 Henry Villard, *Past and Present of the Pike's Peak Gold Regions* (L. F. Hafen, ed.), Ch. 2.
5 *Op. cit.*, Ch. 11.

San Francisco had not risen much more lustily than did the Colorado metropolis. The spring rush of fortune seekers arrived in 1859 to find a discouraged population, for the placer deposits were quickly depleted. Then, on May 8,

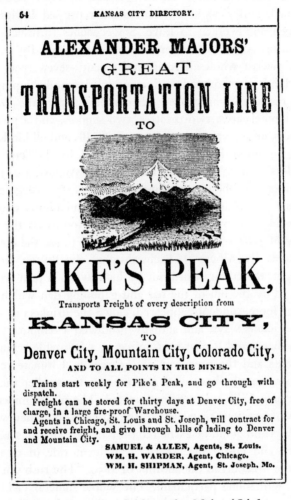

W. H. Russell and Alexander Majors' Link
Colorado with the East.

news reached Denver that John H. Gregory had made a splendid find of lode gold—and hope was reborn. Miners swarmed to the Gregory Gulch diggings and spread out through all the mountain valleys and pockets. Fresh discoveries were made, ensuring the future of the region. By midsummer, fifty or sixty thousand treasure-hunters had arrived and Denver-Auraria had become a thriving city of fully five thousand, its buildings alone representing an outlay of $700,000.

This Colorado population, drawn from all parts of the nation and half the outside world, was remarkably industrious and orderly. Town governments were established, and a vigilance committee repressed lawlessness, warning undesirable men and women to leave. Stagecoaches furnished regular transit from the Missouri River to Denver-Auraria in six days. By the end of 1859, this city had twelve wholesale-retail and twenty-seven retail establishments dealing in all kinds of merchandise, five commission and shipping houses, eight hotels, eleven restaurants, an express office, a newspaper (the *Rocky Mountain News*), four lumberyards, two theatres, two schools, and a plentiful array of doctors, lawyers, architects, and ministers. Sawmills and all kinds of mechanics' shops were to be found. Henry Villard was struck by the "considerable accession of capitalists" during the summer and fall. In August, a so-called constitutional convention of about one hundred and sixty delegates, many self-appointed, drew up a framework of government; and a hotly contested election resulted in sending two rival delegates to Washington to ask the formation of a new Territory of Jefferson. Horace Greeley came to see the country for himself, accompanied by Albert D. Richardson of the Boston *Journal*. On one memorable night, the editor, worn out by his travels, in pain from a wounded leg, and angered by the din of the bar and gambling den which occupied half of the Denver House, suddenly appeared, called the drinkers to order, lectured them on their vicious ways, and actually produced a temporary reformation.[6]

Greeley, Villard, and Richardson united in a favorable report on the mining developments and the prospects of the region. Ultimate results bore out their predictions, but the immediate harvest was far smaller than prospectors, dreaming of a new California, had anticipated. The placer miners found little. Vast treasures of precious metal lay in the Rockies, but they were locked in quartz and galena and could be extracted only by corporations assembling engineers, chemists, and costly machinery. A refluent tide of disappointed men spilled across the Missouri in the autumn of 1859. "The rush got as thick coming as going," writes one participant. The whole mineral yield of the Pike's Peak region that year did not reach three-quarters of a million—far less than the capital sunk in outfits and travel. Yet enough people remained to make Denver, Boulder, and other towns prosperous centers, and in the closing days of Buchanan's term (February 28, 1861) the Territory of Colorado came into existence.[7] The mining thenceforth was of a type which required large investments for machinery and transportation.

6 Villard, *Memoirs*, I, 115–130.
7 Fisk Stone, ed., *History of Colorado*, I, Ch. 6.

[I]

Realms of gold, silver, and copper, of cattle, timber, and fisheries, this trans-Mississippi West opened vistas of strength and daring to the American people. Men's blood flowed faster as they took draughts from the stream of newspaper stories, magazine articles, and books portraying the exuberant life and manifold opportunities of this domain of forests, peaks, and plains. Home-staying youth, to be sure, had plenty of chances. But what hardy young man would not like, in imagination at least, to be a prospector on Cherry Creek? Who would not like to be the pilot who brought the steamer *White Cloud* up to the Omaha landing on April 15, 1857, finding himself overwhelmed by a crowd hilarious over the first arrival of the season? What young fellow worth his salt would not delight in cracking the whip over the six-horse team of Butterfield's Overland Mail as, fording the Arkansas at Fort Smith, it straightened out on the short-cut trail through the Choctaw reservation toward Texas? What young woman would not (in dreams) leap at the chance to spend ten years in pioneering at the Falls of St. Anthony, amid such experiences as Harriet E. Bishop described in *Floral Home; or, First Years of Minnesota*—with lumbermen, hunters, and fur traders as friends, a schoolroom of Sioux children to teach, and a fast-developing frontier community to watch?

The Western adventurer might choose his place and vocation at will. He might be an Indian fighter under Will Harney or Jeb Stuart, anywhere from Fort Pierre to Tucson. He might be a missionary on Puget Sound. James G. Swan portrayed the allurements of that region in *The Northwest Coast*, telling of mines of coal, lead, and gold, incredible forests of fir, spruce, and pine, a soil that produced grain and fruit in perfection, woods filled with elk, deer, and antelope, and rivers almost choked with salmon and sturgeon. He might be a ranchman in Texas, or one of the cattle-drivers now bringing herds of many hundred beeves at a time to cross the Mississippi between Quincy and Rock Island, bound for Chicago. He might be a lumberman floating one of the giant rafts down the Wisconsin, a stream carrying annually a hundred million feet of boards. To form one of these rafts, from fifteen to thirty cribs, each containing from fourteen to twenty tiers of close-packed inch lumber, were fitted together, with spring poles in front to lift the edges of the rafts as they rushed down over foam-mantled rocks, and a heavy oar behind for steering. To shoot the perilous dalles of the Wisconsin just above the sturdy new town of Racine, where the river for half a dozen miles was compressed into a boiling gorge, the rafts were broken up into what were called "rapid-pieces," each consisting of five to seven well-secured cribs. Once out on the smoother Mississippi, the rivermen would gather together an extensive flotilla, on which they erected cabins and cookhouses for the trip to cities downstream. Log rafts, too, were not uncommon.[8]

Real Estate Promotion for Minnesota, 1859.

News of the trans-Mississippi West formed a great part of the intelligence in the American press. Some of it was dreary enough: the eternal Kansas bickering, the murders and vigilante lynchings, the incessant Indian hostilities, or

8 Racine Correspondent, N. Y. *Weekly Tribune*, September 5, 1857, gives a full description.

the riot over slavery in Oregon's constitutional convention of the summer of 1857. Much more of it was constructive. The older sections were constantly being bombarded with statistics exhibiting the wonderful growth of cities and States, railways and factories, banks and colleges. Let a reader open any newspaper in those months in which the Lecompton scheme was hatching, for example, and his eye would light on a story describing some new phase of regional development. He would read Governor Robert M. Stewart's inaugural address at Jefferson City, Missouri, declaring that the coal of the State was inexhaustible, that within a few miles of Iron Mountain and Pilot Knob were ores enough to furnish two hundred million tons of finished iron, and that the lead and copper mines were tremendously rich; or a prediction from St. Croix, Wisconsin, that the town's river trade, new railroad, and farm and timber resources must soon make it one of the largest manufacturing and commercial cities in the Northwest; or a statement upon the swelling commerce of Santa Fé; or a letter from a tourist describing how Omaha, where the first house was built in 1854, had sprung into a city of two thousand, with schools, churches, banks, and newspapers.

The growth of the West was indeed fabulous. It seemed marvellous that Chicago more than doubled its population between 1852 and 1855, leaping from thirty-eight thousand people to eighty thousand. It was marvellous to hear that Milwaukee, which probably counted a greater proportion of foreign-born inhabitants than any other American city, had more than trebled in size within a decade. It was remarkable to find that railroad crews were briskly laying down lines from Chicago and Milwaukee to St. Paul, and that by 1857 no fewer than three railroads were being planned to traverse Minnesota from east to west.[9] Easterners were astonished to learn that, beyond Minnesota, the still inchoate region of Dacotah had settlements. When Congress passed in 1857 an enabling act fixing the western boundary of the State in part along the Red River, news came of a county and town of Pembina left out in the cold and needing some specific government.[10] It was another marvel to find the Oregon legislature in 1856 not only boasting of fifty thousand people, but declaring them the wealthiest fifty thousand on the face of the globe. As for California marvels, they were innumerable. In the mid-fifties that land of gold had ceased to import breadstuffs and was shipping wheat, oats, and barley in increasing quantities to Australia and the Atlantic ports; it had its own paper mill, furniture factories, and large machine shops; and it was erecting a sugar refinery intended to meet the entire West Coast demand.[11]

9 *National Intelligencer*, March 24, 1857, quoting Andrews's recent work on Minnesota and Dacotah.
10 *National Intelligencer*, June 30, 1857.
11 *Ibid.*, May 9, 1857.

The whole West grew like a young giant fed on some magic food of the gods. Down to the panic of 1857 it was a land of speculation—and by 1859 the speculator was again ready to pluck up hope of rich booms. As population flowed outward, the glittering lure of the unearned increment in new cities appealed to investors as better than a gold mine. Douglas was a speculator in farmlands and city lots. R. M. T. Hunter, John W. Forney, and John C. Breckinridge were all involved in real estate transactions at the western end of Lake Superior.[12] Caleb Cushing at the beginning of the fifties owned a seventh part of "Rock Island City" in Illinois. Daniel Webster at an earlier date had held part of this same tract, but, neglecting to pay taxes, had lost possession.[13] Land speculation was one of the motors that drove forward the rapid development of Kansas. Throughout the Middle West, government policies which gave speculators almost unlimited opportunities to buy land fostered the swift rise of tenant farming.[14] Everyone who traveled beyond Ohio was impressed by the materialistic spirit pervading the air. A keen-eyed German, J. G. Kohl, who came over in 1856–57, was struck by the universal preoccupation with business openings, investments, prices, and profits. Traveling up-river from Dubuque to St. Paul in a handsome steamboat, he thought that some of his fellow passengers would take time to look at the enchanting scenery. Not at all; everybody was talking of the cost of farms and the turnover on lots.

The optimism that was a general American trait swelled higher in the West than anywhere else, catching its tempo from the tub-thumping of the boosters. For such men in Wisconsin, Governor Bashford was speaking early in 1857: [15]

Our soil is rich, productive, and easily cultivated; our climate as salubrious and healthy as any on the continent; and with our rapidly increasing facilities for internal communication at home and our direct railroad and water communication both with the Atlantic States and those bordering on the Gulf of Mexico, the cause of our swift advancement and present prosperity, as well as the earnest of their continuance, are alike apparent. . . . The day seems not

---

12 Douglas Papers, *passim;* Henry Harrison Simms, *Life of R. M. T. Hunter,* 100, 101. Douglas obeyed principle in his speculations. "When I became chairman of the Territorial Committee of the Senate, twelve years ago," he wrote August 29, 1857, "I determined never to purchase, or own, or become interested in any land, town lots, or other property in any of the Territories of the United States, whilst I held that position, for the reason that I would not allow an enemy even a pretext for saying that my public interest was influenced or stimulated by my private interest. I have never departed from this rule in any one instance." He visited Minnesota in 1857 to obtain information on that Territory useful to him in his Congressional duties; he was forthwith accused of some connection with the sale of the Fort Snelling military reservation; and he indignantly denied that he had an inch of land in Minnesota or any other Territory. Chicago *Times,* August 30, 1857.
13 William Brackett, Rock Island, July 20, 1850; Cushing Papers, LC.
14 Paul W. Gates, *Frontier Landlords and Pioneer Tenants, passim.*
15 Message of January, 1857.

far distant when, in agricultural and mineral wealth, in commercial advantages, in educational facilities, and all that tends to make us truly great and prosperous as a State, we shall be among the first in the Union.

For realty promoters in western Texas, the San Antonio *Sentinel* was lustily beating the drum:

We have a climate unsurpassed even by the far-famed Italy. . . . The scenery of Western Texas, we venture to say, in point of variety and beauty

BRING OUT THE BIG GUN

GLORIOUS NEWS!!

MINNESOTA A STATE!!!

100 GUNS FIRED AT WINONA:

GENERAL REJOICING,

Minnesotans Exult Over Their Admission,
May 11, 1858.

is second to that of no other country in the world; from the cold and rugged mountain steeps, where the cool clear waters gush from living fountains, interspersed with rich valleys, teeming with luxuriant growths, to the wide-extended prairies, with their gentle undulating surfaces covered with a rich dress of living green. . . . Stock of all kinds are very prolific, and disease among them is almost unknown. We have a varied soil. . . . More produce of almost every kind can be raised in Western Texas with a less amount of labor than in any other State in the Union.

Equal enthusiasm animated the correspondent of the New York *Tribune* in Minnesota: [16]

The new State will very probably number half a million at the census of 1860. No part of the West is receiving a more intelligent or valuable class of

16 Quoted *National Intelligencer*, January 31, 1857.

immigrants than Minnesota. The climate is the delight of the New Englander, the soil is extremely fertile, the beauty of natural scenery is not surpassed in any portion of the Union. The natural productions embrace all the valuable grains, grasses, vegetables, and fruits grown in Wisconsin. Waterpower abounds in every direction, and timber is comparatively abundant. Twenty years hence Minnesota will be gridironed over with railroads, dotted with towns and cities, and will hold upwards of two millions of sober, industrious, intelligent, freedom-loving inhabitants.

Much of this proved true, though the census of 1860 gave Minnesota only one hundred seventy-two thousand people, and that of 1880 only seven hundred eighty-one thousand. Detailed prophecy is risky, as Senator Weller should have remembered when, speaking in Congress for a Pacific Railroad, he boasted of California:

In 1856 there was imported into San Francisco merchandise to the value of one hundred millions, more than the whole amount of goods imported into the United States fourteen years ago. In point of commerce that city is ranked as third in our Union. . . . Although five times destroyed by fire, [she] will now compare favorably with any other city of the republic. In her schools, her churches, her public institutions, in all that dignifies and ennobles human nature, she has made more rapid advances during the last five years than any other city in the world. . . . San Francisco, the greatest city on that coast, before the lapse of a quarter of a century, if this road is constructed, will become the formidable rival of New York. Indeed, I venture the prediction that, within the lifetime of some who now hear me, the American commerce on the Pacific will far exceed that on the Atlantic.

[II]

As the country grew, national authority was necessarily extended over detached and neglected areas of the West. The so-called Mormon war was an episode in this extension. It fell to President Buchanan to write a stern administrative chapter in that Mormon chronicle which had hitherto been so out of keeping with the nineteenth century that, despite its grotesque and ugly sides, it had a touch of romance.

What an epic it was: the brilliant woodland vision seen by the farm lad Joseph Smith in western New York one autumn eve in 1823; the revelation of the buried plates of gold by the angel Moroni; the translation of their engraved contents by the aid of Urim and Thummim; the publication of the Book of Mormon, and the organization of the church; the successive transfers of the devoted adherents to Kirtland, Ohio, to Jackson County, Missouri, and Nauvoo, Illinois; the building of their prosperous church and massive temple on the banks of the Mississippi; the murder of the prophet and his brother, and the accession to power of Brigham Young; the winter flight across the river at the cannon's mouth in 1846; the journey of the intrepid saints, Young like a second Moses at their head, up the arid valley of the Platte, through Echo Canyon and over the Wasatch Range, stoically enduring heat, cold, hunger, thirst, and Indian peril; the triumphant arrival in July, 1847, at their Pisgah, whence they greeted with a shout the spectacle of the gleaming inland sea and fertile Salt Lake Valley—"The Land of Promise! The Land of Promise, reserved by God for the resting -place of his saints!" All the errors and follies which had marked some activities of these unconventional enthusiasts could but slightly mar the splendid chronicle of devotion, heroism, and resourcefulness.

Nor could anyone well deny that Brigham Young was the most command-ing single figure of the West. This rugged Vermonter, who had been given only eleven days' formal schooling before he set to work as carpenter, glazier, and painter, possessed an inexhaustible energy, a domineering temper, and a rocklike will which made him seem truly the Lion of the Lord. The visionary Joseph Smith had been a prophet; he believed in his dreams—he could not have persuaded thousands to accept them had he not possessed a burning faith, even though it was the faith of self-delusion. Young, with only rare flashes of the prophetic spirit, was a masterly organizer, policy-maker, and ruler. Though his sermons were childish, his other writings were shrewd, while his apt practical sagacity, inflexible resolution, and courage against any odds gave him the pro-portions of a statesman. From the moment he took the helm he had never faltered. He had ordered the harassed Nauvoo colony to seek a home in the wilderness, had directed the exodus, fixed upon the goal, and laid out the new metropolis. He had chosen spots for the settlement of Mormon companies sent out from Salt Lake City to various parts of Deseret, the land of the honey-bee. He had made plans for agriculture and industry. He it was who in 1852 announced the doctrine of polygamy, which though to many an abominable institution nevertheless temporarily served a sound purpose in the develop-ment of the colony.

For years, the national government had recognized Young's leadership. Kearny had called on him in 1846 for five hundred men to fight the Mexicans. "You shall have your battalion at once," replied Brigham, and the service of the detachment won him the gratitude of the Polk Administration. Upon the establishment of Utah Territory in 1850, President Fillmore immediately ap-pointed Young as governor, commander of the militia, and superintendent of Indian affairs. In short, he confirmed Young's dictatorship. Visitors to the region were impressed by the business acumen of the theocrat, who estab-lished industries, cooperative stores, banks, and transportation agencies to the prosperity of both the church-state and himself. Mormons chuckled with pride over his personal wealth, for though he lived in simple fashion (except for his costly establishment of wives in the "lion house") he piled dollar upon dollar. As far-flung missionaries sent home recruits, Utah steadily grew. Converts trickled in from Scandinavia, Switzerland, Germany, and above all Great Britain, until the eleven thousand struggling people of the Territory in 1850 were forty thousand ten years later.

Pages of heroic endurance were written into the Mormon record. Crops having failed in 1855 so disastrously that retrenchment was imperative, Young decided to encourage the incoming immigrants of 1856 to make the journey from the Iowa border not with specially despatched wagons and teams, as formerly, but on foot, pushing handcarts. This was simple, ingenious, and feasible, but it gave hostages to fortune. Of five companies which pushed across the plains in this fashion, the first three were successful. The two others met disaster. About five hundred in number, they started late, were crippled by dysentery, a stampede of their cattle and other misfortunes, and finally encountered heavy storms. With inadequate food and clothing, all would have perished had not relief parties reached them on the Sweetwater and near South Pass. As it was, about one-sixth died, while many of the remainder lost toes, feet, or hands. Efforts by the Mormon authorities to put a good face on the situation, and by their enemies to exaggerate the losses, made it difficult to obtain the true story. It was certain that many converts had endured dire sufferings gallantly, that they had complained little, and that the church heads were anxious to conceal their miscalculations. Brigham Young, saying that some members of the handcart companies had expired while singing hymns, and that others, when succor arrived, died while trying to eat the bread in their hands, remarked that nobody should feel a misplaced sympathy; he would be glad if he finally died without a groan or struggle, and with a keen appetite for food! [17] Next year the handcart migrations were resumed with better planning.

Despite his coarse and brutal vein, his egotism, and his frequent pettiness, Brigham Young was popular. He treated his own people with affability, throwing his arm over any Mormon's shoulder and asking cordially about his wives and children. His rough and ready manners, provincialisms of speech ("leetle," "beyond," "disremember," and "they was"), his kindness, and his justice in business dealings, were all assets in that primitive community. Subject as he was to the Quorum of his church, he had to rule by persuasion rather than fiat, and in accordance with the general discipline of the Latter Day Saints; and his policies showed an astute combination of tact and firmness.

17 Deseret *News* quoted in *National Intelligencer*, April 30, 1857.

No man of less strength could have succeeded; he had taken a heterogeneous people, foreign and native, skilled and unskilled, and moulded them into an industrious, orderly, devoted, and homogeneous community. Visitors from the East were struck by the contrast between his meagre intellectual attainments and his indomitable force of personality. They saw, in a house almost destitute of books, pictures or other tokens of refinement, a broad-shouldered, burly, powerful man of more than medium height, his face fringed in wavy hair and adorned with short chin-whiskers. His heavy jaw, tightly shut lips, and suspicious gray eyes proclaimed him a master, and, if need be, a cruel master. He was doggedly determined to remain autocrat of his church state. "I am and will be the governor," he had remarked, "and no power can hinder it, until the Lord Almighty says, 'Brigham, you need not be governor any longer.'" This attitude was the more strongly approved by the Mormons when they found President Pierce appointing political hacks of bad personal character, prejudiced and quarrelsome, to executive and judicial offices in the Territory. Indeed, nearly all the Territories had reason to complain of unfit and rapacious Federal officials. In Utah just before Buchanan entered the White House the friction between the people and the agents of the national government had become even hotter than in Kansas and New Mexico, and the charges and countercharges even angrier. Most Mormons believed they were threatened by an intolerant tyranny.

Several Federal officers, on the other hand, loudly accused the people of criminal and rebellious acts. Is the authority of Washington to be utterly flouted by Utah? they demanded.

This was the question that Buchanan believed he must test. Thunders of the national government, he was told, were rolling unheeded over the heads of a people who wanted total autocracy and were frankly intolerant of the rights of minorities; a people who, after long persecution, desired to be let alone and could not comprehend that they must be incorporated in the national fabric. President Pierce in 1854 had offered the governorship to Lt. Colonel E. J. Steptoe, who was in Salt Lake City with a small body of soldiers; but Steptoe had deemed it imprudent to accept the post, and after a quiet winter he betook himself and his little force to California. Various other civil officers who received commissions from Pierce, arriving after Steptoe departed, were overawed by the hostile aspect of Young, Heber C. Kimball, J. M. Grant, and other Mormon leaders, and found it wise to leave. An act of the Mormon-controlled legislature declared that no law should be valid except those enacted by the governor and assembly, and those of Congress *when applicable*—which meant when sanctioned by Brigham Young. Another act gave the probate courts an authority rivaling that of Federal courts, so that, in effect, one set of courts existed for Gentiles and another for the Mormons.[18] H. H. Bancroft in his *Utah*, which is favorable to the Mormons, quotes Young as saying after Steptoe left that "if they play the same game again, so help me God, we will slay them."

Just before Buchanan was inaugurated, the official Mormon newspaper pealed its defiance of the government. If a majority in any Territory preferred a state of vassalage, it remarked, well and good. But when practically the entire community were known most persistently to prefer officers of their own election to those foisted upon them by arbitrary power, and laws of their own enactment to statutes dictated by unconstitutional authority, then tyranny was intolerable. "How long, think ye, can such oppression be quietly endured? How long, think ye, will any people submit to the dictates, slanders, corruptions, and abuse of officers whom they have no voice in electing, and whose efforts are constantly put forth to the utmost for the destruction of the people?" [19]

This was a challenge which no President could ignore. Nor could Washington ignore the passionate protest of Judge W. W. Drummond of the Federal court in transmitting his resignation on March 30, 1857. Drummond had charged a grand jury in Carson County the previous summer to deal sternly with polygamy under the territorial law against lewdness and adultery.[20] He now posed as hostile to a dictatorship which paralyzed all Federal authority and recoiled not from murder to accomplish its ends; and he appealed loudly to the country. He declared that the judiciary was treated as a farce in Utah; that the infatuated Mormons bowed to but one law, the church law emanating from Brigham Young; that officials were insulted, thwarted, and even slain if they administered any other; and that as the Territory had been governed by Young ever since Fillmore's time, it was noonday madness to try to brook this autocrat's sway. He asserted that after careful investigation he had concluded that his predecessor, Judge Leonidas Shaver, had been poisoned by the Mormons; that the late secretary of the Territory, A. W. Babbitt, had been slain by Indian marauders instigated by the church; and that Captain John W. Gunnison and his party of eight surveyors had been killed in 1853 by savages under Mormon direction. He charged that Young had controlled the action of grand juries on indictments, connived at the destruction of court papers, thrown Gentiles into jail without warrant, and pardoned atrocious murderers simply because they held the Mormon faith.

18 Richardson, *Beyond the Mississippi*, 353; McMaster, VIII, 374, 375; Stenhouse, *Rocky Mountain Saints*, 280 ff.; H. H. Bancroft, *Utah*, 494.

19 *Deseret News*, January 28, 1857.

20 Full text of charge is in *National Intelligencer*, December 23, 1856. Critics of Drummond declare that he was a venal, dissolute gamester, who openly insulted the Mormon community, and whose misrepresentations completely misled Washington; Bancroft, *Utah*, 490, 491.

Another Federal judge, George P. Stiles, whose writs had been defied, who had been threatened with personal violence, and whose office had been sacked, arrived at Leavenworth in May, 1857. With him came Surveyor-General D. H. Burr, who with his clerks had fled under threat of death. Both reported robberies and murders unpunished by law, insolent rebuffs by Young when they asked for protection, and a general defiance of the national government.[21] No Federal officers except two Indian agents remained in the Territory. Meanwhile, a lurid work by an apostate, F. G. J. Margetson's *Horrors of Mormonism*, together with other wildly exaggerated tales, excited popular antagonism. A wave of excited feeling rose against Young and his peculiar people. At least half the charges made by Drummond and Stiles, including all their allegations of murder, were baseless, while the other half were overcolored; but the American people were ready to believe anything of the polygamists.

[III]

Buchanan was prepared to act vigorously. He appointed as governor a capable, courageous Georgian, Alfred Cumming, who had been superintendent of Indian affairs on the upper Missouri; named a new chief justice, two associate justices, a secretary, and a marshal; and deputed a body of twenty-five hundred troops under Colonel Albert Sidney Johnston to accompany Cumming to his post. No man in the army was more highly regarded than Johnston. A West Pointer, he had shown quickness of mind, courtesy, daring (he once killed a puma with his clubbed rifle), and endurance. In the Mexican War, Zachary Taylor called him "the best soldier I ever commanded." When in 1855 he was made colonel of a new regiment of cavalry (with Robert E. Lee as lieutenant-colonel and George H. Thomas a major), Winfield Scott declared the appointment "a godsend to the army and the country." Part of Johnston's troops gathered at Fort Leavenworth and in midsummer of 1857 began their march.

The news of the President's determined action filled Young, Kimball, and their associates with mingled fury and apprehension. It must be remembered that the Mormons had good reason, recalling riot, pillage, assassination, and expulsion, to fear American violence. They were a rigid, earnest, ignorant, and prejudiced people, moulded by sermons, speeches, and newspaper articles which exalted their peculiar system and denounced the American government and people bitterly. Facing an ignorance and prejudice even greater than their own, for few men in the East tried to understand the Mormon outlook, they

---

21 *National Intelligencer*, June 6, August 1, 1857. Chief Justice Stiles, a former Mormon and onetime counsel for Joseph Smith, has also been assailed as a man of bad character; Bancroft, *Utah*, 488, 489. For the official charges by Drummond and others and the reply of the Mormon authorities, see 35th Cong., 1st Sess., *House Exec. Doc.* 71.

were frightened at the prospect of outrage and subjugation. Their leaders, seeing their own authority endangered, whipped up the popular emotion.

Why, demanded the *Deseret News*, should Federal troops come to prey upon the industrious, sober Mormons when they were needed to halt the riots which reddened the streets of Baltimore, Washington, and New York? Why should a horde of Federal officials, the scourings of grogshops and gambling dens, be thrust upon people who wanted their own paternal governors?

Young poured forth a rhetorical incitement to resistance. "I don't profess to be such a prophet as were Joseph Smith and Daniel, but I am a Yankee guesser, and I guess that James Buchanan has ordered this expedition to appease the wrath of the angry hounds who are howling around him." He had sworn in Nauvoo to send any future aggressor to hell across lots, and he would now muster three hundred men who could lap water and help him whip the Midianites. Woe to meddlers! The Mormons would fight to the end ("in the mountains, in the canyons, upon the plains, on the hills, along the mighty streams, and by the rivulets," ran his anticipation of Winston Churchill's phraseology) for their homes and their religion.[22]

Armed resistance was soon a reality. The beginning of October found Colonel E. B. Alexander's forward command of about five hundred cavalry approaching Fort Bridger, a hundred and fifteen miles by direct road from Salt Lake City. The rear of the expedition had not yet reached South Pass and Johnston was hurrying to join the little army, which, all told, hardly numbered fourteen hundred men. At this moment, three supply trains comprising seventy-four wagons equipped by Russell & Waddell of Leavenworth, contractors for the transport of stores and provision of beef, were seized by Mormon bands, pillaged, and burnt. Young had issued an audacious proclamation forbidding armed forces to enter his Territory, mobilized the Mormon militia, scattered parties through the mountains, and fortified Echo Canyon. These events crystallized eastern indignation. Johnston's forces were compelled to go into winter quarters on the Green River near Fort Bridger, which the Mormons had destroyed; and the country echoed with demands that the modern Sodomites, as one editor called them, be brought to terms—though many people began to wonder if Buchanan had chosen the right method.[23]

As infantry and dragoons dragged out the winter, they spoiled for a fight. Johnston roughly declined Brigham Young's gift of salt. Some men, he wrote his family, think the Mormons will submit, but I disagree. "I think their fanati-

---

22 Long speech in *National Intelligencer*, September 17, 1857. See O. G. Hammond, ed., *The Utah Expedition, 1857–58, passim;* John L. Sinn, *The Utah Expedition of 1857.* Harney had originally been asked to lead the expedition, but his duties kept him in Kansas.

23 Full account of bringing trains from Fort Laramie by correspondent, N. Y. *Weekly Tribune,* November 21, 1857.

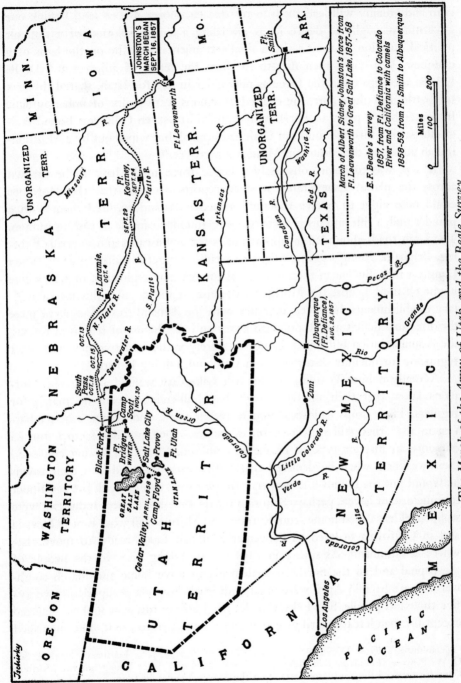

UNORGANIZED TERR.

MINN.

IOWA

MO.

| JOHNSTON'S MARCH BEGAN SEPT. 16, 1857 |

Ft. Smith

ARK.

| March of Albert Sidney Johnston's force from Ft. Leavenworth to Great Salt Lake, 1857-58 |
| E.F. Beale's survey |
| 1857, from Ft. Defiance to Colorado River and California with camels |
| 1858-59, from Ft. Smith to Albuquerque |

Miles
0   100   200

UNORGANIZED TERR.

Ft. Leavenworth

Missouri

Ft. Kearney, SEPT. 24

Platte R.

SEPT. 29

NEBRASKA TERR.

KANSAS TERR.

Ft. Laramie, OCT. 4

OCT. 13

N. Platte R.

Sweetwater R.

S. Platte R.

OCT. 15

Arkansas

R.

R.

Washita R.

Canadian R.

Red R.

TEXAS

Pecos R.

South Pass, OCT. 18

Grande

OCT. 30

Camp Scott NOV. 30

BlackFork

Albuquerque (Ft. Defiance), AUG. 26, 1857

Rio

WASHINGTON TERRITORY

Ft. Bridger WINTER

Salt Lake City

Provo

Ft. Utah

Green R.

Zuni

N E W

M E X I C O

GREAT SALT LAKE

Cedar Valley, APRIL, 1858

Camp Floyd

UTAH LAKE

Colorado R.

Little Colorado R.

Verde R.

T E R R I T O R Y

Gila

R.

U T A H

T E R R.

OREGON

Colorado

R.

Los Angeles

C A L I F O R N I A

PACIFIC OCEAN

The March of the Army of Utah, and the Beale Survey.

cism and villainy will lead them to try one encounter at least; and I think our government ought to desire it, as affording a simple solution of a difficult political question. If they resist, a final settlement would be on the basis of a conquest. We could then dictate to them the terms of adjustment." D. R. Eckels, accompanying the force as new chief justice for Utah, shared this lust for battle. For their part, the excited Mormons were guilty of unhappy acts. In September, a party of one hundred and thirty-seven California-bound emigrants passing through southern Utah had been all but wiped out by a Mormon-Indian attack in the Mountain Meadows massacre.[24]

If war was to begin, obviously a larger force might have to be thrown across the plains. Exaggerated western reports declared that the Mormons could raise eight to twelve thousand armed men, and credited them with a powder mill, a rifle and pistol factory, and a foundry capable of casting cannon. The Utah roads abounded in opportunities for ambuscades and guerrilla fighting. Brigham Young's agents might also enlist vengeful Indian allies.[25] When Congress met, Buchanan therefore asked for ten new regiments, of which five might be used against the Mormons. Because of the popular distrust of military establishments, however, together with the demand for economy to meet the Treasury deficit and Republican irritation over the use of troops in Kansas, the Administration bill failed; Congress merely authorized two new volunteer regiments for quelling disturbances in Utah and fighting Indians.

Actually neither Washington nor Salt Lake City wanted a war. The Mormons knew that their militia, ill-armed and ill-trained, were no match for regulars. Their crops had been poor in recent years, and despite a better harvest in 1857 they still suffered from scarcities. Their powder factory turned out only an inferior type of coarse ammunition.[26] Brigham Young confessed their weakness when he declared that if the army marched into their towns he would put the immovable property to the torch, and go with the remainder to some distant haven, perhaps Sonora, perhaps British America. Industries were stopped, elders called home from Europe, and Mormons in what is now Nevada and in California ordered to concentrate in Salt Lake, ready to move elsewhere at command. As spring in 1858 began, Young directed the people of the capital and all the northern settlements to leave home and march southward. Roads by mid-April were filled with herds, wagons, and perhaps twenty-five thousand people. Salt Lake and the neighboring towns would be deserted except for men left to guard property and if necessary to fire it. The anguished

---

24 Johnston's letter December 12, 1857; *National Intelligencer*, February 18, 1858. See C. W. Penrose, *The Mountain Meadow Massacre, passim.* Neither Young nor the Mormon Church approved this murderous attack on the Missouri emigrant train.
25 Sacramento *Age*, October 16, 1857.
26 N. Y. *Tribune*, May 5, 1858.

Mormons apparently looked forward to the obliteration of their laboriously built state. Fortunately, the Administration had no appetite for costly guerrilla warfare ending in the dispersal of a prosperous and useful people.

At the last moment, one of the few strokes of statesmanship exhibited in this period brought about a happy ending. Although the credit went mainly to Buchanan, it belonged primarily to Thomas L. Kane, brother of the Arctic explorer, and to Governor Cumming. Kane was a vigorous, adventurous man in his middle thirties whose published letters reveal his warm-hearted idealism. Born the son of a Philadelphia judge, he had been educated largely in France, where he knew Auguste Comte, and returning home, had been admitted to the Pennsylvania bar. In 1847 he had gone west to visit the Mormons, had assisted them in their flight to Utah, and had won their enduring friendship. His book on them (*The Mormons*, 1850) was well known. When he heard that the wrath of the government was aroused and that fire and sword were about to be carried into their country, compassion impelled him to try to avert bloodshed. He wished neither office nor salary—merely an opportunity to be useful.

Buchanan consented to his proposal for mediation. Leaving by sea for San Francisco in the first days of 1858, Kane made his way to Salt Lake City, conferred with Brigham Young, reassured him, and reached a tentative agreement. While in temporal matters Washington must be supreme, he said, in church affairs the Mormons would not be molested. Then he hurried on to the dugout quarters which Cumming had been occupying at Black's Fork, arriving after a forced ride in a state of utter exhaustion. Cumming, who desired a peaceful solution, received him cordially. The upshot was that the two men, to the chagrin of army officers thirsting for cheap glory, set off for the Mormon settlement and for new conferences with Young.[27]

In doing this, Cumming, who knew that he would be bitterly assailed by military men and misrepresented in Washington, played a fine part. He realized that force would settle nothing, whereas, if fighting with the fanatical church leaders began, many on both sides would perish, and honest farmers and artisans would suffer most. He had been ready to hurry on as soon as the road was clear of snow, without any military escort or any assurances of a safe reception.[28] Leaving camp on April 5, he was in Salt Lake City on the twelfth. The placated Mormons had kindled bonfires to illuminate his night journey through Echo Canyon; they greeted him everywhere as their governor; Young at once paid him a visit of courtesy; and the territorial seal was immediately delivered to him.

27 Oscar L. Winther, ed., *The Private Papers and Diaries of Thomas L. Kane, a Friend of the Mormons.*
28 J. Forney, Camp Scott, April 18, May 1, 1858; Black Papers.

One of the dramatic scenes of the time was the great public meeting in the Tabernacle on April 25, when Young introduced the governor, and Cumming explained to three or four thousand people his purposes. He was tactful but firm. He had seen the pathetic preparations for general flight. He knew that if the Mormons were driven from their homes by terror the event would be remembered like the expulsion of the Acadians. He was aware that many of his auditors were embittered by the thought of old wrongs, some real, some fanciful; he knew how deeply all English-speaking peoples object to the quartering of troops in their midst. To the respectful audience he said that he had come to vindicate the national sovereignty, and would exact an unconditional submission to the Constitution and the laws. He also said, however, that he had no intention of stationing troops in immediate contact with their settlements, that he would not use military power until all other means had failed, and that he would see that any indicted citizen was tried by a jury of his peers. Above all, he would not interfere with the Mormon religion. When he invited citizens to respond, the scene became uproarious. Speaker after speaker, laboring under marked emotion, dwelt upon their persecutions, the want of national gratitude to the Mormon Battalion, their toils in creating their Western home, and their resolve never to be overrun by a brutal soldiery. Cumming remained temperate, and after the meeting more than one Mormon apologized for his own vehemence.[29]

Already, adverse public opinion and the protests of Kane and others had caused the President to alter his policy. On April 6 he signed a proclamation which, though declaring Utah in rebellion, promised a full pardon to all who would submit to the government. A large additional force had been assembled at Fort Leavenworth for use if needed; but in June two Federal peace commissioners reached a complete agreement with the Mormon leaders. It was arranged that Johnston's little army should march through Salt Lake City, which it found almost entirely deserted, and encamp some distance beyond. In due course it established its post at Cedar Valley, about thirty-six miles south of the city. A disastrous conflict had been narrowly avoided. In this bloodless Mormon War the army had made a demonstration which cost the depleted Treasury millions, which terrified and demoralized the hardworking citizens of Utah, and which accomplished no constructive object that peaceful means could not have attained. Cumming and Kane, supported by a far smaller force, could have brought Brigham Young and his associates to the same terms they now made. This grandiose military display, costly and provocative, could and

29 Cumming, May 2, 1858, to Cass, N. Y. *Weekly Tribune*, June 19, 1858. The governor traveled about the Territory, talked with the people, and tried to reach a mutual understanding. Most people were only too glad to be on good terms. J. Forney, May 6, 1858, to J. Black; Black Papers. For additional matter on the Mormon War, see Appendix II.

should have been avoided. Blame for it rested in part on the Mormons, guilty of unwise words and acts, in part on an excitable public opinion in the East, and in part on the Administration.

Of course nothing could shake the imperious temper of Brigham Young, reduce his prestige as leader of the church, or alter the loyalty of most Mormons to his authority. As church head, he remained chief potentate in the Territory. But from this time forward, the civil governor was given due obedience in his restricted sphere, the laws were respected, and a growing Gentile element was protected in its pursuits. Mail, goods, and emigrant trains could again flow freely from the Missouri to the Pacific, and the development of the West could go on.

[IV]

The mining frontier, the Indian frontier, the cattlemen's and farmers' frontiers, all were fast being transformed. All had to adapt themselves to a nation with a lengthening and thickening network of railroads, a maturing set of business institutions, a shifting balance between agriculture and industry, and a stronger social sense.

No more individualistic figures ever existed than the placer miners who had flocked to the Sierra foothills in 1849–50. Men worked alone, or with but one or two partners. A group might band together to build a dam or ditch, but so long as placers paid handsome returns, the semi-solitary digger predominated. Of the first half-billion dollars in gold taken from California, much the greatest part was recovered with the placerman's simple tools of pick, shovel, pan, and cradle. Even after more elaborate and costly operations were instituted, it was often difficult to find hands for them because men preferred trying their luck as prospectors along bars, riffles, and gulches.[30]

Astute miners quickly perceived, however, that much the richest concentrations of gold occurred in rock veins or in Tertiary "high gravels"—that is, the beds followed by streams in the Tertiary era. The quartz veins along the "mother lode," which runs irregularly through Mariposa County to Amador, were in many instances fabulously large; and capital and associated effort quickly appeared. When tempting outcrops were found in Grass Valley, on Frémont's Mariposa holdings, and at other points, Californians with access to capital began to make large investments.

A Los Angeles company was selling stock as early as the summer of 1850.

---

30 In the period of greatest productiveness, 1850–53, the California placer mines yielded about $65,000,000 a year. If an average of 75,000 miners were at work, they made an average of $8 a day. Some think the average the first year was $20 a day.

Even though none of the quartz mines by 1852 had gone below three hundred feet, the drilling, blasting, and ore-crushing stamps cost more than most individuals could afford. A few early stamp-mills were erected for from $5,000 to $10,000, but this was exceptional. In 1852 California had one hundred and eight mills, representing an investment not far short of six million dollars. As time proved, this was a false dawn for quartz mining. Because the early stamps did not grind the ore to sufficient fineness, because the process of chemical amalgamation to extract the gold was at first inefficient, because for a decade no means of reaching the gold locked up in sulphides was known, because, in short, good engineering knowledge and good apparatus were lacking, most of the metal was lost—sometimes four-fifths of it; while the high costs and low returns quickly ruined companies possessing inadequate capital. Nine in ten of the early plants for extracting rockbound gold failed. Men became so skeptical of quartz mining that the number of mills fell in 1854 to thirty-two. Although the industry soon grew vigorous again, not until after 1860 did it reach significant proportions.

While the Tertiary gravels were more easily dealt with, they too required large investments in labor and capital. They might be covered by hundreds of feet of earth and detritus, together with lava, basaltic crust, or other semi-rocklike material which the miners called cement. To reach the deeper gravel deposits meant tunneling into a slope, timbering and shoring at every step. To wash the gold out of the gravel, rock, and dirt often required the construction of huge dams and flumes. In a rich district, a single hill might have dozens of tunnels sunk into its sides. Where gold deposits lay nearer the surface and were not covered by too indurated a layer of cement, a stream could frequently be diverted to erode the covering and bring the pay dirt into the sluices. That is, water was turned in to strip off the useless layers of the hillside. Somebody quickly perceived that a hose could bring the water more expeditiously and cheaply than a flume; then somebody else placed a nozzle on the hose, got a high pressure, and bored down faster and harder than ever. Bigger and stronger hose came in, fitted with iron collars. Before long, the Sierra foothills were being bombarded with hydraulic artillery which demolished grass, trees, soil, sand, and loose rock, shattering and shearing everything down to the ancient bedrock, and creating havoc with the landscape.

As the fifties wore on, more capital was collected, more companies were formed, and larger bodies of engineers, tunnel-blasters, flume-builders, and hose-men were brought in. The hydraulic operations became gargantuan. Blasting, to loosen refractory rock or cement, was combined with the use of water, and ingenious combinations of tunnels and hydraulic monitors made it possible to wash the very bowels out of seemingly unconquerable mountains. Placer miners downstream complained angrily of the waste washed from the upper slopes. Millions of tons of rubble were dumped into the Sierra streams; sand, gravel, and rocks choked many valleys and ravines; and when spring floods came, the offscourings were carried down to overwhelm valuable farmlands. The once-clear Sacramento flowed yellow. In time, the silt closed the upper channel to navigation and became perilous to steamboats even on the lower reaches. Finally a levee system had to be built to protect the capital city. Passage of legislation to check the grosser mining abuses, however, did not come for another generation.

Until the beginning of 1858, quartz mining had produced only a tiny fraction of California's gold—probably not one percent; the Tertiary gravels had yielded but a modest share; and placer mining remained dominant. But the wheel was turning. Quartz mining required technical expertness for success; and, as it had failed at first for lack of good machinery, experienced technicians, and sound business managers, so in the later fifties it began to revive when these were applied. In Grass Valley in 1856 several rich veins were developed, one yielding more than $400 a ton.[31] Better machinery was landed at San Francisco and Sacramento to be carried into the interior. A convention of quartz operators met at Sacramento in June, 1857, to draw up a code of regulations and to set forth the attractions of their mines to eastern capital.[32] These men believed the "science" of extracting rockbound gold would quickly advance and would make their method supreme. Early mills had been worked by horses or mules attached to an abrasive apparatus, an arrastre or "raster"; later mills were run by steam or waterpower.[33] Butte City in 1856 boasted of a dam and overshot wheel which drove twelve heavy stamps. The Amador County *Sentinel* then predicted that ore-crushing establishments in California would soon employ more capital and labor than the woolen mills in any eastern State.[34] This faith in the future was well founded, for more than three hundred stamp-mills were busy by 1861. If the second half of the first billion of California's gold was furnished chiefly by hydraulic mining, the second billion came mainly from quartz.[35]

After 1858, indeed, the annual output of placer deposits diminished rapidly,

31 *National Intelligencer*, April 26, 1856.

32 *Ibid.*, July 16, 1857.

33 Borthwick, *Gold Hunters*, edited by Horace Kephart, 235, gives a description of the methods.

34 Quoted in *National Intelligencer*, January 19, 1856.

35 John W. Caughey, *Gold is the Cornerstone*, 266, 267. The San Francisco *Bulletin* in its annual review of mining operations for 1856 spoke of five water companies in Columbia County, with canals 27 to 60 miles in length, and capital of $250,000 to $550,000. Placer County had 24 canals. The value of all the canals and ditches in the State at the end of 1856 was placed at $11,000,000. Quoted in *National Intelligencer*, March 3, 1857. Cf. R. G. Cleland, *From Wilderness to Empire*, 255 ff.

falling to $24,000,000 in 1864, while the yield from hydraulic mining rose with spectacular speed, and quartz production increased steadily if slowly. A basic change in the economic pattern of mining ensued. The multitudinous adventurers who had made such places as Hangtown famous—the ravines for eight or ten miles about filled with diggers, the shorn hillsides strewn with buckets, picks, and "long toms," the village stores and gambling houses crowded each Sunday with boisterous young fellows eager for diversion after a week's toilsome isolation—gradually disappeared. Individual effort waned. A few hydraulic mines, and a number of small quartz crushers, were worked by a group of proprietary partners, but in general the corporation took control. The biggest quartz mines soon represented an investment of millions for shafts, railroads, batteries of stamps, and workers' houses. Frémont, who had in Mariposa an estate conservatively estimated to be worth ten millions, lost it to the greedy capitalists he called in to finance his work. Gravel mining also demanded larger amounts, until one twelve-hundred-and-fifty foot tunnel dug into Table Mountain in the middle fifties cost $80,000. Absentee owners, plant superintendents, and companies of wage-hands replaced the versatile and resourceful emigrants who had made immortal "the days of old, and the days of gold, and the days of '49."

Such, in fact, was the story of mining throughout the West. When silver and copper were found in the Gadsden Purchase, not individuals but mining corporations took control. By 1857, the Arizona Copper Mining Company, the Gila River Copper Mining Company, and the Sonora Exploring and Mining Company were busy in the region.[36] A survey of 1861 listed more than a dozen mining corporations in the Arizona country, of which the Santa Rita and the Sapori companies were capitalized at a million dollars each, and the Arizona Land and Mining Company at two millions. Most of this capital came from eastern cities. The sum thus far expended in developing the so-called Heintzelman Mine alone was $230,000.[37]

Colorado was found to be designed not for the creek-trotter but the capitalist. The influx of 1858–59 soon exhausted the limited gulch or surface washings. Attention was then turned to "blossom rock" or disintegrated quartz; the rich strikes of 1859 near Central City and other points, where men found beds of rotten quartz, nuggets, and gold scales, loosed a tremendous rush, with mining camps as feverish as those of California a decade earlier. Yet at the height of the furore Greeley, Villard, and Richardson in their public statement warned enthusiasts that "gold mining is a business which eminently requires of its votaries capital, experience, energy, endurance"—and this was manifestly true.

36 *National Intelligencer*, April 18, 1857.
37 Sylvester Mowry, *Arizona and Sonora, passim.*

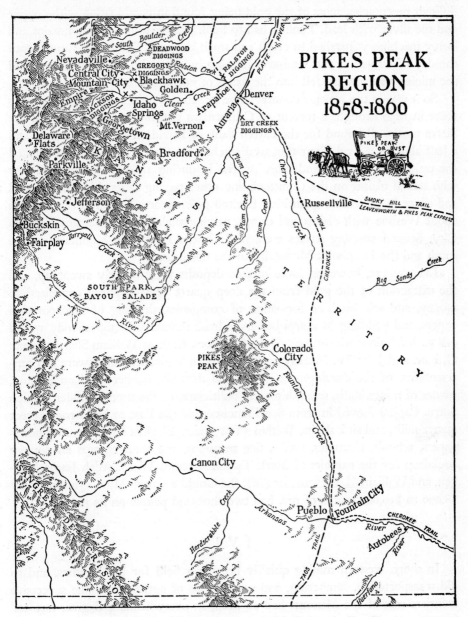

PIKES PEAK REGION 1858-1860

Principal Early Mining Camps of the Colorado Rockies.

The storehouses of precious metals in the mountains were locked in stubbornly difficult receptacles, most of the gold being found in combination with copper and the silver with lead. Tunnels had to be driven deep into the mountains and heavy machinery installed to crush and smelt the ores. Colorado's future, until the day of irrigation and semi-arid farming, was mainly a mining future, and the mining of necessity fell into the hands of corporations.[38]

So it was in the Nevada country. The sensational gold and silver discoveries there in 1859 brought a torrent of Californians pouring eastward through the Sierra passes, all bound for the barren flank of Davidson Mountain a mile and a half above sea level. Four thousand reached the district before snow choked the trails, and ten thousand more poured in during 1860. The fortunate few who staked claims on the Comstock and other paying lodes shipped out gold and silver in incredible quantities. Excited prospectors checkered the districts about Washoe with claims and camps, naming their chief settlement Virginia City. Several amazing strikes were made in the Esmeralda Mountains to the south and the Humboldt Mountains to the northeast.

Everywhere, however, loose surface deposits were quickly swept up, and the extraction of the gold from the deep quartz veins required organization, money, and science. The formation of companies, drafting of incorporation papers, and peddling of shares became a brisk industry. While nobody would call such fabulous adventurers of the Comstock Lode as William Sharon, James G. Fair, and John W. Mackay anything but individualists, they were less representative of the development of Nevada than the banker William Ralston, owner of mines, mills, steamships, and politicians, or the tunnel builder Adolph Sutro. Capital flowed in from San Francisco and the East to build roads, erect quartz mills, and sink shafts. Within a few years, Virginia City, boasting newspapers, schools, churches, banks, fine mansions, and theatres, was an opulent backdrop for the exploits of Mark Twain, Artemus Ward, Adah Isaacs Menken, and William M. Stewart. In 1863, the Gould & Curry Mine, crushing daily $8,000 to $10,000 worth of ore, had two thousand people on its payroll.

[V]

In short, western mining quickly became a field for big business, and so did transportation, lumbering, and some forms of agriculture. The successive frontiers east of the Missouri had all been, in overwhelming degree, farmers' frontiers; the frontiers west of that river were to be more varied—the miners' frontier, the lumbermen's frontier, the ranchers' and sheep-herders' frontier, the bonanza-farmers' frontier. For half a dozen reasons, united planning and capital

38 Bayard Taylor, *Colorado (1887)*, Chs. 7, 8, 9.

counted for more, and individual effort for less, than in the trans-Missouri region.

First, the scale of the land was greater; transportation, a key factor, required more organization and a larger investment.

Second, the surface mineral wealth so quickly garnered in California, Colorado, and Nevada, created towns and cities, with accumulations of capital, almost overnight. Tremendous social power, such as once required decades to create, was generated within a few years. One early arrival in San Francisco was shocked by what he called "the high pressure principle" in evidence everywhere; another wrote that he found everything on a monstrous and perverted scale. As the California historian Hittell remarks: "It seemed impossible that a wealth greater than that of the Indies should flow through such a narrow channel; that such prodigious power should be confined in . . . such an awkward, shambling city." [39]

In the third place, as soon as the loose surface wealth was skimmed off, the remaining riches of the land were found in more refractory form than in the East. Mining required more machinery, lumbering larger sawmills and longer transportation, cattle-raising larger acreages, than in the past.

As a fourth consideration, farming on the great plains and in the San Joaquin Valley faced entirely new conditions; fencing, water-supply, defense, and the processes of seeding, cultivation, and harvesting demanded new inventions (barbed wire, windmills, light rapid-fire weapons, and improved farm machinery) which in many instances meant a heavy outlay.

In the fifth place, labor was costlier in the Far West than it had been on the other frontiers, and the demand for labor-saving machinery was proportionately strong.

Finally, the industrial revolution had now advanced further in America, and improved transportation and communication brought it closer to the frontier. Quite apart from the need for such essential products as mining tools, windmills, and harvesters, the taste of Westerners demanded many of the comforts and conveniences which industrialism was producing. The bales and boxes of merchandise that crowded the Kansas City or San Francisco wharves represented a higher standard of living than the old-time eastern pioneers had known, and one which the population of the trans-Missouri area was determined to maintain.

The romance of the covered wagon with the pioneer family inside can hardly be celebrated too often. But an equally romantic story might be written upon the adventures of a stamp-mill, manufactured in New York, sent around

39 James L. Tyson, *Diary of a Physician*, 51; *Golden Dreams and Leaden Realities*, 74, 75; Hittell, *California*, III, 347.

Cape Horn, uncrated at Sacramento, laboriously carted into some remote mountain valley, and painfully assembled beside a shaft. Nor was it long before good stamp-mills were being manufactured in California. The exploits of the cowboy will never pall. But what of the exploits of a man like T. V. Smith—an enterprising artisan who migrated from Baltimore to Oregon City in Washing Territory, established himself as foundryman and engine-builder, and in 1853 constructed an iron steamboat, *Belle of Oregon City*, which was wholly an Oregon product from the plates of her ninety-foot hull to her boilers and walking-beam engines? The small farmer of Kansas or Nebraska was often a heroic figure. But so were the lumbermen of Oregon and Washington who, cutting cargoes of spars and boards, sold them during the decade to California, the Mexican coast, Hawaii, and China. Indeed, the most lucrative occupation of Puget Sound settlers was lumbering, a type of enterprise requiring considerable capital. By 1858, nineteen sawmills on the Sound had a combined capacity of more than two hundred thirty thousand feet of lumber daily, the two largest steam mills, at Teekalet and Port Madison, producing seventy-five thousand feet a day. The Teekalet establishment, hiring about one hundred and fifty men at $2 to $4 a day with board included, did a general mercantile business and carried a stock of goods worth from $15,000 to $25,000.[40]

Bold men were laying the foundations of large-scale ranching in various parts of the West long before 1860. We have noticed the early cattle drives from Texas to the upper Mississippi between Quincy and Rock Island, and before the war the Morgan steamship line was cramming cattle into its vessels plying from Galveston to New Orleans and Mobile. Some shiploads were even sold in Cuba for the plantations.[41] On the northern plains the western migration quickly created a few large herds. A cattleman near Fort Hall had six hundred head in 1856; and three years later Horace Greeley encountered in the Wyoming country another, whose steers, horses, and other property were worth $75,000. In Washington Territory, one Ben Snipes was in a position to sell cattle to the miners of British Columbia during the Fraser River rush at $100 a head, giving him the money on which he later amassed three large ranches and a hundred thousand beeves. Other bold men were laying the foundations of great timber fortunes. Philetus Sawyer, destined to be a powerful Wisconsin magnate, joined some partners in 1853 in purchasing a sawmill at Fond du Lac, while the elder Weyerhaeuser seized his opportunity after the panic of 1857 to take over, in conjunction with his brother-in-law, the Rock Island Lumber Company of Illinois.[42]

40 *Cong. Globe*, 35th Cong., 2nd Sess., App., 210, 211; San Francisco correspondence in N. Y. *Weekly Tribune*, November 27, 1858.
41 Osgood, *The Day of the Cattleman*, 26, 27.
42 Greeley, *Overland Journey*, 195; Washington Department of Social Security, *Told by the Pioneers*, 155, 195, 211, etc.; R. S. Lillard, *The Great American Forest*, 180 ff., 197 ff.

Capital, in fact, found fertile fields in a hundred directions: in forming the San Francisco Gas Company to light the Western metropolis after 1854 with coal gas; in bringing cargoes of oysters and other shellfish from Puget Sound to Pacific Coast ports; in a huge business of freighting and supply for Indian-fighting troops; in Sacramento's thriving manufactories of California saddles, carriages, and wagons; in the production of California wine and Oregon cider; in the newspapers that sprang up everywhere—Kansas listing thirteen prosperous sheets by the spring of 1858; [43] and indeed, in everything from theatrical troupes to cemetery companies. Congress in 1858 authorized the publication of a digest of manufacturing statistics. As presented soon afterward, the report showed that California on June 1, 1856, had more than a thousand manufacturing establishments, employing almost four thousand hands, and with an annual product worth almost fourteen millions. Her manufactures were already of greater value than those of any Southern (not border) State except Virginia. Even Oregon had fifty-two manufacturing establishments with an annual production much greater than those of Texas, and not far below Mississippi's; even Utah and New Mexico had together thirty-seven manufactories.[44]

Was Minnesota exclusively agricultural? "Two years ago," wrote her first commissioner of statistics in 1860, "Minnesota imported flour to supply the deficiencies in her own product. She has now probably one hundred and forty grist mills." Some of these mills were large, their shipments were growing, and the quality of the flour rivaled the best eastern brands. The new State had plough factories, whiskey distilleries, and breweries. On the St. Croix alone, twenty sawmills cut nearly seventy-five million feet of lumber. The commissioner included a section on the beneficial results of the panic of 1857. Chief of these, stemming in part from a reduction of prices and interest rates and from the stoppage of useless speculation in town lots, was an increase in the active capital of the region. As living costs had declined, the relative profits of industry had increased.[45] And was Utah exclusively agricultural? In the Christmas Day edition of the *Deseret News* in 1852 Brigham Young had written of new pottery and leather works, of an iron industry getting under way in Iron County, of a woolen mill already running, and of plans for a sugar factory. Sugar-making machinery was bought by the Deseret Manufacturing Company in England, landed in New Orleans, and sent by steamboat to Leavenworth. There it was loaded on fifty special wagons drawn by two hundred yoke of oxen. Though five months were needed to drag the equipment to Salt

---

43 N. Y. *Herald*, April 25, 1858. The Portland *Oregonian* was begun December 4, 1850.
44 For the remarkable water-power development of the fifties in Wisconsin, operating grist mills, sawmills, a sash and door works, and an ironworks, see Joseph Schaefer, *Wisconsin Magazine of History*, December, 1934. The Sacramento *Union* for July, 1858, has a series of articles on manufacturing in that city.
45 *Report*, Chs. 8, 12.

Lake City, before the end of 1853 the factory was ready. Beet-sugar making, at first a failure, became eventually a basic industry of Utah.[46]

Above all, the West required transportation. Even California by the end of 1861 had built three hundred and forty-three miles of railroad, a good deal more than Illinois had possessed ten years earlier. The Pacific Mail Steamship Company had been organized in 1847–48 with an outlook that many business-men thought dubious. Could its steamers find an adequate annual traffic? While the first, the *California*, was on her way to the West Coast, full news of the gold discoveries arrived. The vessel had no sooner reached Panama going north-ward than she found a clamorous multitude of gold-seekers waiting to get aboard; and the *Oregon* and *Panama*, following her, were equally crowded. The service had to be rapidly expanded. Late in the fifties, the ships *Adriatic*, *Atlantic*, and *Baltic* of the Collins Line, bought jointly by the Pacific Mail and the Panama Railroad from Brown Brothers & Co., were used to establish a line between New York and the Isthmus. As Brown Brothers took payment in Pacific Mail stock, the company secured the backing of one of the strongest banking houses in the country. Its capital was increased to four millions in 1860. By that date it was a political as well as commercial power, looking forward to the opening of a rich trade with the Orient.[47]

Western river steamboating on the Sacramento, Columbia, and lesser streams was another field for enterprise and investment. Here were conditions far different from those of the slow-rolling Mississippi and placid, well-settled Ohio. The Columbia in particular, fed by Canadian snows and the turbulent Snake and Salmon, offered a new setting for adventure: its majestic gorges, its white rapids and deep dark stretches, its thunderous falls and the solid green of its pines, inspired many rivermen with a lifelong passion. The angry con-flicts of rival steamboat owners, the Indian uprisings, the lawlessness attendant on the abortive gold rushes into the upper valleys of the Snake and Clear-water, and the perils of flood and forest broke many a man; but the steamboat was indispensable to the rise of Portland, Dalles City, and other towns.[48]

One of the features of the industry was its tendency toward monopolistic practices. A combination of steamboat owners plying San Francisco Bay and the inland rivers organized early in 1854 the California Steam Navigation Com-pany, which controlled passenger and freight business—despite many attempts to institute competition—for the ensuing fifteen years.[49] Its profits were nat-

---

46 Nels Anderson, *Desert Saints: the Mormon Frontier in Utah*, 135. The first California refinery was opened by the San Francisco & Pacific Sugar Company, with a capital of $800,000 in 1855. T. F. Cronise, *National Wealth of California*, 608.
47 F. N. Otis, *Isthmus of Panama and Its Commercial Connections*, 149 ff.
48 See the vivid novel by Nard Jones, *Swift Flows the River* (1940).
49 Hittell, *California*, III, 49, 426, 427; H. D. Hubbard, *Building the Heart of an Empire*.

urally enormous. During the eighteen-fifties, the Columbia River was the scene of strenuous activity by numerous small vessels. Then in 1860 the Oregon Steam Navigation Company, pooling a dozen steamboats, was established. Next year it carried some ten thousand five hundred passengers and nearly six thousand three hundred tons of freight between Portland and Dalles; and Indian wars and Idaho mining soon increased its business. It, too, long had a monopoly and made handsome profits—but service was good and its rates did not seem exorbitant.[50]

On the Missouri and its tributaries, as elsewhere, the great days of steamboating lasted until the Civil War. As for the Mississippi, the traffic on the upper reaches of the river, sustained by immigrant travel, quite rivalled that on the lower. The number of steamboat arrivals at upper ports in 1860 almost equalled those of the lower Mississippi, Missouri, Ohio, Illinois, Tennessee, Cumberland and Arkansas rivers combined.[51]

When the whole story of the West is reviewed, much can be said for the thesis that after 1850 its fundamental conditions developed corporate activity on an equal footing with individual effort, and favored the capitalist rather more than the poor man. Mining, whether of iron, coal, copper, silver, gold, or lead, was most profitably carried on by well-financed companies. Railroad-building across the broad plains and into mountain fastnesses was impossible without capital resources, experienced technical skill, and astute business management. Government land policies gave the speculator a fertile opportunity. Ranching in the Southwest offered young Hotspurs a life in which they might find freedom and fortune; but even here the corporation could be a profitable device, as eastern and British capitalists would shortly recognize. The lands beyond the Missouri, full of untouched wealth, beckoned to the hardy farmer, cattleman, and prospector. They beckoned quite as vigorously to the mining-company organizer, town projector, lumber magnate, railroad entrepreneur, and manufacturer in primary industries.

[VI]

As Kansas moved toward statehood, as Oregon and Minnesota entered the Union, as Colorado and Nevada valleys filled with treasure-hunters, and as California in 1860 reached a population of nearly four hundred thousand, the problem of Western communications grew urgent. Until the end of the decade, the Pacific Railroad debate continued sterile. Four routes, examined in detail by expert Federal surveys, had been pronounced practicable. Each had its sedu-

50 Randall V. Mills, *Stern Wheelers up Columbia*, Ch. 4.
51 W. J. Peterson, *Steamboating on the Upper Mississippi 1823-1861*.

lous proponents, and but for sectional rivalry and the slavery issue agreement might easily have been reached on one or even two. The northernmost ran from St. Paul to Puget Sound, the southernmost from New Orleans along a line near the Thirty-second parallel to the Gila River and San Diego. Putting them both aside, Congress could well have fixed upon either the line from the Platte River by way of Great Salt Lake and the Humboldt Valley into California near the Forty-first parallel, or the line from Memphis and Fort Smith through Albuquerque to the coast near the Thirty-fifth parallel. But the lion of sectional jealousy stood in the way.

While men waited, mining discoveries helped to tip the balance. The Nevada gold rush threw a pier of population eastward from central California toward Salt Lake City. More importantly, the Pike's Peak fever threw another pier into central Colorado. The freight and passenger business with Denver-Auraria would obviously help any transcontinental line pay its way. Henry Villard wrote that the prime consequence of the Rocky Mountain rush of 1859 was its influence upon the choice of a railway and telegraph route. "The result of the mining season of 1860 in the Pike's Peak gold regions will definitely settle the long-mooted question of their location and construction. In less than twelve months, no sane mind will doubt the certainty that the first chain of iron and wire, that will render the circulation of the life-blood of our great Republic through the agricultural, industrial, and commercial systems of all its parts, possible and perfect, will be strung across that portion of the Rocky Mountains that has lately been found to abound in mineral wealth." [52]

Only lesser projects could as yet be pushed to fruition, but several were spectacular. Wagon roads became more and more important. The Santa Fé Trail and Oregon Trail, with various alternatives and cut-offs, grew into busy highways. Freighting firms sprang into existence. The largest—Russell, Majors & Waddell—was from 1855 to the Civil War perhaps the most important single business agency in the trans-Missouri West. It sprang to greatness when the government awarded the partners contract after contract for transporting military supplies. Thus, early in 1855, they gained a two-year monopoly of carrying all such stores beyond the Missouri, built offices, warehouses, and shops at Leavenworth, opened a sawmill, lumberyard, and meat-packing plant, and hired a small army of employees. By summer they had five hundred wagons (which alone represented an investment of nearly $400,000), with seven thousand five hundred oxen, and one thousand seven hundred workers. A renewal

---

[52] Villard, *Past and Present of the Pike's Peak Gold Regions*, 147. This statement may be regarded as part of a well-planned propaganda campaign. Actually, when the first transcontinental was built it passed a hundred miles north of Denver, through Cheyenne; though Denver leaders quickly constructed a line connecting with the Union Pacific (1870). See Herbert O. Brayer, "History of Colorado Railroads," in L. R. Hafen, ed., *Colorado*, II.

of the contract early in 1857 gave them a monopoly on the carriage of up to five million pounds of military goods that year. Then, when the expedition against the Mormons took shape, the military authorities served notice that they would have to carry three million extra pounds of supplies to Utah. This was a low estimate. When the army left for Utah, forty-one trains (normally twenty-six wagons each) were scheduled to accompany it with more than four and a half million pounds of supplies.[53]

By 1858 the firm employed four thousand men, and used forty thousand oxen in hauling its three thousand five hundred covered wagons. Army posts, mining camps, and trappers were all dependent on its exertions. The light, strong vehicles, made of white oak, iron-tired, and covered with white osnaburg stretched over hickory bows, could carry five thousand pounds over rough country. Regulations for the bull-whackers stated bluntly (and the rule was enforced), "Swearing, gambling, and intemperance will not be allowed, either in camp or on the plains." Trains moved on a rigid time schedule. Sabbath was observed. At nightfall the wagons formed a circular corral, within which the oxen were turned loose. It is not strange that the "empire on wheels" which Russell, Majors & Waddell built up was treated with great respect. The notes and drafts of the firm were regarded as the equivalent of gold. In Missouri, Kansas, and Nebraska, farmers and stockmen blessed them for their purchases of cattle, hogs, grain, and other products. In every plains fort or mountain camp their wagons were hailed as indispensable to life and comfort. They made Lexington, their first depot, and Leavenworth and Kansas City, their subsequent eastern headquarters, important centers of retail and wholesale trade. It was natural that when the Cherry Creek discoveries brought population flocking into Colorado, William H. Russell should organize (February, 1859) the Leavenworth & Pike's Peak Express Company, with a thousand Kentucky mules and fifty new Concord coaches to operate between the Missouri and Denver. His store and office in the new settlement were the most important business places in Colorado. Alas for the venture! When the surface gold was exhausted, traffic to and from the mountains sank below profitable levels, and as in their work for the army in Utah, the partners suffered heavy losses.

Other firms, while not comparing with Russell, Majors & Waddell, did useful transport service. In 1860, according to the *American Railway Times*, sixty-eight thousand oxen, eight thousand mules, six thousand nine hundred wagons, and about twelve thousand men were employed in freighting in the Far West.[54] Demand for a direct mail road to California, with enough way

53 M. L. and R. W. Settle, *Empire on Wheels*, 17 ff.
54 January 21, 1861.

stations to change horses frequently, became clamorous. Once more sectional jealousy arose. The South stood adamant against a central highway through South Pass as likely to draw the Pacific Railroad after it. A compromise had to be arranged, and Congress appropriated money for various bits of road-building. The War Department in 1858 pushed work on a military road from Fort Smith through Albuquerque to the Colorado, and, in connection with the Mormon operations, greatly improved the roads from Fort Bridger into central Utah. The Interior Department in 1859 completed a road from Fort Kearny through South Pass to Honey Lake, which emigrants found highly useful.[55]

One road survey involved a long-remembered experiment with camels. Lieutenant Edward F. Beale, a Mexican War veteran, was deputed to explore the ground for a wagon road from Albuquerque (Fort Defiance) due west, or nearly so, to California; and he decided to test the desert animal. The idea was an old one; Congress had sanctioned action, and a number of camels had been landed in Texas in 1856-57. Beale picked up twenty-odd camels, with three dromedaries, at San Antonio, loaded them with grain for mules, and covered the thousand miles and more to Albuquerque in forty-five days. Thence he set out (August 28, 1857) for the coast. His journey took him across grassy plains, along the bottom lands of the Little Colorado, over the forested San Francisco Mountain, and across the Colorado River, which the camels swam with ease. Traversing desert sands to the Mohave, and threading more mountains, they reached Los Angeles. Beale was enthusiastic. The camels, he reported, had walked unhurt over ground covered with sharp volcanic rocks, had borne heavy packs up precipitous stretches which unladen mules found difficult, and had carried water for a week at a time without swallowing a drop. They could live on herbage too coarse and scanty for mules, oxen, or horses.[56] In the end, however, most of the camels went to circuses and zoos.

Mail service to the West, too, could be improved. Californians had been glad since 1850 to get monthly mails by way of Independence and Santa Fé, or later through Independence, Salt Lake, and Placerville. They had also rejoiced in semi-monthly mails via Panama, Nicaragua, or Tehuantepec, and the signal gun announcing the mail steamer brought thousands flocking to the San Francisco wharves. During the Mormon War the Independence-Salt Lake-Placerville mail was put for a time on a weekly basis, and then reduced to semi-monthly status.[57] Meanwhile the hearts of Californians were brightened by the announcement of semi-weekly overland mails. At a late hour of the session which expired with Pierce's Administration, Congress provided $600,000

55 Report, Secretary of War, 1858; Report, Secretary of the Interior, 1859.
56 N. Y. *Tribune*, January 24, 1858; House Exec. Doc. 124, 35th Cong., 1st Sess.
57 Report, Postmaster-General, 1858.

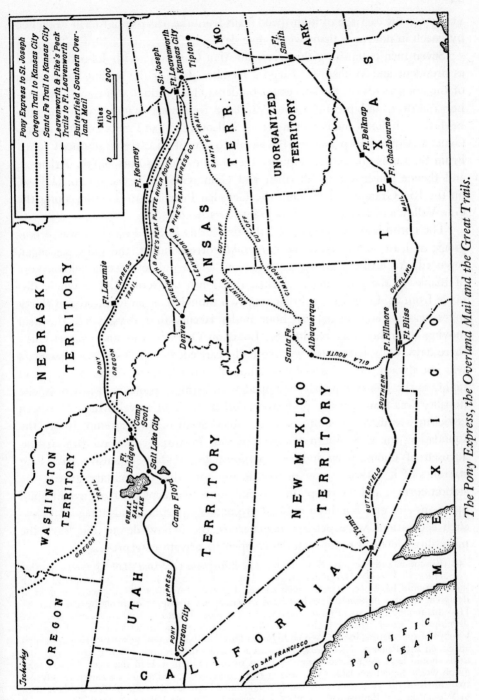

The Pony Express, the Overland Mail and the Great Trails.

yearly for the carriage of high-speed mails from the Mississippi to San Francisco by coach in not more than twenty-five days.

Seven men comprising the Overland Mail Company, with John Butterfield as president and William G. Fargo a member—two of the leading expressmen of the country—were the successful bidders. The contract was signed September 16, 1857, and precisely one year later four-horse stages started simultaneously with pomp and ceremony from St. Louis and San Francisco. Postmaster-General Brown had persuaded Buchanan to accept an extreme southern route. From St. Louis (or rather Tipton) the coaches ran to Fort Smith, Arkansas, and thence southwest to Sherman and Gainesville in Texas, on to El Paso, up the Rio Grande and through the Gadsden Purchase to Tucson, along the Gila Valley and across the Colorado into Los Angeles.[58]

The enthusiasm which greeted the first mails in San Francisco was prodigious; at least so the New York *Herald* correspondent, the only passenger, reported. An artillery salute, a procession, and a public meeting with a vote of thanks to the government marked that tenth of October. The whole distance from St. Louis to San Francisco, two thousand seven hundred and thirty miles, was covered in half an hour under twenty-four days, while the mail moving the other way reached St. Louis on October 9 in just over twenty-three days. Only letter mail was regularly carried; the space for six passengers was not always filled, especially westbound. Indeed, as the stages ran day and night, as the line was poorly equipped with eating stations, and as Comanche hostility was feared, many preferred another mode of travel. Much Northern criticism was directed at the "oxbow route" as an obvious attempt to lay the foundation for a Southern Pacific railroad. Postmaster-General Brown was accused of choosing an indirect, perilous, and unduly expensive line, long stretches of it without water or hay, in the hope that the military guards, the station corrals, and the temptation to emigrants to accept the road would build up towns and give Southern railroad promoters an artificial advantage.[59] While such accusations were perhaps ungenerous, the oxbow detour did leave the more direct central route temptingly open to private enterprise.

58 Roscoe P. and Margaret B. Conkling, *The Butterfield Overland Mail, 1857–1869, passim.*
59 *Harper's Weekly*, December 11, 1858. The N. Y. *Tribune* held that the overland coach service should have been started much sooner. For ten years after the discovery of gold, it declared, about a million a year had been expended on transport of mails by the Isthmus. Had this money been spent on mail service by the most direct overland route, it would have developed a great natural highway across the continent, with settlements and stations. Groups of speculators, including men high in office, had been intent in squandering appropriations on the Panama, Nicaragua, Tehuantepec, and other routes; whereas from 1849 on, mails should have gone direct from St. Louis to San Francisco. Had this been done, a telegraph would have been laid, a safe wagon road constructed, and stages set running daily for two-thirds of the year. And how much would have been saved to the pioneers! Many men in Wisconsin and Illinois had travelled a thousand miles east before undertaking the seven thousand mile sea voyage. N. Y. *Weekly Tribune*, October 16, 1858.

The Overland Mail continued with almost clocklike regularity, its great Concord coaches, staunchly built and swung on leather thoroughbraces instead of springs, with four to six sturdy horses or mules to draw them, sometimes making a hundred miles in twenty-four hours. When winter came on, the El Paso-Tucson route unquestionably had its advantages. But men West and East were irritated by Postmaster-General Brown's assertion that the southern road was alone feasible for all-season travel. Californians doubted this; so did Kansans; and Senator Gwin found it easy to persuade William H. Russell to prove the practicability of the central route. The result was the launching of the Pony Express. In the hope of gaining a lucrative mail contract, Russell and his partners set to work, began hiring fleet horses, riders, and agents, and announced that on April 3, 1860, they would begin a fast service between St. Joseph, Missouri, and Sacramento. They were as good as their word. On the appointed day a rider in the Missouri town sprang into his saddle after the mayor had fastened to it a pouch with forty-nine letters and five telegrams. Amid wild cheers he galloped off to the westward, while far away in San Francisco another mail was started east.[60]

For the eighteen months that the Pony Express continued in operation it was an institution which touched the imagination of the American people. Stations were equipped at fifteen-mile intervals; some one hundred and fifty wiry Indian ponies were kept in readiness; hardy light-weight riders, in darkness or daylight, in storm or sunshine, in peace or amid hostile savages, covered each his stage of seventy-five miles. At first weekly, the service soon became semi-weekly. At every junction point, a fresh rider had just two minutes to fasten the mailbag to his saddle and be off. If a carrier failed to come through, his replacement pushed on empty-handed with the news, which was carried from point to point to the ultimate destination. Fort Kearny, Fort Laramie, South Pass, Fort Bridger, Salt Lake City—this part of the route kept close to the familiar Oregon and California Trail. Then from the southern end of Great Salt Lake the riders pushed through Fort Churchill, Carson City, and Placerville to Sacramento. Americans thrilled to learn of the speed records set. News of Lincoln's election was carried from Fort Kearny to Fort Churchill in six days. The dauntless determination of the riders to get the mail through impressed the nation.

[VII]

If in its practical aspects the Pony Express experiment left something to be desired (for it cost Russell, Majors & Waddell a ruinous sum, while no demon-

60 G. D. Bradley, *The Pony Express*; Leroy Hafen, *The Overland Mail, 1859-1869.*

stration of the feasibility of the central railroad route was needed), in its exemplification of the spirit of the expanding West it was a memorable undertaking. It expressed the enterprise that was converting so much of empty plain and savage mountain into populous and wealthy communities, and that within a dozen years after the peace with Mexico brought four rich trans-Mississippi States into the Union. It was saddening to turn from the boundless constructive energy shown in the West to the dreary quarrel over slavery; a quarrel which, in its failure to achieve any forward constructive steps, contrasted so markedly with the vigorous nation-building beyond the Missouri. And yet it was impossible to look at the West without seeing that its conditions threw light upon the sectional conflict.

For three salient facts stood out in any survey of the Far West. First, this land of plain and peak was natural soil for a free-spirited and highly competitive society, demanding of every resident skill and intelligence. It was, therefore, even in that Gadsden Purchase country which had been bought at the behest of the slave States, a country naturally inhospitable to slavery. Second, when so much energy was steadily flowing into western expansion, and such wide outlets for more effort existed there, it was impossible to think of the country turning to Caribbean areas for a heavy thrust southward. Its main forces moved naturally toward the sunset, where rich opportunities were hardly yet sampled. The cotton kingdom, which realized that the West gave little scope for its peculiar culture, might plan grandiose Latin American adventures; but it would get little support from other regions. And in the third place, conditions in the West demanded capital and organization on a broad scale; if it was a land for individualists, it was even more a land for corporate enterprise—a land for the businessman. Those who pondered these three facts could see that they held an ominous meaning for the South. The nearer Northwest had already done much to upset the old sectional balance, and the Far West, as it filled up, would do still more. Here was a population fronting the future:

Fresh and strong the world we seize, world of labor and the march.

Douglas Under Challenge

EARLY IN August of 1858 Americans felt a thrill of pride to learn of the latest triumph of their inventive genius, the laying of the Atlantic cable. An American and a British warship, the *Niagara* and the *Agamemnon,* had met in mid-ocean the previous month. After dividing the huge coils, they had proceeded in opposite directions; and one end was soon ashore in Newfoundland, the other in Ireland. While there was credit enough for both nations, the inventor Morse and the indomitable organizer Cyrus W. Field deserved special honor. Surely, wrote Benjamin Moran of the American legation in London, "those who accomplished the work of uniting at a throb people divided three thousand miles by ocean have done more for mankind than Alexander and Napoleon." On August 16, President Buchanan and Queen Victoria exchanged congratulations. Alas, service was soon interrupted—but men knew that human ingenuity would shortly perfect this abbreviation of time and space.

This peaceable achievement was the more welcome because, but three months earlier, the United States and Britain had seemed uncomfortably near a breach of relations. British vessels in the Caribbean, commanded by officers excessively eager to stop the slaving business, had begun to board and search vessels flying the stars and stripes. "These aggressions are intolerable," Seward had told the Senate on May 17. "Already eleven vessels have been fired upon in the Gulf of Mexico." Toombs and Stephens, incensed by the first reports, had gone to the White House and urged Buchanan to send a squadron to hunt down the British offenders and seize or sink them. The President, keeping quite cool, had said that he would ask for reparations and then act if they were denied. "Let England have the onus of asking explanations," exclaimed Stephens. "Our flag is insulted and it ought to be resented on the spot. . . . This is the time to act." He and Toombs, staying until near midnight, had made it clear that they actually wanted a war with England. Stephens believed that such a war would stop the sectional quarrel—as Seward was to believe in 1861. "I thought it the most fortunate thing that could have happened to unite the heart of the entire people of the United States and to put down all sectional parties," he wrote his brother Linton. But Buchanan had wisely insisted on a peaceful course, and had easily achieved a complete victory, Lord Malmesbury at the Foreign Office assuring the United States that Great Britain accepted all the principles laid down in the American protest.

The President was able to leave for a short vacation at Bedford Springs without fear of foreign embroilments. Senator Seward, returning to his beloved Auburn, meanwhile diverted central New York by entertaining Lord and Lady Napier and Count Sartiges there, while Jefferson Davis, his health impaired, pleased New Englanders by sojourning amid the cool Maine breezes.

Surely the country, with prosperity returning and the foreign skies clear, could sit down in hope and serenity. Farsighted men, unfortunately, did not think so. They knew that without some change in the spirit of both North and South, the lull was but a truce. Slavery and freesoil, Governor Adams of South Carolina had said, can never be reconciled. We must separate, Edmund Ruffin kept writing his friends—and the sooner we do it the greater the relative weight of the South. Garrison, Theodore Parker, and Wendell Phillips were publicly stating that a bloody termination of the struggle was at hand.[1]

In view of all the trends of nineteenth century civilization, the terrible problem of slavery could be given a final solution only upon the principle which Washington, Jefferson, and Clay had espoused: the principle of gradual emancipation. Obviously, this settlement could not be reached at one stride. It must be achieved by degrees. The first step was to stop the expansion of slavery, and to confine that institution within the fifteen States it already possessed. Such a decision would be equivalent to a decree that slavery was marked for gradual evolution into a higher labor system. Slavery contained would be slavery under sentence of slow death. The second step would be the termination of slavery in the border States. Missouri by 1859 stood near the verge of emancipation. Every advance in the industrialization of the State, every wave of German, British, and eastern immigrants, brought the step nearer. Delaware should soon be a free State. Kentucky had a strong body of ultimate emancipationists. Once the number of slave States was reduced to twelve, and that of the free States proportionately augmented, the fate of slavery would be clear.

The great hope was that if the South could be educated to accept the principle of friendly containment, it would be willing to consider plans for gradual compensated emancipation. When it was ready to entertain such plans, surely a Northern party would arise to offer them. Webster's proposal for using the entire proceeds of the public lands; Clay's hope that emancipation might be

1 N. Y. *Tribune*, September 22, 1858; J. H. Adams, Message No. 1, November 24, 1856; Garrison, *William Lloyd Garrison*, III, Chs. 14-18. For Stephens's course above, see his letters to Linton Stephens, June 1, June 10, 1858; Stephens Papers, Manhattanville.

combined with some measure of colonization abroad; Olmsted's plan for letting the best-equipped Negroes earn their freedom; the Stafford House suggestion that the South educate the Negroes, sanction marriages, and protect slave families——all had elements of statesmanship. Most Northern Democrats would be willing to support a constructive scheme; such moderate Republicans as Hamilton Fish, Lyman Trumbull, Edward Bates, and Abraham Lincoln would certainly do so. But would the South ever ask for aid in giving its peculiar institution a progressive character?

Two groups were aligned against this hopeful possibility that slavery might first be immobilized, then subjected to attrition at the margin, and finally helped by money and migration to evolve into a free labor system. They stood at opposite poles.

One group was the abolitionists and radical Republicans, who wished emancipation attained in a hurry—and many of whom, men of malicious temper, wanted to hurt the South. They thought that the Negro could step from slavery to equality as a man steps from a dungeon into a bright parlor. They did not realize what a dim maze of corridors, anterooms, and halfway apartments lay between. Ever since Birney and Garrison began their intemperate crusade, the abolitionists had accepted a fearful responsibility before history. Now Garrison, Phillips, Higginson, and Theodore Parker seemed positively exulting in talk of disruption, battle, and bloodshed. These men neither knew nor cared anything about the vital question of race adjustment. To most of them it did not exist. The black man, once emancipated, would almost instantly become in all but color a white man; so the *Liberator* and *Independent* implied.

The other group were the Southern extremists, the fire-eaters represented by Yancey, Keitt, Rhett, Porcher Miles, A. G. Brown, Slidell, and Jacob Thompson —a group every month more numerous and influential. They were strongest where Negro population was densest; not so much because slavery was most profitable there as because the problem of race adjustment was most difficult and Negro subordination seemed most imperative. These two groups of extremists were reinforced by politicians whipping up fear and prejudice for votes, editors mongering hate for subscriptions, and millions of devotees of Drift.

The tragic fact was that extremists always possessed the power to catch up the ball and carry it into scrimmage. When the Kansas ball failed, some other would do. Garrison at Framingham on July 4, 1854, burning the Constitution and exclaiming, "So perish all compromises with tyranny!"—Wendell Phillips writing that the Union must sever, and "It is now with nine-tenths only a question of time"—were apparently harmless except to irritate. But John Brown was to give violent application to their preachments upon blood. If the development of the West proved anything, it was that American capital and energy found such broad fields for activity there that Caribbean adventures seemed preposterous. Yet Southern extremists demanded Caribbean grabs and forays. If the growth of the West proved another fact, it was that free institutions must dominate the Terriories of the region and that slavery could never take root in them. Yet the Charleston *News* and Richmond *Enquirer* were raising the sinister demand for a Federal slave code in the Territories and declaring that it must be made the issue in 1860.

Congressional debates had done little to turn men's minds toward a constructive solution. If hope for reason, common sense, and imagination existed anywhere, it was in the Northwest, with its mingled Southern and Northern stocks, practical temper, divorcement from fettering traditions, and idealism. On the prairies of Illinois this summer, a resounding debate on national issues was to take place. Would it point to some road out of the labyrinth, away from the youth-devouring Minotaur of civil war?

[I]

The Douglas of 1858 was a different man from the Douglas who had visited Europe in 1853 to shake off his grief over the death of his first wife. Since in personal affairs he was reticent, writing few letters and confining them to politics and business, we know little of his inner life. But it is evident that his bereavement had been a heavy blow, throwing him for a time into dissipated ways; evident also that his love for Adèle Cutts was an elevating influence and that his marriage restored a lost harmony to his existence. His ambition had been at low ebb in 1855–56; it reawakened when in 1857 he found his wife ready to dispute with Harriet Lane the social primacy of Washington.

His political experience during these years, too, had done much to mature him. With him, the line between rapid decision and recklessness was thin; he had crossed it in 1854, and from the ensuing storm he had emerged with a deeper respect for the convictions of the people of Illinois. Fighting heavy battles in the Senate and on the prairies, he had gained education from the blows he took. If his ambition was to be gratified, he could not flout the sentiment of the growing body of freesoil Democrats in the North.

Above all, Douglas had found his experience with the Southern Democrats a maturing and disillusioning process. How confident he had been in 1854 of a mutually profitable partnership—how sanguine two years later of a friendly alliance—how nonplussed to find Buchanan taken prisoner by Cobb, Thompson, and Slidell—how shocked to discover behind the Lecompton imposture a game of rule or ruin!

Still a young man, only forty-five in the spring of 1858, still using his gifts to educate himself, the Chicagoan was steadily becoming less of a politician and more of a statesman. He had always had a statesmanlike eye to large objects. Only two weeks after he had obtained his license to practice law in Jacksonville, Illinois, he had risen before a large Democratic meeting to fling forth his defense of Jacksonian principles: government by the people, and the expanding role of the republic. The enthusiasm had been intense. He had spoken with heat, and he awoke next day to find himself famous in his prairie world. From these first-enunciated principles he had never deviated. Popular government and national expansion had remained his Arcturus and Aldebaran. He instinctively trusted the people he saw about him. And why not? Some of them were Yankees like himself, some were Southerners, and many were from the Middle States, but they made up a folk of hard sense and sturdy character. The Illinoisans were a self-reliant, honest-minded stock which in one generation developed Lincoln, Douglas, Grant, Trumbull, Yates, Koerner, McCormick, Ogden, Logan, Medill, and David Davis—a proud record for a raw new State.

Let the voice of the people rule! Douglas had never believed that less than the boundless continent could suffice as a theater for American energies. Opposing settlement with England on the Forty-ninth parallel, opposing Trist's peace with Mexico, opposing the pledge in the Clayton-Bulwer Treaty never to annex or colonize any part of Central America, incessantly calling for an honorable acquisition of Cuba, he had made it plain that he wished to see all North America under the starry banner. Make new Territories, carry the flag forward, build railroads, improve harbors, homestead the land, preserve liberty, free the Western Hemisphere from the Old World, and trust to the people—this was his national plan.

As he grew older, he thought less of expediency and more of principle. Looking back, he could see that his championship of the Compromise of 1850 had been based on principle—and it had been a resounding success; his championship of Kansas-Nebraska had been based on expediency—and it was a many-sided failure. Undoubtedly this strengthened his instinctive feeling that principle, in the long run, paid. Yet he was also becoming devoted to principle for its own sake. Some opponents declared that he had fought Lecompton because he saw that otherwise he could never be reelected to the Senate. They did Douglas an injustice. Too powerful to be downed by one blow, he did not overvalue his Senate seat. What he did value was his honor; and Lecompton dishonored the basic doctrine of his political faith—popular sovereignty. He was now showing an increasing adherence to the Jacksonian principle of the Union. As secession lifted its head among Southern extremists, he was to stab and hack at what he considered a dangerous monster.

By the late spring of 1858, he could feel that as a champion of honesty and democratic principle he had won a memorable triumph over the Directory. The Lecompton constitution was as dead as the Yazoo Fraud. His victory was a moral triumph not the less sweet because it was his first thoroughly creditable success since, in the fall of 1850, he had forced the Chicago city council to turn about-face on the Compromise.

But what of the Democratic future? The party had won the narrowest of victories in 1856 when fully united. With Republican strength rising and with the last vestiges of the Whig and American parties slowly disappearing, the Democrats faced certain defeat in 1860 unless they healed their schism. Unfortunately for the party, Douglas and the Administration regarded the problem of unity from divergent standpoints. To Douglas, reconciliation on the basis of popular sovereignty and expansion seemed logical. Let him return to the Senate for six years, let old quarrels be forgotten, and let the party march forward under the banners of Manifest Destiny so popular with most Southerners, and popular control over local institutions so dear to Northern Democrats. To Buchanan and the Directory, however, discipline was the watchword. The Washington *Union* laid down the doctrine that every Democrat must acquiesce in party decisions on great questions, such as the Bank of the United States under Jackson, Texas under Polk, and Lecompton and the English bill under Buchanan.[2] The way to restore the unity of the party was to purge it of traitors and to crush all ideas conflicting with the Dred Scott decision.

The divergence was ineluctable and vital. Douglas had to stick by his principles, not only because they were his breath of life, but because if he did not, half the Northern Democrats would desert to the Republican banner. Cobb, Thompson, Floyd, and Slidell, controlling the President, could not yield to Douglas because that would make him master of the party and logical candidate for 1860; because, too, his type of popular sovereignty meant the containment of slavery, so far as existing American territory went, just as surely as the Republican platform meant it. The breach was unavoidable.

As always in such affairs, personal antipathies deeply tinged the quarrel. Buchanan knew that Douglas regarded him with contempt; Cobb, Thompson, and Floyd knew that Douglas thought them potential traitors. For his part, the Illinoisan was aware that aloof Southern leaders mistook him for a bumptious, ill-mannered upstart. Their talk of him as a recusant, a Benedict Arnold, rankled in his mind. If Jefferson Davis or R. M. T. Hunter could get elected to the Presidency, either man would give Douglas and his friends short shrift. If Douglas were elected, everyone knew that he would make an imperious, self-willed President, that he would fight disunion as Jackson had fought it, and that while he might favor Wise, Stephens, Breckinridge, and a few others who had treated

2 September 1, 1858.

him fairly, the Southerners about Buchanan would walk the plank without mercy. Senator Green of Missouri wrote a friend that Slidell had burned during the winter of 1857–58 to drive Douglas from the party, and that "the Slidell clique" controlled Buchanan and the Senate caucus.[3]

Meanwhile, Douglas had to think of his own seat and his own State, where political war was raging. It was the Directory which had begun the war. It did not have any really compelling reason to oppose his reelection by the Illinois legislature, which would be chosen in the fall and would select a Senator the ensuing January; yet all spring it had been busy trying to undermine him.[4]

The Administration adherents in Illinois, nearly all men presently or prospectively fed from the public crib, were a crew that Douglas detested. Chief among them was Isaac Cook, postmaster of Chicago, who dispensed postmasterships, mail contracts, and postal advertising for political effect, kept in close touch with Washington, and wrote frequently to Buchanan. We have mentioned his associate (and later rival), Charles Leib, Federal mail agent for the State, whose talent for intrigue roused Douglas's special scorn. Leib, a jack of many trades, sometime doctor, lawyer, liquor dealer, Mormon, and an adherent of Jim Lane in Kansas, was a Dugald Dalgetty of politics; Douglas knew that he had been busy for months helping organize the Buchanan machine, getting perquisites for his friends, and making furtive approaches to Republicans for an alliance against the Senator. The notorious John Calhoun, revisiting Springfield, lent the Buchanan men his hand, and so did lesser figures—ex-Governor John Reynolds, John Dougherty, and R. B. Carpenter, who handled large Federal building contracts. These *condottieri* had labored like mad, tempting local politicians with petty offices, trying to buy country editors with printing contracts, and putting every jobholder to work.[5]

They had done him some harm, Douglas knew; but none that he did not feel confident of repairing. The main body of Democrats, especially outside of "Egypt," had remained loyal to the Senator. When the State convention met in Springfield on April 21, just as the English bill was being whipped into shape,

---

3 Green's letter of September 29, 1858, to Judge Samuel Treat, throws light on the plot. He describes how Slidell had frequently reproached him the previous winter and spring for not joining the movement to oust Douglas. Slidell, Cobb, and Bright, he writes, were leagued together for the purpose. Representative Harris of Illinois had been informed in May that Floyd wanted peace because he feared the Douglas Democrats would join in the Republican hue and cry over his incapacity (or worse) in sale of army property at Fort Snelling and Wills Point. He heard too that Toucey and Black, who knew Northern sentiment, were for peace. "But Brown, Cobb, Thompson, and 'Old Obliquity' are for war." He added for the Douglas bloc in Congress: "We are quite indifferent which is chosen, and so tell them." As it would be stupid of the Administration to levy war, he expected them to do it. Green's letter is in the Treat Papers; that of Harris (May 8, 1858) in the Lanphier Papers.

4 For its course see H. S. Foote, *Casket of Reminiscences*, 135.

5 *Cong. Globe*, 35th Cong., 1st Sess., 3055–3058.

nine-tenths of the delegates were for Douglas. The Buchanan men, jeered and denounced, had fled from the hall. Peter Cartwright, roaring like a backwoods exhorter, had choken with the anger of his invective against the Administration tools. John A. McClernand, about to reenter Congress, had been made chairman of the platform committee, and his planks that upheld Douglas, the five anti-Lecompton Representives, and the popular sovereignty cause were carried with a shout. Amid unfeigned enthusiasm, the Senator had been renominated—and of the fifty-nine Democratic newspapers of the State, fifty-five had come down like an avalanche on his side.[6]

This had been a heartening event; and there had been nothing in subsequent Buchananite maneuvering in Illinois to alarm Douglas. To be sure, from the moment the Senator voted against the English bill early in May, Buchanan's weakly resentful attitude had been fixed. He had thought the Senator's course ruinous both to party and country. Had the measure been defeated, he wrote, the country would have been left in a terrible condition; national integrity would have been shaken to its center.[7] The Washington *Union*, in a broadside on May 27, had announced that the Administration would regard Douglas as an outcast.

Perhaps one element in fanning the anger of the Directory was a spiteful story which a Missouri politician, Isaac Sturgeon, a Treasury official in St. Louis, had sent to Washington on May 5. He asserted, with circumstantial detail, that Douglas had assured Frank P. Blair, Jr., that he intended to join the Republicans in 1860. The story was absurd. Douglas meant to bend the Democratic Party to his principles, not abandon it; and the loquacious, bibulous Blair was noted for his ability to garble facts. Nevertheless, gossip regarding this alleged engagement soon filled Washington and Illinois. All summer and fall the question was to be hurled at Douglas: "What about your promise to Blair?" The *Union* charged that he was playing the same part in trying to hamstring the Democratic Party that Van Buren had played in 1848; and during June the tokens of Administration implacability had increased.

Douglas knew that the Administration—through Cobb, Thompson, and Brown—had pulled the strings for the Punch-and-Judy convention of National Democrats which, representing about half the counties of Illinois, met in Springfield on June 9 to organize an opposition. A full ticket for State offices had been nominated. John Dougherty, selected for State Treasurer, had told Lincoln that the Buchanan forces would run a man for every office in every county and district. "If you do this, the thing is settled—the battle is fought," exclaimed Lincoln. The clear evidence that some Buchanan men and some Republican

6 *Fulton Democrat* (Lewiston, Illinois) March-April, 1858.
7 July 31, 1858; Buchanan, *Works*, X, 224–225.

leaders were plotting to exchange advice, labor, and even votes, gave point to a bitter invective which Douglas uttered against Cook, Leib, and their aides just before Congress adjourned. What was this June convention of dissenters? he asked. The true Democratic Convention had been held in April. The cheap Federal placeholder Leib had been touring the State to say that the Administration authorized him to denounce every Democrat who had opposed Lecompton as false to his party. False to his party! Yet this agent Leib had been a member of Jim Lane's reckless Republican gang in Kansas, had done his best there to defeat the Democrats, and had embraced Buchanan's cause only when paid for his dirty work. By assiduous effort, said Douglas, he and his fellow conspirators, after having been voted down twenty to one, had gotten up their convention of jobholders and lickspittles. Their aim was to split the Democratic vote and throw the next Illinois legislature to the Republicans.

Douglas, journeying homeward as the summer of 1858 began, was sanguine that he could prevent this calamity. With all his latent pugnacity aroused, he was prepared to fight desperately for return to the Senate—for popular vindication. Heavy expenses had to be met: travel, campaign quarters, posters, pamphlets, fireworks, marching-clubs' regalia, newspaper advertisements, speakers. Though financially straitened, with many notes outstanding and little income but his salary, he plunged yet deeper into debt. He mortgaged his Illinois property for $100,000, of which $40,000 went to discharge maturing debts, and the rest was for immediate use; according to some reports, he sold his Washington house; he borrowed $13,147 from a friend.[8] At the same time, he mustered all his energies. His health had suffered from the incessant anxieties and exertions of the past four years, from late hours, from occasional drinking, and from neglect of exercise, so that repeatedly he had confessed to the Senate that he was ailing. Fessenden had said at the close of 1856 that he was a dying man unless he mended. While this was exaggeration, onlookers had been struck by his weary if undaunted look.[9] But his fame, his national power, his hope of the Presidency were all at stake, and he intended to sacrifice every dollar and every ounce of strength rather than fail.

The Little Giant's arrival in Chicago on July 9 was a memorable event. All along his route he had met ovations. In Buffalo, followers gathered at the station; in Cleveland they cheered him lustily, with Rhodes, Payne, and Vallandigham in the reception committee, and Governor Salmon P. Chase seeking him for

---

8 Springfield *Republican*, July 27, 1858; Milton, *Eve of Conflict*, 307. The lien on his Chicago estate in 1864 exceeded $64,000; Johnson, *Douglas*, 383. In the first five months of the Congressional session of 1857–58 Douglas franked out 198,600 copies of his speeches, nearly twice as many as any other Senator, and three times as many as Seward. At a cost of $20 a thousand, this meant a bill of about $4,000. N. Y. *Weekly Tribune*, May 22, 1858.

9 Horace White, *Lyman Trumbull*, 89.

a conference; Ohio, Indiana, and Michigan Democrats kept his car crowded. Mrs. Douglas, with her charming smile, enchanted everybody.

His Illinois supporters intended to outdo all rivals. Hiring a special train, four hundred delegates, representing nearly every county and accompanied by a brass band, climbed aboard to meet him at Michigan City, sixty miles to the east. Here a huge crowd of Indianians halted the Senator for a speech. It was late in the afternoon before the special started back. From stations, farmhouses, and fields where men worked, shouting people waved flags and hats. As the train passed slowly along the Chicago waterfront, women shook handkerchiefs from the houses, thousands of men swarmed about the cars, a militia company fired a one-hundred-and-fifty-gun salute from Dearborn Park, and answering guns boomed from the North and South Divisions. The station was filled with a jubilant mob. Douglas, placed in an open barouche drawn by six horses, was escorted by Montgomery Guards and Emmet Guards along Wabash Avenue and Dearborn Street, heavily beflagged, to the Tremont House. Here, two hours earlier, a crowd had begun to form. As the crash of artillery announced the Senator's arrival, others poured in until thirty thousand packed the streets and every roof and window ledge within hearing distance. Chicago had never before witnessed such enthusiasm. As the barouche ploughed through the crowd, the surge and roar were like those of the sea. A moment later, in the fast-gathering dusk, Douglas appeared on the balcony to be greeted by a deafening yell of welcome. Bands blared, fireworks soared, and bonfires threw a ruddy glare upon the scene.

Into his first sentences he threw a note of defiance. This reception, he said, "so great in numbers no human voice could be heard by all the countless thousands who participated in it," was not so much a tribute to him as to the basic American principle which he fought to vindicate. He recalled how he had pledged himself to battle for popular sovereignty. "Have I not redeemed that pledge?" he demanded. And he declared that he would resist to the last the unnatural combination of Buchanan Democrats and Republicans. "I intend to fight that allied army wherever I meet them."

[II]

It was time that Douglas returned home, for already his Republican opponent had been chosen and had opened his campaign with a speech that arrested national attention. Three weeks earlier, when Congressmen were streaming out of Washington to their homes and the country was reading Douglas's final Senate blast against the Administration cabal, a Republican convention had met in Springfield and nominated Abraham Lincoln for the senatorship. Of all rival party leaders, Douglas feared him the most.

Lincoln had fairly earned the honor. Illinois Whigs had respected him ever since he had sat in Congress for their party. His cordiality in stepping aside in 1854 to permit the election of Lyman Trumbull to the Senate was appreciatively remembered by anti-Nebraska Democrats. For nearly three years now he had been the leading forensic champion of the new party in the State, his close-knit arguments against the Nebraska bill, the Dred Scott decision, and Lecompton making him known from Galena to Cairo. Professional politicians liked his humor, his fraternal kindliness, his unfailing sagacity, and his integrity, while they saw in his grasp of ideas and trenchant logic the promise of a doughty champion—the only man in the State capable of meeting Douglas in full onset.

Though almost unknown in the East, Lincoln was in fact as clearly the head of the party in Illinois as Seward was in New York or Cameron in Pennsylvania; and that position he had earned in a way all his own. At a later date, a more tamed and settled American society found a romantic attraction in his rise from backwoods poverty and ignorance. It caught eagerly at certain poignant elements in a story reflecting so many facets of western development—the grandfather slain by Indians while clearing the forest; the father building his slab-roofed log cabin in the Kentucky woods; the work-worn, unnursed, dying mother calling little Abe and his sister Sarah to her bedside for a parting admonition; the removal of the bereaved family to another ill-finished cabin on an Indiana creek, where they lived in the squalor of poor shelter, coarse clothing, shoeless feet, bad water, and ill-cooked food; and the rescue of the children by Thomas Lincoln's new wife, who washed, combed, and fed them, brightened the cabin, and installed good home-made furniture. Americans of later days thrilled to a boyhood of struggle: the hard toil of the bony, fast-growing youth, in homespun trousers and deerskin shirt, helping to till the stumpy acres; his introduction to his first books—the Bible, *Pike's Arithmetic,* the *Kentucky Preceptor,* Noah Webster's *Spelling Book, Robinson Crusoe, The Pilgrim's Progress, Aesop's Fables,* Grimshaw's *History of the United States,* William Scott's *Lessons in Elocution,* and the *Revised Laws of Indiana;* the work of stockdriver, ferryhand, and (in 1828) flatboatman journeying to New Orleans with pork, meal, and other produce. Then came the renewed migration, this time to a better settled area in Illinois, the second river trip to New Orleans, the Black Hawk War, the experience in surveying and storekeeping, the hard study of a few lawbooks, and admission to the bar. In the pioneer West such a story was fairly common, yet there, too, it commanded attention.

Lincoln's neighbors at New Salem and later in Springfield had found his appearance as arresting as a circus poster. The spare muscular frame of six feet four inches, the rugged features, the deep-set, widely spaced gray-brown eyes, and the mobility of the countenance, all melancholy one moment and all mirth the next, caught every eye. But the man's brain and character soon attracted them more. His mind was a countryman's mind; slow, careful, serious, and intensely tenacious; sagacious rather than shrewd, clear rather than clever; given to flashes of humor chiefly because its profound earnestness would have been insupportable without some break. Its quintessential quality was as plain to the unlettered rustic as eventually it became to Lowell and Bryant: it was a dogged desire to learn the exact truth about everything and anything, and a delight in the reasoning process as a means of apprehending truth.

Through his early fascination with Euclid, Kirkham's *Grammar*, and two writers marked by exceptional perspicuity of style, Thomas Paine and Blackstone; through his grappling with the mind of Mentor Graham; through his study of Congressional debates and the editorials of the *National Intelligencer*, both of which he read regularly from his early manhood, ran an intense pleasure in the logical processes of truth-seeking. He accepted no truth at second hand, but reasoned it out for himself; and once it was found, he tried to set a lucid vision of it before others. In seeking a statement of truth, he slowly gained the finest grace of style, a simple accuracy in diction and a logical progression in sentence arrangement which gave everything he wrote the beauty of perfect clarity. One biographer tells us that precise truthfulness and meticulous honesty were his most striking characteristics.[10] This statement pertains to his character, yet it illuminates the fact that the honesty of his mind was of one piece with the honesty of his nature, that a truthful spirit lay back of his intellectual operations and personal acts alike. Being so intensely a truth-seeker, so happy in the task of getting his mind exactly right on every problem, he was also a singularly consistent man. His mind seldom leaped to inspirations or intuitions; his slowness irritated his effervescent law partner Herndon, his fellow politicians in Springfield, and, in the end, half of his Cabinet and more than half of the editors of the North. But once he had laid hold of a truth, stripped it of non-essentials, and fixed it in shining perfection before him, he clung to it.

Next to this delight in truth and logic as a guiding trait was his humanity. Intellect and temperament were often at war in him, for he had the intellect of a cold logician, the temperament of a warm humanitarian. The mast-fed lawyer, as he called himself, took a rich pleasure in Shakespeare, who opened before him a broad world of human nature. He was almost abnormally gregarious in the sense that he loved small social gatherings (not crowds, which he avoided), was an unmatchable funmaker though never without a certain reserve of dignity, and felt instantly at home with men of all sorts—preachers, lawyers, politicians,

10 Beveridge, *Lincoln*, I, 113.

farmers, boatmen, mechanics, newspapermen, anybody with a touch of comradeship in his disposition. Himself simple and good-hearted, he was ready to be
a friendly neighbor to any man worthy of esteem. Out of his delectation in
human society sprang his kindliness, magnanimity, and spontaneous democracy,
which made no account of social distinctions and little even of intellectual differences. He remitted the widow his legal fee; he was the same man to Governor
Bissell and the governor's coachman; *Lear* and the Sangamon County will
litigation illustrated the same values to him. Of the hustling spirit which the
frontier engendered he showed very little; he loved the people about him too
much to like combat or self-assertion; yet in the management of men he had a
skill invaluable to his political advancement. Withal, as his partner Herndon
well knew, he was ambitious of political honors. Brought up in an environment
where political campaigns were personal, he never faltered in his understanding
of the electorate from the time he won two hundred and seventy-seven of the
three hundred New Salem votes for the legislature until he was running
for the Presidency. In his social thinking he was a Jeffersonian, emphasizing
equality and justice; in his economic thinking he accepted the ideal of a free
laissez-faire competitive society.

In the years after Lincoln had formed his law partnership of 1841 with
Judge Stephen T. Logan, and that of 1844 with William H. Herndon, he became
recognized in the West as one of the leaders of the Illinois bar—an attorney who
had built his reputation slowly and soundly on hard work, grasp of the principles of equity, and dexterity in fair-minded appeals to a jury. He was not
widely read in law, nor deeply grounded in precedent. In dealing with most
cases he followed a method both congenial to him and natural under the hard
conditions of circuit practice, where few lawbooks were available and no time
or facilities existed for briefing analogous cases—he based his argument upon
broad considerations of abstract justice, presenting the issues so luminously that
the application of these considerations was plain to the dullest juror.[11] It followed that when his case was bad—when justice lay on the other side—his plea
was listless and feeble. When it was good, however, and when it involved interesting human issues, his logical power, understanding of character, and moral
fervor rendered him almost irresistible. He liked to have time to think his cases
through; he never believed himself fully prepared unless he had gotten up his
opponent's side nearly as fully as his own; and he was thus at his best only
when his mind, as deliberate as it was sure, had time for reflection and study.
The more intricate a case, the more brilliant would seem his lucid presentation
of its elements. Beginning with the kind of litigation that abounded in a rough
new country—land titles, debt collection, tax suits, cattle trespasses, disputed

11 A. A. Woldman, *Lawyer Lincoln*, Chapter X.

boundaries, quarrels over wills—he and the State grew up together, their business becoming more complex, difficult, and important.

As industrial development began, Lincoln became counsel for rich railroad and business corporations; as municipal and State affairs increased, he was called upon for legal opinions on governmental acts. He represented banks, insurance companies, merchants, a gas-light enterprise, and manufacturing concerns. Some of his cases were important. In the famous *Effie Afton* suit of 1857, which grew out of the wreck of the steamer of that name against the bridge built across the Mississippi at Davenport by the Rock Island Railroad, Lincoln joined Norman B. Judd of Chicago and Joseph Knox of Rock Island in arguing the railroad's case. His closing plea was masterly—and the disagreement of the jury was in effect a victory for his side.[12] In the same year he defeated the St. Louis, Alton & Chicago Railroad in a far-reaching case which held the road responsible for the acts of its duly authorized agents, thus establishing a rule cited in many subsequent cases.[13] He was engaged by the Illinois Central Railroad in a still more important case; its resistance to the attempt by McLean County to levy a tax on the railroad's property within the county limits. If the McLean officials succeeded, other local governments would imitate it, and the Central would be thrown into utter bankruptcy. Arguing the constitutionality of the charter exemption of the Illinois Central from taxation, and the interdiction of local as well as State levies by this exemption, Lincoln won his case. Compelled to bring suit for his fee, he easily won a verdict (June, 1857) for $5,000. The sum was important, for it enabled Lincoln the next year to drop his law business for the senatorial campaign. Still other important cases might be mentioned.[14]

Any student of Lincoln's legal career must be struck by the immense variety of cases which he pleaded, the acquaintance his circuit practice gave him with the whole central belt of his rich State, his unvarying industry and competence, and the steadily widening fame of his talents. He appeared in all the State and Federal courts of the area. He dealt with constitutional law, admiralty law, patent law, common law actions, and bills in equity. He was at least once offered an advantageous opening in Chicago. Several State departments, a number of counties, and various towns retained his services. The very month before his

12 Summarized in Beveridge, *Lincoln*, I, 600–604.
13 Woldman, *Lawyer Lincoln*, 164.
14 Douglas was quick to attack Lincoln for his connections with the railroad. "Can you Republicans deny that this day and this hour your candidate, Abraham Lincoln, is the agent and attorney of the Illinois Central Railroad, making stump speeches on its money? . . . Can you deny that he received from the company a single fee of $5,000 for procuring a decree releasing its property from taxation in McLean County, thus taking the side of the company against the people whose votes he is now asking?" Speech at Henry, Chicago *Daily Times*, October 5, 1858.

nomination for Senator, he conducted with brilliant success the defense in one of the most renowned murder trials in the history of Illinois: the trial of Duff Armstrong, son of an old friend and benefactor, whose acquittal he obtained by incisive logic, abetted by an almanac which proved that a witness could not have seen by moonlight the acts which he swore he had seen. His friend David Davis, judge of the State circuit bench, sometimes called upon Lincoln to hold court in his place, and Lincoln always did so to general satisfaction. In all his work as lawyer, his two ruling traits appeared: his earnest, deliberate, inexorably logical search for truth, which when found he presented in luminous terms, and the warm interest in plain humanity, which made him so kindly in administering justice, so modest in his successes, so magnanimous in all his dealings.[15]

His nomination was not untouched by drama. But one rival had appeared, and that a worthy figure—"Long John" Wentworth, just chosen mayor of Chicago by a resounding majority, the first Republican head of any great American city. A scion of the famous New Hampshire family, a graduate of Dartmouth, one of the moulders of the early destiny of Chicago, long editor of its principal newspaper the *Democrat*, an associate of Douglas in obtaining the Illinois Central land grant, a lawyer and politician of shrewd address, Wentworth was a formidable candidate against any man. The morning after the Kansas-Nebraska bill passed the House, he had joined other anti-Nebraska Whigs and Democrats at Crutchet's boardinghouse in Washington, and, then serving his fifth term, had forsaken the Democratic Party to help form a new freesoil organization. People could well respect his versatile abilities and progressive temper. But the imperious will and biting pen of the "Chicago autocrat" had made enemies, and, when the test came, he proved unable to carry the northern counties. Men in and about Chicago, led by State Chairman Norman B. Judd and Charles L. Wilson, editor of the Chicago *Journal*, were determined to defeat him and they made thorough preparations. On April 21 a conference of editors, including C. H. Ray of the Chicago *Tribune*, William Bross of the *Democratic Press*, and George T. Brown of the Alton *Courier*, met in the State library at Springfield to complete their plans. On the appointed day the city delegates marched into the convention hall under a banner reading, "Cook County is for Abraham Lincoln." Still more important than the activities of the leaders just named was a grass roots movement for Lincoln in the county gatherings, where the plain voters demanded his selection. Ordinarily the convention would have

---

15 Woldman, *Lawyer Lincoln*, Chapter XIII. Not merely did Lincoln travel widely. His home in Springfield was a strategic situation for a lawyer-politician, for the legislature brought scores of his friends there every year, while the session of the State supreme court and Federal court attracted lawyers from all over the State. These attorneys held many informal meetings which Lincoln attended. Cf. John G. Nicolay, January 9, 1858, to Trumbull; Trumbull Papers.

nominated men only for State offices, leaving the senatorial preference to be settled later. But to make Wentworth's defeat doubly sure, his opponents and Lincoln's supporters resolved upon the unprecedented step of riveting into the platform a declaration that Lincoln was the party nominee.

Enthusiasm for the freesoil cause and confidence in Republican destiny animated the thousand or more delegates and alternates who met that beautiful June 16 in the little Illinois capital. They gathered in jubilant knots under the maples, elms, and catalpas. They wandered about the Square, with the handsome little Capitol framed in its midst, the post office on the north, and two six-pillared stone structures in the classical style—the courthouse and an insurance building—on the east. They gazed at the new governor's mansion with its cupola, its high windows set in heavy brick walls, and its wide rear porches. When the hour struck, they poured into the Representatives' Hall. Ninety-five counties were represented, and all but five had passed resolutions for Lincoln. Richard Yates pounded for order, launching forthwith into a vigorous prophecy of national triumph. Our party this very hour, he proclaimed, is the most powerful on the continent of North America. Gustave Koerner, the able graduate of Heidelberg who had risen to be lieutenant-governor, was made president of the gathering.

Well might these Illinois Republicans face the future jauntily. Theirs was the united party of hope and fervor, the guardian army of moral progress! So they believed, as they cheered Koerner's ringing predictions of victory, and adopted the platform which Lincoln's friend, Orville H. Browning of Quincy, had drawn up. A little caucus of leaders in the State Library the night before, Lincoln among them, had deputed him to execute the task. It was a platform remarkable for its economic content. Slavery was of course mentioned, with a demand that it be kept out of all Territories; the Dred Scott decision and Lecompton constitution were suitably denounced. Emphasis fell, however, upon the propositions that public lands must be wrested from speculators and corporations and granted to actual settlers; that rivers and harbors must be improved; that the Pacific Railroad must be built; that the rights of free labor must be maintained; and that the national expenses must be reduced. A bold and constructive platform—but it omitted all mention of tolerance, for the Know-Nothing vote had to be won if the party were to achieve its goals.[16]

After naming two men for State offices, the convention passed by acclamation a resolution declaring Lincoln its first and only choice for Douglas's seat. Dislike of "Long John" and wholehearted approbation of the equally long Springfield attorney found vent in cheers which made the State House quiver.

16 Beveridge, *Lincoln*, II, 570, 571. B. Gratz Brown of Missouri had sent Browning the draft of a free labor plank. June 10, 1858, Browning Papers.

Then the convention adjourned, to meet again at eight in the evening to hear its champion deliver the first speech of the campaign.

[III]

Having long known that he would be designated, Lincoln had determined to make his address a memorable appeal to all thoughtful citizens. Thus far he was known (apart from his "spot" resolutions) for only three or four public utterances. He had delivered in 1852, in the Capitol at Springfield, a eulogy upon Henry Clay, commonplace enough except for a glowing endorsement of the purposes of the American Colonization Society. It showed that he still believed in the possibility of ridding America of slavery and restoring the Negro to Africa—"and this too so gradually that neither races nor individuals shall have suffered by the change." [17] He had made his famous reply to Douglas at Peoria in 1854 on the Kansas-Nebraska issue, striking with deadly aim at the central point: the assumption in the Nebraska Act that no moral issue was involved in the spread of slavery. Four months after the Dred Scott decision, he had presented in a Springfield speech a scathing analysis of its moral fallacies, and a telling indictment of the idea that the black man's bondage should be universal and eternal.[18] These three speeches, with a few fragments like the post-election address at the Republican banquet in Chicago in 1856, constituted his contribution to the thought of his time. And he was now almost fifty.

To his new address, Lincoln gave a more careful preparation than to any earlier effort of his life. For weeks, he had been filling stray envelopes and scraps of paper with jotted ideas, throwing them into that wonted receptacle, his hat; and of late he had carefully combined these fragments and had rewritten and polished his argument.[19] The time had come, as he saw, for the Republican Party to take more advanced ground. The hour had struck when, no longer content with an interdiction of slavery in the Territories, the party should assert that even in the South the "peculiar institution" must be viewed as a temporary and transitional system, bound in the course of generations to give way to a better regime. Only by a wise acceptance of this idea could the country be brought to devise bold measures for slavery's ultimate termination.

Lincoln therefore decided to throw into the first paragraph of his speech a flat assertion that a house divided against itself cannot stand; that the nation must in time become all slaveholding (which was unthinkable), or all free. The Biblical phrase, perhaps unconsciously borrowed from Edmund Quincy, had

17 Speech, July 16, 1852.
18 Speech, June 26, 1857.
19 Nicolay and Hay, *Lincoln*, II, 136.

long been in his mind. The fundamental idea he had thought of using earlier that year in a Bloomington speech, but he had discarded it when some conservative friends argued that it would encourage extremists North and South and embitter the sectional struggle. It had been partially stated by George Fitzhugh, but then Fitzhugh was an eccentric radical. Now, convinced that the time was ripe for its enunciation, or at least that the truth ought no longer to be suppressed, he had fixed upon his course.[20]

Just before the convention, he called a dozen or more friends to the library of the State House and read the speech to them. Herndon's recollection was that everyone, as his opinion was asked, condemned the utterance until Herndon himself spoke up: "Lincoln, deliver that speech as read and it will make you President." [21]

Whether this is accurate or not, there is a ring of authenticity in Herndon's report of Lincoln's rejoinder to the group: "The time has come when these sentiments should be uttered; and if it is decreed that I should go down because of this speech, then let me go down linked to the truth—let me die in advocacy of what is just and right."

Lincoln was thinking of Illinois, not the nation, when he made this statement; thinking of the Senatorship, not any larger office; and yet thinking, too, of what the whole country ought to know. From the prairie chrysalis, a winged creature was being born. The speaker who mounted the platform that night appeared to be only the plain circuit lawyer of uneven education and limited reading that his fellow-citizens knew—a provincial figure who, but for one inconspicuous term in Congress, knew nothing of the older sections and had left his State only once since 1849. He seemed to be only a State leader who would now become known to the East, not through his own incontestable merits, but because his opponent was the most redoubtable Democratic chieftain of the nation. Of crudities and limitations, indeed, he still had all too many.

Yet ever since 1849 Lincoln had been steadily taking on stature. Returning from Congress, he had temporarily put aside political ambition, and for five years had devoted himself to self-improvement in general culture, the law, and thought by sustained study and hard desk work. In 1854, when he rose to the challenge of the Nebraska Act, some fruits of that discipline had appeared. Now more were to be revealed. Few in the crowd which sat shirtsleeved, perspiring, and restless in the Capitol hall that hot June night could have had much perception of his still undisclosed intellectual and moral greatness. But all, even the least

---

20 Harvey Wish, *George Fitzhugh*, 150 ff. Fitzhugh had written in the Richmond *Enquirer*, May 6, 1856, that either slavery or free society must be very wrong. "The war between the two systems rages everywhere; and will continue to rage till the one conquers and the other is exterminated."

21 Herndon and Weik, Angle ed., *Lincoln*, 325.

perceptive, could appreciate the courage and the sinewy logical power of his discourse. Without a word of rhetorical embellishment, he drove home in the opening sentences a thesis to whose elaboration most of the remainder of the speech was devoted:

We are now far into the fifth year since a policy was initiated with the avowed object and confident promise of putting an end to slavery agitation. Under the operation of that policy, that agitation not only has not ceased, but has constantly augmented. In my opinion, it will not cease until a crisis shall have been reached and passed. "A house divided against itself cannot stand." I believe this government cannot endure permanently half slave and half free. I do not expect the Union to be dissolved—I do not expect the house to fall—but I do expect it will cease to be divided. It will become all one thing, or all the other. Either the opponents of slavery will arrest the further spread of it, and place it where the public mind shall rest in the belief that it is in the course of ultimate extinction; or its advocates will push it forward until it shall become alike lawful in all the States, old as well as new, North as well as South.

From this courageous beginning, Lincoln had an opportunity to move forward to a statesmanlike examination of the necessity for facing all that was implied in "ultimate extinction." But one radical step was enough; he deemed it wise not to go further. Instead, he made a strictly partisan appeal to the rising fear among freesoilers that slavery would be made lawful everywhere, arguing that the Republican Party must be strengthened as a bulwark against that dire possibility. Slavery, he affirmed, was an aggressive force. Its champions, abetted by Douglas, who cared not whether it was voted up or down, had gained one victory after another in a program of shrewd, unsleeping expansion. First, they had forced through Congress the Nebraska Act opening all the national domain to slavery. Second, they had gained in 1856 what they declared was a national endorsement of this step. Third, they had then obtained from the Supreme Court in the Dred Scott decision a three-headed engine to batter down further walls in their path. One head, declaring that no slave or descendant of a slave could ever be a citizen, was designed to deprive the Negro of any possible benefit from the constitutional guarantee that citizens in each State shall be entitled to all the privileges and immunities of citizens in other States. Another head, asserting that neither Congress nor the local legislature might exclude slaves from a Territory, was intended to facilitate the colonization of the public domain with slaves and thus enhance the chances of permanency for the institution throughout the future. The third head, stating that the Federal courts would not decide whether the transfer of a slave into a free State made him free, but would leave that to be determined by the courts of any slave State into which the Negro might be forced by his master, had a still more sinister intention. Not pushed forward immediately but left to fix itself slowly in the public conscience, it was to be used to sustain the logical conclusion that, as Dred's master had taken him as a slave to Illinois, every other master might take one or a hundred slaves to any free State.[22] This succession of measures, said Lincoln, might not be the fruit of a conspiracy:

But when we see a lot of framed timbers, different portions of which we know have been gotten out at different times and places by different workmen— Stephen [Douglas], Franklin [Pierce], Roger [Taney], and James [Buchanan], for instance—and we see these timbers joined together, and see they exactly make the frame of a house or a mill, all the tenons and mortices exactly fitting, and all the lengths and proportions of the different pieces exactly adapted to their respective places, and not a piece too many or too few, not omitting even the scaffolding—or, if a single piece be lacking, we see the place in the frame exactly fitted and prepared to yet bring such a piece in—in *such* a case, we find it impossible not to *believe* that Stephen and Franklin and Roger and James all understood one another from the beginning, and all worked upon a common *plan* or *draft* drawn up before the first lick was struck.

A fourth step remained, said Lincoln. If the Court decided that the Constitution did not permit a State to exclude slavery (and Judge Nelson had hinted at constitutional restraints upon State power over slavery), then the institution would indeed become national. "Put this and that together, and we have another nice little niche, which we may, ere long, see filled with another Supreme Court decision" of just this purport. This was especially to be expected if Northern voters turned from their Republican guardians to men like Douglas, indifferent whether slavery was voted up or down.

This partisan conclusion, in the eyes of posterity, was pitched on a disappointingly low plane. To be sure, it had some merit as an exhortation to Northerners to maintain a sleepless vigilance lest worse than the Nebraska Act and Dred Scott decision should befall them, and as an appeal to Republicans to stand firm. But its theory of a conspiracy among Douglas, Buchanan, Pierce, and Taney was unfounded. The charge gave Douglas an opportunity—in a speech at Clinton on July 27—to fling at Lincoln the words "infamously false," declaring that he had never exchanged one word with Taney or Pierce on the Dred Scott decision and had not spoken of it to Buchanan until long after it was made.[23] Lincoln's prediction that "we shall lie down pleasantly dreaming that the people of Missouri are on the verge of making their State free, and we shall awake to the reality instead that the Supreme Court has made Illinois a slave State," was an absurd bogey; no court would have dared such folly. He would

22   The Washington *Union*, November 17, 1858, published an article asserting the doctrine that slaves could be brought as slaves into the free States, and kept there. Douglas in his own words, "Branded it at once, and denounced it." Toombs said in the Senate that not a man in any slave State held such a doctrine. See Lincoln, *Works*, II, 454.
23   Carthage *Republican*, August 5, 1858.

have done well to confine himself to the simple facts that Douglas's Nebraska Act, Taney's Dred Scott decision, and Buchanan's championship of Lecompton all outraged the convictions of men who opposed the extension of slavery, and that such outrages would continue unless the voters stood firm behind the Republican Party. Lincoln might have pointed to two very real perils. One was the peril of forcible annexations; the other was the peril of the rising Southern demand for giving slavery positive Congressional protection within the Territories. He did point to the danger of plans for the revival of the African slave trade.

It was not the partisan temper of the speech, for this was a party occasion, but its lack of constructive elements which made it disappointing. Lincoln bravely insisted on the great truth that the nation could not permanently remain half slave and half free; he called for vigilant action to prevent it from becoming wholly slave; but he said nothing as to the means of making it wholly free. This, he plainly implied, had to be done. But how? How much patience, wise counsel, and self-sacrificing help might the South expect from the North in that agonizing process? Nearly three years earlier, he had written a Kentucky leader that no peaceful extinction of slavery seemed in sight. "So far as peaceful, voluntary emancipation is concerned, the condition of the negro slave in America, scarcely less terrible to the contemplation of a free mind, is now as fixed and hopeless of change for the better, as that of the lost souls. . . . The problem is too mighty for me—may God, in his mercy, superintend the solution." This vague hopelessness could not be maintained. From such western moderates as Lincoln and Bates, if from anyone, a constructive attitude might be expected.

The speech was a ringing prologue. Lincoln took characteristic care that it be printed correctly. Giving the manuscript at the end of his address to Horace White of the Chicago *Press and Tribune*, and requesting him to go to the *Illinois State Journal* office and read proof, Lincoln soon followed to con the text himself. He explained that he had taken great pains with it and wished no errors to creep in. Not only the *Journal*, but the Chicago *Press and Tribune* and other western sheets published it. A pamphlet edition was soon issued in Illinois. Would he follow this prologue by a fuller definition of his views?

[IV]

Douglas lost no time in replying. The "house divided" speech was published throughout the East before the Senator left Washington. Printing it in full, the New York *Tribune* and *Weekly Tribune* carried it to millions of readers, with an editorial calling it compact, forcible, and admirable: "Mr. Lincoln never fails to make a good speech, when he makes any, and this is one of his best efforts." [24] The Philadelphia *Press's* Washington correspondent, terming it very ultra, intimated that Douglas would quickly demolish it. At his Chicago homecoming, Douglas shook hands with Lincoln who sat behind him on the Tremont House balcony. His speech, too, had been carefully prepared; and though he delivered it under the exhaustion of two nights' loss of sleep, it was distinguished by the vigor with which it assailed both the Lecompton Democrats and the doctrines that Lincoln had advanced.

The attack upon Lecompton, to be sure, named not a single person, spoke of principles only, and avoided the remotest allusion to the President. Throughout the Senate debates of April, May, and June, in fact, Douglas had uttered not a harsh word (in public) about Buchanan. His Springfield organ, the *State Register*, had essayed during these months (as Lincoln observed to Elihu B. Washburne) to reduce its readers to a drowsy forgetfulness that the two chieftains had ever quarreled.[25] To this extent Douglas was yet holding the door open for reconciliation. But he softened no words in his fiery vaunt of triumph over that "fraud" and "monstrosity" termed Lecompton. He had felt bound in honor to resist, and, with the aid of Crittenden and Bell, of a staunch band of Know-Nothings, and of the manful Republicans, he had won what he boldly called a great moral victory. "We forced them to refer that constitution back to the people of Kansas, to be accepted or rejected as they shall decide at an election which is fixed for the first Monday of August next." While the mode of submission under the English bill did not meet his approval, Douglas was sure that the voters of Kansas would resist its penalties and inducements. "Hence, my friends, I regard the Lecompton battle as having been fought and the battle won, because the arrogant demand for the admission of Kansas under the Lecompton constitution unconditionally, whether her people want it or not, has been abandoned, and the principle which recognizes the right of the people to decide for themselves has been substituted in its place." [26]

Then, turning to the coming campaign, Douglas trenchantly defined his two vital differences with Lincoln and the Republican Party. First, he sharply rejected the "house divided" doctrine, which he stigmatized as an effort to set section against section, and hammer a tyrannous, grinding uniformity of institutions down upon the blessed breadth, variety, and freedom of the American scene. Why should the Union be all free or all slave? Why should its customs and practices not be as diverse as the climate and physiography of the rich domain that stretched from frosty Maine to opulent Louisiana? Tolerance of

24 N. Y. *Weekly Tribune*, July 3, *Daily Tribune*, July 1, 1858.
25 Lincoln to Elihu B. Washburne, May 15, 1858; Ill. State Hist. Lib.
26 Full text, Phila. *Weekly Press*, July 17, 1858.

local differences meant peace; the "house divided" thesis meant war between North and South. In the second place, Douglas emphatically condemned Lincoln's refusal to abide by the Dred Scott decision. He would support the Supreme Court in all matters within its jurisdiction; he regarded a crusade against the highest judicial tribunal in the land as a threat to liberty and security. Moreover, he condemned Lincoln's main ground of complaint (as Douglas misdefined it) against the Court. Lincoln, he said, stood for negro equality; he was against it. He was opposed to every step that recognized the negro or Indian as the equal of the white man; he would give these dependent races every right, privilege, and immunity consistent with the safety of the superior race; but he would stand adamant against equality, political, social, or whatnot.

Readers of this adroit speech could hardly doubt that it was the opening gun of Douglas's contest for the Presidency in 1860. It was written with an eye not only to his senatorial seat but to the White House. He knew well that the Directory—Cobb, Slidell, Thompson, Black—would fight until their thirst for revenge was slaked by defeat or choked by victory; he despised them. He knew that he could expect no votes from those Republicans of rigid principle represented by Seward, Chase, Wade, and Lincoln. But moderate Northern Democrats (with many in the South) would cling to him, while not a few moderate Republicans and Know-Nothings, lovers of the Union and believers in peace, might well join them. The next two years would certainly be a period of political upheaval. Might he not, as a leader who had striven since 1850 for median policies and a natural, unforced solution of problems, rally all those who were tired of perilous extremes? That the Southern radicals led by Slidell and Yancey were a menace to the republic most Northern and border Democrats agreed. That Seward and Chase, with their rejection of Dred Scott, insistence on containing slavery, and higher-law doctrine, were likewise dangerous, conservative Republicans would grant. The nation as a whole, which had voted in 1852 and 1856 for rest and safety, distrusted agitators and wanted a moderate leader in the Presidency. Could not Douglas thrust both sets of radicals aside, and carry the country as a strong, hopeful man typifying the old Jackson-Polk ideas of Union, expansion, and reform?

A fighter who like Sheridan or Patton loved the attack, Douglas was happiest when carrying battle into the enemy lines. To him the foe lay on two flanks. On one side, the more flamboyant men of the cotton kingdom, addicted to juleps, feuds, and gasconade, had shown that they would stop at nothing. They meant to draw an advanced line on slavery and meet any violation of it with secession. On the other side, Seward, still esteemed the almost inevitable nominee of the Republicans two years hence, denounced slavery as a curse, assailed expansion, and hoped to erect a sectional administration. Douglas struck at both. In hailing the downfall of Lecompton he was exulting over the humiliation of Southern fire-eaters. In denouncing the "house divided" dogma and the resistance to Dred Scott he was aiming not so much at Lincoln, who seemed a transient foe, as at Seward. Already Douglas foresaw the triple contest of 1860, with radical Republicans on one side, radical Democrats on the other, and his moderate popular-sovereignty party in the middle. His vision was accurate. He erred only in overestimating his power to take votes away from the radical wings; erred in not foreseeing John Brown's raid, Buchanan's folly, and the impetuous rush of Yancey and Rhett.

From Chicago, Douglas moved to carry the contest down-State, and since "Egypt" was clearly his own, especially into the central counties from Quincy on the west to Danville on the east. He addressed a German delegation in Chicago, boasting that he had made the first speech in the county against the system which proposed to humiliate men on account of birthplace or religion.[27]

Then, on July 16 he stepped into a private car, decorated with bunting. A gay party, including his wife, the young sculptor Leonard Volk, the shorthand expert James B. Sheridan, and various political leaders, took their seats, and the regular train to Bloomington carried them southward. En route, a flat-car with a twelve-pounder cannon was attached, and its boom at every stop reverberated across the flat prairies. At Joliet, the Senator acknowledged the cheers of a throng with dancing banners and blaring band. At Bloomington, a strongly Republican town, he found a drum-and-fife procession, and every preparation for a huge audience. His speech in the midsummer dusk lasted until ten o'clock, when amid flaring torches he and Mrs. Douglas were tumultuously escorted back to the Landon House. He went on to Springfield, where thousands braved a heavy rain to gather about his platform, and thence to Clinton, where he made another long address.

In all these speeches he elaborated upon his Chicago address. He reemphasized his doctrine of white superiority, and repudiated what he called Lincoln's doctrine that the negro should be given equal social and political rights, rights leading to suffrage, officeholding, lawmaking, and in the end racial amalgamation. He reiterated that a division of the American house upon the slavery question was logical and proper; so variegated a nation needed variegated institutions. Very significantly, he restated at length his belief that the Dred Scott decision did *not* mean that slavery would go into all the Territories. Slavery was completely dependent on local support; it would spread just as far as the people wanted it; it could never be forced on an unwilling community. In his Bloomington speech, distributed in eighty thousand copies throughout the State, he quoted a Southern Senator as having said that, without affirmative

27 Phila. *Weekly Press*, August 7, 1858.

legislation to foster it, slavery could no more exist in a hostile community than a newborn infant could survive on a Sahara rock. The local police power would be decisive, declared Douglas: "Slavery will never exist one day, or one hour, in any Territory against the unfriendly legislation of an unfriendly people."

[V]

Both parties had entered the Illinois contest divided. In both, desperate efforts were made to close up the ranks, and in neither was complete success attained. Unity would have been achieved in both had the State been left to itself. But the eastern Republicans and the Cobb-Thompson-Slidell Democrats wished to subordinate party success in Illinois to their own aims.

The position of Greeley, N. P. Banks, Henry Wilson, and others who deluded themselves into thinking that Douglas might take up Republican principles was by no means incomprehensible. Watching the Senator's battle against Lecompton with admiration, they believed that if the Illinois Republicans made no contest against him, a hundred thousand Illinois Democrats might be won over to the Republican cause in 1860. With them would come a host of other Northwestern Democrats—and perhaps Douglas himself. Reject a joint stand against the flagitious Administration, however, and the hundred thousand would be driven back into alliance with the slavery forces.[28] All during the spring, Greeley's *Tribune*, Bowles's Springfield *Republican*, the Hartford *Courant*, and other eastern journals had exhorted Republicans to support the reelection of such anti-Lecompton Democrats as Hickman of Pennsylvania, Adrian of New Jersey, Haskin and Clark of New York, and John G. Davis of Indiana. Douglas seemed to belong in that category. Anson Burlingame was warm for the return of the Little Giant to the Senate, but so were many eastern abolitionists. Be it remembered that the new Republican Party was made up primarily of freesoil Democrats and freesoil Whigs.

Senator Trumbull warned Lincoln on January 3 that the laudation of the Little Giant by seaboard Republicans threatened the success of the party in the Illinois campaign. "Some of our friends here act like fools in running after and flattering Douglas," he wrote. "He encourages it and invites such men as Wilson, Seward, Burlingame, Parrott, etc., to come and confer with him and they seem wonderfully pleased to go. I have had no conversation with him about his course. . . ." This statement was unjust to Seward, who, as his editorial friend James Watson Webb took pains to explain to Lincoln in a long letter, believed

---

28 N. Y. *Daily Tribune*, July 1, 1858. The Robert Todd Lincoln Papers contain many letters to Lincoln on this peril. They indicate that John H. Bryant of Princeton, Illinois, may have done much to keep his brother the editor-poet in line against Douglas.

in Republican men and Republican principles, and was not going to meddle in the Illinois contest. But it was accurate as respected others, and particularly some onetime Democrats who had joined the new party. As David Davis wrote Lincoln this spring, the Republican organization still remained a confederated and not a consolidated party.

Yet this eastern movement seemed to the Illinoisans who knew Douglas best, not only infidelity to principle but the worst kind of practical folly. From the outset, many western Republicans had doubted the sincerity of Douglas's stand, for they deemed his motives selfish. They thought he realized that unless he attacked Lecompton he could never go back to the Senate and never obtain any Northwestern support in 1860; that, as Governor Bissell wrote Lyman Trumbull, his course was dictated solely by fears for his political future. In this they were wrong, but on other points they were right. While it was indeed important to rebuke the Administration, it would be more pointedly and damagingly rebuked by Republican victory than by Douglas's reelection. There was never the slightest chance that convinced Douglasites would embrace Republican tenets, for between them and the new party yawned two impassable gulfs. Douglas had labored for years, as Lincoln said, to prove it a sacred right of white men to take slaves into any new Territories where they were welcome; the Republican Party had been born as a protest against permitting slavery in the national domain. Douglas saw no moral issue in the slavery question; all Republicans did.[29]

Only a few Republicans in Illinois had been infected by the new eastern love affair with Douglas. Jonathan Blanchard, the Vermont-born president of Knox College, who had learned his abolitionism under Theodore Weld at Lane Seminary, had veered early in the year to the Douglas forces. Elihu Washburne of Galena, a former Whig now in the House as a Republican, for some time played an equivocal part. The early spring found him reputedly on Douglas's side; then he wrote a letter to Lincoln's partner Herndon which indicated that he was an honest party adherent; and finally he was reported in Springfield, just before the Republican convention, urging delegates to drop Lincoln and endorse Douglas in his stead.[30] A few other western men were seduced. In

29 Multitudes of Republicans felt with George A. Nourse, who wrote Trumbull January 1: "His course on the Kansas-Nebraska bill is unatoned for, he is just as far off as ever from Republicanism, and is just as big a political scoundrel as ever." They felt with D. L. Phillips, who wrote January 3: "I have no faith in the sincerity of his movements. He is looking to a reelection to the U. S. Senate. We have been cheated enough from that quarter, and when we remember his unstinted abuse, I am willing to let him retire without following him." D. L. Phillips to Lyman Trumbull, January 3, 1858; Trumbull Papers.

30 Washburne sent Lincoln strong protestations of his loyalty. "I have here and in all my letters hence," he wrote May 2 from Washington, "invariably taken the ground that the republican party in Illinois must stand by their principles and their men—that for Senator I was for you against the field—that the party was bound by every obligation of honor and

Indiana, Schuyler Colfax played with the idea that it might be wisest to ensure the Little Giant's return to Washington, and in Missouri Frank P. Blair, Jr., did the same. But the great mass of prairie Republicans had no intention of playing into the hands of the man they had fought for years.

As they marshalled their lines for the campaign, they took steps to put their eastern brethren right. Not only did Joseph Medill's Chicago *Press and Tribune*, Charles L. Wilson's Chicago *Journal*, and other sheets expostulate with Greeley and Bowles, but C. H. Ray and other editors wrote them argumentative letters. From Washington, Lyman Trumbull let his anti-Douglas views be emphatically known. Greeley replied in May with a ringing eulogium of the Little Giant, saying that "no public man in our day has evinced a nobler fidelity and courage," and, while admitting that his future course was unpredictable and that he might soon espouse filibustering and free trade, declaring that Illinois Republicans should at any rate never ally themselves with Buchanan's base cohort of hirelings.[31]

Inasmuch as Greeley's *Weekly Tribune* had about five thousand Illinois subscribers, his stubborn position gave Lincoln pain. Why does he wish the Senator reelected? asked Lincoln. "It is because he thinks Douglas's superior position, reputation, experience, ability, if you please, would more than compensate for his lack of a pure Republican position."[32] Herndon, early in March, had gone east to look at Revolutionary scenes, to make the acquaintance of the New England abolitionists he so much admired, Garrison, Parker, and Wendell Phillips, to get a first-hand view of the Lecompton battle, and to talk with Douglas. Primarily this was a pleasure trip. Perhaps as an additional motive, he was stirred by Lincoln's complaint that "Greeley is not doing me right." More probably a political object did not develop until he reached the East. In Washington he smoked a cigar with Douglas, who wanted him to tell Lincoln that he had crossed the river and burned his boats. He chatted with Trumbull, who expressed his belief that neither the Republicans nor anybody else could put any confidence in the slippery little Senator. In Boston, he saw Governor Banks, Theodore Parker, and several others—cold and rather repellent men, thought Herndon. They inquired whether the Illinois Republicans would accept Douglas, and looked astonished when the vehement response came, "No, never!"

Most important of all, Herndon bearded Greeley in his den and resentfully asked if the editor really wished to see Douglas ride into power with the aid

---

fair dealing to elect you, if it had the strength to elect anybody." Lincoln had already written him on April 26: "I am satisfied you have done no wrong, and nobody has intended any wrong to you." Robert Todd Lincoln Papers. See John M. Palmer in McLean Co. Hist. Soc. *Transactions*, III, 123.

31 N. Y. *Weekly Tribune*, May 15, 1858.
32 Lincoln to C. L. Wilson, June 1, 1858, *Works*, I, 238, 239.

of freesoilers whom he would certainly betray. Do not worry about his future course, responded Greeley. "Douglas is a brave man. Forget the past, and sustain the righteous." Writing to Springfield, Herndon repeated this to Lincoln with a snort: "Good God, righteous, eh?"[33]

Altogether, Herndon's visit probably did a little to enlighten the temporarily bemused easterners as to the real situation in Illinois; and he doubtless used his opportunity to tell Greeley, Parker, and others of Lincoln's true stature. Resentful editorials and letters from the West also had their influence. But what completed the general conversion of eastern Republicans was Douglas's Chicago speech. When Greeley, Bowles, and Bryant read that deliverance, they rent it to shreds.

After Lincoln's formal nomination and Douglas's early speeches, Republicans East and West fell into line. The New York *Tribune*, finally admitting that this was no duel of Hamlet and Laërtes, gave clear if lukewarm support to the party in Illinois. In a succession of editorials it denounced Douglas's squatter sovereignty principle, his expansionist views, his hostility to a broad program of civil rights, and his readiness to let slavery grow. Elihu Washburne made speeches for Lincoln. But, to the very end, nobody knew how many of those anti-Nebraska Democrats who had voted as Republicans in 1856 would turn back to their old hero Douglas, as Napoleon's veterans turned to the Emperor after the landing from Elba. Sheahan of the Chicago *Times*, analyzing the situation early in the contest, believed that while no important leaders could be won over, many of the rank and file would support a Democratic legislature; and Representative T. L. Harris agreed.[34]

If the Republican divisions were largely healed, those in the Democratic ranks rather grew worse. The Senator remained ready for a reconciliation; he had in fact sent explicit word to Buchanan, through James May of Philadelphia, that if the Administration would sustain his Illinois candidacy he would let bygones be bygones. A large body of regular Democrats expressed the view that it would be shameful to rive the party in two on issues that were now as dead as the Continental Congress. Alexander H. Stephens, Vice-President Breckinridge, and Henry A. Wise were among the prominent slave State leaders who hoped ardently for a reconciliation. The St. Louis *Republican*, Memphis *Appeal*, Mobile *Tribune*, New Orleans *Delta*, Richmond *Enquirer*, and Vicksburg *True Southron* advocated mutual forgiveness and forbearance in the cause of party success. Some of these men and journals were thinking of imperiled national union as much as party union.

---

33 Herndon to Trumbull, April 12, 1858; Trumbull Papers; W. H. Herndon and J. W. Weik, *Lincoln*, II, 390-396. According to Greeley, Herndon also praised Douglas.
34 Milton, *Eve of Conflict*, Ch. 20; David Donald, *Lincoln's Herndon*, 112 ff.

But Buchanan, who knew that reconciliation would be construed as defeat, and who called Douglas just what George III called Chatham—"that perfidious man"—made no move. Not for him the statesmanlike tact with which President Jefferson had sought to heal the schism of John Randolph. And the implacable Directory lost no time in taking matters into its own hands. They seized on the Chicago speech as text for a violent editorial in the *Union* of July 16, written without Buchanan's knowledge and padlocking the gates which barred Douglas out of the party. The *Union*, in fact, was now the organ not of the President who feebly disavowed it, but of the Directory ruling in his name. It was members of the Directory who speeded an agent, Francis J. Grund, to Chicago to organize the opposition to Douglas more firmly than ever.

As Douglas continued his heavy work of speechmaking, the National Democrats put forth every effort to defeat him. District-Attorney Henry S. Fitch, one of the most venomous agents, informed Buchanan in mid-August that they were doing better than they had expected. Money had been collected from Slidell and others; nine new Administration papers had just been established in the State; a full speaking program had been arranged. With hundreds rallying daily to the Administration standard, Douglas, knowing defeat was certain, "is becoming desperate in his denunciations and intrigues." [35] Ex-Governor John Reynolds, ex-Judge Sidney Breese, and C. N. Pine of Chicago were helping direct the warfare. The tactics of the National Democrats were to fight on the sly, as the Illinois phrase went. Before long the guillotine was working mercilessly. The Senator's friends were decapitated wherever the patronage-managers could reach them. Postmasters of Springfield, Rock Island, Peoria, Bloomington, Belleville, Galesburg, and many smaller places were summarily removed for no offense but loyalty to Douglas. The Little Giant at times felt as desperate as Cicero proscribed by Octavius at the behest of Antony. When an old friend, Usher F. Linder, proffered his services, an urgent telegram came back: "The hell-hounds are on my track. For God's sake, Linder, come and help me fight them." [36]

This war of the Directory, relentlessly prosecuted by Cobb, Brown, Slidell, Thompson, and Jere Black while Buchanan took refreshment at Bedford Springs, was waged in defiance of the majority will of the party. As the Springfield *Republican* pointed out, most politicians wished harmony restored; and the generality of Democratic newspapers not only ceased their attacks on the Senator but manifested a decided friendliness.[37] James Gardner, editor of the Augusta, Georgia, *Constitutionalist*, voiced his disgust that a test of orthodoxy

35 Henry S. Fitch to Buchanan, August 17, 1858; Buchanan Papers.
36 Linder, *Reminiscences*, 78.
37 Springfield *Daily Republican*, July 27, 1858.

had been laid down upon a question which most voters were willing to regard as extinct. Continuance of the vendetta against Douglas, he wrote, would show a factious and vindictive spirit, and would entail upon its prosecutors the responsibility for all the consequences which would follow division of the party. Perhaps he dimly foresaw how awful those consequences would be! [38]

But the Directory halted at nothing. It acted to found an anti-Douglas newspaper in Chicago. It aroused a wave of resentment in Ohio by dismissing Douglas's friend J. W. Gray, city postmaster and editor of the Cleveland *Plain Dealer*.[39] Veteran politicians expressed amazement at the venom of the Washington *Union*, which spewed epithets and tirades against all Douglas men. Cook, Fitch, and other placeholders scurried about over Illinois, bullying officeholders, arranging meetings, and using Federal printing to bribe newspapers or start new sheets. The whole panoply of Administration influence was set in motion. "For three years," Douglas was to say in 1860, "no friend of mine has been permitted to hold a crossroads postoffice, or even to circulate the public documents under my frank, as a general thing, in my own State." [40]

Alexander H. Stephens, anxious to arrange a compromise, visited Illinois for nearly a fortnight in August, talked with leaders, and came away resolved to use what influence he had with the Administration. He seems to have arranged a brisk peace movement in Chicago. Colonel R. B. Carpenter of that city, who had gotten $500 from the National Democrats for a speaking tour, suddenly gave up his opposition and hurried to Washington. David Stuart, a former member of Congress from the Detroit district and now a prominent attorney in Chicago, whom some regarded as the principal leader of the Douglas forces in Illinois, also visited the capital, his reputed object being to work upon his old friend Cass and others to bring about a friendly readjustment. In alarm, Isaac Cook, Pine, and others hastily appealed to Buchanan to stand firm.[41] They need not have worried. The President had forgiven Representative Montgomery of Pennsylvania his anti-Lecompton course only after the Congressman had written a letter of Uriah Heep 'umbleness. He would get no letter from Douglas, and the Directory would not forgive the man if he did. An earlier effort by George Sanders to patch up a peace had been emphatically rebuked by the President, who bade Sanders withdraw a conciliatory telegram which he had dispatched to Chicago.[42] While expert observers concurred in the view that the Directory had taken the bit in its teeth, they agreed that Buchanan felt

38 Augusta *Constitutionalist*, July 7, 1858; see New York Correspondent, London *Daily News*, October 2, 1858, on Southern protests, Virginia, Tennessee, and Kentucky.
39 N. Y. *Weekly Tribune*, June 26, 1858.
40 *Cong. Globe*, May 17, 1860; 36th Cong., 1st Sess., 2156.
41 Isaac Cook, August 16, C. N. Pine, August 17, 1858; Buchanan Papers.
42 G. F. Milton, *Eve of Conflict*, 327.

a bitter and unrelenting hatred for the man who had defied and defeated him.[43] On this point the Administration would meet no trouble from the President!

The hard-beset Senator could take comfort in the number of national leaders who called for his return to Washington. Senator Green of Missouri, after much wavering, was so impressed by the sentiment of his State that, as summer waned, he frankly declared his willingness to come to Illinois to speak for Douglas.[44] The Democratic candidates for Congress in Iowa, Indiana, and Ohio were, with few exceptions, compelled to declare their support of the Senator, while from Ohio came news that the only way to save the party was to put it back on the Douglas platform.[45] Vice-President Breckinridge finally wrote an open letter (October 4) in which he stated that, while he could not leave home to enter the campaign, he could never forget the courage and ability with which Douglas had repeatedly defended the Union and the rights of the State, and that he wished for his success in the election. Henry A. Wise not only reexpressed his adherence to Douglas, but sternly rebuked the Administration for its course. Could folly be greater? he asked. Douglas's success in Illinois would be the Administration's rebuke; his defeat there would be its death. Buchanan would eventually have to let Kansas enter, wrote the Virginia governor; he might as well have done so on fair terms, for he would lose the Southern Lecomptonites anyway on the issues of the tariff and Pacific Railroad.[46]

It would be the hottest, the closest, the most momentous senatorial campaign in decades; and the announcement that Douglas and Lincoln would engage in a series of joint debates seized the attention of the country.

43 J. P. Heiss (ed. Washington *States*) to Douglas, July 15, 1858; Douglas Papers.
44 Milton, *Eve of Conflict*, 347.
45 Phila. *Weekly Press*, July 21, 24, 1858.
46 Henry A. Wise, October 12, 1858; Buchanan Papers.

14

The Douglas-Lincoln Debates

"WE TRUST," remarked Greeley's *Tribune* in mid-July, "Messrs. Lincoln and Douglas will speak together at fifteen or twenty of the most important and widely accessible points throughout the State, and that the controversy will be prosecuted . . . at every county seat and considerable town. Such a conflict of principles of the gravest public consequences tends to purify the political atmosphere and ennoble the strife of parties."

At first it had seemed that this joint discussion would take place on a purely informal basis. Lincoln spoke in Chicago on the night following Douglas; he sat on Douglas's platform at Bloomington, but kept silent; and in Springfield he followed Douglas's afternoon discourse at Edward's Grove with an evening address in the Hall of Representatives.[1] When Douglas's managers issued a program of engagements covering a long list of towns, the Republican State Committee laid plans to place Lincoln at many of the same points on the same day or the day following. Simultaneously, on July 24, Lincoln challenged Douglas to "divide time and address the same audiences, the present canvass." The Senator reluctantly replied, agreeing to joint debate at one prominent point in each Congressional district save those of Chicago and Springfield, already covered; and he suggested Freeport, Ottawa, Galesburg, Quincy, Alton, Jonesboro, and Charleston. Lincoln assented. It was agreed that the first debate should take place at Ottawa on August 21 and the last at Alton on October 15; that one man should speak for an hour, the other reply for an hour and a half, and the first then conclude in half an hour. Douglas, as the challenged party, seized the advantage of four of the seven openings. Illinois newspapers were quick to appreciate the significance of the encounters.

The arrangement, which followed a pattern familiar in the South and West, was sensible. It conserved the time of busy rural voters, assured both candidates of larger audiences (including Whigs and Know-Nothings) than they might

---

1 For this speech the hall was crowded with what Herndon called "a most enthusiastic gathering of the intellect, and heart, and soul of our town"; and Lincoln's speech was "a whaler." Herndon to Trumbull, July 22, 1858; Trumbull Papers. For the Republican organization in Springfield, see Paul M. Angle, *Here I Have Lived*, Ch. XII.

otherwise reach, and facilitated a true clash of arguments. To Douglas's partisans, the contest seemed to give Lincoln, as the less famous and important man, some artificial benefits. They declared that he could never have collected large crowds of his own, and would gain a spurious prestige from Douglas's renown. They consoled themselves with the belief that the champion of mighty Senate debates would shake this provincial attorney, in full sight of the nation, as a mastiff shakes a terrier. Lincoln, predicted the *State Register*, "will get enough of debate and discomfiture to last him the rest of his life." [2]

Douglas, however, knew well that he had entered upon no light undertaking. Before leaving the East, he had told John W. Forney that he would face the most formidable antagonist to be found in Illinois. To Chicago associates he said frankly that in clarity, force, and dexterity Lincoln was the doughtiest opponent who could be brought against him. At an evening party among friends in the city, just before the debates opened, he betrayed an uneasy preoccupation; when a guest asked if he could entertain any anxiety over his combat with the Springfield lawyer, he replied that he felt deep uneasiness.

Three August weeks remained between the compact of Douglas and Lincoln and their first debate. The Senator spent them in active campaigning, while Lincoln gave the first ten days to preparation and letter-writing at home. On August 11, Douglas spoke at Beardstown, beautifully situated on the Illinois. He had been angered by Lincoln's charge in the "house divided" speech of a conspiracy of Stephen, Roger, and others to thrust the Dred Scott decision on an unsuspecting country; a charge which Lincoln had repeated with emphasis in another Springfield speech on July 17. This accusation was not the less dangerous for being false. At Beardstown, Douglas exploded that it was "an infamous lie." With equal heat he attacked Senator Trumbull for charging that he had been partly responsible for the Lecompton constitution. "The miserable, craven-hearted wretch would sooner have both ears cut off than to use that language in my presence, where I could call him to account." Hardly had Douglas departed, accompanied by his queenly looking wife, than Lincoln arrived on August 12, met at the wharf by two bands and forty horsemen. Speaking for two hours, he once more repeated the conspiracy charge.

The informal contest then moved up the Illinois valley, its broad cornfields basking in the heat. On August 13, Douglas spoke at Havana (center of the Spoon River country which Edgar Lee Masters was later to immortalize). Lincoln in high spirits boarded the steamer *Editor* to follow him. "Several of his old Whig friends were on board," Horace White later recalled, "and the

---

2 For preliminaries of the debate see Beveridge, *Lincoln*, II, 641 ff.; Baringer, *Lincoln's Rise to Power*, 11 ff.; and Milton, *Eve of Conflict*, 328 ff.

journey was filled up with politics and storytelling." His stories were always apropos of some event or idea, and were told with a "facial expression so irresistibly comic that the bystanders generally exploded in laughter" before he reached the point. At Havana, Douglas again lost his temper, called Lincoln a liar, coward, and sneak, and said something about fighting him. Replying the next day, Lincoln remarked that his opponent had been a little excited, and humorously deprecated any idea of a fistic battle. It would prove nothing; besides, "he and I are about the best friends in the world." The judge, he added, was merely trying to stir up political excitement, and "as I find he was tolerably successful in this, we will call it quits." [3]

The two moved on northward, their audiences growing in size. The turn-out for Douglas at Lewistown was especially impressive. Both men found elaborate receptions in Peoria, where they used again the arguments of their Chicago and Springfield speeches. And so, on August 21, they came together at Ottawa.

[I]

This pleasant town of six thousand people at the junction of the Illinois and Fox rivers, eighty-four miles southwest of Chicago, filled up that day with nearly fifteen thousand visitors. Long special trains—decked with banners, their seats packed and one car vibrant with a band—ran in from Chicago and La Salle. Special boats churned down the canal. Towers of choking dust rose from roads which since early morning had been alive with spring wagons, buckboards, carriages, buggies, and horsemen, each vehicle with a plump food basket under the seat. Military companies drew into lines under the bark of impatient officers; peddlers cried their wares; farmers talked of crops and politicians of votes; urchins popped an occasional firecracker. The town had scythed its lawns, dressed its store windows, and flung mottoed strips of canvas across the main street. All morning, citizens were hurriedly tacking flags and bunting to their porches. As the throng thickened, men, women, children, and dogs made Ottawa "one mass of active life"; it became difficult to force a passage through the crowd. Horses neighed, drums thudded, fifes squealed, and knots of men bore transparencies aloft.

Excitement among Democrats rose to a climax as a long cavalcade of horse-men with flags and inscribed ensigns, streaming out on the La Salle highway, met Douglas's four-horse carriage and brought him into town with music, cannon, and resounding cheers. The fervor of Republicans rose in a similar crescendo as Lincoln came in by train from Chicago and was placed in a car-

3 Horace White, quoted in Herndon and Weik, *Lincoln*, 1892 ed., II, 102, 103.

riage decorated with evergreens to be escorted to the home of the mayor. Shortly after one o'clock rival processions formed, and, with much marching and counter-marching, carried the candidates to the treeless public square. Here the crowd was so tightly packed that it took half an hour of rough-and-tumble pushing to get the speakers, committees, and reporters to the platform; and they were no sooner there than a section of the wooden awning, laden with men and boys, collapsed on the heads of the Douglas committee.

Intense feeling was shown. As the candidates took their seats, each was wildly cheered by his followers as the apostle of principles that would save the nation, the preacher of truth that would usher in a bright new era. These hard-headed men of the West, drawn from every section, from Britain and Germany, young in average years and in outlook, had a shrewd realization that the republic indeed stood at the crossroads; that it was girding itself to take mighty decisions; and that the issues under discussion involved the welfare of generations yet unborn.[4]

Never in our history have orators stood in more dramatic contrast. "Everybody knows Douglas," wrote the correspondent of the New York *Evening Post*, "a short, thickset, burly man, with large round head, heavy hair, dark complexion, and fierce bulldog look." As Douglas spoke for an hour, recalling the days when he had been schoolmaster in Winchester while Lincoln was a Salem grocery-keeper, and striving to identify the Republican Party with abolitionism, the crowd frequently interrupted with approving shouts. Then Lincoln rose, getting a long roar of applause. "Built on the Kentucky type, he is very tall, slender, angular, awkward even, in gait and attitude," wrote the *Post* reporter. "His face is sharp, large-featured, and unprepossessing. His eyes are deep set under heavy brows, his forehead is high and retreating, and his hair is dark and heavy." In short, he was ugly. "But stir him up and the fire of his genius plays on every feature. His eye glows and sparkles, every lineament, now so ill-formed, grows brilliant and expressive, and you have before you a man of rare power and of strong magnetic influence. He *takes* the people every time, and there is no getting away from his sturdy good sense, his unaffected sincerity, and the unceasing play of his good humor, which accompanies his close logic and smoothes the way to conviction." The correspondent thought Lincoln the more fluent of the two.[5] As a matter of fact, each candidate had his special virtues and defects as an orator.

4 E. E. Sparks, ed., *The Lincoln-Douglas Debates*, 85-147. In the Ottawa district, radical Republicans were numerous and feeling over Kansas had run high. The district was represented in Congress by the abolitionist Owen Lovejoy, of Princeton, Illinois, a man whose strong convictions, powerful physique, and personal magnetism made him popular. He was renominated and reelected this year, lending strength to Lincoln—who would later clash with him. See Isabel Wallace, *Life and Letters of W. H. L. Wallace*, 73 ff.

5 Chester P. Dewey of the *Evening Post* in Herndon and Weik, *Lincoln*, II, 105-107.

At Ottawa and other points, the advantages of prestige, personal force, platform experience, and intellectual dexterity were all with Douglas. For years he had been one of the most famous of Americans; he had a peculiar magnetism, compounded of dignity, energy, and strength; as he stood up to speak, the victor in a hundred senatorial duels, his square shoulders, broad chest, and leonine head making men forget his shortness, he seemed the very embodiment of thrust, combativeness, and staying power. The defiance, audacity, and restless belligerency of his port irresistibly appealed to the rougher element in every crowd. His well-tailored broadcloth, shining linen, and broad felt hat, his prominent friends and the deference of influential office-holders all over the State who lost no opportunity to lionize him, deepened the impression that a great man had returned home to his people. His voice rolled forth in a fierce if monotonous bulldog bark, never carrying to the out-skirts of a large crowd, but effective wherever heard.

By contrast Lincoln, ludicrously tall, angular, and awkward in gait and gesture, was at first glance unprepossessing. His clothes fitted badly; his stove-pipe hat accentuated his height; his face, sharp, yellow-leathery, and wrinkled, with heavy nose, jaws, and forehead, had a backwoods homeliness; he seemed unsure of himself. It was not until some minutes passed that the audience appreciated the keenness of his gray eyes, the breadth of his forehead, the strength of his chin. He shambled when he walked. His principal movements when talking—clasping and unclasping his hands, first behind and then in front of himself, an uncouth swing of his long arms, or a sudden dip at the knees followed by a sharp upward jerk with much gesticulation of the head—were often indescribably gauche. Three attributes of value, however, he did possess. When he became aroused by his theme, as the *Post* correspondent noted, his face lighted up, his deep eyes glowed, and his uneasy diffidence gave way to a profound earnestness. His voice, always shrill in moments of excitement and sometimes rising to a high treble, had a remarkably penetrating quality, so that the most distant auditor could hear it. Above all, he combined a patent sincerity and common-sense logic with better self-control than his antagonist. When Douglas was angered, his features became distorted, his voice deepened, and he looked like a man in an intense rage. But Lincoln never lost his simple, self-possessed blend of honesty and good humor, which lent persuasiveness to his clear, compact arguments.

The debate under the broiling sun in the treeless, seatless Ottawa square held the audience for three hours. At the end, enthusiastic Republicans carried the embarrassed Lincoln away on their shoulders. Newspapers treated the bout with the partisanship of the time. "Lincoln's Heart Fails Him!—Lincoln's Legs Fail Him!—Lincoln's Tongue Fails Him!" ran part of the headline of the

Chicago *Times*. We think that "since the flailing Senator Douglas received at Ottawa," his friends should "address him as the late Mr. Douglas," declared the Chicago *Journal*. Actually both had spoken well, and with a genuine clash of views.[6]

Douglas had attacked Lincoln's position on two fronts. Up to 1854, he said, the Whig and Democratic Parties, both national, had affirmed the right of the people of each State and Territory to decide their own local and domestic institutions for themselves, subject only to the Constitution. Then, in 1854, Lincoln, Trumbull, and others had brought as many former Whigs and Democrats as possible into a Republican Party which was essentially abolitionist and sectional. Lincoln now declared that the nation would not endure permanently half free and half slave; and he also asserted that he would not submit to the Dred Scott decision because it deprived the negro of the privileges of citizenship. On both heads he was wrong. Touching his first statement, the founders of the nation had willingly seen the country divided into free States and slave States, while it had endured half slave and half free for seventy years. Why should it not continue to exist with the diversity of institutions which fitted a land so huge and varied? Touching Lincoln's second statement, it was plain that the government had been made by white men for the benefit of white men and their posterity. "Do you desire to turn this beautiful State into a free negro colony, in order that when Missouri abolishes slavery she can send one hundred thousand emancipated slaves into Illinois, to become citizens and voters, on an equality with yourselves?" No, the path to concord and progress lay in acceptance of the Supreme Court decision and of Douglas's popular sovereignty doctrine.

Lincoln counterattacked with vigor. First, he cleared up certain misconceptions. The Republican Party was in no sense an abolitionist party. "I have no purpose, either directly or indirectly, to interfere with the institution of slavery where it exists. I believe I have no lawful right to do so, and I have no inclination to do so. I have no purpose to introduce political and social equality between the white and the black races." Nevertheless, the natural right of the negro to life, liberty, and the pursuit of happiness must be respected. He might not be the equal of the white man in mental and moral endowment. "But in the right to eat the bread, without the leave of anyone else, which his own hand earns, he is my equal, and the equal of Judge Douglas, and the equal of

6 Sparks, ed., *Lincoln-Douglas Debates*, 124–147, reprints much press comment. Lincoln was getting a taste of the scurrilous abuse that was to follow him the rest of his life. The Chicago *Times* continued to call him a scarecrow, declared he was so illiterate he could not utter five distinct sentences in succession, and pictured him as utterly discomfited after the principal debates. "Poor Lincoln!" it exclaimed after the Galesburg encounter; October 9, 12, 1858.

every living man." Having made this position clear, Lincoln turned his guns on Douglas.

He agreed that a variety of local institutions was necessary and wholesome in America; but slavery was not one of these desirable variations. It had ever been an apple of discord, and so long as it survived would continue an element of division. The fact that the nation had existed for seventy years in spite of this baneful element could be explained by the position in which the fathers had originally placed slavery. They excluded it from new Territories, and cut off its source in the slave trade, so that the public mind rested in the belief that it was in course of ultimate extinction. But, since of late years Douglas and others had placed the institution on a new basis, looking to the nationalization and perpetuity of slavery, the national discord had become greater than ever. The proper course was to arrest the spread of slavery and place it where Washington, Jefferson, and Madison had placed it—on the way to death. Then peace would come. "The crisis would be past, and the institution might be let alone for a hundred years—if it should live so long—in the States where it exists—yet it would be going out of existence in the way best for both the white and black races." As for the Dred Scott decision, it was no more eternally binding than any other court pronouncement. Had not Douglas once helped add five new judges to the Illinois supreme court in order to reverse one of its decisions?

[II]

The second debate, that at Freeport, might be called the question-and-answer discussion; for here Lincoln replied to certain interrogatories which Douglas had put at Ottawa, and propounded four questions of his own which Douglas answered on the spot. Historically, this was the most momentous of all the debates.

Freeport, close under the Wisconsin line in the Rock River valley, drew an even larger crowd than Ottawa—fully fifteen thousand. The three railroads had offered excursion rates and special trains, one of which, with sixteen coaches, brought a thousand passengers. Spectators poured in from Chicago, Galena, and Beloit. Douglas, arriving the night before, was received with an enthusiastic torchlight procession. Lincoln came in by train the next morning from Dixon, to be greeted by a dense crowd which formed in parade line to escort him to the Brewster House. The weather was cloudy and cool, with an occasional fine drizzle. A grove on the outskirts of town had been chosen for the occasion. For Douglas, a fine carriage had been provided; but when Lincoln clambered into a homely prairie schooner with an escort of weather-beaten farmers, the Senator decided to prove his kinship with the common people by walking to the grounds. Once more the crowd had so closely packed the area that a battering-ram rush was required to get the debaters on the platform. Lincoln was to open. But as he was about to begin, while Douglas sat coolly smoking his cigar, a friend stopped him. "You can't speak yet," he said. "Hitt ain't here"—and they waited until Robert R. Hitt, the Chicago *Tribune's* short-hand reporter, was ready.[7]

Lincoln began by answering a series of Douglas's queries. He had never asked the repeal of the Fugitive Slave Act, for he believed the South entitled to such a law. He was not pledged against the admission of more slave States, for if the people of a Territory on fair vote wanted slavery they would have to be admitted with it. He was not pledged to the abolition of slavery in the District of Columbia, or to the prohibition of the domestic slave trade. But he did believe in the right and duty of Congress to exclude slavery from all Territories. He favored the abolition of slavery in the District of Columbia on condition that it should be gradual, effected with majority consent, and accompanied by compensation. Once more, he declared that he wished slavery put in such a position that it might be regarded as on the road to ultimate extinction. He then turned to Douglas with his own set of questions, of which the second was crucial. How could the Senator reconcile popular sovereignty with the Dred Scott decision?

Lincoln knew well what the answer would be. He had written a Quincy friend, Henry Asbury, two months earlier that it might be hard work to get Douglas to deal directly with the point whether a territorial legislature had the power to exclude slavery. "But if you succeed in bringing him to it—though he will be compelled to say it possesses no such power—he will instantly take ground that slavery cannot actually exist in the Territories unless the people desire it, and so give it protection by territorial legislation. If this offends the South, he will let it offend them, as at all events he means to hold on to his chances in Illinois." Lincoln knew, in fact, that Douglas had already answered. But it was worth while to put Douglas on the defensive; it was worth while to hold up his position plainly in sight of the South. Talking with Medill of

7 Sparks, *op. cit.*, 147–212; Sandburg, *Lincoln, the Prairie Years*, II, 142. It was evidence of the importance of the debates that a corps of newspapermen accompanied the principals. Chester P. Dewey represented the N. Y. *Evening Post;* Henry Villard the Phila. *Press;* Horace White the Chicago *Press and Tribune.* Robert R. Hitt of the *Press and Tribune* furnished a good shorthand report of Lincoln's speeches; and two experts, James B. Sheridan and Henry Binmore, did the same for Douglas in the Chicago *Times.* Various editors, including C. H. Ray and Joseph Medill of the Chicago *Tribune*, appeared at times. David R. Locke, the Ohio journalist later known as Petroleum V. Nasby, talked with Lincoln at Quincy, and Charles F. Browne (Artemus Ward) interviewed him at Springfield for *Vanity Fair.*

the *Tribune* and others on the train, Lincoln had insisted against their objections on posing the question.[8]

The Little Giant answered all four of Lincoln's queries promptly. Three were minor. He would vote to admit Kansas before she had ninety-three thousand people; he believed it impossible for the Supreme Court to commit such "moral treason" as to hold that a State could not exclude slaves; and he would have the United States acquire more territory whenever needed, leaving the inhabitants of each new area to settle the question of slavery as they pleased. Coming then to the major query, Douglas unhesitatingly affirmed that the people of a Territory could, by lawful means, shut out slavery prior to the formation of a State constitution. Despite the Dred Scott decision, the people had the right to admit or exclude slavery, for it could not exist a day or an hour unless supported by local police regulations. "These police regulations can only be established by the local legislature, and if the people are opposed to slavery they will elect representatives to that body who will by unfriendly legislation effectually prevent the introduction of it into their midst." Thus, no matter what the Supreme Court said on the "abstract question," still "the right of the people to make a slave Territory or a free Territory is perfect and complete under the Nebraska bill."

In thus pinning the Senator down, more sweepingly and dramatically than ever before, to the doctrine of control by local police legislation, the Freeport debate caught the nation's attention. Various other men had stated this idea. Speaker Orr had enunciated it in the Kansas debates in 1856. Alexander H. Stephens had asserted it. Senator Cass in his Detroit speech of September 4, 1854, had explained just how at all times "the fate of slavery in these new regions must depend upon the will of the people." But now, forcibly reiterated at a time when men's emotions were keenly sensitive, the doctrine had the naked, quivering, eye-compelling quality of a brandished sword.

[III]

Nearly three weeks elapsed between Freeport and the third debate on September 15 at Jonesboro, a period spent by both men in active campaigning. At Clinton on the 2d, Lincoln perhaps said: "You can fool all of the people some of the time, and some of the people all of the time, but you cannot fool

8 When Medill, shown the question, protested on the train, Lincoln declared that he would "spear it at Douglas" that afternoon. Arriving in Freeport, Medill told Norman B. Judd and Elihu B. Washburne of Lincoln's purpose. They too protested, but Lincoln could not be moved. See Medill's story in Sparks, ed., *Lincoln-Douglas Debates*, 203–206. Cf. Randall, *Lincoln the President*, I, 124, 125. As a matter of fact, Douglas had asserted the doctrine of "unfriendly legislation" in his Bloomington and Springfield speeches, July 16–17; *Illinois State Register*, July 19.

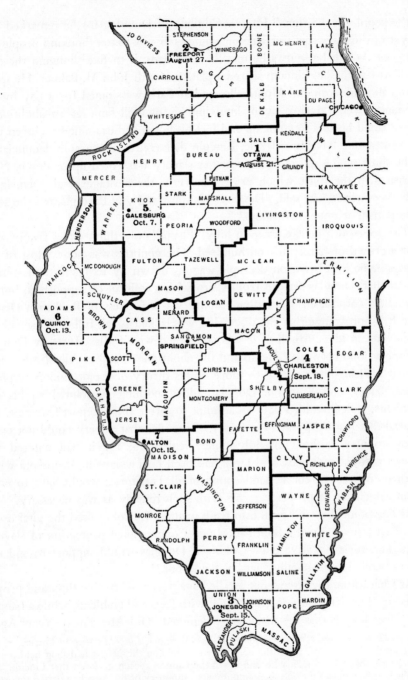

The Seven Douglas-Lincoln Debates

Black lines indicate Congressional Districts; numerals the points and dates of debates.

all the people all the time." He was thinking of Douglas, for he remarked to a lawyer of the place that the Senator would "tell a lie to ten thousand people one day even though he knows he may have to deny it to five thousand the next day." At Carlinville, Lincoln shared a platform with John M. Palmer. He spoke also in Bloomington and Monticello, and at Paris was joined for a day by the eloquent Owen Lovejoy, who, knowing his own ill-fame as an abolitionist, invited timid hearers to come up and feel his horns and examine his cloven foot and forked tail. At Edwardsville, Lincoln delivered a memorable denunciation of the spirit which did not care whether slavery was voted up or down. "Our defense is in the spirit which prizes liberty as the heritage of all men, in all lands everywhere," he said. "Destroy this spirit and you have planted the seeds of despotism at your own doors." [9]

The Jonesboro debate, deep in hilly "Egypt" only thirty miles from Cairo, drew a crowd of hardly fifteen hundred. The country was poor. Most of the farmers came into town on decrepit wagons drawn by ox-teams, and stunted oxen at that. Douglas arrived from Cairo with a trainful of supporters; but he aroused no enthusiasm, for Union County was a fortress of Buchanan Democrats. It is not strange that the discussion was lackadaisical, full of personalities, and lacking in ideas. Much of it was concerned with futile efforts by Douglas to forge a bond between Lincoln and the abolitionists, and equally futile stage-thunder by Lincoln in trying to shore up his theory of a plot among Stephen, Roger, James, and Franklin. Douglas added nothing substantial to his old arguments; Lincoln added only an attempt to refute the Freeport Doctrine. He declared that history proved the falsity of the idea that slavery could not enter a new country without friendly police legislation; for it had entered the colonies without such aids, and Dred had been held a slave in Minnesota without them. Moreover, the Federal courts in all Territories would have to meet any infringement of property rights with such remedy as was necessary.

At one point they did push into fresh ground. Lincoln raised the vital question of an attempt by the South to obtain Congressional protection of slavery in the Territories—a slave code—asking if Douglas would support it; and the Senator replied emphatically that he would not.[10]

At Charleston, the attendance swelled again—ten or twelve thousand people gathering. The flat prairie town was gay with flags and emblems, while a banner eighty feet long across the main street depicted "Old Abe Thirty Years Ago"

9 Sandburg, *Lincoln, the Prairie Years*, II, 142; Baringer, *Lincoln's Rise to Power*, 27, 28. It was not until after 1900, when the epigram about fooling the people had long held popular currency, that several men who had heard the Clinton speech declared that Lincoln had used the words quoted. Our only contemporaneous summary of the speech, a partial report in the Bloomington *Pantagraph* of September 9, 1858, does not contain the epigram. But it sounds like Lincoln and has gained a qualified acceptance as his by good students.

10 Sparks, ed., *Lincoln-Douglas Debates*, 213–266.

driving three yoke of oxen harnessed to a Kentucky wagon. Excitement over the campaign seemed now at its peak. Delegation after delegation rolled in. One train discharged eleven carloads of interested Indianians. The *Evening Post* correspondent wrote that the popular interest in politics was astonishing. "Over long, weary miles of hot, dusty prairie, the processions of eager partisans come on foot, on horseback, in wagons drawn by horses or mules; men, women, and children, old and young; the half-sick just out of the last shake, children in arms, infants . . . pushing on in clouds of dust under a blazing sun . . . talking, discussing, litigious, vociferous, while the roar of artillery, the music of bands, the waving of banners, the huzza of crowds . . . combine to render the scene one of commotion and confusion." Lincoln and Douglas had spent the previous night at Mattoon, and were escorted ten miles along the highway by lines of carriages, wagons full of young people, and prancing horsemen. In Lincoln's procession was a chariot with thirty-two young women, representing as many States.

Both candidates by this time had found the campaign physically gruelling, for it meant lost sleep, bad food, heat, dust, and incessant strain. Douglas suffered the more, though he traveled much of the time in a private car which both impressed voters with his dignity and saved his strength; while on some journeys his wife accompanied him. She was "without exception the handsomest woman I have ever seen," recorded one observer; her charm, good sense, and tact were invaluable politically; and she guarded her husband's diet and rest. But his drinking and his poor physical condition told against him. Mrs. Douglas complained that he lost half his clothes. "I got him four dozen shirts last spring, and two or three sets of studs; he lost all his shirts but two, with one that doesn't belong to him, and all the studs but four, which belong to four different sets."

Lincoln snatched some sleep wherever he could. Traveling by night in a dirty day-coach from Springfield to Clinton, he promised to rouse Horace White of the Chicago *Tribune* at Decatur, where they had to change cars; but both fell fast asleep. Lincoln awakened barely in time to scramble off, and White was carried on to Indiana. Herndon gives us a vignette of Lincoln after the Jonesboro speech: sitting hot, dust-stained, and exhausted in a packed railroad station, still harassed by politicians as he waited for the midnight train north, and worrying over his Charleston speech the day after; then jammed into an overcrowded coach; and finally obtaining a few hours' slumber when a stratagem got him into an empty car.

At Charleston, most of the debate was on the low level of accusation and counter-accusation. The invented conspiracies, that of Lincoln and Trumbull to convert freesoil Whigs and Democrats into abolitionists, and that of Buchanan, Taney, and Douglas to spread slavery over the whole Union, received preposterous attention. This shadowboxing was unworthy of such men. At one point, Lincoln snatched his former colleague O. B. Ficklin by the coat collar to the front of the stand, to testify that in Congress Lincoln had not refused to vote supplies for the Mexican War. Ficklin's astonishment was so comical that the audience burst into a roar of laughter. Douglas vigorously reiterated his old positions. Lincoln, however, did present his conservative views on the racial question at some length. Douglas had accused the Republicans of lacking consistency on the subject. In northern Illinois, he said, their principles were jet black, in the center a decent mulatto, and in "Egypt" almost white. A house divided cannot stand—well, what of the Republican house?

To this witty hit Lincoln answered that he believed the negro must hold an inferior status. "I am not, nor ever have been, in favor of bringing about in any way the social and political equality of the white and black races. . . . I am not, nor ever have been, in favor of making voters or jurors of negroes, nor of qualifying them to hold office, nor to intermarry with white people, and I will say in addition to this that there is a physical difference between the white and black races which I believe will forever forbid the two races living together on terms of social and political equality." Ultimate emancipation, he thought, would take a century or more; but slavery must be put in a position where ultimate emancipation was in prospect. Meanwhile, though Lincoln believed that the States had power to make negroes citizens, he was opposed to the exercise of such a right by Illinois. By the standards of 1950 these utterances lacked courage; by those of 1860 his general stand seemed advanced, and his reservations accurately reflected the views of the vast majority of Illinois free-soilers, who did not want negro equality—or the negro at all.[11]

Nearly three weeks elapsed before the next debate. Douglas spoke in Sullivan, Danville, and Urbana—Lincoln following him. Then Lincoln turned west while Douglas went on north.

[IV]

They met again at Galesburg on October 7, in the most picturesque and impressive of all the debates. The town, founded just over twenty years earlier under the inspiration of the Rev. George W. Gale, who planned it as seat of a

11 This emphatic utterance against racial equality at Charleston brought down on Lincoln's head the abuse of abolitionists. The *Congregational Herald*, edited in Chicago by four clergymen, assailed him (September 30) because he did not go far enough in defense of the negro. "Our standard-bearer has faltered thus soon, while the contest has only begun," it lamented. More than a vague sympathy with freedom was needed from him: "He must adopt its radical principles and stand by them in victory or defeat." This was a foretaste of the Radical attacks which Lincoln would meet in Civil War days.

theological seminary and a rallying point of freesoilers, could boast not only of five thousand people but of some intellectual distinction. Knox College, coeval with the settlement, flourished there. Henry Ward Beecher's brother, Edward, was pastor of the Congregational church. White houses and fine lawns under rising elms gave the town a neat, quiet New England look; but it was also an important rail junction, a line from Burlington and another from Quincy joining here to run northeast to Chicago, and a foundry and farm-implement factory were busy. In the Frémont campaign, Knox County had voted two to one for the Republicans. After a heavy downpour the previous day, the weather was damp and chilly. Nevertheless, twenty thousand people gathered under the snapping flags and bunting and they showed genuine enthusiasm. One delegation carried a great poster depicting Douglas and a flimsy platform labeled "Dred Scott" collapsing together. The Macomb Lincoln Club bore aloft another which gave the answer of Illinoisans to Hammond's mudsill speech:

SMALL-FISTED FARMERS, MUD SILLS OF SOCIETY, GREASY MECHANICS, FOR A. LINCOLN.

This, wrote Horace White later, was Lincoln's best speech of the campaign. Nor did Douglas fail to keep his argument on a high level. Standing on the platform in front of Knox College's "Old Main," they held public attention for three hours in the cold northwest wind, as they had held it elsewhere in blazing heat. Once more Douglas boasted of his fidelity to the banner of popular sovereignty; once more he chided Lincoln for believing in negro equality; and once more he asserted his Freeport Doctrine. Lincoln, responding, again declared that the negro was equal to the white man in his right to life, liberty, and the pursuit of happiness; he again said that while this principle could not be thrust too roughly against the necessities springing from the actual presence of black people and slavery in America, it should be applied to new areas; and he again asserted that the Union would be safe only when slavery was placed in the path to ultimate extinction.[12]

Never had Douglas shown greater intensity of feeling. He taunted the Republicans with their sectional character. "Permit me to say," he thundered, "that no political creed is sound which cannot be proclaimed fearlessly in every State of this Union where the Federal Constitution is the supreme law of the land." Is it a true test of the soundness of a doctrine, rejoined Lincoln, that in some places people will not let you proclaim it? At one time Chicagoans would not let Douglas preach his favorite doctrine. "I ask his attention to the fact that by the rule of nationality he is himself fast becoming sectional. I ask his atten-

12 At Galesburg, Lincoln wore a long cloak instead of his usual shawl, and when he rose to reply to Douglas he handed it to a friend, saying: "Hold this while I stone Stephen," Earnest Elmo Calkins, *They Broke the Prairie*, 277–295.

tion to the fact that his speeches would not go as current south of the Ohio River as they have formerly gone there." Douglas accused Lincoln of infidelity to the Constitution. But Lincoln answered that the Supreme Court followed the election returns. "The Dred Scott decision, as it is, never would have been made in its present form if the party that made it had not been sustained previously by the elections." The grand future of the nation, declared Douglas, lay with the broad principles of the Democratic Party. Yes, responded Lincoln, Douglas stood for annexations, and if Democratic policy were followed, a grab would be made for large parts of Latin America. And as neither the whole people nor the whole government of the United States—merely President and Senate—would have a voice in these annexations, the policy was dangerous.

At Galesburg both men disclosed for the first time a gleam of eloquence. Douglas's contrast between the high national mission of the Democratic Party and the bigoted sectionalism of the Republicans was eloquent. So was Lincoln's echo of one of Clay's finest passages. "I do think," proclaimed Lincoln, "that Judge Douglas and whoever, like him, teaches that the negro has no share, humble though it may be, in the Declaration of Independence, is going back to the era of our liberty and independence, and, in so far as in him lies, muzzling the cannon that thunders its annual joyous return; that he is blowing out the moral lights around us, when he contends that whoever wants slaves has a right to hold them; that he is penetrating, so far as lies in his power, the human soul, and eradicating the light of reason and the love of liberty, when he is in every way possible preparing the public mind, by his vast influence, for making the institution of slavery perpetual and national."

Quincy, too, where they met on October 13, had a New England aspect, though Adams County had been almost equally settled by Yankees and former Virginians and Kentuckians. Here, on the fine bluff overlooking the Mississippi, near some old Indian mounds, was a city well known to young Mark Twain and young John Hay, who had grown up close at hand. The brilliant Carl Schurz, traveling to Quincy for a speech of his own, was on a Chicago train when Lincoln climbed aboard, and has left us a vivid impression of the man. The whole car broke into glad shouts of "Hello, Abe! How are you?" Amid much back-slapping, Lincoln greeted the politicians by their first names. "There he stood," writes Schurz, "overtopping by several inches all those surrounding him." He wore a rusty black dress-coat with inadequate sleeves, black trousers which fell far short of his large feet, and a battered stovepipe hat. His long neck projected from a soft white collar encircled by a black string tie. While his left hand clutched a cotton umbrella and scarred black satchel, and his left arm bore a gray woolen shawl, he kept his right hand free for the endless hand-shaking. When Schurz was introduced, he treated the awed German like a lifelong friend. He explained the points he intended to make at Quincy and asked advice; he told quaint stories to illustrate his ideas; and he talked so simply and familiarly that Schurz soon felt as if they had known each other always.

The day of the debate was fine. Twelve thousand people came by river boat, rail, and highway from Iowa, Missouri, and Illinois; banners and bands were as exciting as ever; and both orators got a rousing reception. Lincoln spoke so persuasively that Schurz, while not crediting him with any distinction of thought, did not see how he could be answered. But when Douglas stood up, natty in well-fitting broadcloth and white linen, the horizontal wrinkle between his keen eyes deep and scowling, the German soon learned. Douglas's baritone voice was hoarse and rough; his tone was angry, dictatorial, and insolent; he used offensive language. "But his sentences were well put together, his points strongly accentuated, his argumentation seemingly clear and plausible." As he sat down, his followers burst into jubilant applause. Lincoln then made the final half-hour speech, and in Schurz's opinion carried off the palm. His arguments were so forcible, his thrusts so piercing, his illustrations so apt, "that the meeting again and again, broke out in bursts of delight by which even many of his opponents were carried away, while the scowl on Douglas's face grew darker and darker." [13]

At Quincy, much old straw was lustily rethreshed, yielding little grain. The most striking passages were those in which the debaters assailed each other for proposing no constructive action regarding slavery, and exchanged divergent views of the Freeport Doctrine. Lincoln asserted that the Republicans did have a plan. Whenever they could get the country to stand and act with them in regarding slavery as a wrong, "then, and not till then, I think, will we in some way come to an end of the slavery agitation." Douglas declared that this "plan" was barren. Lincoln would simply hem slavery into the areas where it existed; and what did this mean? The natural increase of the negroes would soon exceed the capacity of the soil to support them. "He will hem them in until starvation seizes them, and by starving them to death he will put slavery in the course of ultimate extinction." Lincoln pronounced the Freeport Doctrine a fraud. How could a member of a territorial legislature swear to uphold the Constitution and then deny a slaveholding settler rights which Douglas said the Constitution gave him? But Douglas retorted that the Freeport Doctrine was entirely valid, and that such Southerners as Speaker Orr, A. H. Stephens, and Sam Smith of Tennessee said so.

The seventh and final debate at Alton, however unoriginal, was one of the most creditable of the series, pitched throughout on a high level of reason. The

13 Sparks, ed., *Lincoln-Douglas Debates*, 389–448; Schurz, *Reminiscences*, II, 89–99.

crowd was small, but both men knew they would be well reported in Missouri and Kentucky as well as the North. Douglas was in his best fighting trim, though a St. Louis journalist, John F. Hume, who had come on an excursion steamer, was impressed by the painful huskiness of his voice. Lincoln, according to this observer, stood stiff and straight, his countenance immobile; Douglas's countenance was leonine and full of expression, while his manner was excited and he emphasized his speech by almost continuous movement of hands, feet, and face. This auditor was disappointed that Lincoln, standing almost on the spot that had drunk Elijah Lovejoy's blood, spoke without any touch of fiery inspiration.[14]

Douglas showed courageous energy before an audience mainly of Southern sympathies by denouncing the English bill as unjust and assailing Buchanan for following a vengeful course against him. He was full of contempt for the Administration lackeys in Illinois. Appealing for party unity, he said that the life of the nation depended on avoiding a sectional schism. Once more he enunciated his Freeport position, refusing to cringe or evade on the issue. His speech rose to a fervent climax. No principle on earth, he said, was more sacred than that of popular sovereignty. "I will never violate or abandon that doctrine, if I have to stand alone. I have resisted the blandishments and threats of power on the one side, and seduction on the other, and have stood immovably for that principle, fighting for it when assailed by Northern mobs, or threatened by Southern hostility. I have defended it against the North and the South, and I will defend it against whoever assails it, and I will follow it wherever its logical conclusion leads me." That was Douglas's finest hour. However mistaken some men might deem his Nebraska Act, he had shown magnificent consistency in defending its principles.[15]

Lincoln, too, brought his campaign to a telling climax. His speech was full of witty points. He referred to Douglas's old promises that the Nebraska Act would see them at the end of the slavery agitation. "The last tip of the last joint of the old serpent's tail was just drawing out of view." Once more he pointed out that the Republicans, without desire to touch slavery in the States, wished to exclude it from the Territories; and he rehearsed their two chief arguments. One was that the people of the whole nation had a stake in the kind of institutions set up in the common domain. How many men about Alton had left slave States and came to Illinois to get rid of the institution of slavery? A voice shouted: "A thousand and one!" The greater argument was that slavery ought to be placed in the course of ultimate extinction. He quoted Henry Clay. He pointed to the care with which the fathers of the nation had excluded the word "slavery" from the Constitution; for they hoped that, when

14   John F. Hume, *The Abolitionists*, Ch. 12.
15   Sparks, ed., *Lincoln-Douglas Debates*, 449–510, covers Alton in detail.

it was read by patriotic men after slavery had passed away, nothing on the face of the great charter of liberty would suggest that human servitude had ever existed in the republic. Then, adverting to Douglas's refusal to treat slavery as a wrong, he uttered a dozen sentences which indicated why he, rather than his rival, held title-deeds to greatness. That is the real issue, he declared:

That is the issue which will continue in this country when these poor tongues of Judge Douglas and myself shall be silent. It is the eternal struggle between these two principles—right and wrong—throughout the world. . . . The one is the common right of humanity, and the other the divine right of kings. It is the same principle in whatever shape it develops itself. It is the same spirit that says, "You toil and work and earn bread, and I'll eat it. . . ." [A clarification of this issue] will hereafter place with us all men who really do wish that the wrong may have an end. And whenever we can get rid of the fog which obscures the real question—when we can get Judge Douglas and his friends to avow a policy looking to its perpetuation—we can get out from among them that class of men and bring them to the side of those who treat it as a wrong. Then there will soon be an end of it, and that end will be its "ultimate extinction." Whenever the issue can be distinctly made, and all extraneous matter thrown out, so that men can fairly see the real difference between the parties, this difference will soon be settled, and it will be done peaceably, too. There will be no war, no violence. It will be placed again where the wisest and best men in the world placed it.

[V]

Obviously, the debates had shown little logical progression. Had the speakers left slavery and devoted some attention to other topics in the Republican platform—free lands, opposition to monopolies, internal improvements—they might have achieved more freshness. For three reasons this was not done. First, slavery was so much the burning topic of the hour that the public really wanted exclusive attention paid to it. In the second place, Lincoln and Douglas were in rough agreement on most economic topics. Douglas believed in free homesteads; he had been one of the first to introduce a measure on the subject, granting one hundred and sixty acres to any settler who cultivated the land for four years. Douglas believed in internal improvements, and he had been ingenious in plans to finance them by land grants and tonnage taxes. Neither Douglas nor Lincoln was much interested in the tariff, or understood its intricacies, or believed that his supporters cared much about it. In the third place, slavery was the topic best suited to hold disparate elements in the two parties together.[16]

16 Douglas confessed his ignorance of the tariff; *Cong. Globe*, 36th Cong., 2d Sess., 953; Lincoln ignored the subject. Obviously, Lincoln could unite old-time conservative Whigs, old-time freesoil Democrats, and even abolitionists on his freesoil platform; Douglas could unite pro-Southern and pro-Northern elements on his popular sovereignty doctrine.

Yet, for both nation and State, the debates, which were at first over-estimated in value and later underestimated, did contribute to a clarification of issues. Though Douglas had long before stated the essence of the Freeport Doctrine, the debates dramatized it in a way which for the first time arrested the attention of millions. "There was a great deal of sympathy felt for Douglas throughout Kentucky," wrote a Covington man to Alexander H. Stephens, "until his speech at Freeport, where he put forth squatter sover-eignty in all its monstrosity. That speech cooled the ardor of our people." [17] Republicans also seized on it. Horace White suggested to Senator Trum-bull that the Kansas legislature be incited to put the doctrine of unfriendly legislation in force by abolishing slavery and nullifying the Fugitive Slave Act; these measures were to be based on the Freeport speech in an effort to ruin Douglas at the South. Thus, he wrote, they might put Douglas out of the running at Charleston. [18]

Lincoln's speeches, read from the Kaw to the Kennebec, had driven home with memorable distinctness his salient conclusions. What were they? First, that slavery was the one great divisive issue which constantly threatened the disruption of the Union. Second, that it had not been such a threat in earlier times because the nation's founders, by restricting its sphere, cutting off its African source, shamefacedly avoiding any direct description of it in the Constitution, and in numerous instances denouncing it, had led men to believe that it would ultimately perish. Third, that ever since Douglas and others had adopted a new attitude, treating slavery as national and perpetual, the fever aroused by the issue had deepened. Fourth, that the only salvation was to return to the old path, restricting slavery and convincing Americans that it was on the way to disappearance. Finally, that once this new attitude was adopted, its ultimate abolition might take a century or more, but could be achieved without war or bloodshed.

Historically and economically, his argument was subject to sharp emenda-tions. The fathers had not forbidden the expansion of slavery into areas to which it was manifestly suited; the Southwest Territory had been opened to it while the Northwest was closed. Their *expectations* regarding its termination had been much more equivocal than their hopes. The agitation had grown dan-gerous when the nation had first annexed areas in which it seemed an open question whether slavery would be pecuniarily advantageous to settlers, long before Douglas had dealt with Kansas.

17 J. W. Stevenson, October 8, 1858, Stephens Papers, LC. Southerners at the Charleston Convention in 1860 had the Freeport speech with them to use in bombarding Douglas's followers. Murat Halstead, *Caucuses of 1860*, p. 3.

18 December 8, 1858, Trumbull Papers. "A similar broth might be put to boiling in Nebraska," wrote White. For a full account of the indignation which the Freeport Doctrine aroused in the South, see Judah P. Benjamin's speech in the Senate in May, 1860; *Cong. Globe*, 36th Cong., 1st Sess., 2241.

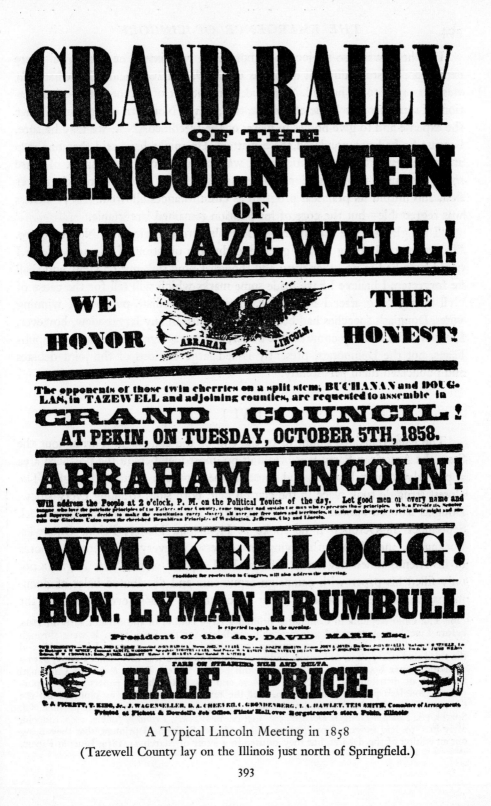

A Typical Lincoln Meeting in 1858

(Tazewell County lay on the Illinois just north of Springfield.)

His thesis was also subject to a more vital criticism. The phrase "ultimate extinction," disregarding all questions of *when*, and *how*, and with what *aids*, was too vague to be helpful. Why did he not speak of compensated emancipation, of some broad scheme of colonization, of the Northern obligation to share the expense and to give homes to many of the freedmen? Not, we may be sure, because he had not pondered these matters. He might have said that one step at a time was sufficient. Politically, it was sound policy not to speak of these social costs until public opinion had been prepared; his party had to gain power first, and unfold its practical program as circumstances allowed. His vagueness was regrettable—but the core of his position remained irrefutable.

"I am glad I made the late race," Lincoln wrote a friend on November 19. "It gave me a hearing on the great and durable question of the age, which I could have had in no other way; and though I now sink out of view, and shall be forgotten, I believe I have made some marks which will tell for the cause of civil liberty long after I have gone." For the immediate purpose of winning votes, Douglas's speeches had been as good as his. In any larger view, however, Lincoln had decidedly come off the better; and it was significant that the Republicans, not the Democrats, presently issued large editions of the joint debates and publicized them persistently.[19]

[VI]

The issue remained doubtful to the end of the campaign. Throughout the State the American Party was breaking up, most members in the northern area apparently joining Lincoln, and those in the southern districts, Douglas. The closest struggle took place in the central belt, both sides straining every sinew. Douglas labored almost to exhaustion there; for example, in the single week September 28–October 4, he spoke at Hennepin, Henry, Pekin, Oquawka, Burlington, and Monmouth, giving set addresses at every point but one. Some of his friends toiled devotedly. Charles H. Lanphier of the *State Register* not only filled his paper with campaign arguments and distributed bales of documents, but visited personally every precinct and almost every voter in the

19 The Ohio Republican Committee printed a large edition of the debates early in 1860, before Lincoln was regarded as a probable candidate for the presidency. It went through numerous editions, the second announcing that fifteen thousand copies had been sold, and the third that thirty thousand copies had been sold. The price was fifty cents a copy, $250 a thousand, paper bound; $350 a thousand, cloth bound. Follett, Foster & Co. of Cincinnati took care of distribution. The N. Y. *Tribune* and other Republican papers solicited purchases. Douglas's protest, June 9, 1860, that the text of his speeches, as reported by the Chicago *Times*, had been altered and mutilated, does not seem to have been justified. Cf. Sparks, ed., *Lincoln-Douglas Debates*, 592–595; N. Y. *Weekly Tribune*, June 2, 1860. Lincoln, early in 1859, had suggested to Johnson and Bradford, Springfield printers, that they bring out an edition of the debates, but they refused in a letter of March 21, 1859; Lincoln Papers.

counties surrounding Sangamon.[20] Lincoln spoke with as much assiduity as his rival. Sometimes he dropped from his high moral level to score a swift hit. For example, late October brought him into Hancock County, speaking to large crowds at Carthage, La Harpe, and other points. One Republican wrote:

I took Lincoln to Dallas on Saturday 2000 persons there he was interrupted often in his speech one Tom Gates called him a liar Lincoln requested him to stand up he done so, great God how Lincoln scored him you could have heard the boys shout a mile. Fitch and others painted a large Negro on a canvass 12 feet square and wrote in a circle over the head Equality this was swinging to a line stretched across the street and we marched under it. Lincoln said in his speech that the democrats had honored them with their favorite banner, that it had been a peculiar favorite banner ever since they had elected Col. Richard M. Johnson to the Vice Presidency and that the motto surrounding the head was certainly his for Col. Dick had shown proof of the fact. [Johnson had lived openly with a Negro woman by whom he had a family of children.] [21]

In a contest of this kind, Douglas was no less in his element than in the senatorial melee, and his inborn gifts of political appeal gleamed brightly against the Illinois cornfields. His unaffected warmth of heart, frank ingenuousness of speech, and bonhomie of demeanor won friends in myriads. With a marvelous gift for names and faces, a genuine interest in the personal welfare of others, and a deep vein of talkative companionship, he addressed Joe and Tom, Squire Rice and Parson Hickham, in just the way which touched their self-esteem; recalled old episodes—the misspelled indictments in McLean County, the reception at Governor Carlin's back in '38, the day the first train ran into Peoria—with just the right felicity of touch; rattled off Washington anecdotes in a fashion which gave little knots of hearers the sense of being on the inside of national politics; inquired after an ailing child or an aged parent. He inspired young men with a feeling of partnership in his great cause. One remembered for decades how he had placed his hand upon a flattered shoulder, saying: "I count very much on your help in this campaign." His boyish appearance, his wonderful memory, the pleasant smile and kind words with which he threaded every crowd, left all those he momentarily touched with a pleased sense that he was their personal friend.[22]

In speaking to his hard-working, hard-living rural audiences, Douglas did not fail to recall his days of boyhood poverty. "I made as good a schoolteacher as I could, and when a cabinet-maker I made a good bedstead and tables, although

20 Chicago *Times*, October 1-9, November 7, 1860.
21 Alexander Simpson to John C. Bagby, October 25, 1860; **Bagby Papers.**
22 Allen Johnson, *Douglas*, 319. His tremendous industry also aroused admiration. The Washington correspondent of the Baltimore *Sun* wrote (August 23) that several Illinoisans had come East full of wonder over his endurance: "He makes two or three speeches a day, and, by reason of the heat, is obliged to change his clothes three times a day at least."

my old boss said I succeeded better with bureaus and secretaries than anything else." In cities, he was adept at making the Germans and Irish feel his good-will. It was no accident that the Emmet Guards had escorted him to his Chicago platform. Everyone admitted that the Catholic vote would be a unit on Doug-las's side.[23] Sheahan's Chicago *Times* appealed vigorously to all foreign-born groups, publishing on election day a long final editorial headed "A Word to Irishmen." The Democratic campaign made the most of the racial issue, con-tending that Lincoln advocated negro equality, and that the Democrats were the only bulwark against the entry of colored men into Illinois to compete with white farmers and laborers. Beyond doubt this racial appeal had potency in special areas.

By his skillful fight, Douglas made the unremitting attacks of the Buchanan Administration seem impotent spleen. The officeholding gang exhibited more fury than ability, and were little helped by such imported speakers as Daniel Voorhees of Indiana, who called the Douglas men white-livered traitors. The executive blade continued to fall on Douglasite postmasters until the Chicago *Tribune* remarked that only one or two were left.[24] In their desperation the Buchananeers adopted outrageous tactics. When Douglas spoke to a large crowd at Hennepin, Fitch and Hoyne appeared with a brass band that played noisily within a hundred yards of the platform; while at Henry the audacious Hoyne mounted a stand about fifty yards from Douglas and began shouting at the top of his voice.[25] Such acts infuriated Douglas.[26] But the Buchananeers faced one insuperable obstacle; they could not meet the argument of loyal Democrats that to defeat Douglas meant electing Lincoln. This ground was much strengthened by the letters of J. J. Crittenden, Breckinridge, and Reverdy Johnson in favor of Douglas, and the speeches of Paine and Steedman of Ohio. A multitude of old-time Whigs in southern Illinois heeded Crittenden's voice. By election day it was evident that the contest was essentially one between Douglas and the Republicans, with the Administration out of the running.

The result was practically a dead heat. On November 2, the Republican leg-islative ticket polled 125,275 votes; the Douglas Democrats 121,090 votes; and

23   See letter of a Jewish gentleman of Quincy, December 26, 1858; Trumbull Papers. He wished to put fifty thousand Jewish votes behind the party in 1860 by getting the Republi-cans to push a Senate protest against Jewish persecution abroad.
24   Chicago *Tribune*, quoted in Indianapolis *Journal*, October 20, 1858.
25   Chicago *Times*, October 1, 5, 1858.
26   James May to Buchanan, October 23, 1858; Buchanan Papers. "The Washington *Union* by its injudicious assaults has created a strong sympathy for Douglas. He is a hero in Ohio." J. W. Stevenson, Covington, October 8, 1858, Stephens Papers, LC. This was true. The Cin-cinnati *Enquirer*, Cleveland *Plain Dealer*, and Columbus *Statesman* all expressed sympathy for Douglas and deprecated the idea of his defeat. Congressman Burns, the only Democratic Representative in Ohio who had voted for Lecompton, was a special object of attack. Madi-son Kelly, Cleveland, September 15, 1858; Buchanan Papers.

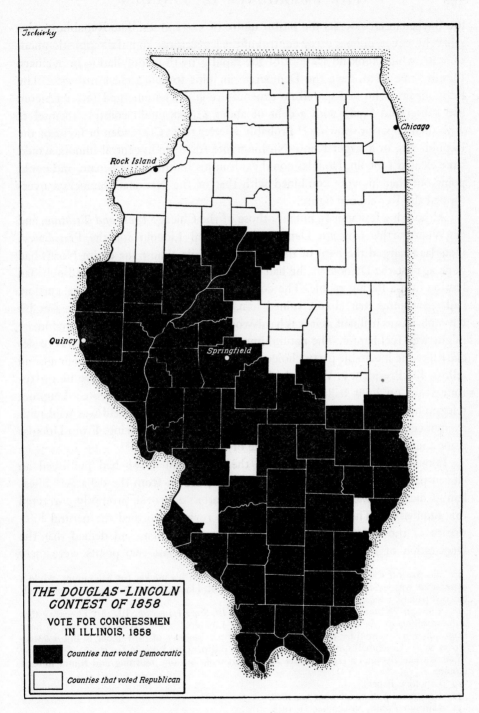

Tschirky

● Chicago

Rock Island ●

Quincy ●

Springfield ●

**THE DOUGLAS-LINCOLN
CONTEST OF 1858**

VOTE FOR CONGRESSMEN
IN ILLINOIS, 1858

Counties that voted Democratic

Counties that voted Republican

the Buchanan Democrats the pitiful figure of 5,071 votes. The Republican plurality, however, did not carry control of the legislature. An unfair apportionment of seats, which took no account of the rapid growth of population in northern Illinois since 1850, gave the Democrats in joint session a clear majority. The Republicans, who had spared no expenditure and who emerged (after Lincoln had subscribed $500) with a debt of about $2,500, could comfort themselves with their superior showing.[27] Probably a letter from Crittenden in favor of the Republicans, or a larger Know-Nothing vote for them in central Illinois, would have elected Lincoln. Douglas could exult in his return to the Senate, and could point out that his vote combined with that of the National Democrats overtopped the Republican figure.

Although a few voices, notably those of the Chicago *Press and Tribune*, and of Wentworth's Chicago *Democrat*, suggested Lincoln for the Presidency, Douglas emerged the hero of the contest.[28] While almost the entire North had gone against the Democrats, he had held his State; he had turned the Buchanan faction into a fleeing rabble. The cost was high: he had worked to exhaustion, had spent sums that almost ruined him, and had made new enemies. But his triumph was as brilliant as it was hard-won, and, as congratulations poured in, he might well feel happy. The natural impulse of friends and foes alike was to declare him the inevitable party choice in 1860—though he tactfully discouraged all talk of the Presidency. When the legislature met in January, it gave him fifty-four votes on joint ballot against Lincoln's forty-six. The devoted Lanphier telegraphed the result to him in the East, adding that Springfield was wild with excitement, guns booming, bands playing, and whiskey flowing. From Douglas came the laconic reply: "Let the voice of the people rule." [29]

Immediately before the election, the Richmond *South* had published an eleven-point summary of Douglas's doctrines, drawn from the debates.[30] Sheahan's Chicago *Times*, doubtless with the Senator's approval, promptly corrected this summary.[31] The first three points, thus revised, affirmed the natural inferiority of the negro, asserted that he was not a citizen, and denied that the Declaration of Independence applied to him. The last two points were mere

27 To pay off the party debt Lincoln had to dive into his pocket for $200 more, while a general tax was levied on Republicans of means. O. M. Hatch, November 22, 1858, in miscellaneous papers, Chicago Hist. Soc.

28 Chicago *Tribune*, November 19, 1858; *Colls. Ill. State Hist. Soc.*, III, 581. The story that a massmeeting in Mansfield, Ohio, had proposed Lincoln for the Presidency seems to have been a fiction invented by the Sandusky *Commercial Register* of November 6. But a letter-writer in the Cincinnati *Gazette* of November 10 did propose Lincoln for the White House. "You are like Byron," a friend wrote him, "who woke up one morning and found himself famous."

29 Lanphier Papers.

30 Richmond *South*, October 30, 1858.

31 Chicago *Times*, November 11, 1858.

statements of fidelity to Democracy. The remaining six were more important. Douglas, according to the *Times*, maintained the possibility of a harmonious union of free and slave States. He asserted the absolute sovereignty of the States with respect to their domestic institutions. He called for a policy of noninterference between free and slave States, and between the Federal government and slave States. He upheld all constitutional guaranties of the rights of the South. He would vindicate the independence of members of Congress against executive encroachment. Not least important, he and his followers upheld the Freeport Doctrine:

> They support the decision of the Supreme Court in the Dred Scott case, in the sense that it guarantees the owners of slave property an equality with the owners of other property in introducing it into the Territories; contending, also, that as slave property is thus placed on an equal footing with other property, it, like all other property, must be subject to all such local laws of the Territory as do not infringe upon the Constitution of the United States; that slave property being thus placed on an equality with other property, if it require higher and further affirmative legislation for its protection and security than is afforded to other property, and the legislature of the Territory should decide not to discriminate in its favor to that extent, then the failure to obtain the higher protection than is afforded to other property is a misfortune attending that description of property for which the Democratic Party have no remedy and are not responsible.

A labored statement! A statement obviously chocolate-coated, too, with the half-dozen conjoined affirmations sweet to the South. The tortuous clauses about "that description of property" and the accompanying emphasis on absolute State sovereignty, non-interference, and constitutional guaranties, pointed to a deep-seated uneasiness on Douglas's part. He might have added a twelfth article of faith. He had said during the debates that the rapid growth of population made it necessary to envisage further annexations, intimating that this might well mean a marked extension of the slaveholding area.

Despite this last article of faith, which he was not anxious to emphasize in Chicago but was soon expounding lustily on a Southern tour, it was far from certain that the cotton States would take kindly to the clarification of Douglas's opinions. When they studied this statement of the impossibility in some Territories of affording slavery the special protection it needed to exist, how would they treat it? Would they not see that it meant containment just as much as the Republican position? In short, what would they think of the Freeport Doctrine? The answer to this question was given with speed and emphasis.

15

Steps Toward Secession

ON THE evening of October 14, 1858, James Buchanan was host at a small bachelor dinner party, his niece, Harriet Lane, being out of town. The private dining room of the White House was cheerful with flowers from the conservatory. Three congenial guests were present—Jeremiah Black, James C. Van Dyke, and James P. Anderson, a courtly Mississippi colonel in the Mexican War who would soon be a Confederate general. This was the night following the crucial Pennsylvania election. As the men dined, telegrams were handed around; and although the President had anticipated losses, they showed an unexpectedly stinging reverse. Nevertheless, the *chef* had provided a good menu; wine circulated freely; and next day Buchanan wrote Miss Lane, "We had a merry time of it, laughing among other things over our crushing defeat. It is so great that it is almost absurd." [1] Seldom if ever has a President taken so sharp a discomfiture with such levity.

Indeed, the early elections proved to be nothing less than a rout for the Administration. In Indiana, an historic fortress of Democracy, seven Representatives would be Republicans, two would be Douglas Democrats, and only two supporters of Buchanan. The next legislature would be Republican. In Pennsylvania, also traditionally Democratic, but two of the twenty-five Representatives chosen were Lecompton men. One of them succeeded in Philadelphia only after his party had mobilized about seventeen hundred "colonized" hands in the Navy Yard. [2] Buchanan's foe, Hickman, was sent back to Congress in triumph.

Particularly bitter to the President was the downfall in the Berks County district of his old friend Glancy Jones, chairman of Ways and Means, and Administration floor leader. Violently attacked for his support of the Lecompton and English bills, the servile Jones had been renominated by a more than servile placeholders' convention. A passionate revolt of the voters had ensued. Despite the use of large sums from Washington, the opposition can-

---

1 To Harriet Lane, October 15, 1858; Buchanan-Johnson Papers.
2 So F. P. Blair, Sr., learned in Philadelphia; letter October 20, 1858, Cameron Papers.

didate was sent to Congress. Buchanan's immediate appointment of the discomfited Jones to be minister to Austria excited indignant comment among those who regarded it as an excessively plain way of setting popular opinion at defiance.[3]

In Ohio, the Republican upsurge left the Democrats with only four Representatives out of twenty-two—and three of them, S. S. Cox, Vallandigham, and George Pendleton, had endorsed Douglas. In upper New England, the Republicans swept Maine and Vermont. In the Northwest, they carried the Minnesota legislature (which would give them a new Senator) and elected the two Congressmen from that State and the two from Iowa. Altogether, October closed in a hubbub of Republican rejoicing. The party was particularly pleased to return to public life a pair of Whig veterans too long out of office: Tom Corwin of Ohio, humorous, shrewd, and eloquent, and Thaddeus Stevens, called by Greeley's *Tribune* the ablest man in Pennsylvania.

And if the October elections staggered the Administration, those of November left it prostrate throughout the North. The remaining New England States chose solid Republican blocks of Representatives. In Massachusetts, the vote was overwhelming. N. P. Banks was reelected governor with a clear majority over both the Democratic and Know-Nothing parties, while only a corporal's guard of Democrats was left in the legislature. Eli Thayer, Anson Burlingame, and Henry L. Dawes went back to Congress, and in the historic Third District Charles Francis Adams, who had just declared that the current issues touched the very essence of free government, was chosen.[4] New Jersey filled its five Congressional seats with three Republicans and two anti-Lecompton Democrats. In Illinois, the victory of Douglas was worse than gall to the Administration, but that was not all. Of the nine Representatives, the Douglas Democrats chose five including John A. Logan and T. L. Harris, the Republicans four. Michigan and Wisconsin kept their places in the Republican column.

To make the result decisive, the Administration lost nearly all its remaining entrenchments in New York. Here the factional quarrel between the Hards under Daniel S. Dickinson and the Softs under Horatio Seymour, together with the personal feud of Fernando Wood and Dan Sickles in the metropolis, had weakened the Democrats. The Republicans nominated a strong man for governor in the merchant Edwin D. Morgan, and the trend of the hour proved irresistible. Morgan gained a decisive plurality over his opponent Amasa J. Parker; his party swept the Assembly; and of the thirty-three Congressional seats, the Republicans or anti-Lecompton Democrats took twenty-nine. In the

3 E. L. Godkin's correspondence, London *Daily News*, November 9, 1858.
4 For Adams's letter, dated October 12, see N. Y. *Tribune*, October 21, 1858.

Westchester district, the President's arch enemy, John B. Haskin, won a smashing victory. Utica sent to the House a tall, handsome young Republican of whom more would be heard—Roscoe Conkling.[5]

The catastrophe, costing the Administration eighteen House seats in all, meant that the Directory had lost control of the House, where the ten or twelve anti-Lecompton Representatives would hold the balance of power.[6] It meant a heavy diminution of Administration prestige. Toucey and Black, who knew Northern sentiment at first hand, were alarmed by the omens for 1860. And what were the causes of this slaughter, heavy enough to choke Scamander?

The central impulse behind the popular uprising was unmistakable; as the Albany *Argus* said, "a Kansas swell" had submerged every other consideration. The North was condemning Lecompton and the English bill. It was significant that nearly all Northern Congressmen who had supported the bill at the Directory's behest had run pell-mell for cover as soon as they faced the voters. English himself had been compelled by Indiana sentiment to promise to vote for the admission of Kansas as soon as the Territory framed and popularly ratified a constitution, without regard for the ninety-three thousand population test. Almost every other Democratic candidate in Indiana, Ohio, Pennsylvania, and New York had been equally explicit.[7] Wherever Lecompton was a direct issue, the popular vote was decisive. In Buchanan's own State, for example, ten Lecompton Representatives went down; two beaten for renomination, eight for reelection. Tremendous enthusiasm attended the victories of Haskin, Hickman, and Harris.[8]

In a few areas, the tariff and homestead issues had played significant roles. In lower New England, the Middle Atlantic States, and Ohio, protection was a popular Republican plank. While Thaddeus Stevens demanded higher iron duties, Yankee candidates called for assistance to textiles. The Northern Democrats, however, did not let their rivals have exclusive use of the tariff issue. Forney told a New York audience that he was for protecting industry in its whole length and breadth, while Ben Butler, running for Congress in the Lowell district of Massachusetts, denounced the low duties of 1846 and 1857 and asked for legislation to save the country from cheap European labor. He proposed a light tariff on the necessities of life and raw materials not produced at home, heavier duties on such raw materials as coal and iron, and an adequate revenue tax on luxuries. Since he also condemned the English bill, critics re-

5 See N. Y. *Tribune* editorial, "Our Elections," November 4, 1858.
6 Nichols, *Disruption of the Amer. Democracy*, 220, 221.
7 So Douglas taunted Buchanan men at Galesburg, October 7, 1858.
8 For John Van Buren's laudation of popular sovereignty see Alexander, *Pol. Hist. N. Y.*, II, 250.

marked that his platform was more Republican than Democratic.[9] The *National Intelligencer* noted that the New England Democrats desired tariffs on textiles, Louisiana Democrats on sugar, Kentucky Democrats on hemp, and Pennsylvania Democrats on iron and steel.

Party lines were similarly crossed on the homestead issue. While the Republicans thought themselves the most active friends of free land grants to settlers, and inveighed against the hostile attitude of the Deep South, many western and border Democrats stood for a rapid disposal of public holdings under a homestead law. For that matter, not a few eastern Republicans continued to pick flaws in the free land program.

Above all, the election was an emphatic Northern condemnation of the Administration's policy in trying to jam Lecompton through Congress and crush Douglas; and, exultant as the Republicans were, the popular sovereignty Democrats were happier still. Forney's *Press* gleefully pointed out that every anti-Lecompton Democrat who sought reelection had been sustained. The party might have won in State after State had it accepted Douglas's policy. If it still clung to the Administration's course, it would be completely wrecked. "Dearly as tens of thousands of honest men love the Democratic party . . . they love the vital principles of free government better, and if the bands of mercenary politicians are not quickly made sensible of their folly, they will be buried deeper than plummet ever sounded." [10] Many Democratic journals remarked that the success of Douglas in Illinois pointed the way forward.[11] Indeed, the general view of impartial men was that the party had two alternatives: they could unite on the Senator's platform with good hope of success in 1860; or they could go forward divided to sure defeat. The *Union* was quick, however, to declare that true Democrats could never surrender to Douglas and to a platform which it pronounced hardly distinguishable from that of the Free Soil Party in 1848.

The amazing fact was that the White House group took the defeat lightly. Behind the *Union's* utterance lay something more than Buchanan's weak vindictiveness, and the arrogant temper of Cobb, Thompson, and Slidell. The Directory believed that mere transient causes had produced the defeat. The economic depression, the mid-term restlessness of voters, exaggerated tales of bleeding Kansas, and the eastern belief that Republican Congressmen would furnish more tariff benefits than such a good friend of industry as Glancy Jones—these were factors which time would erase. Buchanan complacently informed Harriet Lane that he would present Congress, when it met in Decem-

9 *National Intelligencer*, October 28, 1858.
10 Phila. *Weekly Press*, November 6, 1858.
11 For example, Providence *Journal*, November 6, 1858.

ber, such a record of success as had seldom been equalled.[12] The *Union* re-marked that the party always survived disasters, "and gathers new power and strength from each recurrence of them."

But such utterances could not mask the appalling condition in which the election left the country. A feeble President, the captive of a self-willed faction of his party, now repudiated by the North; a divided Congress which faced a certain deadlock on any important legislation; a Supreme Court discredited in half the nation—such would be the government in the next two years. And civil war was already on the horizon. Had the United States possessed a minis-terial constitution, this election would have turned Buchanan out and brought new leaders and new policies forward to meet the crisis; but the American system had all the defects—as well as the occasional merits—of rigidity.

[I]

In one area, however, the blow was not underrated. It rendered the South more conscious of its exposed position, and hence more defiant. Radical slavery men had discounted it in advance; and they understood two great facts—first, that the Republican movement for containment could not easily be checked, and second, that the Northern Democrats were ceasing to be a shield for "Southern rights." All year, a steady rise of intransigence had been visible in the South. This did not spring primarily from the loss of Kansas, the party schism, and the refusal of Northern Democrats to accept Dred Scott at face value. Rather it came from a realization that the balance in area, population, wealth, and power was tipping ever more heavily against the South. This realization gave birth to a sense of angry desperation in many Southerners. The resentment aroused by Douglas's Freeport Doctrine, and the upflare of secession talk which followed the election, cannot be understood unless this alarm of the slaveholding region over the strategic weakness of its overall posi-tion is clearly grasped.

The moment the Lecompton quarrel became implacable, radicals of the cot-ton kingdom had seen their opportunity. With one accord, the fire-eaters had turned their faces toward the annual Southern Commercial Convention opening in Montgomery on May 10, 1858. A. P. Calhoun of South Carolina was chosen

12 October 15, 1858; Buchanan-Johnson Papers. A sufficient commentary on this was fur-nished by the Columbia *South Carolinian*, which expressed its deep regret that Southern rad-icals had pushed the wavering Buchanan into support of Lecompton. "Madly we rushed on under the impulse of this ultra sentiment, which for the time seemed to have inflamed the whole South, until, finally, we found ourselves arrayed against the vast majority of the people of Kansas, a majority of Congress, a majority of States, and a vast majority of the popular vote; and . . . we found ourselves butting with violent collision against our own principles." Quoted in *National Intelligencer*, November 18, 1858.

president, and the usual committees were appointed. The gathering was interested in but two subjects, however: the African slave supply and disunion. L. W. Spratt brought forward a demand for reopening the foreign slave trade which provoked bitter debate, Yancey and others defending it against the attack of such men as Pryor and Preston of Virginia, Hilliard and Harper of Alabama. Although the disagreement was an obstacle to bold action, Rhett, Yancey, and Ruffin privately agreed that the time had come to push their disunion program.[13] The convention showed that the temper of the Lower South, which supplied most of the three hundred delegates, was changing; revolutionary shibboleths were on many tongues, and hatred of the North charged the air. "If you were in this region," a moderate Charlestonian, George S. Bryan, had just written John P. Kennedy, "you would not be considered entirely safe unless you would advocate the slave trade, and declare boldly that you held every man who *worked* at the North as no better than a slave." [14]

The natural center of any disunionist movement would lie in South Carolina, Georgia, Mississippi, and Alabama; the natural leaders of agitation were three nervous, hot-tempered, intractably independent men, Edmund Ruffin, Robert Barnwell Rhett, and W. L. Yancey. They were not young war-hawks. Ruffin was sixty-four this year, Rhett was fifty-eight, and Yancey was forty-four. Not one of them had made a notable mark in politics. Yancey had spent some fitful, unprofitable years in Congress; Ruffin had left the Virginia legislature in disgust with political chicanery; and Rhett, succeeding to Calhoun's seat in the Senate, had resigned it when, after the Compromise of 1850, the secessionists were defeated in his State.

All three, however, were gifted in propagating and organizing sectional sentiment. Ruffin was a proficient journalist and pamphleteer. His defenses of slavery and indictment of Northern aggression were skillfully brought before Southern intellectuals in *De Bow's Review*, the *Southern Literary Messenger*, and the Virginia and Carolina newspapers. Rhett was an able journalist who made the Charleston *Mercury* (of which his son became editor in 1857) an effective organ. He was also a passionately earnest speaker. Yancey, the most striking figure, was *par excellence* the orator of Southern independence. This talented Montgomery attorney, educated at Williams College, who had turned

13 Henry W. Hilliard wrote Buchanan from Montgomery that the Commercial Convention had gone wild on the slave trade, and that the Southern radicals were as bad as the Republicans; May 20, 1858, Buchanan Papers. Edmund Ruffin and Robert Barnwell Rhett had held a long conference on secession a year earlier, May 12, 1857. They then agreed that what was needed was leadership. Rhett, wrote Ruffin in his MS Diary, "despairs of any easy or efficient action by any of the Southern States—and mainly because there are no proper leaders—men who have the will and the ability, and also the necessary influence with the people." Now, in 1858, they thought the omens better.

14 April 10, 1858; Kennedy Papers.

from Jacksonian Unionism when he married into a wealthy planting family and fell under the spell of Calhoun, combined grace of person and melody of voice with logical force. He made hundreds of speeches to audiences always loath to have him close. Beginning in conversational style, he would rouse himself to climaxes worthy of Patrick Henry. All three believed that Southern independence was a necessity, that the Southern people must be awakened to their peril, and that the great hope of secession lay in a Republican victory in 1860.

In midsummer, a letter by Yancey, running through the press and evoking a fusillade of editorial comment, revealed to the nation the fierce intolerance which animated a large body of Southern zealots. In his principal speech at the Montgomery convention, the eloquent if long-winded Alabamian had arraigned the North for its injustice, and told the delegates that unless their enemies showed a change of heart, they must ere long assemble to devise measures for placing their industrial, social, and political relations on the basis of an independent sovereignty. While Ruffin was critical of Yancey's wordiness and dependence on alcoholic inspiration, he had seen that the man's torrential eloquence could be used. He suggested that Yancey organize a spearhead body, called "The League of United Southerners," to apply pressure to leaders, legislatures, and parties. The orator, eagerly assenting, brought out the proposal in the Montgomery *Advertizer and Gazette.* Ruffin forthwith explained it in the Richmond *South* and the Charleston *Mercury*, and began drumming up support in Virginia and North Carolina. Their basic intentions were revealed in the unauthorized publication of Yancey's letter of June 15, 1858, to James H. Slaughter of Atlanta, demanding immediate organization to meet the next aggression:

It must come in the nature of things. No national party can save us; no sectional party can do it. But if we could *do as our fathers did*, organize "Committees of Safety" all over the Cotton States (and it is only in them that we can hope for any effective movement), we shall fire the Southern heart—instruct the Southern mind—give courage to each other, and at the proper moment, by one organized concerted action, we can precipitate the Cotton States into a revolution.[15]

In speeches during July at Benton, Bethel Church, and Montgomery, Alabama, Yancey wrought his hearers up to such a pitch that they forthwith formed bodies of "Leaguers." Their object was to establish local leagues, State leagues, and finally a league of all the slaveholding States; to nominate no candidate, but to vote for such men as would serve their objects; and to inculcate a new Southern motto, "A republic is our only safety." The idea slowly spread. Most Southern comment was dubious or disapproving, most Northern opinion

15   For text and comment see *National Intelligencer*, July 20, 1858.

sneering, but here and there groups took the crusade seriously. Some border men complained that the Alabamian wronged their area by terming it undependable.[16]

In a second and even more extraordinary letter to Pryor of the Richmond *South*, Yancey dealt with these complaints. It was true that he placed but slight trust in the border region, he explained, but he did expect Virginia to play an indispensable role first in protecting, and later in joining, the Southern Confederacy. In Delaware, slavery was but a nominal institution; in Maryland, the free-soiler Henry Winter Davis had been chosen to Congress; in Kentucky, Henry Clay's support of emancipation was bearing fruit in a strong antislavery movement; and in Missouri, where Thomas Hart Benton had so long opposed any extension of slavery, St. Louis was the center of a powerful freesoil agitation. As for Tennessee, one of her Senators, Andrew Johnson, was essentially a free-soiler; the representatives of Tennessee Methodism had opposed striking the antislavery clause out of the church discipline; and the State maintained as judge in its supreme court and professor of law in its university a man who openly declared slavery a moral, social, and political evil. Altogether, Yancey believed that the border States offered little hope to the architects of Southern independence. Virginia, however, could place herself at the head of a buffer tier in defending the nascent Southern republic:

A well-conducted Southern policy (a policy which has been digested and understood and approved by the ablest men of Virginia, as you yourself must be aware), would seem to demand that, when such a movement takes place by any considerable number of Southern States, Virginia and the other border States should remain in the Union, where, by their position and their counsels, they would prove more effective friends than by moving out of the Union, and thus giving the Southern Confederacy a long abolition, hostile border to watch. In the event of the movement being successful, in time Virginia, and the other border States that desired it, could join the Southern Confederacy, and be protected by the power of its arms and its diplomacy.[17]

16 Yancey's organization presumably borrowed its name and part of its spirit from the old-time League of United Irishmen. Already the South had its Southern Rights Associations. Richard K. Crallé of South Carolina, editor of Calhoun's works, was in touch with the Central Southern Rights Association of Virginia. It had been suggested late in 1857 that delegates of all the associations meet in Richmond sometime in 1858 to consult on measures of redress. Floyd, of Buchanan's Cabinet, was to issue the circular call. Meanwhile, a memorial was to be presented to Congress demanding "reparation for the past and security for the future." Crallé, December 4, 1857; Hammond Papers, LC.

17 DuBose, *Yancey, passim;* Yancey's "Speech in Dem. State Convention, 1860," pamphlet. Ruffin's old classmate P. Carr, living in Pike County, Missouri, wrote the Virginian that freesoil St. Louis was a cancer in the body of the State. "I foresee that we may be the Flanders of the Union, and if not of the Union, then the advance guard of the South. There are no truer men than the slaveholders of Missouri." December 16, 1857; C. C. Clay Papers, Duke Univ.

Should this Machiavellian letter be taken seriously? That the proud Old Dominion should play a dissimulant role, that Maryland, Kentucky, and Tennessee should likewise act a double-dealing part to give the cotton principality a buffer zone, that the political heirs of Jefferson, Clay, and Jackson should enter into such tortuous schemes—these assumptions aroused much disgust. Yet, as evidence that a disunion plot was being matured, the letter was important. Whom did Yancey mean by "the ablest men in Virginia"? Readers guessed he meant Wise, Hunter, and Ruffin. Pryor's *South* had often spoken hopefully of dissolving the Union, but it had deprecated any premature step. The iron was to be struck when hot, and not before.[18] When Yancey's first local units of the League of United Southerners sprang into existence, Pryor's journal ridiculed them.

Other radical voices were raised during the summer of 1858. Representative Milledge L. Bonham of South Carolina, speaking at Edgefield on September 2, bewailed the loss of Kansas and saw but one remedy—separation. If the Republicans elected such a man as Seward, Chase, or Hale to the Presidency in 1860, he believed the dignity and safety of the South would demand her departure. "The electric spark which conveys that intelligence ought to be and will be the silent death-signal of the confederacy, come when it may." Bonham made it clear that he thought most Northern Democrats little better than the Republicans. Nine days later an even more defiant speech was delivered by A. G. Brown at Hazelhurst, Mississippi. He was for acquiring Cuba, annexing Tamaulipas and other Mexican states, and taking possession of Central America. All the new territory was to be devoted to slavery; and he would treat a Northern refusal to assist in this aggrandizement, or to admit a new State because it had slavery, as ground for disunion. Congress should pass a territorial slave code. Brown larded his harangue with insults to the North. "That slavery is a blessing to the masters," he shouted, "is shown by simply contrasting a Southern gentleman with a Northern abolitionist. One is courageous, high-bred, and manly. The other is cowardly, low-flung, and sneaking." [19]

As Bonham and Brown spoke, so did others. A strong current of secession talk was running through the general speechmaking of Southern members of the two houses. The time had been when such leaders as Howell Cobb and Alexander H. Stephens fulminated aggressively in Congress so that they might return home to speak moderately to the voters. Those days were past; Southern champions now uttered more radical doctrines at home than in Washington. A competent observer for the New York *Tribune* believed that the disunionists

18 Quoted in N. Y. *Weekly Tribune,* September 11, 1858.
19 Bonham's speech, *National Intelligencer,* September -16; Brown's speech, *idem,* September 23, 1858.

were gaining fast in numbers and power.[20] The Richmond *Enquirer* spoke with irritation of the gallant but excessively radical men who would never be satisfied until slavery was extended to the North Pole.[21] One such figure was Lawrence M. Keitt. In a speech at Whippy Swamp, South Carolina, on October 2, demanding secession if Kansas were admitted with less than ninety-three thousand people or if a Republican were elected President, he sounded the clarion:

Like mildew and blast, like pestilence and famine, abolitionism has swept through the free States, and girdled them round with a belt of deadly influences. If there be any power to stay the ravages of this moral sirocco it has not been exerted. . . . I have seen the Whig Party die; its legions dissolve, its glories melt away, and its proud banner . . . folded over the grave of its great leader; and the Black Republican party, an amalgam of isms, a base conglomerate of opposing elements tied together by fanaticism, step into the field, instigated by hatred to the South, and greedy of sectional power. . . . It has formally announced its intention to abolitionize every department of the government and use them to the overthrow of slavery.[22]

[II]

The Southern feeling thus whipped up during the campaign was intensified when, early in autumn, Seward lifted his voice in an indiscreet interpretation of the crisis. Campaigning for Morgan, the Senator spoke at Rochester on September 25. He wished to define the basic distinction between Republicans and Democrats in a fashion which would bring wavering Know-Nothings and abolitionists into the party. The same unhappy afflatus which had produced the higher-law doctrine descended upon Seward. America, he said, had two radically different systems of labor, one free and one slave, which, as population grew and communications thickened, were brought in some areas into jarring collision. "Shall I tell you what this collision means? . . . It is an irrepressible conflict between opposing and enduring forces, and it means that the United States must and will, sooner or later, become either entirely a slaveholding nation, or entirely a free-labor nation." His phrase "irrepressible conflict" leaped into the nation's consciousness.

In this phrase it was the word "conflict" which rang like a bell, alarming many and angering some, for it bore a connotation of armed strife. To avoid this construction, Seward expressed his belief that the United States would yet in peaceful ways become a land of universal freedom. It would do so through some cooperative action of the several States with the national government, in

20 Washington correspondence, N. Y. *Weekly Tribune*, October 9, 1858.
21 July 30, 1858.
22 Phila. *Weekly Press*, October 30, 1858.

strictly constitutional fashion. In short, his irrepressible conflict was merely a cold war. But other passages had a less irenic tone. Declaring that the sole hope of making a free-labor system national lay in the Republican Party, he seemed to predict a series of drastic measures. The party could not lay down a detailed blueprint, he remarked. "Who would ever have joined even the Whig Party of the Revolution, if it had been obliged to answer, in 1775, whether it would declare for independence in 1776, and for this noble Federal Constitution of ours in 1787?" This had a disturbing ring. Did the Republicans, then, contemplate the possibility of revolutionizing the country within a year after coming to power, and of writing a new instrument of government within a dozen years? Seward's peroration, too, seemed alarming.

"I know, and you know, that a revolution has begun," he asserted. "I know, and all the world knows, that revolutions never go backward. Twenty Senators and a hundred Representatives proclaim boldly today in Congress sentiments and opinions and principles of Freedom which hardly so many men in even this free State dared to utter in their own homes twenty years ago." Under the Democrats the government had surrendered post after post to slavery. But meanwhile the Northern people had been marshalling their hosts to recover these lost forts, "and to confound and overthrow, by one decisive blow, the betrayers of the Constitution and Freedom forever." What did he mean by this one decisive blow?

Although Seward's biographers have compared his "irrepressible conflict" speech with Lincoln's "house divided" address,[23] the New Yorker obviously took the much more radical stand. Lincoln attacked slavery as an institution; Seward also attacked the slaveholders. Whereas Lincoln declared slavery immoral, Seward termed it inhuman as well, and in saying that its legitimate fruits were the poverty, imbecility, and anarchy of Latin America, implied that these traits were being stamped on the South. Lincoln believed that the question would be agitated until a crisis had been reached and passed. He hoped that this would fix territorial bounds to slavery and restore the old view that it was but a temporary institution; whereupon the agitation would cease, and a solution could be left to time. Seward, however, envisaged a conflict intensifying until it reached a climax which would abolish slavery rather than merely put it on the road to extinction. The current strife, he said, marked the inevitable ripening of the conflict; and he spoke not merely of revolution, but of a rising demand that the Republicans, when victorious, should act as the interest of justice and humanity should require.

Lincoln considered the dominant idea of the Republican Party to be the exclusion of slavery from the Territories; Seward declared that its dominant idea

23 Bancroft, *Seward*, I, 461, 462.

was the equality of men before human tribunals and laws. In fine, Lincoln was a Fabian reformer, while Seward stood much nearer the root-and-branch abolitionists. When he spoke of trade in the bodies and souls of men, his phrasing had an abolitionist twang.

That Seward had gone too far was proved by the instant protest of responsible Northern opinion. Gideon Welles published in the New York *Evening Post* of November 15 a criticism which his friends regarded as able even for Welles. The Springfield *Republican* deplored the speech,[24] the Boston *Courier* raised such an uproar that young Henry Adams pronounced it and the conservative Bostonians incredibly terrified, and Raymond's New York *Times* sternly deprecated the utterance.[25] Bennett's *Herald* described the speech as a brutal and bloody manifesto, declared that Seward meant to plunge the country into war, and predicted that if he were elected in 1860, the South would secede. The address was in fact a characteristic piece of impetuosity. Horace Greeley that very spring had written Colfax that, while he liked Seward very much as a man, he was repelled by his selfishness, self-conceit, reluctance to ask the advice of associates, and ingratitude; and that he had ceased to trust the Senator's judgment as a politician. This was the feeling of one of Seward's associates in Washington, the moderate Dixon of Connecticut, who, pronouncing his speech indefensible, said that he was honest, talented—and untrustworthy.

The Senator, distressed by the Nothern outcry, attempted four days later at Rome, New York, to soothe the lacerated feelings of the South. Slaveholders, he declared, were intelligent, reflective men who understood that they could not make America a land of slavery, and who, being a propertied class, were inclined toward moderation; it was only the incitements of Northern Democrats which had led them to take intransigent positions! This was not only absurd, but wholly inconsistent with his previous speech. Having blown too hot, he tried to blow too cold. The inconsistency revealed Seward's greatest weakness, his want of any compelling sense of principle. He would take advanced and even reckless positions with an air of Hotspur courage, but he lacked the profound convictions of Lincoln and Sumner, Jefferson Davis and Stephens. His partial retraction did not mitigate the shock of his Rochester blast. The irrepressible conflict speech frightened many New Yorkers that autumn into voting Democratic, and led many Republicans to feel that Seward was too extreme to lead their presidential battle.[26]

24 Merriam, *Bowles*, I, 243.
25 Adams, Berlin, December 22, 1858, to Sumner; Sumner Papers.
26 Bancroft, *Seward*, I, 464. Greeley was irritated by Seward's self-sufficiency. "That he never said 'I thank you' is very well; but I cannot remember that Gov. Seward ever in his life said to me, 'What do you think of the present aspect of affairs? What is our true course in this emergency?' Do *you* happen to know of his ever consulting and counselling with anybody on terms of equality?" February 5, 1858; Greeley-Colfax Corr.

The Southern uproar over the speech was naturally tremendous. Governor Adams of South Carolina had said the same thing, but Adams was not the leader of a great party. Southern editors never forgot it. Many journals, like the Washington *Union* and its successor the *Constitution,* thenceforth treated it as an avowal of Republican intent to attack Southern institutions in every way possible. Senator Iverson of Georgia, calling it a proclamation of war against slavery, said that it was proof the Southern people would shortly be forced to choose between their special way of life and the Union.[27] After the speech, nervous Southerners felt less safe. The fire-eaters, of course, rejoiced that their antagonist had done so much to unite the section. Senator James H. Hammond had lately made a signally moderate speech at Barnwell Court House, the burden of which was that if the South but stood united it could probably continue to control the government.[28] At the same time, he had declared that, if the Republicans won in 1860, it might be the duty of the South to dissolve the Union. He now read Seward's speech with elation. "It is glorious," he wrote William Porcher Miles. "We have got them dead." Seward had clarified the Republican position for every Southern voter; Hammond had not expected that it would be done so rashly:

But the true issue is now made. The South is to be Africanized and the elections of 1860 are to decide the question. In other words it is emancipation or disunion after 1860, unless Seward is repudiated. If he is not we shall make jelly of him and his party in 1860, if we promptly accept and fight the battle right through on the issue tendered; or, failing in that, we are consolidated, organized, and trained for a Southern Republic.[29]

27   *Cong. Globe,* 35th Cong., 2d Sess., 243.
28   Hammond's speech had largely been realistic in tone. European immigration to the North, he said, was sufficient to form one or two new States every year, while to the South it was negligible. Nor could the South expect to gain much if anything from expansion southward. Slavery seemed to have failed in Mexico and Central America; and what could be done with the millions of Indians and Spaniards in those lands? Calhoun had said that Cuba was forbidden fruit unless plucked in war, and even if it were acquired, it would not restore Southern equilibrium with the North. But the South should not undervalue herself. "She has been lamenting her weakness and croaking about the dangers that beset her when she might glory in her strength and hurl defiance at her enemies." Thirty years earlier the South had been menaced by the tariff, the Bank, the internal improvement system, and abolitionism, all of which had advocates within her own borders. She had united her forces against them; and now the high protective tariff, the Bank, and the brigandage of internal improvements were dead. Why not trust the future? The South had nearly always held control of the general government; "and our history proves that no man and no measure has yet been strong enough to stand against the South when united." But he nevertheless gave warning that the South would accept disunion rather than an abridgement of its constitutional rights. If fanaticism and brute force rode down the slaveholders, the Southerners "will carry with them the pillars of the temple of civilization, and force a common fate on all mankind." That is, they would deprive the world of cotton. The speech, delivered October 27, is largely quoted in N. Y. *Weekly Tribune,* November 20, 1858.
29   November 5, 1858; Miles Papers, Univ. of N. C. Punctuation corrected.

When on the heels of Seward's speech came news of Republican success in the elections, Southern apprehension and defiance rose together. The loss of Kansas, the squatter sovereignty position of the Douglas Democrats, and the growing strength of the Republican Party made it clear that slavery *would* be contained. Hemmed in on the north and west, what chance would it have to expand southward? Very little; and once immobilized, it would begin to die. Adams of South Carolina repeated in a public letter that if the Yankees gained control in Washington, the Southern States would become degraded provinces. Their only safety lay in secession; and it would be more than safe, for the North would soon learn its dependence on the South, and would turn on the Sewards and Giddingses to devour them.[30] With many radicals, the only question now was of ways and means.

Quietly, persistently, efficiently, Ruffin, Yancey, and Rhett were diffusing their ideas (they were primarily Ruffin's) as to a *modus operandi.* Any three coterminous Southern States, acting in unison, could unite to form a new independent nation, safe from Northern aggression. Other States would gradually join these three. It would even be preferable, asserted Ruffin, to dissolve the Union by a series of secessions. If it were done by one general and spontaneous movement, the North might be stung to take up arms, and blood would flow. If, however, a broad belt of slaveholding States were left legally within the old Union, they would serve as a barrier and a safeguard, impregnable against any warlike movement. In time they, too, would secede, for the border States could not hold their property at the mercy of the sixteen or more antislavery States; but the secession would be peaceable.[31] The staid *National Intelligencer* was profoundly shocked at the spectacle of Roger Pryor's Richmond *South* and the *Enquirer,* Wise's organ, debating with impassioned vigor the question whether Virginia would stick to the old Union or join the new Southern Confederacy in that grand breakup which both journals thought at hand. Seaton and Gales published a horrified front-page editorial on the subject.[32] But Ruffin was not in the least disturbed by the debate, for he thought it would be well if Virginia hung back a little before her inevitable decision.

After his sojourn on the Maine coast, Jefferson Davis, returning south in mid-October, halted in New York to speak at Palace Garden. A responsive crowd, largely Tammany men, heard him describe the current crisis as a contest over State Rights and local home rule. Appealing to the Irish and Germans, he declared that Federal encroachments were equally a menace to slaveholders in the South and the alien-born in the North. He was actually cheered as he

30 November 13, 1858; N. Y. *Weekly Tribune,* December 4, 1858.
31 Ruffin's MS Diary, May 12, and his article in Charleston *Mercury,* May 13, 1857.
32 *National Intelligencer,* July 10, 1858.

threatened secession. If one section gained such a predominance that it could override the Constitution and legislate for the other section, he said, the subjugated population would be placed in a colonial position; and they would merely show the spirit of their sires if they struck down this tyranny by revolution. Franklin Pierce had once assured Davis that, if ever a Northern army assembled to march for the conquest of the South, it would have to fight a battle at home before it reached the border. Some New York Democrats now gave him a similar assurance, declaring that the freesoil army would probably be defeated.[33] Another bit of evidence that secession would be safe!

On November 16, Davis addressed the Mississippi legislature on the dangers confronting the South. Much personal vanity and not a little vituperative temper appeared in the speech. Denouncing Seward as a dangerous and powerful man, attacking the irrepressible conflict speech as a threat to amend the Constitution and destroy slavery, lauding Buchanan (with whom he had just talked) as a true friend who would not only maintain his ground but would move another step in advance, Davis gave every sentence a ring of defiance. Repeatedly he threatened secession. If a Republican were elected President in 1860, he said, disunion would be a necessity; and he would tear Mississippi's star from the American flag, "to be set even on the perilous ridge of battle as a sign round which Mississippi's best and bravest should gather to the harvest-home of death." [34] Splendid rhetoric, wildly cheered! There were many thousands of brave, handsome lads in Mississippi at that moment who would rot underground within six years because of such rhetoric, and whose weeping parents would find "the harvest-home of death" an iron and pitiless phrase.

[III]

As radical leaders in the South talked of imminent disunion, they required a fresh issue as a rallying point. Kansas was now as useless for their purposes as for those of the Northern extremists. Particularly did the chieftains of the Southern Democracy need some hurricane demand with which they could confront and defeat Douglas.[35] Within a few weeks after the elections of 1858 they

33 *Works*, III, 332–339; for the Democratic assurances, p. 358.
34 *Works*, III, 339–360.
35 "Take any view of the picture," M. J. Crawford of Georgia wrote Alexander H. Stephens, "and our condition is not flattering for the next race and the next presidency. . . . There is nothing upon which we can go to our own people and rally them, and unless we can *get up* something we are 'done for.' We have made all out of niggers that is to be made, there's nothing left. We have made all out of Kansas that was in it, in fact it was a great investment; it paid handsome dividends to all the Southern stockholders. The charter has expired, however, and all the debts due to and from it are extinguished." September 8, 1858; Stephens Papers, LC. Punctuation corrected.

found it in a sudden revival of the idea of positive Congressional protection of slavery in the Territories, which was a complete rejection of Douglas's Freeport Doctrine. Considering the needs of Davis, Cobb, Thompson, Yancey, and other radicals, this issue was ideal. It would furnish a war cry to "fire the Southern heart," for only aggressive action would keep their ranks intact. At the same time, it would stop bold Douglas. Flushed with his victory in Illinois, and more the idol of most Northern Democrats than ever, he would seize the leadership of the party unless Southern men struck at him instantly. This weapon suited their double purpose completely.

So swiftly did Southern revolutionaries adopt it, and so sharply did some of them change front in doing so, that allegations of a conspiracy were soon bruited about. Very significantly, these allegations were first presented by Southern Unionists. The Nashville *Patriot* presently identified the leaders of the plot as Yancey and Davis.

It declared that Yancey, Ruffin, and other disunionists had conferred at the commercial convention in Montgomery; that the first result had been Yancey's letters to Slaughter and Pryor, and the formation of the Southern Leagues; that he had perceived that his secession scheme must have some immediate basis; and that, knowing that the reopening of the slave trade had too little popularity for the purpose, he had turned to the Congressional protection scheme. The scheme was broached early in September, 1858, in the editorial columns of the New Orleans *Delta*. After the elections, Yancey and his associates disseminated it vigorously, said the *Patriot*. "The calculation was to break up the Democratic Party (as Mr. Yancey intimated in his Slaughter Letter), to excite violent sectional antagonism, to unite the South against the North, and thus to insure the election of the Republican candidate." Governor Wise immediately had the Richmond *Enquirer* espouse it. "But a short time previously he had approved the course of Mr. Douglas in his split with the Administration, and the sudden change of front of his organ shows an undoubted understanding that the doctrine of Congressional protection was to be made, for the first time, an *issue in party politics*." Meanwhile Jefferson Davis also adopted the new issue.[36]

In the eyes of the Columbia *South Carolinian* and the Mobile *Daily Register*, the leaders in the conspiracy were Governor Wise and Senator Albert G. Brown of Mississippi. Within a year, the *South Carolinian* was stating bitterly, and John Forsyth of the *Register* was repeating, a formal indictment:

36 Nashville *Patriot*, "The Conspiracy to Break Up the Union," pamphlet, 1860, HL. John Minor Botts of Virginia also accepted the conspiracy theory; *The Great Rebellion*, 68 ff. Wise stated his position in a letter in the Richmond *Enquirer*, October 28, 1858, demanding "Protection in the Territories and *everywhere*, to all rights of persons and of property."

When Judge Douglas made his famous Lecompton "dodge," it will be remembered that Gov. Wise followed him. Mr. Hunter and his party sustained the Administration. Gov. Wise lost ground fearfully, both in the South and in his own State. It was necessary, therefore, that something be done to effect a restoration of his Southern strength. His dilemma was one of desperation.

In this unpleasant state, Mr. Brown, of Mississippi, happened to hit upon the idea of invoking Congressional intervention to protect slavery in the Territories. Immediately Gov. Wise was up for action. Here was his opportunity. True, the South had been contending for non-intervention. True, she had been demanding of the Federal Government simply to be let alone, to have no restrictive laws against slavery. True, she had never asked for a Territorial slave code, as no one had ever asked for a Territorial horse code. True, there was little territory left to be settled, and therefore no advantage to be derived from such a code. True, under the past history of the country, Alabama, Louisiana, Mississippi, Arkansas, Texas, Tennessee, Kentucky, and Missouri had all been made slave States without a special slavery code, thus demonstrating the uselessness of any such Congressional protection. True, the South when her population was much smaller, both in whites and blacks, than at the present time, had succeeded in colonizing every foot of ground in the confederacy which was adapted to the production of her staple. True, therefore, that the remedy of Congressional protection was being prescribed after the necessity for it was passed. Still, notwithstanding all these practical facts, a Congressional slavery code was an exciting measure which could keep up agitation, and thus keep up politicians.[37]

It is certain that both Wise and Jefferson Davis made a complete *volte-face* on the subject of Congressional protection, and that Davis's change of front was embarrassingly sudden. While in Maine, he was called upon by the Portland Democrats for an address, which they thought needed to dispel the belief of many Northerners that the South was determined to force slavery into the free States. Indignant Yankees were repeating the story that Toombs had boasted he would yet call the roll of his slaves on Bunker Hill; and though Toombs denied it, his disclaimers were treated with incredulity by radical antislavery men. Davis accepted the invitation, and his speech received nation-wide attention.[38] He asserted the familiar Southern dogma that the people of the States had a right to carry their property, including slaves, into any Territory; and this right endured, he said, until the Territory became a State and took the subject entirely under its own control. However, even a Territory could not be compelled to accept slavery if the people did not want it:

If the inhabitants of any Territory should refuse to enact such laws and police regulations as would give security to their property or to his [another migrant's], it would be rendered more or less valueless, in proportion to the difficulty of holding it without such protection. In the case of property in the

37 Mobile *Daily Register,* August 11, 1859.
38 *Cong. Globe,* February 20, 1860; Davis, *Works,* III, 295 ff.

labor of man, or what is usually called slave property, the insecurity would be so great that the owner could not ordinarily retain it. Therefore, though the right would remain, the remedy being withheld, it would follow that the owner would be practically debarred by the circumstances of the case, from taking slave property into a Territory where the sense of the inhabitants was opposed to its introduction. So much for the oft-repeated fallacy of forcing slavery upon any community.[39]

This was the doctrine of Orr, of Cass, of Douglas. At Freeport, Douglas said that if the people of a Territory disliked slavery they would adopt unfriendly legislation, thus excluding it. At Portland, Davis declared that if the people disliked slavery their legislature would withhold laws giving it security, and thus it would "be practically debarred." The one envisaged a positive course, the other a passive course. This was a distinction without a difference. Davis went on to say that the South never asked Congress to extend slavery into the Territories, but instead denied that Congress had any right to do so. Indeed, it held that the general government had no constitutional right to establish or prohibit slavery anywhere. "Hence it is their policy not to interfere on the one side or the other, but, protecting each individual in his constitutional rights, to leave every independent community to determine and adjust all domestic questions as in their wisdom may seem best." Despite the weasel-clause about "protecting each individual in his constitutional rights," this again was substantially Douglas's opinion.

But when Davis reached Mississippi; when he found the Republicans victorious; when he saw Northern Democrats exalting Douglas as the one rock of hope in 1860—then he swung abruptly about. At Jackson, he adverted angrily to Douglas's recent use at Alton of a quotation from the Portland speech. The Illinoisan had no right to treat him as an ally, said Davis. They had differed for years; for while both believed that all property requires protection by the society in which it is held, Douglas thought that this fact conferred a right to destroy, while *he* believed that it "rather creates an obligation to protect." Indeed, Davis added that he found little difference between Douglas and the Republicans. The Republicans asserted the power of Congress to deprive the South of a constitutional right; Douglas denied that Congress held such power, but would confer it on a territorial legislature. Mississippi could tolerate neither position.

Now Davis had not said a word about Congressional protection at Portland —he had disclaimed it. He had not said a word for it in his previous speeches inside and outside Congress. He knew that it was a practical absurdity. He knew that the idea would divide Northern Democrats from Southern Democrats as by a sword of fire. Why did he suddenly adopt it? Why was it so suddenly enunciated by Wise's organ, the Richmond *Enquirer?* Why was it at once taken up

39 Davis, *Works*, III, 299.

throughout the South? It was natural that Unionist journals like the Nashville *Patriot*, Columbia *South Carolinian*, and Mobile *Register* should leap at the word conspiracy, for this seemed the obvious explanation. The word was significantly used by a very different and more important journal, the Washington *Union*. This Administration paper within a few weeks warned the country that some persons unknown were circulating alarmist tales in the South for mere purposes of agitation. "They are only a part of many contemporaneous circumstances, which reveal to the country an important fact. They warn it of a widespread and dangerous conspiracy in the Southern States against the authority of the laws, Constitution, and government, the continuance of the Union, and the integrity of all existing institutions, not only in the Southern States, but in every quarter that can be reached from the Southern States. We see evidences of this movement in the effort to revive the African slave trade against the wish and conviction of nine-tenths of the Southern people." [40] When the *Union* asserted the existence of "a widespread and dangerous conspiracy" in the South, the accusation was startling.

That Davis, A. G. Brown, Yancey, Wise and others actually conspired together to use Congressional protection to check Douglas, split the Democratic Party, and bring about disunion, is nevertheless an exaggerated concept. They had different ideas and aims, they were not personally harmonious, and we have no evidence that they met or corresponded. Yancey, who had more of the conspirator in his blood than the others, later explicitly denied that he had planned to split the Democratic Party and precipitate disunion. He called the charge "an infamous calumny." [41] What had happened was that a long-dormant idea, by a combination of circumstances, was suddenly lifted to prominence in the minds of numerous political leaders and party editors, and spontaneously seized upon by them to achieve certain emergency ends. No conspiracy was required. The times demanded a certain weapon, it lay at hand, and men grasped it. They acted together but without preconcert. What were the main objects which suddenly made the Congressional protection of slavery an ideal engine? They were two. One was to keep the South united on a definite demand. The other was to halt Douglas and his associates—to prevent them from taking control of the party.[42]

40 Washington *Union*, January 6, 1859.
41 Memphis speech, August 14, 1860. But he had declared at Columbia, South Carolina, in 1859, that he had no hope of remaining in the Union, and bided his time only until Southern unity in secession was obtained. If not a secessionist *per se*, he was a unionist only under terms that he knew could never be met. See his "Speech in the Dem. State Convention, 1860," pamphlet. He, Rhett, Ruffin, and Slidell were secessionist intriguers.
42 Judah P. Benjamin told the Senate on May 22, 1860, that the Freeport Doctrine was "the explanation of the sudden change that has been wrought in the relations of the Senator from Illinois with the rest of the Democratic Party." It was not the explanation. But it was made the pretext when a handy pretext was needed; and the natural counter to it was the Congressional-protection idea. *Cong. Globe*, 36th Cong., 1st Sess., 2237.

[IV]

Two overlapping bodies of Southern voters had now determined never to accept Douglas's leadership or adopt the final implications of his popular sovereignty principle. The larger body believed simply that Douglas had betrayed and humiliated them in Kansas. He had first held up to the anxious, harried South a light which proved an *ignis fatuus*. Then in the test on Lecompton, when the section was stumblingly hunting a way by which it might emerge from the situation with credit, he had basely thwarted the Southerners. Even when the English bill offered an easy bridge, he had refused to rejoin his party. A smaller but growing party believed that the Northern Democrats were untrustworthy on the tariff, on the public lands, and on the issue of Caribbean expansion; and that the rupture of the party, as a prelude to disunion, was inevitable. The Cincinnati *Gazette*, just after the election, had pointed to the realities of the day. To the Democratic Party the election was a turning point, it said —for good, if the entire party could reconcile itself to the dictatorship of Douglas as it had once accepted that of Jackson; for evil, if it could not. *"And they cannot. The party is henceforth rent in twain and hopelessly ruined."* [43]

What of Douglas himself? He could afford now to be magnanimous. His first thought after his victory was to conciliate his late opponents.

Turning southward as November ended, he planned to pay a friendly visit to his slave State friends, and to make a series of speeches emphasizing his regard for the welfare of that area. The eleven-point program published by the Chicago *Times* had really been intended to reassure the South. Taking passage at Alton on the *City of Memphis*, he might have pointed to a symbolic element in his passage down the Mississippi. He had done what he could to keep intact the alliance of South and Northwest, of which the great river constituted the binding chain stronger than steel. The waterway was still black with commerce; it was for the South itself to say whether the link should be snapped in twain. At every landing crowds cheered him.

Reaching Memphis on a Sunday, he stayed to address an immense concourse in Exchange Hall the following afternoon. It did not please him to see in a Memphis slave-pen some miserable blacks newly run in from Africa. Introduced by Senator Jones as a friend of the South, he assured his audience that his principles were the same in Tennessee as in Illinois; and he proved it, for his compact, vigorous speech restated the main points made in his debates with Lincoln. The Almighty, he said, had drawn a line across the continent on one side of which

43 November 5, 1858.

the soil must be cultivated by slave labor, on the other by free labor. The peoples of each State and Territory must decide the question for themselves. Once more he reiterated his Freeport Doctrine. "Whenever a Territory has a soil, climate, and production, making it the interest of the inhabitants to encourage slave property, they will pass a slave code and give it encouragement. Whenever the climate, soil, and production preclude the possibility of slavery being profitable, they will not permit it." It was visionary to talk of planting slavery where it was not wanted, and folly to attempt to exclude it where it was desired.[44]

Continuing his southward journey, Douglas met a reception sometimes frigidly polite, sometimes cordial, sometimes enthusiastic. Going ashore at Vicksburg, he found more wretched African savages cowering in the slave-pens—one account says three hundred; a sight which, with current rumors that more slaves had been imported the previous twelvemonth than in any year of the legitimate slave trade, awakened him to the menace in the demand for revival of the traffic. At New Orleans, the followers of Slidell (who called Douglas "the King of the Thugs") and Judah P. Benjamin were openly hostile, but the opposing faction under Pierre Soulé had arranged an imposing reception. Cannon barked as the steamer slid to the wharves; flags and bunting fluttered in the breeze; a brass band poured out music, and a clattering military company escorted Douglas's carriage through dense lanes of cheering people to the St. Charles. On December 6, the Senator delivered another address, reiterating his political creed with an additional article—the acquisition of Cuba. This rich island belonged by nature to the continental power which it flanked, he said; it must be acquired; but the acquisition must be on terms honorable to all. He did not go as far as the slippery Caleb Cushing, who, in a recent address in Richmond, had urged the annexation of both Cuba and Mexico with no fastidiousness about methods; but he did prove that he still held the expansionist views of Young America.[45] Obviously, he was not for popular sovereignty in Cuba, for he did not suggest for a moment that the will of the people should be consulted upon the transfer.

The Senator was anxious to avoid any appearance of pressure upon the party or of discourtesy toward the South. Far from letting his followers press his name for the Presidency, he was boldly stating that the South was entitled to the next Chief Executive. Of course he had no use for Cobb, Slidell, or Davis among the Southern aspirants, but he spoke in high terms of Breckinridge.[46] All the Ad-

---

44 Memphis *Avalanche*, November 30, 1858. Before leaving Chicago, Douglas had told friends that he would take decided ground against a territorial slave code; Weck to Lyman Trumbull, November 22, 1858, Trumbull Papers.

45 A. Dudley Mann wrote Buchanan: "Those supposed to be most in the secrets of Judge Douglas give out *sotto voce* that during the first days of the session he will make a peace offering demonstration, with respect to Mexico and Cuba, which will be cordially accepted by the slaveholding States." November 29, 1858; Buchanan Papers.

46 And also of Wise; Chicago *Tribune*, November 13, 1858.

ministration regulars and the Southern extremists, however, believed that if they met him as a friend he would quickly establish his domination. They had assailed him as a traitor, they had said repeatedly that the breach with him was final, and they feared him too much to take his extended hand.

Hence it was that, while he pushed down the Mississippi and proceeded to Cuba, some Southern leaders who knew perfectly well that the Freeport Doctrine was an old story and who had accepted it without protest from the mouths of Cass, Douglas, Orr, and Stephens, suddenly turned about, denounced it with seeming anger, and proclaimed the Congressional protection dogma. The breach between Northern and Southern Democrats was to be made total. Scores of editors dipped their pens in the ink furnished by Davis, Brown, and the Richmond *Enquirer*. That journal, which was Wise's organ, stated that Congressional protection was an issue raised above the platforms of parties, that it could not and must not be compromised, and that the South could take nothing less than the legislation needed to validate its rights under the Constitution—"rights sanctioned and judicated by the Supreme Court." [47]

The response to this extraordinary demand was certain to come with vigor. Northern Democrats would no more submit to it than Republicans; that is, all Democrats except those represented by the New York *Day-Book*, a proslavery sheet which echoed the *Enquirer* and the Charleston *News*. Even many Buchanan men, predicted the New York *Tribune* on September 22, 1858, will raise the indignant inquiry: Is thy servant a dog that he should do this thing? While Davis's speech and the ultimatum of the *Enquirer* were still being reprinted, Governor William F. Packer of Pennsylvania, who had supported Buchanan's nomination two and a half years earlier, was writing his annual message. He denounced the new dogma as a menace to the Union. It "will shake the very pillars of our constitutional fabric," he declared. "It would compel every Territory to elevate property in slaves above every other description of property, and to establish a slave code in its early municipal regulations, or else it would convert the Congress into a theatre of crimination and confusion, and fill the country with strife; and all this without securing a single advantage to the North, or protecting a single right of the South." [48] Great numbers of hitherto moderate Northern Democrats began to think that much truth attached to Republican talk about the aggressions of slavery.

If ever there was a pernicious abstraction, it was this new Southern demand. The history of Kansas, Nebraska, Oregon, and Minnesota had illustrated anew the truth that slaveholders would never migrate to any region where slavery was unprofitable. These Southerners were uniting in a preposterous appeal

47 November 11, 1858.
48 Packer's full message is in *National Intelligencer*, January 9, 1859.

which they knew would never be granted, and some of them were plotting secession once it was refused.[49]

[V]

It was one of the heavy misfortunes of the nation not merely that it elected small Presidents, but that the potentialities of the Presidency as an instrument of democratic leadership were so little recognized. The Chief Magistrate executed the laws; now and then he proposed one; but he knew little about rallying public opinion behind some great new policy. The value of the Presidential speechmaking tour in arousing sentiment, the use of interviews or public letters in focussing attention on an issue, the feasibility of appointing an executive commission to investigate and report—all this remained to be discovered. The discovery did not lie far in the future. Lincoln was to employ the public letter and interview with great effect; Andrew Johnson was to make a momentous speechmaking "swing around the circle," and to use special investigative agents. Had Buchanan possessed more imagination, energy, and elevation of outlook, he might have used them to divert the nation's attention from jarring quarrels to constructive tasks.

The message which he laid before the new session of the Thirty-fifth Congress when it met on December 6, 1858, evinced a desire to place the country upon new roads. An upward revision of some tariff rates, with a substitution of specific for *ad valorem* duties; Congressional action for a Pacific railroad; a national bankruptcy law; and a bold series of moves in Mexico, Central America, and the West Indies—these made up a program argued in several thousand words. At the same time, Buchanan rejoiced that the Kansas question had been settled—as it had. The republic could turn to new questions. A fighting President with a talent for dramatizing his views might have persuaded it to do so; but not a President who was widely despised, who made but a single limp statement without following it up, and who confessed that he had not an ounce of pugnacity. He remarked, for example, that his tariff suggestions were "the fruit of my own observations, to which Congress, in their better judgment, will give such weight as they may justly deserve."

Had he been an aggressive President who meant to enforce his ideas, his statements on foreign policy would have created an angry international sensa-

---

49 Nor would a Congressional slave code work. The Louisville *Democrat*, staunch warrior journal of the Douglas clan, remarked: "No act of Congress or decision of the Supreme Court will make or unmake the institution of slavery anywhere. The local public sentiment will always dispose of the case. . . . If any other party than the Democrats has power in a Territory they will legislate slavery out somehow if its advocates are in a minority; and there will be found no practical remedy. The power is complete and uncontrollable," Quoted in *National Intelligencer*, November 25, 1858.

tion. What he said of Cuba was essentially outrageous. Spain and Mexico had recently been on the brink of hostilities. Filibustering circles had talked of using a Spanish-Mexican war as an excuse to grab Cuba; the Washington *States* had asserted that the last chance of acquiring the island was at hand; August Belmont had written Slidell that the hour for action was approaching; and during November the Cabinet had held protracted sessions on foreign relations.[50] Buchanan now announced that our relations with Spain were highly unsatisfactory. Spanish officials in Cuba, he said, had insulted our flag, injured the persons and property of our citizens, and refused redress. He asserted that Cuba in its colonial condition was a standing threat to all trade issuing from the Mississippi, and a constant source of injury to the American people. We should like to acquire that island peaceably, he declared, but circumstances might so shape themselves that it would have to be taken by force.

Equally extreme were his statements regarding Mexico. The President described the civil war which was again raging in the republic; the war of Benito Juarez and other liberals against the dictator Comonfort, who, supported by the large landholders, the church, and much of the army, had suspended the constitution. The struggle was destined to continue for three years before the forces of reform triumphed. Meanwhile, the reactionary regime in Mexico City had treated Americans and other foreigners with arrogant brutality. Buchanan said flatly that abundant cause existed for a resort to hostilities against it, and that, if Comonfort crushed Juarez, all hope of a peaceful settlement would be gone. The frontier, too, was so disorderly that the President requested Congress to let him send the army into Chihuahua and Sonora, to set up a temporary protectorate supported by military posts. This came close to a proposal for war and seizure. It was reinforced by another urgent recommendation that Congress authorize him to use forces on the Isthmus of Tehuantepec, blockading the coast and moving troops into the interior for the protection of transit rights. This would mean placing American bayonets in other Mexican states.[51]

The President likewise dealt unmercifully with Nicaragua. This little country he assailed on the ground that, early in 1856, the Rivas government had summarily revoked the grant and charter of the Transit Company, though he knew that the regime was but a facade for William Walker and his filibusters. Since

50 Belmont's letter, June 5, 1858, was forwarded to Buchanan; Buchanan Papers.
51 Senator Judah P. Benjamin had been interested in the Tehuantepec Company, which planned the construction of transit facilities. Our minister, John Forsyth, had been instructed to demand full transit rights, but made no headway. He remained in Mexico City until June, 1858, when with Buchanan's approval he first suspended and then broke off diplomatic relations. No intercourse existed until the spring of 1859, when Buchanan sent down Robert McLane of Maryland, with authority to recognize the Juarez government if he thought proper. Buchanan, *Defence*, 267 ff.; Bemis, *Amer. Secretaries of State*, VI, 324–347.

then, the government had failed to ratify a treaty signed by its minister in Washington guaranteeing to all nations the use and protection of the Transit Route, for it objected to a provision empowering the United States to keep the line open if Nicaragua ever failed to perform that duty. Under the circumstances, Buchanan recommended that Congress allow him to employ the army and navy to prevent obstruction of the route, and to safeguard American travellers. The same proposal was made with respect to the Panama route, traversing the territory of New Granada (Colombia). Finally, a sharp cause of quarrel was specified with Costa Rica. A party of unarmed Americans had been fired upon there in 1856 by Costa Rican troops, with some casualties.[52]

Three views might be taken of these aggressive proposals. The first was that armed invasion and occupation all around the Gulf were the only proper answers the nation could make to intolerable injuries. If Buchanan held such an exaggerated opinion of our sufferings and the proper remedy, he stood almost alone in doing so. The second was that, as four years earlier the Nebraska bill had been brought forward partly to end Democratic dissensions, so now the President's expansionist program had the same object. But his hostility to Douglas jarred with such an interpretation. The third and likeliest view was that the Southern annexationists, eager to gain new lands and just now anxious to out-Douglas Douglas, were guiding the President's pen.[53]

Jacob Thompson, according to press reports, had been insisting in Cabinet on an extreme policy with respect to Mexican and Central American affairs.[54] For some time, with the Southern press commenting resentfully on the movements of foreign warships in the Gulf, a stir of hope had been visible in expansionist circles. One of the largest American fleets ever sent out had just gone southward to help persuade stubborn Paraguay to make amends for an attack on the warship *Water Witch* and other offenses. Some observers supposed that this squadron might arrive home at an opportune moment to assist in gaining territory in the Caribbean or Gulf.[55]

Moreover, it was now or never with the expansionists. Congress was still briefly Democratic, but after March 4 the House would be in hostile hands. It was now or never, too, with any Democratic-sponsored scheme for a Pacific railroad.

[52] Buchanan had asserted his intention of enforcing the neutrality laws of the United States. Nevertheless, a certain sympathy seemed to exist between his Administration and William Walker, as was shown in the rough treatment of Commodore Paulding after his arrest of Walker. R. P. Meade, *Hiram Paulding;* Bemis, *op. cit.,* VI, 356, 357.

[53] "This is in my judgment the worst and most dangerous document ever originating from a President of the United States," observed Ben Wade. It "would make the people of the United States no better than a nest of Pyrates." December 8, 1858; Wade Papers.

[54] Wash. correspondence dated November 30, 1858, N. Y. *Tribune.*

[55] See Edward Bates's letter, N. Y. *Weekly Tribune,* April 23, 1859. For additional material on foreign affairs, see Appendix III.

[VI]

Public attention was instantly snatched from the President's forcible-feeble utterances to a melodramatic episode: the deposition of Douglas from his chairmanship of the Senate committee on Territories. Both governmentally and politically, this was one of the three most important committees of Congress. With Kansas waiting outside the door, with Colorado and Dakota requiring nurture, with Arizona's ten thousand people demanding a separate territorial government, it had highly important work on hand. Everyone knew that it had been the scene of Douglas's hardest work, and the theater of some of his greatest achievements. Year after year, since 1847, he had been reelected by unanimous vote in caucus. The position was the one in which he had taken the keenest pride, for it identified him with the growth of the West, where his heart had always lain.

Not since the Senate had defeated Martin Van Buren's appointment as minister to England had such a blow been struck in the face of a Democratic leader. Douglas, resolved not to take his seat in Washington until after the Illinois legislature had reelected him, had proceeded with his beautiful wife to Cuba. His enemies had arrived in Washington determined to cast both him and Senator Broderick into outer darkness. They were encouraged by the Directory, and cheered by news that the Virginia Democratic convention had administered a rebuff to his friends by tabling a resolution congratulating the Illinois Democracy on their victory. The nomination of John Letcher for governor of Virginia was also regarded as a victory for Buchanan-Hunter forces against the Wise-Douglas group. Jefferson Davis and Slidell placed themselves at the head of the cabal against the absent Illinoisan.[56]

On Thursday, December 9, the caucus handed down its vindictive decree: Green of Missouri was to be chairman in Douglas's place. Over all opposition, Davis, Slidell, Hunter, Iverson, and the other radicals had ridden implacably. Bigler had opposed the step because he thought it unfair to attack Douglas in his absence; Toombs had denounced it as dictated by vengeful hostility toward an individual; A. G. Brown had objected that it was impolitic and ungenerous. Douglas's close friends, Shields and Stuart, had made indignant protests, terming the action suicidal. Besides these men, Clingman and Green had voted against any change. This made seven opponents in all, Broderick not having been asked to the caucus. The debate, beginning at ten-thirty, had raged until noon. Then, after being adjourned for a brief session of the Senate and for lunch, upon its resumption it had grown steadily more acrimonious until the final vote late in the afternoon. At the height of the battle Toombs walked out in disgust. As

56 N. Y. *Weekly Tribune,* December 11, 1859.

word of the decision flew around Washington it created intense excitement and its significance was instantly grasped.[57]

The extreme proslavery wing of the Democratic Party was determined not only to overthrow Douglas but the principle for which he stood. It meant to take the advanced step which Davis had said Buchanan was ready to support: it intended to force the demand for a territorial slave code, and this implied the destruction of the Freeport Doctrine, to which all anti-Lecompton men would subscribe. A leading Southern Senator declared that the South had temporized long enough and would tolerate no halfway position.[58]

The response among Douglas's followers was immediate. Rumors had been current that he had prepared, and would soon issue, a declaration that he would not be a candidate for the Presidential nomination in 1860. If this were true (and he certainly had said that the South was entitled to the nomination), the Cobb-Thompson-Slidell-Davis group had taken the one step that would force him to make a desperate and indomitable battle for the nation's leadership.

As for the Republicans, they were openly exultant. Seward grimly remarked that the truth of his statement about an irrepressible conflict between slavery and freedom was now evident. To such impartial observers as yet existed in Washington and the country, the caucus blow indicated a most alarming refusal of proslavery Democrats to tolerate any diversity of opinion upon the measures they wanted, including their inordinate demand for the Congressional protection of slavery in unwilling Territories.

From that fateful December day, the lists were cleared for the onset; the combatants, in three groups, took station; the trumpeters prepared to blow their signal. The Southern irreconcilables maintained an air of sullen determination. The Douglas group burned with pent-up resentment; and those who had complained of late that their chieftain had been too conciliatory would now have no reason to doubt the savage energy behind his blows. The Republicans, seeing their star in the ascendant, were ready to fight hard and seize fast every gain that fortune threw into their grasp. Their own Senate caucus had decided unanimously against falling in behind Douglas in his contest with his fellow-Democrats. With the great prize now in full view, the Republican Party was resolved to battle its own way to victory.

[57] Senator Green of Missouri wrote that the "chief worker" (probably Slidell) expressly said he regarded Douglas as still a Democrat, and that he justified the move on other grounds: "That the Territorial Committee was the great leading committee of the Senate, and that to satisfy the majority, they must elect one without doubt or suspicion." Green warned that the change would excite public indignation. To Samuel Treat, December 14, 1858; Treat Papers.
[58] The man is not named; Wash. correspondence dated December 9, 1958, N. Y. Tribune.

16

Deadlock in Congress

THE GATHERING of Congress, always a diverting spectacle, was rendered more interesting in December, 1858, by the fact that except for the dome, the Capitol was at last practically completed. This would be the first full session which Senate and House could spend in their handsome new quarters. After the British raid in 1814, Benjamin H. Latrobe had supervised the rebuilding of the old central portion of the Capitol, with its freestone walls and small Bulfinch crown. From the Administration of J. Q. Adams to the death of Zachary Taylor, the legislative and judicial branches had been satisfied with that quaintly attractive structure. Then, in 1851, the great north and south wings of New England marble, designed by Thomas U. Walters, had been begun and were rapidly pushed forward. In 1856, the larger dome, adapted from the immortal creations of Michelangelo and Wren, had been undertaken. Senators and Representatives had been elated to leave their outworn chambers. Thirty years later, S. S. Cox vividly recalled the gaiety of the House as it marched from the old shadowy and murmurous hall into the new apartment with its ornate gilding, lights shining through the varicolored escutcheons of thirty-one States in the roof, and richly carved oaken furniture.

Year by year now, the House seemed to gain upon the Senate in ability and influence. To be sure, it had only a few veteran leaders. On the Democratic side James L. Orr resumed the gavel as Speaker, while Galusha A. Grow and Joshua Giddings among the Republicans were rich in experience. But both sides of the chamber exhibited young men of brilliant promise. The Republican roster included John Sherman, Elihu B. Washburne, F. P. Blair, Jr., Schuyler Colfax, and Henry Winter Davis. Among the Democrats were J. L. M. Curry, L. Q. C. Lamar, S. S. Cox, a weatherbeaten Texan named John H. Reagan, and a quick-witted, somewhat boisterous North Carolinian, Zebulon B. Vance.

Yet, if by a diminishing margin, leadership still rested with the Senate. The Nestor of that body was John J. Crittenden, who had entered it on the day Monroe was inaugurated. His bushy eyebrows, stern countenance, and severely earnest speech gave a misleading impression of his personality, for he was emi-

427

nently a man of peace. In ability no one compared him with Clay, whose mantle he had inherited. He was an acute and learned but not profound lawyer, a forcible but not eloquent orator, a political tactician always patriotic but often clumsy. His negligent dress and rustic manners pointed the contrast with the elegant Harry of the West. Nevertheless, he was loved for his affability, and heard with respect for his sense and moderation. With him could be ranged a few other temperate men. The judicial-minded John Bell, a wealthy slaveholder who hated proslavery extremists and who had opposed the Nebraska Act and Lecompton bill, was conspicuously national-spirited. Sam Houston, the hero of Texas history now mellowed by years, was not so much a moderate as a national-ist; for on sectional issues he was a roughly eloquent battler for the Union. But circumstances threw him into the compromise group. Pugh of Ohio could fairly be termed moderate in temper and tenets.

By general agreement, the most brilliant Southern speaker was a man of alien birth and Jewish blood, Judah P. Benjamin of Louisiana. At first glance no member was less prepossessing. His short body, thick and ill-proportioned, his heavy-jowled, swarthy face, shrewd and even cunning rather than intellectual, his excessively suave manner—all this told against him until he began to speak. Then his deeply musical voice, the grace of his delivery, his exquisite diction, and the keen plausibility of his argument produced an irresistible impression. As the bar, first of America and later of Britain, was to testify, he was an admirable advocate. The Senate gallery stirred with expectation when he rose, and sighed with regret when he sat down.[1]

Equally a type, but antipodean in character, was the fine old Virginia aristo-crat, James M. Mason. Brought up among large slaveholders, this grandson of George Mason looked down upon middle-class folk without pretense or snob-bery but in the manner of a genuine patrician. Elegant in shining broadcloth and white linen (though later he turned to Virginia homespun), he had natural dis-tinction of manner; even in taking a chew of tobacco he lifted it from a velvet pouch with Attic gesture. Though without oratorical power, he was heard with attention, for he had sound judgment; his rigid integrity was admired (some-thing which could not be said of the gamester Benjamin); and he was a man of principle.[2] He had been too proud of his standards to say a word for Lecompton, or to vote for the claim of Bright and Fitch to Senate seats. Members equally respected R. M. T. Hunter, a Virginian of commonplace parts but tireless in-dustry, who was a conservative in natural temper and a radical in his attachment

---

[1] Buchanan on August 31 had offered Madrid to Benjamin, who declined it because he could not afford the expense and preferred the Senate. Benjamin to Buchanan, September 7, 1858; Buchanan Papers.

[2] G. M. Towle, *Continental Monthly*, II, 156 ff.; C. F. Adams, Jr., *Autobiography*, 59, 62, 82.

to Calhoun's memory and Southern Rights ideas. Rather shrill and awkward in speaking, he could display, when really interested in a subject, a clear logical power. Because of his natural moderation and grasp of finance he was now often mentioned for the Presidency. That far more brilliant debater, Robert Toombs, whose grasp, terseness, and salty wit were almost worthy of Charles James Fox and who was equally a watchdog of the Treasury, was too extreme and capricious to inspire any such trust.

Next to Douglas, of course, the two strongest Senators were Seward and Jefferson Davis. The personalities of both, long familiar to the country, were becoming better understood every year—yet neither was genuinely popular in a national sense. Neither had much eloquence or epigrammatic force. Seward adopted a conversational, monotonous delivery, and when he took his favorite stand, leaning against a Senate pillar, his left hand twirling his glasses while his right delivered occasional brief gestures, he might have been talking to a drawing room. His coolness, mental alertness, and balance won admiration, but of a restrained kind. Then, too, he continued to display an impish, mocking, ironic vein, which alternately delighted and enraged his friends but which the public did not understand. Few saw that beneath it lay a calm, patient nature, too philosophical to be capable of unflinching combat, too reasonable to treat any issue as having but one side. As for Davis, his chief fault was an excessive severity and nervous tension. Now at fifty just rising to the height of his powers, he was growing moodier, harder, and more austere. He was almost the beau ideal of a Southern leader—but he lacked the requisite imagination, warmth of heart, and faith in the people. His chiseled features, unaffected courtesy, and fluent conversation masked a proud reserve. In debate he was increasingly apt to give way to sharp sarcasm, and to betray his fanatical devotion to the slaveholding culture. If only he were less polished and rigid!

It was Douglas who had wonderful gifts of popularity; and he returned to the Senate flushed with his recent honors. In Cuba, the Spanish authorities had shown him great deference. When he reached New York, a civic reception was tendered him at City Hall, and, despite a cold rain, throngs gathered outside to cheer him. In Philadelphia, he spoke to five thousand people; Baltimore gave him another ovation; and a crowd at the Washington station roared its welcome.[3] No other political figure in the country could have aroused such enthusiasm. When he entered the Senate chamber, however, he was treated coldly by most Southern leaders. Slidell was insolent, Davis loftily frigid, and Toombs frankly hostile.

The backdrop of the Congressional session was again a busy social season.

3 N. Y. *Herald*, January 1, Philadelphia *North American*, January 4, *National Intelligencer*, January 6, 8, 1859.

Once more Miss Lane and Mrs. Douglas were the two reigning hostesses. Prominent among the foreign visitors were Sir William Gore Ouseley and his wife, London friends of the President, and the prima donna Piccolimini, who created a sensation at a White House levee on the arm of the Sardinian minister. Daniel Sickles was at that levee with a beauty (not his wife) at his side. The President came in, escorting Mrs. Gwin; he had aged and his head drooped more perceptibly, but hostile observers thought his eye as shrewd as of old. Four roughly dressed Pottawatomie Indians attended, emitting an aboriginal odor. The White House was scarcely an adequate setting for the sparkle and color of these personalities. Its faded frescoes and gilding, threadbare curtains and rugs, and worn-out chairs looked increasingly shabby, while it lacked enough pictures, bric-a-brac, and other ornaments to make it attractive. But although Congress was being asked to pay for a renovation, many members were cool to the project. Buchanan was unpopular throughout the North, the South wondered who would be the next occupant, and some critics grumbled that the President had used the White House not for a national hospitality, but for the gathering of votes.[4]

The Cabinet group still made a cheery, congenial circle, which despite thickening troubles gave its rather insouciant tone to the capital. Governor Cobb, as everybody called him, was fond of a good dinner and an evening at cards, and as Mrs. Cobb stayed in Georgia with her babies a good deal ("she knows her duties," wrote Jeremiah Black), he was often a house-mate of the President. Everyone liked Jacob Thompson and still more the sprightly Mrs. Thompson, with her gay laugh and warm, frank manner. It was "Jere" Black, however, who was the life of Cabinet gatherings. He wrote Hattie, as Miss Lane was affectionately termed by her intimates, notes touched with delightful humor, addressing her as "Most Excellent and Thrice Illustrious," and signing himself the humblest of her servants. Once when he, Cobb, Gwin, and a few others accompanied Buchanan on an excursion to Baltimore, they had an amusing day. "We spent the morning shopping and sightseeing," Mrs. Thompson reported to Hattie. "We had dinner at three o'clock, and a very good dinner it was. We sat at table a long time, eating, drinking, telling jokes, etc. I never saw the President in better humor, and Governor Cobb was more than himself on this occasion—and you can account for it when I tell you they had some old wine they said was worth $10 a bottle." The group, sometimes enlivened by John Appleton and that courtly Virginian, Ambrose Dudley Mann, enjoyed their drives, receptions, and suppers. Cass, to be sure, was something of a problem, but Buchanan's letters showed a fondness for him, praising his benevolence, his ability, and his readiness to forget his dangerous fainting

4 *Harper's Weekly*, February 19, 26, March 5; N. Y. correspondence January 11; London *Daily News*.

attacks. Both men liked a brisk morning walk, and a Southern journalist depicts them encountering each other:

As I pass to my breakfast every morning about nine o'clock, I meet an old gentleman in a suit of black, with white hair and white cravat, and a gold-headed consequential walking-stick; his countenance, generally austere, is rendered doubly so on these occasions by an air of troubled thought; his step is firm and rather decided, and anon the pompous cane plumps testily into the gravel promenade which connects the executive mansion with the Department of State, for here I always fall in his way. The old gentleman is the President, full of weighty matters of government. . . . As he enters the portico in front of the State Department he meets another old gentleman, and they salute each other with a ceremony befitting the days of the *ancien régime* in France. This second old gentleman wears a rusty old suit, with a tough old stick and an old brown wig. He is chunky and robust, and walks erect as a soldier. He once was one, for it is General Cass, the Nestor of American politics.

A minor ripple rolled through the press when Buchanan made James Gordon Bennett and his wife (ignored in the best New York society) his guests at dinner and the last White House reception. This was well-earned pay for valuable services. Bennett's *Herald* had been so fulsome in praise of Administration policies that Republicans called it the New York organ. Another minor ripple emanated from Mrs. Douglas's last ball of the season, crowded with select guests from the eastern cities as well as Washington. Douglas stood beside her as she received seated, for she was indisposed. Half a hundred Southern members of Congress attended—but not a single Cabinet member or presidential intimate.

By common consent, the greatest social event of the season took place on February 17, 1859, when friends of Lord and Lady Napier, the retiring British minister, gave them a ball. No foreign envoy had ever been more popular than the young Scot and his wife. The gathering in the one hundred and fifty-foot ballroom at Willard's drew groups of guests from distant cities, and twelve hundred people kept up the gaiety and feasting until early morning. Secretary Cass escorted Lady Napier into the room, Lord Napier following with Mrs. Justice Wayne. Everybody of importance seemed present under the flashing chandeliers and the portraits of Washington and Victoria. Seward was seen dancing a quadrille; Sam Houston stepped forth with a Massachusetts belle; Burlingame of Massachusetts and Keitt of South Carolina stood *vis-a-vis* in a set. The armed services were represented by dozens of officers, from General Jessup and Commodore Kearny down; the press, by such sages as Seaton of the *National Intelligencer* and Schouler of the Boston *Atlas;* the diplomats, by Sartiges escorting his Boston-reared countess, by the bachelor Spanish minister so attentive to a Western belle that some thought he favored annexation after all, and by dozens of lesser figures. If in part distinguished, the company was also mixed, and one guest long remembered James Gordon Bennett, Jr., capering through a set with Dan Sickles. Yet the newspapers were no doubt right in saying that no earlier Washington gathering had beheld so many beautiful women, costly toilettes, and important men.[5]

Then fell upon Washington the shock of the murder of Philip Barton Key—district attorney, son of the author of "The Star-Spangled Banner," and nephew of Taney—by Congressman Sickles. Washington was an enlarged village, busy with gossip; it had gossiped much about the dashing Sickles, the vivacious and feather-headed Italian girl, Teresa Bagioli, whom he had married (she then only seventeen) in 1853, and the attentions shown her by the handsome, fine-mannered "Phil" Key. The smitten pair carried on their intrigue so openly that they seemed never to have entered their place of assignation on Fifteenth Street without a cloud of admiring witnesses at the windows of neighboring houses.

A melodramatic climax was inevitable. In March, the whole country was reading of it: The quiet Sunday afternoon in Lafayette Square; the emergence of Key from the Washington Club house; his sudden confrontation by Sickles, drawing his derringer; the three shots; the retreat of Sickles, as Key's body was borne away, to the residence of Attorney-General Black; and the rapid ventilation of the whole sordid story. Equally inevitable was Sickles's acquittal, a crowd carrying him on its shoulders to his carriage. He was a favorite of Buchanan, Black, and Slidell, but many people had thought it unseemly for the President of the United States to visit him in his cell.

One happier incident received less notice from the press. On the last evening of the session, the Senate galleries noticed a tall, distinguished-looking gentleman entering the eastern door of the chamber. Members hurried to greet him. First Mason, then Douglas, took his hand, while Seward, Hammond, Clay and others clustered about. Someone brought up Simmons of Rhode Island, who had begun life as a farm-and-factory boy—for the stranger was Richard Cobden, who had gone from the Manchester factories to Parliament. Next morning the Liberal statesman, after breakfasting with Senators Hunter and Mason, hurried off to talk with Gamaliel Bailey of the *National Era*, and to accompany Robert J. Walker to Brady's gallery, where they had their photographs taken. That evening Cobden dined with Lewis Cass, and the following day breakfasted with the President, who asked him to stay at the White House when he returned to Washington. His impressions of Buchanan are interesting. "Found him looking much older, and apparently out of spirits, and not so happy as when I knew him in London. Having attained the highest object of his worldly ambition, he is disappointed with the result."

Cobden, disposed to think the best of American democracy, was a friendly

5 *National Intelligencer*, February 19, 1859; Mrs. C. C. Clay, *Belle of the Fifties*, 118.

observer. After visiting Chicago, he was soon on the *War Eagle* descending the Mississippi to Cairo, and pleased both with crew and passengers:

The company on board the boat comprised a great many rough bearded men with coarse dresses of uncouth fashion, some with loose trousers tucked into their dirty boots, others with their pantaloons rolled up above their shoes like our "navigators." These men, most of them young and full of animal spirits, were on their way to the new gold mines at Pike's Peak, all of them carrying the baggage and provisions and small firearms required for a journey across the plains to the foot of the Rocky Mountains. I was struck with the orderly sober and forbearing demeanor of these men. Not a rude or boisterous word fell from any one of them. This I attribute to the sobriety of all on board. With only one exception I observed that nothing but water was drunk at the table.[6]

[I]

The Congressional session had begun amid gloomy omens of rising sectional irritation. Southerners were exasperated by the sale of Helper's *Impending Crisis*, which went from printing to printing and continued to inspire editorials and speeches. Republicans were of course aware that it reached few of its intended audience, the slaveless whites of the South. Whether they would respond to Helper's thesis if it were brought to their attention was a moot question. J. F. H. Claiborne, a Mississippi editor, had written that although the poor whites were regarded as the vulnerable bastion of the Southern fortress, he thanked God that they were thoroughly republican, well educated, and sensible of their superior position in the existing order.[7] At the same time, he admitted that the efforts of the abolitionists to incite the slaveless majority against the slaveowning minority were of necessity closely watched, and year by year that watch had to be sharpened. Republicans, anxious to sow Helper's seed, realized that few could pay a dollar for it. Frank P. Blair, Jr., Cassius M. Clay, Lewis Clephane, William H. Anthon, and others therefore arranged to print a hundred thousand copies of a pamphlet compendium costing only sixteen cents each. This two-hundred-page version contained all the essential matter in the regular edition, and the Republican press was soon giving umbrage to the South by calling for subscriptions.

The North, meanwhile, found new provocation in the clandestine slave trade. While Buchanan was berating Cuba for maintaining the traffic, the Southern clamor for reopening it was growing, slave-ships fitted in American ports were being captured off the African coast, and worst of all, Southern juries were refusing to enforce the national laws.

6 Richard Cobden, MS Journal, March 5–28, 1859, Midhurst, Sussex.
7 Undated memorandum, Claiborne Papers, Univ. of N. C.

Late in the summer of 1858, the brig *Echo*, captured in Cuban waters by the U.S.S. *Dolphin*, was brought into Charleston. She had cleared from New Orleans, shipped about four hundred and fifty Negroes at the Guinea port of Kabenda, and recrossed the Atlantic in a painful forty-seven-day voyage which cost about one hundred and forty blacks their lives. The survivors, landed at Castle Pinckney wharf, presented a pitiable sight. Some were in a dying condition, others were walking skeletons.[8] While arrangements were made to convoy the negroes to Monrovia as wards of the Colonization Society, the Federal authorities undertook to prosecute the motley crew—Spaniards, Portuguese, and other nationalities. These sixteen desperate-looking scoundrels were guilty of the deaths of nearly ten times their own number.[9] Under the law of 1820 the crime was piracy, its penalty death; and severity was obviously more than justified. South Carolina sentiment, however, condemned the law. Pronouncing it despicable, the Charleston *Evening News* expressed a hope that the grand and petit juries would do their duty and then ask for executive clemency. When the grand jury did bring in an indictment, resolutions were introduced in the State Senate declaring the law unconstitutional, null, and void, and members roundly applauded the assertion that the slave trade was as innocent and legitimate as any other.[10]

The result was the complete breakdown of the case. The jury in the Federal circuit court in Charleston, sitting under Justice Wayne and Judge Magrath, brought in a verdict of not guilty. While the *Mercury* showered them with compliments, Senator Hammond proudly told the Senate that South Carolinians were unconquerably opposed to enforcement of the statute. The government then brought Captain Townsend of the *Echo* to trial at Key West in the spring of 1859. Here the Southern judge interposed every possible obstacle. The Federal attorney proved that the *Echo* was a slaver, that she was an American ship, that Townsend was her master, and that he was an American citizen. But the judge held it necessary to prove, in addition, that the vessel was owned or fitted out by an American. When the prosecution produced from the New Orleans custom house a certified copy of the ship's registry, representing Townsend to be the owner, the judge decided first that, being a copy, the document could not be admitted as evidence, and second, that it did not really prove Townsend the owner. The prosecution then offered in evidence the original bill of sale of the *Echo* to Townsend. This the judge rejected because the handwriting of the men

8 *National Intelligencer*, September 2, 1858.

9 See the interesting diary of officer of the *Niagara*, N. Y. *Weekly Tribune*, October 27, 1858.

10 Charleston *Evening News*, August 30, Charleston correspondence, N. Y. *Tribune*, November 26, 1858.

who had executed it was not proved. At this point, Northerners concluded that judges and juries in the South were acting to nullify the laws against the slave trade.[11]

The heinous case of the ship *Wanderer*, caught bringing slaves not to Cuba but the United States, went far toward proving this true. Her story was one of the most extraordinary of the time. The *Wanderer* was a one-hundred-and-four-teen-foot yacht built at Setauket, Long Island, in the winter of 1856–57, remarkable for speed and seaworthiness. Sailed southward, she gained admiring attention in Charleston and Savannah, particularly attracting a young businessman, interested in planting, banking, and the cotton trade, named Charles A. L. Lamar. Returning to Long Island, the yacht was sold, nominally to a recently elected member of the New York Yacht Club, "Captain" William C. Corrie of South Carolina, but actually to Lamar. From that moment the craft began to arouse suspicion. Corrie shipped a hard-looking crew, installed huge iron water tanks, and made curious interior changes. Federal Marshal Rynders of New York, apprised of her queer character, had her stopped by a revenue cutter in Long Island Sound and searched; but the captain talked so plausibly that she was not detained. The yacht then proceeded to Charleston. Here no secret was made in select groups that she was intended for the "trade," and that Lamar was her principal owner. Before long she made for the African coast; fell in with one of the British fleet watching for slavers; entertained some of the naval officers, Corrie laughingly asking them what sort of a slaver they thought the *Wanderer* would make; anchored at a well-chosen spot; took aboard an estimated six hundred slaves; and cracking on all sail, turned about for a Southern port. Many of the negroes were buried at sea.

Reaching Cumberland Island below Brunswick, Georgia, on a night in late November, 1858, the *Wanderer* landed about three hundred surviving negroes at the Du Bignon estate on Jekyll Island, where preliminary preparations had been made. Thence they were hastily distributed to customers in the interior. Since news of the episode could not long be suppressed, the Federal marshal from Savannah was soon on Jekyll Island searching for evidence. Early in December the yacht was seized, and, while the North expressed indignation, the Department of Justice took steps to prosecute. Lamar wrote a friend that "things are in a hell of a fix," that the yacht "will be lost certain and sure," and that it would be necessary to bribe witnesses. Half a dozen ailing slaves had just died. "I think the whole of them now sick will die," he wrote; "they are too enfeebled to administer medicine to." The character of the business may be inferred from the fact that he later admitted that he had lost two out of three negroes. He

11 N. Y. *Weekly Tribune*, June 4, 1859.

did attempt bribery, offering two of the chief witnesses five thousand dollars not to testify.[12]

The grand jury in the Charleston district refused to find an indictment against Captain Corrie, popular in that area. When the government instructed the Federal attorney to enter a *nolle prosequi* with a view to removing Corrie to Georgia where the slaves had been landed, Judge Magrath refused to permit such action. He offered three arguments. First, he said, although the slaves had touched soil in Georgia, Corrie had been found in South Carolina where process was served on him, and was therefore answerable to the South Carolina tribunal. Second, the President had no power to interfere with the course of the law, or to use his discretion as to discontinuing a prosecution when once begun. Finally, the offense of carrying off a negro who had been a slave did not amount to piracy, the law of 1820 being applicable only to the abduction of a negro who was a freeman when taken! Corrie's detention in the Charleston jail thus served merely to prevent his trial in Georgia. Federal law ought to be enforced, wrote Magrath privately to Hammond; but could it be? "Why in South Carolina the jurisdiction of the U. S. does not prevail in the Court House itself!" [13]

In Savannah, the Federal attorney and judge were represented by the press as men determined to permit no child's play; yet here too the issue was farcical.[14] A Savannah jury which found indictments against the owner, captain, and others accomplished nothing. Indeed, the jurors shortly recanted. They published a protest saying that they had acted under compulsion of the court, for they regarded the law against the slave trade as a gross injustice. "We feel humbled, as men," they asserted, "in the consciousness that we are freemen but in name, and that we are living, during the existence of such laws, under a tyranny as supreme as that of the despotic governments of the Old World. . . . Longer to yield to a sickly sentiment of pretended philanthropy and diseased mental aberration of 'higher law' fanatics . . . is weak and unwise." [15] Nobody was tried. The *Wanderer* was sold by government order on March 12, 1859, at Savannah, but only one other person had the courage to bid, and Lamar got the vessel for $4,000. He was determined to go ahead with the trade. "To be sure," he wrote another Georgian, "at first I knew nothing of the business. I have learned some-

---

12 See "A Slave Trader's Notebook," *North American Review*, November, 1886; articles in *The Rudder*, Vol. XV, February–March, 1904; W. M. Thompson, "The Slave Ship Wanderer," *National Intelligencer*, January 4, 1859; Savannah *Republican*, December, 1859.

13 Robert Bunch to Lord John Russell, May 3, 1860; FO 115/230. Pamphlet, "Slave Trade Not Declared Piracy by Act of 1820; United States vs. W. C. Corrie, Opinion of Hon. A. G. Magrath." Magrath to Hammond, January 21, 1859; Hammond Papers, LC. Magrath wrote that a plot was afoot to defy the nation by giving an imported African to certain desperate men, widely publicizing the fact, and then supporting these lawless characters.

14 Savannah *Republican*, December 30, 31, 1858.

15 *Harper's Magazine*, 1859, p. 255.

thing since, and I hope can put my information to some account. I have been in it for 'grandeur,' and have been fighting for a principle. Now I am in it for the dollars." [16]

Other men, too, regarded the slave trade as a matter of principle. Judge Magrath presided in the Federal district court at Charleston when, early in 1859, the case of the captain and crew of the ship *Brothers*, captured off Africa under suspicious circumstances, came up. The Federal attorney presented evidence and asked for indictments. Magrath responded with a charge which, while calling for enforcement of the law, consisted largely of laudation of slavery with an allusion to the rapid change of Old World opinion in its favor. Naturally the jury, after retiring for an hour, refused the indictments.[17] The British consul was an alert observer of the proceedings on the *Echo* crew and Captain Corrie of the *Wanderer*. Judge Magrath's conduct in the latter case he thought "a melancholy instance of that which in this country is too common, the overwhelming power of public sentiment." [18] The jury in the *Echo* trial, he reported, paid no attention to the evidence, and had the defense asked them to do so, would have declared that not one of the accused had ever been aboard the *Echo*. He also reported that plenty of money for the defense came from Havana; that the pilot of the captor ship, the U.S.S. *Dolphin*, was shortly murdered; that a man ready to turn state's evidence was threatened with assassination; and that everybody in the trade was assured that those who got into trouble would be safeguarded. The Federal attorney said privately that the failure of the case would give a fresh impetus to slave-running.[19]

[II]

The question of the proportions reached by the slave trade we treat elsewhere; but it may be said here that what most alarmed Northerners was that the long-hesitant movement to make the traffic legal was now reaching full-blown proportions. Originally, its advocates had appealed chiefly to the large planters who found their labor supply too costly. Some Southern leaders still frankly advocated it as certain to benefit wealthy landholders and foster an aristocratic culture. Thus William H. Trescot assured Porcher Miles that the trade would lead to the development of a hierarchical Southern civilization in contrast with the Jeffersonian theory of government.[20] But now the movement was

16 June 29, 1859; *North American Review*, November, 1886, "A Slave Trader's Notebook."
17 *National Intelligencer*, January 15, 1859.
18 Bunch to Lord John Russell, May 3, 1860; FO 115/230.
19 Bunch to Lord Malmesbury, April 21, 1859; FO 115/216.
20 W. H. Trescot to W. P. Miles, February 8, 1859; Miles Papers, Univ. of N. C.

pressed on two very different lines: as an appeal to a democratic diffusion of slavery, and as a contribution to Southern defiance of the North.[21]

John Mitchel in his *Southern Citizen*, just established in Washington, adopted what he called the honest human flesh program, declaring that the trade would soon reduce the price of a robust fieldhand from $1,000 to $100, enabling every Southern farmer to buy one. No longer would a line be drawn between, nabob and poor white; the monopolist would be put down; every citizen could belong to the grand family of slaveholders. Daniel Lee preached the same doctrine in his *Southern Cultivator*.[22] John J. McRae, who succeeded to Quitman's seat, espoused this plan for equalizing the dignities of Southern citizenship. Some estimates of the number of slaves needed if they became a "democratic" possession were extremely high. A Texan wrote the New York *Express* that half a million of the "black rascals" were wanted in his State, while Daniel Lee computed that it would take a million Africans to till the seven hundred thousand square miles of unimproved land in the South. Then, too, talk of heavy slave importations was coupled with talk of territorial annexations. Martin J. Crawford of Georgia told Congress that unless the war upon slavery was stopped, within fifteen years the South would have reopened the trade and extended its dominion as far as Guatemala or farther.[23]

A similar defiance of the North was expressed by other men. Such leaders as A. G. Brown of Mississippi emphasized State sovereignty;[24] the South had a right to meet its own labor problem, declared Davis, and Federal intervention was improper if not unconstitutional.[25] To many Southerners, the phraseology of the Act of 1820, terming the importation of slaves "piracy," seemed to throw a slur on the whole institution. They forgot that the law so stigmatizing the trade had been advocated by President Monroe, with the support of such Cabinet members as Calhoun and W. H. Crawford, and that the measure, introduced by Mercer of Virginia, had received the vote of the whole South Carolina delegation, including Poinsett and McDuffie. Since then, the sensitivity of slaveholders had increased.[26]

21   And other reasons as well. Three had been brought forward in the Southern Commercial Convention at Savannah just after Buchanan's election. They were (1) that abundant negroes would overflow into the Territories, expanding the institution; (2) that cheap slaves would safeguard the cotton kingdom against Brazilian and Indian competition; and (3) that it was more humane to bring negroes from Africa than to break up families in the border States by purchasing them there.
22   *Southern Citizen*, December 4, 1858, *et seq.*; *Southern Cultivator*, August, 1858.
23   Amer. Anti-Slavery Society, *Annual Report* year ending May, 1859, pp. 40–42; *De Bow's Review*, October, 1858, "African Slavery Adapted to the West and Northwest."
24   A. G. Brown quoted in New Orleans *Picayune*, July 3, 1859.
25   Speech of July 6, 1859; *Letters, Papers, and Speeches*, IV, 61–88.
26   Jefferson had called the slave trade "an execrable commerce"; Madison had pronounced it "infernal"; Hayne had said in 1826 that any South Carolinian concerned in it "would be indignantly driven out of society." Yancey to A. Alison, August 11, 1861, Yancey Papers.

It was true that, as Slidell said, the great mass of Southerners condemned the foreign slave trade. In Texas, for example, despite some planters who wanted cheap hands, Sam Houston assailed any revival, while John H. Reagan after attacking it was reelected to Congress by an unprecedented majority.[27] In Louisiana, many citizens expressed a sense of shock when early in 1858 one house voted for the importation of twenty-five hundred Africans to be indentured for not less than fifteen years; and the *Picayune* declared that the movement would meet the utter repugnance of five-sixths of the population.[28] Albert Pike of Arkansas had said that he would be torn apart by wild horses before he would consent to renewing so cruel a traffic.[29]

Yet it seemed to be true that the movement was growing, and that many, like Ruffin, were confessing a conversion to it. Had not the majority of the South Carolina legislative committee to which Governor Adams's message was referred reported in favor of it? Had not one prominent figure after another taken it up? Did not eighteen Mississippians advertise in the spring of 1858 that they would pay $300 a head for a thousand Africans landed between Pensacola and Galveston? [30] It seemed also to be true that much of the opposition rested on grounds of mere expediency. Many men did not want slaves made cheaper. Many held that importation would not pay, for too many blacks would die before being acclimated. Many thought the agitation ill-timed because it divided Southern sentiment in the face of Northern menaces.[31]

To Northern reproaches over the nullification of slave-trade laws, the South could reply with reproaches over Yankee nullification of the Fugitive Slave Act. It could point to such episodes as the mob disorders in the neighboring towns of New Albany, Indiana, and Brandenburg, Kentucky, when the seizure by slaveholders of an alleged underground railroad agent, Horace Bell, and his rescue from a Kentucky jail, caused whole communities to rush to arms. For a week, parts of southern Indiana and northern Kentucky seethed with mutual hostility.[32] Of course the danger of a reopening of the African slave trade was small. Of course the actual loss of the South (and especially the Deep South) from runaway slaves was easily bearable. But dread of future peril does most to harrow men, and North and South had grown deeply apprehensive of each other's policy. Misunderstanding made fear, fear made hatred, hatred made hysteria. Helper, the *Wanderer*, the Bell riots, were but indications of a

27 *National Intelligencer*, August 25, 1859.
28 New Orleans *Picayune*, March 5, 1858.
29 Southern Commercial Convention, 1856, *Proceedings*.
30 Enterprise *Weekly News*, April 14, 1859; *De Bow's*, August–November, 1858.
31 *National Intelligencer*, October 30, 1858; Ruffin to Mitchel, June 14, 1859; Ruffin Papers, Univ. of N. C.
32 October, 1858; New York, Louisville, and Cincinnati press.

massive trend. "What is Kansas or any similar question," Representative Willoughby Newton of Virginia asked, "but the drift on the surface of the stream over which politicians are madly contending, regardless of the steady current that is steadily sweeping them to destruction?" [33]

[III]

It was again in an atmosphere of emotional unreason that Congress began its deliberations. Lecompton was no more; the pending questions were nearly all economic—the Pacific Railroad, the homestead bill, the tariff, and internal improvements; yet they too tended to arouse sectional passion. For one reason, the old issue of local rights and State activity against centralized national power was involved. For another, all the proposed economic legislation seemed likely to take dollars out of Southern pockets and put them into Northern. Above all, however, the pending bills threatened to upset the sectional balance more violently than ever. The South desired to bind the Northwest to itself in continued enjoyment of a low tariff and cheap European goods, in the use of the Mississippi as a grand North-South artery of trade, and in the production of complementary agricultural staples. All the pending proposals tended rather to bind the Northwest to the East.

Buchanan, as everybody expected, had renewed his Pacific Railway recommendations in emphatic terms. He suggested a route traversing a temperate latitude, where trains would not be impeded by the ice and snow of winter, or the tropical heats of summer. This left a wide field of choice open, for towns all the way from Dubuque to Baton Rouge would naturally assert that they enjoyed a beatifically ideal climate. Time had not lessened the rivalry of cities and sections. Men of Chicago and St. Louis found the extreme southern route, which Jefferson Davis had favored when Secretary of War, incredibly repulsive; men of New Orleans and Memphis viewed a road through Minnesota and Dakota with stupefaction; while a route west from St. Louis would receive few Southern votes and very grudging Northern support. Nobody liked the idea of having to pay for three railways to get one, but nothing less seemed likely to satisfy all areas.[34]

Debate was opened by the hopeful Gwin of California as soon as the session began. The pending measure, held over from the previous session, provided that the western terminal should be in San Francisco and the eastern at some point between the Big Sioux and the Kansas rivers as they emptied into the Missouri,

33　Va. Military Institute speech, *National Intelligencer*, July 24, 1858.
34　Cf. Foot of Vermont, *Cong. Globe*, 35th Cong., 2d Sess., 75; N. Y. *Weekly Tribune*, December 4, 1858.

the contractors being required to make their choice on grounds of feasibility, directness, and economy. The government was to grant alternate sections of land in a strip twenty miles wide on each side, and to lend $12,500 a mile for every section of twenty-five miles completed, the loan to be repaid with interest in mail service and military transportation. Gwin, Douglas, Harlan of Iowa, and many others were satisfied with this plan. The contractors, they said, would know best. They might decide to push their line from the Missouri southwestward to Texas and New Mexico; they might follow the Thirty-fifth parallel (roughly the Memphis, Fort Smith, and Albuquerque line); or they might push northwest up the Missouri River and then across to Puget Sound. Any attempt to restrict the choice could readily exclude the best route of all. Whatever the eastern terminal, it could easily be connected by radiating lines with many cities North and South. And why should Congress delay? The broad West awaited communications and development, while British competition by a Canadian transcontinental was all too possible.[35]

But enthusiasts for the bill were taken aback by the formidable strength of two opposition elements. The larger was a Southern bloc which urged that the road would tax the whole nation and deplete the national domain for the benefit of Northern interests. The smaller was a group of hard-headed realists, chiefly New Englanders, who declared that the pending scheme would attract irresponsible speculators, line the pockets of crafty promoters, and, after tens of millions had been expended, result only in throwing a half-built road upon the government. This second group might have been placated by a few safeguarding amendments, but the Southern dissenters would run no risk of a northern or central line.

Jefferson Davis objected that a terminus between the mouths of the Kansas and the Big Sioux would be a terminus on the borders of the Great American Desert. Within a hundred miles, the railroad would enter a region of arid and utterly worthless land, and it would remain isolated unless it turned sharply south to strike the road which Texas was constructing westward. While he denied any sectional bias in the matter, he made it clear that he thought the southernmost route (from Fulton, Arkansas, to San Diego near the thirty-second degree and then to San Francisco) much the most practical, and doubly desirable because of the readiness of Texas to build the line to the Rio Grande.[36]

Iverson of Georgia, in a stirring speech, also attacked the central route on the grounds of its injustice to his section. This contractors' bill, he said, would rob the South to benefit the North. The two prizes of twenty-five million acres of public land, and twenty-five million dollars to be taken out of a quarter-

35 *Cong. Globe*, 35th Cong., 2nd Sess., 49–56; 333, 334, etc.
36 *Ibid.*, 72–78.

century mail contract, would be irresistible to Wall Street. The moneyed interests which were financing the northern and western roads would seize the new opportunity. They would infallibly adopt a northern route, pouring all the freights of the Far West over the Pennsylvania, New York Central, Erie, and other lines into the Northern cities and States. What Northern capitalist would invest in a Southern railway? It was notorious, said Iverson, that hardly a Yankee dollar had gone into any enterprise in the slaveholding area; if Senator Hammond tried to raise ten thousand in New York on his half-million-dollar estate in South Carolina, he would be refused. I protest, said the Senator, against any scheme of government aid which will heap untold benefits upon one section, and give hardly sixpence to the other.

Other Southerners, such as Brown of Mississippi and Mason of Virginia, argued against both the constitutionality and the necessity of the proposed Federal-aid scheme. Not a few slave State members felt that they could hold out for the El Paso-San Diego line or nothing—for by government surveys it was the shortest and cheapest of all routes. Texas proposed to subsidize her own road for six or seven hundred miles across the State, and, at the moment, the prospects of this Texas Pacific Railway seemed bright. The charter had been granted; a generous State subsidy (no less than 10,240 acres of land and a loan of $6,000 for every mile built) had been promised. Efficient officers had been elected, who, late in 1858, persuaded J. Edgar Thomson, widely regarded as the best railroad engineer in the land, to take charge of construction. The bi-weekly government mail service along the projected route had done much to clear the way for builders. Efforts were being made to induce some eminent Southerner (William C. Rives was approached) to take the presidency.[37]

The objections of Fessenden, Henry Wilson, and other New Englanders were very different from those of the South. They wanted a railroad built; they favored the north-central route; but they deplored the financial arrangements of the pending measure. On the one hand the bill offered too little incentive to responsible capitalists, and on the other held out too easy a prize to thieves and charlatans. It would be easy for speculators, these Yankee realists declared, to build that part of the road which ran through fertile land, collect the government bounties, and, when the semi-arid region was reached, stop short. Dishonest contractors would need only to raise half a million as security, set to work at Sioux City or Council Bluffs, construct the line through six hundred miles of the best country within reach, take six millions in cash and six or seven million

<hr>

37 *Ibid.*, 242-244, for Iverson; *De Bow's* July, 1858, contains Beale's favorable report to the War Department on the survey of a wagon road from Fort Defiance to the California line near the Thirty-fifth parallel.

acres of fertile land, and when they touched the rattlesnake and prairie-dog belt, abandon the road to the government.

Wilson's own plan had great merit—as the history of the Credit Mobilier later taught. The government itself, he argued, should forthwith build a central railroad as a grand national enterprise, reserving all the adjacent lands as a sinking fund to pay off the bonds sold for construction purposes. If, subsequently, Southern interests wished to build along the Thirty-second parallel and Northern interests near the Forty-ninth, he would give them adequate land grants; but these roads could wait. The initial railway was a national necessity, while those which followed it would be commercial enterprises, dependent for their prosperity upon the growth of population.[38]

Advocates of the Pacific Railway bill had counted, as Harlan of Iowa plaintively remarked, on the twelve New England Senators. They had counted, indeed, on all the Northern Senators except those of New Jersey, and on the eight Senators of Missouri, Iowa, Minnesota, and California. This would give them thirty-four votes, a clear majority. The defection of Wilson, Fessenden, and others was a heavy blow. In vain did Douglas expend his most forcible arguments on the question; in vain did Bigler and Green reason with their Southern colleagues; in vain did the California Senators lobby with frenzied energy. John Bell was ready to submit to any ordeal of prolonged hours to reach a vote. But the combination of New England and the South sealed the fate of the bill. It was a disappointment all the bitterer to Douglas, Gwin, and Harlan because they had cozened themselves with dreams of a large majority.[39]

It was soon evident that the debate had merely thrown a searchlight from a new angle into the widening chasm of sectional animosity. Jefferson Davis remarked that he had foreseen from the beginning that they would finally run into the poverty-stricken sectional quarrel, a thing from which he always turned with loathing. With visible rancor, Henry Wilson accused the Southerners of a secret plan to place the western terminal at Guaymas on the Gulf of California, where it would serve a coming Southern Confederacy. This was untrue, and was hotly denied. But, with equal acerbity, Iverson avowed an attitude which gave some ground for Wilson's suspicions. "Sir," he exclaimed. "I believe that the time will come when the slave States will be compelled, in vindication of their rights, interests, and honor, to separate from the free States, and erect an independent confederacy; and I am not sure, sir, that the time is not at hand. . . . And, sir, it is because I believe that separation is not far distant . . . that I am unwilling to vote so much land and so much money as this bill proposes, to build

38 *Ibid.*, 35th Cong., 2nd Sess., 304–315.
39 *Ibid.*, 333, 334.

a railroad to the Pacific, which, in my judgment, will be created outside of a Southern confederacy, and will belong exclusively to the North." [40]

As Wilson and Iverson spoke in these terms, Sam Houston delivered the finest single utterance of the debate. He naturally wished to see the railroad hammered down in Texas, traversing the fertile trough (as he called it) from the mouth of the Red River to El Paso. But, spurning sectional name-calling and secession doctrines, he denied the right of any man to talk of disunion. "Disunion, sir! You might as well tell me that you could have a healthy patient and a whole man, if you were to cut the main artery of his life. Have gentlemen ever reflected as to when, where, and how they are to begin disunion; and where it is to end? Who will cut the great Mississippi in two? Who is to have the mouth of it? Who is to command its source? Will it be those who agitate the subject, or who are ultra upon it? Never, never! Look at the great West, rising like a giant." To this outburst Iverson replied with new threats of disunion. [41]

Amid jeers and laughter on one side, reproaches and lamentations on the other, the bill failed as on January 27, 1859, the Senate by the overwhelming vote of 38 to 20 carried an amendment which reduced it to nullity. Party and sectional lines were thrown into confusion as Fessenden voted *no* with Slidell, and Preston King *aye* with Hammond. Gwin, red with anger, moved that as the Senate had turned six weeks' labor into a farce, it should adjourn for the day; and it did so, the members aware that the transcontinental railroad was dead until after the election of 1860. The victory lay with the South.

[IV]

Would homestead legislation, which the previous session of the Senate had postponed by a vote of 30 to 22, fare any better? Its advocates hoped so. Since the bill of 1854 had been slain outright in the Senate, the situation had radically changed. While Southern opposition had solidified, most of the old Northern antagonism had melted away. The long struggle of Greeley, Galusha A. Grow, Andrew Johnson, and others was achieving some of its ends. Originally, the seaboard States had stood in the main against the Ohio and Mississippi valleys. [42] But logical argument, Republican Party solidarity, and the results of the panic of 1857 had told in favor of the measure until only a conservative Northern minority, with the New York *Herald* as chief mouthpiece, was against the bill. Seward of New York professed as much ardor in the cause as Richard Yates of Illinois, or Doolittle of Wisconsin.

40 *Ibid.*, 242–244.
41 *Ibid.*, 334.
42 Helene Zahler, *Eastern Workingmen and National Land Policy, 1829–1862,* 178, 179.

The panic had taught the North a manifold lesson. It had shown manufacturers that apprehension of a future labor shortage arising from migration westward was exaggerated. Burning the fingers of land speculators, it had taught these gentry that they would do well to give small holders a better opportunity. It had placed before eastern cities the spectacle of unemployed multitudes crowding the breadlines and soup houses, when (theoretically) they might be growing food. Above all, it had suggested to industrialists and traders that nothing was more important than the rapid development of Western markets for goods—and homesteaders would furnish markets and fat profits.

Since House passage of the bill was certain, Southern Senators would have to fight against it with their backs to the wall. They were aware that the rapid colonization of the West by small farmers would stimulate Yankee industrialism, that it would hasten the emergence of more Northwestern States dedicated to free soil, and that it would strengthen the Republican Party. But some Southern leaders hesitated to avow a naked sectionalism, while nearly all were reluctant to emphasize the old cry of unconstitutionality, which John Bell had recently told a Nashville audience was too sophistical to impress anybody.[43] It was necessary to fall back upon other staple arguments. Senators from slaveholding States contended that the grant of free homesteads would destroy land values in the older areas, and would soon result in glutted crop-markets and ruinous farm prices. They predicted that it would swell the immigration from European slums. They argued that it would penalize the slaveholder, for he found it so difficult to remove to the common domain that he would get nothing out of the law. Above all, they declared that it would throw the door wide open to class legislation, for a government which gave land to the landless might soon vote money to the moneyless.

Making a sudden bold thrust, Grow and his friends on February 1, 1859, carried the bill through the House by a vote of 120 to 76, with thirty-seven Northern Democrats among the majority.[44] It was significant that only three slave States cast any votes for it, and only seven free States any votes against it. The hopes of friends of the measure rose with this House passage. Let Congress press on, wrote Greeley, to give the nation this new Declaration of Independence, emancipating and elevating the poor but industrious worker.[45]

Hardly had the struggle opened in the Senate, however, than it became inextricably involved in another and fiercer battle over the pending bill to appropriate thirty million dollars for Buchanan to use in negotiating the purchase of Cuba. The South was almost a unit against the Homestead bill; the North was

43 Speech of July 18 in *National Intelligencer*, August 6, 1857.
44 Roy Nichols, *Disruption*, 232.
45 N. Y. *Weekly Tribune*, February 12, 1859.

almost unanimously against the thirty-million grant; and as they came up simultaneously, sectional feeling was certain to spin a connection between them. Buchanan, with Slidell, Belmont, and other expansionists prodding him, had set his heart upon making the annexation of Cuba the grand achievement of the Administration. Thus he would placate the South, appeal to the nationalist feeling of Young America, and place his name beside those of Jefferson, Monroe, and Polk as leaders who had broadened the national domain. Immediately after his inauguration, he had begun secret negotiations with an American financial agent of the Spanish Queen-Mother, one Christopher Fallon. The two men revived the old scheme of Belmont for combining bribery, banking influence in Europe, and the pressure of Spain's hungry creditors upon her half-bankrupt government, to bring about a sale of Cuba at a good round sum—say one hundred millions. Fallon hastened to Europe, where he devoted some busy weeks in Paris, Rome, and Madrid to conferences and intrigue. Among others, he saw the avaricious Queen-Mother Christina. Although vexatious delays ensued, the grand plan was kept alive. In accordance with it, Buchanan, late in 1858, had sent William Preston, lawyer, former Representative, and scion of a wealthy Louisville family, as minister to Madrid, and Slidell had arranged the bill for dangling before Spain this initial bait of thirty millions.

So preposterous was the idea of any immediate purchase of Cuba that nearly everybody regarded the thirty-million scheme as a device for the campaign of 1860 rather than for serious negotiations. To persuade Spain to part with the rich island in which its pride, its easiest revenues, and its hopes of power were centered would be difficult to achieve, even by the nicest combination of solicitation, cajolery, secret pressure, and weighty financial inducements. Cuba was the brightest remaining jewel of a nation which had all the haughty jealousy of a decayed grandee. The melange of insult, abuse, and bullying in Buchanan's December message had been resented by Madrid as a blow in the face. That message was intended primarily for expansionist elements at home, and Slidell's bill was meant to satisfy the desires of Southern annexationists and perhaps give the Democrats a unifying issue in 1860 as Texas had given them one in 1844. Caleb Cushing, writing Franklin Pierce of the utter demoralization of the party, had declared that the problem of rallying it seemed baffling. "We may have to intervene in Mexico. In fine, I live in hope that something will turn up to animate and justify the party"—and now Micawber Cushing could see Cuba turning up.[46]

46 April 9, 1858; Pierce Papers, LC. Buchanan thought that if Slidell would go as minister to Paris, where he might be far more effective than Mason, he could help get Cuba; but Slidell was reluctant to go unless he saw a strong chance of success. See their correspondence, May–June, 1858; Buchanan Papers. Cf. Sears, *Slidell*, 152.

Spanish resentment over Buchanan's affront was expressed by all parties of the Cortes on the last day of 1858, in a debate whose dignity and moderation contrasted with the rodomontade often heard in Congress on foreign affairs. The colonial minister referred scornfully to the philanthropic pretensions of Buchanan's passages on the slave trade, strange enough from a country where slavery was preserved in a harsh form and Negroes were punished for the crime of getting a little instruction. Spain, he said, would confront the Americans defiantly: "If you want Cuba, come and take her!" The leader of the opposition predicted that the nation would stand as a single phalanx in defense of Spanish rights all over the globe. Before rising, the Cortes voted unanimously to defend the integrity of the empire against any assailant. The Spanish press would have been more scorching but that, like the European press in general, it connected the President's outburst with the coming elections.[47]

Spain was no longer the faction-torn, decrepit nation she had been when Buchanan helped draft the Ostend Manifesto. Marshal Leopold O'Donnell, a former governor-general of Cuba, was now at the helm and giving the country fresh optimism and strength. If Spain was not strong enough to menace others, he told the Cortes, the nation could at least defend its own name from stain.[48] Demonstrations of loyalty also broke out in Cuba.[49] Needless to say, they were largely inspired by the authorities, and one Havana observer wrote Preston that among the numerous groups which had spirit enough to resent the tyranny of the regime, Buchanan's proposals had made a most favorable impression.[50] A great part of the Cuban population, however, actually did spurn the message, for the efforts of officials during recent years to prejudice the people against American annexation had met with considerable success. Among the Spanish-born elements, perhaps a fifth of the people of the island and half those of Havana, few would support any scheme of purchase.[51]

The general belief that the thirty-million bill was nine-tenths politics found reflection in Washington gossip. Edmund Ruffin spent some time in the capital, as 1859 opened, quietly preaching secession. He was there when the Democratic caucus on January 15 gave three or four hours to the bill, with opinion much divided. Hunter and Shields thought the proposed action impolitic, while Douglas, though willing to place the money in Buchanan's hands, believed the prospects for gaining Cuba gloomy. He declared that only one chance of success existed; if another *Black Warrior* affair took place, the island should instantly be seized. Ruffin regarded the President's message as ill-advised, for it had

47 London *Times, Daily News,* December, 1858.
48 *National Intelligencer,* January 25, 1859.
49 *Ibid.,* January 22, 1859.
50 G. W. Madan, December 24, 1858; Buchanan Papers.
51 C. J. Helm, January 1, 1859; Buchanan Papers.

not only angered Spain but aroused apprehension in Britain and France. He entered in his diary:

January 17.—At night went to see Hammond. He thinks that neither the President nor others of the members in Congress, are sincere in their proposed measures to acquire Cuba—but that each wants only to cultivate popularity by pretending to be foremost in the move—that all of them would be horrified if the bill should, by possibility, be enacted. Hammond thinks that war would certainly be made on us by France and England, if we were to acquire Cuba, even by purchase. He ascribes this evil political move, and most others, to the aspirants to the Presidency, of whom he enumerated and named eighteen in the Southern States, as understood by the public (and among whom he counted himself), and of them eleven who were active in the pursuit. They were Hunter, Wise of Virginia, Breckinridge and Crittenden of Kentucky, Orr of South Carolina, Bell and Johnson of Tennessee, Toombs of Georgia, Houston of Texas, Davis of Mississippi, and Slidell of Louisiana.[52]

Yet the real basis of the move lay not so much in Presidential ambitions as in a desire to anneal the party—a commendable desire—and give it a winning issue. As such, and as a means of avoiding a national crisis in 1860–61, it met the covert hostility of determined secessionists. They now saw clearly that Democratic unity must be shattered before the Union could be rent in twain. "Don't touch Cuba," William Gilmore Simms exhorted Porcher Miles. "It is the bait which the Democratic Party holds out to the South. Beware how you enter this field. The Democratic Party has but one chance left for life, that of involving us in foreign war. It is a mere delusion to suppose that our chances of getting Cuba are less, if we separate, than as a whole. *If separate, we can control the whole commerce—all the shipping of the North! It is better to be separate before we take Cuba.*" [53]

Altogether, the thirty-million bill was utterly unrealistic, and, since it could not possibly pass the House, no statesmanlike reason existed for pressing it. Southern speakers, tacitly admitting its worthlessness for diplomacy, tried to justify it as an instrument for arousing expansionist sentiment. The President, remarked Mallory of Florida, had touched a popular chord, and the spirit that had given the country Louisiana and Texas was reawakening.[54] Others adopted the argument that if the United States exhausted peaceable negotiation, it could more easily justify summary measures if they became necessary. At a later date, Jefferson Davis gave his own complete rationalization of the annexationist case. In the first place, he said, the moral effect of the Senate's passage of the thirty-

52 Edmund Ruffin, MS Diary, LC; abbreviations spelled out. Yet John A. Dix wrote the President of strong feeling even among Republicans for the Cuban bill; January 22, 1859, Buchanan Papers.
53 W. G. Simms to W. P. Miles, February 3, 1859; W. P. Miles Papers, Univ. of N. C.
54 *Cong. Globe*, 35th Cong. 2nd Sess., 1189.

million bill would have fortified the Executive in his negotiations. In the second, the Administration would have been put in a better position to fish in troubled European waters; for the war of Napoleon III against Austria was about to begin, and Spain might be involved. Finally, a victory for the bill would have rebuked British meddling in Cuba, and warned Victoria's government to cease its demand for measures of emancipation.[55] Actually it may be doubted whether it would have achieved any one of these very dubious ends.

It was easy for opposition Senators, supported by the whole freesoil press, to riddle the bill. As Seward said, it was not a giant in armor but a crazy windmill. They argued that for Buchanan to pledge thirty millions in negotiating for the island, at a time when the national revenue had sunk to fifty millions, would be reckless extravagance. If he gave the thirty millions as advance payment on a treaty promising $250,000,000, said Seward, then the Senate must either ratify the bargain or lose the money. And what other promises might Buchanan not make in his negotiations? Would he agree to make Cuba a State, or several States? What status would he assign to the two hundred and fifty thousand free Negroes and four hundred thousand slaves in the island? Wilson, Collamer, Doolittle and others ridiculed the idea that annexation would help in the suppression of the slave trade; they expatiated on the difficulty of assimilating a half-million Spanish creoles; and they prophesied that other annexations would necessarily follow—Jamaica, Santo Domingo, Central America. Toombs, said Collamer, wished to annex the whole tropical belt of the Western Hemisphere; and Toombs interjected, "It is true; the whole of it!" [56]

[V]

By the last week of February, a variety of events had wrought Congressional tempers to a savage pitch. The expansionists were angered by the taunts of the Republican press, daily reiterating that the Buchanan regime was bankrupt, that the Cuban bill was the last desperate dice-throw of unscrupulous gamesters, and that the South, having failed to extend slavery in the Northwest by fraud, was trying to push it in the Caribbean by force. They were angered also by the refusal of many Republicans to debate the merits of annexation. Many leaders

55 Speech of July 6, 1859, Mississippi Democratic Convention. Open aggression was preached by several Southern leaders. Governor Wickliffe of Louisiana had said in his annual message that if this mode of freeing the island should fail, he hoped "some more potent one will be used." Judah P. Benjamin was for three steps: first to support Buchanan's offer of purchase; second to offer Spain a large sum to make Cuba independent; and finally to inform Madrid that whenever an opportunity should occur the United States would give Cubans the same aid that Great Britain had lent to other revolting Spanish colonies. *Cong. Globe*, 35th Cong., 2nd Sess., 960–964, 1186. A. G. Brown made a swashbuckling speech in Tammany Hall; he was ready to fight Spain, Britain, and France all at once for Cuba.

56 *Cong. Globe*, 35th Cong., 2nd Sess., 1187.

of the new party carefully refrained from saying that the United States should *never* acquire Cuba; they simply opposed the Buchanan-Slidell method. Seward, Fessenden, Dixon, and others took the view that they would not discuss the question whether new Caribbean areas (say Cuba with the Wilmot Proviso applied and Catholicism disestablished) were not desirable; they should merely denounce the infamy of the pending scheme. To Slidell and Toombs this was dishonest.[57]

Republicans for their part were irritated by Buchanan's veto, February 24, of the long-desired measure to grant public lands or land scrip to the States for the support of colleges of agriculture and the mechanic arts. The general idea of this legislation had been in the air for years, taking a wide variety of forms: Greeley's grandiose project for a People's University; the plan of Jonathan B. Turner of Illinois for industrial universities founded on land grants; the proposal of the Massachusetts legislature in 1855 for a national agricultural college, and so on. It was fitting that Justin S. Morrill of Vermont, the son of a horny-handed blacksmith who had often lamented the lack of more than six weeks' schooling, should crystallize these current ideas into a practical measure. It was also better strategy to put the bill in the hands of an easterner than in those of (say) Trumbull of Illinois, for many people felt that the western States had already gotten too much of the common domain. Behind the bill rallied an impressive array of Northern farming, labor, and professional supporters, while two border Senators, Crittenden and Pearce, lent their aid. Opposition came from various groups —from people who distrusted book-larnin', from enemies of class legislation, from Westerners who feared land speculation by absentee scrip-holders, and, most stubborn of all, from Southerners who stressed the constitutional argument and who saw that, since the lands would be distributed in proportion to Congressional representation, the measure would benefit one section more than the other.[58]

Something like a farm bloc seemed arising—and it would yet be aligned with the Republican Party. An Agricultural Congress meeting in Washington under Patent Office auspices helped supply pressure. The bill had passed the House the previous session 105 to 100; it now passed the Senate 25 to 23. Slidell, who had reason to know, predicted that the President would veto it. Despite the fact that even Toombs said that no veto could be justified "by a damned sight," despite Dan Sickles's intervention for it, and despite protests from loyal Pennsylvania Democrats, Buchanan killed it. Federal aid to agricultural education could never

57 James Dixon to Welles, January 24, 29, 1859; Welles Papers.
58 See W. E. Sawyer, "Evolution of the Morrill Act of 1862," MS doctoral dissertation, Boston Univ., 1948. No connection has been found between Jonathan B. Turner's bill and Morrill's, but it is not impossible that it existed; Mary T. Carriel, *Turner*, 152–165. State agricultural colleges were still extremely weak.

become law while he sat in the White House. In a futile vote on reconsideration, Morrill kept his House strength intact, 105 to 96.[59]

Though Buchanan was undoubtedly sincere in his constitutional objections, his veto message irritated many Northern commentators. To his arguments that the public lands should be safeguarded, that the States should not look to the Treasury for gifts, and that the grant would probably not benefit agriculture or mechanic arts, they replied that the bill did not donate one-sixth as much land as that given in the previous decade for railroad and military bounties, that it was merely a plan for dividing a small part of the common domain, and that experts had offered impressive evidence of its benefits. Actually, in the existing state of agricultural science, a delay of a few years was not harmful. Politics and sectional jockeying had probably motivated Morrill quite as much as an interest in scientific education. But the veto gave Greeley an opportunity to berate the President as a "Slave Power tool." Another veto, that of the bill for eliminating the dangerous shoals in the St. Clair channel connecting Lakes Huron and Erie, aroused the ire of Northwestern commercial interests, for the cost was trifling and the prospective benefits were immense. Again Buchanan's constitutional position was tenable, and doubtless taken in all sincerity. But Michigan and Wisconsin politicians, reacting to public sentiment, swore to support any Presidential candidate who would promise river, harbor, and lake improvements. Some even said that this would be the cardinal issue of 1860 in the Northwest.

Meanwhile, the quarrel between the Douglas Democrats and the Administration men had broken into the debates like the regular eruption of Old Faithful geyser. Since his arrival, the Illinois Senator had suffered contumely and insolence. While some Southerners were haughtily freezing, others sought a personal quarrel. Again we have to remember the venoms of the period. In mid-January, Slidell published a provocative card in the *Union*. He had denounced Douglas, on the authority of some talebearer, as a calumniator; Douglas had replied that he was nothing of the kind; and now Slidell repeated that he *was*, for the Illinoisan had inspired anonymous attacks upon him. Rumors spread in Washington that a Southern plot had been formed against Douglas's life. Men even said that Slidell had agreed to insult him in the Senate bar, force him into a duel, and kill him.

On the advice of a Washington correspondent, Douglas sent for a well-known Kentucky marksman, Tom Hawkins, to be his bodyguard. The Senator was nearly maneuvered into an encounter with Fitch of Indiana, but managed to avoid it. When Buchanan, still determinedly hostile, sent the Senate another

59   W. B. Parker, *Justin S. Morrill,* 267. John A. Norton, February 22, 1859, wrote Buchanan that in a recent Southern tour he had found much sentiment for the bill, that Philadelphia feeling strongly favored it, and that his signature would soften the antagonism of many Pennsylvanians who had condemned his Lecompton policy; Buchanan Papers.

list of Danite appointees for Illinois, Douglas attacked many of them as corrupt. Fitch's son held a place on the list, and the Indiana Senator chose to resent the speech as an affront; but in the end he withdrew his challenge.[60] Seven notes passed between the two men in four days! [61] The dudgeon of Douglas's follow-ers was intense. After he was murdered, they declared, the Southern fire-eaters planned to assassinate other opponents! [62]

It was impossible to keep this flaming quarrel between Northwestern and Southern Democrats confined to committee rooms, lobbies, and newspaper offices. On February 23, Senators Hale, Seward, and Chandler adroitly tossed the issue of slavery protection in the Territories into the tiltyard of the full Senate. Instantly the two Democratic factions rushed into battle. All the more resolute Southerners—Jefferson Davis, A. G. Brown, Gwin, C. C. Clay, Judah P. Benjamin—repudiated popular sovereignty, and demanded an efficient pro-tection of slavery in the Territories by enactment of Congress. Under the Dred Scott decision, they contended, slavery had a right to obtain the shield and buckler of Federal law in all instances in which a Territory denied it a proper defense.[63] These tenets were ferociously (the word is not too strong) rejected by Broderick, Stuart, Pugh, and above all by Douglas, as ever a host in himself. Congress, thundered the Illinoisan, has never yet enacted a criminal code or a property code for any organized Territory of the United States; why should it begin with slave property? I am obliged to the Senator from Mississippi, he remarked with an ironical bow to Davis, for assuming that I would never vote for fastening a slave code upon a Territory; "and I have yet to learn that there is a man in a free State of the Union, of any party, who would." [64]

The debate, running on till midnight, committed the opposing groups to positions which they declared they would never surrender. The schism was fundamental, and could end only in the total defeat of one side. Davis, Brown, and other Southerners served notice, in effect, that if the party convention which had already been fixed for Charleston in May, 1860, should adopt Douglas's Freeport doctrine, they would leave the hall in revolt. With equal intensity of conviction, Douglas and his associates made it plain that if the convention were forced to adopt the slave-code demand, they would attack that black flag.

60 Milton, *Eve of Conflict*, 364. In Illinois the Buchanan men were hostile as ever to Douglas; and Isaac Cook, losing no opportunity to assail and besmirch him, reported regu-larly to Buchanan. In Missouri, Isaac Sturgeon and others were equally vindictive, and also kept in close touch with the White House. Meanwhile, Douglas's organ the Chicago *Times* continued to castigate the Directory (Cobb, Slidell, Black, Jacob Thompson) as "political hucksters" who made Buchanan their "tool." This group, it said, had stooped to acts from which Bomba of Naples would have turned in disgust.
61 *National Intelligencer*, January 27, 1859.
62 Washington *States*, January 26, 1859.
63 *Cong. Globe*, 35th Cong., 2nd Sess., 1241, 1242.
64 *Ibid.*, 1244.

In some of the exchanges on that fatal February day, Davis and Douglas snarled at each other like panthers. Moderate Democrats perceived that the party was being torn in two. The sober, canny, somewhat timid Hunter, occupying a seat midway between the two chief combatants, was almost ludicrous in his dismay. His afflicted visage, as he turned during the four-hour battle, first to the bellicose Illinoisan and then to the icily cutting Mississippian, seemed to one observer to recall poor old Adam in the quarrel of Orlando and Oliver: "Sweet masters, be patient; for your father's remembrance, be at accord." [65]

The Union no less than the party was involved, and everybody knew it. Davis, Mason, and Brown uttered their hot words in behalf of an abstraction; but some of the bloodiest pages of history have concerned abstractions, which are peculiarly unsusceptible of compromise. If Douglas was resolved to follow his Freeport road, said Davis, "I wish him godspeed and a pleasant journey"; but, "not the breadth of one hair would I follow the Senator." [66] With like finality, the Little Giant retorted, amid applause from the galleries: "Allow me to inform him [Davis] that I stand on the platform, and those that jump off must go out of the party." Each side warned its opponents that they would receive no votes in the opposite section. No party embracing the popular sovereignty creed could carry a single Southern State, for this meant containment. No party clinging to the slave-code doctrine could win one electoral vote north of the Ohio, for this meant a coercion of freedom. The drama of the encounter was enhanced by an interruption:

Mr. Greene. Will the Senator permit me to give him a little information I have just received?
Mr. Davis. Certainly.
Mr. Greene. The legislature of Kansas has passed a law, declaring that from and after the passage of the act, slavery shall cease to exist in Kansas.[67]

So Horace White's scheme to give the slavery-protection question practical shape, and thus make the Freeport Doctrine more divisive, had succeeded! Republicans did not conceal their elation over the Democratic quarrel. The differences are so vital, trumpeted Greeley's *Tribune*, as to forbid all hope of Democratic unity in 1860.[68]

With tempers sharpened by these events, Republicans and Buchanan Democrats on February 25 flung themselves into the final battle on precedence for the

---

65 N. Y. *Weekly Tribune*, July 2, 1859.
66 *Cong. Globe*, 35th Cong., 2nd Sess., 1247.
67 *Ibid.*, 1255. It is significant that Douglas's friend James W. Singleton of Quincy, a man of Virginia origin, wrote him that public sentiment in Illinois required a firm stand. "We are not in a condition to carry another ounce of Southern weight, and I say so with the most painful reluctance." February 25, 1859; Singleton Papers, Ill. State Hist. Lib.
68 N. Y. *Weekly Tribune*, March 5, 1859.

Cuban grant or the Homestead bill. Slidell declared that since all argument on Cuba had been exhausted, before the Senate adjourned that night he meant to get a vote or have an hour fixed for one. The Democratic caucus had aligned itself behind him. Republicans, however, persisted in obstruction; they urged that while it was admittedly impossible to get the Cuban bill through the House, the Senate might within ten minutes send the Homestead bill to Buchanan's desk. Douglas, who supported both measures, was in despair. Let us, he said, agree to act on each of them, the Cuban bill first, before we take up the indispensable appropriation bills. Very well, rejoined Lyman Trumbull: we shall permit a vote on the Cuban proposal if Senator Hunter, who always has an appropriation bill ready whenever any measure comes up to which he is opposed, will promise not to block us.[69] Hunter, his eye upon Southern support for a Presidential nomination, refused.

It was now past nine o'clock: the Senate, which had sat the two previous nights until twelve, was weary; nerves were ready to snap. Seward, remarking bitterly that this was the last hour of the last day on which a motion could be made to take up the Homestead bill, arraigned the South for preferring Cuban adventures to a great constructive enactment. Toombs, flushed with anger, took the floor. His seat being near those of Seward and Wade, he directed his declamation full in their faces, betraying his passion by gestures and language. He smote his own desk and that of Seward; he thrust his chair against Wade's; he waved his fist. I despise the paltry tricks of tuppenny demagogues to prevent a vote, he shouted; they use their cry of land for the landless to evade a plain issue; shivering in the wind, they are afraid to take up a great national policy which appeals to the patriotism of the whole American people.

The instant he sat down, Seward, Wade, Fessenden, and Wilson were on their feet. Blunt Wade obtained the floor. "Skulk, eh? Shiver, do we?" he ejaculated as he brought his fist crashing down on Toombs's desk. He threw the Georgian's reproach for obstruction back in his teeth. It was the South which was obstructing the most glorious measure that had ever come before Congress. "The question will be, shall we give lands to the landless, or niggers to the niggerless?" [70]

As the debate thus reached a paroxysm of sectional passion, both the Cuban and Homestead bills failed. Other men spoke. Toombs, returning to the fray, said that Georgians were proud not to ask a single favor from the government: not land, not tariffs, not fishing bounties, not steamship subsidies. At one in the morning, Slidell and Brown gave up their fight. They won a hollow victory on a test motion to lay the Cuban bill on the table, which its adherents defeated 30 to 18.

While they could point to this as evidence that the Senate favored the bill, the measure was left just where it had been. It was clear, in fact, that while the Democratic Senate would have passed the Cuban bill, the Republican and Know-Nothing vote in the House would have killed it. The Senate would have defeated the Homestead bill, for the decisive motion for taking it up, made by Pugh of Ohio, was beaten 29 to 26. Only two members from the slaveholding States, Bell and Andrew Johnson, voted for the motion, and only six members from the free States against it. Sectional lines held firm.[71]

Even as these bills died, the heritage they left was all too evident. Buchanan's message, the Senate debate, and the newspaper discussion had imbued many Southerners with a stronger determination to expand the national domain toward the tropics. When the thirty-million proposal was denied even a clear-cut vote, radical proslavery men saw fresh evidence that the North was determined never, under any circumstances, to allow slavery another rood of land. The contest had meanwhile excited in countless Northern minds a new suspicion of Southern aims. Henceforth many Northern publicists constantly drove home their suspicion that the South intended to annex Cuba, Mexico, and Central America, spreading its own type of slavery throughout this domain; and that its leaders would not hesitate, once the scheme was consummated, to break away from the North and form a separate nation.[72]

[VI]

The tariff, meanwhile, had thrust a new lever into the widening sectional chasm. Never, said Simon Cameron early in 1858, had there been such distress among the ironworkers of Pennsylvania. Wide parts of that State were dependent directly or indirectly upon iron, for when furnaces went out of blast, coal mines, railroads, and canal boats felt the blow. Luzerne County, for example, a principality in itself, had thousands of miners, blacksmiths, woodcutters, machinists, hardware merchants, and railwaymen who responded to the pleas of ironmasters for more tariff protection. While the cost of making rails was at least $45 a ton, the spring of 1858 found fifty thousand tons of English rails offered in New York at $41. A parallel situation existed in textile areas of New England. Wool manufacturers grumbled that the existing tariff on raw wool was practically a bounty to the English manufacturer, who got his wool free. They pointed to idle mills and hungry workmen. The recent elections had shown

71 *Ibid.*, 1363 ff. Earlier the vote had stood 28 to 28 to take it up, and Vice-President Breckinridge had cast the deciding negative; pp. 1074–1076. Republicans knew that Buchanan would veto the bill, but they believed that if they could force it to a veto their chances in the campaign of 1860 would be improved.

72 N. Y. *Weekly Tribune*, April 16, 1859.

Northeastern Democrats that if their party was to survive, it must adopt the cry for greater protection. Particularly were the Keystone Democrats, who had just lost ten seats in the House, determined to insist on a revision.[73] They whole-heartedly approved of Buchanan's proposals for new schedules. But Secretary Cobb was for keeping the *ad valorem* duties, and once more was quoted as saying: "Old Buck is opposing the Administration." [74]

The struggle began on the opening day of the session, when Representative W. M. Dewart of Pennsylvania moved to instruct the Ways and Means Committee to report a bill increasing the coal and iron duties. Although this failed of the required two-thirds vote, various tariff measures were immediately tossed into the hopper. The most important were three: a bill prepared by the Pennsylvania Democrats, another written by Chairman Phelps of the Ways and Means Committee in consultation with Secretary Cobb, and a bill of Justin S. Morrill of Vermont, spokesman for the Republicans. The Pennsylvania group proposed a general return to the rates of 1846; the Phelps bill slightly increased the schedules of 1857; and the Morrill bill was a fairly strong protectionist measure. Though the committee strove earnestly to reconcile conflicting views and bring out a measure commanding general support, it fell into hopeless disputes.

Everyone knew, meanwhile, that the Senate would almost certainly block any tariff increases, for its Southern bloc would stand immovable. The Democratic caucus, on January 29, determined that it was inexpedient to raise duties or put them on the specific basis—a rebuff to Buchanan. Even yet, however, House revisionists did not despair. They brought renewed pressure to bear on the Ways and Means Committee. In that body, three Southern Democrats wanted no increases whatever; three Republicans wanted generous increases; and two members stood in a median position. The protectionist Democrats now threatened to join hands with the Republicans.[75] They threatened, too, to block vital appropriation bills unless the Southern members consented to some increases. Montgomery of Pennsylvania tried to tack an amendment for specific iron duties to the post office appropriations. At every point, Southern Representatives, using ingenious modes of delay, blocked these efforts.[76]

73 "I cannot see how you are to get Pennsylvania back in rank and file by 1860 unless this Congress will give them protection for coal and iron." Rev. John Chambers to Buchanan, Philadelphia, November 8, 1858; Buchanan Papers. Between Harrisburg and Columbia, eleven out of fourteen furnaces had shut down, throwing a thousand men and their families into poverty. Officers of the Phoenix Iron Companies, Paxton Furnace, and other corporations were bombarding Congressmen; see Cameron Papers, 1858.

74 Nichols, *Disruption of the American Democracy*, 234. For the demands of wool manufacturers see the anonymous pamphlet, "Free Trade in Raw Materials Considered in Its Effect upon All Classes of the People," New York, 1855.

75 N. Y. *Weekly Tribune*, January 29, 1859.

76 Nichols, *op. cit.*, 235, 236.

Greeley was vigorously scolding the Republican dissenters on the tariff. At least fourteen members of the party, and perhaps nineteen, he thought, were at heart free traders; they included Nichols, Mott, Edward Wade, and Bingham of Ohio, Leach of Michigan, Curtis of Iowa, Lovejoy of Illinois, Potter and Billinghurst of Wisconsin, and Frank Blair of Missouri. "I do think," he burst out at one point to Colfax, "you fifteen bolters ought to be whipped." The sectional alignment was thus, in large part, the Northwest and South against the East. In the end nothing was done. On February 26, with the end of the session at hand, Chairman Phelps moved a suspension of the rules to let him introduce a bill for reinstating the Walker tariff of 1846—with its duties higher than the existing schedules—for a limited period. His motion received a heavy majority, 128 to 88, but failed for want of two-thirds. The slave State members voted 66 to 17 against it, and the free State members were 111 to 22 in its favor.[77]

The irritation of Northern industrial areas over the failure of revision was trenchantly expressed. Pennsylvania manufacturers declared that a failure of Congress to act would give their State to the Republicans in 1860.[78] At a meeting of the Iron Masters Association in Philadelphia on New Year's Day, James Cooper of Pottstown had significantly called for united action to control the next Presidential election in various States. Proper organization in Pennsylvania, New Jersey, Maryland, Ohio, and other States, he declared, would suffice to secure a large majority for adequate protection to the iron interest and other manufactures. It had often been said that Buchanan had carried Pennsylvania only because of a vague but universal impression that he sympathized with the iron industry, and Cooper repeated the statement. "A glance at the election returns of 1856 will show that the general election in October of that year, which controlled the presidential election a month later, was carried by this interest without organization." Already Simon Cameron, John Covode, and other Pennsylvania Republicans were making the most of the tariff issue; already the New York *Herald* was slyly boosting Cameron for the Republican nomination in 1860 as a conservative man of Democratic antecedents for whom the Pennsylvania coal and iron districts would pour out a vote that would surely elect him.[79]

[VII]

Once more, members could look back on an utterly barren session, spent mainly in wrangling. The whole Thirty-fifth Congress, to which men said adieu

77 *Cong. Globe,* 35th Cong., 2nd Sess., 1409–1412; Greeley, February 4, 14, 1859, in Greeley-Colfax Corr.
78 N. Y. *Weekly Tribune,* February 12, 1859; J. M. Hopkins, November 24, 1858, Buchanan Papers.
79 *National Intelligencer,* January 22, 1859; N. Y. *Herald,* June 24, 1858.

on March 5, 1859, had been a Congress of deadlock and fission. Apart from the passage of the English bill, the admission of Minnesota and Oregon were the only forward steps of consequence. Even the making of these new States was a compromise process; for if both were freesoil, both were also initially Democratic, and sent Democratic Senators to Washington.

Superficially, the deadlock in Washington merely expressed the old antagonism of slavery and freesoil interests. The progress of the inexorable revolution, which in both sections was replacing moderate men by radicals, was dramatically revealed when the Senate of the Thirty-sixth Congress met for a short special session. Nineteen members had been newly elected or reelected. Tennessee, Kentucky, and Texas had replaced three conservative nationalists, John Bell, J. B. Thompson, and Sam Houston, with three proslavery sectionalists, A. O. P. Nicholson, Lazarus Powell, and J. W. Hemphill. Rhode Island, Michigan, and Iowa had dismissed three moderate-minded Democrats to fill their seats with radical-minded Republicans, Henry B. Anthony, the slashing owner-editor of the Providence *Journal*, Kingsley S. Bingham, who had won his spurs as a freesoil Representative, and James W. Grimes, who, like the others, had been an early organizer of the Republican Party. The reelected Senators were without exception men of granite opinions and belligerent energy: Fessenden, Henry Wilson, and Douglas among the Northerners; Toombs, A. G. Brown, and Judah P. Benjamin among the Southerners. The Senate would hear less, in the next two years, of the cooings of the dove of peace.

In a less superficial view, the session showed that a new element had intensified the old hopes and fears regarding slavery. A third section was involved, the teeming Northwest. Its destiny was not yet firmly settled. It was still linked with the South by the busy Mississippi, by Southern markets for its corn and pork, by the common interests of two agricultural regions, and by the ties of sentiment binding countless thousands of settlers to their ancestral homes in Virginia, Carolina, Kentucky, and Tennessee. It was linked with the Northeast by equally powerful ties. While it could no more give up either set of bonds than it could give up its life, a preponderance of interests would always express itself in lines of political preference; and that effort would sway the balance between the North and the South. The session also showed that economic issues were becoming more prominent. They were not dangerous in themselves, and the fact that such Northwestern men as Nichols of Iowa, English of Indiana, and Hodges of Illinois voted with the South on the tariff proved that they were not clearly sectional; but they might seriously reinforce the central element of cleavage.

Half-way mark for the Buchanan Administration! One misfortune had followed another: the Dred Scott decision, irritating millions and settling nothing; the Lecompton struggle, dividing the Democratic Party; the costly and needless

Mormon War; the panic and the depletion of the Treasury. The temper of both North and South had grown worse. At this eleventh hour, could the conservative forces of the nation be awakened? It did not seem likely. The country might yet regain the partial concord won in 1850—or it might slip swiftly toward disunion and war.

Index

INDEX